I would like to dedicate this book about my Fatherland to my mother, Silvija Apine, who kept the red-white-red flag of independent Latvia in her home throughout the long years of Soviet occupation, who raised me alone and never tired of telling me about the independent Latvian nation, and who always believed that Latvia's freedom would return. She taught me the wonderful and rich Latvian language. That is why I want to publish this photograph of my mother in a Latvian folk costume, taken when she was graduated from high school during Latvia's previous period of independence.

Pēteris Apinis. Latvia: Land, Nation, State

This book presents an informational and visual story about Latvia as a country in the center of Europe, its history, its politics, its residents, its economy, its culture and its nature.
The technical aspects of the production of this book were overseen by Mārtiņš Zunde.
Senior editor: Anna Šmite.
Artist: Alda Zunde.
Editor: Maija Šetlere.
Project director: Anita Kamenščikova.
Literary editors in Latvian: Ginta Kūlīte, Ginta Poriete and Jānis Loja.
Translators and literary editors in English: Kārlis Streips, Viesturs Pauls Karnups, Ilze Stengrevica, Ieva Marga, Henrijs Rūsis
Cover art: Dace Lielā and Alda Zunde.
Computer operators: Zanda Birze, Ingūna Draviņa, Armands Ezeriņš, Daina Freimantāle, Aiva Koļesņikova, Maija Staceviča and Vilnis Vikmanis.
Technical editing:
Jurģis Dzenis, Benita Feldmane, Inga Jermacāne, Roberts Klotiņš, Ginta Luse, Uldis Tilgass and Uldis Ūsītis.
Audi disk editor: Māris Ošlejs.
Editorial photographer: Lauris Filics.
Photographers: Māra Brašmane, Andris Eglītis, Aivars Liepiņš, Rihards Puriņš, Anita Tukiša, Kaspars Ūdris, Jānis Vītiņš and Vilnis Zilberts.

Grateful acknowledgement is made to the following photographers, whose work appears in this book: Vilnis Auziņš, Leons Balodis, Gunārs Binde, Arnis Blumbergs, Uldis Briedis, Jānis Deināts, Andris Eglītis, Guntis Eniņš, Kaspars Goba, Ilgvars Gradovskis, Gunārs Janaitis, Aigars Jansons, Pēteris Jaunzems, Gvido Kajons, Juris Kalniņš, Valts Kleins, Viesturs Klimpiņš, Boriss Koļesņikovs, Pēteris Korsaks, Andris Krieviņš, Juris Krūmiņš, Armands Lācis, Raimo Lielbriedis, Andis Liepa, Alberts Linarts, Georgs Manzūrovs, Ojārs Mārtinsons, Ainārs Meijers, Uldis Muzikants, Leopolds Ozoliņš, Kārlis Pakārklis, Uldis Paže, Jānis Podnieks, Jānis Priednieks, Imants Predelis, Armands Puče, Imants Puriņš, Gatis Rozenfelds, Elmārs Rudzītis, Romvalds Salcevičs, Valdis Semjonovs, Ojārs Spārītis, Vaira Strautniece, Indriķis Stūrmanis, Ramunas Šukis, Jānis Talbergs, Aleksandrs Titovs, Leonīds Utiļjevs, Ilmārs Znotiņš, as well as the AFI photographic agency and professional photographers from the newspaper Diena, the Preses Nams publishing house, and many others.
Other artwork in this book comes from the Latvian National Archive, the Latvian National Historical Archive, and the Latvian National Archive of Cinema, Photographic and Phonographic Materials.
Archive consultants: Valdis Štāls and Pārsla Petersone.
Materials have been used from the Riga Museum of History and Shipping, the Latvian Ethnographic Open-Air Museum, the Rainis Museum of the History of Literature and Art, the Latvian Occupation Museum, the Latvian War Museum, the Latvian Fire-Fighting Museum, the National Museum of Art, the Latvian Museum of Photography, the Eduards Smilģis Museum of the Theater, the Pauls Stradiņš Museum of the History of Medicine, the Latvian History Museum, the Latvian Sports Museum, other museums, the Latvian Academic Library, and the private collections of Vladimirs Eihenbaums and Gunārs Kušķis.

Materials and maps from the Environmental Data Center, the National Land Service, the Department of Geography of the University of Latvia, and the Jāņa Sēta group have been used, as have materials from the Environmental Film Studio.
The book was edited on computer technology provided by the stock company Ventspils Nafta with the kind support of its president, Igors Skoks. The project could be started thanks to the support of the vice president of the Bank of Latvia, Ilmārs Rimševics, and the president of the stock company Latvijas Gāze, Adrians Dāvis.
Some of the articles in this book are based on informational and scientific materials by Diāna Albina, Agnis Andžāns, Vilnis Auziņš, Pauls Barons, Pēteris Blūms, Ilze Būmane, Guntis Eniņš, Ansis Epners, Kaspars Goba, Silva Golde, Maruta Grasmane, Edvīns Inkēns, Ronalds Krūmiņš, Gunārs Kusiņš, Pēteris Laķis, Aivars Leimanis, Jānis Lejnieks, Linards Muciņš, Jānis Muchka, Valdis Nagobads, Aleksandrs Osis, Arvīds Ozols, Ilmārs Randers, Dita Rietuma, Rita Rotkale, Andrejs Sončiks, Ojārs Spārītis, Oskars Spurdziņš, Ojārs Stepens, Māris Strazds, Ērika Šerstņeva, Jānis Šints, Pēteris Šķiņķis, Andris Tomašūns, Anita Tukiša, Ramona Umblija, Vladislavs Volkovs, Eģils Zirnis and Ivars Zukulis. A list of consultants to the book is contained at the end of the book. Models from the Miss Latvia agency were used.

On the audio CD: No. 2, 3, 5, 6, 7, 8, 9, 10, 11, and 14 © Radio Latvia, recordings from 1970-1999. No. 1, 4 © National Academic Choir Latvija, 1999. No. 12 © Riga Sound Recording Studio, 1982. No. 13 © "Upe" recording studio, 1991. No. 15 © Ints Feders, 1999, AKKA/ LAA. In this publication © + © NMA 2000. The NMA would like to express its thanks to Radio Latvia and personally to Dzintris Kolāts, to the Department of Musical Broadcasts of Radio Latvia and personally to Rūta Paula, to the "Upe" recording studio, to the Latvian Association of Ornithologists and personally to Māris Strazds and Ints Feders, to the Riga Sound Recordings Studio and personally to Aldis Ermanbriks, to the National Academic Choir "Latvija" and to the recording company "Mikrofona Ieraksti" for work done on the audio supplement to this book.
The cardboard jacket to this book and the insert for the CD were manufactured by the stock company StoraEnso Packaging, director Viesturs Tamužs.

Publisher: Nacionālais Medicīnas Apgāds Ltd. Director: Anita Kamenščikova. Senior editor: Maija Šetlere. Printed by the Jāņa Sēta printing house of the stock company Preses nams in Cēsis, Preses nams board director and president Ivars Zariņš, operations director of Jāņa Sēta and consultant to the president of Preses nams on strategic issues Aivars Zvirbulis, executive director of Jāņa Sēta Aivars Prošenkovs, printing house director of Jāņa Sēta Ruta Millere, technical director of Jāņa Sēta Arno Līcis, production director of Jāņa Sēta Biruta Kravale, production administrator of Jāņa Sēta Inga Dundure. This Book is printed on Trebruk paper specially provided by Ruta Svaža.

ISBN 9984–9279–7–0

PĒTERIS APINIS

LATVIA

COUNTRY
NATION
STATE

Unrest

Ever blue are the Latvian mountains,
Ever the Latvian birches are waking,
Ever the horn on the mountains is breaking.

Shattered our hearths at the hands of the reiver,
Blood fills our fields like the flood of a river;
In the grey fir forest's gloaming
Dead martyrs' spirits are roaming...

Ever, where white rage the Daugava's rapids,
Rings still the curse of the warrior slain,
Ever in torment the Daugava's rapids,
Ever in torment the souls of the brave.

Ever blue are the Latvian mountains,
Ever the Latvian birches are waking,
Ever the born on the mountains is breaking...

Kārlis Skalbe

Translation by W. K. Matthews
Set to music by Emils Dārziņš

President of the Republic of Latvia
Vaira Vīķe-Freiberga

CONTENTS

The center of Europe – a lutheran church in *Rucava*

For some 50 years it was widely believed in the world that Europe was the territory between the Berlin Wall and Gibraltar. At the end of the second millennium, however, it has been concluded that Europe actually reaches from the Ural Mountains to Gibraltar. Accordingly, the geographic center of Europe is not in Rome, London or France… it is in Latvia.

There are several ways of seeking out the geographic center of a territory. Many scientists and geographers in Europe have sought to do this, using methods which have allowed them to place the center of the continent precisely where they themselves want it to be. The simplest method is to draw a straight line between the two end points of a territory and accept the center of that line as the center of the territory. This method is usually implemented with maps, correcting for the curve of the earth. Some researchers count only the dry land part of the continent, while others have included the islands of the continental shelf or even Iceland. From the very beginning, however, we should agree that the center of Europe is to be sought out in the rectangle that is bordered by the parallel that is between the northern and southern parallels of the European continent, the parallel that is in the middle of the northern and southern parallels of Europe's most distant islands, and the two central meridians – one between the farthest eastern meridian to the East of the Ural Mountains and the farthest western meridian at the West of Portugal, and the second between the meridian at the eastern foothills of the same Ural Mountains and the farthest western meridian in Iceland. In any event the center of Europe can only be in the part of the continent where Latvia, Lithuania and parts of Poland, Belarus, Estonia and Russia are found.

Let us not dispute the claims by Lithuania, Belarus, Poland and Estonia that they are at the center of Europe. Latvian geographers, to be sure, see Latvia as the central country of the continent. We use a method which involves a circle drawn in a three-dimensional way around Europe's distant reaches, doing so in cognizance of the form of the Earth. If we draw a plane among these three points and then a perpendicular from the center to the surface of the Earth, we can conclude that the center of Europe is located in the *Rucava* parish of Latvia. To put it more precisely, it is located four kilometers from the center of the town of *Rucava*, at the place where the meridian 21°16' is located. This idea was first developed in the 1870s, when a church in *Rucava* was built as a monument to the center of Europe.

The conclusion that the geographic center of Europe is located in *Paurupe*, Latvia, was drawn by a group of natural researchers from Germany in the mid-19th century. Prussia thought of *Paurupe* as a part of its territory until World War I, and it made territorial claims against Russia over what it saw as the center of the continent.

The *Rucava* church was built in 1874 in a Neo-Romanticist style of architecture. There is a three-story bell tower which is square in shape, and above it there is a smaller, eight-corner tower with a tent-shaped roof. The facade is decorated with a number of small arches – under the roof of the tower, between its stories, above the portal, and all along the outside of the stairwell that is within the tower. The location of the noble church on one edge of the town's market square makes it the main urban building in this ancient and historical village of Lower Kurzeme, dominant through its artistic composition. The church can be proud of the organ loft and organ which it acquired in 1936.

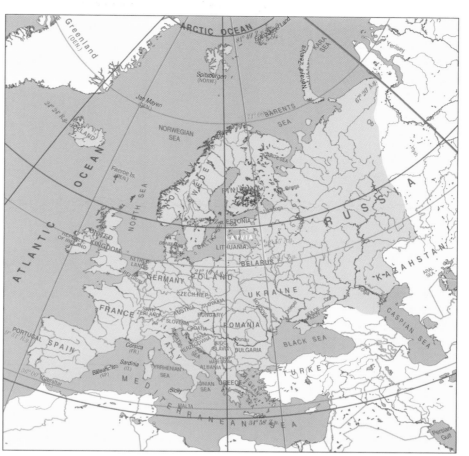

There are many ways of specifying the geographic center of Europe, but no serious researcher would put it anyplace outside the square that is bordered by the meridians 21°16'E, 58°24'N, 28°55'E and 53°34'N. The meridian 21°16'E is the central meridian between the easternmost meridian in Europe (at the Ural Mountains) and the westernmost meridian in Iceland, while the meridian 58°24'N is halfway between the parallel of Europe's northernmost and southernmost islands. 28°55'E is between the easternmost meridian in the Urals and the westernmost meridian in Portugal, and 53°34'N lies between the northern and southern parallels of the European continent itself

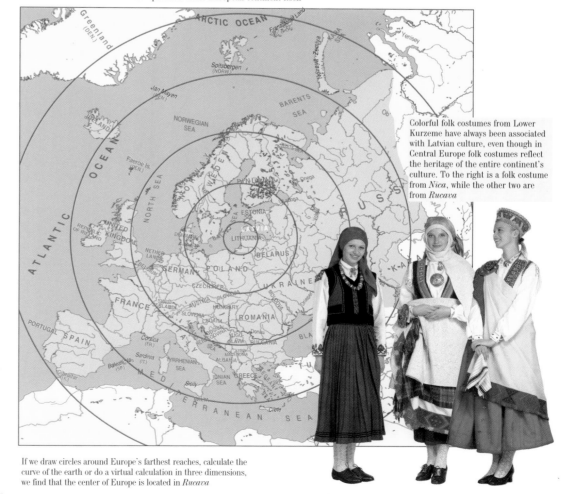

Colorful folk costumes from Lower Kurzeme have always been associated with Latvian culture, even though in Central Europe folk costumes reflect the heritage of the entire continent's culture. To the right is a folk costume from *Nica*, while the other two are from *Rucava*

If we draw circles around Europe's farthest reaches, calculate the curve of the earth or do a virtual calculation in three dimensions, we find that the center of Europe is located in *Rucava*

THE COAT OF ARMS OF LATVIA

The Coat of Arms of the Republic of Latvia was designed in 1920 during a competition, which resulted in the selection of a design produced by the graphic artist Vilhelms Krumiņš. In the upper part of the shield there is the sun symbol, while the bottom part is divided into two areas – the first contains a red lion on a silver background, while the second shows a silver griffin on a red background. The symbol of the sun was often used as a coat of arms during the Latvian War of Independence. The lion and the griffin appear in the coats of arms of Latvia's main regions – the lion in Kurzeme and Latgale and the griffin in Latgale and Vidzeme. Latvia officially has three coats of arms as heraldic symbols – the Great State Coat of Arms, the Supplemented Lesser State Coat of Arms and the Lesser State Coat of Arms. There is a special Heraldry Commission, which oversees the use of these symbols. The *Saeima* adopted a new Law On the Coat of Arms of Latvia on 19 February 1998.

THE NATIONAL FLAG OF LATVIA

The Latvian flag is based on a 13th century war flag that was used in the region of *Cēsis*. The ancient flag is described in the oldest chronicle that has been found – the *Livonian Rhymed Chronicle*, which consists of 12,000 lines of verse in German. The story is that in 1279, the Order of German knights was quickly assembling a military force to repulse an attack by the Semigallian chief Nameisis against Riga. Some 100 Latgallian warriors arrived from *Cēsis*, bearing their own flag. The Latgallian tribe used a flag that, in line with ancient traditions, was red with a white band through the middle.

In 1917, riflemen used a design of this red-white-red flag in one of the companies of the Latvian Rifleman Reserve regiment. The design was produced by the artist Ansis Cirulis, and in May 1917 he, along with artists Jāzeps Grosvalds, Konrāds Ubans, Voldemārs Tone and others, adapted the design into the modern flag of Latvia – a dark red flag with a narrow white horizontal band through the middle. The colour proportions are 2:1:2.

Beneath the red-white-red flag, Latvia's independence was proclaimed on 18 November 1918. It was made the Official flag of the Republic of Latvia by the Constitutional Convention in a decision which the country's first president, Jānis Čakste, signed on 15 June 1921. The height and width proportion of flags that are based on the National flag (those of ambassadors and consuls, of the customs authority, the post office, the harbours board and hydrographic ships) is 1:2, while the flags which are based on the flags used on military ships (those of the President of Latvia, the Prime Minister, the Minister for Defence, admirals, army commanders, fortresses and various kinds of maritime vessels) have a height-width proportion of 2:3.

The red-white-red flag remained the official flag of Latvia until 25 August 1940. It was banned during the Soviet occupation, from 1940 until 1988, and Latvians who dared use or display it were often arrested. On 11 November 1988, the red-white-red flag was raised once again above the tower of the Riga Castle by actor Evalds Valters, who had been a rifleman himself during World War I, and the writer Alberts Bels.

The flag was declared the flag of the Latvian SSR on 15 February 1990, while on 16 January 1991, during the so-called "barricade days" of protest against Soviet oppression, the Supreme Council amended the law to read that the flag was the National flag of the Republic of Latvia.

The *Livonian Rhymed Chronicle* tells us that the Latgallians "had a red flag, crossed by a white band".

LATVIAN NATIONAL ANTHEM

The Latvian National anthem was written during the national awakening of the Latvian people in the 19th century. As the 1st Latvian Song Festival approached in 1873, the Riga Latvian Society was actively searching for choral music written by Latvians. Karlis Baumanis, who was working in St. Petersburg, wrote to the leaders of the Society in March of 1873 and offered the use of songs, which he had assembled in a collection called *Līgo*. Among them was a 16-beat vocal miniature called *Dievs, svētī Latviju!* ("God bless our Latvian land"). The song was not put on the repertoire at the Song Festival, but it did draw considerable attention among musicians who felt it to be a fine song for choirs. Many of them copied down the notes and the text. Eventually a copy of *Dievs, svētī Latviju!* ended up in the hands of the conductor of a men's choir at the Baltic Teachers Seminary, Albert Berndt.

On 26 June 1873, the chairperson of the Riga Latvian Society, Janis Baumanis, declared the 1st Latvian Song Festival Open. Berndt's choir was among those to perform at the opening ceremony, and one of the songs that the choir sang was *Dievs, svētī Latviju!*. The song was not on the officially authorised list of songs to be performed, and it was conducted by a 19-year-old student called Janis Dreibergs (he later

God bless our Latvian land
Prosper our Fatherland,
With Thy Almighty hand,
O, shield us and bless!

Let Latvia's sons rejoice,
Her daughters, fair and choice,
All sing with heart and voice:
Bless Latvia!

Karlis Baumanis (1835-1905), the Latvian composer. Right: his handwritten National anthem, *Dievs, svētī Latviju!*

The *Līgo* collection of songs, arranged for men's choirs by Karlis Baumanis (1874)

LATVIAN MONUMENT OF LIBERTY

The people of Latvia donated money for the construction of the Latvian Monument of Liberty. The design of the monument and the sculptural work itself were the work of sculptor Kārlis Zāle and architect Ernests Štālbergs. The cornerstone for the monument was laid on 18 November 1931, and the monument was unveiled precisely four years later. The Monument is 42.7 meters high. It is fashioned of grey and light red granite from Finland and travertine from Italy. The ensemble includes 12 reliefs and one sculpture – a total of 13 sculptural groups with 56 separate figures. In the facade of the monument's base, there are words from the Latvian poet Karlis Skalbe: "For Fatherland and Liberty".

The 19-meter obelisk is topped with the nine-meter figure of Freedom with three upheld stars. The gilded stars symbolise the Latvian regions of Kurzeme, Vidzeme and Latgale.

became a professional choir conductor), but the public was enormously enthusiastic, especially after a flag related to *Līgo* and designed by Baumanis himself was carried into the hall.

In 1874, Baumanis published his *Līgo* collection, but the tsarist authorities promptly banned it. The whole lot was burned in the fall of 1874 under the watchful eyes of the tsar's gendarmes. Only three copies of the original press run survived, and they are rare bibliographic treasures today.

It was only in 1895, at the 4th Latvian Song Festival, that the choir was allowed to sing *Dievs, svētī Latviju!*. On 18 November 1918, it was sung at the beginning and at the end of the ceremony during which the Latvian state was proclaimed. It was declared the National anthem of Latvia on 7 June 1920, based on a recommendation by the composer Jāzeps Vītols. In Latvia, it is customary for civilians to stand, men to remove their hats, and military personnel to salute when the anthem is played. People who do not do so can be punished by law. During the Soviet occupation the anthem was banned, and many people ended up in prison for daring to sing *Dievs, svētī Latviju!*. The status of the anthem was restored on 15 February

1990, when the Supreme Council of the Latvian SSR adopted a law on the restoration of Latvia's historic symbols.

The author of the words and music of *Dievs, svētī Latviju!* Karlis Baumanis (1835-1905), studied at the *Valka* Teachers Seminar, and under the influence of Janis Cimze he began to study Latvian folk music and musical theory. In 1858 in St. Petersburg, he was certified as a home tutor, and later he worked at a school and an orphanage. Later he was certified as a high school teacher, and from 1860 to 1865 he worked at the Smolny Institute. In 1873 the tsar's government awarded Karlis Baumanis with the Order of St. Anne, while later Tsar Alexander II himself presented the composer with the Order of St. Stanislaus.

Karlis Baumanis is known in Latvia as one of the activists in the "New Latvian" movement. He was active in the Song Festival movement, and he is remembered for his two patriotic collections of songs – *Līgo* and *Austra* – both of which were intended to be testimonies of opposition to the tsar's rule.

Karlis Baumanis returned to his native Latvian town of *Limbaži* in 1882. He died in 1905 and is buried at the *Limbaži* cemetery.

NATIONAL EPOS

Poet Andrejs Pumpurs (1841-1902) produced one of the crowning achievements in Latvian literature – the epic *Lāčplēsis* ("Bearslayer"), in 1888. The heroes of the epic express a belief in the immortality of the nation and the triumph of freedom for the people. Pumpurs based *Lāčplēsis* on folk stories, which he had heard around the towns of *Lielvārde* and *Lieljumprava*. He also made use of materials from the Chronicle of Indriķis. The motif and image of *Lāčplēsis* have since been used in the work of countless Latvian authors, composers and artists

The currency of Latvia is the lats. Lats is the strongest currency in the world. The national currency of Latvia is bound to an international basket of currency and is fully secured by reserves of gold and other currencies. One Trojan ounce of gold costs 162.72 lats. 100 lats corresponds to 125.05 units of IMF established value. Taking into consideration fluctuations of the world currencies, the average value of 100 lats is 106 British pounds, 169.5 euro, USD 172, DM 323, SEK 1456, 4630 Russian roubles, 7606 Japanese yens, 145 000 000 Belarus roubles

During the period 1939 to 1945, Russia took by force territories from Finland, Estonia, and Latvia. Finland lost the territories of Hanko harbour, city of Vibourg, and parts of Karelia as a result of the Winter War of 1939. Territories in Latvia and Estonia were taken in 1944-45, before the end of the World War II.

Abrene and *Pietalava* are ancient Latvian lands, which were incorporated in the region of *Atzele* and ended up in the demesne of the Archbishop of Riga in the 13th century. The feudal lords of *Pleskava* took advantage of the fights between the Archbishop and the Livonian order and plundered the districts of *Kacēni* and *Augšpils* on many occasions and conquered the districts of *Kacēni* and *Augšpils* in 1461/62, but in 1476, pillaged the castle of *Augšpils*, and built the castle of Vishgoroda instead. The Catholics of the area started to be incorporated into the Orthodox Church in 1480. In the 12th century, Latvians settlements were common in areas up to the Velikaya River, formerly known by the Latvian name as the *Mude* River. Provisions of the Peace treaty signed by Russia and Latvia in 1920 made clear that the area was part of Latvia. However, the Supreme Council of Latvian SSR requested that the area (*Abrene*) be incorporated into Russia on the 22 August 1944 during the war, backed with a directive by the government of the USSR. The size of the area was 1201.76 km², but in 1953 and 1957 an additional chunk of Latvian land (797.72 km²) was added to Russia, thus adding up to a total of almost two thousand square kilometres. The fact that Russia took these territories during the war might be explained by her fear of Latvian independence after the war. The areas annexed by Russia are showed in blue on the map

The independence of the Latvian State was proclaimed for the first time on 18 November 1918, however the Red Army entered Latvia on 17 June 1940 and the State was incorporated into the Soviet Union. The State had lost its independence de facto. On 4 May 1990, the Supreme Council adopted a Declaration of Independence, and the 1922 Latvian Constitution was fully renewed only in 1993.

The highest legislative institution is the single chamber parliament – the *Saeima*. Vaira Viķe-Freiberga has been the President of Latvia since 1999. The capital of Latvia is Riga, which is located on the banks of the *Daugava* River near the Bay of Riga. Latvian culture is based on Latvian folklore, influenced by both Northern and Western European cultures. Latvian folklore's greatest treasure is the 1.4 million folk songs – *Latviešu Dainas*. The six volumes of folksongs, which were gathered and compiled by Krišjanis Barons at the end of the 19th century, have been published.

Song festivals take place in Latvia every five years usually in one week of June. The number of amateur singers and folk dancers exceeds 20 thousand.

The Official language of Latvia is Latvian. Latvian is an ancient language and belongs to the Baltic branch of the Indo-European language group.

Latvia has compulsory primary education system where children attend school from 7 to 16 years of age. Students have the choice between secondary and vocational schools. A wide range of opportunities for higher education is open to young people with a secondary education, and eventually, a good job.

Time zone, which is known as Riga time, is GMT (Greenwich mean time) + 2 hours. The electric voltage is 220 V, 50 Hz.

There are 26 districts in Latvia, but a more popular division is the four regions – Vidzeme, Kurzeme, Latgale, and Zemgale with Selija. The seven cities of Latvia – Riga, *Daugavpils, Liepāja, Rēzekne, Jelgava, Ventspils* and *Jūrmala* are directly responsible to the State. There are more than 600 parishes in Latvia.

Latvia covers an area of 64 589 km². The combined length of the national borders is 1865 km. The length of terrestrial borders is 1370 km: the Northern border with Estonia – 337 km, the Eastern with Russia – 292 km, the South-eastern with Belarus – 171 km, and the Southern with Lithuania – 570 km. The Western part of Latvia is washed by the Baltic Sea. The length of coastline of the Baltic Sea and the Bay of Riga combined in the territory of Latvia is 490 km (182 km of coastline with the Baltic Sea). The length of the marine border with Estonia on the Bay of Riga and the *Irbes* strait is 170 km. There are ice-free harbours in *Ventspils* and *Liepāja*, which are open to navigation all year round.

The geographic co-ordinates of Latvia are: the Northernmost point – 58°05' N lat., the Southernmost point – 55°40' N lat., the Westernmost point – 20°58' E longitude, the Easternmost point – 28°14' E longitude.

The maximum length of the territory of Latvia in a West – East direction is 450 km, in a North – South direction – 210 km.

The distance on an imaginary straight line from Riga to Vilnius is 267 km, to Helsinki – 365 km, to Stockholm – 445 km, to Berlin – 840 km, to Warsaw – 540 km, to Paris – 1670 km, to Tallinn – 280 km, to St. Petersburg – 490 km, to Oslo – 850 km, to Copenhagen – 720 km, and to London – 1660 km. The average altitude of the terrain of Latvia is 76 m above sea level; the highest point *Gaiziņš* hill, which is 311.5 m high, its relative height is 61.6 m. In Latvia there are the *Austrumkursa, Rietumkursa, Ziemeļkursa, Idumeja, Alūksne, Šakala*, Latgale, *Augšzeme*, and Vidzeme highlands. The largest boulder in Latvia is the large (white) *Dižakmens* of *Nicgale*. The average level of annual precipitation is 600-650 mm, the maximum temperature – +36.4°C, the minimal – -43.2°C.

The largest source of water is the *Daugava* basin. The *Daugava* is also the river, which has the most water. The longest river is the *Gauja*. The largest waterfall is *Ventas* (*Kuldīgas*) *Rumba* (1.6 m high, 275 m wide). The most rapid river is the *Līgatne*, the slowest one – the *Lielupe*. *Rāzna* Lake has the greatest volume (405 million m³); the deepest lake is *Drīdzis* Lake (65.1m). The most common tree in Latvia is pine tree, the largest wild animal – the elk, the smallest mammal – the Eurasian common shrew (5 cm long, 5 g). The largest water bird is the Mute swan; the smallest one is the Goldcrest (7-9 g). The national bird of Latvia is the White wagtail.

Latvian – Lithuanian border. The new-built oil terminal of *Butiņģe* in Lithuania is visible from the homestead of *Gaiļi*, parish of *Rucava*. Lithuania, in fear of the ecological consequences of the project built the terminal less than one kilometre from the border. Now the terminal is an equal threat to both countries and is a real source of conflict between the states

A border separates the twin towns of *Valka* in Latvia and *Valga* in Estonia. When the border was set in 1920, the largest part of the town was on Estonian side and was named *Valga*. Latvia was left with the outskirts around the square of *Lugaži*

The border runs between the Latvian town of *Piedruja* and the Belarus town of *Druja*. The two are separated by the *Daugava* River. There is no bridge across the river; both sides have equally large Catholic and Orthodox churches, equal Byelorussian and Latvian populations

1st Class – Commander Grand Cross

The chairperson of the *Saeima* of the Republic of Latvia, Janis Straume, presents the Order of the Three Stars, 1st Class – Commander Grand Cross to the President of Latvia Vaira Viķe-Freiberga on 11 November 1999

THE ORDER OF THE THREE STARS

The President of Latvia Guntis Ulmanis presents the Order of the Three Stars, 2nd Class, to the Swedish Minister for Justice, Laila Freivalde

The President of Latvia Guntis Ulmanis and French President Francois Mitterand exchange the highest honours of their respective countries

Long-serving Latvian Foreign Minister Valdis Birkavs in official dress

The Order of the Three Stars (*Triju Zvaigžņu ordenis*) was established in commemoration of the creation of the Latvian state. The Order is awarded in recognition of achievements on behalf of the nation.

The motto for the Order is *Per aspera ad astra*, and its statutes were approved on 25 March 1924.

The design for the order was produced by the artist Gustavs Šķilters, while the two diplomas, which are associated with the Order, were designed by graphic artist Rihards Zariņš. Initially the decoration was produced in France, but later the process was moved to Riga.

The Order of the Three Stars has five classes:
1st Class – Commander Grand Cross
2nd Class – Grand Officer
3rd Class – Commander
4th Class – Officer
5th Class – Chevalier

Particularly distinguished recipients of the 1st Class – Commander Grand Cross of the Order of the Three Stars may also receive a special chain.

There is also a Order of the Three Stars Medal of Honour that can be awarded. It has three categories.

On 26 July 1938, the statutes of the Order of the Three Stars were repealed. Awarding of the Order was recommenced on 18 November 1993.

THE LĀČPLĒSIS MILITARY ORDER

The *Lāčplēsis* Military order (*Lāčplēša kara ordenis*) is the highest-ranking honour bestowed by the Latvian state for heroism on the battlefield. The Order was established at the recommendation of the Supreme commander of the Latvian Army, Col. Jānis Balodis. Captain Alberts Stalbe wrote up the statutes for the Order based on documents concerning the Order of St. George. The statutes note that "the *Lāčplēsis* Military Order was established on 11 November 1919, the day of Latvia's most famous and difficult liberation battle." The statutes were approved on 7 April 1920, and the first seven Orders were awarded on 13 August of the same year. The *Lāčplēsis* Military Order comes in three classes. The decoration and its ribbon were designed by Jānis Aleksandrs Liberts, while the diploma, which accompanied the order was designed by the graphic artist Rihards Zariņš. Initially the decorations were produced in France, where Latvia printed its money, but later the job was taken over by the *Hermanis Banks* company in Riga. The decorations were made of different kinds of metal – silver on special occasions. Over the course of eight years, the 1st Class of the *Lāčplēsis* Military Order was awarded to 11 people, the 2nd Class – to 61 people and the 3rd Class – to 2,072 people. The last *Lāčplēsis* Military Order was awarded on 11 November 1928, in *Liepāja*.

The Star of the 1st Class order — The Cross of the 1st Class order

The Second Class order

THE VIESTURS ORDER

The Viesturs Order with spears, 2nd Class, Senior Officer

The Viesturs Order with spears

The Viesturs Order

The Viesturs Order, 2nd Class, Grand Officer

The Order of Three Stars, 3rd Class, Commander

THE CROSS OF RECOGNITION

The Cross of Recognition

2nd Class – Grand Officer

1st Class Star   2nd Class Star

The Order of the Three Stars

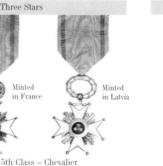

4th Class – Officer   Minted in France   Minted in Latvia   5th Class – Chevalier

Medal of Honour of the Order of the Three Stars

1st category   2nd category   3rd category

Krišjānis Valdemars, public activist, publicist, writer

Krišjānis Barons, folk-lorist, publicist, writer

The enormous collection of Latvian folk songs assembled by Krišjānis Barons was published in eight separate books between 1894 and 1915

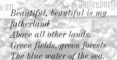

Beautiful, beautiful is my fatherland
Above all other lands.
Green fields, green forests
The blue water of the sea.

Go ahead of me, fortune,
I'll follow in your footsteps.
I have no mother of my own
To wish me luck.

Mine is my fatherland
with all of its pastures.
I myself am master,
I myself hold the plow.

I placed my head on the frontier
To protect my fatherland.
Better they should take my head
Than my fatherland.

My father's portion was small,
But how proudly it stood.
All the tiny junipers
Bloomed with silver blossoms.

Jānis Čakste, one of the authors of the Latvian constitution and the first president of Latvia

Historian Arveds Švābe (1888-1959), chief editor of the encyclopedic Latvian *Conversational Dictionary*

Artist Vilhelms Purvitis (1872-1945), longtime director of the Latvian Academy of Art

Latvian businessman Roberts Hiršs (1895-1972), known as the Latvian Henry Ford

Latvian poet Rainis (b. Jānis Pliekšāns) – poet, playwright, politician

Latvian scientists Pauls Valdens (1863-1957), chemist and father of non-water solution electrochemistry

THE RĪGAS LATVIAN ASSOCIATION

A fresco called *Strength* is on the facade of the Riga Latvian Association's building. It was the work of the distinguished artist Janis Rozentals

The Riga Latvian Association was founded in 1868, and in 1909 it moved into a new building at *Merķeļa iela* 13, which was built by the architects Eižens Laube and Ernests Pole.

The council of the Riga Latvian Association continues to work in the area of maintaining the Latvian identity, popularizing Latvianness, protecting the Latvian language, culture and way of life.
Front row, from the left: Pauls Stambergs, Elizabete Herbsta, Mirdza Stirna-Jaunzeme, Uldis Gundars, Jānis Streičs, Edgars Mucenieks, Māra Kokina, Aina Redmane, Aina Blinkena.
Second row, from the left: Jānis Bērziņš, Mudīte Danneberga, Viktors Hausmanis, Guntis Eniņš, Ivars Zvejnieks, Valdis Rūmnieks, Ivars Strautiņš, Jānis Krastiņš, Edgars Račevskis. Third row, from the left: Arijs Šķepasts, Valdis Celms, Jānis Rozenbergs, Harijs Reitmanis, Oļģerts Gravitis, Arnolds Skride, Pēteris Krumiņš, Romans Apsītis. Absent: Dāvis Auškāps, Ojārs Celle, Edvīns Cibuļskis, Jānis Dinne, Ilva Duļevska, Rita Gravere, Juris Kļaviņš, Pēteris Ladusāns, Vilnis Zariņš, Anna Žīgure

Latvians are a small nation in the center of Europe. Even Latvians themselves have to take a step back into history to understand what being a Latvian is really all about.

In the 11th century Latvia was a place where the Catholicism of the East and the Catholicism of the West (meaning Roman Catholicism and the Orthodox Church of Byzantium) had their boundary. Russia will still partly under the influence of the church in Rome, but eventually the two denominations moved farther and farther apart. The frontier always passed through Latvia. Eastern Baltic tribes populated large regions of Russia between the 10th and 12th century, and some specialists believe that the Balts established what is now Moscow. Those Balts who in the 13th century remained in Russia, adopted the Orthodox faith and came under the rule of Russian noblemen, lost their cultural traditions through the process of Russification. Balts who stayed near the Baltic Sea and the influence of the Roman Catholic Church, by contrast retained their national identity. In the 13th century, when the German Crusaders seized control of a large territory at the shore of the Baltic Sea (reaching approximately to where Latvia's Eastern boundary is located now), a boundary was drawn among the Baltic tribes, and the Balts lost the territory that was locate to the East of that line.

The Latvian nation was formed through a merger of the ancient Baltic tribes – Latgallians, Semigallians, Selonians and Courlandians, as well as the Finno-Ugric tribes – the Estonians and the Livonians. Of considerable importance in the emergence of the Latvian ethnos, too, were the various nations which crisscrossed Latvia with weapons and with goods for sale. In the first millennium BC there were colonies of Goths, Vikings, Russians and Danes in Latvia. Latgallians often went to war in Russia, while Courlandians pillaged coastal areas all around the Baltic Sea. In the 13th and 14th century, when soldiers from Germany, Denmark, Sweden and Lithuania were all present at various times in Latvia, there was a considerable mixing of the nations. Later Latvia's territory was crossed by Swedes, Saxons, Poles and Russians, as well as Mordovians and Tatars from the armies of the Russian Empire. French soldiers left their surnames to children in the 19th century, while the wars of the 20th century led to massive shifts in the Latvian population. All of these factors influenced the Latvian ethnos. Throughout the ages Riga has been an international city, one with a German majority until the 18th century and with a Russian majority at the end of the 20th century. The culture of these two nations has influenced not only public life and the economy, but also the language and culture of the Latvian nation.

Despite all of this, Latvians have managed to maintain their national identity, language, culture, folk songs, characteristics and life content in the face of multicultural pressure. In a book called *Lands and Nations* that was published in 1898, the German author wrote: "Through a few characteristics Latvians differ positively from Estonians. they beat the Estonians with their sharp and flexible minds, they are witty, good-hearted, hospitable and peaceful. Ongoing oppression, however, has left its mark on the Latvians. Their gentility and good-heartedness

often borders on weakness of character and a lack of will. The Latvian has become faithless, closed off and suspicious."

The most important thing which Latvia can bring to the world's culture and history is Latvianness. Latvians tend to be orderly, proper and consistent. Latvians are creative, hard-working, handsome, wise and merry. The Latvian folk songs list a number of Latvian virtues, first and foremost the virtue of hard work. Latvians are proud of work that has been done well and properly. Latvia's harsh climate and the battle of Latvians for many centuries for their very existence have created great working abilities and durability in Latvians. Latvians are honest workers who want to receive proper pay for the work which they do – in cash or in barter. Latvians hold three things holy – work, family and homeland. Latvians have a sense of obligation toward other people, including their parents and families. Latvians love their country, they are clean in flesh and clothing and they live in tidy homes. The Latvian tradition holds that the father does practical work and raises the children, while the mother in the family maintains and shapes the spiritual atmosphere of the family. Latvian colors are those of nature – the brown of the earth, the green of leaves, the changing blue of waters and clouds, the inconsistent gray of fog and rainy days. Latvians retain peace of heart and balance in nature.

The nature of the Latvian nation is inborn and passes from generation to generation. Of course, the characteristics of any nation change over the course of time, and people take on new characteristics, depending on the time and its circumstances. Under conditions of complete oppression, the nature of a nation shapes differently than is the case in freedom. Periods of rapid change are very dangerous for nations, because previous behavioral models can come into conflict with new situations. There can even be splits in the ethnos. Unlike other nations, Latvians have faced so many different periods of rapid change that they have become accustomed to adapting to change. What's more, Latvians seem never to have been fully prepared for a long period of peace and economic growth.

From a socioanthropological perspective Latvians are an open nation. They lack tolerance and they do not trust alien activities. The existence of Latvians to a certain extent is dictated by the fact that for millennia Latvians have held on to their land with such strength that no force has been able to chase them away. Latvians have chosen to suffer centuries of oppression rather than leave their land. There is no gold in this land, no jewels, no metal ore, no oil or coal. It is not particularly fertile land. People can carve out a living only through relentless work. This indicated that since ancient times Latvians have relied on their abilities and their hard work. These are the highest moral conclusions which a nation can achieve. Those who have these characteristics own land and history.

Over the course of the centuries, Latvians have transferred their understanding of life and their national philosophy through folk songs. The *dainas* reflect the spiritual treasures of the Latvian nation. Latvians – just a bit more than one million souls – have created more than 500,000 folk songs. Other nations around the Baltic sea had folk songs, but only Latvians

Male visitors of Latvia regardless the home-country admit that Latvian women are the most beautiful in the world.
Mrs. Globe '98 Ieva Bondare

maintained them in the oral tradition, transferring them from generation to generation. To a certain extent that is because between the 16th and 18th centuries the Latvian language was not particularly affected by the religious upheavals of the rest of Europe or by modern literature, which led to the death of folk songs in Germany, Sweden and Denmark under the burden of the printed word and the nihilistic approach of the church. It must also be said that the survival of the Latvian folk song to this very day can in large part be attributed to two amazing people who lived in the mid-19th century – Krišjanis Valdemārs and Krišjānis Barons. Valdemārs was an important economist in Russia, a father of maritime education and an advisor to Russia's financial system and the family of the tsar. Valdemārs understood the cultural and historical importance of the folk song. Barons was a pedantic, educated and creative man who systematized tens upon tens of thousands of folk songs and published them in a massive collection. The content of Latvianness can be found in the wisdom of the *dainas*, with their inner conviction in defense of the nation, the language and the people.

Latvians, unlike many other nations, always sing at various ceremonies. Ancient traditions of costumed festivals in the wintertime and vast celebrations at the summer solstice have been preserved. National food such as gray peas, rye bread, carrot rolls and porridge are given prominence at ceremonial events.

The centuries of oppression which the Latvian nation faced created a considerable amount of enviousness in the nation. Those people who have been torn from their land have always proven quite able to adapt to the market economy. Emigrants after World War II had no problem in integrating into the economic structures of the United States, England and Australia. One economic study said that of all of the nations that immigrated into the United States after World War II, the Latvians were second behind the Jews in terms of making a living and achieving public status. Those who have remained in Latvia have always had problems in achieving wealth, because over the centuries Latvians have constantly had to deal with war, revolutions and the violence of other nations. The best period for the Latvians was the early 19th century, when Latvians in Rīga became distinguished builders, industrialists and tradesmen. Kristaps Morbergs and Kristaps Bergs built some of the most outstanding buildings in Rīga's *Ring of Boulevards*, and many of them are now architectural monuments at the European scale.

During the 20th century Latvians did not really lose their yearning for, as one poet put it, "my corner, my piece of land". After the collapse of the Soviet Union, Latvians were less prepared for the market economy than were Russians, Jews and Belarussians in Latvia. Latvians continued to fight for their little gardens and farms.

For Latvians, faith is a deeply hidden and intimate matter, and they go to church rarely. Latvians do not demonstrate their religion theatrically – at best they fall to their knees in church. Latvians also hide their everyday emotions. Except for the legendary highway robber Kaupēns who in 1999 was immortalized in a musical play, there have been no famous cheats or robbers. Latvians usually resolve disputes calmly, and brutality is less common than among other nations. Fans at Latvian sporting events do not break their chairs or run out on the field to argue with the referee. Latvians will instead bang their drums to express their emotions in a more or less musical way.

Rīga could be considered a European capital in the field of chemistry. Scientific work which resulted in a Nobel Prize was done in Rīga by Swante Arrhenius and Wilhelm Oswald. Two others who were surely deserving of a Nobel Prize were Pauls Valdens and Gustavs Vanags, and one who did get the prize was the American inventor of the laser, Arthur Shawlow, who won the prize in physics in 1981. His parents emigrated from Latvia in 1905.

Latvia contributed the world of the permanent circus to Europe. A 10-year-old boy called Kristaps Bars ran away with the circus in Latvia and later, as *Christopher de Bach*, he established circuses in Vienna, Paris and Berlin. Rīga brought a new understanding of Art Nouveau into the world. No other city in the world can demonstrate such extensive and vivid Art Nouveau architecture. In 1510 Rīga was among the first cities to decorate a fir tree for Christmas. The world's leading encyclopedias cite Rīga as the place where the Christmas tree originated.

Latvians have survived 700 years of rule by German barons, 62 years, 200 years of rule by the Russian tsars, and 50 years of the Communist occupation.

The younger generation of Latvians has successfully integrated into the European educational system, economy and labor market. Books are gradually being replaced by the Internet. Young people are studying computer science and software design. Latvians speak foreign languages, and in place of the traditional German and Russian languages, English is now in vogue. When European Latvians are asked about what Latvianness is, they answer – a Latvian sense of life, folk songs, freedom, the Latvian language and song festivals. Latvians come together in song once every four years at the main stage in *Mežaparks* in Rīga. The choir movement has always been an important element of unification for the small Baltic nations, allowing them to express their identity in an alien and imposed cultural environment, to maintain self-understanding and to awaken pride among singers and audiences alike. The first song festival in *Dikļi* (1864) and the first national Latvian Song Festival in Rīga (1873) were symbols of the nation's community. At all song festivals, whether in Latvia or abroad, the folk song has been the nucleus around which the Latvian nation has been able to withstand the centrifugal force of time. Latvians have managed to preserve their traditions and the land, nation and state which we are proud to call – Latvia.

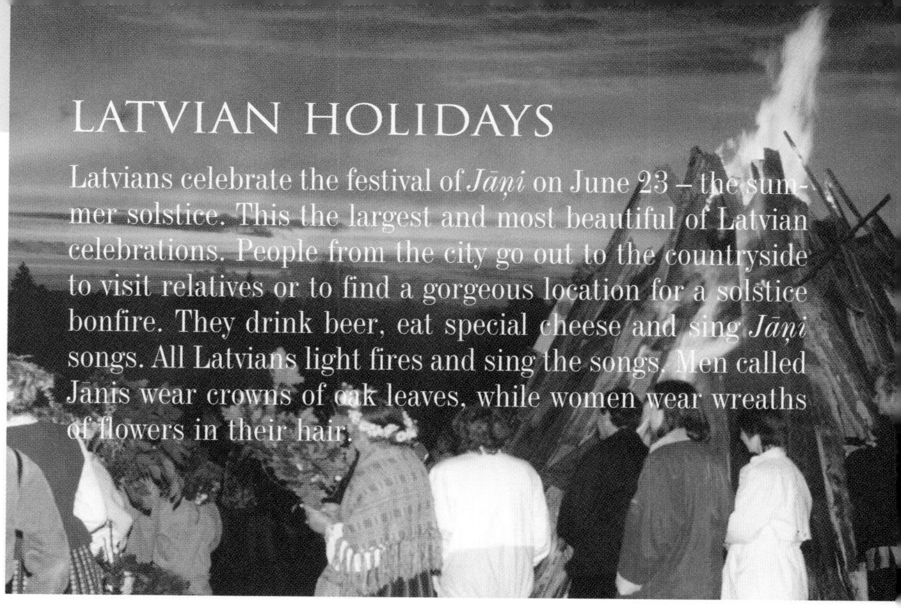

LATVIAN HOLIDAYS

Latvians celebrate the festival of *Jāņi* on June 23 – the summer solstice. This the largest and most beautiful of Latvian celebrations. People from the city go out to the countryside to visit relatives or to find a gorgeous location for a solstice bonfire. They drink beer, eat special cheese and sing *Jāņi* songs. All Latvians light fires and sing the songs. Men called Janis wear crowns of oak leaves, while women wear wreaths of flowers in their hair.

Despite the fact that Latvians have been subject to various forms of rule over the centuries, they have always preserved their holiday traditions. Among the most important festivals in the Latvian mentality are family celebrations and festivals held to mark the seasons of the year.

The most important festivals for Latvian families have traditionally been Christenings (when a baby gets his or her name), weddings and funerals. A person's life begins at birth and a ceremony to give him or her a name. Relatives near and far gather for this event, and godparents are chosen. The godfather and godmother lead the entire Christening ceremony. In ancient times there were as many as nine godparents for children – mostly godfathers for boys, mostly godmothers for girls. Godparents undertook to protect the interests of the child for the rest of their lives, especially if something happened to the parents. The most important elements of the Christening ceremony were the feast that was consumed and the ceremonial hanging of the baby's cradle. The basis for this celebration was a belief in the idea that rituals could have a favorable effect on the future life of the individual. People dressed in their finest clothes, decorated themselves with silver jewelry, set tables groaning under bountiful food and drink, celebrated with great joy, generosity and good-heartedness. All of this was supposed to guarantee a wealthy and happy life for the child. During ceremonial dances the baby was lifted toward the windows of the room and toward the table so that the life of the child might be full of light and generosity. The baby was lifted toward the sun so that he or she might grow up as loved, as sincere and as good as the sun.

Weddings, however, were truly the most ornate celebration for families over the centuries. Krišjānis Barons, in arranging Latvian folk songs, devoted a special place to wedding songs, bringing together traditions from various regions of Latvia and grouping folk songs that were relevant to the various aspects of courtship and marriage in three volumes.

Latvian wedding traditions even today maintain distant echoes from the past – the stealing of the bride, a *battle of songs* between the relatives of the bride and the relatives of the groom, the setting of a rich table at the home of the new husband. New families are celebrated with elements of a game. The young couple is ceremonially sent to bed for the wedding night. Before that there is a process known as *mičošana*, in which the crown which unmarried women traditionally wear in Latvian folk costumes is removed from the bride, to be replaced with the headscarf that is traditional for married women. The bride's dowry is inspected, and the skills of the bride and groom are tested in various activities.

Funeral traditions have to do with the relationship between life and death in Latvia. There are deeply philosophical and unusually harmonic ceremonies which relate to nature and eternity. Funeral ceremonies involve the imagined participation of the deceased person, with his or her relatives and friends engaging in a serious dialogue with the deceased person. Outward desperation and exaggerated sorrow are not the norm at Latvian funerals. Latvians speak of the deceased person with a good word, and funerals are strictly ritualized. Until the person is laid to rest in his or her grave, others listen to quiet music and to words of farewell from a clergyman or a lay person. The funeral concludes with a feast at the home of the person who has died, and the people who have remained behind reach the peaceful and philosophical understanding that the strength of life – the principle of activity and work – is incomparably more powerful than the weight of death.

Traditions which have to do with the seasons of the year in Latvia mark the paths of the sun and the moon, the most important times in a farmer's year, and hopes for success and welfare in the family, in the granary, the threshing barn, the livestock barn, the garden and the pasture. For centuries Latvians observed the uninterrupted rhythms of nature, and from these observations there came the traditions of feeding deceased relatives during the autumn season known as *veļi*, of greeting and honoring God on Christmas Eve, of watching the starry skies of the New Year carefully and then engaging in a loud celebration.

The traditions of Roman Catholicism have been brought together with ancient Latvian traditions at Easter and at the summer solstice. Latvians color eggs in a traditional way and set rich tables at Easter, and the main form of activity is swinging in a swing that is set up in every farmyard. The *Jāņi* festival of the summer solstice affirms the conclusion of the very active spring phase of farming and the launch of summer work. "Jāņi" is the most important celebration for Latvians, bringing them together to drink beer, eat special cheese, sing songs, leap across the fire and then go off two-by-two to seek the *fern blossom* of legend. It is said that the fern in the forest blossoms only during the night of *Jāņi*, and only for two people who are in love. People are not supposed to go to sleep before sunrise at *Jāņi*, because one who sleeps on *Jāņi* night will sleep throughout the summer, says tradition.

The *Mārtiņi* festival on November 10 allows Latvians to think back on the joys and difficulties of the past year. People work hard to finishing all of their outdoor and threshing work before the festival. After *Mārtiņi* comes the seasons of the winter solstice. Latvians participate in a process called *ķekatas* which involves dressing up as birds, bears, Gypsies, death itself, etc. Costumed people in the countryside go from house to house, demanding food and drink, dancing in the rooms of the house and chasing away evil spirits. *Ķekatas* are an ancient ritual which guarantees success in the following year.

The start of the *Jāņi* night festival on the shores of the *Daugava* River and near the ruins of the old Dinaburg castle

The archbishop of the Latvian Lutheran Church, Janis Vanags, with the oak-leaf crown that is worn by everyone called *Jānis* on the night of the summer solstice festival. Latvianness involves an understanding an love of the nation's traditions, as well as a Christian world view. Here the archbishop is being interviewed by Indira Ozola

In every farm, the host for the *Jāņi* festival becomes known as *Jāņu tēvs* (Father Janis), even if, as in this case, his real name is not Janis. This is sculptor Ojars Feldbergs who, as *Jāņu tēvs*, is destined to pour beer and treat the *Jāņu bērni* (*Jāņi* children) who have gathered at his home

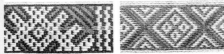

Liv ornamental designs. Latvian folk costumes represent a merger of Latvian and Liv national designs and colour senses.

This drawing by J.K. Brotze shows hired workers of various nationalities

This illustration shows residents of Riga in the late 18th century. From the left: A Greek woman; a saleswoman in typical garb; a Russian gardener; a farmwoman from the *Turkalne Ikšķiles* congregation. The drawing is by J.K. Brotze.

Residents of Riga in the late 18th century, as depicted by J.K. Brotze. From the left: a German trader; a German servant woman; a Jewish woman; the son of a Russian tradesman.

The first time that Latvian folk costumes were described in detail was in the work of Johann Christoph Brotze, who produced a 10-volume series on "monuments" in Latvia with a handwritten table of contents.

A young farm girl and an older married woman from *Lielvārde* in ceremonial folk costume. The married woman is the one with the cap. Drawing by J.K. Brotze.

Maruta Grasmane is the founder and director of *Sena klēts*

SENA KLĒTS ("THE ANCIENT GRANARY")

Latvian folk costumes are a unique aspect of the Latvian national heritage, comparable in importance to Latvian folk songs.

In order to preserve this treasure for future generations, the Latvian Folk Costume Research and Practical Manufacturing Centre *Sena klēts* was established in 1991. Support for the Centre was provided by the Latvian Cultural Fund and the Ministry of Culture. The centre produces ethnographically authentic folk costumes, using unique museum examples. Since 1991, the Centre has established a collection of folk costumes from all regions of Latvia, which form a permanent exhibition of folk costumes at its premises in Riga at *Kr. Barona iela* 28a. Enormous interest in the collection has been demonstrated both by Latvians and by people in other countries.

At *Sena klēts*, one can purchase a full folk costume from any region of Latvia or any part thereof. Wonderful presents – knitted mittens and socks, as well as ethnographic jewellery produced by masters of the art – are also available.

Sena klēts organises conferences, seminars, courses and lectures, and consultations are available to anyone interested in Latvian folk costumes. *Sena klēts* helps Latvians and others to study Latvia's cultural history, and this has a clearly positive influence on the present-day cultural environment in Latvia. The folk costumes that were photographed for this book all came from the collection. The models are the men and women of the Miss Latvia agency – the best-looking Latvian young people of the 1990s.

There are two kinds of Latvian folk costumes – archaeological ones and ethnographic ones. Archaeological folk costumes date back to from the 7th to the 13th centuries, when the territory that is now Latvia was populated by Baltic tribes – the Latgalls (Latgallians, Letts), the Kurs, the Semigallians, the Sels and a Finno-Ugric tribe - the Livs. Clothing has been found in burial grounds that have been discovered during archaeological digs. Thanks to heavy bronze ornamentation, some fragments of cloth have been preserved for centuries, and these fragments can be used to determine the materials from which clothing was made, the techniques that were used, and even the colours that were used.

There is very little information about clothing from the 13th to the 16th century. More concrete information is available about folk costumes from

Jete Užane, who lives in *Dzērbene*, knits splendid Latvian mittens.

the 16th to the 19th century – there are both drawings and written records. Ethnographic folk costumes are those which come from the 17th to the 19th century.

Latvian farmers were serfs during much of this period, and most people spent their entire lives in a specific part of the country. People made their own clothing from local materials and with relatively primitive tools. In such circumstances, each region of Latvia developed its own ethnographic traditions in terms of the cut of clothing, the composition of decorative elements, etc. Nature itself influenced the selection of colours.

Eventually five historical ethnographic regions emerged in Latvia – Vidzeme, Latgale, Augšzeme, Zemgale and Kurzeme – and each had its own type of clothing complex.

Vidzeme is the largest region in terms of folk costume design – there are six distinct folk costume areas here. Each area has unique and different folk costumes, and when such costumes are prepared and worn today, the respective traditions must be observed.

In Latgale, specific aspects in folk costume design have survived around the cities of *Daugavpils*, *Rēzekne* and *Ludza*. Older traditions concerning the wearing of folk costumes such as the fact that jackets or bodices are not worn with ceremonial costumes have also been preserved.

Folk costumes in Kurzeme can be divided into nine distinct ethnographic areas. This is also the region in which the oldest types of clothing and ornamentation, such as shawls with metal ornaments, are still used today. Here, too, long-standing traditions were preserved for centuries. Even as late as in the 1950s women in central Kurzeme wore their folk costumes when they went to church.

In the 1920s, folk costumes became a sign of "Latvianness" and national pride. Latvian women wore their folk costumes not only at Song Festivals and such, but also when they went to church and to celebrations at the homes of friends and relatives.

During the Soviet occupation, Latvian folk costumes were used for propaganda purposes to demonstrate the "care" which the Communists had for Latvia's national culture. Stylised forms of folk costumes were developed. Such folk costumes were used for various ceremonies such as the event in this photograph, the young people are greeting the best workers from the *kolhoze*.

In the 1970s, Latvian girls wearing colourful Latvian folk costumes marched at the head of parades at propaganda-based ceremonies honouring the October Revolution and the first of May.

Song festivals allowed Latvians to preserve their national identity. Latvians are proud of their regional folk costumes, and choirs always perform in their local regional folk costumes.

The largest collection of regional folk costumes in Latvia is found at the Latvian Museum of History, which is located in the Riga Castle.

The folk costumes of Augšzeme were worn in the land of the Sels on the left shore of the *Daugava*, where the *Ilukste* and *Jēkabpils* districts are located today. Red striped skirts were given a white sparkle through white yarn woven into the cloth. An ornate shawl typical of Eastern Latvia was worn on ceremonial occasions. Married women wore a complex head cover that was 4 meters long. Unmarried women wore a unique crown of acorns with red woven roses. Similar crowns have not been found anywhere else in Latvia.

The region of Northern Latgale – the *Abrene*, *Balvi* and *Viļaka* districts. This is the only one of Latvia's traditional folk costumes where wool from a sheep has maintained its white colour throughout the costume. Woven patterns decorate the bottom of the skirt with flax thread lace and woven red lines.

An archaeological folk costume from Latgale, 10th-13th century

An archaeological costume of a Liv woman, 10th-13th century

The most ornate shawls in all Latvia were found in the *Krustpils* district, and the lovely design still serves as a textbook example on composition and mastery in weaving. The basic principles of these woven patterns can also be found in other areas of Eastern Latvia.

These Latgale costume complexes in Eastern Latvia can be divided into two specific regions. Latgale is farthest away from the sea and from traditional trade centres in Latvia, and ancient traditions persisted longer there. The head covers of married women – complexly tied – as well as delicate and very ornate Eastern Latvian shawls attest to this.

The district around the town of *Lielvārde* is renowned for its unique, four-meter woven belt, in which no single design element is repeated more than once. Ethnographic specialists have long been interested in unravelling the mysteries of these lovely belts. *Lielvārde* women wore extremely ornate bride's shirts with approximately 365 star designs. These designs, too, have never fully been explained.

These folk costume complexes from Zemgale were worn in the *Jelgava* and *Bauska* districts. These were particularly ornate costumes, especially the skirts with flower patterns or large checks and tree motifs. The elaborate design of shirts worn with the costumes, which involves very difficult sewing techniques, is not seen anywhere else in Latvia. Also unique are the decorations on the shawls worn in this region. Silver jewellery was very popular in Zemgale.

Costumes from the Western Vidzeme region were worn around Riga, *Cesis* and *Valmiera*. The development of these costumes was influenced by Riga's status as a centre for trade and craftsmanship. A white shawl was soon replaced with a silken one, and aprons replaced belts.

In the Northern Vidzeme districts of *Valka* and *Valmiera*, women wore unique short jackets with small "ears" on the back. Estonian influences, especially stylised depictions of flowers, can be seen in head covers — especially the hair ribbons of unmarried girls and the caps of married women.

Winter folk costumes from Northern Vidzeme

Folk costumes from the centre of the *Piebalga* district — *Vecpiebalga* and *Jaunpiebalga* — were very simple with extremely long shawls. Black was a common colour in skirts, caps and other elements of the costumes.

Northern Vidzeme region folk costumes

Costumes from the *Madona* district of Eastern Vidzeme. Skirts were ornately patterned. The skirt that looks crosshatched is unique, because the folds of the skirt hide square designs. The round hats of women are thought to be the most ancient element in these costumes. Visually these are reminiscent of the round crowns that were worn by unmarried girls.

Folk costumes from the *Dienvidtirza, Alūksne* and *Jaungulbene* districts of Northern Vidzeme

Northern Kurzeme folk costumes were worn in the northern parts of the *Talsi* and *Ventspils* districts. This is a coastal region long populated by Livs. Liv costumes are reticent, with few decorations. Women wore a unique, two-part head cover because it was considered dishonourable for a Liv woman to appear in public with her chin revealed. Northern Kurzeme was home both to Latvians and Livs, and the two types of costumes display mutual influences. The lines in Northern Kurzeme skirts are wider and brighter than in other places, because that part of the country picked up the use of chemical dyes faster than did other parts of the country. The white shawls have little decoration, but women often wore brightly coloured scarves with great pride

Folk costumes from the district of *Ventspils* were distinguished by the simultaneous wearing of several shawls — a dark blue one with bronze ornaments on the bottom and a white ceremonial shawl on top. In cold weather older women sometimes wore a third shawl, too. All of the shawls were fastened in front with a large, ornate brooch. The unique bodice skirt with its high waist was fastened with a metal belt.

The *Alsunga* district is on the sea and includes the northern parts of the *Aizpute* district. These costumes have an interesting history. In the 17th century, a rich Polish woman married into an *Alsunga* family, bringing along her servants and craftsmen. She was responsible for the arrival of red skirts, specific types of blouse collars and armbands of great colour. Women in the region wore several shawls, of which the upper one is most interesting. The vivid checks on the shawl led it to be known popularly as "crazy cloth". An unusually elaborate headdress was worn by women —a small, flowered woven cap with two silk scarves tied on top. This is the only district of Kurzeme where woven belts survived

Kuldiga district folk costumes were found in the western part of the region. The unique aspect of the costumes — extremely elaborate shirts, several shawls and — for unmarried women — metal crowns

Southern Kurzeme folk costumes were worn in the *Liepaja* region, and traditions there are not as uniform as is the case in other parts of Kurzeme. Costumes worn around *Vainode*, *Kaleti*, *Asite* and *Perkone* are quite similar to costumes from Eastern Kurzeme. *Nica*, *Barta* and *Rucava* parish costumes were particularly unique, so ethnographic specialists consider them to be individual districts

Costumes from the Eastern Kurzeme region were worn around *Kuldiga*, *Aizpute* and the eastern parts of the *Liepaja* district. They are very similar to Northern Kurzeme costumes. Their specific aspect — new techniques used in the decoration of caps and shirts, including crocheting.

Nica district costumes were worn in the parish of the same name. They are among the most vivid of Latvian folk costumes, with colourful skirts, an ornate shawl connected to the right shoulder of the wearer with a "pile" of brooches, the high crown of an unmarried woman decorated with brocade ribbons and glass pearls — all of this has long since made the *Nica* costume one of Latvia's most popular

Barta region costumes were distinguished by the way in which shawls were worn — connected on the right shoulder by a "pile" of brooches, and passing the shawl under the left arm. A simple black skirt with a red bottom and a jacket decorated with red brocade ribbons — these made the *Barta* folk costume different from any other. Shirts were decorated with elaborate ornaments of black thread

Folk costumes in the *Rucava* district were covered with three shawls. The first was a white sewn shawl, the second was a checked shawl, and the third was a roughly women one. The three shawls were gathered at the waist so that the tops reached just below the wearer's breasts, and at the side they were fastened with a "pile" of brooches held up by the elbow of the right arm. *Rucava* women wore particularly ornate blouses, and their headdress was unusual

THE LATVIAN LANGUAGE

Dr. Juris Bārs
(1808 – 1879)

Kārlis Mīlenbahs
(1853 – 1916)

Jānis Endzelīns
(1873 – 1961)

Jānis Loja, Sr.
(1896 – 1969)

Marta Rudzīte
(1924 – 1996)

The Latvian language is the official language in the Republic of Latvia. It is an Indo-European language which, together with the Lithuanian language and the Ancient Prussian language that disappeared in the 17th century, makes up the Baltic group of languages.

There are approximately 1,565,000 ethnic Latvians in the world, according to the 1989 census of the USSR – 1,388,000 in Latvia, 47,000 in the Russian Federation, 7,000 in the Ukraine, 4,000 in Lithuania and 3,000 apiece in Estonia, Belarus and Kazakhstan. Elsewhere in the world, there are some 110,000 persons of ethnic Latvian descent.

The Latvian language emerged from the languages of the ancient Baltic tribes – the Latgalls (Latgallians, Letts), the Semigallians, the Sels and the Kurs. The Latvian language has also been influenced strongly by the Liv language – one of the Baltic Finnish languages that served as the foundation for the formation of the modern-day Liv dialect.

The Lithuanian language is older than the Latvian language, and the latter language has many new elements. The Latvian language has sounds and forms, which mostly developed from those sounds and forms that exist in the Lithuanian language to this very day.

Most of the sounds in the Latvian language have been inherited from other languages, and there are both short and long vowels. The short vowels that used to appear in the final syllables of Latvian words, except for *u*, have disappeared, long vowels have been shortened, diphthongs have become simple vowels, and the diphthongal combinations *an*, *en*, *in* and *un* have become *uo*, *ie*, *ī*, and *ū*, respectively. The most ancient Baltic consonants, *š* and *ž*, correspond to the sounds *s* and *z* in the Latvian language. Latvian has both a broad and a slender pronunciation for the letters *e* and *ē*; there are no nasal vowels or aspirated consonants. There is also a specific group of consonants pronounced with the tongue against the roof of the mouth – *ķ*, *ģ*, *ļ*, *ņ* and *ŗ*. The consonants *f*, *h*, and *ch* are found only in derivations of foreign words.

The vast majority of Latvian words are stressed on the first syllable. There is no neuter gender, no duals, and the old degrees of comparison of adjectives have been replaced with new forms. Adjectives have both a definite and an indefinite form. The Latvian language has a variety of forms of declination, including many prefixes and suffixes. The genitive form also has an ablative function. Verbs can be expressed in the present, the past and the future, in simple and perfect forms. The conjugation of verbs is the same in the third person singular and the third person plural (viņš, viņa, viņi, viņas *iet* – meaning he goes, she goes, they (men) go and they (women) go). There is a debitive mood – *jāiet* (I must go) and, as in the Lithuanian language, a subjunctive mood – *ietu* (I would go). There are many participles, some of which can be declined and some of which cannot – *ejošs* (going, as in "I am going now"), *ejot* (while going, as in "While going, he sang a song"), *ejams* (to go, as in "There is still a long way to go"), *iedams* (similar to *ejot* – "While he was going, he…"), *iets* (has been walked, as in "A long way has been walked"), *iešot* (claimed going, as in "He says he is going tomorrow"), and *gājis* (a form meaning has gone). The Latvian language makes it possible to express oneself briefly and precisely, and the same phrase in Latvian takes up much less room than it does in German or Russian.

Closest to the Baltic languages are the Slavic languages. The influence of the Russian language is felt in borrowed words, most of them very old indeed – *bagāts* (rich), *baznīca* (church), *dabūt* (to obtain), *gads* (year), *grēks* (sin), *kristīt* (to christen), *nedēļa* (week), *sods* (punishment), *strādāt* (to work), *svētki* (holiday, festival). The Slavic languages – Russian, Polish and Belarussian, have had a strong influence on the phonetics, vocabulary and morphology of the Latvian language in the broad territory in which the *augšzemnieku* ("High") dialect of the language was developed.

Latvians and Livs have long lived together, and there has been a melding of the two languages to a certain extent. Some 80 modern Latvian words originated in the Liv or Estonian languages – *allaž* (always), *Jelgava* (the name of a city, which in Latvian was known as *Mītava*), *joma* (area, as in area of activity), *kaija* (seagull), *kāzas* (wedding), *laulāt* (to wed), *liedags* (beach), *loms* (catch, as in a good catch of fish), *paisums* (high tide), *pīlādzis* (mountain ash – the tree), *puisis* (young man), *puķe* (flower), *selga* (the open sea), *sēne* (mushroom), *vaba* (pole or stake), *vimba* (a species of fish), etc.

The Germanic languages have also had an important impact on the Latvian language. The earliest Germans to arrive in Latvia before and during the Crusades spoke Middle Low German, and from them the Latvian language obtained such words as *āmurs* (hammer), *bāka* (lighthouse), *bikses* (trousers), *brīvs* (free), *brokastis* (breakfast), *bumbieris* (pear), *dambis* (dam), *ēvele* (plane – the carpentry tool), *grāvis* (ditch), *kastrolis* (pot – for cooking), *kleita* (dress – the woman's garment), *krelles* (necklace), *krūze* (cup), *ķemme* (comb), *lievenis* (porch), *līme* (glue), *masalas* (measles), *mērkaķis* (monkey), *nagla* (nail), *odere* (lining – of apparel), *zāģis* (saw – the tool) and *zārks* (coffin). Later the Latvian language adopted words from modern High German, but most of these were later declared "barbarisms" and replaced with proper Latvian words. A few of these words refused to die out, however, including *feldšeris* (a medical profession similar to a paramedic), *grants* (gravel), *šachta* (shaft) and *štābs* (headquarters), for example.

There are three dialects in Latvian – the Central, the Liv, and the *augšzemnieku* dialect, which can be divided into 512 sub-dialects. These sub-dialects are classified in sub-dialect groups – Kurian, Latgallian, Livian, Selian, Tamnian (a word used to describe one part of the Liv dialect in Northern Kurzeme; prior to the 20th century, the word *tāmnieki* was used to describe all Livs), and Semigallian. The Central dialect is at the basis of the literary Latvian language, because it has best preserved the most ancient sounds of the Latvian language, as well as the three intonations that are used in the language – the stretched, the broken and the falling intonation. The *augšzemnieku* dialect features a great many phonetic transformations, words and morphological specifics. In the Liv dialect, short vowels in final syllables have disappeared, and the male gender is often used in place of the female gender. Latvian is an inflected language with several analytical forms. There are 50 phonemes – 12 vowels, 10 diphthongs and 28 consonants.

Some Latvian names, especially the names of people and places, have been found in chronicles and in historical documents in other languages since the 13th century. The first book in the Latvian language that has survived to this day was printed in 1585. The written Latvian language can be divided into three phases – the Old Latvian (from the 16th to the 18th century), the New Latvian (from the mid-19th century to the 1880s), and the modern literary phase (from the late 1880s and early 1890s to the present day).

The first authors (or, to put it more precisely, translators) of Latvian texts were German clergymen, and the "Latvian language" which they wrote was a fairly erroneous language strongly influenced by the orthography of Middle Low German. Gothic letters were used in printed texts, while Latin letters were used in handwritten texts. In the 16th century, written Latvian was close to the Central dialect, reflecting the language that was mostly spoken in Riga.

In the 17th century, the Baltic German writer and theologian Georg Mancelius transformed the written Latvian language based on the High German orthography, introducing the principles of etymology into the process. He marked the short vowels in final syllables in accordance with their pronunciation, indicated long vowels by adding an *h* after the vowel, designated palatalised consonants by crossing the respective letter with the line, marked some sibilants and affricatives with the so-called "heap letters", and differentiated between the slender and the broad *e* (*e* and *ä* or *ae*). Mancelius used the Semigallian versions of the Central dialect as the foundation for the written language. The orthography that he developed survived, with a few changes, for more than 200 years.

Until the mid-19th century, the written Latvian language which German clergymen used, when compared to the people's language as revealed in folklore, was much poorer and alien – similar to a bad translation today.

In 1847, a *Dundaga* physician, Juris Bārs, proposed a significant change in orthography. He recommended that Latin letters be used in printed versions of texts, that the "heap letters" be abandoned in designating a single sound, that long vowels should be signified with a horizontal line atop of the letter, and that the sibilants *š*, *ž* and the affricative *č* be written with a small hook above the letter. Bārs also recommended that no written differentiation be made between the slender and the broad *e* and *ē*.

The so-called New Latvians laid the foundation for modern Latvian literary language. They rejected unnecessary borrowed words (which they called "barbarisms"), developed new words, introduced various international words, and brought the written Latvian language closer to the popularly spoken language. The views of the New Latvians were reflected in the work of the writer Juris Alunāns, who produced the book "Songs Translated for the Latvian Language" in 1856, as well as a series of articles about language, in a collection of articles called "Household, Nature and the World" (1859-1960), and in the newspaper *Pēterburgas Avīzes* (1862-1865). Latvian writers proved that Latvian was a cultural language with an artistic form that could be used to express any concept and image, as well as the conclusions and concepts of science in every area of life. Alunāns coined a number of new words that have survived to this very day – *ārzemes* (foreign countries), *atkārtot* (to repeat), *burts* (letter, as in the letters of the alphabet), *ceļinieks* (traveller), *cilvēcība* (humanity), *dziesminieks* (bard, singer), *dzimte* (gender), *kareivis* (soldier, warrior), *rokraksts* (handwriting), *veikals* (shop), the names of the months, starting with *janvāris* (January), the names of many countries, including *Anglija* (England) – all ending with the suffix *-ija*, etc. Another of the New Latvians, Atis Kronvalds, was responsible for *aizbildnis* (guardian), *burtnīca* (notebook), *izglītība* (education), *izloksne* (sub-dialect), *līdzeklis* (resource), *nākotne* (future), *pagātne* (past), *priekšmets* (object, as in "That object is a chair"), *pilsonis* (citizen), *skābeklis* (oxygen), *varonis* (hero), *vēstule* (letter), *zīmulis* (pencil), *zinātne* (science), etc.

The New Latvians sustained the idea that Latin letters should be used in written Latvian. Kronvalds felt that the Latvians should create their own, appropriate orthography instead of borrowing principles from other languages.

In the 19th century, several authors promoted the use of the Russian alphabet for the Latvian language. A Latvian primer with Russian letters was published in Vilnius in 1864, and calendars with Russian letters were published in Vilnius, Moscow and Riga alike. The same can be said of a collection of Latvian folk songs by Jānis Sproģis and several other books. After World War II, in addition, there were efforts to impose the Russian alphabet on the Latvian language, but luckily, these efforts did not succeed.

When the modern phase of the literary language developed, the Latvian written language – largely corresponding to spoken language – was in place. The language developed along with society. A great deal of help in the development of the written language was provided by authors such as Reinis and Matīss Kaudzīte, Apsīšu Jēkabs, Rudolfs Blaumanis, Eduards Veidenbaums, Anna Brigadere, Jēkabs Janševskis, Andrievs Niedra, Rainis and Andrejs Upītis. Rainis alone was responsible for a number of words that are used today, many of them poetic derivations of other words – *atjaunināt* (to renew), *atveldze* (relief), *augsme* (growth), *ausma* (sunrise), *brīve* (freedom), *dāsns* (generous), *degsme* (eagerness), *dvesma* (breeze), *dziņa* (passion), *ilgas* (yearning), *malds* (erroneous temptation), *plūsma* (flow), etc.

In 1876, the Riga Latvian Society set up the first Latvian orthography commission, which partially supported the proposals by Bārs previously referred to. In 1907, Kārlis Mīlenbahs and Jānis Endzelīns published a Latvian grammar, which addressed literary language forms and constructions, and also made it quite clear to readers which forms and words should *not* be used.

Modern Latvian orthography was adopted in 1908 by the second orthography commission of the Riga Latvian Society, although the orthography was fully put into practice only in the 1920s. In order to reflect the phonemes of the Latvian language, Latin letters were supplemented with several diacritical marks – a small hook above sibilants (which is derived from the Czech language and is also used in Lithuanian, Slovenian, Croatian and other languages), a horizontal line to indicate long vowels, etc. Palatalised consonants were marked with a comma under the letter – something that is found only in the Latvian language.

There are also a few departures from the principle of rationality in the Latvian alphabet. Although generally speaking each phoneme has a letter and each letter has

Janis Loja, Jr.

Rasma Grisle

only one proper pronunciation, there are exceptions. The letter *o* is used to designate the diphthong *uo*, as well as the short and long vowel *o* and *ō*; the letters *e* and *ē* refer to both the broad and the slender pronunciation of the two letters; and two letters are used to designate the affricatives *dz* and *dž* and the palatal fricative *ch*.

Although the work which Endzelins did between the 1920s and the 1940s on the Latvian written language was outstanding work, the effect has been spoiled by several thoughtless periods of reform in 1938, 1946 and 1957, when the palatalised letter *ŗ*, the combination *ch* and the letter *ō*, for the long *o*, were rejected. There are now basically two systems of writing. One was used until 1946 in Latvia and is still used both sporadically in Latvia and in much of the writing of the émigré Latvians; it involves a pronunciation of international words as closely as possible to the Greek and Latin pronunciations of the words from which they are derived and the use of *ch*, *ŗ* and *ō* in pursuit of this. This form is used in the Latvian language dictionary that was published in the United States in 1993. The second system is the one that is in official use in Latvia today. It was adopted in 1957 and is reflected, e.g., in the orthographic and orthoepic dictionary of the Latvian language published in 1995.

A second written language – the Latgallian written language – emerged in the 18th century based on the *augšzemnieku* dialect of the Latvian language. The first known publication in Latgallian was a Catholic hymnbook in 1730. The Latgallian written language books were usually printed in Latin letters with elements of Polish orthography, such as *sz* for *š*. Until 1865, most of the books that were published in Latgallian were religious publications, as well as grammars and primers.

After the crushing of revolts in Poland in 1863 and 1864, tsarist Russia imposed restrictions on printed materials which included the rule that in the Vitebsk Province, of which Latgale was part, no books, newspapers or magazines could be printed in the Latgallian language with Latin letters – Russian letters had to be used instead. Schools in what is now the Latgale region of Latvia used only the Russian language in lessons. The goal of the Russian Empire was complete russification of the Latgalians. Censors in the Baltic region were ordered to prohibit all books in the Latgallian language. For 40 years, the region made do with books that had been published in earlier times. There were people who copied entire books by hand, as well as secret publishing houses in Helsinki, Klaipeda and St. Petersburg that, over the course of 40 years, produced an equal number of clandestinely published books.

In 1900, one Francis Trasuns published a Catholic calendar in Latgallian using Latin letters, but a true renaissance in Latgallian writing occurred only in 1904, when the ban on Latgallian publications was lifted. Francis Kemps published the "*Daugava* Calendar", which was printed by one Janis Ozols in Cesis. The calendar proved enormously popular, and income from it was such that Kemps could begin publishing the newspaper *Gaisma* (Light), which was published in 1905 and 1906.

After the lifting of the publication ban, books, newspapers and magazines could once again be printed in the Latgallian written language. The principles of the written language were revised several times, most recently between 1927 and 1929, when the Latgallian Orthography Commission met to do its work. The use of the Latgallian written language ceased in Latvia in 1958, and it was only in the late 1980s, when the Popular awakening began, that it once again appeared in books, newspapers and magazines.

During the first period of Latvian independence, from 1920 to 1940, the Latvian language became the source of communication, both written and spoken, in all areas of life. A dictionary of scientific terminology with some 7,000 entries was published in 1922. In the 1930s, there were terminological dictionaries in such areas of activity as anatomy, construction, trade, mathematics, physics, cosmography, civil law, electrical engineering, etc. Of fundamental importance in the development of the Latvian language was the four-volume dictionary of the language that was begun by Milenbachs and then continued, supplemented and edited by Endzelins between 1923 and 1932. Later Endzelins and E. Hauzenberga supplemented and revised the dictionary twice – in 1934 and in 1946. The dictionary stands to this very day as a masterpiece of Latvian lexicography. It is both a Latvian-German dictionary and an explanatory dictionary with beautifully written definitions and examples. It is a dictionary of the norms of the literary language of the day, a dictionary of toponyms, a dictionary of proper pronunciation and an etymological dictionary.

An academically produced grammar of the Latvian language appeared in 1922 (*Lettische Grammatik*). The author, Janis Endzelins, also proposed a series of new words such as *aptumsums* (darkening or eclipse), *attieksme* (attitude), *dotumi* (skills, abilities), *ietekme* (influence), *izcils* (outstanding), *labestība* (kindness), *laimests* (prize) and *senisks* (ancient).

Lessons in schools and at universities were taught in Latvian, and the Latvian language was a specific subject of study. A Baltic Philology Department was established at the University of Latvia in 1920, and under Endzelins' leadership it trained distinguished teachers and linguists. The number of people who used proper, literary Latvian increased all the time, and government policies were aimed at encouraging this. On 5 January, 1935, a law On the official language was adopted.

The fate of the Latvian language after the Soviet occupation of 1940 has been contradictory indeed. In 1940 and 1941, there were no significant changes to the language. During the Nazi occupation, in 1942 and 1944, two editions of a dictionary focused on the proper written Latvian language were published, and these put an end to debates about the proper writing of various foreign words. However, then came a decision by the Council of Ministers of the Latvian SSR on 5 June, 1946, which had a highly deleterious effect on the way in which the Latvian language is written. The letter *ŗ* was eliminated, as was the marking of long vowels in most foreign words.

During Stalin's rule, there was an active fight against "Bourgeois Nationalism", and the lifelong work of Janis Endzelins – a rich and proper Latvian language – was scorned and damaged. Endzelins was fired from the university in April 1950, his Baltic Philology Department was closed, and his students were persecuted.

The Soviet Union and the Communist Party were two-faced about language issues. There were constant articles in the press, which praised the blooming of the Latvian language in the community of brotherly nations during the period of Communism, and the great and lively influence of the Russian nation and its language on the Latvian language was proclaimed. In truth, however, the situation was quite different. As large numbers of Russian-speaking colonists flowed into Latvia, the Latvian language quickly disappeared from official documents, correspondence and various meetings. In order to promote "the brotherhood of the peoples", mixed language schools were set up, and Latvians were invariably in the minority in these schools. In Latgale even today, there are civil parishes in which there are no Latvian schools, and Latvian children are forced to study at Russian language schools.

The Latvian language was taught insufficiently in schools – much less than the Russian language. Latvian language textbooks were so complicated that students came to hate their native language. In many areas of science, it was possible to publish only in Russian. Many university instructors who arrived from other Soviet republics made no effort at all to learn the Latvian language, and students at such institutions as the Riga Institute of Medicine had to study and take their examinations in Russian. The height of this absurdity came in the 1980s, when the leadership of the medical institute ordered that Latvian instructors deliver lectures to Latvian students in Russian so that graduates could work in any corner of the Soviet land. No such procedure existed in Lithuania, Estonia or any other university in Latvia.

The goal of the Soviet occupants was to ensure that Latvian would be a form of communication only in the family. Russification was a banned word, and any talk of such a process was hotly denied. Latvians, according to Soviet propaganda, freely chose Russian as their language for "international communication".

The Russian language had a negative effect on the Latvian language – a number of barbarisms entered the language, but that was the least of it, because barbarisms can quickly be spotted and rooted out. Far worse were the many "new" words that appeared in Latvian as direct derivations from Russian – *aizrobežu* instead of *ārzemju* for foreign (the latter means "of foreign lands", while the former is a direct translation of the Russian word for "beyond the borders"), *atgriezt* instead of *atdot* for to give back, etc. The Russian language has also contributed to shifts in the way Latvian is pronounced (especially in terms of an excessively hard *l* and *i*), as well as in syntax (improper order of words in sentences).

Despite this, the Latvian language has survived. The Academy of Sciences of the Latvian SSR was established in 1946, and it had an Institute of Language and Literature (today it is known as the Institute of Latvian Language of the University of Latvia). Several important books were published – an introduction to Baltic philology (1945), a book on the sounds and forms of the Baltic languages (1948), a Latvian grammar (1951), and a dictionary of toponyms in the Latvian SSR in two volumes (1956 and 1961) by Janis Endzelins, as well as a modern grammar of the literary Latvian language in two volumes (1959 and 1962), and a dictionary of the Latvian literary language in eight volumes (1972-1996). A terminology commission was set up at the Academy of Sciences, and Rasma Grisle of that Commission has suggested a number of new words such as *spriedze* (tension), *mazspēja* (failure, as in heart failure) and others. The writer Zigmunds Skujiņš is the author of *vaļasprieks* for hobby and *tālrāde* and *tāldzirde* for television and radio, although the latter two words have never really caught on.

On 26 December, 1957, the Council of Ministers of the Latvian SSR once again tinkered with the written Latvian language, reinstating the use of long vowels in foreign words, but rejecting the use of *ch* unless it was used to designate two specific sounds, as in the word *Chinvali*. A vowel in an emphasised syllable in a foreign word, when pronounced with the Russian emphasis, was compared to a long vowel in the Latvian language, and this led to a series of vowel uses that were not typical in the pre-war literary Latvian language – the word for literary person, for example, is *literāts*, while the word for literature is *literatūra* – the long and the short *a*, respectively. The same is true with *revolucionārs* (revolutionary) and *revolūcija* (revolution).

The Latvian language was taught in Russian language schools both insufficiently and, in many instances, at a very poor quality. There was no real reason for Russians to learn the Latvian language anyway, because they could make do perfectly well and in all instances with their own language. The idea of proletarian internationalism and bilingualism, it seems, applied only to Latvians.

At the turn of the millennium, there are still many thousands of people to the East of Latvia – in the former territory of the USSR – who consider themselves to be Latvians. The 1989 census of the Soviet Union showed that there were 46,000 ethnic Latvians in Russia. One half of them considered themselves to be Latvians, but only one-quarter could speak the Latvian language. This large number of people are not only those living in organised colonies of Latvians in Bashkiri, Georgia and the *Omsk*, *Tomsk* and *Krasnojarsk* districts of the Russian Federation, but also those Russian and former Soviet Union citizens living in many other large cities and remote corners of the rural tundra and taiga.

In 1776, when the Russian Tsar travelled through Vidzeme, farmers near *Cēsis* and *Valmiera* asked him to protect them from the violence of German landlords. In response, the landlords punished the complainers, and they were sent in chains to Siberia in 1777, forced to walk all the way. After a few months of torturous travel they ended up in a town called *Tobolsk*, which was already a prominent place for deportation under the reign of Peter the Great, Empress Elizabeth and Catherine the Great.

The first colony of Latvians in Siberia emerged in 1802 in *Rizhkov*, which is now a village in the *Krutinka* region of the *Omsk* district. Taking advantage of a law on colonisation of the Trans-Baikal region of Russia, the Lutheran pastor of *Tobolsk* asked that a colony be set up for the Lutherans of the town. Later *Rizhkov* became the home of revolutionaries and people convicted of crimes in the territory of Latvia. Eventually the population ballooned to the point where the local land could no longer sustain everyone, so a new colony was set up in what is now the *Krasnojarsk* district – *Lejas Bulāna*.

The number of Latvian colonies in Russia increased in the late 19th century, when during a phase of agricultural reform, the Tsar's government encouraged people to take over untouched areas of land. Many servants, as well as younger children in large households who had no prospect of obtaining land at home, left their homes and took over freely available land, first in Latvia itself, but later also in all of Russia, including Siberia and the Far East. There were some 600 larger and smaller Latvian colonies in Russia in 1914. After 1905, revolutionaries who had participated in the revolution of that year and were either deported or went into voluntary exile also arrived at the colonies.

On the eve of World War I, there were more than 200,000 Latvians and their descendants in the territory of Russia. Beginning in 1915, their number was doubled by World War I

refugees from Latvia. When the independent Latvian state was established, Latvia and Russia concluded an agreement on the repatriation of refugees, and between 1919 and 1927 Latvia registered 223,572 people who came home from Russia. In a 1926 census, Russia found 151,500 people who identified themselves as Latvian, and more than 200,000 Latvians were registered in all of the Soviet Union. Some 50,000 people from Latgale were probably not included in that number.

The period after World War I was particularly important in terms of the development of major Latvian colonies. After the Bolshevik revolution, many men from the legendary Latvian Riflemen's Divisions remained in Russia. They were given important government posts or made leaders of industrial factories, and they helped to shore up Soviet authority in the more remote regions of Russia. Revolutionaries who had been deported in 1905 and refugees from 1915 differed from other residents of Russia in that they were well educated, knew foreign languages and were hard workers by nature. Prior to the revolution, the Latvians who lived in small colonies in Russia were seen by local authorities as the successors of Finns or Germans. As the Latvian Riflemen proved their heroism during the October Revolution, however, Latvians were emboldened to declare themselves as such. The economic and social activity of Latvian colonists, never idle to begin with, increased even more during this period. Among Latvians there were many shopkeepers and tailors. Contemporaries reported that Latvians were much more likely to be engaged in such work in Siberia than Jews or Poles – nations known for their affinity for trading. The first private dairies in Russia, for example, were all founded by Latvians.

In 1933/1934, there were 119 Latvian language schools, including 17 high schools, in the territory of the USSR. In 70 schools lessons were taught in the Latgale dialect of Latvian. There was a Latvian sector at the Moscow University for Western Nations, and a Latvian pedagogical school existed in Leningrad. Another pedagogical school was located in *Achinsk*, while an agricultural technical college in *Bitz* had a Latvian sector, as well. In 1936, Latvians had 173 educational institutions in the USSR.

Prior to 1936, there were several publishing houses in Russia that specialised in Latvian books and newspapers. Periodicals were also ordered from Latvia.

Because Latvians were highly educated, many were appointed to senior posts. In many places Latvians supervised the highly lucrative businesses of gold and diamond mining. In many villages there were well-developed small industrial facilities and crafts shops, and export goods were produced of a high quality. Agriculture was very well developed among Latvians, who used progressive management methods and the latest equipment. Some Latvian villages even had electricity produced with steam engines. Latvians also made an important contribution to the colonising of the Far North of Russia. One Eduards Bērziņš

arrived at the Bay of Nagajev in 1932, and his company, *Dalstroj*, did much of the construction work of the new city of *Magadan* and the Kolim highway. Indeed, before Stalin began his "reforms" and his "ethnic cleansing", Latvians were a popular and influential part of the Russian population.

It all came to an end in 1936, when forced collectivisation began in the Soviet Union. Latvians were used to farming in single-family farms, but they were forced to join *kolhozes*. Their equipment and property was turned into common property or distributed to other *kolhozes*. Many Latvians responded to this policy by burying their agricultural equipment or sinking it into swamps. Those who protested most actively were arrested, their property was alienated, and they were sent to work in coal, gold and uranium mines. Latvian schools, clubs and libraries were shut down. Many Latvians were basically illiterate in Russian, because there had been no need for the language in Latvian settlements, but now everyone was required to speak and write in Russia in everyday work. Many Latvian villages were liquidated or merged with Russian or multi-national villages. Latvian newspapers and publishing houses were closed down. In fear of repression, many Latvians began to hide their true ethnic identity. By 1938, virtually all of the Latvians who had been working in the Soviet government had either been shot or deported to places from which they never returned.

1940 and 1941 were merciless years in the relationship between Latvians and Russians. The Soviet Union occupied Latvia, and the independent state ceased to exist. 15,000 people were deported to Siberia on the night of June 14, 1941. Even greater numbers arrived in Russia in another round of deportations on March 23, 1949. Most of these people were sent to *Kolim*, the *Magadan* district, *Norilsk* and *Vorkut*, as well as the cities of *Dobovk* and *Karagand* in Kazakhstan. The deportees and their survivors often tried to return home when Khruschev's "thaw" occurred, but quite a few people remained behind in Siberia. Some had married locals, others found good work in Siberia, and still others had nobody left in Latvia to go home to. Deportees and their children were often surprised to find that Latvians had been living in Siberia for many decades before Soviet repression began, but Latvians really became organised only after the Soviet Union collapsed. With the help of the independent Latvian state, Latvian cultural centres and associations were formed. People who were forced into collectivisation and the merging of villages still tried to stay together. Most Latvians who live in Russia today live in the cities of the Russian Federation.

In the 1970s and 1980s many Latvians volunteered for the so-called "lightning construction" projects in Russia's various regions. People who worked to build the Baikal-Amur railroad, for example, and those who laboured in the Tjumen oil fields, received far better wages than did people in Latvia. What's more, people who worked on

these projects had access to industrial and food products that were not as readily available back home. During the Soviet period, meat, shoes and clothing were often not available at all in Latvia. The Soviet Union was a place of ideological terror, and young people who were willing to go to work in newly populated territories or the natural gas fields of Siberia were promised the equivalent of mountains of gold.

The author of this article worked in Western Siberia, not far from the Arctic Circle, in the 1980s as a doctor. A Latvian colony called *Dzintari* was established there. Latvians lived together in friendship and tried to preserve their culture. They had access to Latvian music from the West. Most of them returned to Latvia in the late 1980s, when the likelihood of independence called them back home. Few Latvians remained in Russia.

In the post-war period, there was little information about Latvian colonies in Latvia, because the authorities did not want to publicise the fact that at one time Latvians – a minority nation – had helped in governing much of Russia's territory. Early information about Latvian colonies was collected by the photographer Uldis Briedis and the documentary filmmaker Ingvars Leitis. In 1975, the two men bicycled all over Russia, visiting many Latvian villages, meeting Latvians and trying to provide information about them back home through the pages of the magazine *Zvaigzne*. The Communist Party did not like this, and after two stories were published, the party boss, Augusts Voss, had this to say at a Communist Party congress: "Two adventurers have gone on a questionable trip across Siberia, and *Zvaigzne* is writing about their experiences at the level of the bourgeois press." The articles were banned, and an issue of the magazine that was already being printed was destroyed. The editors printed it again, suffering enormous losses. Uldis Briedis was not allowed to work under his own name when he returned to Riga, and so he worked under a pseudonym – Matiss Perkons. On 1 July 1977, the documentary filmmakers

Andris Slapiņš and Vaira Strautniece turned up at the village of *Lejas Bulani* in the *Krasnojarsk* district, and over the course of two weeks they filmed the everyday lives of people in this Siberian village. The film was released under the title "The Night Before Song". The film was not recognised officially, and it was not widely shown. These activities were of enormous importance later, however, when in the early 1990s Latvia began to understand its global educational mission. Teachers from Latvia have worked in the Latvian settlements of Russia almost without interruption, and several Lutheran congregations have been restored. This is of key importance in maintaining Latvian culture and historical links. The Latvian villages are also an important source of cultural, historical and folklore heritage. Ethnographers and folklorists have visited many of the settlements to study treasures that have disappeared altogether in Latvia or have been changed under the influence of other cultures.

Latvians who live in Russia today are once again influential people, heading bank branches, medical clinics and major construction companies. The Latvian Diaspora are almost alone in shaping a positive image for Latvia in Russia and other republics of the former USSR. The Latvian embassy in Moscow is important in maintaining links between Latvians in Russia and their fatherland. Imants Daudišs, who was ambassador to Russia beginning in the late 1990s, has many relatives who were deported to Siberia in the 1940s and are now important scientists and professors in that region.

[Research for this article was done by the journalist, photographer and documentary filmmaker Kaspars Goba.]

LATVIANS IN THE WEST

A colony of Latvians in Brazil in 1938

Janis Tupesis, standing in front of an old Latvian cemetery in Wisconsin

Jekabs Zebergs (1863-1963), an editor and public activist who emigrated from Latvia to the United States in 1888, establishing the first American Latvian organization and church congregation in the United States

Skandava – Dievsēta in Viskonsina

Kārlis Reinholds Zariņš (1879-1963), a diplomat who from 1940 until the end of his life was the bearer of the rights of the independent Latvian government in London

A class of nurses in Germany in 1946

A construction brigade in 1959

Arnolds Speke (1887-1978), a philologist and historian who represented the rights of the independent Latvian government in the United States

The passport of the Latvian citizen E. Epermane, issued in *Valmiera* in 1938 and registered in 1950 in the Latvian Embassy in London, later to be extended until 1991. Many Latvians refused to adopt citizenship in other countries and remained citizens of the Republic of Latvia throughout the long period of Soviet occupation

Pauls Reinhards, first secretary at the Latvian Embassy in London

A building, *Straumēni*, owned by the *Daugavas Vanagi* organization

The *Daugavas Vanagi* in Milwaukee in 1983

The church of the Latvian Lutheran congregation in Washington, D.C., also serves as the home of the American Latvian Association, the Latvian Museum and Collection of Antiquities, the World Federation of Free Latvians and the Latvian Freedom Fund

Colonists from Livonia are known to have arrived in the North American colonies of Delaware and Pennsylvania in 1640, and in 1687 Courlandians from Tobago settled for life in Boston. The organizer of a religious movement among Latvians in Vidzeme, Bishop Georg H. Loskios, moved to Pennsylvania in 1802. There was a very serious wave of emigration from Kurzeme to the American state of Wisconsin, where loggers settled. In the mid-18th century, iron ore miners and cannon manufacturers settled in Connecticut in an area which became known as Riga Hill. Locals called them *Rīgieši*, or people of Riga. In the mid-19th century many Latvian sailors settled in the United States, and missionaries began their work. On August 15, 1888, the first true Latvian colony was established at the recommendation of one Jekabs Zibergs in Boston, Massachusetts.

There have also been Latvians in Brazil since the 19th century. The first Latvian organization in Brazil was founded in Rio Novo in 1890. Latvian Baptists began to move to Brazil in the early 20th century, and in 1928 the Latvian Association of São Paolo was established. In 1941 the Brazilian Red Cross established a Latvian Assistance committee which helped Latvians who had suffered in the war.

Today there are some 25,000 Latvians in Brazil. Those who arrived after world War II worked very hard to obtain their own homes. There are several families which own large factories and companies. One of Brazil's leading writers is a man called J. Korps, who has published more than 15 books in Portuguese. Talis Sigulda is a prominent and well known artist. There are five Latvian church congregations in Brazil, and the newspaper *Zem Dienvidu Krusta* (*Under the Southern Cross*) is published in São Paolo, edited by Janis Lepste.

There are also some 25,000 Latvians in Australia, but most of their children have been born in mixed families and do not speak Latvian any more. Noted Australian Latvians have included the historian Edgars Dunsdorfs, who was a professor at the University of Melbourne, Dr. Muižnieks at the University of New South Wales, Jānis Priedkalns, a professor of anatomy and histology at Adelaide University, a coronary care specialist and professor at the University of Melbourne, Professor Saltups, the director of a psychiatric center in Sydney, Dr. J. Kariks, an instructor in dentistry at the University of Melbourne, A. Verniece, and the head of the Veterinary Surgery Clinic at the University of Melbourne, Dr. V. Šloss. Australian Latvians have more influence in their adopted country than do Latvians in other countries, because they have a great many academically educated and important people in their midst.

The largest numbers of Latvians in the West live in the United States and Canada, and most of them arrived after World War II. In 1944, when the Soviet army reinvaded Latvia, many people fled to the West in fear of a repeat of the animalistic behavior of the occupants during 1940/1941 – the period known as the Year of Terror. The intelligentsia, businessmen, wealthy farmers and medical personnel headed for Germany on foot, by horse-drawn cart or on German ships, or else for Sweden via fishing boats from Kurzeme. This latter process was organized by the Latvian Central Council, an illegal organization which was run by Konstantīns Čakste. Despite fall storms on the Baltic Sea, some 3,000 well-known politicians and intellectuals reached Sweden. In 1945 the trip became even more dangerous, because the unprotected fishing boats were bombed by Russian aviators just as though they were enemy troops.

There are differing reports on how many Latvians ended up in Germany. Professor Dunsdorfs has calculated that there were some 200,000, some of whom were taken there by the Nazis as forced laborers, some who were members of the Latvian Legion, but most who were civilian refugees. Some 40,000 Latvians disappeared in Eastern Germany in 1944/1945. Members of the Latvian Legion who defended Germany fell or were taken prisoner. Many refugees died in Allied bombing raids, particularly in Dresden. Others were caught by the Red Army and declared traitors against the Soviet motherland. Many were shot, others were deported to Siberia.

At the end of the war, there were some 160,000 refugees in the so-called displaced person camps which were run by the United Nations Refugee Relief Organization in Western Germany. They were scattered all over West Germany in some 2000 camps. Some lived in apartments that had been taken away from Germans, but many lived in old army barracks, where families tried to gain a little bit of privacy by attaching blankets to ceilings. Life without work was boring, and people lived modestly, but there was a great deal of public and cultural activity. Theater performances and concerts were staged, and there was even an opera in Oldenburg. Writers gathered for meetings and helped to keep up the spirits of the refugees, many of whom lived with the hope that their refugee status would be short-lived and they would be able to return back to Latvia. In 1947 people began to leave Germany. Some 20,000 refugees were taken in by Great Britain, and about one-half of them later went to Canada and Australia. Some 20,000 refugees went directly to Australia, and approximately 1,000 traveled to South America.

The major wave of emigration to the United States began in 1950, when some 90,000 refugees went to that country and another 20,000 departed for Canada. Approximately 10,000 Latvians remained in Germany, and 5,000 stayed in Sweden.

Latvians who remained in Europe were given a certain amount of social aid, but they had problems in finding work in their professions. The musicians Mariss Vētra, Janis Mediņš and Teodors Reiters were greeted with enormous enthusiasm at the Stockholm Opera before World War II, but after the war they sat in the cellar and attic of the opera house and transcribed notes.

The situation in America and Australia was better, because both countries are basically countries of immigrants. A local clergyman preaching before a newly arrived group of Latvians congratulated them as *new Americans*. Few were able to find work in their specialties, however. Professors worked as roofers, their wives worked as maids. Post-war America, however, was a place of enormous economic growth, and Latvians were clever in accessing that growth. The first Latvian millionaires appeared 10 or 15 years after the war, as did university professors, wealthy doctors and engineers.

While still in the German refugee camps, Latvians set up local governing bodies to work with the occupant Allies. The Central Council of Latvians, led by Karlis Kundziņš and Arveds Švabe, was set up in 1946. In England Latvians established the European center of the Committee for the Restoration of Latvia. American Latvians set up the American Latvian Association, and their compatriots in other parts of the world established the Latvian National Association in Canada, the Latvian Association in Australia and New Zealand, and the South American Latvian Association. Eventually delegates from these structures formed the World Federation of Free Latvians, which initially was chaired by Peteris Lejiņš. In 1970, however, a 32-year-old activist named Uldis Grava took the helm of the WFFL, and under his leadership it became an active fighter for Latvian freedom. At the Helsinki Summit in 1973, Grava managed to get close enough to Soviet Foreign Minister Andrei Gromyko to exchange words with him. Grava and several other delegates from the association were arrested. Later chairmen of the organization were Ilgvars Spilners, Oļģerts Pavlovskis, Linards Lukss and Gunārs Meierovics. Delegations from the WFFL attended security conferences in Geneva, Belgrade, Madrid, Ottawa, Budapest and Vienna, and delegates were often arrested for demonstrating against the Soviet occupation of Latvia. Young people organized demonstrations in Helsinki and

A demonstration in Stockholm

The Rev. Maris Ķirsons cut his veins in Madrid in order to attract the world's attention to the destiny of Latvia

A scene from the Latvian demonstration in Madrid, where Balts loudly reminded the world of the Soviet occupation

On June 14, 1983, American President Ronald Reagan, in the presence of representatives from the three Baltic nations, signed a law which declared June 14 to be Baltic Freedom Day in the United States

A demonstration in Venezuela

US President Gerald Ford (left) met with the chairman of the World Federation of Free Latvians, Uldis Grava, before departing for the Helsinki Summit in 1975. Ford promised Grava that the United States would not recognize the incorporation of the Baltic States into the Soviet Union

Worship at a Latvian military cemetery in Belgium. From the left: Lutheran pastor Zilgme Eglīte, P. Dupats, and Lutheran Deacon Klāvs Bērziņš

From the left: Janis Ritums, Ilgvars Spilners and Janis Muchks in Visby

WFFL chairman Andrejs Ozoliņš, a mathematics professor at the University of Lester

An organization of Latvian military officers in Canada

The main concert of a song festival in London, at Albert Hall

The parade of a Latvian song festival in 1984

The global song festival in Munster

The parade of the global song festival in Munster in 1987

Some 5,000 Western Latvians gathered at the two song festivals that were held in Munster. Because a Latvian high school was located there, the German city became a true center for the world's Latvians

Madrid and ended up in local jails. A clergyman called Maris Ķirsons cut his own veins in the central square of Madrid during he security conference there. There was an enormous slew of publicity about this, and the issue of Latvian independence was covered in detail in newspapers and on television.

One of the main accomplishments of Western Latvians during the period of the Soviet occupation was the so-called Baltic Tribunal in Copenhagen, where the Soviet Union was accused of violations of international law in the Baltic States. Four internationally known lawyers heard 12 witnesses and issued the Copenhagen Manifesto, which was widely discussed in the Western media and provoked the soviet foreign ministry to issue an angry reaction. The Latvian National Fund in Stockholm, led by the poet Andrejs Eglītis, also did extensive political and information work in exile.

An organization of war veterans, the *Daugavas Vanagi* (Hawks of the *Daugava*), was established by a group of war prisoners in Belgium under the leadership of Col. Vilis Janums. Eventually it became one of the most important organizations among Latvian exiles, with some 10,000 active members at one point. Western Latvians generally agree, however, that the backbone of Latvian life abroad was the church, with its congregation halls. Youth groups on four continents were also very active, organizing meetings and congresses.

One priority among Latvians, beginning in the time of the refugee camps in Germany, was always education and the maintenance of the Latvian identity. There were elementary schools in almost all of the DP camps, as well as 10 high schools. Children went to local schools in other countries, but in major Latvian centers there were always Saturday or Sunday schools where young people learned the Latvian language and the Latvian way of life. In some cases these schools were held in private homes. Summer high schools, as well as various youth groups and seminars, were organized. American young people themselves organized 2x2 Latvian summer camps, from which activists later developed the idea of the 3x3 summer events – Latvian programs for the representatives of three generations at once. There was a full-time Latvian high school in Munster, West Germany. In early years of the exile, there was even a Baltic University in Hamburg.

Many Latvians remember their careers in Saturday schools as being nostalgic places. While other children played baseball, Latvian youths spent time learning about the number of cows in Latvia in 1939.

Book publishing was a very active industry among Latvians in exile – nearly 7,000 titles

The mixed choir *Straumēni*, with conductor Z. Aboliņš at the center of the front row

Lilija Zobens and Jānis Muchks

were published, including 500 collections of poetry. In all of the countries where Latvians lived there were Latvian newspapers – *Latvju Vārds* and *Latviju Ziņas* in Sweden, *Londonas Avīze* in England, *Latvija* in Germany, *Universitas* for Latvian student fraternities, *DV Mēnešraksts* for the *Daugavas Vanagi* and their supporters, *Ceļa Biedrs* for Latvian Lutheran congregations, and *Treji Vārti* and *Jaunā Gaita* – literary magazines. At the turn of the millennium only four newspapers remained – *Brīvā Latvija* in Europe, *Laiks* in the United States, *Latvija Amerikā* in Canada and *Austrālijas Latvietis* in Australia.

Professor E. Dunsdorfs collected a great deal of data about social and cultural life among Latvians in exile. In 1970 alone, there were 1,782 different events – 218 lectures, 193 memorial events, 289 annual events, 234 concerts, 122 exhibitions, 81 congresses, 190 balls, 151 theater performances and 92 athletic events.

Song festivals were organized regularly, and each lasted between 3 and 8 days. The repertoire included concerts, meetings of writers, arts exhibitions, balls and crafts sales. The first song festival in exile took place in June 1946 near Nuremberg in Germany. England saw its first Latvian Song Festival in 1949 in London, while the first festival in America took place in 1953 in Chicago. There were seven different song festivals in the Eastern United States in the 50 years of the Soviet occupation, and 11 on the West Coast. The first song festival in Canada was also held in 1953, in Toronto. Until 1991, there were eight more festivals – one for every four years. The American and Canadian song festivals were always the largest in the world, with at least 10,000 visitors.

In Australia song festivals were part of a larger cultural festival which took place every year between Christmas and New Year's in Sydney, Melbourne, Adelaide, Brisbane or Perth, beginning in 1951.

The first European Song Festival was organized in 1964 in Hamburg, followed by festivals in Hannover in 1968, Cologne in 1973, London in 1977, Leeds (UK) in 1982, and Helsingborg (Sweden) in 1989. In 1979 a global song festival was held in the town of Visby, which is located on the Swedish island of Gotland in the Baltic Sea and was the closest geographical point to Latvia in the free world. This event was political in nature – "We'll build a bridge across the open sea", sang participants. All of the events were held outdoors. There were two more global song festivals – in Munster, Germany, in 1984 and 1987.

The Latvian national renaissance of the late 1980s and early 1990s was greatly helped by Latvians in exile. The Latvian Popular Front and, later, the first post-war Latvian government leaned on the contacts of American and Australian Latvians to develop their initial political activities. Latvians in America, Germany, England, Australia and especially Sweden helped young Latvians to find study opportunities in the free world.

Some Western Latvians have returned or moved to Latvia. The development of the market economy in Latvia was assisted by Western Latvians, among them an enormously successful businessman from Venezuela, Vilis Vītols. Western Latvians who have served as ministers in the Latvian government have included the brothers Oļģerts and Valdis Pavlovskis, Gunārs Meierovics, Jānis Tupesis, Jānis Ritenis, Indra Samite, Vita Terauda and Egils Levits. Parliamentary deputies have included Inese Birzniece, Pēteris Elferts, Pauls Kļaviņš, Aristids Lambergs, Juris Sinka, Maris Graudiņš, Vaira Paegle and others. In 1999 Vaira Vīķe-Freiberga, a psychology professor who until 1998 lived in Canada, was elected president of Latvia.

Dr. Visvaldis Dzenis patented several cheese processing machines in 1957 and 1961

Dr. Edvīns Vedējs, a chemist from the United States, has been a foreign member of the Latvian Academy of Sciences since 1992

Professor Pēteris Liepiņš

The chairman of the *Daugavas Vanagi* in the United States, Andrejs Sparniņš, the editor of the newspaper *Latvija Amerikā*, Ingrīda Vīksne, and Velta Sparniņa

The chairman of the Association of Latvian Physicians and Dentists, Ansis Muižnieks, and his wife Ingrīda – both tireless organizers of Latvian cultural life on the West Coast of the United States

Poet Andrejs Eglītis in Gotland, Sweden. The head of the Latvian National Fund and author of the legendary Latvian poem *God, Your Earth is Burning* returned to Latvia in 1998

The most well known Latvian painter in America, Raimonds Staprāns, and his wife, Ilona

Johanna Benjamiņa celebrates the summer solstice festival at the restored *Valdeķi* baronial estate with the Rev. Anita Gaide and the Rev. Ivars Gaide of Canada

A sculpture of a crocodile that is now housed in the Latvian town of *Dundaga*. The American Latvian businessman Norberts Klaucens dedicated the sculpture to the courageous people of Kurzeme

Flags in the streets of Munster greet the Latvian song festival in 1984

Arvīds Blumentals lives in Australia and studies the jungle and Aboriginal tribes there. He also hunts crocodiles

Aleksandrs Laime (1911-1994), spent most of his life in the jungle of Venezuela, and he discovered and named a number of rivers, including the *Rio Gauja*, which includes the world's highest waterfall – Angel Falls

Gunārs Meierovics, son of Latvia's first foreign minister, served as minister for European Affairs in the restored Republic of Latvia, and Aina Nagobads-Abola, who was the first post-occupation Latvian ambassador in France

Ella Jurevics, an activist at the Church of Zion in Chicago, Zigrīda Stile, and an American Latvian who is a deputy in Latvia's Parliament, Inese Birzniece

Justs Karlsons and Ieva Laukers inherited the downtown Riga property of the Bergs dynasty; they are in the fourth generation of the Bergs family

Construction company owner Vilis Vītols from Caracas now owns the *Māra* Bank in Latvia

Painter Laris Strunke

Actress Ausma Kantāne, the Latvian ambassador to the United States Ojārs Kalniņš and his wife, Irma Johnson, and the poet Imants Ziedonis. In 1999 Kalniņš was appointed director of the Latvian Institute in Riga

Vaira Vīķe-Freiberga and Juris Kronbergs in 1999

The reburial of the clergyman, writer and literary specialist Ludis Berziņš (1870-1965), who died in Denver, Colorado, and whose remains were brought back to Latvia in the fall of 1997

The head of the Council of Europe's Cultural Heritage Committee, Jose Maria Ballester, Latvian President Guntis Ulmanis and his wife Aina, Minister for Culture Jānis Dripe, and the director of Latvia's Cultural Monument Protection Inspection, Juris Dambis, at the Latvian Ethnographic Open-Air Museum

A WEALTHY RURAL HOMESTEAD

Braki, the homestead of the Latvian playwright and novelist Rūdolfs Blaumanis in Vidzeme. The building is now a branch of the *Madona* Local History Museum

Clusters of etnographic houses can still be seen in *Vecpiebalga*

AN AESTHETICALLY ATTRACTIVE CULTURAL-HISTORICAL RURAL COUNTRYSIDE

The cultural heritage of a nation is represented both in material and non-material form, but it is always the result of the work of people. It includes the work of artists, architects, musicians, artists and scientists, as well as anonymous artisans who express the spirit of humanity and its value system. All of these provide a meaning to the life of a nation.

The preservation of Europe's cultural heritage is seen as the protection and study of material and spiritual cultural monuments, researching, listing, maintaining and using the facilities and involving them in modern life.

Latvia's cultural heritage contains 3,364 architectural monuments, 2,495 archaeological monuments, 2,414 artistic monuments, 44 territorial and urban construction monuments, and 111 historical monuments. These make up the aggregate of the architecture, archaeology, monumental, sacral and applied arts, science, technology, as well as underwater Latvian heritage.

Jūrmalciema houses in *Pape* on the seacoast of Kurzeme

A hedge typical of Northern Latvia

The only Stork Museum in the world is in *Staicele*. Latvians consider a stork as a symbol of welfare. A stork nest on the roof means one can expect a great number of kids in that house

This farm, designed by architect Lauris Gundars, was built in the 1990s in *Piebalga*, using architectonic elements from the classic Vidzeme homestead

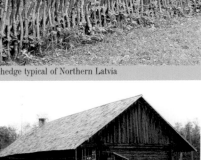

A residential building, formerly used as a threshing barn, at the *Melturi* homestead on the shores of the *Amata* River

Coastwise fishery with small motor vessels is traditional in Latvia

CULTURAL-HISTORICAL SEA COAST COUNTRYSIDE

Since ages Latvians used to go to sea on boats. The fishermen craf was as respected as ploughmen. Latvian folk songs call fishermen the ploughmen of the sea

A seafarer's home, *Kapteiņi*, near the village of *Ķurmjrags* on the Vidzeme coast

The *Talsi* parson's manor house, dating back to the turn of the 18th and 19th centuries

The *Mēri* manor house near *Smiltene*

Latvia's uniqueness from the perspective of Europe's cultural heritage is represented by:
• Evidence that the territory was once occupied by a wide variety of ancient Baltic and Finno-Ugric cultures;
• Archeological heritage, some of them underwater;
• A large proportion of military buildings from many periods in history;
• The sacral and lay buildings of the Hanseatic League;
• An aesthetically attractive cultural and historical countryside in rural areas and along Latvia's seashore;
• Sacral architecture involving all denominations of religion from the 13th to the 20th century;
• A cultural countryside network of manor houses and associated churches;
• Rural construction built on the principle of single-family farms;
• A large proportion of wooden buildings in cities and rural areas alike;
• A multi-cultural spiritual and material environment throughout Latvia.

The *Stukmaņi* manor house near *Pļaviņas*

The *Dobele* Lutheran Church, which was built in 1495

LATVIA'S SACRAL ARCHITECTURE COVERS A WIDE RANGE OF RELIGIOUS DENOMINATIONS

A Catholic church in *Pasiene*, built between 1861 and 1770

An 18th-century Orthodox church in *Jelgava*, designed by the architect Bartholomeo F. Rastrelli. The building was severely damaged in World War II, but its congregation has now restored it

The Reform Church in Riga, built between 1727 and 1731 based on a design by architect Kristof Meinert

The Old Believer's church in *Rēzekne*, built in 1895

A synagogue built in *Rēzekne* in the late 19th century

A Uniate church in *Jēkabpils*

A new Baptist church in *Dundaga*

WOODEN BUILDINGS IN CITIES AND RURAL AREAS

A Vidzeme threshing barn, now housed at the Ethnographic Open-Air Museum

The *Vecborne* Church is considered to be the oldest wooden church in Latvia

The mid-18th century *Ungurmuiža* manor house in *Cēsis* District

The "eight-corner" threshing barn in *Taurene* Parish, *Cēsis* District

The *Bērzgale* Church in *Preiļi* District

The protection and administration of Latvia's cultural monuments is overseen by the State Cultural Monuments Protection Inspection, which is under the supervision of the Ministry of Culture. Latvia has devoted particular attention to the study, preservation and restoration of wooden buildings. Together with Sweden, Finland, Norway, Russia, Estonia and Lithuania, Latvia is engaged in an international co-operation project called "Wooden Cities". Latvia has interpreted the project as involving care for sacral and national wooden architecture. Among the monuments that have been registered are wooden churches, manor houses, farms, threshing barns, the wooden buildings of Riga and *Jūrmala*, as well as structures in small towns such as *Līgatne*, *Piltene* and *Pāvilosta*.

Restoration of wooden architecture in Riga

Residential buildings attached to a Russian Old Believer's church in *Židino*, *Daugavpils* District

The *Indrica* Church in *Krāslava* District

Workers' houses built in the 1880s for men from the *Līgatne* paper factory and their families. The site is located in *Cēsis* District

The home of a wealthy landowner in *Jelgava* District

The *Jāņskola* school in *Piebalga*, which now houses a museum dedicated to the lives of composer Emīls Dārziņš and the poet Jānis Sudrabkalns

The *Laucese* Catholic Church in *Daugavpils* District

A residential building put up in the first half of the 20th century in the village of *Koniņciems*, *Rucava* Parish, *Liepāja* District

A late-19th century summer house in the *Jūrmala* village of *Dubulti*

The *Kombuļi* Church in *Krāslava* District

A VARIETY OF EVIDENCE CONCERNING ANCIENT CULTURE

Ancient signs engraved in the *Dinamarkas* border stone

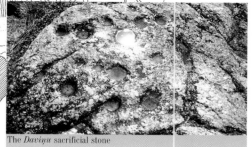
The *Daviņu* sacrificial stone

A headdress used by latgall woman in the 11th century – a crown found at a burial site at *Guģeri*

A sacrificial cave used by ancient Livs in what is now *Liepa* Parish

THE ARCHEOLOGICAL HERITAGE – SOME OF IT UNDERWATER

Archeological digs conducted in the 1970s at the *Araiši* lake castle of the 9th and 10th century

An ancient Latvian soldier (model designed according to archeological finds from an 11th century burial site at *Guģeri*)

Remains of 12th – 13th century ship from Rīga

CULTURAL MONUMENTS FROM MANY CULTURES

"The devil's boats" – ancient burial places

The seaside *Nida* cemetery in *Rucava* Parish, *Liepāja* District

A monument to residents from the *Ventspils* District town of *Jūrkalne* who perished while refugees during World War I

A monument to Swedish soldiers, who fell during the 30-Years War, located at *Vilce*

A Jewish cemetery in *Ludza*

The graves of Polish soldiers from World War I in *Krāslava*

The graves of British soldiers who died during World War I in *Jelgava*

Gypsy and Russian cultural elements at the Rainis Cemetery in Riga

A monument to Lithuanian soldiers who died in World War I at *Eglaine*

A monument in *Jelgava* dedicated to German soldiers who died during World War I

A World War I War cemetery in *Pašuliene*, on the *Ilūkstes-Šarlotes* road

THE CENTER OF RIGA, FEATURING A WEALTH OF ART NOUVEAU AND FUNCTIONALIST ARCHITECTURE, HAS BEEN LISTED IN THE WORLD CULTURAL AND NATURAL HERITAGE LIST

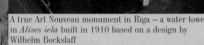

A true Art Nouveau monument in Riga – a water tower in *Alises iela* built in 1910 based on a design by Wilhelm Bockslaff

A building at *Smilšu iela* 1/3, designed in 1906 by architect Nikolajs Proskurnins

The residential building at *Tērbatas iela* was put up in 1900, and its architect was the distinguished Konstantīns Pēkšēns

The National Art Museum of Latvia, at *Krišjāņa Valdemāra iela* 10a, was built in 1905 on the basis of a design by Vilhelm Neumann

Riga's historical centre, including the Old City, was included in the World cultural and natural heritage list on 4 December 1997, and this indicates the extraordinary and universal cultural value of the area. The will of the Latvian people and their sense of cultural belonging motivate its protection. By December 1997, UNESCO's World cultural heritage list included 506 natural and cultural objects from throughout the world. Riga's centre has thus been compared to the pyramids of Egypt, the Taj Mahal in India, the Galapagos Islands, America's Grand Canyon, the Swedish island of Visby, and many other globally famous objects. In order to engage in international co-operation in the field of cultural heritage, the three Baltic States have set up a joint cultural heritage committee, and the 11 countries of the Baltic Sea region have also developed a co-operation program. The chairperson of the Baltic committee, Juris Dambis, represents Latvia at the European Council's Cultural Heritage Committee.

USE OF ETHNOGRAPHIC MOTIVES IN ARCHITECTURE

Rudolfs Donbergs designed this apartment building at *Lāčplēša iela* 21, and it was built in 1910.

A residential building at *Marijas iela* 26, designed by Professor Eižens Laube and built in 1905

A 1906 residential building at the corner of *Lāčplēša* and *Brīvības ielas*, designed by architect Aleksandrs Vanags

In the 1980s, architects Ausma Skujiņa and Anita Marinska designed a series of apartment buildings in *Mārupe*

From the old churchyard known as *Konventa Sēta*, one sees a romantic view of the tower of St. Peter's Church, as well as the apse of what used to be St. George's Church

These buildings, which are behind the castle of the Order of the Brotherhood of the Sword, were built in the 18th century

Skārņu Street was the main trading street in ancient Riga

The yard of the three buildings known as the "three brothers" – *Pils* Street 17, 19 and 21

A VARIETY OF CULTURES IN LATVIA'S CITIES

Three major churches stand near one another in *Daugavpils* – the Virgin Mary Catholic Church (1905), the *Daugavpils* Lutheran Church (1893), and the St. Boris Gleb Orthodox Cathedral (1907). The first two buildings were put up by architect Wilhelm Neumann. *Daugavpils* is the only large city in the world where the churches of all three leading confessions are so close to one another

A temple to the wind god in *Alūksne*

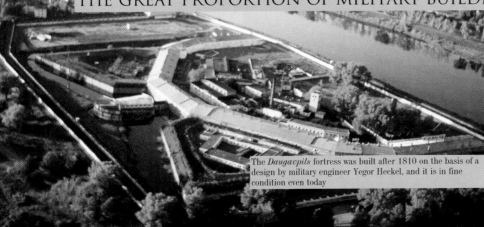

A Lutheran church in the mostly Jewish-populated *Gostiņi* Parish is a significant architectural monument

THE GREAT PROPORTION OF MILITARY BUILDINGS IN LATVIA

The *Daugavpils* fortress was built after 1810 on the basis of a design by military engineer Yegor Heckel, and it is in fine condition even today

The *Liepāja* fortress was one of the largest seashore forts in all of Eastern Europe. It was blown up in 1915

The *Liepāja* military port which was built in the late 19th century and early 20th century today is a strange monument to the armed forces of the Soviet Union. Abandoned submarines are being broken down and used in metallurgy

The Robežnieki castle mound, Krāslava District

The image of Mother Latvia at the Cemetery of the Brethren in Riga. Sculptor Kārlis Zāle, architects Peteris Feders and Aleksandrs Birzenieks

The *Krūte* lutheran church in *Liepāja* District, built in 1642

Latvia's cultural heritage is guarded by the law "On protection of the cultural heritage". The country's list of cultural monument lists 474 castle mounds, 1,233 ancient burial grounds, 76 Medieval castles or their ruins, 136 baronial estates, 134 Lutheran churches, 48 Catholic churches, 33 Orthodox churches, and 29 homes of prominent individuals.

The majority of Latvia's cultural heritage is made up of cultural and historical landscapes and individual territories – the historical centers of towns, ancient burial grounds, cemeteries, parks, locations of historical events, places where prominent people lived and worked, groups of buildings or individual buildings and structures, works of art, equipment and objects of historical, scientific, artistic or other cultural value, etc. The preservation of these entities serves the interests both of the Latvian nation and of the international community.

The ruins of a castle in *Dobele*

The *Krāslava* Orthodox Church

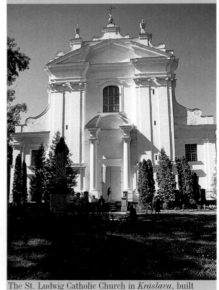

The St. Ludwig Catholic Church in *Krāslava*, built between 1755 and 1767, is one of the most vivid monuments of late Baroque architecture in Latgale. The architect was Antonio Paraco

The *Kazdanga* baronial mansion, built in 1800 by the architect Johann Berlitz

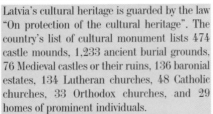

One of Latvia's historical symbols is the *Staburags* cliff, over which a stream used to run. Today the cliff is located under the waters of the *Daugava*, in the reservoir of the *Pļaviņas* hydroelectric station. In order to ensure that other cultural monuments are not submerged, the entire *Daugava* River valley is under national protection

The home of composer and teacher Janis Cimze in *Rauna*

The *Kalna Kaibēni* homestead in *Piebalga*, where the authors of the first Latvian novel, Reinis and Matiss Kaudzite, lived

The *Ilmāja* Church in *Liepāja* District, built around 1640

THE PRESERVATION OF LATVIA'S CULTURAL HERITAGE. MANAGEMENT OF CULTURAL WORK IN LATVIA. COOPERATION WITH THE COUNCIL OF EUROPE AND UNESCO

The most important aspect of the arts and culture in Latvia at this time is integration into the European artistic and cultural life, promoting the creation of outstanding works of art by talented artists, and supporting research into the history of Latvian art, culture, education, traditions and folklore. The preservation of the cultural heritage for future generations is equally important.

Cultural life in Latvia is headed by Culture Minister Karina Pētersone. Cultural life in Latvia involves more than the contributions of unique painters, sculptors and composers, more than concert life and exhibitions. In Latvia the term "cultural life" is also held to mean the preservation of the cultural environment for future generations and the creation of a European cultural environment. The village of *Slutiški* in *Daugavpils* District is an ancient territorial and architectural monument. The village is located in the *Daugava* River valley, and a project called "*Daugava* Valley" is being implemented with the help of the Council of Europe. During the last years of the Soviet occupation, there were plans to built a new hydroelectric station on the *Daugava* that would have flooded much of the river valley. Latvia's cultural workers went to war against the plan, and the preservation of the ancient shores of the *Daugava* was one of the key achievements that brought the Latvian nation together in the 1980s

Cultural life in Latvia is headed by the Ministry of Culture. Most major artistic and cultural projects in Latvia are organized with financing from the Latvian Cultural Fund or the Latvian Cultural Capital Fund. The three people who run the three structures are the true leaders of Latvian cultural life.

The chairman of the Latvian Cultural Fund, Pēteris Bankovskis, seen against the ancient shores of the *Abava* River. Latvia law provides for tax relief for companies which sponsor important cultural, educational and artistic projects in the country. Pēteris Bankovskis has helped writers to write books, educators to bring the educational system into order, and researchers to study cultural life and cultural history. A pilot project on the *Abava* River valley, financed in cooperation with the Council of Europe, is helping to protect a unique landscape. The *Pedvāle* sculpture park, which has been recognized by UNESCO, is also located in the valley, run by its organizer, the artist Ojārs Feldbergs. Also in the valley are the beautiful small towns of *Kandava* and *Sabile*

The director of the Cultural Capital Fund, Māris Bērziņš, seen against the background of the Latvian town of *Talsi*. A program of cooperation among countries of the Baltic Sea in the area of cultural heritage helps Latvia to study, maintain and restore the architectural treasures of small towns. The Culture Capital Fund helps to promote cultural and artistic projects. The fund is a non-profit state-owned company that is charged with promoting cultural and artistic innovation, financing cultural and artistic work by natural and legal persons, and sponsoring cultural research projects. The Culture Capital Fund also pays lifetime stipends to outstanding cultural and artistic personages in return for their contributions to the arts. The fund also helps people to obtain an education or further professional development in the arts, to popularize Latvian art and culture in the world, to disseminate newly created cultural projects, and to make works of art and culture available to broader audiences. The Culture Capital Fund has devoted particular attention to the development of traditional culture. The fund organizes a projects competition four times a year, and resources are divided up among projects that are approved. The Culture Capital Fund is financed from a tax on alcohol and tobacco, with total funding of approximately Ls 2.5 million per year

THE GOETHE INSTITUTE

The library of the Goethe Institute in Riga. The institute was opened in 1992 and expanded considerably in 1999

The Goethe Institute is a German-founded institution which supports the German language and culture in Latvia. The opening of the Goethe Institute in Riga is in part a recognition of the 800-year presence of German culture in the city. The Riga branch of the institute helps to promote German culture, as well as to develop creative cooperation with cultural specialists in Latvia, preparing and organizing scientific conferences, discussions, concerts, cinema showings, theatrical performances and exhibitions. The institute has worked in Riga since 1992 and is located in Old Riga. The historical building in which the institute is located was carefully modernized and expanded in 1998. The offices are the most beautiful of any of the Goethe Institute's locations in Europe.

The Goethe Institute provides all kinds of professional assistance to German language teachers in Latvia, ensuring abilities for people to pursue a further education in German either in Latvia or in Germany. The institute also works in close cooperation with the education ministries of the three Baltic States in developing new teaching curricula and in providing consultations on German language examinations. The library of the Goethe Institute in Riga was opened in 1995, and it provides extensive learning opportunities.

The building of the Latvian parliament was designed by architects Jānis Baumanis and Robert Pflug. The building once housed a German military organization. With the help of the Council of Europe, Latvia's Parliament is working to improve Latvian laws on the protection of culture and the natural heritage

A meeting of the board of the Culture Capital Fund

The consecration of the new offices of the Goethe Institute in Riga, May 21, 1999. Delegations from Germany and Latvia attended the ceremony. From the right: President Guntis Ulmanis of Latvia; President Roman Herzog of Germany and Mrs. Herzog; and the director of the Riga branch of the Goethe Institute, Ronald Ruprecht and his wife

EDUCATION IN THE TRADES IN LATVIA

The Riga Trade High School trains restorers, metalworkers and carpenters. The school was established by former Education Minister Jānis Gaigals (center)

Chairs built by young men from the Trade High School are found in the castle of the Swedish royal family and at the Cabinet of Ministers of Latvia

An old picture frame is being restored here

Education in the trades in Latvia is supported by the Council of Europe's Committee on Cultural Heritage. Particular attention is devoted to the training of restorers

Restorers from the Trade High School worked on old wood carvings from a church in *Liepna*

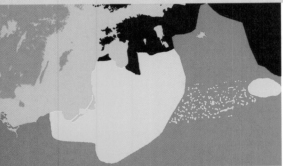

The *Kņāvi* hill castle in *Jēkabpils* District. Hill castles were fortified settlements built on high hillocks or on landscapes at the meeting point of rivers. The archeologic findings provide broad knowledge about the residents of Baltic in the last 10 thousands of years

The distribution of Baltic tribes and their neighbouring peoples – the Balts are shown in yellow, the Slavs – in red, the Finno-Ugric peoples – in blue, and the Germanic nations – in green

Archeological work at the ruins of the *Ikšķile* castle

The *Pilišķi* hill castle in *Preiļi* District

This is where the ancient town of *Naujene* stood, complete with the *Dinaburg* castle

The *Jersika* hill castle in *Preiļi* District

Approximately 13,000 or 14,000 years ago, the massive glaciers of the Ice Age retreated from the territory that is now Latvia. Tundra stretched all along the Baltic Sea, the boundaries of seas, rivers and lakes were established, and the kingdom of plants and animals appeared. It is thought that human beings appeared on the shores of the Baltic Sea in the 12th millennium BC, but there is clear evidence of human settlements in Latvia, which date back to the 9th millennium BC. The most ancient settlements were found at an archeological site near the town of *Salaspils*. These were the homes of nomadic huntsmen toward the end of the oldest phase of the Stone Age.

From the late 9th millennium BC to the mid-4th millennium BC, the middle part of the Stone Age prevailed, and all of the territory of what is now Latvia was populated.

From the mid-4th to the mid-2nd millennium BC, Latvia experienced the late Stone Age. The territory was quite densely populated, especially around Lake *Lubāna*. Archaeologists have found tools and household objects, which suggest that these ancient residents were most often occupied with fishing and hunting. There were contacts with other tribes to the North, because objects of shale have also been found.

In the 2nd millennium BC, the first objects made of bronze began to appear in the region, and people began to turn to farming and livestock breeding. Wheat, barley, peas, beans and flax were all grown. The significance of cattle increased, because cows and bulls could be used for food, skins and, through their bones, various household objects. People also raised pigs and horses. As livestock breeding and farming developed and people began to accumulate wealth, it became necessary to develop fortified settlements. These were built on high hillocks or on protuberances of land at the meeting point of rivers. Such hill castles (or hill forts) were located in *Tērvete*, *Koknese* and *Daugmale*. Societies moved from matriarchal to patriarchal structures.

From the 2nd to the 4th century AD, people began to obtain iron ore from local swamps, using it to produce axes, awls, knives and scythes, as well as ornaments and jewellery. People expanded their economic activities and trade developed. Archaeologists have found Roman coins and other objects, which suggest that the trading process was wide indeed.

Between the 5th and the 9th century, residents built increasingly fortified hill castles. These were settled by noblemen and their armies. Wider settlements often sprang up around the castle walls, with people who engaged in various crafts and trade activities. Lake settlements, the most widely researched of which is found at *Āraiši* (9th and 10th century AD), sprang up. This was the period of the middle Iron Age in Latvia. In place of clan-based communities, territorial ones were established, and some of these communities proved to be busier than others. Economic inequality increased, and war came with it. Captives in wars were sometimes used for forced labour, but slavery, as an institution never took hold in Latvia.

The most ancient residents of Latvia were not the ancestors of the Latvian ethnos. In the 9th millennium BC, the region was occupied by hunting tribes from Southern Europe, while in the 6th and 5th millennium BC people came from the East. It was only in the 3rd millennium BC that the ancestors of Livs, Estonians and Finns – people from the so-called Finno-Ugric tribes – began to appear. Early Baltic tribes – the ancestors of the Latvians and Lithuanians – arrived in the 2nd millennium BC. They populated vast territories all over Eastern Europe, gradually moving toward the North and the East. In the 1st millennium BC, the Balts populated Russia all the way to Moscow, as well as most of what today is Latvia and Lithuania. Various groups of tribes emerged from the ancient Balts – Kurs, Semigallians, Latgalls and Sels, and these tribes, along with the Livs, eventually merged into the Latvian nation.

The ancient Baltic nations did not have a common name. Herodotus referred to them as *Neurs* and *Budins*, while Tacitus, speaking of a nation that lived in the land from which amber came, wrote of the *Aists*. History suggests that the only part of Latvia that Tacitus really knew was the region around what is now Liepāja, his word stuck with the Estonians, who call their country Eesti – not far from *Aist*. The word "Balts" appeared only in 1845, and was acquired from earlier writings of a monk, Adam of Bremen, who had dubbed the Baltic Sea, *Mare Balticum*.

Historical sources suggest that the Balts maintained contacts with neighbouring nations, especially the Scandinavians and Russians. Scandinavian burial mounds, metal products and coins have been found in Latvia. Scandinavian sagas and Runic writings also speak to the Baltic nations. The best known evidence of these contacts is the "History of Denmark" which was written by a scribe known as the Grammatician of Saxony. People from Gottland and Sweden traded with the Balts and some-

times tried to subjugate them.

Archeological sites around the town of *Grobiņa* show that around the mid-7th century this area of Kurzeme was the site of a colony, known as *Jūrpils*, of Swedish and Gottlandian traders which survived until the early 9th century. The marauding Vikings often visited the territories of the Kurs, both to trade and to pillage. In 855 AD the Swedish king Olav attacked the Kurs, took *Jūrpils*, and demanded that the Kurs pay annual tribute to the king. Around 925 AD an Icelandic adventurer called Egil, son of Skalagrim, turned up in Kurland and, according to legend, he first concluded a trade agreement with the locals and then turned to thievery and destruction. The Kurs captured him and locked him up in a cellar pending a trial on the next day, but Egil managed to get free and was never seen again.

The Kurs did not remain in debt to the Vikings when it came to pillaging. Kurland boats plied the shores of Sweden and Denmark, and the ancients knew how to build seagoing vessels that were appropriate for long voyages. The Danes had a prayer – "God, save us from the Kurs!"

In the Sermland region of Sweden there is an old Runic stone from the 11th century with this text: "Siegrid asked that this stone be put up in memory of her husband Sven. He often sailed to Zemgale in an ornate ship along the Horn of Kolka." The Vikings tried to take control of rivers that led to southern lands – the most convenient mode of travel at that time. The Semigallians had to fight off attacks from the Vikings several times, but because they were rich and unified, they did not have much difficulty in protecting their territories.

During the era of the Vikings, the Scandinavians also maintained contacts with Latgale, which was a territory of trade and transit at that time. The Latgalls had the most trouble with their eastern neighbours – the Kriviches, who were a Slavic nation. Information about the Baltic tribes, especially the Latgalls and Semigallians, can be found in the historiography of the ancient Russians – the Chronicle of Nestor, the Chronicle of Pleskau and the Chronicle of Novgorod, specifically. Noblemen from Polock and Pleskau often tried to strengthen their positions near major waterways, and they often attacked the lands of the Latgalls and Livs. Russian armies were found in the towns of *Jersika* and *Koknese*. The Orthodox version of the christian faith began to spread in Latgale in the 11th century, but most of the residents of Latvia, like all ancient farming nations, believed in a variety of deities, especially Mother Earth, Mother Forest and Mother Fortune.

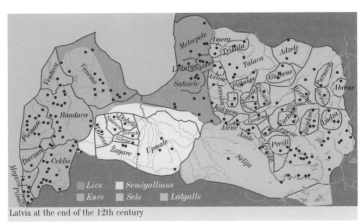

Latvia at the end of the 12th century

Liv woven belt designs from the 11th century, found at *Salaspils*

Writing tools from the Middle Ages, recovered from the *Cēsis* castle

Archeological excavation was begun in Latvia in the mid-19th century, but archaeology as a science rapidly developed only after World War II. Many extremely valuable finds have been made over the last 50 years. Thus, for example, researchers of the Stone Age have concluded that the most ancient settlements in the territory of Latvia appeared in the 9th millennium BC. Extensive archeological work has been done at such notable Stone Age monuments as the *Zvejnieku* burial grounds (by a team led by Francis Zagorskis), the *Sārnate* swamp settlement (Lucija Vankina), and the *Lubāna* lowlands Neolithic settlement (Ilze Loze). Bronze Age monuments include Latvia's chronologically oldest hill castles – *Ķivutkalns* near Dole and *Vīnakalns* at *Lišķile*, as well as the unique *Ķivutkalns* burial grounds, which has yielded anthropological materials that have made it possible to conduct more detailed research into the way in which the Baltic ethnos was formed. These Bronze Age sites have all been studied by Janis Graudonis.

The most important revelations from the Iron Age have come after a thorough examination of a number of hill castles and burial grounds, as well as lake castles. Much digging was done under the leadership of Elvira Snore at the *Asote* hill castle, while other work was done at *Tērvete*, *Daugmale*, *Ķenteskalns*, and others. Research into burial grounds at *Salaspils*, *Ķivti* and *Gūģeri* has allowed archaeologist Anna Zariņa to reconstruct the clothing of ancient Latgalls and Livs. One of the most important archeological finds from the Iron Age has been the *Araiši* lake castle, where a team led by archaeologist Janis Apals has set up an open-air museum.

Over the last few decades Medieval archaeology has been developed as a completely new field of study. Evalds Mugurevičs has made a particularly significant investment in this process. Much work has been done at castles in *Cēsis*, *Bauska*, *Turaida*, etc. Urban archaeology has also been an area of busy activity, and for the last four decades there have been sites in Old Riga every summer. Andris Caune has directed this process, and new knowledge has been obtained about the appearance of Riga in the Middle Ages and the lifestyles of people who lived there at that time.

Fragments of the fortifications around a hill castle at *Jersika*, 12th century

Dr. Andris Caune is a distinguished researcher of archaeology in Old Riga. We see a site in what used to be City Hall Square

Some of the walls of the Medieval *Araiši* castle (14th century)

These amber ornaments are 5,000 years old and were found at *Siliņupe*, near *Lapmežciems*

Latvia's most ancient residents used these flint tools 11,000 years ago

A reconstruction of the clothing of a Selian woman from the 12th century near *Sēlpils*

A reconstruction of the clothing that would have been worn by a Latgall woman in the 13th and 14th century near *Drabeši*

Dendrochronologist Maris Zunde studies a cross-section from oak that was found in one of the cultural strata of City Hall Square

Archeological work at ancient Semigallian burial grounds from the 8th to the 11th century near *Bauska*

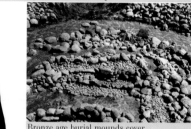

Jewellery worn by Liv women in the 11th century, as found at *Salaspils*

Bronze age burial mounds cover stone caskets near *Limbaži*

Students from the University of Latvia work at reconstructing a 2,500-year-old boat-shaped grave known as "Devil's Boat". The site is located near *Lube*

The walls of the *Dinaburg* castle

A ducat of Maximilian II, which was cast in 1571 in Hungary. It was found at the Medieval *Cēsis* castle

The Chronicle of Indriķis, or Henry

"Destiny's Horse", a painting by Arturs Baumanis. The artist based his painting on a story in the Chronicle of Indriķis about the monk Dietrich, who was captured by the Liv. The direction in which the white horse moved determined whether the monk would live or die. He lived, and christianity took root in Latvia

A 1901 postcard titled "Bishop Albert founds Riga". In 1201, Albert launched a settlement at the place where the *Ridzene* river flowed into the *Daugava*, establishing a convenient port. A Liv village had existed at the site since time immemorial, and they had built up a port, too. Albert used trickery to conquer the land, which he needed for his town and castle. He invited Liv leaders to dinner, and during the festivities, he took them hostage. In order to save their own lives, the elders had to turn their sons over to German captivity, as well as to yield their claim to several areas of land around the *Ridzene* river

Artist Voldemars Vimba's "The Battle at *Saule*". The first important victory for the Latvians and Lithuanians against the German invasion took place at *Saule* in 1236. As the Germans slowly pushed into Semigallia, they gradually became interested in going on to conquer Lithuania. The Brotherhood of the Sword launched a major drive against Lithuania, taking advantage of a large number of young Crusaders who had recently arrived from Germany. The knights made their way through the land of the Lithuanians, pillaging and robbing, while the Lithuanians busied themselves with drawing up a proper military force. When the Germans were heading back to Riga with their booty, a Lithuanian and Semigallian force lay in wait for them at *Vecsaule*. It was a terrible rout. The master of the order, Folkwind, was killed, as were numerous knights, German noblemen and Crusaders. The Semigallians chased the Germans through all of Semigallia and killed virtually all of the brethren. This was the end of the Brotherhood of the Sword

A written version of Latvia's history first began to appear in the 11th century, and the earliest known recordings of events were produced in Latvia itself. Adam of Bremen (1043-1072), who gave the Baltic Sea the name of *Mare Balticum*, produced a chronicle called *Gesta Hammaburgensis ecclesiae pontificum*, in which he described the Kurs as stubborn and barbaric pagans. The largest amount of historical information regarding Latvia at the beginning of the last millennium comes from the 13th century document known as the Chronicle of Indriķis. This history covers the period between 1180 and 1227. It was followed by the Chronicle of Rhymes, which brings the events reported in Indriķis' chronicle up to 1290 AD.

Indriķis was a Catholic clergyman who accompanied the German Crusaders on their journeys. He was a good storyteller, and in 1225 and 1226 he wrote the Livonian Chronicle. The document was written in Latin and described the way in which the Brotherhood of the Sword conquered Latvia. The chronicle is very much written from the victor's point of view. The Chronicle of Rhymes, by contrast, is written in a Middle German dialect. It praises the heroic battles of German knights who fought against the ancient Latvians. The document also contains a wealth of factual information.

The Christian faith spread in Latvia quite quickly in the 12th century, arriving mostly from the Orthodox East. Archeological sites on the shores of the *Daugava* River have found Orthodox crosses, grave sites and building ruins which date back to as early as the 11th century AD.

It is known that in 1140 there was already a stone church in *Koknese*, and christianity began to spread into Latvia from the West around that time. A Catholic church is known to have existed in *Kolka* in 1148. Danish historians have written that a Danish scholar called Ernemondus was the first bishop of Kurzeme. He served under the archbishop of Lund, Absalom, at the Lund Cathedral, and he participated in an attack which the Danish king Abel waged against the now-Lithuanian town of *Palanga*. On 24 June 1161, he was appointed bishop of Kurzeme. In 1169, he went to Rome to receive a papal affirmation of his bishop's title, which he ended up holding for 15 years and four months. During Ernemondus' reign, the Kurs attacked the Danish town of Skone (in 1170). In 1175, the Danish king Sven Estridson built a church in *Kursa*.

The next bishop of Kurzeme, serving from 1176 to 1185, was called Hermanus.

German traders who had good contacts with traders in Gottland and Denmark, had been plying the Baltic Sea since the early 12th century. Toward the end of the century, they followed the traders of Gottland along various trade routes that led to Russia and the Baltic region. The Germans quickly came to understand the importance of the *Daugava* river. In 1164 a monk called Meinhard, who had served as a chaplain and bookkeeper to a group of German traders, arrived in the land of the Livs. Meinhard learned the Liv language and began to proclaim the christian faith. In 1185 and 1886 he brought builders from Gottland to the region, and they built a stone castle and church in *Ikšķile*. After the death of Meinhard in 1196, Pope Celestine III decided to continue the promotion of christianity on the shores of the *Daugava*. Leadership of this mission was entrusted to an abbot called Berthold. He arrived in the Bay of Riga with a group of soldiers in 1198. A battle broke out, and a Liv warrior known in Latvian history as Imauts or Imants killed Berthold.

The third clergyman sent to the Baltic lands was Albert, who convinced Pope Innocent III to proclaim a second Crusade to Livonia. After careful preparations, Albert took 23 ships and 500 Crusaders to the Liv lands. In 1201, he began to build a settlement at the place where the *Ridzene* river flowed into the *Daugava*.

The Crusaders arrived in the spring and returned back to Germany at the beginning of the winter, and so Albert, now a bishop, encouraged that an order of knights patterned after the example of the Crusades in the Holy Land be established. The Brotherhood of the Sword, known in Latin as *Fratres militie Christi*

de Livonia was founded in 1202. The brethren in this order swore to reject family and property and to serve only God and the church. The knights carried a white tunic with a red cross and a depiction of the sword.

Albert was a sly politician, and he shored up his power in Livonia both through treacherous tactics and through military force. Albert quickly drove a wedge among various Baltic ethnic groups who had been at loggerheads to begin with. The Liv ruler Kaupo fell victim to praise and extravagant gifts and shifted his allegiance to Albert. At a battle near *Salaspils* in 1205, Kaupo fought against his own people and defeated them. The Germans took *Turaida* in 1206, and in 1207, they began to build a stronghold in *Cēsis*.

Once the Liv had been vanquished, Albert turned his considerable energies to ensuring that he could have full control over the *Daugava*, which by then was already an important trade route. Albert promised the ruler of *Koknese*, Vetseke, help against attacks from the Lithuanians if Vetseke would give Albert title to some of his land. Vetseke considered this to be an offensive proposition, burned down his castle together with the Germans and departed with his people to Russia.

In 1208 the settlement of *Sēlpils* surrendered to the Germans. One year later the Brotherhood of the Sword launched a surprise attack against *Jersika*, sacking and burning the settlement and taking the wife of the local ruler Visvaldis hostage. As ransom, Visvaldis was made to surrender several parts of his territory and to become a vassal of the bishop's. Albert won *Tālava* by encouraging battles between Estonians and the Latgalls of *Tālava* – a process that, of course, weakened both sides.

On 12 July 1210, a group of Kurs sailed for Riga with the aim of chasing out the Germans. They had been promised Liv, Semigallian, Estonian and Lithuanian support. The aid never materialised, and the Kurs had to retreat. At a battle at *Durbe* in 1260, the Kurs joined with Lithuanians to defeat a German force and, for a brief period, to liberate Kurland. However in 1267, the entire region fell under German control.

Albert's biggest headache was Zemgale. Initially he billeted a German force at *Mežotne*, drawing out the Semigallian ruler Viestards to liberate the settlement. Soon enough *Mežotne* fell back to the Germans. In 1228, Semigallians sacked a cloister at *Daugavgriva* and, soon after, the settlement of *Aizkraukle*. In a legendary battle at *Saule* in 1236, Semigallians and Lithuanians conquered a German force, vanquishing one of the best military units of the Brotherhood of the Sword and killing the master of the order, Folkwind. The remnants of the Brotherhood merged with the Teutonic Order in 1237, and the new organisation was named the Livonian Order. The Semigallians kept up their fight against the German knights for many years to come. In 1287, they attacked Riga, sacking *Ikšķile* and beating a much larger German force, killing every man. This was the last major battle between the indigenous peoples of Latvia and the German knights. Many Semigallians left their native lands and headed for Lithuania. The Germans had all of what is now Latvia under their control by 1290. They remained for more than six centuries.

There are two different ways of looking at the events of the 13th century in Latvia. Baltic German historians have seen the Brotherhood of the Sword as a force, which brought Christianity and European culture with it. Latvian historians, by contrast, have seen the events of the 13th and 14th century as something which primarily concentrated on expanding German economic interests into the Baltic region. It is true, however, that it was precisely in the 13th century that the boundary between Eastern Orthodoxy and Roman Catholicism was created, and it ran right across the Baltic lands. Those Baltic tribes, which fell under the control of the Roman Catholics, maintained their languages and eventually merged into what is now the Latvian ethnos. Those tribes, which ended up on the Orthodox side of the line, came under the rule of Russian princes and eventually underwent russification.

THE LIVONIAN PERIOD

When Germans began to conquer the lands of the Baltic territory, the rule was that one-third of all conquered land went to the military order that did the fighting, while two-thirds went to the local bishop. In the 1260s, when Kurzeme was divided up, however, the process was reversed. The bishop got one-third of the land, and the Livonian Order took over two-thirds. Several tiny states were set up in the area that is now Estonia and Latvia, and the most powerful of them was the state of the Livonian Order, which was ruled by the master of the order, and the Archbishopric of Riga, which was controlled by the archbishop. The two states fought over political hegemony in Livonia for nearly a century. The Livonian Order sought independence from the archbishop, because the German Order of which it was part was directly subordinated to the pope in Rome. Only after the German Order was defeated at *Valka* in 1422 did the first meeting of the Riga archbishop's *Landtag* come together, with bishops and representatives of the order meeting to discuss the important issues of the day. The *Landtag* met once a year, and in later years, representatives of the local knighthood, as well as of various cities in the region, also participated. The *Landtag* dealt with various economic issues, declared war, and settled disputes among Livonian nobles.

As the Germans consolidated their power in the region, Latvians lost all political rights, even though initially some of the rulers who had yielded to German rule willingly were allowed to keep some of their land. These leaders stayed on their lands and participated in the conclusion of peace treaties with the Order and the bishops, but their power was sharply circumscribed, and they were basically nothing more than vassals of the new rulers. Some of the Latvian rulers were germanised, while others preserved their ethnicity and took titles such as freeman, *leimanis*, or *ķoniņš*. Several *ķoniņš* dynasties in Kurzeme (the Kaleji, Ziemeļi, Peņiķi, Vidiņi, and others) even had their own coats of arms.

The freedom and property rights of the Medieval Latvians were ensured on paper, but not in real life. The Germans were often violent against indigenous populations and behaved in all manner of unlawful ways. The first serious battles between the two sides occurred in 1212, when farmers in the region of *Autīne* rebelled against the Brotherhood of the Sword after the brethren confiscated the beehives of the farmers. The rebellion was put down, but not before it drew in farmers from several different regions. Initially farmers did indentured work for the local nobleman for only a few weeks each year, and farmers had the right to own their own land and homes. As the properties of the landed gentry expanded, however, the duties extracted from locals increased, too. Farmers who fell into debt were prohibited against leaving the lands of their rulers. Noblemen concluded agreements with each other to ensure the return of farmers who fled.

The largest German castles were located along good traffic routes. There were large settlements of traders and craftsmen, and cities began to emerge. Riga gained the rights of a city in 1225, followed in the 13th and 14th centuries by *Aizpute*, *Cēsis*, *Kuldīga*, *Limbaži*, *Valmiera* and others. Riga's economy was based on trade. Initially various professions in Riga were open to indigenous populations, too. The first school in Riga – the Dom School, which trained clergymen – was opened in 1211. In 1226, the School of St. George's Church followed in 1226, and the School of St. Peter's Church was opened in 1353. Riga was an important crossroads for trade between the West and the East. Large numbers of traders who acted as middlemen in trade operations settled in the city, and in the 15th century Riga already boasted some 8,000 permanent residents. The city's status was increased by its membership in the Hanseatic League, which provided various rights and benefits to its members. Riga was a rich city, because trade was a lucrative business indeed. In 1354, wealthy traders set up the Large Guild, which later won various concessions from the local government in Riga.

Craftsmen of various kinds set up their own guilds, and eventually these merged into what became known as the Small Guild. Only Germans were allowed to become members of the guilds, and only people who were in the guilds were allowed to engage in various professions and to open their own workshops. Locals were prohibited from engaging in trade or any of the professional crafts. Instead they were carriers, weighers and loaders, and they organised their own groups – the Brotherhood of Beer and Wine Carriers, for example, which was formed in the 13th and 14th century by carriers who worked in the transportation sector. Another group was organised by grain carriers. These brotherhoods organised leisure activities and worked to defend the interests of their members. They all had their own altars at local churches. Most of the members of these organisations were Latvians. The most successful Latvians studied and became wealthy, and some of them took part in the political governance of the city. All of them, however, were forced to germanise in order to be able to join the major guilds and to rise through the city's ranks.

In the 14th and 15th centuries, Livonia was made up of approximately 40 different regions, and they did not always get along with one another. In the mid-15th century, the Livonian Order was weakened through battles with Lithuanians. The Order restored its authority over the region when a man called Walter von Plettenberg (1494-1535) became the master of the order. This wise and thoughtful ruler managed to bring discipline into the Order and to restore its authority. In 1503, von Plettenberg won an armistice with the Russians after his forces beat a Russian military force on the shores of Lake Smolin in 1502. The armistice was extended several times, thus protecting the Livonian Order against Russian attacks for more than 50 years.

Ethnic Latvians accepted the Catholic faith in the 13th century only insofar as appearances were concerned. In fact, most Latvians were baptised forcibly. One of the problems with the new faith was that German clergymen seldom learned the local language, and so there were communication problems. In 1422, the *Landtag* in *Valka* decreed that members of the gentry must ensure that all of their vassals go to church regularly so that the clergy could teach them about the Christian faith, the Lord's Prayer and the commandments. Martin Luther's Reformation won great resonance in Livonia, where many people were disgusted with the Catholic Church's selling of indulgences, the cult of the saints, and the lifestyle of clergymen who were far too focused on the material world. A clergyman called Andrejs Knopkens began to proclaim Luther's teachings at St. Peter's Church in 1521, followed by Silvestrs Tegetmeijers at St. Jacob's a year later. Many members of the landed gentry supported the Reformation, as did the Riga city council. Most historians feel that Walter von Plettenberg did not support the Reformation openly, but he did allow events to proceed at their own pace. The so-called Icon Riots erupted in Riga in 1524, and images of the saints were stolen from Catholic churches and burned outdoors. Monks were ejected from their cloisters. In 1524, a Latvian Lutheran congregation was established at St. Jacob's Church. The clergymen at the church had learned the Latvian language, and worship was held in Latvian. Many noblemen and ordinary people converted to Lutheranism. Latvian farmers, who were ordered to join the same church as their lords, also converted. Many Lutheran services initially were almost identical to Catholic worship rites, because German clergymen continued to refuse to learn the Latvian language, and local farmers simply did not understand what they were saying when they tried to speak a few words in Latvian. Many Latvians ignored the shift in denominations and stuck to their ancient, local traditions. Walter von Plettenberg's farsighted approach to the denominational matter created a tradition of ecumenism in Latvia, which survives to this very day. Save only for the aforementioned Icon Riots, Latvia has never been the site of violent differences of opinion on matters of faith, and never has one denomination been able to win firm control over the country.

One of the essential tenets of Martin Luther's Reformation was that church services must be held in the language of the congregation. Religious texts quickly had to be translated into Latvian. The first books in the Latvian language were published in Germany in 1525, but no copy of these books has survived to this day. This did, however, lead to one of the most important events of the 16th century in terms of Latvia's history – the emergence of written Latvian. The oldest known printing of the Lord's Prayer in Latvian is found in a Prussian chronicle that was written between 1529 and 1531. It is clear from the text that the author, Simons Grunavs did not understand the text himself. There are linguistic mistakes, which can occur only when one is copying a language that one does not know. Grunavs later claimed that his text was used by Ancient Prussian priests for all kinds of mystical and even satanic purposes, but an analysis of the text clearly shows it to have been written in Latvian, not Ancient Prussian.

The library of Uppsala University has a book called *Agenda*, which was published in 1507 in Latin. It is a Catholic book which sets out the procedure for worship, complete with the necessary texts. In the margins, someone wrote some of the texts by hand in Latvian, including the Lord's Prayer and various phrases from the liturgy. These make it clear that even when rites such as baptism were held in Latin, the clergyman was forced to address participants in the language that they knew. Examples of the hand-written phrases include "Do you wish to christen these children?" and "Tell me the names of the children". It is known that the book in question was used by clergymen in *Suntaži* and Riga in the 16th century, and the annotations were made between 1507 and 1540. Documents from Latvia's various trade-based organisations contain not only lists of Latvian members, but also phrases and even complete pages of text in Latvian. One of the documents which has survived is a 1497 text written by the Latvian leader of a salt carrier and loader association, Stagers. It is written in Latvian.

In the 1530s, the Reverend Johann Eck completed a manuscript of the Lutheran *Enchiridion* in Latvian, and he also translated fragments of the gospels. One of the oldest known written recordings of the Lord's Prayer was written by a travelling German writer and musician called Johann Hazentäter, who visited Livonia in 1547. He sent a copy of the Lord's Prayer as an example of the language which people spoke in Vidzeme to the distinguished German scientist Sebastian Munster (1489-1552), along with other information about Livonia at that time. Munster was a theologian, mathematician and geographer in Heidelberg and Basle, and he wrote the book *Kosmogrāfija* (Cosmography) in 1550 – the first known printed text in the Latvian language.

THE 16TH AND 17TH CENTURIES IN LATVIA

Protocols of the "plough audit"
in Vidzeme, 1624 and 1629

Riga, 1605

The *Blümentale* agreement on the division of spheres of influence among the Riga archbishop, the city of Riga and the Livonian Order

Labour agreements with servants signed by officials from the Large Guild between the 15th and 17th centuries

A document from Livonian Order master Walter von Plettenberg granting certain privileges to the city of Riga, 1525

A document referring to accounts with shippers in *Ventspils*, April 18, 1655

A document signed by King of Poland and Lithuania, Stefan Batorius granting privileges to the city of Riga, January 14, 1581

Livonian Order master Gotthard Kettler signed this document, which grants privileges to the city of Riga, on January 24, 1560

In the 16th century, Russia began to pose a serious threat to the territory, which is now Latvia. At that time Russia was still known as the land of Moscow, and its rulers needed access to the Baltic Sea in order to maintain contacts to the West. The Livonian states stood in the way.

Ivan the Terrible, Russia's tsar, demanded the Livonian Order to pay the tribute to his court, which at one time the region of *Tērbata* (Tartu) had paid to the Russian princes. The Order's refusal to do so provided Ivan with the excuse that he needed to launch a war against the Order. Weakened by internal disputes, the Order was in no way ready for war when 1558 Ivan's forces attacked Livonia. The Livonian wars lasted from 1558 until 1583, and the greatest of suffering was visited upon the local people in the region. Russian forces, unopposed, moved on *Tērbata*, *Narva*, *Rēzekne*, *Viļāni* and *Alūksne*. Seeing how easily his forces were advancing, the tsar refused to accept an offer from the *Valmiera Landtag* to pay the sums that had been demanded. In January 1559 the forces of the Riga archbishop and the Livonian Order suffered a heavy defeat at *Cesvaine*. The Russian army, leaving completely destroyed areas in its wake, advanced on Riga, but failed to take the city. The soldiers returned to Russia along the shores of the *Daugava* River, burning, pillaging and murdering all along the way. On 2 August 1560, the armies of Ivan the Terrible routed the forces of the Riga archbishop and the Livonian Order in Sweden.

Denmark, Lithuania, Poland and the Livonian Order did not want Russia to gain a foothold on the Baltic Sea, and so it was decided that Livonia must be put under the rule of other countries. The Livonian Order was disbanded in 1561. Master Gotthard Kettler was given control of Western Latvia to the *Daugava*, and he named this area the Duchy of Kurzeme and Zemgale. Kettler became a vassal of the Polish-Lithuanian king Sigismund II Augustus. The Duchy of Trans-*Daugava* was set up in Latgale, Vidzeme and Southern Estonia, and this duchy was under the direct control of the Polish-Lithuanian Empire. In 1569 Poland and Lithuania went to war against Russia. In 1577 Ivan the Terrible attacked the Duchy of Trans-Daugava once again, attacking with an enormous military force from Novgorod to *Trikāta* and *Valmiera*. The Russians sacked the regions around *Nītaure*, *Sigulda* and *Turaida*. Soldiers from a garrison in *Cesvaine* were tortured mercilessly for their refusal to surrender to the tsar. A similar fate was visited upon the defenders of castles at *Ērgļi* and *Aizkraukle*. Defenders of the *Cēsis* castle blew the building up, thus committing suicide, when they decided that it was impossible to stand against the Russian forces. By the autumn of 1577, Russia controlled all of Vidzeme. Most of the soldiers withdrew back to Russia, leaving a number of military garrisons behind in the various castles. The territory was completely devastated, and travellers in the region reported that between Riga and *Valmiera* one heard no barking dogs, no crowing roosters. The owner of the *Bērzaune* manor, Tiesenhausen, wrote of the devastation: "The enemy of my estate was so wild that only the walls of *Kalsnava* remain standing, while in *Grostona* not even a fence post remains. Only one threshing barn is left in *Mārciena*. 150 farms have been burned, and many of the farmers have been killed or taken hostage. In *Radava* Parish, only 15 farms of 50 remain. Of 26 farms in *Silciems* – only three. *Mārciena* had 30 farmers before the war. Only six remain after the war."

In 1579, the Polish king Stefan Batorius and the king of Sweden launched a counteroffensive against Russia, which had been weakened by the long war. In 1582 Moscow was forced to conclude an armistice with Poland. One year later it followed suit with Sweden. In 1583 the 25-year Livonian war finally drew to an end.

The terms of the peace treaty left Sweden with control over Northern Estonia, while the Polish-Lithuanian Empire won control over the Duchy of Trans-*Daugava*. The first governor of the duchy was Gotthard Kettler, and in 1566 he was replaced by Jan Karol Hodkevic. In 1561, Poland's king, Sigismund II Augustus, had promised the German barons that their privileges would be preserved, that freedom of religion would be maintained, and they would be given control over the land, as well as all authority over the farmers who lived in the region. The original document whereby Sigismund granted these privileges has not survived, and historians feel that the document never got past draft form. Still, German barons insisted on the privileges and tried to win the rights, which they had supposedly been promised. The condition of farmers was difficult, indeed, not only on the German estates (70% of all of the manors), but also on Polish lands. Farmers were placed under indentured servitude, and they had to pay duties that were assessed based on the size of the various farms. Farmers were not allowed to sell anything without the permission of their lords, and corporal punishment was common. Polish king Stefan Batorius wanted to improve the situation of the farmers, but he did not live long enough to issue a law that would limit the arbitrary behaviour of the German barons. When he died, the situation remained unchanged.

In 1582, Pope Gregory XIII recommended that a new calendar (the so-called Gregorian calendar) be adopted by all Catholic territories in place of the old Julian calendar. Stefan Batorius ordered that the calendar be implemented in Riga and in the Duchy of Trans-*Daugava*. Lutheran Riga opposed the move, fearing that it represented some Catholic treachery. In 1584 the king repeated the order, and the Riga city council yielded. Building owners in Riga, led by attorney Martiņš Gize took advantage of the situation to extract promises from the Riga city council that local citizens would be allowed to participate in the governance of the city. When the city council refused, the so-called Calendar Riots broke out. In 1589, military units were brought in to oppress the rebellion. The leaders were executed, but the council was forced to yield at least a little bit. Representatives of the guilds were invited to participate in the governance of the city.

In 1620, a nine-year war broke out between Poland and Sweden, basically over the future of the Swedish throne, but also because both countries wanted to control the lucrative trade routes of the Baltic Sea. In 1592, Polish king Sigismund III Vasa, who was a devout Catholic, inherited the Swedish throne. This was not acceptable to the Lutheran noblemen of Sweden, and the Swedish parliament proclaimed Sigismund to be an interloper. The king refused to yield, and war broke out between Sweden and Poland. The war took place mostly in Estonia and Vidzeme. Both armies crossed Vidzeme several times, and farmers were forced to feed soldiers from both sides. Many farms were burned and looted. To make matters worse, the harvest failed in 1601, and famine ensued. The Black Plague was close on its heels, and its effect was devastating. Every single resident of *Alūksne* reportedly died, and *Limbaži* reported that only eight people had survived. The land went to fallow, and fields grew over.

Peace was achieved for several years in the 1620s after Swedish king Gustavus Adolphus (the son of Karl IX) conquered the city of Riga, even though it was well fortified and held out against the Swedish army for six weeks. The Swedish army also took all of Vidzeme and part of Kurzeme. In 1629 an armistice was concluded between Poland and Sweden at the Prussian city of Altmark. Poland was given the duchies of Kurzeme and Zemgale, as well Latgale, which the Poles dubbed Inflantia. Sweden took Estonia and Vidzeme. This division proved to have lasting consequences. Vidzeme, Kurzeme and Zemgale remained Lutheran territories. The literacy of the population increased, and the level of education in these areas was much higher than in other parts of the region. Latgale remained Catholic, and when it was later absorbed into Russia, forced russification took place.

Swedish king Karl XI began to reduce the rights of the manors in Vidzeme when he came to understand that free farmers would provide greater income to the state. A process known as "plough audit" was launched. The size of fields was registered, people of working age and livestock herds were counted, and the value of land was assessed. Data from this audit were used to determine levels of indentured servitude and duties to be paid in the future, and these were carefully recorded in special books. Once a farmer had paid all of his duties, he was allowed to sell his land. Farmers were also allowed to pay extra in order to get rid of servitude obligations, and they became free farmers. Economic regulations issued in 1696 which, among other things, said that any punishment more severe than six lashes must be approved by the courts.

The Swedish government promoted educational development in its lands. In Livonia, the Swedish authorities, led by the theologian Johann Fischer, worked intensively in this area. A school for Latvian children was opened in Riga, and rural areas were not forgotten either. Officials at churches were ordered to teach children to read, sing and write. After the power of the barons had been reduced, the king issued a decree, which granted a certain amount of farmland to each congregation, and income from the land was used to keep up the local school.

The first university in Sweden was Uppsala University, which was founded in 1477. The first university in the Baltic was the Königsberg Prussian University, which was founded in 1544, followed by Vilnius University in 1579. Gustavus II Adolphus opened a school in Tartu, which in 1632 was transformed into the Academie Gustavina. Tartu University became the first university in the Lutheran part of the Baltic region. During its first 24 years of existence, it had 1,056 students – 476 from Sweden, 115 from Finland and 303 from Livonia. Admission to the university was open to the children of farmers, too.

The first ethnic Latvian whose academic education and scientific achievements were of true note was Janis Reiters (1632-1695), a Latvian theologian, lawyer and writer who was the son of a Riga builder called Indriķis Jatnieks. Reiters studied at the Dom School in Riga, and it 1650 he was admitted to Tartu University, where he studied theology. In 1654 he published a dissertation on meekness that was written in Latvian. In 1656 he successfully defended another dissertation, this time on Holy Communion. Reiters spoke Latvian, German, Estonian, Swedish and Finnish, and later he also learned Russian, Polish, French and Italian. He was also able to read Ancient Latin, Greek and Hebrew.

Janis Reiters worked as a Lutheran pastor at a church in *Rauna*, and he quickly made friends with local farmers, defending them against the excesses of the local baronial administration. He became famous for his sermons, and he often criticised the teachings of Martin Luther.

In 1662 Reiters published a book containing the Lord's Prayer in 40 different languages. Hoping to win a commission to translate the Bible into Latvian, in 1664 he published a Latvian translation of the Gospel of St. Matthew (no copy has survived). In 1665 Reiters converted to Catholicism and travelled to Braunsberg, Bromberg, Vienna and Rome. In 1666 Pope Alexander VIII paid him a significant sum of money. According to Reiters himself, he later worked at Vilnius University as a professor of civil justice with the recommendation of the papacy. Later he taught law in France. In 1675 Swedish king Karl XI reinstated Reiters' rights as a Lutheran pastor and assigned him a church near Pernau in Estonia.

A second edition of Reiters' book of the Lord's Prayer was published in Rostock in 1675. Between 1676 and 1677 he served as a garrison pastor at the fortress of *Koknese*. He delivered sermons in German, Swedish, Finnish and Latvian and became enormously popular among local Latvians as a defender of the oppressed. For this, he was fired from his job at the garrison. Reiters went to Riga, where soon after his arrival a huge fire broke out. Reiters lost his entire library and was falsely accused of arson. He was forced to move to Sweden and then to Finland,

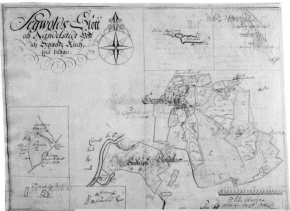

A map of the *Sigulda* castle and the *Nandelstedt* manor – *Segewolds Slott och Nandelstedt Hoff uti Segewoldz Kirchspiel beläget*. The map was drawn by Oloff Kvist in 1681

where he worked as a pastor and a doctor.

Swedish king Gustav Adolphus II ordered that the Lutheran church in Vidzeme become the state church, and Catholicism was prohibited. The king appointed a senior clergyman, Hermanis Samsons as the local superintendent. Attendance at church was mandatory, and people who did not turn up suffered corporal punishment. Nevertheless, many farmers continued to pray to their agrarian-based pagan gods. The superintendent launched a vicious battle against them. A massive hunt for witches ensued, and trials that were common in Europe in the Middle Ages were held in Latvia, too. Superintendent Samsons produced a handbook, *Hexen Pedigten* ("Sermons About Witches"), which was published in Riga in 1626.

In 1673, two German theologians, Johann Fischer and Ernst Glück, moved to Riga. Fischer was appointed superintendent of the local church, and soon he travelled to Stockholm with a long memorandum on the status of the church in Livonia in hand. King Karl XI ordered him to hurry up with the translation of the Bible into Latvian and gave the theological permission to open another book printing facility in Riga. Reiters at this point had already translated part of the Bible, and he had also published several segments of the Gospel of Matthew without any censorship from the superintendent. The sole sur-

viving copy of his translation is housed at the Carolina Rediviva library in Uppsala. When it came time to find a translator for the whole Bible, however, Glück was chosen. He spent five years learning the Latvian language and brushing up on his Ancient Hebrew and Ancient Greek. The translation, he felt, had to come from the original. It took Glück eight years to translate the Bible. The translation was examined by a council of clergymen from Vidzeme and Kurzeme, assembled by Fischer. The Bible was printed in 1,500 copies between 1685 and 1694. One half of the copies, by order of the king, were distributed to churches and schools. It was a good translation. Glück, who served as a pastor in *Alūksne*, was active in establishing so-called people's schools throughout Vidzeme. In his town alone he founded three schools. Around 1683 a primary reader thought to have been written by Glück was published for schoolchildren. In 1687, congregational schools began to be opened at various churches. Buildings were constructed for the schools, and teachers were given land. Initially attendance was compulsory, but soon enough farmers were perfectly happy to send their children to school.

Glück had an interesting destiny. During the Great Northern War, the Russians took him to Moscow, where he worked as a teacher, editor and translator of classic literature into Russian. His foster daughter, Marta Skovronska (Rahbe), became the favourite of Peter the Great, and later she became Empress Catherine I of Russia.

The Swedes ruled Vidzeme for nearly a century. The Swedish government was particularly concerned about the condition of roads in the region. Barons were ordered to build inns along the roads, which ran through their lands, and to provide everything that was necessary for travellers. Judges known as "pavement lords" supervised the condition of the major roads. Gustav Adolphus introduced a new judicial system in Vidzeme, setting up a number of land courts, which had jurisdiction over all local residents. The highest court in the region was attached to the royal court at Tartu.

Farmers in Vidzeme enjoyed a relatively good life during Swedish rule, and the period is known to this very day as the "good times of the Swedes". After the conclusion of the Altmark treaty, Latgale remained under the control of the Polish state. The landed gentry in Latgale had great power, but the barons spent most of their time quarrelling with one another over property rights. The noblemen also sought to extract as much money from their farmers as possible. Farmers in Latgale lived in villages that were divided up into narrow strips of land. Each farmer was given one of these pieces of land, and when a farmer died, his heirs divided the land up into even tinier portions. There were also linguistic specifics. The Latvian language in Vidzeme was influenced mostly by Germanic and Finno-Ugric languages, while the language in Latgale was affected mostly by the Slavic tongues.

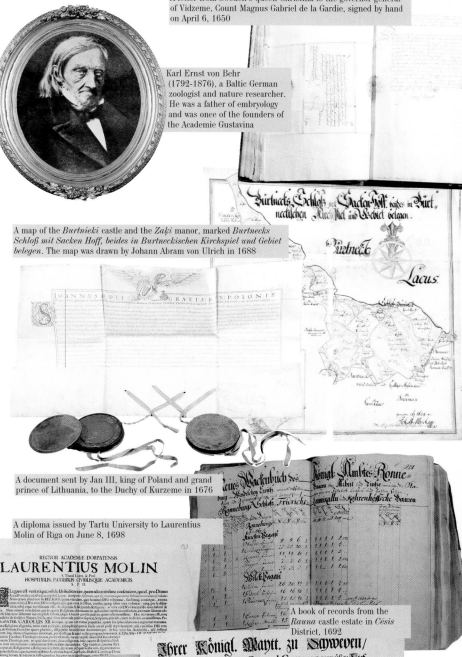

An order issued by the dukes of Kurzeme and Zemgale, Friedrich and Wilhelm, on the division of the duchy, 1595

Privileges issued to the city of Riga by Swedish king Gustav Adolphus on September 25, 1621

King Gustav II Adolphus of Sweden (1594-1632, crowned in 1611). He won control over part of Vidzeme and over the city of Riga in 1621

A letter from Sweden's queen Christina to the governor general of Vidzeme, Count Magnus Gabriel de la Gardie, signed by hand on April 6, 1650

Karl Ernst von Behr (1792-1876), a Baltic German zoologist and nature researcher. He was a father of embryology and was once of the founders of the Academie Gustavina

A map of the *Burtnieki* castle and the *Zaķi* manor, marked *Burtnecks Schloß mit Sacken Hoff, beides in Burtneckischen Kirchspiel und Gebiet belegen*. The map was drawn by Johann Abram von Ulrich in 1688

A document sent by Jan III, king of Poland and grand prince of Lithuania, to the Duchy of Kurzeme in 1676

A diploma issued by Tartu University to Laurentius Molin of Riga on June 8, 1698

A book of records from the *Rauna* castle estate in *Cēsis* District, 1692

An atlas of 17th century roads that was published in Riga in 1695 by Johann Abram von Ulrich – *Neue Einrichtung der naccurat gemeßen Landstraß Brücken im Rigischen Kreyße durch Johann Ab: v: Ulrich, Geom. et Revis: Reg: jur. ao 1695*

An order issued by the governor general of Vidzeme, Erich Dahlberg, on the transfer of Tartu University to Pernau, June 17, 1699

THE DUCHY OF KURZEME
(COURLAND)

The Coat of Arms of the Duchy of Kurzeme

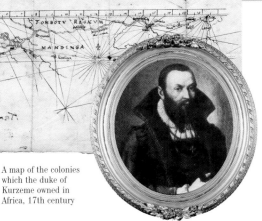

A map of the colonies which the duke of Kurzeme owned in Africa, 17th century

Gothard Kettler (1517-1587), the last master of the Livonian Order, laid the foundations of the Kettler dynasty and was the first duke of Kurzeme and Zemgale

Jēkabs (1610-1682) was the mightiest of the dukes of Kurzeme and Zemgale. During his reign, there was extensive development of trade and industry. The Duchy held colonies overseas and had a mighty fleet

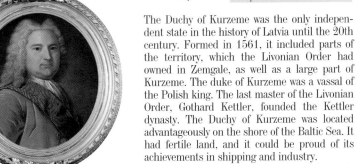

Ernst Johann Biron (1690-1772), the duke of Kurzeme, was, according to history, partly Latvian. He was the *de facto* ruler of Russia for a period of time, and he was responsible for the construction of the magnificent castles of *Rundāle* and *Jelgava*

The Duchy of Kurzeme was the only independent state in the history of Latvia until the 20th century. Formed in 1561, it included parts of the territory, which the Livonian Order had owned in Zemgale, as well as a large part of Kurzeme. The duke of Kurzeme was a vassal of the Polish king. The last master of the Livonian Order, Gothard Kettler, founded the Kettler dynasty. The Duchy of Kurzeme was located advantageously on the shore of the Baltic Sea. It had fertile land, and it could be proud of its achievements in shipping and industry.

The 30-Year War, which wreaked great havoc in Europe, caused enormous losses, and there was a great demand for industrial and agricultural products from the independent Duchy. Particularly in demand were wood materials, textiles for sails, hemp rope, pitch, tar, cannons and gunpowder. For this reason, the most important phase in the history of the Duchy was the period during which Duke Jēkabs reigned.

Duke Jēkabs ruled from 1642 until 1682. His aim was to transform Kurzeme into a state similar to Holland. One after another, he had new factories, sawmills and tar-making plants built. During his reign, 15 iron and 7 copper smelters were built, along with many glassmaking facilities, paper mills and soap factories. There were several textile making facilities and factories that produced weapons. The ports of Kurzeme, especially Ventspils, were the sites of shipbuilding yards that worked without interruption. The swamp ore that was found in Kurzeme did not meet the duke's needs, and so he leased iron and copper mines in Norway.

Duke Jēkabs concluded trade agreements with France, Portugal, Spain and England. He was rich enough to loan money, ships and cannons to the Stuart kings Charles I and Charles II of England. The two rulers lost the throne of England, however, and their debts to Kurzeme were never repaid. Jēkabs sold some of his ships to France and England, but Kurzeme had a much larger fleet than France at that time. In Ventspils alone, 120 ships – more than 40 of them warships – were built, and *Jelgava* became the Duchy's leading trade centre. The *Baldone* and *Emburga* iron smelters began to produce cast iron between 1650 and 1658, and most of it was exported. One of the largest steel smelters in the Duchy was found in *Jelgava*. Iron was transformed into steel, or iron tools such as axes, swords, guns and cannon parts were produced. Most of these things were exported to France and Holland. There was also a copper smelter in *Jelgava*. Ore was imported from Sweden and Norway and floated down the *Lielupe* River.

Between 1675 and 1780 the Duchy had a mint which produced shillings, thalers, florints and ducats. Duke Jēkabs held several colonies from which gold was obtained, and gold coins were produced in *Jelgava* until 1660. Between 1646 and 1701, there was a major sawmill in *Jelgava*. Until the mid-18th century, there were at least three textile manufacturing plants in *Emburga*, as well as a fulling-mill, which produced wallpaper.

Between 1642 and 1658, a textiles plant in *Vircava* was the most important sail making facility in all Europe.

There was a glassmaking kiln near the *Svēte* River in *Jelgava*, which produced table glass, crystal glass, glass beads, glass panes for windows, coloured glass and mirrors. Most of the mirrors were exported to Gambia and the West Indies. Another interesting business, which was run by the duke, was a farm where falcons were bred. Hundreds of hunting birds were raised each year, and many were presented to foreign rulers as gifts.

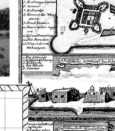

The duke's fortress in Gambia, 17th century

Jelgava was the capital city of the Duchy of Kurzeme. Duke Ernst Johann Biron invited the Italian architect Rastrelli to *Jelgava*, and he built one of the most ornate palaces in Northern Europe there

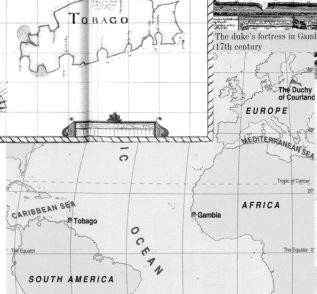

Tobago – the colony of the Duchy of Kurzeme

The island of Tobago was a colony of Kurzeme

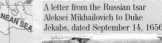

A letter from the Russian tsar Aleksei Mikhailovich to Duke Jēkabs, dated September 14, 1656

A letter from Duke Jēkabs to Governor General Christer Horn, 1655

Propsals of Master *Bengt Ström* to improve the iron manufacturing in Kurzeme, year 1687

A glassmaking kiln in *Jelgava*

The double deck of Duke Jēkabs *Die Pax*, which carried the colonists to Tobago in autumn 1656

A kiln in *Vitiņi*, *Dobele* District

A kiln at *Nigrande*

King Karl XII of Sweden (1682-1718)

War broke out among Russia, Poland and Sweden in 1654, but Tsar Alexei concluded a peace with the Poles in 1661 so that the two countries could join forces against Sweden.

In the late 17th century, Sweden faced a joint military force composed of Denmark, Poland and Russia. A nobleman from Vidzeme, Johann Reinhold Patkuls was of key importance in setting up this coalition. He encouraged noblemen in Vidzeme to oppose the Swedish king and to surrender to Poland. Patkuls also encouraged Polish king Augustus II to go to war with Sweden, because the 17-year-old ruler in Stockholm, Karl XII, had no experience in military affairs. War broke out in 1700. Denmark also participated in the war, but Karl XII made short work of beating it. He then turned against the Russian forces that were preparing to besiege Narva. In the summer of 1701 Karl XII beat a Saxon force in fields near Riga and took over Kurzeme. Over the next several years Karl XII battled in Poland and Saxony, finally forcing Augustus II to sue for peace. The traitor Patkuls was turned over to the Swedes, and in 1707, he was sentenced to death by torture.

The Russian armed forces, meanwhile, were marauding through Vidzeme. In 1702, a Russian military leader, Boris Sheremetyev, beat Swedish forces several times in Vidzeme, leaving destroyed fields and cities behind and taking local residents hostage. The Russians also forced the defenders of *Alūksne* to surrender. All of the city's residents were taken hostage and taken to Russia. Among them was the pastor of the *Alūksne* church, the translator of the Bible into Latvian Ernst Glück. He was taken with his entire household. In 1705 Sheremetyev reported to the tsar: "Nothing is left in the land of the enemy. From Pleskau to Tartu, 38 *versts* (1 *versts* = 1, 066 km) to this side of Pernau, and from Riga to *Valka*, everything has been destroyed; all of the castles have been torn down. Nothing is left but Pernau and Revel, and a few estates along the sea."

The Russians also invaded Kurzeme, but in 1705, the Swedes beat the Russian army at *Mūrmuiža*. The Russians withdrew into Vidzeme in the conviction that Karl XII would hasten after them. For this reason, Vidzeme was also completely sacked. Karl XII, meanwhile, was in Ukraine, hoping to win the support of local Kazakhs. Having failed to do so, he was forced to begin a decisive battle against the Russians at Poltava. The young Swedish king lost. In the same year, the Russian army besieged Riga, and on 4 July 1710, the city surrendered, because famine and the Black Plague had

The Privileges and Regulation of the Green Guards of Jelgava, years 1790–1799

returned to the city. The Russian era began in Vidzeme. The Northern War continued, but no more were the battles waged in Latvia.

After the war, Vidzeme was empty. The pre-war residents had all been killed, taken hostage or died of the Black Plague. Tsar Peter I reinstated all of the privileges of the landed gentry that had been taken away by Sweden, returning their lands to them and declaring that henceforth only representatives of the nobility could own manors. Catherine I in 1783 declared the manors to be the absolute property of the noblemen, thus in effect presenting the barons of Vidzeme with a gift of 188 manors.

The condition of farmers deteriorated. Indentured servitude was put back into place, and farmers were banned from selling their produce on the open market. Many farmers began to drink heavily – breweries and vodka stills provided a great deal of income to the nobility. The Russian government put the Latvian farmers under a new form of slavery. People were impoverished, and they had no rights at all. Many of the free farmers who had obtained these rights during the Swedish rule now lost the privileges once again. Countless Latvian men sought to enlist in the Swedish army.

In 1729, a group of missionaries from the Herrnhutian colony in Saxony arrived in Vidzeme, hoping to teach the Latvians of Vidzeme about Christ, to promote a clarity of the heart and love among brothers. Latvians were responsive to the call and happily gathered for church services on Sunday mornings. The Herrnhutian brethren spoke in simple words, which the farmers could understand, proclaiming the love of Christ. The Herrnhutians quickly learned the Latvian language, and, as simple artisans themselves, they had a better understanding of the farmers than Lutheran clergymen did. Meetings of these brotherhood congregations in *Valmiera* were attended by farmers from *Cēsis*, *Trikata* and *Rauna*. Later the brotherhood began to put up buildings in other parts of Latvia, too. An inviolable part of church services was singing. The Herrnhutians soon enough produced a hand-written book of hymns, which were sung both in church and in everyday life. Close links among the congregations drew Latvians together in the national sense, too. Most of the members of these congregations learned to read so that they could read the Bible and the hymnal. Initially Lutheran clergymen supported these brotherhood congregations, but soon enough, they changed their minds, fearing that the Herrnhutians might alienate Latvian farmers from the Lutheran church. In 1743, Empress Elizabeth banned the activities of the Herrnhutians, and persecution began. When Catherine the Great came to the throne of Russia, however, freedom of religion was reinstated, and the Herrnhutians renewed their work in Vidzeme. During the time when the feudal system was collapsing all over Europe, the period of indentured servitude in Latvia reached its apogee. In 1739, a local official called Rosen issued a declaration which claimed that the lord of a manor had property rights to all of his people and that he could sell or trade them. Noblemen were allowed to charge duties from their farmers as they saw fit, and they were given free reign over the properties of farmers, too. Farmers were understandably dissatisfied with this, and rebellions broke out. Empress Catherine II, worried about the situation, decreed that farmers in Latvia and Estonia would have the same rights of governance as existed in Russia. Courts were set up in the various districts of Latvia to hear petitions from farmers. Noblemen were banned from increasing servitude requirements and duties arbitrarily, corporal punishment was limited, and farmers were allowed to sell the produce that was left over when they had made their contributions to the nobles.

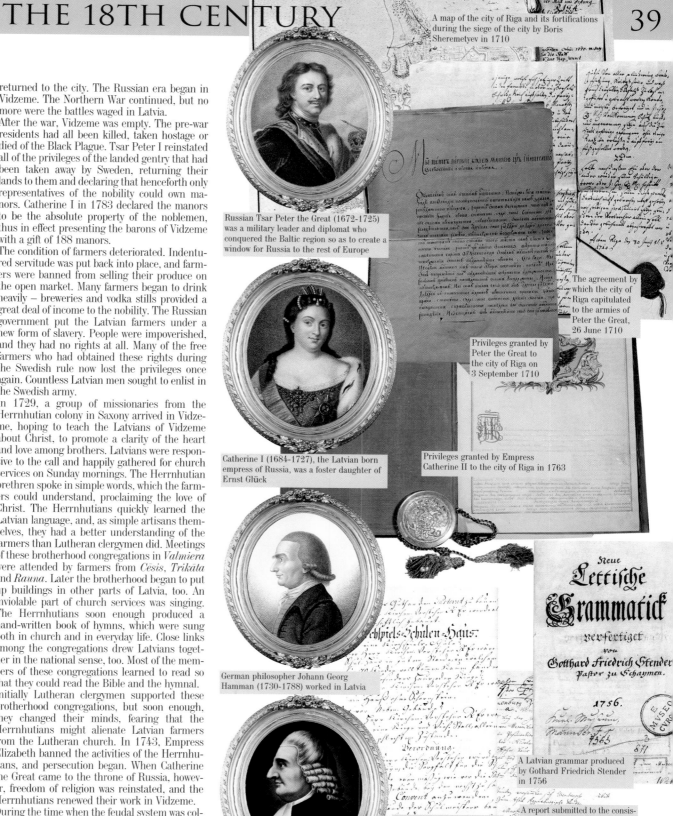

A map of the city of Riga and its fortifications during the siege of the city by Boris Sheremetyev in 1710

Russian Tsar Peter the Great (1672-1725) was a military leader and diplomat who conquered the Baltic region so as to create a window for Russia to the rest of Europe

The agreement by which the city of Riga capitulated to the armies of Peter the Great, 26 June 1710

Privileges granted by Peter the Great to the city of Riga on 3 September 1710

Catherine I (1684-1727), the Latvian born empress of Russia, was a foster daughter of Ernst Glück

Privileges granted by Empress Catherine II to the city of Riga in 1763

German philosopher Johann Georg Hamman (1730-1788) worked in Latvia

Neue Lettische Grammatick verfertiget von Gotthard Friedrich Stender Pastor zu Schaymen. 1756.

A Latvian grammar produced by Gothard Friedrich Stender in 1756

A report submitted to the consistory of Vidzeme about the work of the Herrnhutian brotherhood in *Cēsis* District, 1742

A visitation protocol from the *Araiši* congregation in *Cēsis* District and a description of the school of the congregation, 29 January 1766

Gothard Friedrich Stender (1714-1796) was a monumental figure in Latvian literature. He was a clergyman in Linde and Žeime, a professor of geography in Copenhagen, and a pastor at churches in *Sēlpils* and *Sunākste*. Stender wrote books that focused on the spiritual world of the Latvians, beginning with the first steps in reading and ending with the highest religious and scientific idea. Stender sought to educate farmers, writing several kinds of new readers – *Jauna ABC* (The New ABC) in 1782, and the first illustrated reader, *Bildu ābice* (The Picture Reader) in 1787. He also wrote the popular book *Augstas gudrības grāmata* (The Book of High Knowledge) in 1774, that described the world's understanding of the sciences at that time. Stender was active in Latvian linguistics, and he produced two Latvian grammars, *Neue vollständigere lettische Grammatik* and *Lettisches Lexicon* (1789)

An agreement presenting the *Rauna* castle and manor to Count Keiserling by Catherine the Great on 26 July 1762

An educational certificate issued to butcher Georg Heinrich Heising on 3 February 1788. The seal attached to the certificate represents the butchers of Riga

Tsar Alexander I of Russia (1777-1825), repealed servitude in Kurzeme and Vidzeme, reopened the University of Tartu

A declaration from Tsar Alexander I, prohibiting the construction of stone buildings in suburbs, July 1811

A list of doctors who volunteered for service in the Russian army, 1812

A list of Latvian farmers who were mobilised under the command of Lt. General von Sievers for the fight against Napoleon, October 14, 1812

A document describing the defences which the Riga garrison mounted against an attack by Napoleon, 25 May 1812

A report on the battles of the Riga garrison against Napoleon's army in defence of the city, 14 September 1812

Garlieb Helwig Merkel (1769-1850) was a Baltic German publicist and writer and a supporter of the ideas of the Enlightenment. He published a book *Latvieši* (The Latvians) that was released in 1796 and 1800 and was translated into English and Danish – but it was written in German and translated into Latvian only in 1905! Merkel also wrote a story called *Vanems Imanta*, and he was of great importance in the Latvian national awakening. Merkel wrote in German about the fact that Latvian farmers had no rights. He called for justice and humanity and for the repeal of indentured servitude. His writing did a lot to inform the world about the pitiful lives of Latvians

Illustration for G.H. Merkel's book "The Latvians"

The 19th century began with economic difficulties in the entire Russian province of Vidzeme. Capitalism expanded very rapidly, and a consumer society emerged. Noblemen lacked the money for agriculture, and they lived in fear of farmer rebellions. The promoters of the ideas of the Enlightenment convinced many people of the need for reform. One person who was critically important in promoting a repeal of indentured servitude was the teacher Garlieb Merkel (1769-1850), who worked as a home teacher at several manors in Vidzeme and saw clearly the pitiful condition of farmers and the heartlessness of their lords. In 1796, Merkel published the book *Die Letten, vorzüglich in Livland, an Ende des psiholosophischen Jahrhunderts*, with the aim, Merkel himself said, "of showing the noblemen and clergymen of Vidzeme a mirror, which would show them a reflection that would cause them to be afraid of themselves". Under the influence of Merkel and other activists of the Enlightenment, a relatively liberal group of noblemen who supported the idea of agrarian reform slowly emerged. Rebellions among farmers occurred from time to time. A revolt against the so-called head tax erupted in 1784, when the Russian government began to demand that local farmers pay this tax. In 1802

farmers at the *Kauguri* manor rebelled against their masters.

In 1801, a man with humane and liberal views ascended to the Russian throne. Tsar Alexander I in 1804 approved a new law on farmers in Vidzeme, specifying property rights for farmers, as well as various obligations for them. Noblemen were no longer allowed to sell farmers or to evict them from their homes. Neither could they increase the level of servitude arbitrarily. The farmers wanted more, however – they thought that the government would grant them true freedom.

Between 1812 and 1814 the Russian Empire was at war with Napoleon's France. Napoleon's forces attacked Latvia and occupied Kurzeme. The soldiers came from Prussia, which was a French ally, as well as from Poland – 32,500 men in all. General von Gravard commanded the Prussians. The Russian forces in Latvia, commanded by Governor General N.G. Essen, had only 18,500 troops. The city of Riga was prepared for a French attack. Large stores of grain were deposited at the St. John's, Dom and St. Jacob's churches, and flammable materials were brought out of the Riga Castle. Buckets of water were placed in the attics of many buildings. Craftsmen were prohibited form leaving the city. Soon panic erupted among the denizens of Riga, including General Essen, who ordered that the suburbs of Riga be burned down. 782 buildings perished, and 6,500 people lost their homes. The suburbs were burned down primarily for political reasons. The rulers of Riga felt that the residents of the suburbs were supporters of the French Revolution and might come out in support of Napoleon's forces.

Jelgava fell to the French on 21 July. The Prussians who arrived in Latvia announced that nothing would be changed, and farmers who had hoped that indentured servitude would be repealed were disappointed. The Prussians, of course, only served to strengthen the hand of German barons. They formally restored the duchy of Kurzeme, which on 1 August was named the Union of the Duchy of Kurzeme and Zemgale and the *Piltene* Region. Local noblemen led by Count von Medem were appointed the new government of the Duchy.

The French never did get to the fortifications of Riga, and it turned out that the burning of the suburbs had been unnecessary. Essen was sacked from his post, and, one year after the date of the fire, he shot himself in *Baldone*. The Marquis F. Paulucci was appointed in his stead. The French and Prussians ruled in Kurzeme and Vidzeme for five months, and both urban and rural residents alike suffered no losses during the war. For quite some time the Russian armed forces were present in the country, however, passing through *Jelgava* on their way to France. The war ended in 1814.

In 1816, indentured servitude was repealed in Estonia. On 30 August 1817, in the presence of Tsar Alexander, the same was announced at a ceremony in *Jelgava*. The farmers of Kurzeme were free. Governor General Paulucci demanded that the Vidzeme *Landtag* liberate that region's farmers, too, but many noblemen objected. The tsar himself had to sign a declaration to repeal indentured servitude in Vidzeme, on 26 March 1819. This meant that farmers in Kurzeme and Vidzeme obtained personal freedom and could select their own place of life and work. The fly in the ointment was that they also lost all of their land. Land had to be either bought or rented from the local barons.

In 1841, famine broke out in Vidzeme, and by 1845, it covered the entire Baltic region. Many farmers who hoped that the Russian tsar would help them to get land converted to the Russian

Orthodox faith. In 1849, the tsar approved new farming laws which specified that noblemen had to lease or sell to farmers plots of land that were declared as a special category of land alongside baronial and quota lands. These latter territories remained under the free control of the nobility. In 1860, Tsar Alexander II issued another round of laws for the farmers of Vidzeme, setting out the relationship between noblemen and farmers for the next 50 years. In 1861, indentured servitude was repealed in Russia and Latgale.

In Vidzeme in the 1860s, farmers began to buy their farms and to improve their agricultural activities. Meadows were drained, and farmers began to till numerous fields at once. There was more time for recreation and education. The people began to awaken to a new life. The purchase of farms took place most actively in Kurzeme in the late 1870s and early 1880s. Farmers in Latgale won the opportunity to buy land in 1863, when the Russian government decreed mandatory land purchases with the support of the National Land Bank. Farmers throughout Latvia learned new self esteem, and they felt sovereign.

The few Latvians who had managed to get a university education helped to awaken the nation's thirst for education and spiritual life, calling on people not to be ashamed of their belonging to the Latvian nation. Activists in the so-called National Awakening included Krišjanis Valdemars, Juris Alunāns, Krišjanis Barons and others. Valdemars was a student at Tartu University, and he, along with Alunāns and Barons, established the Latvian newspaper *Pēterburgas Avizes* (1862-1865). The newspaper carried articles about the latest achievements in economics and science, as well as about international events. The activists called on people to increase their national self-understanding and to tend to the Latvian language. On Valdemars' advice, 10 maritime schools were established in Latvia. Among them was the first maritime school used by the Russian trade fleet, in *Ainaži*, as well as schools in *Ventspils*, *Liepāja*, *Rīga*, *Ģipka* and other places. Valdemars also called for someone to begin collecting examples of Latvian folklore. Krišjanis Barons did the work, collecting no fewer than 217,996 folk songs, which he published in six volumes.

Information written in *Bolderāja* about ships entering the *Daugavgrīva* port, 1811

So-called teacher seminaries were established to train teachers. In 1839 a seminary opened in *Valmiera*, directed by Jānis Cimze (1814-1881). In 1841 the Kurzeme teachers seminary was opened in *Irlava*, although all courses there were taught in German.

Urban development in the first half of the 19th century proceeded slowly in Latvia, but in the latter half of the century, there was very rapid growth. This was due mostly to industrial development, but also to the newly won freedom of farmers. Rural residents became wealthier, and new traffic routes, including railroads, were installed. In 1861 the first rail line was opened between Riga and *Daugavpils*, and several local lines were set up, too. This promoted port development in Latvia, and in terms of the volume of goods transported, the port in Riga was second in all of the Russian Empire.

Bernhards Dīriķis (1831-1892), a journalist and activist, was the first chairman of the Rīga Latvian Society

Rihards Tomsons (1834-1884), a public activist and writer, was one of the most active people in the establishment of the Rīga Latvian Society. Later, he was its chairman

Fridrihs Grosvalds (1859-1924) was a public and political activist, spokesman and chairman of the Rīga Latvian Society. He was a deputy in the first Russian Duma in 1906

Krišjānis Kalniņš (1847-1885) was a specialist in legal matters who served as the chairman of the Rīga Latvian Society from 1875 until 1885. Under his leadership the work of the Society expanded greatly. Kalniņš was among the first to fight for the right of Latvians to participate in Rīga's local government

Jānis Fridrihs Baumanis (1834-1891) was a distinguished Latvian architect who served as chairman of the Rīga Latvian Society and as a member of the Rīga City Council

Several major industrial enterprises opened in Rīga, including the machinery plant *Felzers and Co.*, which produced bicycles, the rubber products factory *Provodņik*, and others. Telephones were first installed in Rīga in 1882, and by the end of the century, the Rīga Electro-Technical Factory was producing phones. The owners of the companies were mostly non-Latvians. Latvian entrepreneurs invested their money in building construction and smaller enterprises. Latvian communities began to be established in Rīga and other Latvian cities, and the need for social activities emerged. A "Friends of Latvians Society" had been in place in *Jelgava* since 1824, and it was active in researching the Latvian language, literature, history and ethnography. A group of Latvians in Rīga on 19 February 1868, asked for permission to set up a committee to collect donations for famine victims in Finland and Estonia. The authorities granted permission, and various events were organised by the Latvians to collect the money. The campaign to raise funds included the first-ever Latvian theatre performance in Rīga, and soon enough, it occurred to people that a permanent Latvian organisation could be established. The most active supporters of the idea were civil servant Bernhards Dīriķis, architect Jānis Baumanis and factory director Rihards Tomsons.

In 1868, the interior minister approved the statutes of the Rīga Latvian Society. An active cultural life emerged, with lectures, theatre performances and choir concerts. Societies sprang up in other cities and parishes, too, and regional song festivals were held – in *Dikļi* in 1864, in *Matīši* in 1866, and in *Dobele* in 1870. The first nation-wide song festival was organised by the Rīga Latvian Society in 1873, and the festivals thereafter became a tradition, one, which promoted the development of Latvian choral art and unified the Latvian nation.

Various economic societies were set up – one for savings and loans, several for dairies, several for consumers, etc. The Rīga Athletic Society opened its doors in 1862, with membership only for wealthy people. The first Latvian athletic organisation in rural areas was the *Palsmane* Amateur Chess Society, which was founded in 1898.

The relationship between Germans and Latvians worsened around this time, and both sides complained to the Russian government. A Russian senator was dispatched to Latvia and ordered to get a detailed understanding of the existing situation and to conduct a full audit of all of the institutions in Latvia. This process began in Many 1882 and concluded in August 1883. The Baltic Germans in Latvia were terrified of what the senator might report, and the documents, which he sent to St. Petersburg, disappeared along the way. Legend holds that one copy of the report was even stolen from the desk of the tsar himself. The senator concluded that the entire system of courts and agriculture in Latvia was incomplete, adding that few people in the province spoke Russian, and government interference would be needed. A process of russification was promptly launched. Lessons could be taught in Latvian only in the first few grades of parish schools; everywhere else lessons were taught only in Russian. Between 1887 and 1890, this system was introduced in all of Latvia's schools, including high schools. The police and the courts system were restructured to conform to the Russian principles, which underpinned these institutions.

The process of russification hit hardest in Latgale. In 1865, printed texts in the Latgall dialect that were produced with Latin letters were banned. During the first years of this ban Latvian language books could still be published in Rīga and Tartu, but in 1871 a nation-wide ban which lasted for nearly 40 years was imposed.

In the late 1880s and early 1990s, a movement known as the *New Current* was established, beginning in Tartu, where a group of Latvian theology students in 1888 founded a scientific and literary association with the purpose of promoting self-education and of friendship with students at other universities. On the basis of the last name of the founder of the group, the members were known as *pipkaloņi*.

The ideas of the New Current appeared openly first of all in literature, where the Western European fashion of Realism was quickly being adopted. Activists in the movement emphasised the importance of science, especially Darwinism. In philosophy they tended toward materialism in the sense that Marx used the word. The activities of the New Current movement were very much supported by the newspaper *Dienas Lapa*, which was first published in 1886. After Pēteris Stučka and Jānis Pliekšāns (later known as Latvia's national poet Rainis) took over the editorship of the paper, it became a key promoter of the ideas of the New Current movement. Extensive debate arose after the publication of an article, "Thoughts about modern literature" by Jans Jansons-Brauns. The New Current movement imported Marxist literature and distributed it among the working class. *Dienas Lapa* was banned in May 1897. Some of the New Current members were arrested, while others managed to escape to foreign countries. The New current movement closed down in 1899.

The 19th century ended with a rebellion of workers in Rīga, *Liepāja* and *Daugavpils*. The revolt in Rīga began after women working at a linen factory demanded higher salaries. Employees from the *Fēnikss* and *Union* factories joined the disturbances, which quickly expanded. Many workers were arrested and convicted, while many others were killed or injured in conflicts with the authorities.

Active scientific work had been going on in Rīga since the beginning of the 19th century. In 1803, a man called Dāvids Hieronīms Grindelis (1776-1836) established the Rīga Chemical and Pharmaceutical Association and published the first scientific journal in this area of activity. Historians, natural scientists and other groups established their own groups. Wealthy Latvian families could send their children to Tartu, St. Petersburg and Moscow for a higher education. A very large number of Latvians studied and later worked at the Tartu Veterinary Institute, gaining global attention for their research in microbiology. In 1862, a technical institute was opened in Rīga, and in 1896 it was reformed into the Polytechnical Institute. Students from all over the Russian Empire studied at the institute, and there was important research work in mathematics, geology and chemistry there. A particularly important event was the 10th All-Russia Congress of Archaeologists in Rīga in 1896. Among the delegates were chemistry professor Pauls Valdens, linguist Kārlis Mīlenbahs, composer Andrejs Jurjāns and other prominent Latvians.

The first Latvian novel written in the style of Realism, *Mērnieku laiki* ("The Days of the Surveyors"), was published by the brothers Reinis and Matīss Kaudzīte in 1879. Another author who produced a rich body of work during this period was Rūdolfs Blaumanis. The husband-and-wife team of Rainis and Aspazija began to write, too.

Painters including portraitist Jānis Roze, landscape masters Jūlijs Feders and Vilhelms Purvītis, and Realist artist Jānis Rozentāls were among those Latvian artists who won prominence in Russian and German art galleries. The most distinguished architect in Rīga was the Latvian Jānis Baumanis.

In 1873, at the first Latvian song festival, composer Kārlis Baumanis premiered his composition *Dievs, svētī Latviju!* ("God, bless Latvia"), which later became the Latvian national anthem.

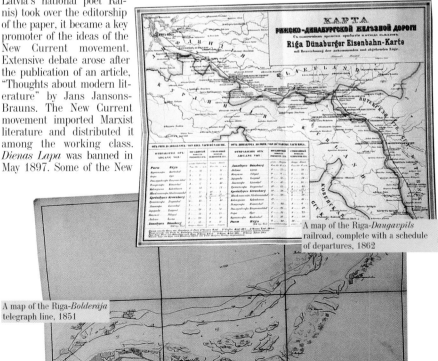

A map of the Riga-*Daugavpils* railroad, complete with a schedule of departures, 1862

A map of the Riga-*Bolderāja* telegraph line, 1851

LATVIANS AT TARTU UNIVERSITY

Krišjānis Valdemārs (1825-1891), an economist, philosopher and politician. Wishing to improve the welfare of Latvian farmers to Western European levels, he was a supporter of the principles of private property and free competition. As a realist in politics, he opposed the economic and political superiority of the Baltic German nobility, which in his view was a major obstacle in the way of Latvian land ownership and the emergence of an upper stratum in Latvian society. Valdemārs was a diplomat who could debate in a highly gentlemanly style, and he was a forceful persuader who knew how to speak with a Latvian farmer just as well as with a Russian prince. Valdemārs was known throughout the Russian Empire as an authority on economics and maritime affairs, and for a time he served as the *de facto* maritime minister for the empire. Under his leadership, a number of maritime training schools were opened in Latvia, the abilities of young people from rural Latvia to gain an education were expanded, the newspaper *Pēterburgas Avīzes* was launched, and publication of Latvian folklore materials was begun. In 1848 Valdemārs opened a public Latvian library in Ēdole, calling on Latvians to write their own history and to avoid the false interpretation of events which the Germans were producing. He also said that it was the obligation of every Latvian to look after his or her national language. A Russian-Latvian-German dictionary was published at Valdemārs' suggestion. Valdemārs' key tenet in life was that "the Latvian culture must be established by the Latvians themselves. [..] A well-educated Latvian is not ashamed to show the world that he is a Latvian."

Krišjānis Barons (1835-1923), was the most distinguished representative of the Latvian national awakening and enlightenment. Barons was a man of universal knowledge, and he possessed colossal working abilities. In *Mājas Viesis*, *Pēterburgas Avīzes* and other newspapers, he informed Latvian readers about nature and the cosmos and explained the laws of the natural world. In 1859 he wrote a textbook on the physical geography of the Baltic provinces of the Russian Empire. Barons is best remembered, however, for the enormous amount of work which he did in collecting and publishing Latvian folk songs. During his studies he came across folklore and ethnographic materials from various nations. In 1857 he published Estonian legends and explanations of Estonian folk songs in the Latvian press. In 1878 Barons took over a project from Fricis Brīvzemnieks which was aimed at collecting and recording folk songs. Barons developed a fantastic and phenomenal system for keeping track of the huge number of folk songs, and this system can be used to reconstruct the true world of the Latvian folk songs and the Latvian understanding of life which produced them. The multi-volume collection *Latvju dainas* (Latvian folk songs) is encyclopedic in its scope and precision, revealing the living and work conditions of Latvians, the various types of communities which they established, their cares and their joys, their life understanding, and their ethical, aesthetic and religious values. Thanks to the work which Barons did, our culture has an ethnic foundation upon which the Latvian nation can increase its self-esteem and take advantage of the weapons of folklore that strengthen the Latvian community

Atis Kronvalds (1837-1875), a teacher who laid the foundations for Latvia's national educational system. Kronvalds emphasized schools as a center of national culture, encouraging learning from the lowest to the highest level of education. Kronvalds felt that courses and lessons must be taught in Latvian and that schoolchildren must be raised in a spirit of national consciousness. Kronvalds waged war against the educational system of tsarist Russia and, in so doing, laid the foundations for Latvia's professional aesthetics. He was the first Latvian to explain art and literature in terms of aesthetic categories and functions

Auseklis (b. Miķelis Krogzemis, 1850-1879) was a poet who studied at the Valka Teachers Seminary run by the Reverend Jānis Cimze. In 1873 he published the collection *Dzejas no Auseķļa* (Poems from Auseklis), and the collection was instrumental in awakening the Latvian spirit. In 1876 an educational annual was published which contained a speech that Auseklis had delivered to a teachers conference in Rīga – "How to raise students in a proper spirit". Auseklis taught that the school is a matter of honor, power and wealth for any nation, and so schools should be appropriate for the needs of the nation. He counseled the introduction of special systems of lessons and training, and he recommended a new curriculum for what he called "people's schools"

Latvian students at Tartu University in the 1860s. This is the only known photograph of Juris Alunāns (1832-1864). He is seen second from the right in the second row of the photograph. Alunāns was an active member of the New Latvian movement, correlating its ideas and laying the foundation for the art of Latvian national poetry. Alunāns also sketched in the main contours of the Latvian national ideology. As a student of economics at Tartu University, Alunāns translated the work of foreign poets into Latvian, and in 1856 he published 48 of these translations in a book called *Dziesmiņas* (Little Songs). A second volume of *Dziesmiņas* was published after the poet's death, in 1869. *Dziesmiņas* was as seminal work in terms of Latvian poetry. The texts may have been produced by poets in other European countries, but Alunāns cemented them into the cultural constructs of the Latvian nation. Alunāns was an active writer who published no fewer than 150 popular and scientific articles in the newspaper *Mājas Viesis*. Alunāns was a rationalist, but he could also be a national romanticist. He laid the foundations for Latvian satire, he railed against dishonest judges, lawyers and noblemen, and he denounced the so-called "osier-Germans" – Latvians who pretended to be Germans and thus refused their own national identity. Alunāns began work on a book on the national economy. He did not manage to complete it himself, but it was published three years after his death, in 1867, by his brother, Indriķis Alunāns. Among the sentences which Latvians could read in their own language in this book was this: "If communism is considered with the mind, then it is seen as pure nonsense. The communism wants equality among nations, but he leads them to even greater inequality."

Fricis Brīvzemnieks (1846-1907) dedicated his life to Latvian culture. In 1867, encouraged by Krišjānis Valdemārs, he began to collect Latvian folklore. Brīvzemnieks traveled all around Latvia, setting up expeditions to collect folklore and ethnographic materials and calling on the masses to participate in this process. Brīvzemnieks maintained close contacts with those who were collecting examples of folklore, as well as those who were the tellers of folk stories and folk songs. He met people, corresponded with them, never failed to say thanks for things that were sent in, presented people with gifts, encouraged people and inspired them. In 1878, Brīvzemnieks asked Krišjānis Barons to bring some order to the folk songs that he had collected. With the support of the Royal Association of Friends of the Natural Sciences, Anthropology and Ethnography of Moscow University, a book of 1,118 Latvian folk songs, sayings, riddles, stories and spells was published in Latvian and Russian. Brīvzemnieks actively published articles in Moscow's Russian newspapers about the difficult economic, legal and cultural aspects of the lives of Baltic farmers

Main building of Tartu University, built in 1809

The movement which had the greatest significance in the Latvian national awakening of the mid-19th century was the New Latvian movement (the *jaunlatvieši*, as they are known in Latvian). In the 1840s, quite a few Latvian rural residents – especially those who were no longer linked to noblemen through indentured servitude – were able to improve their material situation considerably. People worked as saloonkeepers, millers, estate overseers and forest rangers. When indentured servitude was replaced with leasing fees, farmers could improve the standing of their farms, and the wealthier farmers could send their sons not only to better parish or congregational schools, but also to universities. A Latvian intelligentsia emerged, and a Latvian national self-understanding came with it.

Beginning the mid-19th century, some 40 young men went to study at Tartu University each year. Latvians also studied at other universities. In Tartu, student Krišjānis Valdemārs organized a discussion group which was active in developing new ideas and new forms of thinking. The Valdemārs group defended the interests of Latvian farmers and opposed the landed German gentry. The Latvian movement thus quickly took on a nationalist flavoring. As is known, Germans in Latvia saw ethnic Latvians as nothing more than peasants, but Krišjānis Valdemārs defiantly attached a sign to the door of his dormitory room: "Krišjānis Valdemārs, Latvian". The New Latvians were representatives of the ideas of the Enlightenment, and they felt that if Latvians could develop a greater self-understanding and self-esteem, this would help society to move forward. They sought to teach people about various aspects of science and to increase their national self-esteem. Valdemārs frequently said that the foundation for the welfare of a nation and its ability to develop upward was work. The New Latvians brought the national together, taking a stand for national rights and a national culture. They published materials in which they talked to Latvians about their difficult economic and political situation. They sought to promote the development of the Latvian language and literature, and they began to collect examples of folklore.

The most active members of the New Latvian movement were Krišjānis Valdemārs, Juris Alunāns, Krišjānis Barons, Atis Kronvalds, Jēkabs Zvaigznīte, Juris Caunītis and Kaspars Biezbārdis. They helped to develop a new style of writing which came to be known as National Romanticism. Its most talented representatives were the poet Auseklis and the writer Andrejs Pumpurs. A folklore specialist called Fricis Brīvzemnieks was of a like mind with the New Latvians when it came to his political activities.

Juris Alunāns published a book called *Dziesmiņas* (Little Songs) in 1856. The government-appointed curator of "Latvian affairs", the Reverend Gustav Brasche, denounced the book and, in so doing, was the first to use the term "New Latvians" in public. The students at Tartu were delighted and appropriated the term for their own use.

In 1860 Alunāns organized the publication of a three-volume almanac called *Sēta, Daba, Pasaule* (The Farm, Nature and the World), writing the first two volumes himself. The first book contains a wide range of household advice, geographic and historical information, and even a section containing jokes and anecdotes. The second volume was devoted to Russia – its territory, highlands, mountains, rivers, lakes, canals, climate, etc. The book also contained information about actual economic matters such as the expenditures of the tsar's family and the state's income and spending. The most important article in the third volume was a treatise on Latvian folk songs that was produced by Jēkabs Zvaigznīte. The almanac's fourth volume was published in 1873 by Atis Kronvalds. In the 1890s the almanac was used by the student fraternity *Letonija* as a form of publicity.

Tartu University was of critical importance in the education of Latvia's intelligentsia. The Academie Gustavina was opened in Tartu in 1632 and existed until 1710, when the Northern War and an epidemic of the Black Plague broke out in the region. Tartu was chosen as a university city because of its geographic location – almost exactly at the center of the Baltic provinces of the Russian Empire and in close proximity to the Russian capital of St. Petersburg. Tartu University was reopened in 1802, and it soon became a special institution among Russian universities. Tartu had extensive autonomy and received considerable government subsidies. Lots of construction work was done in Tartu, modern equipment and technologies were purchased abroad, and highly distinguished professors were hired.

When Tartu University reopened its doors, it was with four traditional faculties of study – medicine, law, theology and philosophy. Tartu, unlike other universities in Russia, taught courses in German, while examinations and dissertations until the mid-19th century were prepared in Latin. In 1893 the town of Tartu was renamed Jurjev (it had been called Jurjev between 1030 and 1224), and Russian was imposed on the university as the language of instruction.

Among those who worked at Tartu University over the years as professors and instructors were the distinguished astronomer and geodesic specialist Wilchelm Struhwe, mathematician Martin Bartless, chemist Karl Klauss, chemist Wilhelm Ostwald, physicist Boris Jakobi, and surgeons Nikolai Pirogov, Ernst Bergmann and Mikhail Burdenko. One of the first natural scientists of Latvian origin to work as a professor at Tartu was the physician, pharmacist and chemist Dāvids Hieronīms Grindelis, who was a professor of chemistry at Tartu and served as the university's rector from 1810 until 1812.

The first known ethnic Latvian student at Tartu was Kārlis Viljams, who was the son of a farmer in *Lugaži* and who studied mathematics at Tartu from 1803 until 1809.

Along with the New Latvians Krišjānis Valdemārs, Juris Alunāns, Kaspars Biezbārdis and Krišjānis Barons, a member of the Latvian group was medical student Jānis Jurjāns, who became the first physician in Latvia to be paid from the budget of the parish in which he worked. Also in attendance at some of the Latvian discussion evenings was theology student Jānis Zakranovičs, who later became a clergyman in Lielauce.

Tartu University also saw the emergence of student groups which promoted the ideas of materialism. A Latvian group called *Pīpkalonija* was among them, and it published a collection of articles, *Pūrs* (Dowry), which was authored by the law student and poet Eduards Veidenbaums, as well as Kārlis Kasparsons and Jēkabs Alksnis. The founders of the Latvian Social Democratic movement, Jānis Jansons-Brauns and Fricis Roziņš-Āzis, were also Tartu students.

From 1802 until 1914, more than 1,300 students were graduated from Tartu University. 62 of them defended doctoral dissertations. In 1919, the newly established University of Latvia employed no fewer than 40 Latvian professors who had trained at Tartu, among them Jānis Endzelīns, Fricis Blumbahs, Francis Balodis, Pauls Jurevičs, Aleksandrs Dauge, Pauls Mincs and Kārlis Balodis.

Mowing of rye in the *Pušas* village, *Andrupene* Parish, *Rēzekne* County

The people of a farm at lunch in the *Pauliņi* village, *Ozolaine* Parish, *Rēzekne* County

An old woman at the spinning wheel at the *Vecboski* homestead, *Laši* Parish, *Ilukste* County

Lunch out in the fields

Growing flax at the *Jaungaiļi* village, *Stirniene* Parish, *Rēzekne* County

The period of time during which the Latvian nation has been self-confident has not been long. Latvians began to see themselves as representatives of an actual nation only in the early 19th century, and it was only in the middle of the 19th century, thanks to such leaders as Krišjānis Valdemārs and other "New Latvians", that the people became proud of their nation. This means that the various forms of national self-understanding such as literature, music, folklore collections and academic research of language have not existed for a very long time either.

Latvians have been writing and publishing books for a long time, but Latvian literature as such really emerged only in the late 19th century, when writers such as Rudolfs Blaumanis, Anna Brigadere, Apsīšu Jēkabs, Jēkabs Janševskis, Ernests Birznieks-Upītis and the Kaudzīte brothers, Reinis and Matīss, with their realistic novel *Mērnieku laiki* ("The Times of the Land Surveyors"), appeared on the scene.

All of these classic authors were people who loved the land. They romanticised the farms of their youth, and they created beautiful stories about the patriarchal farming structure that had prevailed in Latvia for centuries. Every Latvian has rural relatives, and many have ancestral homesteads in beautiful regions of the country. Every Latvian from childhood has been taught that each person must have "a corner, an area of land". This is something, which Latvians have sought to achieve for centuries. Some bought land when serfdom was repealed. Others were granted land in return for their meritorious service in the rifleman brigades of World War I.

Today Latvian schoolchildren all read late-19th century novels and stories, which are set in the countryside. Most of the Latvian folk songs, which are known as the *dainas* have a rural setting, as well. Nostalgia for single-family farms and individual farming was strengthened among Latvians by the long Soviet occupation, which forced people into *kolhozes* (collective farming) that stripped the land bare. The collective system of farming was an empty one, full of slogans and not much else. Piety for the single-family farm was also preserved among Latvians who lived in exile. Generations of Saturday and Sunday school Latvians in exile linked the idea of "Latvianness" to the farms of the 1930s.

Given all of this, it is no wonder that the average Latvian today still takes a spade in hand from time to time to plant a little garden outside the back door, to raise flowers or carrots. In the summertime, even urban Latvians go out into the hayfields to do some work with a scythe and rake. Latvians so very much love the homesteads of their forebears that these farms represent freedom, a wealthy and prosperous country. So when one talks about the Latvian nation and the land of Latvia, one must never forget that the spirit of the farmer is still very much alive in many Latvians.

Mowing clover at the *Kazaki* homestead, *Gaiķu* Parish, *Kuldīga* County

A carpenter's workshop at the *Druviena* manor in *Druviena* Parish, *Cēsis* County

Spreading fertiliser on the fields at the *Jumji* homestead, *Snēpele* Parish, Kuldīga County

Gathering fertiliser at the *Vilkates* homestead, *Saikava* Parish, *Madona* County

Brewing beer at the *Kangares* homestead, *Saikava* Parish, *Madona* County

The interior of a living room at the *Dejas* homestead, *Rucava* Parish, *Liepāja* County

Pottery salesmen in the *Ezernieki* Parish, *Rēzekne* County

A woman fashions woven footwear known as *vizes* at the homestead of Juris Zalāns, *Stirniene* Parish, *Rēzekne* County

A weaver and her loom at the homestead of Šakaļevs Nikifors in the *Jasnova* village, *Brigu* Parish, *Ludza* District

Baking bread at the *Diņģekalni* homestead, *Bebrene* Parish, *Ilukste* County

Threshing grain by hand at the *Luborži* village, *Rundēni* Parish, *Ludza* County

Dollying of the laundry at the *Dzērbeņi* homestead, *Tirza* Parish, *Madona* County

Weaving fishing nets in *Plieņciems* village, *Engure* Parish, *Tukums* County

A man carves a spoon at the *Riteļi* homestead, *Raņķi* Parish, *Kuldīga* County

Water carrier at the *Vaičuki* homestead, *Ciecere* Parish, *Kuldīga* County

Shearing a sheep at the *Jaunzemji* homestead, *Kalsnava* Parish, *Madona* County

Making butter in a barrel at the homestead of J. Grebežs, *Kristobas* village, *Galēni* Parish, *Rēzekne* County

Rinsing laundry in the "shirt barrel" at the *Kupči* homestead, *Nīca* Parish, *Liepāja* County

A LATVIAN HOMESTEAD

The oldest form of settlement in Latvia was the village, which was gradually replaced by single family homesteads. This process occurred more quickly in Vidzeme, Kurzeme and Zemgale. Villages survived along the coasts of the country, where people engaged in fishing. In the Eastern Latvian region of Latgale, farms continued to be associated with specific villages for a longer period of time.

The average Latvian family farm had several buildings – a residential building, a livestock shed, a threshing barn, a granary and a bathing house or sauna, known as the *pirts* and an outhouse. In poorer farms, single buildings could house more than one function – the livestock shed, the barn, the granary, etc. The residential building was usually placed in the centre of the farm – at the highest and driest location. The other buildings were usually arranged around the residential building, while the *pirts* and the outhouse were located at some distance.

The arrangements differed a bit from region to region. Thus, for example, buildings in Vidzeme tend to stand rather far apart, while in Zemgale a hedge or a fence surrounds them all. In Latgale, farmyards were rectangular, with buildings and a high hedge all around. Homesteads in Kurzeme usually had scattered buildings, with the residential building in the centre of the yard. At one end of the yard was the "working yard", which connected the residential building to the livestock shed and the stalls, while on the other side there was the "clean yard" with a flower garden and a granary.

The pride of every Latvian homestead was a carefully tended fruit orchard. A specific aspect of farms in Vidzeme was the fact that farmers often lived not in a separate residential building, but in the grain-threshing barn or, later, in a room or rooms built as annexes to the threshing barn. In Vidzeme and in some places of Kurzeme, people also lived in the *pirts* and their adjacent rooms. Hired hands and older farm workers who were no longer capable of work lived most often in such facilities.

Residential homes on farms had different kinds of roofs, depending on the region in which they were found. Roofs were usually covered with straw, reeds or shingles. Windows were small to promote the retention of warmth indoors. The stove was a central focus in the interior of living facilities. It was located next to the main door of the room and was used to bake bread, to prepare meals and to heat the building. Benches

attached to the walls were often the oldest objects in the room. At one time they were used for sitting and sleeping alike. Somewhere in the room was a table with benches or chairs. Benches could also be used as cots or beds. Alongside the beds of married people there was a cradle – a hung cradle in Latgale and Vidzeme, a cradle set up on a stand in Kurzeme. Alongside the bed of the owners of the farm there was often a shelf, on which traditionally, Latvians put the Bible and a calendar.

Clothing was stored in various containers, including dowry chests, which were kept in the granary. Wardrobes began to appear in rural Latvia in the 18th century, and initially they were considered a sign of considerable wealth. Many farmers placed their wardrobes in as conspicuous place in the room as possible. The size of buildings on a farm was also an indicator of prosperity, because buildings were always built with an eye toward the number of people, the head of livestock and the amount of grain and other agricultural products that would require housing and storage.

As production processes developed and the structure of Latvia's society changed, there were also changes on the Latvian family farm. In the 20th century the residential building of farmers were large houses with several rooms, some of which were meant for the owners, some for married farm workers and others for single farm workers. As the furniture industry developed, Latvian farmers began to purchase ready-made furnishings, and new types of furniture such as writing tables, cabinets for dishes, installed furniture, etc., began to appear.

Farms in various regions were unique in different ways, but everywhere in Latvia, farmers took pride in maintaining good order and cleanliness within the territory that was surrounded by the farm's trees. Latvian women were justifiably proud of their beautiful flower gardens, and yards were always carefully swept. On holidays, Latvians decorated their farms (and not just the residential buildings) with birch-boughs and with various items from the national art forms. Latvians hold their farms to signify a great deal about the power and strength of the respective family and dynasty.

A young boy tends to the pigs at the *Spugova* village, *Istra* Parish, *Ludza* County

Sowing grain and harrowing the land at the *Tiltapurvs* village, *Vipe* Parish, *Daugavpils* County

A blacksmith called Rutkis at his shop at the *Lestene* manor, *Lestene* Parish, *Tukums* County

Ploughing fallow fields at the *Gaiļi* homestead, *Snēpele* Parish, *Kuldīga* County

Working with a swingle-staff on flax at the *Jaunzemji* homestead, *Kalsnava* Parish, *Madona* County

Crushing of pearl-barley with a pole-pestle at the *Stikoni* village, *Preiļi* Parish, *Daugavpils* County

A scythe is used to process animal skins at the *Puraki* village, *Galēni* Parish, *Rēzekne* County

LATVIA AT THE BEGINNING OF THE 20TH CENTURY

The "House of the Blackheads" (*Melngalvju nams*) was once the most important building in the square which also housed the Riga City Hall. It was first mentioned in the literature in 1334 as a new building of the city's Carge Guild. In the 15th century, the building was leased to unmarried foreign tradesmen who were known as the "blackheads" because their symbol was the head of a black man. In 1713, the tradesmen's association took ownership of the building, and thus it acquired its name. The building has been rebuilt many times, most notably between 1619 and 1625. The building was destroyed in 1941 and rebuilt in the late 1990s

Before World War II, Riga had 64 synagogues and prayer buildings. The largest and most ornate of these was a synagogue in *Gogoļa iela*, which was built between 1868 and 1871 on the basis of a design by architect Paul von Hardenack. The synagogue was a Renaissance-style building with a rounded facade that featured three portals. The interior was enormously ornate with a beautiful altar. During the first days of the Nazi occupation, the synagogue was burned down with hundreds of Riga Jews inside. Today a memorial has been built on the site

A pier for river steamboats at the *Daugava* shore market

The first vacationers arrived at the *Ventspils* seashore in the 1830s, and a spa building was put up in the early 20th century

This electrical engineering factory, *Unions*, was a branch of the German company *Union*, which was founded in 1898. The workers of the building and much its equipment were evacuated to Charkov in 1915, and work soon began in that city. In 1927, the empty buildings of the *Unions* factory were taken over by the State Electrical engineering factory VEF. Some of the buildings were put up in 1898 based on a design by architect Heinrich Scheel, while the remainder were the work of architect Peter Behrens and built in 1914

The original building of the Riga Latvian Society, built in 1869 after a design by architect Janis Baumanis, burned down in 1908. The present-day building of the Society was built a year later based on a design by architects Eižens Laube and E. Pole

At the beginning of the 20th century, the economies of liberal Europe were in full bloom. Government expenditures were low, budgets were balanced and they were not encumbered with heavy social expenditures. Capital and the labour force were mobile, and governments interfered little in the economies. The only protectionist country in Europe was Russia, but even Russia had been reached by the investment boom at the end of the 19th century. Communications were free, Europe was unified. At the beginning of the 20th century, European countries posted growth rate indicators of 5% per year. As the most mobile and economically developed city in the Russian Empire, Riga closely followed the world's economic and philosophical trends.

At the beginning of the 20th century, Latvia could not be imagined without its rapidly growing cities, its factories, workers and trams, without the restless, teeming and international environment of the larger cities. More than 40% of Latvia's residents lived in cities, and the proportion of ethnic Latvians in urban areas increased significantly. The wave of industrialisation and modernisation that hit all of Europe carried all of Latvia with it. As a country on the crossroads of the world, Latvia enjoyed specific benefits, which ensured adequate living standards not only in urban, but also in rural areas. Workers and agricultural employees earned much more than their compatriots in Russia, and some of the money could be deposited in savings banks. New kerosene, petrol and electrical motors made the work of workers radically easier and increased productivity.

Latvia's educational system operated in three languages, and the percentage of residents attending school was higher than in Western Europe. The number of girls in gymnasia exceeded the total number of boys studying at gymnasiums, high schools and commercial schools. There were hundreds of libraries and educational associations. Latvian workers spoke several languages, went to the theatre and read works of literature in German – Social Democratic tracts among them. Farmers sent their sons and daughters to universities. Agricultural societies sprang up to teach Latvians to manage their farms better. People happily sang in choirs. Latvian, German, Jewish and Russian architects and engineers built a second Riga in just 15 years – an ensemble of architectural styles that does all of Europe proud. In the late 19th century and early 20th century, Art Nouveau buildings were put up which make Riga the most distinguished Art Nouveau monument in the entire world. Construction work proceeded at such a pace that in 1901 Riga was almost certainly the most important city in the world in terms of capital turnover. Under the leadership of landscape architect Georgs Kufalts, Riga became a garden city.

Art exhibitions and salons became an everyday experience, and foreign exhibitions were also organised. Several professional Latvian theatres operated successfully. These soon became centres for revolutionary thought, bringing together the Latvian nation. The theatre public was mature and demanding. Musical life hit many high notes, and professional Latvian musicians began to emerge. There were music schools and a Latvian opera. Riga hosted world-famous conductors, orchestras, performers and musicians from all Europe. New books were printed at a rate of three per day.

As welfare and the boundaries of tolerance were expanded, there were people who felt that liberal democracy was too vulgar, materialistic and individualistic, and that it provided no room for heroism, collectivism and faith. Until 1905, however, the Russian Empire and its Baltic German aristocracy thought that the Baltic regions were a harbour of peace. The standard of living in Latvia, as well as the nation's everyday life, traditions and cultural specifics, brought Latvians close to Western Europe. The Latvian nation particularly keenly felt the darkness of the repressive Tsarist regime and its policy of Russification.

Socialism seemed to be a perfect idea to enormous numbers of workers, members of the intelligentsia, farmers and young people. Latvian Social Democrats were intelligent people with extensive knowledge in economics and foreign languages, and in this, they differed considerably from Social Democrats in Russia.

The revolution of 1905 in Latvia turned upon two enemies – the Tsar's government and the German aristocracy. Initially it was a workers' revolution, but it reached its apex in rural areas. Teachers, who made up one-half of Latvia's literary establishment and who were respected as great authorities, led the nation into revolution. Latvian men of letters such as Rainis, Jānis Asars, Jānis Jansons-Brauns, Janis Akurāters and Kārlis Skalbe were the tribunes of the revolution and became extremely popular. People demonstrated, disarmed local police officers, burned down baronial estates, fought against arbitrary arrest and oppression, went into the forests to fight a guerrilla war and founded new local self-government institutions. The revolution in 1905, for the first time brought to the fore ideas regarding freedom. For the first time in many centuries, the Latvian nation was dictating its own history.

There were many victims in the revolution, many buildings destroyed or burned down. Nearly 13,000 people were killed, deported or forced into emigration. Nearly half of the baronial estates in Kurzeme and Vidzeme, as well as hundreds of farmhouses were reduced to ruins. Because of the burning of aristocratic properties and the arrest of many members of the aristocracy, followed by a merciless repression of the revolutionaries, the revolution turned into a tragedy the relationships between the Baltic Germans and Latvians. The Latvian farmers had historical justice on their side, but also the Baltic Germans felt Latvia to be their homeland.

Another consequence of the revolution was increased colonisation of Latvia by Germans and Russians – a process that was very dangerous to the Latvian nation. On the other hand, the revolution also put much greater freedom in place. The Russification of Latvian schools was stopped, the press could breathe more freely, and Latvian organisations could work with greater liberty. The year 1905 was the first rehearsal of the ideas of statehood, self-governance and agrarian reform – ideas that the Latvian state would put into place 15 years later.

The Maritime School at *Mangaļi*

The Riga police headquarters in the late 19th century. The building was built between 1889 and 1891 after a design by the Riga architect Reinhold Schmelling. Today the building at *Aspāzijas bulvāri* 7 houses the main headquarters of the Riga City Police

The City of Riga's second theatre was built between 1900 and 1902, and today it houses the Latvian National Theatre at *Aía Kronvalda bulvāri* 2. The architect was Augusts Reinbergs

The post and telegraph building of Riga was built in 1901 after a design by architects Julius Pfeiffer and L. Novikov. Today the building at *Aspāzijas bulvāri* 5 is owned by the University of Latvia, which uses it for lecture halls for the Management and Economics Faculty

The *Milgrāvis* Gymnasium (also known as the Green School) was founded in 1908 by philanthropist and public figure Augusts Dombrovskis (1845-1927). Dombrovskis was born into a poor family in Riga, and from early childhood, he accompanied his father on fishing boats. Dombrovskis' mother taught him to read, and he picked up other knowledge on his own. After spending some time as a worker in a relative's sawmill, Dombrovskis founded his own mill at *Milgrāvis* in 1887. Dombrovskis used the money that he earned through the mill to establish various cultural and educational institutions in the neighbourhood. In 1900, he opened a two-year elementary school and kindergarten. The gymnasium was opened in 1908. In 1902, a building for a friendly society was opened, and one year later, the group formed the Latvian Temperance Society *Ziemeļblāzma*. In 1904, Dombrovskis put up another grand public building with an enormous hall that could seat 2000 people. In 1906, the building was burned down by the punitive expedition in the wake of the 1905 revolution. By 1913, Dombrovskis had erected a new building for the public. In 1907, he turned one of his buildings into a home for writers, and the legendary folklorist Krišjānis Barons was among those to live there for a time. Dombrovskis was chairperson of the Riga Latvian Society's Security Commission for many years. People in the *Milgrāvis* neighbourhood of Riga still remember Dombrovskis with kindness and respect, because he did so much to promote the welfare of workers in the area

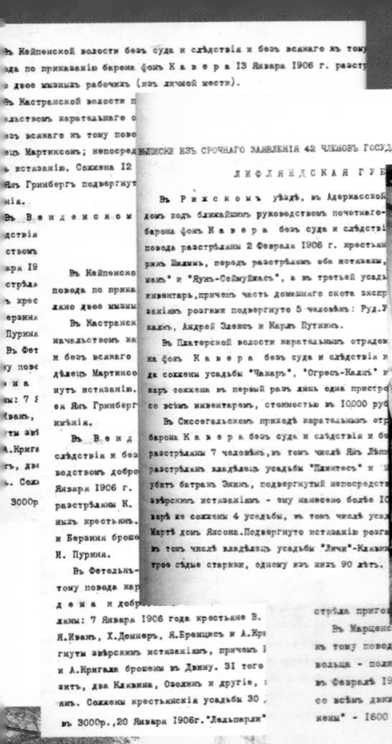
ВЫПИСКИ ИЗЪ СРОЧНАГО ЗАЯВЛЕНІЯ 42 ЧЛЕНОВЪ ГОСУДАРСТВЕННОЙ ДУМЫ О ЗАПРОС...

ЛИФЛЯНДСКАЯ ГУБ...

Working people in Latvia in 1905 were strong and organised. In the photograph, we see workers from the *Salamandra* mechanical workshop

Textile workers in the *Pārdaugava* area of Riga

A meeting in January 1905 attracted workers of various nationalities in Riga, and Latvian businessmen joined them, too

A meeting in *Dundaga* in November 1905 attracted farmers, agricultural workers and landless people from *Talsi* to *Ventspils*

Revolutionary events in Latvia forced the tsar to implement democratic reforms. The first Russian Duma was assembled. In the photo, we see the Latvians who were delegates to the Duma – Frīdrihs Grosvalds, Kārlis Ozoliņš, Jānis Kreicbergs, Francis Trasuns, A. Bremers and Jānis Čakste, 27 April 1906

The revolution of 1905 was the first important step, which the Latvian nation took toward freedom and democracy. Latvia was a part of the Russian Empire at this time, and divided into several different provinces. Riga had relatively better living conditions than did other cities in the Empire, but the chaos which prevailed in tsarist Russia involved a complete lack of responsibility among business people and the nobility; most of them acted completely arbitrarily. Workers earned very little and worked 14 hours a day. There was no kind of job protection, there was no insurance, and medical assistance was scant. Children were used in many workplaces.

In 1903, an economic crisis began in Russia. Factories were closed and unemployment increased. The situation among Latvian farmers was even worse – although land reform had been completed, half of the land still belonged to the nobility. Farmers who had bought their own farms had to pay high interest rates on the bank loans which they took for this purpose, while those who leased their farms had to pay high rents set by the nobility. The farmers also suffered because of certain privileges that were enjoyed by the noblemen – only they had the right to go fishing and hunting. Farmers had no right to open manufacturing enterprises, to distil spirits, or to organise markets for their produce.

Russia and Japan went to war in 1904. Latvia was the scene of anti-war demonstrations. Unlike in other Russian cities, the bourgeoisie in Riga stood side-by-side with the working class. The revolution soon took on a nationalist tone. The idea of a free and independent Latvian state had not yet been formulated, but the rebellion turned against the German barons and the administration of the Russian tsar.

A labour strike began in St. Petersburg on 2 January 1905, and the authorities fired upon a demonstration in that city on 9 January. The strike spread to Riga on 12 January, reaching truly grandiose levels on 13 January. The police and the Russian armed forces opened fire on demonstrators without any warning. 70 people were killed, 200 were injured, and many more drowned in the *Daugava* River when the ice beneath them broke. The strike spread to other cities in Latvia and lasted for eight days. Farmers went on strike in Kurzeme in March. Churches were the sites of demonstrations in rural areas, with revolutionary farmers taking the pulpit to make speeches. The landed gentry fought against the strikers without any mercy – people were arrested, tortured and beaten to death. Many revolutionaries were convicted of crimes. Baron Meiendorf persuaded the tsar to declare a state of war in Latvia.

On 7 September 1905, Latvian workers broke into the central prison in Riga and set a number of political prisoners free. Among them were Jānis Lācis and Jūlijs Šlesers, who had been sentenced to death. Railway workers went on strike on 12 October. On 19 October the newspaper, *Dienas Lapa* was published for the first time without being vetted by the censors, and it took on a Social Democratic tone. Workers formed their own militia unit. The tsar's government responded with violence by the so-called "black hundred" paramilitary units. The Riga militia units and the "black hundred" squared off against one another.

Latvian teachers in November began to teach lessons in Latvian. The Governor of Vidzeme, Zvegincev, called in supplementary military forces from St. Petersburg, and an armed battle began when they arrived. On 28 November, Latvian farmers defeated a group of dragoons near *Skrīveri*. The dragoons marauded through Latvia, shooting people at the slightest suspicion and burning down the homes of farmers. Latvian farmers responded by setting fire to the country's manors. There were a few successful moments of negotiation, such as an instance when the barons Rosen and Wolff negotiated with Janis Jansons-Brauns and achieved the release of hostages on both sides.

In *Tukums*, by contrast, barons Raden and Reke took to terrorist methods and used the dragoons as murders. Workers held *Tukums* and *Talsi* for several days, but then General Shoruzhenkov promised that all of the demands of the workers would be met if they ended the armed struggle. The general did not keep his promise and, treacherously sneaking into the city with a large group of soldiers, he wreaked his revenge. Many workers were killed. Armed battles later broke out in *Piebalga*, *Aizpute* and *Cēsis*.

The tsar's government sent a variety of punitive expeditions to the Baltic provinces. The largest were an expedition led by General Orlov in Vidzeme and one led by General Meinhard in Kurzeme.

In March 1906, the Governor General of the Baltic provinces, Sologub, had 20,000 troops and 32 cannon at his disposal. Baltic German barons also led bloody punitive expeditions, which engaged in monstrous activities in Latvia. People were shot without trial just because a baron or clergyman pointed to them as revolutionaries. A popular form of punishment was 400 lashes, which of course killed many of the women and children that underwent the process. There were no trials; no effort was made to determine guilt or innocence. People were hunted and shot, beaten with sticks of wood and the stocks of guns. Corpses were left hanging as a warning to others. In nearly all of Latvia's parishes, teachers were shot because they had helped farmers to write petitions to the tsar. Artillery was used to fire upon *Rūjiena*, *Dobele*, *Lielauce*, *Vecauce*, *Kuldīga* and other cities. When European democracies protested against the violence in the Baltic provinces, Stolipin ordered that military trials be begun. Governor General Mellert-Zakomelski, himself a baron, set up the trials and appointed fellow noblemen to chair them. In fact, these were courts at which Baltic Germans tried Latvians. More than 2,000 people were sentenced to death.

The revolution had countless victims, wrecked buildings and burned-out ruins. More than 13,000 people were killed, deported or forced into emigration. Nearly one-half of the manors in Kurzeme and Vidzeme, as well as hundreds of farm homes, were reduced to ruins. The revolution of 1905, with the burning of manor-houses, the arrest of noblemen, and heartless repression against working people and farmers, became a tragic phase in the relationship between Baltic Germans and Latvians. The Latvian farmers had historical justice on their side, but the fact is that the Baltic Germans, too, thought of Latvia as their home.

Another consequence of the revolution, which was extremely dangerous for Latvians, was the increased colonisation of Latvia by Germans and Russians alike. The revolution did, however, bring a certain amount of freedom with it. The russification of Latvian schools was halted, the press was made more free, and the right of assembly was guaranteed to a somewhat greater extent. 1905, in fact, was something of a first rehearsal for the ideas of statehood, local governance and agrarian reform – programs which were later implemented by the Latvian state.

The revolutionary events in Latvia forced the tsar to launch democratic reforms. A Duma (Parliament) was assembled, and Latvia sent Karlis Ozoliņš, Fridrihs Grosvalds, Janis Čakste, Janis Kreicbergs and Latgale clergyman Francis Trasuns to the Duma as its delegates.

A 1906 postcard called "Hands Up!" shows repression in Riga after the revolution. Any person could be arrested arbitrarily, and military courts punished people for their role in the rebellion

Russian punitive expeditions sentenced more than 2,000 Latvian schoolteachers, parish officials and farmers to death without trial. Here we see a death sentence being carried out at what was known as the punishment pine tree in *Talsi*. Among those to die was the poet and parish schoolteacher Jūlijs Dievkociņš, and people always put flowers at his gravesite in *Zalve*

A refugee camp during World War I, 1915

Jānis Zālītis (1874-1919) was a delegate to the Russian Duma and one of the key organisers of the rifleman battalions. To the left – a Latvian rifleman battalion heads from Riga to Daugavgrīva, 1915

The Latvian riflemen of the tsar's army – recipients of the Cross of St. George, 1915 - 1916

The funeral of the first fallen riflemen moves along Suvorov Street in Riga, 1915. In the foreground are riflemen bearing funeral wreaths. The catafalques on which the caskets were carried follow them

Latvian riflemen celebrating the summer solstice festival, 1917

Latvia was a prosperous place at the beginning of the 20th century. The revolution of 1905 had been survived. Latvians became more self-confident, practical, educated and organised, dreaming of a dictatorship of the proletariat – a global movement of workers and worker solidarity. The dictatorship of the Bolsheviks was still off in the future. Latvia's citizens and Social Democrats proved unable to come up with a specific, transnational goal, however. The people were split along political lines. Nevertheless, in 1913, it was precisely the workers of Riga, Liepāja and Valmiera who provided the strongest support for the Latvian nation.

The government of tsarist Russia had been afraid of the Latvians ever since the 1905 revolution because of the high level of organisation in Latvian society. Six knowledgeable and intelligent Latvians were delegates to the Russian Duma (Parliament), and they were respected both at the Duma and in Latvian society.

When World War I began, Latvia's society was loudly patriotic. With their patriotism, Latvians sought to convince the Russian state and its government that they were loyal subjects of the state and that they should receive greater rights in return. Initially many people in Latvia felt sure that Russia would win the war and that this would lead to an elimination of the great influence, which local Germans had in the country. A wave of hatred began to wash over the Germans. The events of 1905, including the fact that Baltic Germans killed many schoolteachers and revolutionaries, were not forgotten. Some activists called on Latvians to come to their senses on the issue, but Latvia's population, and especially the Social Democrats, were overtaken by centuries of hate against the Germans. Every historical injustice dating back to the Crusades was dragged up. The phrase "Hit the German!" coincided well with Russia's official position toward Germany. In 1914, Russia lost a number of battles in Eastern Prussia, and some 20,000 Latvian soldiers lost their lives. By 1915, the front lines were in Latvia. Germany occupied Kurzeme. The Latvian language was banned, the region's economy was drained completely, and people were put into concentration camps. The nobles of Kurzeme, now enjoying the support of Germany itself, tried to colonise the region and to wreak revenge against the Latvians for the events of 1905. Mass hysteria broke out. People allowed themselves to be carried away by what was basically mass psychosis, and the results were catastrophic. Before the war, there were 800,000 residents in Kurzeme. In 1915, no fewer than half a million people lost their homes and lost everything that they had owned. This was a perfect gift for the local Germans and their colonists. Kurzeme was empty – an excellent place for Germans to fill up. Riga was evacuated with unnecessary haste and without any real purpose. In the summer of 1915, 30,000 train wagons were used to take away machinery and equipment from the city's factories, as well as monuments, transportation vehicles, church bells and brass roof covers. Government institutions and schools were moved to inner Russia. A quarter million residents of Riga had to leave their city.

The Latvian refugee became a symbol of the times. The refugees were in a very difficult situation, because Russia's governing institutions did not care for them at all. Poverty, illness and despair were widespread. 800,000 Latvian refugees covered a vast territory from Smolensk to Vladikaukaz. They represented fully one-half of the Latvian population. A central committee to handle the refugees was set up, and its first chairman was Vilis Olavs (1867-1917). He set up a refugee care system that set a good example for all of Russia. Tens of thousands of lives were saved.

The Russian army gave up Kurzeme without a fight, and Latvia's society became increasingly convinced that only Latvian military units could free Kurzeme and protect Riga and Vidzeme. Two delegates to the Russian Duma, Jānis Goldmanis and Jānis Zālītis, in 1915 called on people to "rally under the Latvian flags!" Latvian rifleman battalions quickly sprang up. Latvians were establishing an army of the type, which they understood. The military unit was distinguished even by its external appearance – a noble bearing, uniforms sewn to measurement, flags, songs, medals, literary groups, orchestras, theatrical troupes, newspapers, flowers, cleanliness, and order, whether in the trenches or on the farm. The relationship between commanders and soldiers were friendly, the men studied and

trained diligently, and true fighting abilities were quickly developed. The riflemen fought on their own land and for their own land. They were closely linked to the nation, and they were loved by it. The same could certainly not be said for the military commanders of Russia, who gave the Latvian riflemen no support at all. Legendary battles at *Nāves sala* ("Death Island"), *Smārde*, *Ložmetējukalns* ("Machine Gun Hill") and *Mazā Jugla* were unsuccessful, but the riflemen became legends in their own time. The Latvian nation was spoken of not only in Russia, but also in Western Europe.

When the Latvian rifleman battalions and later regiments were formed, their abilities were exaggerated. The riflemen did not retake Kurzeme, they did not protect Riga or Latvia. Because of incompetent commanders from the Russian army, thousands of Latvian soldiers perished needlessly.

Most of Latvia's riflemen eventually joined the Bolsheviks in Russia, for a variety of reasons – their hatred for tsarist Russia, the pointlessness of the battles in which they had engaged, and the indecision of influential Latvians. The riflemen were active in the Russian civil war, believing the Bolsheviks and their leader Lenin when they said that Latvia would be allowed to become independent. Neither the tsar's government or the provisional "white" government under Kerensky had ever promised anything of the sort. By making that promise, Lenin gained the support of the strongest and best-organised unit in the Russian armed forces – the Latvian riflemen. Why were the Latvian riflemen of such critical importance in the Russian armed forces during World War I and the Russian civil war? Perhaps it was because of the high level of education among Latvians. The Latvian riflemen were all able to write and read in three languages, while Russia's own soldiers, many of whom came from Siberia and the vast steppes of the Russian hinterland, were almost always illiterate. It would be a mistake to say that without the so-called "red" riflemen of Latvia the tsar's Russia would not have collapsed, but it is a fact that the riflemen were the one unit in the Soviet armed forces which Lenin could send to the most critical parts of the front lines. They always carried out their duties admirably. True, they did not have a country to call their own, but they were alight with the ideas of the universal workers' paradise, and so they were merciless in their attacks.

The Latvian Refugee Committee, which was established in St. Petersburg in 1915, provided money to refugees and helped them to find housing and work, as well as medical care, schools and cultural opportunities. The main purpose of the Committee, however, was to gather Latvians together and to keep them from getting lost in the vastness of Russia. The Committee became the parliament and government of the scattered nation. Leaders included some of the best politicians of the day – Vilis Olavs, Jānis Čakste, Kristaps Bahmanis and Arveds Bergs, among others. It was precisely at the various refugee centres that the idea of an autonomous and independent Latvia really took hold.

The two countries in Europe that suffered the greatest material losses during World War I were Latvia and Belgium. Those that lost the greatest number of people were Latvia and Serbia.

World War I transformed Europe. It became pacifist, democratic, nationalistic and revolutionary. Empires collapsed, nation states emerged. On 18 November 1918, the Republic of Latvia joined their ranks.

In the trenches near *Olaine*, 1918

Rifleman & artist Kārlis Baltgailis (1893-1979). Self-Portrait

Prisoners of war during World War I

The "red" riflemen

A monument to German guardsmen who fought against the Bolsheviks in Latvia. Known as "The Iron Guardsman", the monument was located at the corner of *Tērbatas iela* and *Brīvības bulvāris* in Riga

The war graves of Finnish soldiers at *Klapkalnciems*

The war graves of men who fell during World War I

The proclamation of the independent Latvian State at the National Theater in Riga, November 18, 1918.

The declaration of independence of the Republic of Latvia

A letter of support sent by Foreign Secretary Balfour of Great Britain in which the independence of Latvia was favored, November 11, 1918

A document offering *de iure* recognition to the Latvian state, January 26, 1921

Zigfrīds Anna Meierovics (1887-1925), politician, diplomat and first foreign minister of the Republic of Latvia. He promoted the establishment and international recognition of the Republic of Latvia and died in an automobile accident

Miķelis Valters (1874-1968), author of the idea of an independent Latvian state and one of the founders of the Republic of Latvia. He served as the country's first interior minister and was later Latvia's ambassador to Italy, Poland, France and Belgium, where he remained after 1940

Pauls Kalniņš (1872-1945), a political activist and Social Democrat, one of the founders of the Republic of Latvia. He was a member of all of the sessions of Latvia's independent Parliament and emigrated form the country in 1944

Pēteris Stučka (1865-1932), attorney and political activist, one of the organizers of the Latvian Communist Party. He led a Communist government between 1918 and 1920 that is remembered as a period of merciless terror

Fricis Roziņš (1870-1919) stood alongside Stučka in founding the LCP. In 1919 he was the agriculture minister of the Soviet Latvian government

Andrievs Niedra (1871-1942), a Latvian writer and political activist. From April until June 1919, he headed a government propped up by the German military

Riediger von der Goltz (1865-1946), commander of a division from the Landeswehr

Pavel Bermont-Avalov (1881-1936), an adventurer who was one of the leaders of the counterrevolution in Latvia

Hans Manteuffel (1894-1919), a Baltic German baron and Landeswehr officer who helped in staging a coup in Latvia in April 1919. He fell during an attack on Riga

Linards Laicens (1883-1938), Latvian poet, author and political activist. He was the first author to call openly for an independent Latvian state in the press. He moved to Moscow 1932 and was killed during Stalin's purges

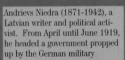

The idea of a free and independent Latvian state first arose among a small group of Social Democrats who were political émigrés in the early 20th century. They were led by Miķelis Valters, who in late 1903 issued the radical demand "Down with arbitrary governance, down with Russia", promoting the idea of a division of the Russian Empire into national states. This marked the beginning of Latvian political nationalism.

In the spring of 1915, volunteer Latvian military units succeeded in their battle against the Germans, and this brought the issue of political autonomy for Latvia onto the front burner. The most active in popularizing and defending this idea were Latvians Ernests Blanks and Linards Laicens in Moscow, as well as other educated Latvians who gathered around the newspaper *Dzimtenes Atbalss*. In July and August 1917, they actively propagandized the idea of an independent Latvian state. Russian military failures and the yielding of Riga to the Germans in 1917 provided fertile ground for these ideas. Latvia's intelligentsia understood that Latvia, with a country split by the front lines of the war, with thousands of refugees and with a collapsed economy, could only aim itself toward the Western democracies. The poet Kārlis Skalbe put the idea into words: "Let us stand with both feet in Europe."

In April 1917, America joined the war. President Woodrow Wilson was an active defender of the ideas of democracy and self-determination. The United States declared that one of its goals in the war was the defense of the interests of small nations. Wilson's ideas became political gospel for Latvians and other small European nations. A major role in ensuring Latvia's independence was played by the Latvian Temporary National Council (LPNP in the Latvian acronym) and the Democratic Bloc. In Valka in 1917, the LPNP declared that Latvia "is an autonomous and indivisible state." On January 30, 1918, in St. Petersburg, the LPNP distributed an announcement in which it declared that "Latvia must be an independent, democratic republic which joins together Kurzeme (Courland), Vidzeme and Latgale." Under German occupation, the Democratic Bloc sought to preserve and actualize the idea of self-determination.

In 1918 there were favorable geo-political and international legal conditions for the establishment of the Latvian state. On November 7 and 8, 1918, the Baltic Germans formally established the Duchy of the Baltic, which was supposed to include Courland, Vidzeme and Estonia. This was a move of no political realism whatsoever. LPNP representative Zigfrīds Anna Meierovics convinced Great Britain of the need for an independent Latvian state. On October 23, 1918, British Foreign Secretary Arthur James Balfour told Meierovics that London had decided to grant provisional recognition to the Latvian National Council as the Latvian government. On November 17, 1918, a People's Council was set up, and Kārlis Ulmanis was chosen as Latvia's first prime minister. The independent state was proclaimed at a ceremony on the very next day. This was made possible largely by the daring of four distinguished people – Ulmanis, Valters, Pauls Kalniņš and Fricis Menders. During the course of a single night, the four men created a philosophical basis for the new state which was acceptable to virtually all of the political groupings in the country. The temporary government was established spontaneously. Hidden and open enemies of the state responded immediately, and a period of great chaos followed.

The Latvian state was proclaimed at the National Theater in Riga on November 18, 1918. Riga was controlled by the German Landeswehr, most of Latvia was controlled by the Bolsheviks, and even those who attended the proclamation ceremony had great doubts about the viability of the new state.

Kārlis Ulmanis was selected as the first head of the temporary government, which immediately devoted much of its attention to the relationship with Germany – the country which continued to hold most of the reins of power in Latvia. The German government immediately decided to establish relations with the Ulmanis government, and a few days after November 18, the German Cabinet of Ministers recognized Ulmanis as the provisional highest authority "in the Latvian ethnographic territory". The People's Council was deemed the controlling institution in that territory.

The German military, however, was not disciplined on this matter at all. The major powers of the Entente were unable to force Germany to fulfill Article 12 of the *Kompjeņa* armistice that had been signed on November 11 and to halt the further movement of the Russian Bolsheviks into the Baltic States. Soviet Russia denounced the Brest peace treaty of March 3, and in early December, a few days after the proclamation of the independent state, the Bolshevik armed forces entered Latvia. The country's battle for freedom was launched in earnest.

The temporary government faced a hopeless situation early in 1919. On January 13, the Bolsheviks entered Riga, and in a very short time thereafter they took over most of Latvia. A government headed by Pēteris Stučka began to run affairs, and the temporary government was forced to decamp to *Liepāja*.

In 1918 and 1919, there were in fact three different governments in Latvia. Latvia's independence, too, was proclaimed three times – on December 2, 1917, on January 30, 1918 and on November 18. It was only on the latter of these dates that true democratic foundations were established for the Latvian state, ensuring the people's unity and their ability to win against the Red Army and the forces of counterrevolutionary leader Pavel Bermont. Only when the Latvian nation took to its weapons to beat the country's enemies and the institutions which they had set up could the state really be established. Victory was ensured by democratic potency and by the true interests of the Latvian nation. The Republic of Latvia chose a democratic model of development that won support among the population when the Constitutional Convention was elected in April 1920.

Russian, German, British and Latvian historians have shed different light on the events of 1918. British historians claim that Latvia won its freedom from Russia only thanks to the special support which it was given by Foreign Secretary Balfour. While we must not discount the achievements of Sir Arthur, we must also remind readers that an announcement from London which was issued on November 11 and which British historians cite frequently contained not a word about the Latvian Temporary National Council and Latvia's independence from Russia. Rather, the document focused on the state's independence from the German occupation. Latvia's independence occurred at the end of World War I, when all of the countries that were involved in the conflict were focused on their own interests. In the context of these interests, Latvia's independence was merely a secondary issue, and it won its independence largely because Europe needed a barrier against a military invasion by the Bolsheviks. The new states which broke away from the Russian Empire became fence posts in this barrier. British hatred against Germany was so deep that London automatically and fiercely opposed any political or military steps which Berlin took, especially if those steps posed a threat to British interests. In order to scuttle the idea of a German-Russian union, British diplomats reached for all of their skills to help in the establishment of the new Latvian state, but then the Latvians were left to battle against the Russians and Germans alike. At a time when the Latvians were fighting side-by-side with the Landeswehr in opposing the Bolsheviks in Vidzeme and the Germans were feeling strong and able, the British turned Latvia's military units against the forces of Bermont near *Cēsis*. The fact that the Latvian and Estonian armies took a stand against Bermont put an end to the counterrevolutionary's plans in the region, but it also allowed the Bolsheviks to hang in there for a while longer. It is hard to say that Bermont himself would have beaten Lenin's Bolsheviks, but the number of men who could stand against "Red terror" after this event was smaller.

The first attempt by Latvians to form their own state was known as the Iskolat Republic, taking the name from the relevant Russian province. This structure was never completed. The achievements of the Bolsheviks could not be seen as any affirmation of the idea that Latvians yearned for socialism. Latvians did not vote for communism, they voted against war and against the military policies of the Russian tsar. This marked a brief enthusiasm among Latvians for an anti vote, because only the Bolsheviks promised Latvians peace. The moral and political prestige of Russian citizenship had lost its luster quite a bit during the war, but socialism, as a democratic system, was described only in theoretical articles. The administration of Pēteris Stučka was propped up by military force in 1918. The councils of the administration quickly flowed together with the institutions of the Bolsheviks, and a party-based dictatorship was the result. The administration was able to govern only with open terror. The so-called "red troikas" engaged in horrific repression against anyone who did not yield to the Bolshevik ideology. The red terror cost thousands of people their lives. The idea of self-determination for nations was more a social issue than a national program for the Bolsheviks, and they declared their stand for the "proletariat of the nations".

Latvia's own people were not unified during this period. There was a conflict with the Baltic German minority, even though in the battle against the Bolsheviks in 1919 the Germans were an important ally. The alliance with the Germans, however, did nothing to improve the status of the temporary governments among the population at large. The orientation toward Germany also allowed German and Baltic German colonizers who were hostile to the idea of an independent Latvian state to operate more freely. In December 1918 they forced the temporary Ulmanis administration to sign a promise that any foreign soldier who spent a month on the front lines against the Bolsheviks would automatically be granted citizenship in Latvia. The German military forces which fought against the Bolsheviks in Courland rapidly changed into a Latvian military contingent. The Baltic Germans expressed their readiness to integrate into the new country, demanding guarantees of their property, rights and culture in return. The temporary government and the remnants of the People's Council ignored these demands in the winter and spring of 1919. Any compromise with the Baltic Germans would have been seen as a betrayal. On April 16, 1919, the men of the Landeswehr violently put an end to the activities of the Ulmanis government. The barons Manteufel, Recke and Brimmer joined with military officer Riediger von der Goltz to stage a coup. Ulmanis and several of his ministers sought refuge in a British mission, and later the entire temporary government was forced to reside on a military ship, the Saratov, which was anchored in the *Liepāja* port. Germans in *Liepāja* tried to set up another, more loyal government. Under pressure from the diplomats of the major allies, a compromise was found in the person of Andrievs Niedra.

Niedra was a dedicated anti-Communist, and in the name of a defeat of Bolshevism he was willing to settle for extensive Latvian autonomy within a citizenship-based Russian state. The Germans like Niedra, but his government was recognized only by von der Goltz and Germany itself. The Bolsheviks were already camped outside of *Liepāja*. The Soviet government, however, could do little to help Stučka's Bolsheviks, because it was busy with Russia's internal problem. The Bolsheviks were chased out of Courland. In just a few months the Latvian Soviet government proved completely unable to battle external and internal enemies alike. Increasing the prestige of the Niedra government, von der Goltz's forces – the so-called Iron Division and the Baltic Landeswehr — on May 22, 1919, ejected the Stučka government from Riga. Forces commanded by the Latvian military officer Jānis Balodis also entered the city. The Germans proceeded to expand into Vidzeme, from which the Bolsheviks had been routed by Northern Latvian and Estonian military units. Von der Goltz, of course, wanted these units to yield to his command, but the commander of the Estonian forces, General Johann Laidoner, replied firmly that a line of demarcation had been drawn in Vidzeme.

British diplomacy stood against the yearnings of the German military to join up with Russian monarchists, and taking advantage of Estonia's annexation-related intentions in Northern Latvia, it provoked the *Cēsis* battles. In these battles Latvian and Estonian forces joined up under the leadership of Johann Laidoner against the Landeswehr and several units of Pavel Bermont's forces. The Landeswehr joined the provoked battle, and on June 22 the Latvian army beat Bermont's forces at *Cēsis*. The Niedra government fell on June 27. A peace treaty was signed at Stazdumuiža which provided for a withdrawal of the German forces from Riga by July 5. Northern Latvian military units entered the capital city on July 6, and the Ulmanis government returned two days later. The German military, however, refused to obey the request of the Allies that it withdraw from Latvia altogether. The German forces became part of the Russian army under the command of a former Russian military officer, Pavel Bermont-Avalov, who called himself an earl and who had a very shady past. On October 8 von der Goltz and Bermont-Avalov attacked Riga once again from the Kurzeme side. On November 3, the Latvian army began its liberation of Riga from the Iron Bridge across the *Daugava* River, and Allies contributed artillery fire from warships in the Bay of Riga in their support. The city was liberated on November 11, and ever since then November 11 has been Latvia's memorial day, known as *"Lāčplēsis"* Day. On November 28 German forces were forced out of Latvia altogether.

What remained, however, was the Bolshevik force in Latgale, and to deal with it Latvia's government concluded a military agreement with Poland. Marshal Juszef Pilsudski demanded only that the Latvian side pay for the accommodations of 20,000 Polish men in return. On January 3, 1920, a joint Latvian-Polish force went on the attack near *Daugavpils*. *Rēzekne* was liberated on January 21, and by the end of January the joint force was in *Zilupe* – the easternmost town in Latvia. Peace negotiations with Russia continued for a long time, even as the battles were still raging. On August 11, 1920, Russia and Latvia signed a peace treaty in which Russia promised to recognize Latvia's sovereignty and the refuse all claims on Latvia's nation and land "for time eternal".

Troops from the Northern Latvian brigade of the Latvian armed forces, commanded by Col. Jorģis Zemitans, entered Riga on July 6, 1919. Here we see them parading down Alexander Boulevard (now Riga's *Brīvības bulvaris*). The Latvians beat the forces of Pavel Bermont at *Cēsis* on June 22. The Niedra government fell on June 27 as a result of the complex political and military conflict. A treaty was signed at *Strazdumuiža* which provided for a German withdrawal from Riga on July 5. This was the only time in the history of Latvia that the Latvian armed forces themselves liberated Riga militarily to march into the city as heroes

A temporary treaty between Latvia and Germany on the restoration of contacts, July 15, 1920

A conference was held in Helsinki in 1920 at which new ideas for European development and cooperation were considered. Latvia was among the participating countries

An agreement signed by representatives of the Baltic States during the *Bulduri* Conference, August 31, 1920. The first attempt to establish a Baltic Union took place at that conference. An agreement was signed, but no real union was ever established. The failure of the Baltic States to implement the ideas that were developed at *Bulduri* was a key reason for the loss of independence by the three countries in 1940

The personal file of Karlis Frikhofs, recipient of the Order of *Lāčplēsis*, 1924

A rifleman from the Riga Student Company

The first female rifleman, Lina Čanka

The armored personnel carrier *Kurzeme* at the Rome Hotel in Riga, 1919

Latvians in Latgale successfully fought behind the lines of the Bolshevik army. Lt. Col. Jānis Skujiņš is at the right of this photograph

The tanks of Bermont-Avalov's army after the liberation of Riga

The peace treaty of 1920 between Latvia and Russia in which Russia promised to recognize Latvia's sovereignty and independence "for time eternal"

The signing of a peace treaty between Latvia and the Soviet Russia. The Soviet delegation was headed by Adolf Ioffe. Riga, August 11, 1920

The ratifying document of a non-aggression treaty between Latvia and the Soviet Union that was concluded on February 5, 1932, July 28, 1932

A church confirmation, 1930s

A Latvian farm family outside its home in the early 20th century

An armored personnel carrier, *Sargs* (Guard) on the Esplanade square in Riga in the early 1920s

In the 1920s and 1930s, Latvian farms made great advances in dairy and cattle farming, and they produced dairy products and meat that satisfied the Latvian market and were exported abroad. Latvia for a time was Europe's leading exporter of cheese and butter

Poet Aleksandrs Čaks outside a bookstore in Riga

Latvia's approach to the world involved energetic but peaceful diplomatic activities. Between the two world wars, Latvia was an active member of the League of Nations, and it had particularly close relations with Lithuania and Estonia, as well as Sweden, Finland and Denmark from the Scandinavian countries.
In this photo we see Swedish King Gustav V on a state visit to Latvia in 1928

President Alberts Kviesis and Prime Minister Kārlis Ulmanis at a harvest festival in 1933

"Latvian money for Latvian products", says this sign

Members of a workers' athletic association, *Ciņa* (Battle) on a march in the *Grīziņkalns* neighbourhood during an athletic festival in October 1926

The non-aggression agreement signed by Latvia and the USSR on February 5, 1932

The President Kārlis Ulmanis with Latvian ambassadors in 1939

Latvian home guards entering their headquarters building in Riga (at Home Guard Street 29) in May 1934

Prime Minister Kārlis Ulmanis outside the Cabinet of Ministers building while his coup was going on, May 15, 1934

The signing of the first Latvian-Soviet agreement. Soviet representative Mikoyan is at the left. Moscow, 1928.

Prior to World War II, there were only three parliamentary republics in Europe, while after the war there were sixteen. Most of them adapted their basic constitutional principles from the liberal constitution which France had after 1875, with a parliamentary political system at the center of the process.

On January 18, 1919, at the Paris peace conference that was chaired by the French head of government, Georges Clemenceau, a Latvian delegation headed by Jānis Čakste was in attendance. On September 30 of the same year, the foreign ministers of the three Baltic States and Finland met to discuss a joint approach to negotiations with the Communist government in Russia, as well as with the Entente. On August 11, 1920, Russia became the first country to grant *de iure* recognition of Latvia's independence. England, France, Italy and Japan followed suit on January 26. The Baltic countries were admitted to the League of Nations on September 22, 1921.

In 1920, the consequences of the recent war were still very much in evidence in Latvia. 10% of homes had been destroyed completely, while 14% were left uninhabitable. Of the 2.5 million people who lived in Latvia before the war, only 1.8 million remained. A quarter of arable farmland had been allowed to go to fallow. In 1915, when the Russian army withdrew from Latvia, it took all of Riga's factories with it. Much of the equipment was destroyed during the chaos of the Russian civil war, and Latvia eventually regained only some 10% of the value that had been removed. When von der Goltz's army withdrew in 1919, for its part, it stole a great many cultural treasures and burned down the *Jelgava* castle and the Peter Academy. Germany has ever since refused to talk about the marauding which its soldiers did in rural Latvia during that time.

Elections for the Constitutional Convention were held in 1920, and the convention met for its first meeting on May 1 of that year. Jānis Čakste was chosen as the chairman of the convention. The panel completed its work in 1922, when the Latvian constitution was approved, specifying that Latvia was an independent, democratic republic in which sovereign authority belonged to the nation. Parliament was given legislative and major leadership functions. Parliament, known as the *Saeima*, was elected by adult citizens of the Republic of Latvia. The head of state was the president, elected by Parliament. The president's authority was limited mostly to representative functions. The Cabinet of Ministers was assigned the task of handling the everyday life of the state. The survival of the Cabinet depended on the confidence of Parliament.

The vast majority of people in Latvia – everyone except committed Communists and the few remaining supporters of Niedra's government – celebrated not only their independent country, but also the process of parliamentary governance. Latvia's people were enormously energetic in the post-war period. Political life was active, and there were virtually innumerable political parties. Everyone wanted a piece of freedom. Governments came and went, but after the great damage of war, Latvia recovered remarkably quickly nonetheless. Universities were opened. Artists went forth in bold new directions. At the same time, however, there were many state-owned companies and monopolies, as well as a growing army of civil servants, and these caused enormous losses to the national budget. Latvia was governed by neoliberal economic principles, and trade was free. After a brief period of enchantment with the idea that Latvia might be a bridge for transit from Russia to the West, the country found its place in post-war Europe was as an agricultural country with a growing industrial sector. Latvia's main trade partner was England, and British pounds

The Ulmanis government on a visit to the Latvian Ethnographic Open-Air Museum in the 1930s. From the left: Agriculture Minister Janis Birznieks, Interior Minister Vilis Gulbis, War Minister Janis Balodis, President Karlis Ulmanis, Public Affairs Minister Alfreds Berziņš, Justice Minister Hermanis Apsitis, Communications Minister Bernhards Embergs and Education Minister Augusts Tentelis

were used to buy cheaper and more qualitative goods from Germany. Latvia's own currency, the lats, was the result of hard work by Finance Minister Ringolds Kalnings, who held the post from June 1921 onward.

The Constitutional Convention also adopted a law on land, which confiscated the former lands of the baronial estates and proclaimed them to be state property. The former owners of landed estates, provided that they had not fought against Latvian independence, were given 100 hectares of land apiece, while the remaining land was divided up among what were known as *jaunsaimnieki*, or "new farmers." Each new farmer received a parcel of land not larger than 22 hectares. Finally Latvia's servant and landless classes could satisfy their dreams of having, as a poet put it, "my own corner, my own patch of land."

Latvia's successful foreign policy was led by Foreign Minister Zigfrids Anna Meierovics, who improved relations with Estonia, Lithuania, Poland, Finland and Germany and Russia, too. His ministry ensured that Latvia was respected and recognized in other countries. The friendship was not easy to maintain among the Baltic States themselves, however. Arbitration was necessary to settle border issues, and Latvia lost half of the town of *Valka* to Estonia, as well as the entire city of Palanga to Lithuania.

Democracy in Europe came under threat almost from the very beginning of the 1920s, and the philosophies of totalitarianism began to spread. Fascist, anti-liberal Italy seemed peculiarly tempting in 1922. In May 1926 Poland fell to authoritarianism. Lithuania followed suit six months later. Latvia's egalitarian process of agrarian reform, which led to the creation of a great many small and economically inefficient farms, inevitably led to a need for ongoing government subsidies. Political demands for a system that would unquestionably fulfil promises in this area were rife. In 1927 the Latvian Farmers Union proposed that the country's parliamentary system be replaced with a more authoritarian regime. The main problem of parliamentary Latvia lay in its structure. There were too many farmers, and there was too little in the way of a democratic bourgeoisie. The bourgeoisie was too weak, it had no traditions in terms of parliamentarianism, and the structure was not rooted in the mentality of the nation.

On May 15, 1934, Prime Minister Karlis Ulmanis staged an authoritarian coup in Latvia which was an act of political and legal violence. Democracy died in Latvia. Parliament was disbanded, political parties were banned, a state of military emergency was declared, local governments were eliminated, the democratic press was prohibited, the mass media were censored, political opponents were arrested and, to top it all off, in 1936 the authority of President Alberts Kviesis was arbitrarily taken away from him and given to Ulmanis instead. The coup was bloodless, and no political opponents were executed. The fact is that the period of Ulmanis' authoritarianism was interesting and wealthy in nature.

The "Latvia of May 15", as the authoritarian country came to be known in the regime's lexicon, had three main values: Leadership, Unity and Nationalism. Ulmanis implemented the process of leadership by taking over the entire decision-making process in the state, presenting himself as the highest authority on all matters. A personality cult quickly sprung up – wherever Ulmanis went, there were ceremonial gates for him to pass through, he

was showered with honorary titles, and the flattery which he had to hear cannot be described through words. Yet the leader managed very successfully to present himself as an understandable, strict but just and proper farm man – an image which was perfectly acceptable to the mentality of most Latvians.

The basic motivation for the Leader's (as he insisted that he be called) idea of unity was this: "There are only two million of us, and in order to reach goals in many areas, we must not break up. We must build our state in unification and agreement." The authoritarian regime particularly supported the country's farmers – "guarantees of the nation state and eternal Latvia", as they put it. The period of Ulmanis' rule is still remembered today as a period when Latvia exported bacon and butter – a process which ensured a steady flow of hard currency into the country's coffers and freed up local resources for developmental needs.

Latvia for Latvians – this was the basic principle of Ulmanis' nationalism. Pretending either that all of the minority problems in Latvia had been resolved or that there were no minorities in Latvia in the first place, Ulmanis limited the educational and linguistic rights of non-Latvians in the country. The economy was "Latvianized", and the rights of German, Jewish and Russian industrialists and tradesmen were limited to a certain extent. The Ulmanis regime did not, however, cultivate national hatred or anti-Semitism. National minorities retained the right of cultural autonomy, and they were never seen as anything less than fully vested citizens of the country.

The propaganda of "Latvian Latvia" veered close to farce at times, but Ulmanis' powerful personality, as well as his ideology, did a great deal to increase the national self-esteem of the Latvian nation in just a few years' time. Ulmanis' time was a period of a great many empty nationalistic and patriotic slogans, but his work was based on realistic and practical approaches to economic and social problems. Ulmanis was fanatic in his support for a job well done. The idea of work done properly was lifted to the level of government policy. This, too, was not strange to the Latvian mentality.

Many people in Latvia, especially among the intelligentsia, did not recognize the coup of May 15, 1934, to be lawful, and they did not think much of the Leader's form of leadership. The economic achievements of Ulmanis' Latvia were not to be denied, however. The standard of living in Latvia increased, cities grew, and the regime became more and more acceptable, if not completely attractive, to the country's residents.

Ulmanis' regime engaged in a vast program of construction – hydroelectric plants, bridges, highways, administrative buildings, public halls, hundreds of schools, all built in just six years. Industry developed successfully, and the country's greatest manufacturing achievements lay in radios, telephones and the Minox camera. Roberts Hiršs gained great success in textiles. The VEF electronics factory produced several airplanes, as well as automobiles on a license from Ford. Ulmanis was a true patriot. Latvia was always the point to his life and work, the only content of his approach to life. He loved Latvia, tended to it and nurtured it as he was able, and he demanded that the citizens of his state follow suit. Foreshadowing John F. Kennedy's famous phrase 20 years later, Ulmanis said: "Ask not what the country will give you. Think first what you can give to the country."

The exaggerated nationalism which existed during Ulmanis' reign actually helped the Latvian nation to survive the military occupations that were visited upon it for the next half century. People still remember the Ulmanis period as one during which people worked hard and at a good quality, when they enjoyed an acceptable standard

of living, when there was an independent state and government, when human relationships were heartfelt and simple, and when society and the state functioned normally.

In November 1938, Latvia marked the 20th anniversary of its independence. As is the case in any country, Latvia did not lack for problems, but people were proud of the fact that "this land is ours". True, the political regime was dictatorial, but it was never bloody or aggressive. Had Latvia encountered a different fate, it would have passed through the period of dictatorship like Portugal and Spain did, and perhaps today it would be just as wealthy and successful a member of NATO and the European Union as those two countries are. Unhappily, Latvia found itself squeezed between Hitler and Stalin – the two bloodiest and monstrous dictators in the history of human civilization with their Fascist Germany and Socialist-Fascist Soviet Union. Latvia's authoritarian government, it must be said, was completely inappropriate for putting all available diplomatic and military resources to bear against the Soviet Union's plans for annexation.

The signing of a mutual aid pact between Latvia and the USSR. The pact is being signed by Soviet Foreign Commissar Vjacheslav Molotov. Standing – I. Zotov, Stalin, Latvian Foreign Minister Vilhelms Munters, Fricis Kociņš, and the deputy Soviet foreign commissar, Vladimir Potjomkin. Moscow, October 5, 1939

5. oktobri Savstarpējās palidzības paktu starp Latviju un Padomju Socialistisko Republiku Savienibu, kurš skan šādi:

Caurskatijuši un pārbaudijuši šo paktu, esam to apstiprinājuši saskaņā ar Ministru Kabinetā 1939. gada 10. oktobri pieņemtā likuma noteikumiem, paziņojam un apliecinam, ka šis pakts ir pieņemts, ratificēts un apstiprināts, un apsolam, ka tas tiks stingri izpildits.

So apliecinot, esam izdevuši šo ratifikacijas grāmatu, uzspiežot tai Republikas zimogu.

Rigā, 1939. gada 11 oktobri

K. Ulmanis

The document of ratification for the mutual aid pact, October 11, 1939

An agreement between Latvia and the Soviet Union concluded in 1939 which allowed Moscow to bring its military forces into Courland. The document was presented to Latvia as an ultimatum

Policeman's uniform in 1935

A parade march of a policeman's company on November 18

Rīgā, 1939.g.7.novembrī.

Pārskats
par Baltijas vāciešu repatriaciju.

Baltijas vāciešu repatriacija jau norisinājās ļoti intensīvi. Pašu šī jautājuma gaita ir šāda.-

Germans began to emigrate from Latvia in 1939, after the conclusion of the infamous Molotov-Ribbentrop Pact. This is a report on the repatriation of the Germans

VOLLMACHT

Den Reichsminister des Auswärtigen Herrn Joachim von Ribbentrop bevollmächtige ich hierdurch, mit dem Bevollmächtigten der Republik Lettland über einen Vertrag zur Sicherung

A non-aggression agreement between Latvia and Germany, concluded in 1939

The Song Festival in *Daugavpils*, 1940

21 July 1940. An order from President Ulmanis on the transfer of the President's functions to Prime Minister August Kirhenšteins

On 18 June 1940, several Communists who had been imprisoned in Latvia's central prison for actions deemed dangerous to the State were liberated. Criminals who agreed to support the new Soviet regime and to join the KGB were also released

A demonstration in *Ķemeri* in the summer of 1940 calling for the sacking of the local government

20 June 1940: Andrei Vishinski and the Soviet ambassador to Latvia, Vladimir Derevjanski, greet demonstrators. In the first row of the demonstration are agitators sent in from the Soviet Union with posters prepared in Moscow

On 7 June 1939, Latvia and Germany signed a non-aggression pact. Germany promised Latvia that its war with Poland would not affect Latvia, while Latvia undertook not to participate in any guarantee systems aimed at Germany, or to permit the Russians to attack the Baltic republics. It later turned out that this was a tactical move for Germany, because when the situation changed, Hitler put all of Europe's small countries on the chopping block. The fate of the Baltic States was decided on 14 August 1939, when Hitler and Stalin divided Europe.

On 23 August 1939, the Soviet Union and Nazi Germany signed a pact in which they agreed on the division of Poland, as well as the inclusion of Latvia, Estonia, Finland and Transylvania (part of Romania) in the Soviet "sphere of interest". This was all set out in a secret protocol that was attached to the larger agreement. Soviet representative Vjacheslav Molotov and German representative Joachim von Ribbentrop signed it in secret in Moscow. The first article in the protocol said that in case of territorial restructuring, the northern boundary of Lithuania would mark the border between the German and Soviet spheres of interest. Lithuania's interest with respect to the district of Vilnius was recognised by both parties to the agreement.

On 28 September 1939, the Soviet Union signed a friendship treaty with Germany, thus becoming an official ally for Hitler. Germany and the Soviet Union marked a precise boundary between the occupied parts of Poland. This agreement, too, contained secret protocols concerning territories, as well as the ability of ethnic Germans to leave those areas, which fell into the Soviet sphere of interests. Germany was promised that Sovietisation in the Baltic States would take place gradually and in full cognisance of Germany's economic interests. Baltic Germans from Latvia and Estonia would be allowed to leave. It was very clearly specified that the Baltic States would later be incorporated into the Soviet Union. The Germans sold Lithuania to Stalin for 2 million gold roubles, and it, too, was included in the Soviet sphere of interest.

On 27 September, Estonia's foreign minister, Karl Selter, was summoned to Moscow, where officials demanded that he sign a mutual aid agreement. Latvia did the same on 5 October, and Lithuania yielded on 10 October. Soviet military bases were set up in *Piltene*, *Edole*, *Kuldīga*, *Cīrava*, *Durbe*, *Grobiņa*, *Liepāja*, *Paplaka*, *Priekule* and *Vaiņode*. Latvia had become a protectorate of Moscow.

The Finnish foreign minister was also summoned to Moscow and given an ultimatum of signing a humiliating agreement or facing the consequences. The Finns stood up to the threat, flatly refusing to turn over any of their territory, to lease the Hanko harbour to the Russians and to demilitarise the Soviet-Finnish border. Moscow responded with loud threats against Finland. On 26 November, Soviet Foreign Commissar Molotov claimed that Finland had fired upon the village of Mainil in Russia and, ignoring Finnish protests, on 29 November the Russians went to war. Helsinki was bombed. Moscow Radio announced that in the region of Karelia, the "people's government" of Finland had been established. Finland fought heroically. The League of Nations denounced the Soviet aggression, and on 14 December, the USSR was expelled from the League.

Despite the great heroism demonstrated by Finnish soldiers during what has come to be known as the Winter War, Finland ended up having to turn over some of its territory – Karelia, the city of Viborg, and the naval base at the Hanko port. 25,000 Finnish soldiers fell during the war with the Soviet Union, as did between 2 and 3 million Soviet soldiers. Some historians feel that the Soviet Union attacked Finland as a practice run so that it would later be ready for war against Germany or, possibly, the United States in Alaska.

When news of the Hitler-Stalin agreement and the Molotov-Ribbentrop pact – both of which sounded the death knell for Latvia – reached the rest of Europe, the Ulmanis government demonstrated a complete lack of seriousness by predicting confidently that there would be no war. Information about threats against the State and its citizens were kept from the population. Foreign passports were confiscated, and only very wealthy people with extensive contacts could keep their passports and flee the coming conflagration.

At dawn on 15 June 1940, Soviet Interior Ministry forces attacked a Latvian border control station at *Masļenki* and two other border sites. Three border guards and the wife of a border guard were killed at *Masļenki*, and 17 civilians were captured and taken into Russia. In order to find cause for aggression, the Soviet Union also staged a conflict in Lithuania, accusing the Lithuanian government falsely of having taken Soviet soldiers hostage.

On 15 and 16 June 1940, the Latgale Song Festival was held in *Daugavpils*. Participants expected President Ulmanis to attend, but the Soviet Union had already begun military aggression against Lithuania and the President could not leave Riga. His speech to the song festival was transmitted on the radio. After the president spoke, the festival choir sang the Latvian national anthem, *Dievs, svētī Latviju!*, three times. On 16 June, the Latvian government received an ultimatum from Moscow, and a response was demanded in six hours' time. There were two demands in the ultimatum – that a new government is established immediately and that the Soviet military be granted free access to Latvia's territory without delay. There was nowhere to turn for help. The German army had occupied Paris two days earlier.

Latvia was occupied on 17 June. The chairperson of the Soviet Union's Council of Commissars, Andrei Vishinski followed the Soviet military, and he led the effort to destroy the Latvian state and to put the Soviet occupation in place. In Lithuania Vishinski's deputy, Dekanazov led the process, while in Estonia the secretary of the Central Committee of the Russian Communist Party, A. Zhdanov, did it.

On the evening of 19 June Vishinski arrived in the office of Latvian President Ulmanis to present to him a new list of Cabinet ministers, as prepared in Moscow. On 21 June Vishinski spoke from the balcony of the Soviet embassy, promising that Latvia's independence would be honoured. Vishinski spoke in Russian, but he concluded his speech in Latvian, saying "Long live free Latvia! Long live the friendship between the Republic of Latvia and the Soviet Union!"

The Soviet regime had prepared very carefully for the occupation. A large ship dropped anchor in the Riga port, and on 17 June 600 agitators came on shore with posters that had been printed in Moscow and, accordingly were rife with grammatical mistakes. 10,000 security officials were also sent into Latvia, and they, too, brought slogans into the streets on 17 June to "celebrate" the arrival of the Soviet military. The occupants were also greeted by those who thought Communism would bring good times with it, the non-loyal segment of the minority community that had never accepted Latvia's independence, and a series of collaborationists who were entirely prepared to work with anyone

The secret protocol on the division of spheres of interest that was signed by Molotov and Ribbentrop on 23 August 1939

Soviet Union's People's Commissar Andrei Vishinski speaking to demonstrators in Riga

The secret protocol of an agreement signed by Molotov and Ribbentrop on 28 September 1939

This issue of *the New York Times* carried news about the Soviet occupation of the Baltic States on June 17, 1940

Latvijas Republikas valdības deklaracija.

Stājoties pie augsto valsts pienākumu pildīšanas, valdība paziņo Latvijas Republikas tautai:

Vecā valdība kritusi. Tā nebija taisnīga pret visiem, tā negribēja izprast tautas intereses, nespēja nodrošināt ar Padomju Savienību 1939. gada 5. oktobrī noslēgtā savstarpējās palīdzības līguma godīgu pildīšanu un slepeni no Padomju Savienības bija -slēgusi militaru savienību ar Igaunijas un Lietuvas bijušām valdībām.

Jaunā valdība uzskata par savu uzdevumu veicināt un celt tautas materialo un -rīgo labklājību, nodrošināt brīvību un tautas tiesības, nodrošināt valsts un visu pilsoņu -tereses, neatkarīgi no viņu mantas stāvokļa, ticības, izglītības vai tautības.

Ievērojot šos uzdevumus, Latvijas Republikas valdība izsludina amnestiju visiem, -s cīnījušies par brīvību un mūsu tautas laimi, visiem, kam savas politiskās demokra-kās pārliecības dēļ bijušā valdība ņēmusi brīvību.

Par savu vispirmo uzdevumu jaunā valdība uzskata nodrošināt Latvijas un Pa-mju Savienības 1939. gada 5. oktobra savstarpējās palīdzības līguma godīgu pildīšanu, -matojoties uz šī līguma pilnīgi izveidot ciešu savienību starp Latviju un Padomju Sa-nību, un ar visiem līdzekļiem novērst katru šī svarīgā valsts uzdevuma traucējumu.

Tas, ka Latvijas Republikas teritorijā atrodas mums draudzīgās Padomju Savienības -ņotie spēki, ko Latvijas tauta saņem ar prieku un sirsnību, ir labākais pierādījums -ūsu tautas patiesai draudzībai ar šiem spēkiem. Tas ir arī pierādījums mūsu lielā kaimiņa Padomju Socialistisko Republiku Savienības — draudzīgajām attiecībām ar mūsu zemi.

Valdība ir stingri un nešaubīgi pārliecināta, ka Latvijas tautas un Padomju Soci-stisko Republiku Savienības draudzība vēl vairāk veidosies un stiprināsies un ka tikai -ā veidā iespējams nodrošināt tālāku mūsu tēvijas attīstību un uzplaukumu.

Valdības stingra pārliecība ir, ka lielās Padomju Savienības un Latvijas Republikas -tu nesatricināmā draudzība arī uz priekšu būs varens un reals spēks, kas nodrošinās -tvijas valsts neatkarību, savstarpējo drošību un mierīgu, sekmīgu abu valstu sadar-.

Savā ārējā politikā valdības princips ir mierm̄īgu un draudzīgu attiecību nodro-

The government declaration of the Kirhenšteins government, printed in the government newspaper *Valdības Vēstnesis*, 22 June 1940

Lācis (1904 -1966), the collaborationist – the Council of the Latvian SSR

of People's Commissars of the Latvian SSR in August 1940. t, front row: the people's commissar for national control, rubiņš; the people's commissar for agriculture, Jūlijs people's commissar for justice, Andrejs Jablonskis; the the council, Vilis Lācis; the deputy chairman, Fricis Deglavs; le's commissar for the interior, Alfons Noviks. In the second ple's commissar for social welfare, Alfrēds Nurža; the missar for light industry, Kārlis Šics; the people's or labour, Ludvigs Kažemaks; the people's commissar for al economy, Jānis Jagars; the people's commissar for the stry, Jānis Gustsons; the people's commissar for trade, ; the people's commissar for local industry, Kārlis Karlsons; le's commissar for finance, Arnolds Tabaks

who had strength and power. Ulmanis not only ordered Latvia's military to stand down and avoid a fight, he did not even lodge a diplomatic protest against the occupation. Many people were distraught. The fact is, however, that it was the Soviet Union, not Kārlis Ulmanis, which destroyed Latvia, first occupying it in a very brief military campaign, and then annexing it six weeks later.

Soviet "comrades" dubbed the incorporation of Latvia into the Soviet Union a "Socialist revolution", and the entry of the Red Army was proclaimed to be "Latvia's protection against the war". The people were promised that democracy would be restored and that there would be free elections. Farmers, retailers and industrialists were told that private property would be inviolable.

In June 1940 the Soviet puppet regime staged a parliamentary election in which, on the evening of 10 July, it was announced that only one list of candidates – that of the Working People's Bloc – met all of the legal requirements to stand for election. A former education minister, Atis Ķeniņš, tried to file the list of the Democratic Latvian Bloc, and he printed a campaign program. When the new rulers came to understand that they would not be able to stop the opposition candidates lawfully, Ķeniņš and most of the candidates on the list were simply arrested, and their materials were confiscated. Catholics in Latgale also managed to publish a campaign platform, but after threats were levelled against them, they declined to submit a list of candidates.

The elections were held under strict occupation control on July 14 and 15, and the most basic principles of democratic elections were ignored. People who voted had their passports stamped to indicate that they had voted. Those who did not were threatened with punishments.

Moscow announced the "official" results without delay – 97.6% of the voters in Latvia, 98.2% in Estonia and fully 99.5% in Lithuania had voted for the only list of candidates.

On 21 July 1940, the new Latvian *Saeima* met for its first session, and right away it decided to ask the Supreme Council of the USSR to make Latvia a republic of the Soviet Union. That evening there was a demonstration which was amply attended by KGB men from Moscow who were dressed up as working people and who cheered on behalf of the USSR. Vishinski spoke: "May I congratulate you on the great, historic day when you joined the Soviet Union!" Odd: Nothing had been said about joining the Soviet Union before, but now Latvia was already proclaimed as a member republic!

A group of Baltic representatives was dispatched to Moscow to ask the Supreme Council for the right to join the USSR. Large demonstrations were staged in Moscow to greet these delegations.

On 5 August, the Supreme Council of the USSR unanimously "admitted" Latvia to the Soviet Union as the 15th republic of the union.

On 18 May 1940, the Latvian government had granted emergency powers to its ambassadors abroad, saying that if the government were unable to fulfil its duties, Latvian Ambassador Kārlis Zariņš in London and Ambassador Alfrēds Bīlmanis in Washington must represent the country's interest in the free world. Bīlmanis launched an immediate protest against the incorporation of Latvia into the Soviet Union. In a note prepared on 23 July Zariņš explained the anti-constitutional nature of this occurrence. The Latvian Constitution of 1922 specifies that Latvia is an independent democratic republic and that sovereign power in Latvia belonged to the people. Had the *Saeima* wanted to amend these provisions, this would have been possible only after a national referendum. A few days after the incorporation, the government closed all foreign offices and companies in Latvia, and all foreigners, including journalists, were expelled.

The Soviet Union sought to eliminate all of those Latvians who had any authority, respect of knowledge, those who were leaders, government officials or businessmen. Thousands of people were repressed, including the Latvian government ministers and the directors of various institutions. The year from June 1940 until June 1941 – the year of the first Soviet occupation – remains known in Latvian history as the Year of Terror.

The Soviet Union had already set up its *gulag* network of concentration camps. Within Russia, representatives of several professions – railway workers, journalists – as well as representatives of such nationalities as Latvians, Ukrainians and Finns, had already been dispatched to the camps before World War II. Latvians were sent to Siberia from various places in the Soviet Union in 1937, 1938 and 1939, and many were killed.

President Ulmanis was arrested, and on 21 July 1940, he was deported. He died on 20 September 1942, in a prison in Krasnovodsk.

War Minister Jānis Balodis was arrested and deported on 31 July 1940.

Foreign Minister Vilhelms Munters was deported to Voronezh in July.

Finance Minister Jānis Kaminskis was deported in 1941.

Interior Minister Kornēlijs Veitmanis was deported in 1940.

Education Minister Jūlijs Auškāps was deported in 1940 and executed in Sverdlovsk on 3 August 1942.

Transportation Minister Artūrs Kaposts was deported in 1941.

Justice Minister Hermanis Apsītis was executed on 19 January 1942, at the Astrahan prison.

Agriculture Minister Jānis Birznieks died under deportation in 1955.

Former Interior Minister Arnolds Bergs was executed in December 1941 in Orenburg.

Former Agriculture Minister Markus Gailītis was deported in 1941 and last seen alive in the autumn of that year in Astrahan.

Vilis Gulbis, who had served as the Agriculture, Education and Interior Minister, was shot on 19 January 1942, in Astrahan.

Former education and agriculture minister Jānis Kauliņš was executed on 30 April 1942, in Novosibirsk.

Former Prime Minister and Interior Minister Marģeris Skujenieks was executed in July 1941 in Moscow.

Public Affairs Ministers Alfrēds Bērziņš managed to escape to the West.

A few days after Latvia's incorporation into the Soviet Union, the government of the Latvian SSR began to liquidate all forms of private property. Real estate, private industries, banks, private shops and other companies were nationalised, and land was proclaimed to be the property of the people.

Public thought, as well as the national economy and all other aspects of the nation's life, were subject to a unified system of governance and ideology. The repressive mechanism, with its interior structure and its militia, worked hand-in-hand with the courts and the prosecutor's office to ensure that people obeyed orders without objection and that any socially "dissatisfied" people were isolated. Typical elements of the process of sovietisation included centralised management and planning of the economy, a move toward collectivisation, and the establishment of a bureaucratic system of control, and full censorship of the mass media. Praise for the "great leader" Stalin became an automatic part of every celebration and party anniversary.

A few days after the incorporation of Latvia into the USSR, all youth organisations, including the Boy Scouts, the Girl Scouts and the *Mazpulki* (a local organisation analogous to the Scouts), the Red Cross, all student and many public organisations were shut down. The Soviet occupation regime took over all of the property of those organisations.

Culture was now meant to support the policies of sovietisation, and it was ordered to denounce the previous period of democracy. Soviet culture was loud and pushy – "Red corners", mass demonstrations in the streets, the strictly controlled press, the poetry that was written in flattery of Stalin and the Communist Party, etc.

"Creative unions" made up of writers, composers, filmmakers and other artists were set up in order to control what they did, to support those who toed the line, and to punish those who did not. It was mandatory for the leaders of these creative structures to work with the KGB.

A basic element in sovietisation was the imposition of Communist thinking on the educational process. Students from kindergarten to university were taught about the battle of the classes and the ideas of Marx, Stalin and Lenin. New teachers could not be prepared in time, so the government of the Latvian SSR issued instructions to existing ones. The Pioneers and Komsomol organisations were set up. Agitation was an everyday factor in schools, and children were made to participate in pro-Soviet demonstrations.

The first signs of national opposition to the system appeared in the early fall of 1940. There were active nationalist teachers all over Latvia who flatly refused to teach the tenets of Communist ideology. There were active illegal groups in *Dobele*, *Bauska*, *Cesvaine*, *Jēkabpils*, *Kārsava*, *Rauna*, *Cēsis* and *Daugavpils*, as well as at teachers' institutes at *Rēzekne*, *Jelgava* and Riga. An 11th-grade student from the *Jelgava* No. 1 High School, Fricis Skurstenis, organised a patriotic youth group, "Free Latvia", which opposed the policies of the occupants. The KGB found the

Atis Ķeniņš (1874-1961) was a poet and teacher who served as Education and Justice Minister between 1931 and 1933. He tried to file a list of candidates for the 1940 parliamentary election to stand against the Working People's Bloc, but for his pains he was arrested on 19 September 1940. In 1941 he was deported to Kazakhstan. He returned to Riga in 1955

Nepadodieties musinātājiem, kas grib graut Latvijas darba tautas vienoto fronti

Daži turīgu aprindu pilsoņi, aktīvie 1934. gada 15. maija fašistiskā apvērsuma dalībnieki ar ģen. Jāni Balodi priekšgalā Ata Ķeniņa vadībā sākuši organizēt saeimas vēlēšanām savu demokratisko latviešu sarakstu, neraugoties uz to, ka visi patiesi demokratiskie Latvijas iedzīvotāji jau pievienojušies Latvijas darba tautas blokam. Šie politiķi savu pasākumu acīm redzot organizējuši, cerēdami, kā tas bija iespējams agrākos laikos, iegūt sev kādus labumus un taisīt politiku — pēdiņās. Viņi vākuši iedzīvotāju vidū parakstus, lai gan pats kandidātu saraksts nav sastādīts. Daži lētticīgi pilsoņi tā devuši savus blanko parakstus.

Mūsu drošības sargi šo politisko avantūru ir laikā atklājuši un nodevuši lietas noskaidrošanu un atrisināšanu prokuraturai.

Pilsoņi! Esiet apzinīgi, nepadodieties musinātājiem, kas grib graut Latvijas darba tautas vienoto fronti! Vienīgi patiesi demokratiskais un progresīvais kandidātu saraksts ir Latvijas darba tautas bloka saraksts, kura vēlēšanu platforma pasludināta, no visām progresīvām organizācijām pieņemta un kurā ievesti pārstāvji no visām iedzīvotāju aprindām.

Pilsoņi un pilsones! Dodiet pienācīgu atbildi visiem demokratiskās Latvijas ienaidniekiem 14. un 15. jūlijā. Visi kā viens ejiet pie vēlēšanu urnām un balsojiet par Latvijas darba tautas bloka sarakstu.

An article in the newspaper *Jaunākās Ziņas* in opposition to Ķeniņš' efforts to file a list of candidates for the parliamentary election in July 1940

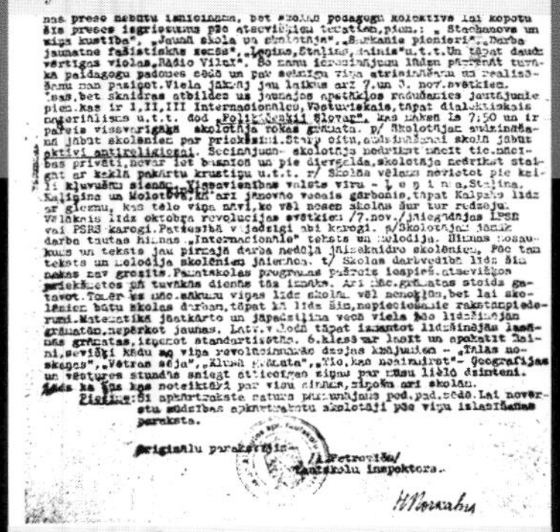
Instructions from the inspector of schools, A. Petrovičs, on Soviet propaganda in schools, 1940

Automobiles in a demonstration before the parliamentary election on 14 and 15 July 1940

The National Opera in 1940 – the entire Soviet agitation arsenal and every resources were used for propaganda purposes

Many of the agitators who were sent in from the USSR did not have posters in Latvian, so they brought along ones that were written in Russian

A pro-Soviet demonstration in 1940

The declaration adopted by the People's Parliament of the Republic of Latvia on 21 July 1940, concerning the country's accession to the Union of Soviet Socialist Republics, published in *Valdibas Vestnesis*, 1940

Par Darba tautas bloku

95 proc. vēlētāju

Vakar centrālā vēlēšanu komisija saņēma iepriekšējas ziņas par Saeimas vēlēšanu iznākumu. Pavisam nodota 1.179.643 balsis, no kurām par vienīgo sarakstu — Latvijas darba tautas bloka kandidātiem — 1.157.730 balsis (97,6 proc.) Stripotu sarakstu ir 27.919. Salīdzinot ar 1931. gada Saeimas vēlēšanām, par Darba tautas bloku nodotājo balsu skaits ir gandrīz par piekto daļu lielāks nekā toreiz nodoto derīgo balsu kopskaits par visiem sarakstiem. Ar to tauta devusi savu spriedumu par veco iekārtu, iejot jaunajā vēstures posmā disciplinēta un vienota.

Par Latvijas darba tautas bloka kandidā-

An article about the results of the 1940 parliamentary election. The article was written and printed before voting was completed

A pro-Soviet demonstration in 1940

A demonstration in *Liepāja* in 1940

ПРАВДА

Pioneers from the No. 40 Elementary School in Riga prepare a wall newspaper for Red Army Day

An article in *Pravda* about Latvia's admission to the Soviet Union, 6 August 1940

Augusts Kirhenšteins, shortly before his departure to Moscow with the request of the collaborationists that Latvia be admitted to the USSR, August 1940

Journalists interviewing Prime Minister Kirhenšteins in his train car as he and other collaborationists travel to Moscow to ask Stalin for permission to join the USSR. To the right of Kirhenšteins is the director of the LETA news service, I. Kaģis

group, and only one of the 14 schoolchildren who had been members of the group ever returned from the Siberian camps.

A group of military officers led by Lt. Col. Janis Upitis, who had been the deputy commander of the Latvian military headquarters' Operations Unit before the war, organised more serious opposition. The officers helped to explain to people what had happened and to encourage them not to lose faith. Opposition groups were also organised among members of the National Guard, the police, and university students, but many of them were caught, tried and deported. The church and christianity as such were also repressed. Schools were banned from teaching religion, and atheism was taught instead. The University of Latvia shut down its Faculty of Theology. The church was prohibited from engaging in its traditional social role – marrying people, registering births and deaths, supervising cemeteries, etc. Church properties were nationalised. Such real estate that was left to the church was taxed heavily. The faithful were per-

secuted, many clergymen were deported. Forty church pastors were deported in 1940. Some were shot.

The Latvian army was first renamed the People's Army, and then it became a territorial corps of the Red Army. On 11 July 1940, the Latvian SSR ordered the establishment of the Baltic Military Region. This was done at a time when Latvia was still formally an independent country. Since 4 July, the army had been subject to the ideological control of the Red Army's political leadership. Latvian officers were replaced with Soviet commanders. One day Latvian officers were all told to go to *Litene* for additional training. They were disarmed and put into trucks, told that they were going to be doing field training. Once out in the woods, most of the officers were shot, while others were arrested and sent to Siberia. Senior officers, including all of Latvia's generals, had earlier been sent to Moscow, and they had met the same fate.

The KGB's duty was to monitor all of the people who were not satisfied with the new regime. A broad network of informers was set up, and the bosses of the KGB, Semjon Shustin and Alfons Noviks, had unlimited power. They signed documents sealing the fate of thousands upon thousands of people, and one of the signatures was sufficient to sentence a person to death. Arrests began on 5 August 1940. Over the course of a year 7,020 people were convinced of crimes, including 404 women, 17 children and 172 pensioners. 980 people were shot, the remaining ones were deported.

In basements throughout the country the KGB took to its grisly task of torturing people. In order to force innocent people to admit to untrue accusations, victims were interrogated and tortured mercilessly and for weeks on end. A commissar of the KGB called Serov had prepared instructions as early as 11 October 1939, on how mass deportations were to be organised in Latvia, Lithuania and Estonia. On the night of 13 June 1941, more than 15,000 people, including 1,200 children younger than 7, were deported to the farthest reaches of Siberia. People were woken up in the middle of the night, given one hour to get ready, and allowed to take only what they could carry. Everything else was confiscated by the Communist regime. The victims were pushed into previously prepared cattle railcars. Men were separated from their families and were sent to Siberian camps that were surrounded by barbed wire fences. Women and children were sent to various settlements in Siberia. The cattle railcars journeyed for weeks and months. Many people, including infants and the sick or the elderly, did not survive the trip.

Not a single word appeared in Latvia's newspapers about these events. Families were told nothing about those who were deported. The railway tracks were covered with notes that people threw out of the barred windows of the cattle railcars for their loved ones. Eventually very few people came back from the deportations. On the same night, 21,000 people were deported from Lithuania and 11,000 from Estonia. Those were the first, but not the last mass deportations.

A few days before Germany went to war against Russia, as well as in the first few days of the war, the KGB became particularly monstrous in its activities. People were shot without trial and based on a commissar's order alone, scribbled on a small piece of paper. Members of the intelligentsia and the businessmen class were killed in great numbers.

A document listing people to be deported. There was one denunciator in every parish responsible for making such a list

The declaration, which the People's Parliament adopted on 21 July 1940, asking that Latvia, be admitted to the USSR

A decree from the Supreme Council of the Latvian SSR on 12 April 1941, concerning "nationalisation of the property of large land owners and speculators"

The first congress of the Writers Union of the Latvian SSR

An order from the Cabinet of the Latvian Soviet Socialist Republic calling on newspaper correspondents from the Latvian SSR to halt all activities abroad and to return home and ordering the expulsion of all foreign journalists from the Latvian SSR, published in *Valdibas Vestnesis*, 20 August 1940

Acts on the new ownership of nationalized real estate from 1940

A decision by the Cabinet on closing a Jewish organisation in Riga, published in *Valdības Vēstnesis*, 23 June 1940

A decision signed by the people's commissar for the interior of the Latvian SSR, Semjon Shustin, on the arrest of the director of the British Institute, Jānis Šmits, for "anti-Soviet activities".

This book, "These Names Accuse", lists the thousands of people who were deported to the Soviet Union during the Year of Terror

Augusts Kirhenšteins at the podium in Moscow on 5 August 1940, asking that Latvia be allowed to join the Soviet Union. A delegation of Latvian Communists is in the foreground. Loud displays were common in the Soviet Union, and that's why the Latvian folk costume was dragged into this process

On 5 August, the Supreme Council of the Soviet Union unanimously admitted Latvia as the 15th republic of the USSR. At the far right at the podium is Stalin, while at the far right in the foreground in Andrejs Upītis, a prominent writer is the Latvian SSR

The Red Army demonstrates its power after the incorporation of Latvia into the Soviet Union on 5 August 1940

A family split apart, seen here in March 1941. This is the Lindiņš family – Rudolfs and Anna, with their children, Sigurds, Elga and Tristans. Rūdolfs Lindiņš was shot during the occupation of Latvia. When the KGB knocked on the door on 14 June 1941, the elder son jumped out of a window and escaped. Later in life he became a prominent member of the Latvian community in Australia. Daughter Elga was not at home that night and was not deported. She later became the director of the Latvian Geology Administration. The younger son and his mother were deported. The boy died in Siberia, while Mrs. Lindiņš died shortly after returning from the deportation. She had been gone for 16 years

A hall in the main headquarters of the Riga KGB with cell doors. Latvia's intelligentsia and members of the independent country's government languished here. Three-person troikas held trials, and the accused were usually sentenced to death

The first chairman of the KGB in Latvia was Semjon Shustin, a Jewish Communist who was certainly one of the greatest murderers in the history of the Latvian state. When the German Nazis occupied Latvia in July 1940, they pointed to Shustin's rampage as an excuse for their own annihilation of Latvia's Jewish communities, seeking to attach blame for Shustin's monstrosities to all Jewish people

The people's commissar for the interior in the Latvian SSR was Alfons Noviks, a Latvian Communist from Latgale who sent thousands of people to their death. He was known as a hero during Soviet years, and he often spoke to Pioneer groups in schools about his battle against what he called the counterrevolution. The "hero" was sentenced to life in prison for crimes against humanity after Latvia regained its independence and died in prison

Hermanis Apsītis (1893-1942), Riga regional prosecutor from 1927, Judicial panel prosecutor from 1933, Justice Minister from 1934-1940, arrested and executed in 1940

The KGB occupied the building on *Stabu iela*, which used to house the Latvian Interior Ministry during Soviet years. It was universally known among the population as "the corner house"

26 June 1941. An order from Semjon Shustin concerning prisoners in the central prison: "Because of social dangerousness, all are to be shot". 78 people were killed as the result of this piece of paper

Victims of Soviet terror in the yard of the Riga central prison, 1941

General Kārlis Gopers (1876-1941) was chairman of the Latvian Boy Scouts. He was arrested in 1940 and executed a year later

Father Pēteris Apšenieks of the *Baltinava* Catholic Church (1897-1941), arrested and killed on 13 June

Jānis Kruze (1891-1941) was drafted into the army of the Russian Empire in 1915, joined the Latvian army in 1919, received the Order of the Three Stars and, in 1937, the Estonian Order of the Eagle, and worked as an investigator in the Political Board of the Interior Ministry. He was arrested in 1940 and shot at *Baltezers*, Latvia, in 1941

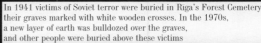

In 1941 victims of Soviet terror were buried in Riga's Forest Cemetery, their graves marked with white wooden crosses. In the 1970s, a new layer of earth was bulldozed over the graves, and other people were buried above these victims

The Nazi army occupies *Liepāja*, June 28, 1941

The ruins of Old Riga in 1941. Russian forces blew up some of the most beautiful buildings in the old city as they retreated

The arrival of the German army in Riga, July 1, 1941

After the atrocities of the Soviet occupation in 1940 and 1941, many Latvians greeted the Nazi army as liberators

The ideological methods of Nazi Germany were quite similar to those of the Soviet Communists. "Supporters" were made to participate in demonstrations, dressed in Latvian folk costumes but carrying both Nazi and Latvian symbols

On June 22, 1941, the German army attacked the Soviet Union and the countries which it had occupied. Thanks to their high level of organization and their appropriate tactics, the Germans moved very rapidly deep into Soviet territory. The Soviet army proved to be unprepared for lightning attacks and fully unable to defend itself. Because the Latvian city of *Liepāja* was home to a military port, army airports and warehouses, the German army bombed the city on the morning of the very first day of the attack. By June 24, *Liepāja* was encircled by German military units. *Daugavpils* was taken on June 26, while *Krustpils*, *Jelgava* and *Liepāja* fell on June 29. Riga was occupied on July 1, and all of Latvia's territory was in German hands a few days later. As the Soviets retreated, the KGB blew up parts of the old city in Riga and set fire to the tower of St. Peter's church. Before leaving Latvia's territory, the KGB managed to arrest and kill many people. Many others were forced to leave Latvia along with the fleeing Soviet military units. The commissar for the interior, Shustin, ordered that political prisoners all be shot. Demonstrating unbelievable duplicity, the Communists did not let Jewish residents of Latvia to flee from the country and into the Russian interior, thus leaving them victim to the German Fascists. During the first days of the war, partisan units were formed all over Latvia to attack the departing Soviet military. National partisans were particularly active in Vidzeme where, after the murder of Latvia's military officers at Litene, virtually the entire membership of the 24th communications battalion fled to hide in the forests of the region.

A nationalist Latvian organization called *Pērkoņkrusts* (Thunder Cross) issued this call for Latvians to join local defensive units.

the Germans. Thousands of members of the intelligentsia, as well as economic and political leaders had disappeared or been deported. Latvians detested Stalin's regime and saw the arriving Germans as liberators from the abhorred Bolshevik government and its policy of terror. Soon enough, however, it became clear that the Germans were an occupying force, too. Industrial raw materials were removed from Latvia, and important companies were placed under the direct control of similar enterprises in Germany. Farms were ordered to turn over specific amounts of produce. The wearing of Latvian army or home guard uniforms was banned, the Latvian hymn and flag were prohibited, and people were ordered to turn in all of their weapons. Latvian army officers had organized self-defense units in Riga and its environs, ready to hunt down those Soviet soldiers who had remained behind the withdrawing army and were hiding in the forests, as well as those people who had collaborated with the Soviet regime and had not managed to get away with the army units. The self-defense force also searched for criminals who had been released from Latvia's prisons by the Communists. The work was coordinated by the Latvian Organizational Center, headed up by former finance minister Alfrēds Valdmanis. The Germans did not trust

the Latvians, however, and the volunteer organizations were disbanded.

Along with the German army, representatives of the operative division known as Einsatzgruppe A also arrived in the country, and their mission was to destroy communists and Jews. Latvia, Lithuania, Estonia and Belarus were subordinated to Germany's ministry for occupied Eastern regions, which was led by a Baltic German Nazi called Alfred Rosenberg. The ministry's headquarters in the Baltic region were placed in Riga. The first clear evidence of the fact that the newly arrived Germans were an occupying force came on July 4, 1941, when many Jews were herded into the Riga synagogue and left there while the building was set on fire. The Nazis explained that this was revenge for the Germans who had been shot in Riga's prisons by the KGB, arguing that most KGB officers were Jews. The genocide against the Jews continued. Several ghettos were set up in Latvia, Jewish people were forced to wear the yellow star of David on their clothes. Similarly murderous policies were implemented against Latvia's Gypsies. All of the patients in the country's psychiatric hospitals, as well as those who were listed in the files of various psychiatrists, were exterminated. Germany killed not only Latvia's residents. During the war more than 70,000 Jews who were citizens of Latvia were murdered, but the total number of Jews who died in the country, according to authoritative reports, was 314,000. Germans brought Jews from Germany, Austria, Czechoslovakia and other countries to Latvia. Jews were shot by security officers from the SS, but there were also Latvians with unbalanced psyches and sadistic yearnings who guarded Jewish camps and brought people to the extermination sites; in other words, they, too, participated in the genocide. Latvians for centuries had lived in harmony with Jews and Gypsies, and there were many people who tried to come to their rescue. Jews and Gypsies were hidden in people's homes and in other places. Those who helped were, of course, risking their own lives. Latvian sailor Žanis Lipke alone hid 55 Jews from the Riga ghetto. Since 1987 dozens of Latvia's residents have been awarded a special order of merit for their work in helping Jews during the war.

The German terror was waged against the indigenous population, too. Long-term German plans were to ensure that ethnic Germans would make up the majority of the population in Latvia, and Latvians were to be second-class residents once again. There were several concentration camps in Latvia, the largest at Salaspils. People were imprisoned for opposing the German regime, for failing to pay the taxes that were levied, or for failing to register with a labor board that was set up. Many Latvians were taken to Germany where, without any explanation, they were put to forced labor. Many young Latvian girls were also taken, and in most cases nothing was ever heard of them again.

As losses began to mount on the Eastern front, Germany began to run out of soldiers, and men from the occupied territories were forced to enlist. A Latvian volunteer group was formed into the 15th and 19th divisions. Authoritative members of the Latvian intelligentsia were used for propaganda purposes, ordered to tell everyone that the so-called Latvian Legion would be fighting for a free Latvia. Latvian men were in no hurry to sign up for these units, but the German regime interpreted this as hostility against the Nazis. This could result in punishment both for those who were of draft age

A celebration to mark the 1st anniversary of the arrival of Germany's army in Riga, July 1, 1942

A Nazi propaganda meeting under the slogan "A protest demonstration of Latvian workers against the decisions of the Moscow Conference", Riga, November 13, 1943

The minister for occupied Eastern territories of the German regime, Alfred Rosenberg, visits Latvia and meets schoolchildren in Dobele, May 17, 1942

A regional song festival in Riga on July 11, 1943

Guests of honor at the song festival included (front row, from the left), a general commissar for Latvia and national adviser Otto Drechsler, a commissar for the Riga District, Joachim Fust, and the general director of the self-governing organization of the Latvian territory, General Oskars Dankers, Riga, July 11, 1943.

The first 1,000 men drafted into the Latvian Legion march toward the Dome Square in Riga to take their oath of service, March 29, 1943

The inspector general of the Legion, SS *Gruppenführer* and SS weapons Lt. Gen. Rūdolfs Bangerskis inspecting a parade of legionnaires, Riga, September 4, 1944

A parade of the Germany military in Riga in honor of Adolf Hitler's 53rd birthday, April 20, 1942

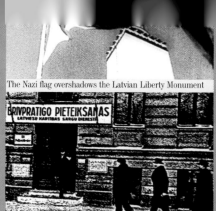
The Nazi flag overshadows the Latvian Liberty Monument

A location where volunteers could join the Latvian Home Guard, 1941

Latvian legionnaires in Courland

The German occupying force published the newspaper *Tēvija*, which allowed the German propaganda machine to denounce the Soviet Union, praise Hitler and sow anti-Semitism

German police in the streets of Riga

A ceremony marking the 25th anniversary of the date when the Baltic Landeswehr took Riga on May 22, 1919. Here we see a memorial ceremony in a cemetery where many soldiers of the Landeswehr are buried.

An order issued on October 31, 1943, which sets out a list of ranks for police officers in Latvian

Latvian Legion Lt. Daugavietis, July 1944

The highest-ranking SS and police commander in the Ostland and Northern Russian, SS *Obergruppenführer* and SS weapons and German police General Friedrich Jeckeln in 1944

Latvian sailor Žanis Lipke hid 55 Jews from the Riga ghetto and saved their lives. He has been awarded a global order of merit for his work

Initially Germans did not trust Latvians, and most Latvians were dispatched to work units. Only later was the Latvian Legion formed. Here we see men who were drafted into labor units marching near the Liberty Monument in 1943

Young people who were drafted into the labor services of the German occupation are seen here in Dome Square before being taken to Germany, March 26, 1942

Latvian schoolchildren being trained as assistants to the German air force, late July or early August, 1944

and members of their families. The Latvian divisions which were formed operated under the command of German officers.

The most vicious battles toward the end of World War II were fought by the 19th division in what has become known as the Fortress of Courland in 1944, especially from December 23-31, the so-called Christmas battles. Latvian legionnaires carried the brunt of the battle, refusing to retreat in the firm belief that they were fighting for their fatherland. The fact that these brave men held on in the Fortress of Courland allowed countless Latvians to emigrate, thus avoiding Russian revenge which began as soon as the war was over. Under the command of Colonel Kurelis, the legionnaires sought to fight both against the Germans and the Russians, but they were ground up by the war machines of the major powers. After Germany's final capitulation on May 8, 1945, several thousand of the legionnaires went into the forests to continue their fight as guerillas. It was a true tragedy for the Latvian nation that the Soviet Union, too, established two divisions of Latvian riflemen, and Latvians ended up fighting against one another on both sides of the front lines. Latvia's soldiers died in the fight over Moscow, when Russian commanders sent them into battle as cannon fodder. Latvians earned medals for bravery in both armies. The first commandant of occupied Berlin was a Latvian – General Nikolajs Berzzariņš. There was an opposition movement in Latvia during the German occupation – the Latvian Central Council, which was led by Konstantīns Čakste, a son of the first Latvian president. The council hoped that the Allies would lend their support in opposition to a second Soviet occupation. The council worked with the Swedish government to organize boat lifts of refugees to Sweden. As the Soviet army neared once again, many people got into small fishing vessels to evade a repeat of the events of the Year of Terror. Countless people left behind everything that they owned. some 250,000 refugees headed for Germany and Sweden. Many perished along the way.

All in all, World War II was a devastating tragedy for the Latvian nation – weakened by two military occupations and, at the end of the war, scattered across the globe, their fatherland left to many years of Soviet occupation, complete with deportations and all manner of humiliation.

The Red Army entered Latvia in 1944 and 1945, behaving fully like an occupying force. The Russians marauded, murdered and raped, and they were followed by the KGB's armed units, which repressed people, killing and deporting those who had sympathized with the German occupation or had failed to oppose it. For Latvians, World War II did not end until 1991, when they finally got rid of Lenin's, Stalin's and Brezhnev's occupation.

A Soviet tank amid the ruins of *Jelgava*, 1944

A disabled German personnel carrier alongside the *Riga-Ērgļi* road after the withdrawal of the German army, 1944

Soviet soldiers have broken through to the sea at *Klapkalnciems*, fall 1944

The funeral of civilians who died in *Ķemeri* when the Soviet army was moving toward the Bay of Riga near *Klapkalnciems*, 1944

German soldiers surrendering at *Tukums*, May 1945

More than 100 people crowded aboard this boat, which the Latvian Central Committee send from the Swedish island of Gotland to bring refugees out of Latvia, 1944

The graves of German soldiers in *Saldus*

Graves near the town of *Blīdene* mark the final resting place of soldiers from the 19th division of the Latvian Legion who fell in 1944 and 1945.

The grave of a soldier from the Latvian Legion who fell in 1944. The grave is located in *Bauska*

The German army killed many people in the village of *Audriņi* on charges that they had been supplying food to Soviet partisans. This monument was sculpted by Alvine Veinbaha and set up in 1973. The architect was Gunārs Asaris

The graves of victims of genocide against Jews in the town of *Subate*. Jews in Latvia's small towns were exterminated completely by the Germans

The *Salaspils* memorial (1967) is located where the *Salaspils* concentration camp once stood. The monument was sculpted by Ļevs Bukovskis, Oļegs Skarainis and Jānis Zariņš, while the architects were Oļģerts Zakamennijs, Gunārs Asaris, Oļģerts Ostenbergs and Ivars Strautmanis

A monument to soldiers who fell during World War II that is located in *Vietalva* (1967). Latvian riflemen in the Red Army fought pitched battles here. The architect was Edgars Šēnbergs, while the sculptors of the monument were Valdis Albergs and Zenta Zvāra.

THE YEARS OF THE SOVIET OCCUPATION

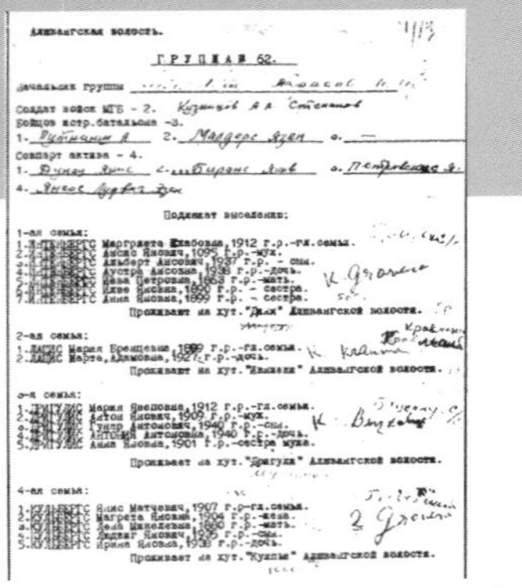
Алшвангская волость.

ГРУППА № 62.

Начальник группы

Солдат войск МГБ – 2.

Бойцов истр.батальона – 3.

Совпарт актива – 4.

Подлежат выселению:

1-ая семья:

Проживает на хут. "Дзах" Алшвангской волости.

2-ая семья:

Проживает на хут. "Ивыкаи" Алшвангской волости.

3-я семья:

Проживает на хут. "Дригули" Алшвангской волости.

4-ая семья:

Проживает на хут. "Кулпы" Алшвангской волости.

A list of families to be deported on March 25, 1949, from the *Alsunga* parish. On the list were hard-working farm families that were called kulaks by the collectivizing Soviet regime

The deportation of local residents from Latvia in the late 1940s. People were rousted from their beds in the middle of the night and allowed to take along only what they could carry. People who resisted were hauled before the courts and ended up in concentration camps

Cattle cars at the *Stende* railway station, waiting to carry deportees to Siberia on March 25, 1949. The cattle cars were filthy, and many people were not fed along the way. Children and the elderly died in large numbers

A celebration of the *Jāņi* summer solstice festival in 1956 in Siberia. Latvians did not forget their ethnic roots even on the tundras, and under very harsh conditions they grew vegetables, raised livestock, worked hard and preserved their traditions

The funeral of a deported Latvian in Vorkut, 1955

The Lutheran church in the town of *Lestene*, seen here in the 1950s or 1960s. The church was used by the Soviet armed forces as an observation post during World War II, and so it was fiercely bombed by the Germans. More than 100 churches were wrecked during the war – and then the Soviets arrived with their state-sponsored policy of atheism. 124 churches from several denominations were shut down. Warehouses were set up in 34, another 22 were adapted for various cultural needs, 20 were torn down, and 21 were left to slowly go to ruin

For most of the world, World War II ended in 1945 or 1946. The soldiers of those countries which prevailed in the conflict returned in triumph, the countries which had been part of the Fascist Axis licked their wounds and turned to the rebuilding of their ravaged economies. Those countries which fell under the influence of the Soviet Union but retained some level of freedom, entered a long period which can only be seen as a remarkable balancing act – trying to bring the Socialist world view together with the desire to survive and to engage in economic activity.

For the occupied Baltic States, however, the war did not end for another 50 years. Franklin Roosevelt and Winston Churchill sold the three countries out to Stalin at a conference in the Crimea, although this, of course, was not proclaimed loudly, and for a long time after the war the Baltic nations continued to hope that the Western democracies would come to their rescue, keeping the Russians from killing, deporting and Russifying local people, destroying local economies and making a mockery out of the process of education. Immediately after the German capitulation, thousands of Latvian, Estonian and Lithuanian men went into the forests, weapons in hand, to continue the war against the occupants in guerilla fashion. These national partisans fought until 1956, and the very last Estonian guerillas left the forests only in 1988. The occupants sent tanks and bombs against the national partisans. 13,000 relatives of men who had gone underground were deported to Siberia. Children were killed, wives were raped. The fight of the national partisans in Latvia was yet another page in the tragic history of the country and its nation. The special services of the United States and Sweden provided moral and material support to some extent. It's hard to say how many partisans there were, but we known that 2,420 fell in the battle against the Bolsheviks. In return, the partisans killed more than 2,000 Communist Party activists, many of whom were Latvians. Russian soldiers and militiamen also lost their lives in the process.

Once the Russians began to arrive in Latvia, they were amazed at what they saw. Russian women who took up residence in the apartments which Latvian refugees had left behind were often seen in the streets and even at the opera clad in nightgowns – garments which they took to be a fine evening wear.

The first to be destroyed fully under Soviet rule was the agricultural industry. Anyone who had salaried help on the farm, who had more than 22 hectares of land, or who had held land during the German occupation – all were dubbed kulaks by the Soviet authorities. Their taxes were increased to ridiculous levels, and those who could not pay were hauled before the courts for tax evasion. Prison and deportation to Siberia were the punishments. In 1946, the first kolhoz, *Nākotne* (Future) was established. The first collective farms, of course, received massive amounts of support for the state so that everyone could see how good life was on the collective farm and how hard it was for people on individual farms.

On March 25, 1949, thousands of farm men, women, senior citizens and children were packed aboard cattle cars and sent East. 12,990 families with 42,133 people ended up in Siberia in these deportations. Soon after the newspaper *Cīņa* reported that "voluntarily and with great joy, farmers have begun the establishment of kolhozes". The choice certainly led to all of this voluntarism – it was either the kolhoz or the Siberian gulag.

The kolhozes did not take off, however, because people turned to drinking, and nobody wanted to undertake any responsibility for collective property. In 1939, when Latvia was still independent, the average yield of grain in Latvia was 20 centners (a centner is a unit of measurement that was used in independent Latvia and in Soviet times; it is equal to 100 kilograms), while in the first year of mass activity by the kolhozes, the figure was 3.5 centners. Cows which yielded up more than 2,000 liters of milk during the period of independence now averaged only 421 liters.

Immediately after the occupation in 1945, the Soviet rulers began to flood Russians and Russified groups from other parts of the Soviet Union into Latvia. Former soldiers were turned into factory workers, and they arrived *en masse* in the 1940s. The bosses were all Russians too, because senior positions in the Soviet Union could be held only by members of the Communist Party, and in Latvia there were only some 4,000 Latvians who were members of the party – most of them Latvians from Russia. Communists who knew nothing at all about agriculture and who did not speak Latvian were chosen to head the collective farms.

Industrial development began in Latvia in the late 1940s, but the aim was not to produce consumer goods. Instead, Latvian companies manufactured heavy machinery, train wagons, turbines and other industrial products. The planned economy was based on a unified system in which one part of a machine was perhaps produced in Ukraine, another in Russia and a third in Georgia – and then they were all sent for assembly in Latvia. Once ready, the machine was sent on to Siberia. If any part of the chain stopped working (as happened in 1989, when the Baltic States withdrew from the Soviet economy), the whole system fell apart.

Stalin died on March 5, 1953, and in the subsequent battle for power in Moscow, Nikita Khruschev arrested and executed Stalin's main henchman, Lavrenti Beria. A period known as Khruschev's thaw began. In February 1956 Khruschev admitted that Stalin's regime had been criminal in its pursuit of terror, declared that Stalin's purges had been a mistake and that the principles of Marxism had been crippled, and allowed many Latvians to return home from Siberia.

There was a corresponding thaw in Latvia between 1956 and 1959, when men like Council of Ministers deputy chairman Eduards Berklavs, Communist Party second secretary Vilis Krumiņš and Economics Institute director head Pauls Dzērve sought to protect the Latvian environment in Latvia, to stop the senseless increase in Latvia's non-Latvian population, and to order the Bolshevik chauvinists who were running the kolhozes and factories of the republic to learn Latvian. Even leading collaborationists such as Communist Party boss Jānis Kalnbērziņš and Council of Ministers chairman Vilis Lācis did not object.

In 1959 Khruschev visited Riga, and opponents of the reforms soon enough turned him against Berklavs and Dzērve. At a Communist Party plenary session in July many Latvians were dubbed "national Communists" and sacked from their positions. Berklavs was deported. Another man who lost his post was the Russian scientist Alexander Nikonov, who was the minister of agriculture in the Lācis-Berklavs government and, after being tarred with the "national Communist" brush, ended up at an agricultural institute in Stavropol. There, he became one of Russia's leading scientists, and eventually his friend Mikhail Gorbachev asked him to become one of the leaders in designing the transformation of the Soviet economy from a planned to a market economy.

In 1959 power in Latvia was taken over by Arvīds Pelše and his trusted colleague Augusts Voss. Both of them were Latvians from Russia. They resisted speaking Latvian and they hated everything that was Latvian. All government offices were ordered to conduct all of their business only in Russian, and not even minimal skills in the Latvian language were demanded of anyone who worked in the system. The traditional Latvian summer solstice festival was banned, and, typically of the Soviet process of overkill, the government ordered a rewriting of cookbooks so that beer and cheese named after the festival (*Jāņi*) could be called something else. That was not enough. The firefly, known as *jāņtārpiņš*, was renamed by zoologists, and the red currant (*jāņoga*) was renamed by agricultural specialists. One of the most popular plays of the Latvian writer Rūdolfs Blaumanis, "Tailor's Days at *Silmači*", was banned, because one of the scenes in the play

National partisans. In the back, from the left – Galvans Antans-Zemitāns, Kārlis Mareckis-Kļaviņš and Jānis Romans-Bitīte. In the front, from the left – Edvards Rižais-Paegle and Jāzeps Ruze-Nātriņš (the second name behind the hyphen in each case was the code name used by the respective guerilla). This photo was taken in 1947

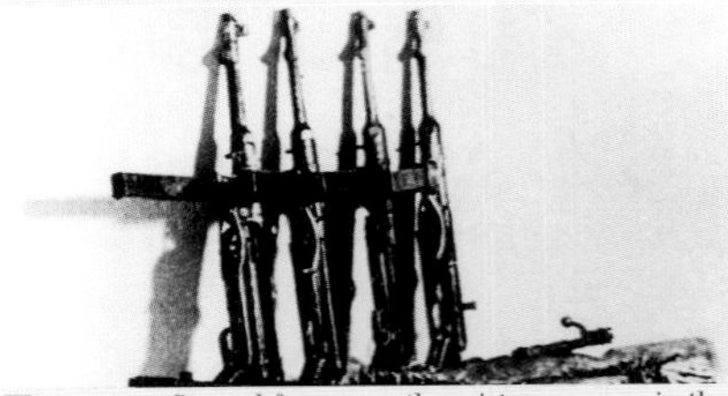
Weapons confiscated from a youth resistance group in the city of *Liepāja*. The weapons were found at the home of a member of the resistance, Žanis Megnis, in the *Dunalka* Parish in 1947

A celebration in commemoration of the Soviet victory in World War II in *Daugavpils*. (Russians typically saw women dancing together at festivities because their men were already drunk.) Children's choirs were usually a part of the ceremony

Elections for the Supreme Soviet of the Latvian SSR, February 27, 1955

Children at the military victory commemoration in *Daugavpils*

Graduation day at the Riga No. 2 High School in 1949

People queuing outside a store in the town of *Saldus* in the 1960s. They were waiting for milk or butter. Similar lines were seen at shops which sold meat or vegetables. If you didn't want to starve, you spent many long hours in those lines

Nikita Khruschev (1894-1971), a senior official of the Soviet state and the Communist Party, in Riga in 1959. As a result of this visit, Eduards Berklavs was sacked from his leadership post in Latvia and Arvīds Pelše was appointed in his place. What followed was Russification and centrally planned planting of corn

The unveiling of a Lenin monument in Riga in honor of the 10th anniversary of the founding of the Soviet Latvian state, 1950

A Soviet military parade at the Lenin monument

People arriving from other parts of the Soviet Union at the Riga train station in 1955 or 1956. Every day hundreds of people arrived in town and went running right off to the local department store, which had much better products than stores in Russia itself. Many people came to like Latvia. Thousands stayed

Military veterans in *Daugavpils*. An unfailing part of Soviet life was a passion for all kinds of honorary titles, medals and military orders

Newspapers published in the Latvian SSR in 1955

features people celebrating the Jāņi festival.

Other decrees issued during this period banned theaters from staging any plays with a sad ending. Indeed, all plays and books had to have happy endings in which workers or revolutionaries won the day. The government ordered that "world literature" be enriched with vivid images of workers. To satisfy these requirements, Latvian authors found themselves rewriting not only their own books, but also those of Latvian writers who were already dead.

In 1961 the CPSU formally declared the goal of Russifying all of the nations in the Soviet Union. Communists in Latvia were astonishingly responsive to this demand. Thousands upon thousands of people from other Soviet republics were flooded into Latvia, most of them going to work at the large Soviet factories that were built in Riga, *Liepāja*, *Daugavpils* and other places. A chemical fiber factory was built in *Valmiera*. *Ogre* got a textiles factory which employed only young women, thus wrecking the demographic balance in that region.

Between the late 1930s and late 1980s, the population of Riga doubled, but only because of the mechanical process of migration. Latvians were a convincing majority in the city in 1939 (70%), and they were a convincing minority in 1989 (just 36%).

All planning took place in Moscow. Khruschev decided that agricultural output could be improved in the Soviet Union if everybody were to grow .. corn. This particular plant fared well in Ukraine and Moldova, but not in Latvia. No matter – field after field of grains and clover were plowed under so that corn could be sown.

A massive process of land reclamation was also launched. Fields with excessive moisture were to be drained, but, as usual, the Soviet government asked not for quality, but for quantity – a certain number of hectares had to be drained, no matter what kind of land it was. Of course, it is sloppy to work in a wet field, so the "draining" was mostly done in bone-dry fields that did not need any draining at all.

Around the same time, the government ordered that old oak trees – the kind which every self-respecting Latvian farm had one of at a corner of the farm – be chopped down. This liquidated a tradition that had been in place for centuries.

Individual farmers in Latvia were allowed to keep 5-6% of the land which they had once owned for personal use as "household plots". Unbelievably enough, these tiny plots of land in 1967 produced 42% of the milk, 44% of the meat, 61% of the potatoes and 65% of the vegetables in Latvia. This makes it quite clear how inefficient the kolhozes were. There were exceptions – Edgars Kauliņš, a Latvian, ran a very successful kolhoz called *Lāčplēsis*, in *Lielvārde*. Kauliņš in the 1940s managed to keep nearly all of his people from being deported, and as a result of this he had honest, hard-working personnel. The kolhoz flourished.

In 1964 Khruschev was deposed, and Leonid Brezhnev came to power in the Soviet Union. One of his aims was to expand a large-scale industrial production. In 1960 the government began to build a hydroelectric station on the *Daugava* River at *Pļaviņas*, and the site was selected partly because the work would submerge under the river's waters one of the most sacred places in traditional Latvian thinking – the cliff known as *Staburags*. The cliff, along with the *Pērse* waterfall and the foundations of the *Aizkraukle* castle ruins, went under.

The power station was built by 4,000 Russian workers who were brought in from other parts of the Soviet Union, and for whom a new town was built outside of *Aizkraukle*. They arrived with their families, and very few departed when the hydroelectric station was done. The village was dubbed *Stučka*, in honor of the leader of the Latvian Communist Party in 1919, Pēteris Stučka.

In 1976 a hydroelectric station was built near Riga, and it flooded a key World War I battleground known as *Nāves sala* (Death island), as well as parts of another island, *Doles sala*. The site of the *Ikšķile* church – the first Christian church in Latvia – was cut off and turned into an island.

The massive increase in Latvia's population led to extensive residential building in the country's cities. Of course, all of the buildings were centrally planned, and they were not known for their architectural design innovations. Also of course, new workers were flooded into Latvia to build these structures. The population increased more quickly than did the number of apartments, however, and very soon a queue for apartments was established which, in revised form, survives to this very day. People in Latvia had to wait for decades to get out of their "communal" apartments, because housing could be obtained quickly only by retired Soviet military officers. Thousands of such men arrived in Latvia with their families.

The communal apartment was one of the more interesting phenomena of Soviet thinking. Large apartments in the center of Riga were divided up, and even if there was just one kitchen and one bathroom in the apartment, between three and eight families were moved in – one for each room.

In the 1970s, the government turned in earnest to eradicating the Latvian way of life. Single-family farms were liquidated. A ban was issued on the renovation of any rural buildings that were not in villages. Owners of single-family farms were told that their homes were in the way of land reclamation or land clearing processes, and countless homes were torn down with bulldozers. Latvians were herded into villages of the kind that were traditional in the tsar's Russia, but never in Latvia. When the Latvian farmer lost his land, he also often forgot how to work.

Two other unfailing hallmarks of the Soviet system were queues for everything and the system of favors that was universally known as a *blat*. In the 1950s people queued for bread and milk. In the 1970s, the Socialist economy provided only one kind of sausage or one kind of cheese at the store – and people stood in long lines for those. Two times a year, after surviving a queue of six hours, you could buy two kilograms of oranges.

If you had a *blat*, though – which meant that you knew someone who could do something for you, such as the director of the store or, holy of holies, the manager of a warehouse – you could get lots of things that were not available to ordinary mortals. There were also special stores for the Communist elite, where even better things could be bought for special prices.

Soviet industries were not known for their care for the environment, and enormous damage was wrought. Unpurified sewage went into rivers, an acidic lake of tar developed in a sandy depression near *Inčukalns*, and a chemicals factory in *Olaine* simply dumped all of its waste in local swamps, leaching all kinds of poisons into the groundwater. Urban air became particularly polluted, because Soviet industry was never required to put any kind of smoke-cleaning equipment in place. Agricultural equipment which was meant for the steppes of Russia and not for the fields of Latvia destroyed the earth. Weeds emerged, and poisons were dumped on them to kill them. DDT was used extensively as a pesticide, but it also killed bees, butterflies, ground-nesting birds and hares. Any objection to this devastation was deemed as nationalism or anti-Socialist agitation.

The true villain in terms of the destruction of Latvia's ecology, however, was the Soviet army, which set up a number of facilities in the republic. *Zvārde*, for example, had the good "fortune" of being the site of a bombing test ground, where 24,500 hectares of land were bombarded with aviation ordnance and rockets every day. The Soviet military had a network of bases all across Latvia. Rockets and airplanes were in place for attacks against Germany and England. Rocket fuel was dumped into rivers and lakes. Special towns were built for military personnel near Riga and *Dobele*, and there were no Latvians at all in these areas. The vast majority of Russian officers did not consider the possibility of leaving Latvia after demobilization for even one minute. They went to work as schoolteachers, political officials and company bosses.

Signs like these were seen all over the Soviet Union. This one, which says "Our work for peace and the flourishing of the fatherland", stood opposite the Latvian Liberty Monument in the 1960s, 1970s and 1980s. On the other side of the *Daugava* River a big sign proclaimed that "The next generation will live in Communism"

A song festival in Riga, 1950

A ceremony at the Latvian Red Riflemen's Museum, with red rifleman Pēteris Griško front and center

A plenary session of the Supreme Council of the Latvian SSR. In the first vote, loud applause greeted the suggestion that seats on the Presidium be reserved for members of the Central Committee of the CPSU, headed by Comrade Leonid Brezhnev, but in truth the seats were taken by local Communist leaders led by Augusts Voss. Nearly all senior politicians were Russian or Russified Latvians from Russia, and the Latvian language was hardly ever heard at the Supreme Council

August Voss (1916-1994), a functionary of the Communist party

A Soviet military parade was held on the embankment area of the *Daugava* River twice a year – on May 9 and on November 7 in Riga

Instructions are given to a militia patrol in 1951. The militia in the Soviet Union was a repressive force which was aimed mostly at defending Communist interests, so inevitably virtually all of the militiamen in Riga were Russians

A Soviet demonstration in *Daugavpils*, which was almost completely Russified during the Soviet occupation. Soviet-era migrants had no traditions, no roots in a native land, no friends, and so they gathered around the Communist Party. Latvia's Russian Communists and their collaborators were often more Communist than the Russian Communists themselves

Communist training began from childhood, but the most important part of the party's work with young people was the Komsomol youth organization. here we see a congress of the Komsomol of the Latvian SSR in Riga, with all of Latvia's big Communist bosses up on the dais

Rural "architecture" – huge apartment buildings that replaced the traditional Latvian single-family farm

Typical features of the Soviet period are huge and dirty farms. Latvia was producing meat for Moscow and Leningrad. The farms were built on the banks of beautiful rivers and all the waste went right there

Traditional livestock feed – grains and clover, as well as hay – was rejected during Soviet times, and new kinds of feed, produced in containers that were fully inappropriate for Latvia's conditions, were developed

Communism means Soviet power plus electricity for the whole country, Lenin said

Soviet soldiers outside the Latvian president's castle. Of course, during Soviet times it was known as the Castle of the Pioneers

Several Soviet military bases were built near *Dobele*, and soldiers from several tank divisions lived there, prepared to attack the West when needed. This is a monument in *Dobele* which, like other Soviet-era monuments was supposed to glorify the Soviet armed forces

During the senseless war in Afghanistan in the late 1970s and the 1980s, several hundred Latvian youths went to their deaths. This is the funeral of a fallen Latvian soldier in *Gulbene*

The Soviet army took over a Medieval castle in *Ventspils*, covering up its failings with quasi-artistic masterpieces like this one

The Soviet naval port in *Liepāja* was home to a series of submarines that were past their usefulness and were left there to rust. Many sank in the harbor

The Soviet military victory over Fascist Germany was glorified ceaselessly in the Soviet Union, and hatred of the Germans was cultivated actively. There had to be a Lenin monument, or at least a memorial to the fallen heroes of the Soviet army, in every city, town and hamlet

Men from Latvia were sent all over the Soviet Union for military service, and the authorities made sure that two Latvians were never put into the same military unit. Larger numbers of Latvians were dispatched only to the wars in Vietnam and Afghanistan, where many lost their lives.

In the economy, instructions about what to produce and how to do it better arrived from Moscow on a very regular basis. Once the Western democracies began to move ahead of the Soviet Union in terms of technological developments, manufacturing output and product quality, the Communist Party began to issue orders in all areas of life. The most peculiar instructions came in the area of science, where the teachings of Lisenko denied the teachings of Mendel. The Soviet Union officially "proved" that you could transform rye into wheat and that the science of cybernetics was all a lie. When the era of computerization began, the Soviet Union was quick to announce that "Soviet computers [are] the largest computers in the world!" The Soviet Union needed to be first or biggest in everything – the first words that children were taught to pronounce in kindergarten were Lenin and Gagarin.

There were some positive aspects to the industrialization of Latvia. Latvian workers maintained their high level of work discipline, and this allowed Latvia to reach much better production indicators than any other place in the USSR. The *RAF* factory produced the Soviet Union's first vans, named *Latvija*, and they were popular throughout Eastern Europe. The VEF company in 1961 began to manufacture the first transistor receivers in the Soviet Union. Little Latvia represented 0.3% of the Soviet Union's population and 1% of its territory, but it produced all of the Soviet Union's electric and diesel trains, 65% of its mopeds, 21% of its radios, and 20% of its trams. Latvia had better per capita agricultural and industrial indicators than any other place in the Soviet Union. The industrial and manufacturing level was higher than in other republics, there was a higher work culture, and workers lived at a higher standard of living. The CPSU may have tried to turn Latvia into a Russian backwater and to drag the standard of living in Latvia down to the Soviet average, but it did not ever manage to do so.

In the 1970s, the Soviet Union entered a serious arms race with the United States, and it began very rapidly to run out of money. Soviet leaders turned their eyes to Siberia, where there were enormous deposits of oil, iron ore, coal and gold. But the problem was – how to get to those riches. The resulting project was typical in its Soviet grandiosity – the Baikal-Amur road,

Gunars Astra (1931-1988) was a tireless campaigner for human rights in the Soviet Union. Tried for anti-Soviet activities, he began his speech of defense with the words, "I believe that this time will disappear like an evil nightmare." Astra spent years in prison and in concentration camps, which destroyed his health. He did not live to see the restoration of Latvia's independence

A Soviet armed personnel carrier near the Lenin monument in Riga in 1988, flying the flag of the Latvian SSR – white and blue sea waves against a red background, with the ever-present hammer and sickle and red star in an upper corner. This kind of activity represented threats by the Russian army against the desire of Latvians to fly their national flag

US President Ronald Reagan and Soviet leader Mikhail Gorbachev meet in Iceland on October 12, 1986. A new era had begun in the world

On February 7, 1987, the general secretary of the Central Committee of the CPSU, Mikhail Gorbachev, visited Riga, where he was greeted with divided emotions – both as a hope for the future and as a representative of the occupation. Unlike other Communist Party leaders, who often came to Latvia to relax, to hunt and to entertain themselves in saunas, Gorbachev came to work. He only visited Latvia once

Mikhail Gorbachev, greeting a veteran Latvian Communist, Ieva Paldiņa, in Riga. She is said to have been one of the organizers of the deportations of the 1940s

The first informal organization in Latvia was the Environmental Protection Club, and its first major event was a demonstration against the building of an underground metro in Riga on April 27, 1988

Former political prisoner Verners Krisons, seen here in the far North of Siberia in October 1990. Not all Latvians returned from deportation during Khruschev's thaw in 1956

Russian tanks in Riga – *Dzirnavu iela* on September 10, 1989

Helsinki 86 leader Juris Ziemelis at a protest demonstration on August 23, 1987

The protest of August 23, 1987. The only ones who were not afraid of Soviet repression at this time were old men who had nothing more to lose. They placed flowers at the Liberty Monument and were then arrested

Some people discarded their Soviet passports as a form of protest

A demonstration at the Liberty Monument devoted to the 48th anniversary of the Molotov-Ribbentrop Pact. Militiamen here are seen beating up and arresting participants. August 23, 1987

On June 14, 1988, Latvians held the first official meeting in memory of the victims of mass deportations that had ever taken place in occupied Latvia

Capt. Pāvils Ceriņš and Lt. Osvalds Ķezberis – Latvian military officers who were forced to become officers in the Soviet military, repressed and deported to Siberia in June 1941 from the train station in *Gulbene*. In the fall of 1998, they were the only two people left from the group which was deported with them, and here they are seen reminiscing at the place from which they were sent East

Voldemārs Sveiferts, a recipient of the *Lāčplēsis* military order of Latvia, placed flowers at the base of the Liberty Monument on June 14, 1989

During a meeting of the Supreme Council of the Latvian SSR in 1988, Latvians expressed their views with this sign: "Down with the occupation!"

aimed at reaching oil and gas deposits in Western Siberia. All of the Soviet republics were ordered to contribute to this effort. Hundreds of young people from Latvia were sent to build roads, railroads, buildings and oil pipelines. Latvians built several towns in Siberia.

The late 1980s brought changes to the map of the world that were just as significant as the changes that occurred in the 1940s, only this time the shift was made with much less in the way of war and victims. The history of the world was influenced by two powerful and wise men who had been chosen for key posts, who hated Communism, and who worked together. They were American President Ronald Reagan and Pope John Paul II, who was previously a Roman Catholic cardinal in Poland and whose family roots can be found in the Latvian region of Latgale. The Soviet Union in the early 1980s faced not only a stagnant economy, but also a frequent replacement in leadership positions. One after another, three secretaries general of the CPSU died – Brezhnev, Yuri Andropov and Konstantin Chernenko. On March 15, 1985, the Central Committee chose as its new general secretary a man called Mikhail Gorbachev. He was a relatively young man, skilled in economic thinking and intelligent. Gorbachev began to introduce reform almost immediately – on May 16 he announced an anti-drinking program. Opponents worked hard to discredit the plans – vineyards in the Caucasus were destroyed, routes for the importation of narcotics were opened. But Gorbachev prevailed. The late 1980s was a period in which there were very few alcohol-related crimes, accidents and suicides in Latvia.

On July 15, 1985, during a Latvian song festival in Riga, the first public expression of free thinking emerged. The poet Imants Ziedonis published an article in the cultural weekly *Literatūra un Māksla* (Literature and Art) in which he decried the fact that the repertoire of the song festival was rife with Russian and Soviet songs. This was the first relatively free press article by a Latvian after 40 years of censorship. Ten days later, on July 25, what was known as the Baltic Peace and Freedom Ship began top sail across the Baltic Sea. An activist called Juris Sinka used a radio link on board the ship to tell Latvians about what was happening in the world, ignoring Russian propaganda in the process.

The Chernobyl nuclear catastrophe took place on April 26, 1986. Contrary to years of Soviet tradition, Gorbachev decided to announce the catastrophe to the Soviet Union and to the world. From that moment forward, the press and the residents of Eastern Europe knew that they could, albeit quietly, albeit incompletely, begin to speak the truth. In Brezhnev's day the nuclear incident would undoubtedly have been claimed as a triumph for Soviet science or as a provocation by evil capitalists. Now, however, the Soviet Union admitted that it was a catastrophe. Many of Latvia's best workers were sent to clean up the mess. There were no safety considerations in place, doctors were put to work digging the earth with shovels, engineers swept up radioactive dust. Many of the "saviors" of Chernobyl died on the spot, others contracted various cancers that killed them later.

On July 10, 1986, three very brave men called Linards Grantiņš, Raimonds Bitenieks and Mārtiņš Bariss established the group *Helsinki 86* in *Liepāja*. On June 14, 1987, they held an open demonstration in commemoration of the thousands of Latvians who had been deported on that date in 1941. On August 23 they protested against the Molotov-Ribbentrop Pact. On November 18 they went to place flowers at the base of the Liberty Monument in Riga in honor of Latvia's independence day. The revolution which convulsed the Soviet Union in the late 1980s was begun by the *Helsinki* group in Latvia.

Of enormous significance in the awakening movement in Latvia was the Environmental Protection Club, led by Arvīds Ulme. It used the principles of non-violent revolution to stop plans to build an underground metro in Riga.

The Soviet Union in 1988 was a place where *glasnost* and *perestroika* – openness and transformation – were in full swing. Among those who became interested in a free economy were the Soviet secret services, which saw economic liberalization as a way to improve the welfare of the KGB and its members. Not really knowing how to move in this direction, the functionaries of the Communist Party and the KGB allowed the people a certain amount of freedom in terms of speech, thought and publication. They obviously could not foresee that even the slightest breath of freedom would break open the gates, that people were yearning for freedom and that they would jettison the "ideals" of Communism without the slightest hesitation.

On March 24, 1988, Latvians held a demonstration at the Cemetery of the Brethren in Riga in commemoration of the deportations of 1949. The Communist Party did not stand in the way of this event, but it did ban people from gathering at the Liberty Monument. The next break in the wall came at the beginning of June, when the Latvian Writers Union met in emergency session to hear historian Mavriks Vulfsons announce publicly that in 1940, Latvia was occupied. Vulfsons is a unique personality in the history of Latvia. He was a Communist youth group activist in 1940 who celebrated the arrival of the Soviet Union. He promoted the Sovietization of Latvia and read lectures about it to students at the Latvian Academy of Art. But then he became a leading defender of Latvia's freedom and independence. It is hard to say in retrospect whether he was linked to the KGB and whether he was perhaps ordered by the powers above to make his pronouncement so as to keep a true Latvian nationalist from doing the same. It is more likely that Vulfsons took advantage of the far-sightedness that he had brought into his old age as a Jew who survived the century. Perhaps he, better than Latvians, felt the way in which the situation was developing, and Mavriks Vulfsons pushed the first stone of the avalanche that followed. Latvia woke up.

The period between 1988 and 1991 was a time in Latvia's history when Latvians felt united, proud and happy. Latvians breathed one breath, they were joined by patriotic songs, and they had one common enemy – the military occupation. The process led to increased fertility and reduced mortality. There were fewer incidences of cancers, ulcers and heart disease. Positive emotions strengthened the immunity of the Latvian nation, and since the days of the Latvian Riflemen there had never been such an uplifting time. The Latvian was proud, creative, strong and collegial. For the first and only time in the history of the Latvian SSR, the Latvians believed in their statesmen and supported them.

On October 8 and 9, 1988, the Latvian Popular

VEF worker Modris Lujāns, carrying a poster denouncing employees of the Communist Party and the KGB on June 14, 1988. He was arrested. Later he turned to politics and was elected to Parliament several times. There, he replaced his working man's sweater with a black suit

Politicians of two generations – at a demonstration on October 6, 1988, in Mežaparks, the last first secretary of the Latvian Communist Party, Jānis Vagris (left) was interviewed by journalist Edvīns Inkens. Inkēns later became a leading supporter of Latvia's membership in the European Union and served as the chairman of Parliament's European Affairs Commission

On March 23, 1988, Latvians walked from the Liberty Monument to the Cemetery of the Brethren to lay down flowers in memory of those who perished due to Communist terrorism

The Russian army in Riga after a massacre of civilians in Tbilisi, Georgia, on April 9, 1989. The protester here is a man called Dambitis, a "professional protester" who once tried to put a crown of thorns on a statue of Communist lead Arvīds Pelše and another time sought to put a coffin at the base of the Lenin monument in Riga. He was often arrested and beaten

The first congress of the Latvian People's Front on October 8, 1988. The congress was opened by actor Ēvalds Valters (1894-1994), who had served as a rifleman in World War I. Valters was a legendary actor who lived to see his 100th birthday and, at the age of 94, was able to stand in front of a crowd, calling people to freedom, to raise the flag of Latvia above the president's castle and, above all, never to lose his style

On October 6, 1988, at a mass demonstration in *Mežaparks*, Ieva Akurātere sang a hymn-like song called "Please, dear God, help the Latvian nation", which raised the emotions and the self-understanding of the Latvian nation to a new height

The Latvian Popular Front was founded on October 8 and 9, 1988. Here we see chairman Dainis Īvāns (far right) after his election

The stars of the most popular television program in the early 1990s on Latvian State Television, *Labvakar* (Good evening) – Ojārs Rubenis, Edvīns Inkēns and Jānis Šipkēvics. They were courageous and professional journalists who led the way at Latvian TV. Behind them in this collage, the dismantling of the Lenin monument on August 21, 1991. Lenin waves good-bye – a sign of the times

The *Baltic Way* on August 23, 1989 – a human chain linking Tallinn with Riga and Vilnius

When it became clear that the Russian military would have to leave Latvia, a period of open theft began. The partly abandoned military bases were soon visited by children and the curious, and soldiers sold off everything that moved, including weapons, in return for "the liquid currency" – vodka

On May 9, 1990, when a relatively free election to the Latvian Supreme Council had taken place and a new Latvian government had been set up, the Soviet military still paraded its strength in the streets of Riga. True, here it looks like they're departing

A symbol of the Russian military in Latvia was the radar detector in *Skrunda*, and as long as it stood, the armed forces were still present in Latvia. Above, Prime Minister Māris Gailis addresses a crowd gathered to watch the detector being blown up, May 4, 1995

Front was founded. The LPF was an organization which put generals next to the rank and file, and it brought the people together in strong unity. The first chairman of the LPF was a 33-year-old journalist, Dainis Īvans. Latvians from the leadership of the Latvian Communist Party, including Anatolijs Gorbunovs, Imants Daudišs and Ivars Ķezbers crossed the lines to join the new group.

One day before the Latvian Popular Front held its first congress, the Soviet organs of power put new people into place. Jānis Vagris became first secretary of the Communist Party, Anatolijs Gorbunovs was made chairman of the Supreme Council, and Vilnis Edvīns Bresis became chairman of the Council of Ministers. All three men proved to be loyal to the Latvian state. The independent Latvian flag was raised in 1988 and remained raised. It is not quite sure who was the very first to raise the red-white-red flag – hundreds of people now claim to have done so. It is a certain fact, however, that the flag rose above the Tower of the Holy Spirit of the Riga Castle on November 11, 1988, and it was raised by actor Evalds Valters (who had been a rifleman in World War I) and author Alberts Bels.

A very interesting episode in the decline of the Soviet Union was the election of a new Soviet Supreme Council on March 26, 1989. Candidates supported by the Latvian Popular Front won 30 seats, and as soon as they got to Moscow they began agitating. Led by Dr. Vilens Tolpežņikovs, they managed to get the Soviet Congress of People's Deputies to declare that the Molotov-Ribbentrop Pact was unlawful, thus in fact admitting that the Baltic States had been occupied.

Events in 1989 and 1990 moved forward with dizzying speed. The Baltic people felt the taste of freedom, they sang their national hymns and they wrote in their native languages. They denied the leading role of the Communist Party, they organized demonstrations and sent petitions to the leaders of the world. On May 31, 1989, the Latvian Popular Front formally announced its support for the political and economic independence of Latvia, and on August 23 of the same year, the people of the Baltic States came together in an unbelievable demonstration of unity, faith and dedication – the "Baltic Way", which was a chain of hand-holding people which stretched, unbroken, from Tallinn to Vilnius.

Elections for the Latvian Supreme Council were held in 1990, and the Latvian Popular Front won a handsome victory. The newly elected Supreme Council met for its first session on May 3, electing Anatolijs Gorbunovs and Dainis Īvans as its chairman and vice chairman. The next day the Supreme Council declared Latvia's independence and appointed Ivars Godmanis as the first postwar prime minister of the Republic of Latvia.

There were two important counterattacks to this revolution. On January 13, 1991, Russian tanks encircled the buildings which housed the Lithuanian Supreme Council and Lithuanian TV. The Lithuanian people had built a human wall around these structures, and 14 people

were killed, while another 110 were injured. The next night, half a million people gathered in Riga to protest the Soviet Union's military attack in Lithuania. Barricades were put up around major public buildings in Latvia. Boris Yeltsin took the side of the Baltic States. He flew to Tallinn, where he met with Anatolijs Gorbunovs and signed an agreement on relations between Latvia and the Russian Federation.

The second counter-revolution took place in the Soviet Union itself on August 19, 1991. On August 21, the Latvian Supreme Council approved a constitutional law on the independence of Latvia. The country's independence was recognized by Russia (which was not yet a sovereign state itself) on August 23, followed by Iceland on August 24. It became the first Western country to recognize Latvia's independence. Latvia owes a great deal of thanks to Boris Yeltsin, a democrat who took a stand with the right of small nations to self-determination. Yeltsin visited Riga, met with parliamentarians in Latvia, and recognized the country's independence.

The United States recognized the restoration of Latvia's independence on September 5, the Soviet Union – on September 6. Over the course of just a few weeks, nearly all of the countries of the world recognized Latvia's independence. The prime ministers of the three Baltic States were received in Washington by President George Bush. The first American ambassador to Latvia was an émigré Latvian called Ints Siliņš – a member of the American diplomatic service. The withdrawal of the Russian armed forces from Latvia began on March 19, 1992, and concluded in 1995. On June 5 and 6, 1993, Latvians elected their independent parliament (the *Saeima*). On July 6 Parliament reinstated Latvia's constitution, and on July 7 a new president – Guntis Ulmanis was elected. The first legitimate Cabinet of Ministers of the post-war Latvian state took office on July 20, headed by prime minister Valdis Birkavs.

Ivars Godmanis and his guards during the period of barricades in Riga

A demonstration organized by the Popular Front on January 13, 1991, gathered more than 500,000 residents of Latvia on the shores of the *Daugava* River

At a meeting of the "International Front" near the Victory Monument commemorating the Soviet victory of World War II. Here we see Communist Party boss Alfreds Rubiks, who ordered the OMON forces into the streets, sending them to take over the Interior Ministry and to shoot up Riga's streets

On January 16, 1991, a driver for the Transportation Ministry, Roberts Mūrnieks, was shot and killed on the *Mangaļi* bridge near Riga. He became the first victim of Latvia's revolution against the soviet occupation

The Riga barricades on *Dome* Square in January 1991. For seven days, all of Riga was on the barricades, protecting the television and radio stations, the telephone central, the government and Parliament. On January 20, the OMON forces of the soviet Union attacked the Latvian Interior Ministry. Militia Lt. Vladimir Gomonovich, inspector Sergei Kononeko, film producer Andris Slapiņš, and schoolboy Edijs Riekstiņš were killed in the battle. Cameraman Gvido Zvaigzne, seriously injured, died a few days later

The funeral of the victims of the Soviet attack on the Interior Ministry, January 25, 1991

Barricades in *Dzirnavu* Street were put up to protect a telephone and communications central from the Soviet Union's special OMON forces

Children and adults
on the barricades

Difficult but successful negotiations between
Latvia and Russia concluded with the full
withdrawal of the Russian military

American Secretary of State James Baker presents
a flag which flew above the embassy of the Latvian
government-in-exile in Washington, D.C.,
to Foreign Minister Janis Jurkans and Supreme
Council chairman Anatolijs Gorbunovs

The Baltic foreign ministers in Reykjavik, after Iceland became
the first country in the world to recognize Baltic independence

Empty shells found around
the Interior Ministry on
January 20, 1991

The place where film producer
Andris Slapiņš died. The
morning of January 21, 1991

Modern history in Latvia has been written only since 1991. The state had to
build itself up from virtually nothing.
Prior to 1991 Latvians did not have
much knowledge about foreign affairs, democracy and
justice in the democratic understanding of the world as
well as about social guarantees, management or marketing. Modern history in Latvia was not a smooth
affair. In a few years, the country cast off the planned
Socialist economy and turned into a growing democracy. Exports which once went only East moved to the
West, and especially to the European Union. Raw materials and energy – cheap in the Soviet Union – became
expensive. Industrial output, which was the basis of the
Soviet Latvian economy, ceased to exist, for the most
part, because markets were lost for the backward technologies, clunky automobiles and seriously out-of-date
electronics that were the Soviet standard of output. The
massive Russian food market disappeared, and agricultural output declined.

These problems, however, were all part of the history of a free country. On the day when the last Latvian ambassador to the United States (which did
not recognize the Soviet occupation of Latvia and
maintained a Latvian legation in Washington for
50 years) arrived in Riga to transfer the authority
of the Latvian government back to a free Latvian
government, the freedom of the small nation was
restored after half a century of its having been lost.
Modern history in Latvia involves a lot of foreign
policy activity – the recognition of Latvia's independence by other countries, the withdrawal of
the Russian military, the dismantling of the Soviet-era radar station at Skrunda. Latvia is returning to Europe in foreign policy terms, in economic terms, in social terms and in geographic terms.
As the 20th century ends, Latvia is also entering
Europe as a candidate member of the European
Union. Of course, modern history in Latvia is
being written with certain errors, but
only the person who never does anything
can say that he never makes mistakes.
Modern Latvian history involves our own
army, our own bureaucracy, our own
journalism, our own parliament, our
own changes in government, our
intrigues and our songs, our politicians
and those who describe this history.

An order (*ukaz*) from Russian President Boris
Yeltsin on the recognition of the independence of
the Republic of Latvia on August 21, 1991

The first Danish diplomat in Riga;
Denmark was the first country to restore
diplomatic relations with Latvia

Anatols Dinsbergs, Latvia's ambassador to the
United States during much of the occupation,
returned to Riga in 1991

Sweden's Justice Minister, émigré Latvian
Laila Freivalde, opened the Swedish
embassy in Riga

Latvian soldiers carry sacks of documents
from KGB headquarters in 1991

An agreement between the
Republic of Latvia and the Russian
Federation on the full withdrawal
of the Russian armed forces from
Latvia, April 30, 1994

The first Russian military unit departs
from Latvia. *Bolderāja*, March 1992

The withdrawal of Russian
military equipment from Latvia

A letter of support from the
British Foreign Secretary,
Douglas Hurd, August 1991

The sister and brother of
Swedish politician Olof
Palme at the *Skangaļi*
baronial estate in Latvia.
Palme's mother was born
on the estate, and he spent
his childhood here

A communique on the restoration of diplomatic relations between Latvia and France
and the exchange of accredited diplomats,
August 30, 1991

Riga, le 30 août 1991

COMMUNIQUE

La République Française et la République de Lettonie ont décidé de
rétablir leurs relations diplomatiques et d'accréditer des Ambassadeurs.
L'ouverture des Ambassades de France à Riga et de Lettonie à Paris
interviendra dès que les modalités pratiques d'installation seront réglées.

Un programme bilatéral sera mis en oeuvre afin de développer
rapidement entre les deux pays des liens de coopération dans les domaines
économique, culturel, scientifique et administratif.

La France, en liaison avec ses partenaires de la Communauté européenne,
favorisera l'entrée rapide la République de Lettonie dans les différentes
instances internationales, notamment dans l'Organisation des Nations Unies,
et l'établissement de relations étroites entre la Lettonie et la Communauté.

M. Janis Jurkans   M. Roland Dumas

Ministre des Affaires   Ministre d'Etat,
Etrangères de la   Ministre des Affaires
République de Lettonie   Etrangères de la
                                Republique Francaise

courage and determination. It is now time to economy will not be we can.

My dear

I am delighted that at
states at last have regained their independence. It
gives me particular pleasure that Douglas Hogg is
visiting Latvia so soon after our recognition of your
independent statehood to start discussions about the
re-establishment of diplomatic relations. I am sure that
relations between our two countries will flourish as they
did in the past.

with best wi

sincere

I also look forward to welcoming you soon as a
colleague in international bodies in which the Baltic
states may now take their rightful place. As you know,
membership of the United Nations is agreed by the General
Assembly on the recommendation of the UN Security
Council. Roland Dumas and I have agreed, as the two
Pers
hel
p.

Douglas H

THE WHITE HOUSE
WASHINGTON

August 31, 1991

n people, please accept
ou and all the Latvian
erved freedom and

Sincerely,

[signature] G Bush

c of Latvia

Dear Mr. President:

I am delighted to announce that the United
States is prepared to resume diplomatic ties
with your government.

As you know, American recognition of the
Republic of Latvia has continued without
interruption since 1922. The United States
never recognized the forcible incorporation of
Latvia into the Soviet Union, and we are proud
that we stood with the Latvian people during the
many difficult times of the last fifty-one
years. I am thus especially pleased that recent
developments have made it possible for you to
resume your status as an independent state and
for us to exchange diplomats. The United States
looks forward to the development of warm and
mutually beneficial relations between our two
nations.

Over the past year, the courage and
determination of the Latvian people have been an
example and inspiration to all of us who love
freedom. The world will not forget your own
courageous and disciplined leadership during the
dark days of January and during the recent
attempted coup. I look forward to meeting you
in the future and to regular and fruitful
contacts between our two governments in the
months and years ahead.

A letter from American President
George Bush to Latvian leader Anatolijs
Gorbunovs, reemphasizing the American government's refusal to recognize
the violent incorporation of Latvia into
the USSR, August 31, 1991

On December 13, 1995, the man who
was minister of security during the "Year
of Terror" in 1940 and 1941, Alfons
Noviks, was sentenced to life in prison

The grave of Andris Slapiņš (1944-
1991) in the Forest Cemetery in Riga

The grave of film producer Juris
Podnieks (1950-1992) at the Forest
Cemetery. Podnieks filmed Soviet
soldiers shooting peaceful demonstrators
in Tbilisi and the violence of the Soviet
army in Vilnius and Riga

Zigfrīds Anna Meierovics (1887-1925), the first foreign minister of the Republic of Latvia

Latvian Foreign Minister Vilhelms Munters (1898-1967) and Ambassador Kārlis Zariņš (1879-1963) at the Latvian embassy in London, 1937

The Latvian embassy in London for many years was the only legitimate bearer of the authority of the Latvian state in the free world. Here we see advisor Voldemārs Punga, secretary Jānis Kalniņš, Ambassador Kārlis Zariņš, agricultural attaché E. Zelmenis and consul J. Biriņš

American Professor George Kennan was the last pre-war American ambassador to Latvia. An outstanding authority on diplomatic matters, he is seen here with Soviet Foreign Ministry official Nikolajs Neilands (right) in Riga in 1987

The first German ambassador to post-war Latvia was Count Haagen von Lambsdorff, whose ancestors were Baltic Germans

Latvian Foreign Minister Jānis Jurkāns and former American President Ronald Reagan in 1991

Jānis Jurkāns and German Foreign Minister Hans Dietrich Genscher at a press conference in Riga

The deputy secretary general of the Council of Europe, Dr. Hans-Christian Krieger, Latvian Foreign Minister Valdis Birkavs, and Latvia's ambassador to the Council of Europe, Georgs Andrejevs, at the ratification ceremony for the European Human Rights Convention, which prohibits the use of the death penalty during peacetime, in Budapest on May 7, 19993

The flags of Latvia (seventh from the left) and other countries above the headquarters of the Council of Europe

Latvian Finance Minister Elmars Siliņš and President George and Mrs. Barbara Bush at the White House

President Guntis Ulmanis addresses a session of the European Parliament

Latvian Prime Minister Andris Šķēle and Foreign Minister Indulis Bērziņš at an EU summit meeting in December 1999, where Latvia was invited to begin membership negotiations with the EU

The general secretary of the Council of Europe, Daniel Tarshis, and Latvian Foreign Minister Valdis Birkavs at the signing of the Council of Europe Agreement

Delegates from the three Baltic States at the White House in the United States, September 17, 1991

President Bill Clinton and Latvian Prime Minister Valdis Birkavs. Behind them are American Secretary of State Warren Christopher (behind Clinton) and Latvian Economics Minister Ojārs Kehris, 1994

US President Bill Clinton addresses the residents of Latvia in Riga. Behind him are Estonian President Lennart Meri, Latvian President Guntis Ulmanis and Lithuanian President Algirdas Brazauskas, 1994

Latvia's foreign policy has always been based on the community of the Baltic States, on closeness with the Nordic Countries, on close cooperation with all of the democracies of Europe, on good and friendly neighbouring relations with Russia and Belarus, on active work in international organizations such as the UN, the OSCE, the Council of Europe, the Council of Baltic Sea States, etc. Latvia has always sought to become a fully vested part of democratic Europe. This mission was begun by the Latvian Foreign Ministry in 1918, when the Latvian state was founded. The first foreign policy victory was a letter from Lord Balfour to Latvian Foreign Minister Zigfrīds Meierovics on October 23, 1918, in which Great Britain's recognition of the Latvian National Council as the legitimate government of Latvia was expressed. Diplomacy and foreign policy also played an important role in winning recognition of the independent Latvian state in Europe in 1919 and 1920, which concluded with the recognition of Latvia's independence *de iure* on January 26, 1921.

From the very beginning of the existence of the Latvian state, despite severe financial difficulties that existed at the start, the government devoted a great deal of attention to foreign policy, opening a series of embassies in Western Europe, Russia and (later) the United States. Latvia was particularly active as a member of the League of Nations, to which it was admitted on September 15, 1921. Latvia faced a very complicated foreign policy situation in the late 1930s, when two totalitarian dictatorships – the Soviet Union and Germany – divided up the world. In a secret protocol attached to the infamous Molotov-Ribbentrop Pact of August 23, 1939, Latvia was turned over to the Soviet Union's "sphere of interests".. The foreign service in Latvia at that time was run by a complicated person called Vilhelms Munters. On October 5, 1939, Munters was summoned to Moscow,

where the Russians insisted that he sign a mutual aid agreement. Under the auspices of the treaty, Soviet military bases were established in *Piltene, Edole, Kuldīga, Cīrava, Durbe, Grobiņa, Liepāja, Paplaka, Priekule* and *Vaiņode*. Latvia, Estonia and Lithuania became *de facto* protectorates of Moscow. When news of the death sentence which the agreement between Hitler and Stalin represented for the three Baltic States was already circulating in Europe, President Kārlis Ulmanis and Vilhelms Munters felt that they had to keep up a show of optimism. People were not told of the threats which existed against the state and its residents. Nothing was done to ensure the legal continuity of the state, or to set up a government in exile. Foreign passports were confiscated, and only very wealthy and well connected people could hang on to the documents which in many cases saved their lives.

On May 18, 1940, the Latvian government granted emergency authority to its ambassadors abroad, saying that if the government were to become unable to carry out its duties, then the Latvian ambassador to London, Kārlis Zariņš, and the Latvian ambassador to Washington, Alfrēds Bilmanis, would have to take over the defense of Latvia's interests in the free world.

After the Soviet Union invaded Latvia, Ambassador Zariņš, on July 23, submitted a note of protest to the Foreign Ministry in London, arguing that the activities of the puppet government which the Soviets installed in Latvia were illegal, given that the Constitution of Latvia specified that sovereign power in Latvia belonged to the nation of Latvia. That, said the ambassador, could be changed only through a national referendum. A few days after the occupation, the collaborationist government of Augusts Kirhenšteins closed down all foreign embassies and companies in Latvia, and ejected foreign correspondents and other foreigners.

A meeting of the Baltic Council in *Jūrmala*, Latvia, June 6, 1990

The Baltic Assembly, meeting in Tallinn, Estonia, in November 1998

A meeting of the three Baltic presidents and the president of Poland, June 28, 1999

President Ulmanis at the United Nations headquarters in Geneva, April 1996. Here he is seen with the director general of the European headquarters, Vladimir Petrovski

President Ulmanis and the royal couple of Sweden during a state visit to Stockholm in October 1995

President Ulmanis and the future prime minister of Great Britain, Tony Blair, November 1996

The president of the European Commission, Romano Prodi, and the commissioner on the enlargement of the European Union, Günther Verheugen, with Latvian Foreign Minister Indulis Berziņš in Riga in 2000.

President Ulmanis and Israeli Prime Minister Binyamin Netanyahu during Ulmanis' state visit to Israel, February 1999

Latvia's ambassador to the Holy See, Aija Odiņa, at her accreditation ceremony with Pope John Paul II

Latvian Foreign Minister Indulis Berziņš greets Polish Foreign Minister Bronislaw Geremek at the Riga airport, October 27, 1999

Foreign Minster Berziņš (right) with the Dutch minister for European Affairs, Dik Benshop, 1999. The UN's permanent representative to Latvia, Jan Sorensen, is in the middle

President Ulmanis and Prince Charles of Great Britain in Latvia, November 17, 1995

President Ulmanis on a state visit to India in October, 1997. Here he is seen at a greeting ceremony

President Ulmanis in Samarkand, Uzbekistan, in May 1996

Latvia's new president, Vaira Viķe-Freiberga, paid a state visit to Finland and is seen here with President Marti Ahtisaari

Between 1940 and 1990, the interests of the independent Latvian state were represented abroad by Ambassadors Zariņš and Bilmanis and, after their deaths, by heads of the respective diplomatic legations – Teodors Ozoliņš, Pauls Reinhards and Anna Marija Zariņa in the UK and Julijs Feldmanis, Arnolds Speke and Anatols Dinbergs in the United States. Neither America nor Britain, nor Germany, ever recognized the Soviet occupation of Latvia.

Latvia's diplomats managed to maintain the diplomatic interest of the world until the restoration of the independence of the three Baltic countries in 1991. On the eve of the collapse of the Soviet Union, a man who was loyal to the idea of Latvia's freedom, Vilnis Edvīns Bresis, became chairman of the Council of Ministers of the Latvian SSR, and he appointed Eižens Počs as head of the local branch of the Soviet Foreign Ministry. After the relatively democratic Supreme Council elections of 1990, which were won by the Latvian Popular Front, Ivars Godmanis took over as head of government, and Jānis Jurkāns was appointed the country's first foreign minister. The first country to recognize the restoration of the independence of Latvia, Lithuania and Estonia in 1991 was Iceland. The first foreign head of state to visit Latvia, also in 1991, was French President François Mitterand.

The restoration of independence required that the consequences of the Soviet Union be eliminated. This could be done after Boris Yeltsin took power in Moscow after the 1991 coup. He recognized Latvia's independence, visited Latvia's Parliament, and rested in the resort town of *Jūrmala*. In April 1994 Latvian President Guntis Ulmanis and Prime Minister Valdis Birkavs paid a state visit to Moscow, where they signed an agreement on the withdrawal of the Russian armed forces from Latvia. On May 4, 1995, the last remaining Russian military facility in Latvia – the *Skrunda*

radar detector – was blown up.

When Latvia's independence was restored, Latvia's politicians, not least those who led its foreign ministry, had a lot to learn. Immediately after the recognition of Latvia's independence in 1991, the chairman of Parliament, Anatolijs Gorbunovs spoke at a meeting of the General Assembly of the United Nations in New York. In 1993, President Ulmanis participated in a meeting of the heads of state of the countries of the OSCE. Since 1993, meetings of the Baltic Assembly have been held regularly. In 1994 Riga was visited by Pope John Paul II and American President Bill Clinton.

Before World War II, Riga was visited by a former American president, Herbert Hoover, as well as a future president – John F. Kennedy. Richard Nixon visited Latvia in 1993. Since 1991 Latvia has opened embassies in many of the world's countries – Russia, the United States, Germany, England, France, the Netherlands, Sweden, Denmark, Belgium, etc.

At this time Latvia is recognized throughout the world, and all over the globe it has partners in politics, trade and economics. President Ulmanis went on state visits to many different countries in Europe and North America, as well as to China in 1994, Ukraine in 1995, Uzbekistan in 1996, Turkey in 1997, Israel in 1998 and Japan in 1999. In 1996 Guntis Ulmanis received an award of recognition for the Institute of East-West Studies from American Secretary of State Madeleine Albright. In 1997 Latvia was one of the initiators of a conference on good neighbourly relationships among countries that was held in Vilnius. In January 1998, Latvia, Lithuania and Estonia signed a Partnership Charter with the United States. In February 1999 Latvia became the first of the Baltic States to join the WTO.

Latvia links its future to the European Union and participation in Transatlantic security structures. The European Commission recognized Latvia's

independence on August 27, 1991. Latvia was admitted to the Council of Europe in 1995; in the same year it also became an associated member of the European Union. A Commission on European Affairs was set up in Parliament in Latvia, and on October 17, Latvia submitted its official application for membership to the government of Spain, which was presiding at that time. Since 1996, a delegation of the European Commission has been at work in Riga. Also in 1996, the Cabinet of Ministers approved Latvia's first program for integration with the EU.

In 1998 there was a summit meeting of the Council of Baltic Sea States in Riga, which was attended by Russian Prime Minister Viktor Chernomyrdin, German Chancellor Helmut Kohl and other senior leaders. Also in 1998, the first official meeting of the Association Council of Latvia and the EU was held in Brussels. In December 1999 the EU officially invited Latvia to begin membership negotiations.

The Latvian Foreign Ministry has, since the restoration of Latvia's independence, been headed by four ministers – Janis Jurkans until 1992, Georgs Andrejevs from 1992 to 1994, Valdis Birkavs from 1994 to 1999, and Indulis Berziņš since 1999. The state secretary of the Ministry since 1993 has been Maris Riekstiņš. Latvia has embassies and diplomatic missions in 41 countries.

THE LATVIAN FOREIGN POLICY INSTITUTE

The Latvian Foreign Policy institute is a private non-profit organization which researches the security of the Baltic States. The institute was established in 1992 with the financial support of the Swedish government. Since then, 30 major publications have been issued in English and Latvian, and 20 international conferences have been organized. In this photo, the director and founder of the institute, Atis Lejiņš (right), is seen with American political scientist Zbigniew Brzezinski at a conference on the Baltic States on the road to the European Union.

The conference "The Baltic States on Their Way to the European Union", organized by the Latvian Foreign Policy Institute on December 3, 1994. The meeting was chaired by Swedish Prime Minister Karl Bildt

THE POLITICAL SYSTEM AND THE CONSTITUTION

THE POLITICAL SYSTEM

The Latvia's Way party has been represented in the *Saeima* longer and more extensively than any other. The party's economic policies are liberal. Seen here is party member Ivars Godmanis, who was Prime Minister from 1990 until 1993 – a period when the country underwent its most significant period of reform toward a market economy

Latvia's Way has consistently supported Latvian membership in the EU.
The chairperson of the *Saeima*'s European Affairs Committee, Edvīns Inkēns, and the chairperson of the party, Andrejs Panteļejevs, are seen in this photograph

Latvia's Way stands for a socially responsible market economy. Here we see the chairperson of the *Saeima*'s Economics Commission, Kārlis Leiškalns, and the chairperson of the parliamentary faction, Kristiāna Lībane

The Fatherland and Freedom/LNNK party is a nationalist party, which defends the primacy of the Latvian language, a strict and unyielding citizenship law and an unchangeable constitution. The deputy chairperson of the *Saeima* in its last session, Aigars Jirgens, party chairperson Māris Grinblats and the current chairperson of the *Saeima*, Jānis Straume, are seen here

Fatherland and Freedom/LNNK is a conservative party, which stands for a balanced budget and has a strict position on various social issues. Roberts Zīle (left) has been Minister for Finance and Minister for Special Assignments – for co-operation with international financial institutions in several governments. Here he is seen with the chairperson of the parliamentary faction, Andrejs Požarnovs, party chairperson Māris Grinblats, and Minister for Welfare Roberts Jurdžs

The first Article of the Latvian Constitution declares that Latvia is an independent, democratic republic. A country, which is a democratic republic, is one in which power belongs to the people, and power is expressed either directly or through elected representatives. The Latvian Constitution provides for both possibilities, and there are two sources of legislation – the *Saeima* and the people.

The Constitution allows the body of citizens in Latvia to propose draft legislation in the *Saeima* or to adopt laws through national referendums. This means that the people have the right to express their will on various issues. The mechanism, which the Constitution sets out for this procedure, however, is not simple, and in practice, this means that the people take advantage of this power only in very important cases.

The authority, which the Constitution gives to the *Saeima*, the Cabinet and the President, is structured appropriately for a parliamentary republic. The Cabinet remains in office as long as the *Saeima* maintains confidence in it. The government is to a certain extent independent from the *Saeima* in its work, but if the balance of power in the *Saeima* shifts, the same usually happens in the Cabinet, as well.

The *Saeima* also elects the President of Latvia. The Presidency in Latvia is largely a representative office, but the President has the right to summon extraordinary sittings of the *Saeima*, to summon and chair extraordinary meetings of the Cabinet, and to proclaim war. This means that the influence which the President has on important decisions in the State depends more on the President's force of personality than it does on any constitutionally mandated powers.

The first publication of the constitution of the Republic of Latvia in 1922

The authority of the Constitution was specified in temporary regulations concerning the system of government of the Republic of Latvia which were published on 1 June 1920, and by the Standing Orders of the Constitutional Assembly, which were accepted on 12 October 1920

THE CONSTITUTION

The first elected legislative body in Latvia – the Constitutional Assembly, which was elected in April 1920, adopted Latvia's Constitution, known as the *Satversme*. The main duty of the Assembly was to prepare and then to accept Latvia's basic law. The Constitution was adopted on 15 February 1922, and it came into force on 7 November of the same year. Latvia's *Satversme* is one of the oldest and shortest constitutions in Europe.

In the 1990s, the Constitution was reinstated in phases. The declaration regarding the renewal of the independence of Latvia on 4 May 1990 by the Supreme Council, reinstated only those articles which set out the constitutional and legal basis of the State (Articles 1, 2, 3 and 6). The full Constitution was reinstated when the first freely elected post-Soviet 5th *Saeima* took office, on 6 July 1993.

Initially the Latvian Constitution had seven chapters, regulating the country's political system, the institution of the Presidency, and the main operational principles of the legislative, executive and judicial branches of the State. A second part On the Rights and Obligations of Citizens was drafted in 1922, but it was not adopted. This situation was rectified on 15 October 1998, when the *Saeima* adopted a new chapter to the Constitution, "Fundamental Human Rights".

The People's Party (*Tautas partija*) is associated with considered economic policies and an understanding of cultural issues. Here we see the chairperson of the parliamentary faction, Gundars Bērziņš, and the deputy chairperson of the *Saeima*, Rihards Pīks

The World Federation of Free Latvians is represented in the People's Party by Vaira Paegle, who is a former chairperson of the organisation, and the former Mayor of Valmiera, Kārlis Greiškalns

Jānis Lagzdiņš and Dzintars Ābiķis worked together in the Latvian People's Front and then in the Latvia's Way (*Latvijas ceļš*) political party, but today they are both members of the People's Party

The For Human Rights in a United Latvia (*Par cilvēktiesībām vienotā Latvijā*) association represents five political parties which focus on the interests of Latvia's minorities and have left orientation in economic policy. In the photo we see the chairperson of the association, former Foreign Minister Jānis Jurkāns, and Jakovs Pliners

The leader of the New Party (*Jaunā partija*) is the famous composer and public figure Raimonds Pauls. The party boasts a number of economists, among whom are two former economics Ministers, Ainārs Šlesers and Ingrīda Ūdre (above)

The Latvian Social Democratic Workers Party (*Latvijas sociāldemokrātiskā strādnieku partija*) is Latvia's oldest. The party was founded in 1904, and early congresses were attended by the leader of the Russian Bolshevik revolution, Vladimir Lenin.
The newspaper *Cīņa* was the oldest social democratic newspaper in the world

Chairperson of the parliamentary faction, Egīls Baldzēns (right) and former Minister for Agriculture, Pēteris Salkazanovs

The *Saeima*'s most important function is to adopt laws. Draft laws (Bills) may be submitted by the President, the Cabinet, committees of the *Saeima*, groups of no fewer than five members of the *Saeima*, and groups of no less than one-tenth of the nation's voters. Most draft laws (approximately two-thirds) are submitted by the Cabinet.

Before a draft law is considered by a full sitting of the *Saeima*, it is submitted to the relevant committees. The *Saeima* itself decides which committees are to review each draft proposal, as well as which committees is to take the main responsibility for each proposal.

The *Saeima* examines draft proposals in three readings. In the first reading, one of the members of the responsible committee provides a report on the draft, and debates are held on the general principles in the proposal. If conceptual agreement is given at the first reading, the *Saeima* sets a deadline for the submission of proposals concerning the document. On second reading, the responsible committee provides its conclusions about the proposals that have been submitted, and the draft is considered article by article. After the second reading, too, a deadline is set for the submission of proposals. Only those articles with respect to which proposals have been made are considered on third reading. The *Saeima* can declare a draft law to be urgent, in which case it is heard only on two readings. The State budget and international treaties are approved on two readings, for instance.

The Constitution may be amended only if at least two-thirds of the members of the *Saeima* are present at the relevant meeting of the *Saeima*. Amendments are heard on three readings and each must be approved by a two-thirds majority. Articles 1, 2, 3, 4, 6 and 77 of the Constitution may be amended only after a national referendum, because these are the articles, which are concerned with Latvia's status as a nation and the main principles for electing the *Saeima*.

After the *Saeima* adopts a law, the President of Latvia must proclaim it not sooner than seven days and not later than 21 days after the vote in the *Saeima*. Urgent laws must be proclaimed no later than on the third day after the law was adopted. Laws take effect 14 days after their proclamation, unless the specific law provides otherwise. In some cases, the President can postpone the proclamation of the law so that the matter of organising a referendum can be considered.

The Green Party (*Zaļā partija*) was formed on the basis of Latvia's Environmental Protection Club, and today it battles actively for a proper environment and against projects which have not been considered from an ecological viewpoint. Members of the Green Party have protested the building of the Būtinge oil terminal near the Latvian border in Lithuania, and their tactics have included chaining themselves to a pump that the terminal uses out in the sea. The Green Party has also protested against environmental pollution. The party is headed by long-time environmental protection Minister Indulis Emsis and publisher Askolds Kļaviņš

The work of Latvian *Saeima* is supported by the Chancellery. Director Māris Steins (middle) and his deputies Guntis Beņķis and Valdis Ziemelis

Legislation is the basic responsibility of *Saeima*. Outstanding lawyers provide their consultations. Here: head of the Legal Bureau Gunārs Kusiņš and the Parliamentarian Kārlis Leiškalns

Latvian *Saeima* has established groups for collaboration with Parliaments of other countries. Here: Andrejs Panteļējevs meeting Vice-minister of Foreign Affairs Sieou-Je-Hoang and external trade manager K.H. Wu from Taiwan

The Latvian Farmers Union (*Latvijas Zemnieku savienība*) was founded in 1917 as a party to defend the interests of farmers. During the first period of Latvian independence, it was one of the country's largest political parties. The honorary chairperson of the party is former President Guntis Ulmanis, while the current chairperson is Rīga City Council deputy Maija Rubīna

Saeima delegation in the White House. From left: Edvīns Kide, Filips Strogonovs , Aida Predele, Aleksandrs Kiršteins, US Vice-preSident Al Gore, Aivars Kreituss, US Ambassador in Latvia Ints Siliņš, US president Bill Clinton, State Secretary of the Ministry of Foreign Affairs Māris Riekstiņš, the Minister of Foreign Affairs Georgs Andrejevs, Andrejs Panteļējevs, Vice-minister of Foreign Affairs Mārtiņš Virsis, Latvian Ambassador in US Ojārs Kalniņš, Latvian diplomate Maira Mora, Māris Grīnblats, Councillor to the Latvian Embassy in US Ints Upmacis, Andris Rozentāls

CHAIRPERSONS OF THE SAEIMA

Jānis Čakste (1859–1927),
president of the Constitutional
Assembly

Fridrihs Veismanis (1875–1942),
chairperson of the 1st *Saeima*

Pauls Kalniņš (1872–1945),
chairperson of the 2nd, 3rd
and 4th *Saeima*

In Latvia, the nation vests its sovereign authority in 100 elected members of the *Saeima*. The Latvian *Saeima*, or parliament, is elected once every four years by general, equal, direct, secret and proportional elections. Elections are held while the previous session of the *Saeima* is still in office, which means that the institution functions on an ongoing basis. Elections are held on the first Saturday of October.

Suffrage in Latvia is extended to citizens who are 18 years old or older on the day of the election. Members of the *Saeima* must also be citizens, and they must be at least 21 years old.

The *Saeima* has a number of functions, including the legislative function, the function of adopting the national budget, and the function of appointing or dismissing the President, the Prime Minister, the Auditor-General, members of the judiciary, etc. The basic rules, which govern the work of the *Saeima*, are set out in the Constitution, but the *Saeima* also has its own Standing Orders. These address the status of deputies, the procedure for reviewing draft laws and other proposals, as well as other issues.

The *Saeima* works in sessions – three each year. Sittings of *Saeima* have a quorum if at least one-half of the Members of the *Saeima* are present. Plenary sittings are usually held once a week, on Thursdays.

THE SAEIMA AND POLITICAL PARTIES

At the request of the President of Latvia, the Prime Minister or at least one-third of the members of the *Saeima*, the Presidium of the *Saeima* must convene an extraordinary sitting of the *Saeima*.

Decisions by the *Saeima* (except in a few instances that are provided for in the Constitution) are taken by a majority vote among those members of the *Saeima* who are present. Sittings of the *Saeima* are open, although a sitting can be declared closed if two-thirds of the members of the *Saeima* agree. The work of the *Saeima* is conducted by a Presidium, members of which are elected by the *Saeima* at the start of every new term. The Presidium works even when the *Saeima* is not in session. Its members are the chairperson of the *Saeima*, two deputy chairpersons, the secretary and the deputy secretary. The Presidium determines matters of internal order in the *Saeima*, compiles the agenda and performs other organisational functions.

There are 16 permanent committees in the *Saeima*, and the *Saeima* determines their duties. Committee memberships are composed immediately after the *Saeima* meets for the first session of each new term. Members of the *Saeima* may be members of no more than two permanent committees at the same time. Committees review all matters that are to go before the *Saeima*, and they also review various proposals submitted by members of the *Saeima* and members of the Cabinet. Committees have the right to submit draft laws and other proposals to the full sitting of the *Saeima*. Committee meetings are open, but they may be closed by virtue of a decision by the relevant committee or by the *Saeima* as a whole. Special committees can be set up for specific functions if one-third of the members of the *Saeima* so request. In specific cases, the *Saeima* must set up investigative committees.

Anatolijs Gorbunovs (b. 1942),
chairperson of the Supreme Council
of the Republic of Latvia and the
5th *Saeima*

Ilga Kreituse (b. 1952),
chairperson of the 6th *Saeima*

Alfrēds Čepānis (b. 1943),
chairperson of the 6th *Saeima*

Jānis Straume (b. 1962),
chairperson of the 7th *Saeima*

SECRETARIES OF THE SAEIMA

Roberts Ivanovs (1883–1934),
secretary of the Constitutional
Assembly

Jānis Veismanis (1878–1942),
secretary of the 1st *Saeima*

Pēteris Juraševskis (1872–1945),
secretary of the 2nd *Saeima*

Jānis Breikšs (1887–1965),
secretary of the 2nd
and 3rd *Saeima*

Jānis Kauliņš (1889–1941),
secretary of the 4th *Saeima*

Adolfs Bļodnieks (1889–1962),
secretary of the 4th *Saeima*

Imants Daudišs (b. 1945),
secretary of the Supreme Council
of the Republic of Latvia and the
5th and 6th *Saeima*

Indulis Bērziņš (b. 1957),
secretary of the 6th *Saeima*

Silvija Dreimane (b. 1962),
secretary of the 7th *Saeima*

The official visit of a delegation of the Kuwait National Assembly to Latvia 26-28 September, 1995

The official visit of the Speaker of the Israeli *Knesset* (Parliament) Dan Tichon to Latvia, 11-13 January, 1999

During the official visit of the President of the Norwegian *Storting* (Parliament) Kirsti Kolli Grendal (left) to the *Saeima*, she met with the President of Latvia, Guntis Ulmanis. Centre – the official interpreter Eva Eihmane

The 9th Session of the Baltic Assembly in Riga, 5-6 October 1996

The official visit of the Speaker of the Swedish *Riksdag* (Parliament) Birgitta Dahl and a Swedish parliamentary delegation 14-16 February, 1995

The speaker of Israelian Parliament *Knesset* prof. Schewah Weiss speaking to Anatolijs Gorbunovs during an official working visit in Riga in August 30 - 31, 1994

The official visit of the Speaker of the Finnish *Eduskunta* (Parliament) Riita Uosukainen 20-21 February, 1995

The visit of the Vice-chairman of the National People's Congress of the People's Republic of China Wan Hang Bin to Latvia, 6 June 1995

The visit of the Speaker of the House of Representatives of the Commonwealth of Australia Steven Martin and an Australian parliamentary delegation to the *Saeima*, 4-7 September 1994

The official visit of the speaker of the Danish *Folketing* Dr. Erling Olsen and the presidium of the *Folketing* to the Republic of Latvia, 12-13 February, 1996

President of the Parliamentary Assembly of the Council of Europe Mr. Miguel Anjel Martinez talking to the member of *Saeima* Mr. Andrejs Panteļējevs 17 November, 1995

Jānis Čakste (1859-1927) was the first President of Latvia, serving from 1922 to 1927. He was born near *Jelgava* and later graduated from the Faculty of Law of Moscow University in Russia. Returning to Latvia after graduation, Čakste became actively involved in the region's political life, organising and leading a number of public organisations. In 1917, he was appointed Governor of Kurzeme. As a member of the People's Council, he organised the defence of Latvia's independence in international forums, including the Paris peace conference. After 1919, he was the chairperson of the People's Council. In 1920, Čakste was elected chairperson of the Assembly, and in 1922, he was elected as the country's first President. Čakste treated everyone objectively and fairly, establishing the authority of the Presidency and its traditions. Čakste proclaimed 402 laws while in office. Among the most important were the law on military service, the various laws on annual budgets, a law on associations, unions and political organisations, etc. The rapid development, which Latvia underwent in the 1920s, could not be imagined without the achievements of this distinguished public figure.

Gustavs Zemgals (1871-1939) was the second President, serving in office from 1927 to 1930. He was also born in the *Jelgava* region and, like Čakste, graduated from the Faculty of Law of Moscow University in Russia. Once back in Latvia, he became active in political life, gaining prominence as a liberal and democratic promoter of Latvian interests and as a publicist. Zemgals was one of the initiators and founders of the independent Republic of Latvia in 1918. He was among the leaders of the People's Council, a member of the Assembly and a Minister, serving in Parliament from the Democratic Centre Party. He was elected to the Presidency in 1927. Zemgals was a convinced democrat and rejected political extremism in any form. Following the example set by his predecessor, he represented the Latvian nation with honour.

Alberts Kviesis (1881-1944) was Latvia's third president, serving from 1930 until 1936. Also born in the *Jelgava* region he was a graduate of the Faculty of Law of Tartu University in Estonia, later becoming actively involved in Latvian political life and chairing a number of public organisations. After 1917, he became the deputy chairperson of the Tartu Division of the All-Russian Union of Cities. Later he served as the head of the Legal and Organisational Division of the Kurzeme Temporary Land Council's executive committee. In 1918, he became a member of the People's Council. Other posts which he held was the chair of the Latvian Courts chambers, member of the first three *Saeimas*, deputy Speaker of the *Saeima* and Minister for the Interior. Kviesis was a delegate in Latvia's peace delegation in 1920, when diplomatic relations between Latvia and Germany were restored at a meeting in Berlin. He was elected to the Presidency in 1930 and 1933. Kviesis continued the best traditions of his predecessors, but his status in the Presidency changed radically following the coup d'etat by Kārlis Ulmanis on 15 May 1934. Kviesis formally remained in office until 1936, but he was forced to become a mask and a cover for the new regime.

Kārlis Ulmanis (1877-1942), the fourth President of Latvia, was also born in the *Jelgava* region. He studied agriculture in Switzerland, Germany and the United States. Until 1913, he pursued various business interests in Latvia, but gradually he became more and more active in Latvia's political life, establishing Latvia's largest political party – the Farmers' Union – in 1917 and becoming its leader. After 1918, he was one of the most influential politicians in Latvia. He was the first Prime Minister of Latvia and later held a variety of Ministerial portfolios. He was a member of the Assembly and of all four *Saeimas*. In 1934, as Prime Minister he staged a coup d'etat and, while retaining the office of Prime Minister, became the sole ruler of the country, dismissing the *Saeima* and banning all political parties including his own. In 1936, he appointed himself to the Presidency of the country. During what has come to be known as the Ulmanis era, the country's economy was strengthened considerably, the welfare of the people increased, and the self-confidence of the Latvian nation was given a considerable boost. The ability of the Latvian state to represent itself in the increasingly complex international situation, however, deteriorated. Ulmanis' period of office ended when Latvia's independence was lost. In 1940, he was forced to turn over power to a Prime Minister appointed by the occupying Soviet forces, and in 1941, he was deported to Siberia. Ulmanis died in 1942, in a prison hospital in Turkmenistan, in the Soviet Union.

Guntis Ulmanis (b. 1939), the fifth President of Latvia, served in office from 1992 until 1999. Guntis Ulmanis is a nephew of the pre-war President Kārlis Ulmanis. He was born in Riga and studied in the Economics faculty of the University of Latvia. Ulmanis is an economist by profession. After the restoration of Latvia's independence, he served on the Council of the Bank of Latvia. In the first post-war *Saeima* elections, in 1993, he was elected to the *Saeima* as a member from the Latvian Farmers' Union. Shortly thereafter, he was elected to the Presidency. In 1996, the *Saeima* re-elected Ulmanis as the President of Latvia. During his two terms, Ulmanis devoted considerable attention to foreign policy – Latvia's integration into international organisations, facilitation of co-operation with European and other countries, etc. An important achievement during his Presidency was the conclusion of an agreement with the Russian Federation on the withdrawal of the Russian Army from Latvia. Ulmanis was an active supporter of cultural, artistic and athletic events.

Vaira Viķe-Freiberga (b. 1937), the sixth President of Latvia, was elected in 1999. Born in Riga, Viķe-Freiberga spent most her life abroad. She earned a Bachelor's degree in English in 1958, a Master's degree in psychology in 1960, and a Doctorate in experimental psychology in 1965. Viķe-Freiberga speaks Latvian, French, English, German and Spanish. From 1965 until 1998, she was a professor of psychology at the University of Montreal in Canada. She is the author of 7 books, 160 articles, 250 speeches and papers, and of a major database of Latvian folk songs, which are known as *Dainas*. She has chaired the French section of the Canadian Academy of Sciences and has represented Canada at a NATO forum on human factors in Brussels. As a representative of Canada, she provided consultations to a commission that reformed Brazil's parliamentary constitution in 1989. Vaira Viķe-Freiberga is an Officer of the Latvian Order of Three Stars at the fourth degree. Upon her elevation to the Presidency, she was automatically awarded the Order of Three stars at the first degree with chain.

President Alberts Kviesis and Prime Minister
Karlis Ulmanis at a harvest festival in 1933

Three Presidents of the Baltic States: (from left)
Lennart Meri (Estonia), Guntis Ulmanis (Latvia) and
Algirdas Brazauskas (Lithuania)

Latvian president Vaira Viķe Freiberga and Lithuanian
president Valdis Adamkus are opening the exhibition
"Latvia Between Two World Wars"

Accreditation of the Malaysian ambassador
Dato' Syeed Sultan bin Seni Pakir on
16 November 1999

Opening of the final choir concert of the Latvian Song Festival on 5 June 1998

Meeting of the Presidents of the Baltic States, Poland and
the Ukraine in Tallinn, Estonia on 26-27 May 1997

Guntis Ulmanis reaches agreement with the
President of the Russian Federation, Boris
Yeltsin, on 30 April 1994 in Moscow, regarding
the evacuation of the Russian Army from Latvia

Accreditation of the Nuncio from the Holy See

Vaira Viķe-Freiberga together with the *Bashkir
(Russian Federation)* Latvian folklore ensemble
during the Latvian Song Festival in 1998

The laying of the foundation stone for the *Islice* SOS
Children's Village in July 1996

Traditional basketball match contest for
the President's Cup in *Valmiera* in July 1998

The Constitution of Latvia determines the role and responsibilities of the President in conformity with the principles of a parliamentary democracy. The President is not politically responsible for his or her actions.

In order to become a candidate for the Presidency, a person must be a Latvian citizen enjoying full rights, and to have reached the age of forty years. Persons who are Latvian citizens and also the citizens of another state may not be candidates for the Presidency. Following election, the President may not also have other offices or positions. If the person who is elected President is also a member of the *Saeima*, he or she must give up his or her parliamentary mandate. The President is elected by the *Saeima* for a four-year term, if by secret ballot he or she receives at least 51 votes. The President may be re-elected for a second term.

The term of a President ends in the following circumstances: if the term for which he or she were elected ends; if he or she voluntarily resigns from the Presidency before his or her term has ended; if he or she dies in office; if he or she has recommended the dismissal of the *Saeima*, but the ensuing referendum results are against this action; if he or she have been relieved of his or her duties by the *Saeima*.

The President takes part in the formation of State legislation. He or she has the right to initiate legislation. The President may not necessarily present his or her legislative initiatives in the form of a Bill, but may informally suggest an idea to the *Saeima*, the realisation of which the *Saeima* may give to the relevant Standing Committee of the *Saeima*. Similarly, the President may give to the *Saeima* a Bill, which has been submitted by at least 1/10th of the electors. The President may express his or her opinion regarding legislation that the *Saeima* has adopted, and with a substantiated argument request that

the law be re-examined a second time. However, if the *Saeima* does not take notice of the objections of the President and adopts the law unchanged a second time, the President may not object again.

The President proclaims laws adopted by the *Saeima* or at referenda. Nevertheless, the President may suspend the publication of a law himself or herself or, if requested to do so by 1/3rd of the members of the *Saeima*. In this case, a referendum in respect of the particular law must be organised, if, after the suspension of the publication of the law, at least 1/10th of the electors have expressed their wish for a referendum on the law.

If the President is not satisfied with the work of the *Saeima*, he or she cannot dismiss the legislators himself or herself, but can only recommend that the people make a decision about this at a referendum.

One of the important Presidential functions in respect of domestic politics, is the invitation to a person to form the Cabinet.

The President has a somewhat wider role in the field of defence and military administration. He or she is the Commander-in-Chief of the national armed forces and appoints a Supreme Commander in time of war. On the basis of a decision of the *Saeima*, the President may declare war.

In terms of international relations, the President has representative functions.

The President has a right to pardon sentenced persons, as well as several regulative functions, for example, if necessary, to summon a session of the *Saeima*, or the right to convene and chair an emergency meeting of the Cabinet.

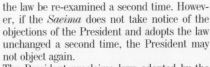

Guntis Ulmanis at the ceramics workshop of
Peteris Ušpelis in Latgale in the summer of 1995

During a State visit to Iceland
(19-21 May 1999), President
Guntis Ulmanis visited a fish
processing plant. On the right,
the President of Iceland Olafur
Ragnar Grimson

Opening of rural sports games
in *Valmiera* in July 1998

Official visit to Germany 11-15 December
1995. Guntis Ulmanis with the Burgomaster
of Frankfurt Mrs. Petra Rota. Signing in the
city's Gold Book

In the room where the Latvian Cabinet meets, there is an engraved sign on the wall: "One Justice for All". The Prime Minister, the President of Latvia and the director of the State Chancellery sit at one end of the table in the room. The places of Ministers is determined by their age and experience, more experienced Ministers sit closer to the Prime Minister.

In the photo: At the head of the table – Prime Minister Andris Šķele, President Vaira Vīķe-Freiberga and the director of the Chancellery, Alvis Vītols, with the 1999 Cabinet (from the left) – Minister for Agriculture Aigars Kalvītis, Minister for Welfare Roberts Jurdžs, Minister for Special Assignments for Co-operation with International Financial Institutions Roberts Zīle, Foreign Minister Indulis Bērziņš, Minister for Education and Science Silva Golde, Minister for Special Assignments for Local Government Reform Jānis Bunkšs, Minister for Transport Anatolijs Gorbunovs, Minister for Justice Valdis Birkavs, Minister for Culture Karina Pētersone, Minister for Economics Vladimirs Makarovs, Minister for Finance Edmunds Krastiņš, Minister for Defence Ģirts Kristovskis, Minister for Environmental Protection and Regional Development Vents Balodis and Minister for the Interior Mareks Segliņš.

Kārlis Ulmanis (1877-1942), Prime Minister 1918-1921, 1925-1926, 1931, and 1934-1940

Zigfrīds Anna Meierovics (1887-1925), Prime Minister 1921-1923 and 1923-1924

Jānis Pauļuks (1865-1937), Prime Minister 1923

Voldemārs Zāmuels (1872-1948), Prime Minister 1924

Hugo Celmiņš (1877-1941), Prime Minister 1924-1925 and 1928-1931

Artūrs Alberings (1876-1934), Prime Minister 1926

Marģers Skujenieks (1886-1941), Prime Minister 1926-1928 and 1931-1933

Pēteris Juraševskis (1872-1945), Prime Minister 1928

Adolfs Bļodnieks (1889-1962), Prime Minister 1933-1934

Ivars Godmanis, Prime Minister 1990-1993

Valdis Birkavs, Prime Minister 1993-1994

Māris Gailis, Prime Minister 1994-1995

Andris Šķele, Prime Minister 1995-1997, 1999

Guntars Krasts, Prime Minister 1997-1998

Vilis Krištopans, Prime Minister 1998-1999

The Prime Ministers of Latvia have their own banner – a special Prime Ministerial flag. With every change of government, the former Prime Minister attaches a silver nail to flag staff. In the photo: the former Prime Minister Māris Gailis after attaching a silver nail, and Valdis Birkavs and Pēteris Bankovskis

The Latvian Prime Minister, a member of the national conservative party *Tēvzemei un brīvībai (Fatherland and Freedom)*, and the Russian Prime Minister Viktor Chernomyrdin meet at the CBSS summit, January 1998 in Riga

The Cabinet of Ministers in *Brīvības bulvāris* 36, built as the Palace of Justice in 1938 by the design of architect Frīdrihs Skujiņš

Latvian Prime Minister Vilis Krištopans meets the Foreign Investors' Council (FICIL), 1999

Prime Minister Guntars Krasts and NATO Secretary General Javier Solana in Riga, 18 June 1998

Prime Minister Andris Šķēle and the Prime Minister of Sweden Göran Persson in Riga, 3 June 1996

The Prime Minister Māris Gailis, Foreign Minister Valdis Birkavs, Council of Europe General Secretary Daniel Tarschys, and the President of the Council of Europe Parliamentary Assembly Miguel Martinez at the ceremony marking the admission of Latvia to the Council of Europe in Strasbourg, 10 February 1995

Prime Minister Vilis Krištopans and the Vice-Premier of the Peoples Republic of China, Wu Ji in Riga, 1999

The Prime Minister meets once a week with the President for a working breakfast. In the photo: the President, Vaira Vīķe-Freiberga and the Prime Minister, Andris Šķēle, 1999

Deputy Prime Minister (later Prime Minister) Māris Gailis, the US President Bill Clinton, and US Ambassador to Latvia Ints Siliņš at a press conference in Riga, 7 July 1994

Prime Minister Andris Šķēle with the President of Estonia Lennart Meri in Riga, 23 October 1996

Prime Minister Guntars Krasts with the Italian Prime Minister Romano Prodi (final 1999 – the President of the European Commission) placing flowers at the Latvian Liberty Monument in Riga, 2 February 1998

Any Ministry has its political employees and its permanent employees. Political employees are assistants and advisors who handle specific tasks and whose authority is set by the relevant Minister. Among them is the press secretary, who is responsible for relations with the media, as well as a Parliamentary Secretary, who is responsible for relationships with the *Saeima*. Other Ministry employees are civil servants – specialists in their field. The highest-ranking civil servant in any Ministry is the State secretary.

Departments and divisions handle work in Ministries. Several divisions make up a department, and the departments, when taken together, form the ministry. If there are many departments, the State secretary has the right to choose a deputy to manage the various departments. Ministries are responsible for government poli-

cy in their sectors. Often Ministries have to implement programs or take specific steps, and that is why most Ministries have structures that are outside of the Ministry but co-operate with it. Such institutions are more or less dependent on the relevant Ministry. A Ministry may impact on the work of such structures in a very direct way – appointing its director, telling it what to do, and taking decisions on what should be done in any specific situation.

Institutions that are under the supervision of Ministries operate in the relevant sphere of interests, but they have a certain amount of independence in their work. The work of such institutions is specified by law, and the Ministry can recommend candidates for leadership positions (decisions are taken by the *Saeima* or the Cabinet). A Ministry can influence the work of such

an institution only by proposing that the director be replaced or by influencing the amount of money that the institution receives.

Co-operation institutions, which are set up by the government and public or private organisations or structures, are even more independent. This is a new type of structure in public administration, and so far it had been used seldom. The State participates in the work of a co-operation institution by designating its representatives to the council of the institution and by subsidising its work. There are decision-making rights for the representatives of the relevant public or private organisations, too. Financial sources for these institutions can be highly varied. The government can influence the work of these co-operation organisations through its representatives on the council.

Dāvids Rudzītis (1881-1939) was director of the Latvian State Chancellery from 1918 to 1938

Senior officials at the State Chancellery on 22 October 1999. From the right: Alvis Vītols, director; Agnese Kveska, director of the Legal Department; Edvīns Andersons, director of the Department for Co-operation Projects; Sarma Krīvena, director of the Personnel Division; Daina Vaivare, director of the Documents Preparation Department; Aivis Freidenfelds, director of the Press Department; Andris Saranovičs, director of the Operational Division; Anita Sinta, director of the Registration Department; Sarmīte Mazura, director of the Correspondence Department; Tālivaldis Zamozdiks, deputy director for economic affairs; Līga Peiberga, director of the Documents Provision Department; and Aija Pūpola, director of the Finance Department

THE NATIONAL ADMINISTRATION SCHOOL

The director of the National Administration School, Gunta Veismane

Training at the National Administration School

Examinations at the National Administration School

The National Administration School (*Valsts administrācijas skola – VAS*) was founded on 7 December 1993, and its goal is to ensure that people who work in the State public administration are honest and effective service providers for Latvia's society. The school provides training for candidate members of the civil service. It develops training programs, leads and co-ordinates the training process throughout the country, tests candidate civil servants on their qualifications, and develops a strategy for training which aims to improve the knowledge and professional skills of State administrative personnel, to train civil servants who are appropriate for government work in line with EU requirements, and to develop people who are capable of participating successfully in the process of European integration.

Among the topics which are covered at the school are management, psychology, ethics, various legal aspects, computers, languages, finances, basic knowledge about the EU, etc. – more than 80 subjects in all.

THE STATE CHANCELLERY

After the independence of Latvia was proclaimed on November 18, 1918, it was decided that the country's highest institution of public administration would be the temporary government. The institution that underpinned its work – the temporary government chancellery – was formed by December 2. The first director of the chancellery was Dāvids Rudzītis. The first official Cabinet meeting, the minutes for which were taken by the director, took place on November 26, and it is on that date that the founding of the chancellery is now commemorated.

Today there is a State Chancellery, which is attached to the Cabinet and which is directed by a person recommended by the Prime Minister and approved by the Cabinet. The chancellery has two main missions – to handle the correspondence and other work of the Cabinet and the Prime Minister, as well as to supervise the acceptance and publication of laws, the publication of the official newspaper, as well as the work of the relevant printing facilities, library and archive.

The Cabinet adopted its rules of procedure on August 8, 1919, and in 25 brief paragraphs it set out the procedure for Cabinet meetings and the taking of minutes at those meetings.

Meetings are summoned by the State Chancellery on orders from the Prime Minister, and each Minister has the right to vote at those meetings. Deputy Ministers and experts can attend meetings with advisory rights. The meetings are chaired by the Prime Minister, who specifies the order for and duration of debate. Participants must be told of the agenda for a Cabinet meeting at least six hours in advance. There is a quorum if more than one half of the members of the Cabinet are present. When there are opposing views on a matter that is before the Cabinet, an open vote is taken. Proposals or objections must be announced immediately after a vote, and they must be submitted in writing to the State Chancellery within two days after the respective meeting. The minutes of each meeting are taken by the director of the chancellery. The minutes must be in their final version within two days' time, and they are signed by the chairperson of the session and by the person who took the minutes. Objections to the content of the minutes must be submitted within three days after receipt of the minutes.

The chancellery also supervises the paperwork of the Cabinet and the Prime Minister. The director of the chancellery also handles credits for the Cabinet and the chancellery.

The work of the State Chancellery is regulated by its by-law, which was approved by the Cabinet.

THE STATE CIVIL SERVICE BOARD

The State Civil Service Board is responsible for overseeing civil service policies in Latvia. The Board provides consultations and oversees all processes that have to do with the implementation of the Law on the State Civil Service and with the work of the civil service.

The long-term goal for Latvia's civil service is to ensure that relevant law is implemented properly and that it becomes an effective part of the State's system of administration. A second goal is to establish a professional, politically neutral and loyal civil service to provide stable, efficient, open and transparent administration of the State in a way, which conforms to the public interest.

The main strategic goals of the board include analysing the work of the civil service and developing prognoses concerning its development, preparing draft laws and other regulatory enactments in accordance with the Law on the State Civil Service, developing a unified registration system for State administrative institutions and personnel, developing and implementing a personnel management system, engaging in informational and educational activities, and participating in other projects aimed at developing the system of public administration. The Board co-operates with other institutions and co-ordinates relevant work.

The development of the civil service involves the need to achieve greater effectiveness and operational results, consistently delegating authority to institutions and officials and specifying authorisations in job descriptions and relevant regulatory documents.

The staff of the State Civil Service Board (director Armands Kalniņš is at far left)

ELECTIONS AND NATIONAL REFERENDUM

The Republic of Latvia as an independent State has, from its foundation, always had a voting system based upon proportional representation for elections. When Latvia regained her independence after the Soviet occupation, the system was again incorporated into the Election Law. The system applies to both parliamentary and local government elections. Voters have a

right to make internal changes in candidate lists. The Law also provides an opportunity for Latvian citizens who live abroad to participate in elections. All citizens of Latvia who are 18 years of age or older may participate in elections, while candidates for Parliament must be at least 21 years old. *Saeima* (the Parliament) and local government elections are held once every four years. To gain seats in the *Saeima*, a list must receive at least 5% of the total vote. An important form of democracy is the national referendum. Since the restoration of Latvia's independence, there has been one referendum. On 3 October 1998, citizens were asked to vote on Amendments to the Latvian Citizenship Law, which had been approved by the *Saeima*, but suspended by the President of Latvia. Voters particularly focused on a provision in the amendments, which provided an opportunity for children born in Latvia after 21 August 1991, to non-citizen parents, to receive automatic citizenship. In other words, the Latvian State had decided to grant citizenship to all children born in Latvia. A majority of voters did not support repeal of the amendments, and the modern citizenship norm was left in place. Internationally, the results of the referendum in Latvia were welcomed, stressing that this represented another step toward the European Union.

CENTRAL ELECTORAL COMMISSION

Elections in Latvia are organised by the Central Electoral Commission, an independent State authority comprised of nine members. Eight of the members are appointed by the Latvian Parliament and one is appointed by the Supreme Court of the Republic of Latvia. The chairman, deputy chairman and secretary of the Commission may not work in other employment or hold any other elected or appointed office. The duties of the Commission include the management of funds granted by the State, the issuance of instructions, the review of complaints and work in the field of public information and public relations. The work of the Latvian Central Electoral Commission in providing information to voters has been praised both inside Latvia and abroad. The Chairperson of the Commission has, on several occasions, addressed international conferences of the organisers of elections, and in May 1999, the Chairperson was one of five lecturers who participated in a program of information exchange in Bosnia-Herzegovina. Since 1994, the Commission has been a member of the Central and Eastern European Association of Professional Organisers of Elections.

EU observers consider the Latvian electoral system to be one of the most fair and safe in Europe. The Director of Saieima Chancellery Maris Steins transfers the electoral-bulletins to the Chairman of Central Electoral Commission Arnis Cimdars

THE STATE CONTROL

The State Control is the supreme constitutional control institution. The Auditor-Generale and the Council of the State Control are elected by the Parliament. The Latvian State Control has a collaboration with all supreme auditing institutions of Europe.
Right: Raits Černajs, the Auditor-Generale (middle), signing an agreement of collaboration with Lithuanian and Estonian Auditors - Generale.

THE CONSTITUTIONAL COURT

The Constitutional Court is an independent national body apart from the general system of juridical system. It is authorised to judge about the conformity of laws and legal acts with the Constitution. It operates according to Article 85 of the Constitution. The seven judges are elected by the *Saeima* with 51 vote at minimum for a period of ten years. The President, a group of 20 or more Parliamentarians, the Cabinet of Ministers, the Plenary of the Supreme Court, the Prosecutor - Generale, the Council of State Control, the Bureau of Human Rights, a municipal council and a minister authorised by the government can submit a case to the Constitutional Court.
The Constitutional Court: Ilze Skultane, Ilma Čepāne, Romans Apsitis, Aivars Endziņš, on duty of the Chairman of the Constitutional Court, Anita Ušacka, Andrejs Lepse

Since May 1999 the Latvian Constitutional Court is an associated member of the Conference of European Constitutional Courts. Here in the Vilnius session A. Endziņš together with the Chairman of Poland's Constitutional Tribunal Marek Safjan, judges of the Lithuanian Constitutional Court Vladas Pavilonis and Juozas Žilis, the Lithuanian Primeminister Algirdas Vagnoris, the President of the Austrian Constitutional Court Ludwig Adamovich and the Estonian Judge of the European Court of Human Rights Rait Maruste

Aivars Endziņš has assisted in the elaboration of basic legal acts for the constitutional courts of Armenia and Georgia. Here together with Gaguik Haritunyan, the Chairman of Armenian Constitutional Court, Avtanandil Denetrashvily, the Chairman of Georgian Constitutional Court and the Vice-Secretary-Generale of EC Commission *Democracy through Law* Christos Giakoumopolus

The first Prosecutors-General of post-occupation Estonia, Latvia and Lithuania: Indrek Melak (Estonia), Janis Skrastiņš (Latvia) and Arturas Paulauskas (Lithuania)

The oath of a Latvian prosecutor: "In undertaking the obligations of a prosecutor, I am cognisant of the responsibility that has been entrusted to me, and I swear that I will be honest and just, faithful to the Republic of Latvia, always in search of the truth, never betraying the truth, and fulfiling my prosecutorial obligations strictly in accordance with the Constitution and the law."

The Estonian and Latvian Prosecutors-General, Indrek Melak and Janis Skrastiņš, play chess at Estonia's Sangaste Castle

Prosecutors Juris Pēda and Jānis Vilders are prosecuting a case against former officials of the failed *Banka Baltija* bank

The Chief prosecutors of the Office of the Prosecutor-General: Rudite Aboliņa, Marite Kučinska, Biruta Ulpe, Janis Vilders and Jazeps Ancans (front row, from the left); Janis Osis, Gunars Bundzis, Eriks Zvejnieks, Oļģerts Šabanskis and Edvins Ziediņš (second row)

The Justice sculpture – a beautiful girl bearing a sword and a legal code. Sculptor Karlis Zemdega (1894-1963) said that his design was inspired by the ancient Latvian deity *Laima*, who, in Latvian folklore, determined people's fates, administered justice and divided things up fairly

THE OFFICE OF THE PROSECUTOR OF THE REPUBLIC OF LATVIA

The Office of the Prosecutor of the Republic of Latvia was established on 26 September 1990. Prosecutor-General Janis Skrastiņš held that office from the beginning of that period until early 2000. The Law On the Office of the Prosecutor sets out its structure, status and authority. In Latvia, the Office of the Prosecutor is part of the judicial branch, and it ensures that laws are observed.

The Office supervises the work of inquiry institutions and the investigative field-work of other institutions; it organises, manages and conducts pre-trial investigations; it engages in criminal prosecution and sustains charges filed by the State; it supervises the way in which punishments are carried out; and, when the law so provides, it protects the rights and lawful interests of individuals and the State.

The Office of the Prosecutor is a unified, centralised and hierarchically constructed three-level system of institutions that is headed by a Prosecutor-General or, in his or her absence, one of the departmental chief prosecutors. The Prosecutor-General leads and supervises the work of all of the institutions of the Office of the Prosecutor, determining their structure and staff. The Prosecutor-General is also the direct manager of the Office of the Prosecutor-General. The various departments of the Office supervise work in all of the related institutions, while regional Offices of the Prosecutor monitor the work, which is done by district Office of the Prosecutor.

Norms have been elaborated in the Law On the Office of the Prosecutor, which guarantee the independence of the Office of the Prosecutor when investigating matters. The prosecutor is independent of influence from State institutions and officials and follows only the law. A prosecutor has the right to accept any case for further consideration, but no institution has the right to order a prosecutor to do anything that runs contrary to his or her convictions. In a multi-party society, membership in a political party may create the impression of political bias or at least doubts about objectivity, so the law in Latvia prohibits prosecutors from being members of political parties or being active therein. The Law On the Office of the Prosecutor also includes various guarantees that reduce the Prosecutor-General's dependency on political shifts. The law says that the Prosecutor-General must be a person who has had at least five years of experience in an Office of the Prosecutor. The nomination is made by the Chief Justice of the Supreme Court and is approved by the *Saeima*

for a five-year term. The Prosecutor-General appoints all other prosecutors after qualification exams, apprenticeships and an opinion from a special attestation commission. Chief prosecutors are appointed for five-year terms, while other prosecutors are appointed for unlimited terms. The Council of the Prosecutor-General is an advisory institution, which reviews various matters concerning the organisation and work of the Office of the Prosecutor. It also establishes attestation and qualification commissions and approves the by-laws of these commissions. The attestation and qualifications commissions administer candidacy examinations for prosecutorial candidates, adjudge the appropriateness of individuals for specific jobs in the system, specifies the duration of apprenticeship, and reviews major violations of discipline. The appointment of a chief prosecutor by the Prosecutor-General is possible only with the consent of the attestation commission.

The Chief Justice of the Supreme Court of the Republic of Latvia, Andris Guļans

THE SUPREME COURT

The highest-standing judicial body in Latvia is the Senate of the Supreme Court, and it was established on 19 December 1918. The first senators were Karlis Ozoliņš, Voldemars Zamuels, Kristaps Valters, Miķelis Gobiņš, Augusts Lebers and Janis Graudiņš. The work of courts in the early days of the Latvian state was hindered by the absence of a national system of rights, as well as a lack of trained judges. Between 1918 and 1940, however, the Senate gained acceptance as the highest-standing judicial institution in the country.

After the Soviet occupation, when Latvia was incorporated into the Soviet Union, a judicial system, which corresponded to the laws of the occupants, was imposed on Latvia. Only three of Latvia's 23 Supreme Court senators died in Latvia. Seven died while in deportation in the Soviet Union, while another 13 were forced to flee to the West.

When Latvia renewed its independence after 50 years of occupation and it became possible to reinstate the structure of the State that was set out in the 1922 Constitution of Latvia, judicial reform was immediately begun. The goal was to create an independent court system, to reinstate appeals and cassation procedures, and to engage in other reforms in accordance with the requirements of the European Union. The Law On Judicial Power was adopted on 15 December 1992. The Supreme Court has two separate divisions – the court that hears final appeals in cases, and the Senate, which is the absolute forum of last resort.

The first level of the Supreme Court's appellate system is also divided into two divisions – the Civil Matters Court and the Criminal Matters Court. The Senate of the Supreme Court has analogous departments.

The Supreme Court also has a Plenary and Judicial Practice Division, which analyses and researches judicial practice and drafts rulings for the plenary session. There is also a Rehabilitation Division which, in accordance with the law *On the Rehabilitation of Unlawfully Repressed Persons*, researches and prepares opinions about the criminal cases that were filed against people during the

Judges of the Supreme Court: First row: Zigmants Gencs, Ruta Zaķe, Martiņš Dudelis, Pāvels Gruziņš, Andris Guļans, Gunars Aigars, Gunars Bičkovičs, Zaiga Raupa, Astrida Kazarova un Leontine Pluksna, Second row: Eduards Pupovs, Voldemārs Čiževskis, Aiva Zariņa, Ausma Kalvane, Skaidrite Lodziņa, Georgijs Kuzņecovs, Imants Fridrihsons, Rita Saulite, Ludmila Poļakova, Aija Branta, Marija Goldšmite, Anita Nusberga, Arturs Freibergs un Raimonds Gravelsiņš, Third row: Ausma Keiša, Māra Katlapa, Marite Zaģere, Vilnis Vietnieks, Valdis Salmiņš, Ojars Druks-Jaunzemis, Ilgvars Zigfrids Šepteris, Rolands Krauze, Fricis Jaunbelzējs, Irēna Vinkšno, Ramona Nadežda Jansone, Vanda Cirule and Valda Eilande

Soviet occupation by military tribunals and courts. More than 25,000 unlawfully repressed persons have been rehabilitated through this process so far.

The Supreme Court of the Republic of Latvia provides for the strengthening of a democratic society, human rights and the principles of a law-based state. Since the renewal of Latvia's independence and the adoption of the Law On Judicial Power, five regional courts have been renewed as the first level of the appellate process.

THE RĪGA REGIONAL COURT

The Riga Regional Court returned to its historical building at *Brīvības bulvāris* 34 in Riga after the Soviet occupation ended. The building, constructed by the Latvian architect Janis Fridrihs Baumanis (1834-1891) in a Renaissance style with Baroque facades, was built for a regional court of the Russian Empire between 1887 and 1889. The architect won high praise for his ability to place the building successfully into its surrounding environment

Janis Fridrihs Baumanis designed the building for the Riga Regional Court at *Brīvības bulvāris* 34. From above, it looks like the crown of the Russian tsar

and to provide not only for a highly respectable exterior, but also for a very comfortable interior. Regional courts were set up in Imperial Russia in the late 1880s, when radical reforms were instituted in the Baltic provinces of the Empire, and a completely new system of courts was being put in place. When viewed from above, the building of the Riga Regional Court does look a bit like the tsar's crown.

The Riga Regional Court of the Republic of Latvia was founded on 5 December 1918. Fricis Gailitis was appointed Chief judge of the court, while Ernests Grinbergs was named Chief prosecutor of the court. On 30 March 1994 – nearly half a century later – the Riga Regional Court was renewed, and Parliament appointed Janis Muižnieks as the first Chief judge of the renewed court. The court began full operations on 31 March 1995, with 11 judges. Today the Criminal Matters Department and Civil Matters Department of the Riga Regional Court employs 30 judges and 74 other court employees. The work of the Riga Regional Court covers a territory which contains approximately one-half of the country's population – the city of Riga and its six districts, the city of *Jurmala*, and Riga District and *Ogre* District.

THE LATVIAN BAR ASSOCIATION

The Latvian Bar Association (*Latvijas Juristu biedrība*) was founded on 17 December 1988, as a non-governmental professional organisation. Its initial aim was to promote the restoration of Latvia's independence through various legal mechanisms and instruments. Members of the organisation helped to develop legal and judicial arguments, which enabled the occurrence of one of the phenomena of modern history – the renewal of Latvia's national independence in 1991 through non-violent means.

The goals of the association have remained unchanged. A law-based state and society must be established. The principle of the distribution of power must be observed. The legal profession must be responsible before society, and it must enjoy prestige in society. A full-fledged and hierarchical system of laws and norms must be established in Latvia. Human rights must be observed, public life and private life must be seen as distinctly separate fields, the market economy must be developed, and correct and lawful regulations must be put in place.

The Latvian Bar Association seeks to promote public thinking about these issues, which is in line with the Association's understanding of a law-based state.

Members of the Latvian Bar Association come from a variety of legal specialities, they belong to different political parties and religious denominations. The Presidium of the Association meets weekly to discuss laws, draft laws and concepts. Special committees are set up to deal with concrete aspects of the law. Seminars and conferences are organised.

The presidium of the Latvian Bar Association that was elected on 12 December 1998. First row: Vija Jākobsone, Kalvis Torgāns, President of the Latvian Bar Association Aivars Borovkovs, Valentīna Elksne, Uldis Petersons. Second row: Jānis Birzulis, Uldis Papans, Imants Rudolfs Plīčs, Edgars Meļķisis, Zenons Indrikovs, Ilmārs Kalniņš. Third row: Gunārs Kusiņš, Andris Bunka, Jānis Rozenfelds, Arvīds Dravnieks. Absent: Signe Terihova, Linards Muciņš, Tālavs Jundzis, Ivars Bičkovičs

THE LEGAL PROFESSION AND NOTARIES PUBLIC

Within the composition of Latvia's judicial sector, operate such democratic institutions as the legal profession and notaries public. Both professions are centuries old in Latvia, but it was only in the 19th century that ethnic Latvians were given an opportunity to join these professions. Members of the legal profession in Latvia's history include Jānis Pliekšāns (better known as the great Latvian national poet Rainis) and Pēteris Stučka, as well as Latvia's first three presidents – Jānis Čakste, Gustavs Zemgals and Alberts Kviesis.

During the first period of Latvian independence, both the legal profession and notaries public continued to do their work based on the laws of the Russian Empire. It was only in 1935 that the Latvian law on the country's judicial structure was amended to include a chapter on the legal profession, and only in 1938 did the government adopt a law on notaries public.

The Council of Latvian Sworn Advocates in 1938

New lawyers just after their oath-taking ceremony in 1998

During the Soviet occupation the legal profession in Latvia SSR was by no means independent, because the Communist Party and its executive bodies interfered in legal processes constantly, and "untrustworthy" people were kept out of the profession altogether. The work of notaries public was also circumscribed – they were basically nothing more than clerks who worked for the executive.

Many members of the legal profession were active participants in the effort to restore Latvia's independence in the late 1980s and early 1990s. Linards Muciņš, Andris Grūtups, Andrejs Krastiņš, Rūta Marjaša and Jānis Lagzdiņš were all members of the Supreme Council of the Latvian SSR which declared the country's independence. Members of the legal profession have served as ministers and members of the *Saeima* ever since. In 1993, Latvia adopted new laws on the legal profession and on the profession of notary public. The statutes of the Council of Sworn Advocates, as well as an ethics code for the legal profession, were approved.

There were 540 practising sworn advocates in Latvia at the time of this writing, as well as 76 assistant advocates. Most of the advocates worked in law firms, while a few had individual practices. Sworn advocates and their assistants are present in all of Latvia's judicial districts, but a sworn advocate has the right to work in any of the districts. Advocates participate in the judicial process by bringing criminal, civil and administrative cases before the courts and before various pre-trial investigation institutions. Advocates also provide other kinds of legal assistance. They are independent in their work, and their work is subject only to the law.

The Latvian Council of Sworn Notaries is an independent organisation, which brings together the country's sworn notaries and their assistants. All of the country's sworn notaries are members. Both of the organisations mentioned above are autonomous subjects of public rights. The executive institutions of the Council of Sworn Advocates and the Council of Sworn Notaries are the general meeting, the Council and the Auditing Commission. General meet-

The Council of Latvian Sworn Notaries in 1999

ings are convened once a year, and delegates discuss major operational issues. Councils are elected once every three years, as are the auditing commissions. At the time of this writing, the chairperson of the Council of Sworn Advocates was Dr. Aivars Niedre, and his deputy was Vija Jākobsone. Members in the Council of Sworn Advocates are both advocates and assistants to sworn advocates. An advocate is authorised to practice in Latvia only after the taking of an oath before the Chief Justice of the Supreme Court. The organisation is a member of the International Advocate Association, and it also co-

operates with similar organisations in Estonia, Lithuania, Germany, Finland, Norway, Denmark, the Netherlands, and other countries.

The ethics code of Latvia's sworn advocates is based on the ethics codes approved by the International Advocates Association, as well as the code of the international group which governs the behaviour of lawyer. The code sets out basic ethical principles that must be observed by all advocates who work in Latvia and abroad.

The Minister for Justice appoints notaries public in collaboration with the Council of Sworn Notaries. Notaries must

Assistants to sworn advocates take their oath in 1999

Barrister and Parliamentarian Linards Muciņš and Mrs. Inga Muciņa, a sworn notary

Lawyer (and American First Lady) Hillary Clinton greets lawyer Vija Jākobsone in 1994

These lawyers were the first to take the oath of a sworn advocate in post-Soviet Latvia. They did so in 1993

A ceremony at which the Latvian Council of Sworn Notaries was admitted to the International Society of Latin Notaries in Berlin in 1995

pass an examination before they are licensed to work. The Minister has the right to punish notaries and to dismiss them from their post.

Both advocates and notaries in Latvia are members of free professions, which means that they receive no salary and perform their work in accordance with their economic risk. Some categories of residents in Latvia enjoy free legal or notary services that are financed by the State.

The Council of Latvian Sworn Notaries in 1938

LATVIJAS ARHĪVI

The main building of the Latvian State Historical Archive

Compared to other countries in Eastern Europe, Latvia was lucky in that the two World Wars did not do much harm to its national archives. On the contrary – both in 1918 and in 1940, when the Communists undertook their nationalisation measures many valuable documents from the libraries of manors, castles and cities and towns ended up in the archives. It can be assumed that Latvia's archives are among the most important in the world, and they excellently illustrate the way in which Europe's life was documented in the last millennium. Specialists from Poland, Sweden, Russia and even the Vatican have come to Latvia to study authentic documents in the collection.

The institutions, which make up the Latvian National Archives, operate on the basis of the Law On Archives, which was adopted in 1991. This law sets out the way in which materials are collected, preserved, made available and administered in the system.

Both institutions and individuals can submit requests with the archives with respect to social and legal issues, as well as with respect to matters concerning Latvia's public life, politics, economy and cultural history.

Documents with limited availability are reserved for academic or scientific study, and they can be accessed only with special permission. The General Directorate of the Latvian National Archives actually operates 15 different archives, as well as a laboratory and a special library. In the reading rooms of the archives, any interested party can learn about the registration system that is used, as well as about the documents that are stored in the institution. This does not cost the visitor anything.

The history archive of Latvia was founded in 1919, and today it has a collection of more than six million items of documentation from the period between 1220 and 1944. Among the enormously valuable documents in the archives are papers from the chancelleries of the Vidzeme Knighthood and the Kurzeme Knighthood, the office of the Governor General of the Baltic provinces, and the offices of the governors of Vidzeme and Kurzeme. There are also documents from the archives of manors, churches, religious congregations and individuals. There are documents from the masters of the Livonian Order, the archbishops of Riga, the kings of Poland and Sweden and the tsars of Russia. Documents from the Nazi occupation regime are here. A significant share of the documents has come from the institutions of the independent Latvian state that existed between 1920 and 1940.

The Latvian State Archive was established in 1961 as the Central State October Revolution and Socialist Development Archive of the Latvian SSR. The archive contains nearly 2 million documents from the State institutions of the Soviet occupation regimes of 1917-1920

and 1940-1944, as well as documents from the State and local government institutions, enterprises and organisations from Riga and *Jūrmala* in the period between 1944 and 1994. After the independence of Latvia was renewed in 1991, the archive was charged with supervising the archives of the State's central institutions, as well as the archives of the cities of Riga and *Jūrmala*. In 1991 and 1992 the archive took over documents from the Latvian Communist Party and the KGB of the Latvian SSR. Personal documents from various people in the field of culture in Latvia also represent a significant share of the collection.

The archive co-operates with public organisations in Latvia and abroad to preserve valuable documents.

The Latvian State Archive of Cinema, Photographic and Phonographic Documents was established in 1963, and today it holds some 24,000 films, 289,000 photo negatives and 28,000 sound recordings which concern the public, economic and cultural events which have taken place in Latvia since the late 19th century. The archive continues to update its collection in co-operation with the mass media and with other producers of audio-visual materials. The State Archive of Personnel Documents was established in 1992, and today it has nearly 1 million documents from the personnel files of companies in Riga and *Jūrmala* that have been liquidated, that have gone bankrupt or that have been privatised. The archive's purpose is to preserve the documents so that they can be used as evidence in social insurance and social welfare cases.

The Central Laboratory for the production of microfiches and for restoring valuable documents is an independent institution. It researches, restores, binds and photographs documents. It also oversees climate and microbiological conditions in places where archival documents are stored.

The Special Library of the archives system has been an independent system since 1984. Its collection is available to archive employees, researchers and other interested parties. The collection includes methodological literature from the fields of archival sciences, history and public science. There are also numerous reference and encyclopaedic materials. The library also contains rare publications about European and Baltic history, heraldry and genealogy from the 16th to the 19th century.

The General Director of the National Archives, Valdis Štāls, and a senior specialist from the Documents and Publications Division of the historical archive, Dr. Pārsla Pētersone, evaluate documents that have been selected for this book

Latvian President Guntis Ulmanis attends the archival exhibition *Riga and Prague – the capital cities of two independent states in the 1920s and 1930s* in Prague, May 1999

A delegation of Baltic archivists is seen visiting the storage facility of the personnel documents archive at *Ata iela* 1 in Riga. At the centre of the photograph – the director of the facility, Dace Ozoliņa

The director of the *Sigulda* zonal archive, Felicita Roslava, receives a government award on the 35th anniversary of her facility in 1999

The director of the Latvian State Historical Archive, Nikolajs Rižovs.

The oldest storage facility of the Latvian State Historical Archive at *Palasta iela* 4 in Riga is 110 years old

The director of the Latvian State Archive, Daina Kļaviņa, a representative of the Council of Europe, George Vitiello, and the secretary general of the International Council of Archives, Charles Keczkemeti

Senior officials from the archives at the celebration of the system's 80th anniversary in March 1999

THE ENTERPRISE REGISTER OF THE REPUBLIC OF LATVIA

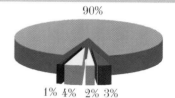
90%

1% 4% 2% 3%

- enterprises
- public organizations
- media
- mortgage
- foreign companies

The rate at which companies and enterprises have been founded in Latvia. The graph shows data from 1 January 1991 to 11 October 1999

The various kinds of structural entities that were registered in the Latvian Enterprise Register in 1999

The Enterprise Register of the Republic of Latvia was established in 1991. Its task is to register enterprises, branches, representative offices of foreign enterprises, mass media enterprises, public organisations, commercial pledges and marriage contracts. The Register also registers all changes that are made to enterprises, and it stores information regarding the financial status of enterprises, which they provide in their annual reports. A significant achievement for the Register was the establishment of the Register of Commercial Pledges which, since its establishment in March 1998, has registered 4,946 instances of commercial pledges for a total amount of 1.37 billion lats.

All of the information that is collected in the register is publicly available, and information about any registered object can be accessed from anywhere in the world via the Internet. In 1992, the Enterprise Register opened its information system, and today it is recognised as one of the most modern systems of its kind. The system is consistently updated to reflect changes in Latvian law, as well as to take into account the development of the Register itself and related registers elsewhere in Europe.

The Enterprise Register of the Republic of Latvia was the first in Eastern Europe to link up with the European Business Register.

The chief notary of the Enterprise Register of the Republic of Latvia, Maris Gulbis

THE LAND REGISTER

The Land Register is used to register immovable property and related rights. The Land Register is available to anyone, and its records can be trusted. Article 994 of the Latvian Civil Law specifies that an owner of immovable property can only be a person who has been recorded as such in the Land Register.

Regional branches of the Land Register were established at the country's regional courts in 1993, when the Law On the Land Register which initially had been approved in 1937 was reinstated. Today there are 28 such branches, and decisions on Land Register matters are taken by 68 Land Register judges. An important

The Land Register Department of the Ministry of Justice and judges and sworn notaries from the regional Land Register branches meet in a task force to talk about mutual co-operation. At the far right is the chairperson of the Riga Regional Court Land Register branch, Ilga Neimane

A working meeting of judges from the regional Land Register branches in Latvia. They were discussing the establishment of a pilot model for the computerised Land Register system

shift in the development of the system of Land Registers in Latvia occurred at the end of 1999, when amendments to the relevant law were adopted which provide for the complete computerisation of the system. The amendments envisage the establishment of a unified and computerised Land Register.

As the databases of the regional Land Register branches are integrated into a single system and the electronic data are given legal effect, the effectiveness of the Land Register system, as well as the servicing of clients in that system, will improve. The Land Register law now provides that the State unified and computerised Land Register following its establishment will be the only computerised Land Register, which contains legally recognised information.

The building which houses the Riga City Land Register branch

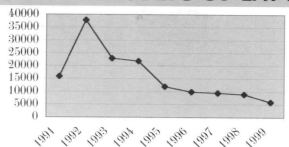

The director of the Latvian State Archive of Cinema, Photographic and Phonographic Documents, Inta Kaņepāja, receives the Badge of Honour First Class of the Order of Three Stars

The directors of the Latvian, Lithuanian and Estonian archive systems, Valdis Štāls, Vidas Grigoraitis and Jaak Rand, sign a protocol of co-operation for the year 2000 in *Vilnius*, September 1999

A delegation of employees from the Latvian archives attends the opening of an exhibition in honour of the 80th anniversary of Latvia's independence at the Finnish National Archive in November 1998

The executive board of the Latvian Association of Archivists in June 1999

An exhibition of archival documents, *The Heritage of the Archives of the Soviet KGB in the Baltic States*, in *Limbaži* in 1997

The commander of the National Police, Juris Rekšņa, who is a collector of police headgear from around the world

Escorts in Latvia are accompanied by policemen on motorcycles. These policemen also engage in the work of the Traffic Police

In Latvia the police are a structure of the Interior Ministry, serving the state and its inhabitants. The basic job of the police is to guarantee individual and public safety, to avert crimes and other violations of the law, to solve crimes and to find the people who have committed them. The police must help individuals, institutions, companies and organizations to carry out their duties and protect their rights. The police have the right to levy administrative fines in some instances.

The work of the police is based on the Constitution of the Republic of Latvia, several international treaties, the law "On the police" and the law "On operative actions".. The police may not be involved in processes that are banned by the laws of the Republic of Latvia, and when the police are doing their work, no one may interfere in that process.

The Police Department of the Interior Ministry has four specialized divisions – the Security Police, the Criminal Police, the Transportation Police and the Immigration

Police. The job of the Security Police is to ensure public order. It runs a Public Order Protection Department which has patrol services in Latvia's cities and districts, a Preventive Department with inspectors and minor affairs inspectors in cities and districts, a Licensing and Permit Department, the Traffic Police, the Apsardze security service and other structures.

The patrol service of the police ensures order and guarantees public safety on the streets and roads of the country, as well as in parks, squares and other public locations. Patrol employees are assigned to specific posts, and they walk or drive concrete routes. Usually the police are dressed in uniform, but when required they can also be in civilian clothing. The main job for the Traffic Police, of course, is to ensure order and safety on streets and roads. The Criminal Police prevent, solve and investigate crimes such as banditry, smuggling, armed attacks, forgery, blackmail, murder, rape, theft, drug-related crime, etc. The Criminal Police also fight against organized and economic crime, search for people who are hiding or missing, etc. Each employee of the Criminal Police has a numbered badge. The Criminal Police cooperate with the border guard, the Home Guard, the Customs Service and other institutions.

The Transport Police provide for order on the railroad, at airports and at ports.

The Immigration Police fight against illegal immigration in Latvia.

Officers from the Latvian police are always ready to speak to the press. From the right: the commander of the Traffic Police, Alnis Jirgens; the commander of the National Police, Juris Rekšņa, and Gen. Aloizs Blonskis, commander of the Criminal Police

After lectures at the Latvian Police Academy – police Col. Imants Pliès, the academy's director, Zenons Indrikovs, Interior Minister Andrejs Krastiņš, and the parliamentary secretary at the ministry, Kārlis Leiškalns

Pope John Paul II and the commander of the Riga Traffic Police, Voldemārs Hmeļevskis (center)

At an exhibition on the archives of the Soviet KGB in *Limbaži* in 1997. From the left: Interior Minister Dainis Turlais and the head of the European Commission delegation in Latvia, Günther Weiss

Policemen on parade

US First Lady Hillary Clinton (right) and the director of the Operative Management Center of the Riga Police Headquarters, Linda Hajenko

Police training

Dogs participate in police work. This dog is being trained for the needs of police

APSARDZE

Apsardze employees – ready to respond to a call

Work at the central *Apsardze* headquarters

The *Apsardze* security company is a structure of the National Police of the Interior Ministry. *Apsardze* guards buildings and facilities, including apartments and private homes, installing centralized alarm systems, responding to alarm calls, averting crimes, transporting and guarding money and dangerous cargo (including medications that contain narcotic or psychotropic substances), and guarding individuals and objects.

Apsardze and its various units employ more than 1,000 certified police employees who are actively involved in ensuring public order and battling against crime. 68 automotive response teams are on duty at all times, including 15 in Latvia. There are places in Latvia where only an *Apsardze* unit is available to protect the public peace at night. In cities where there is no patrol service, the job is done by *Apsardze*. *Apsardze* units are found in all of the country's district cities, as well as in other major populated areas.

Apsardze provides centralized guard services with modern alarm systems, radio communications and a modern radio telephone signal processing central at its main headquarters. Personnel at the headquarters respond operatively to alarm calls from protected objects, dispatching patrol units as needed. The teams which respond to these calls are mobile, well trained, supplied with radio communications resources and armed. Today *Apsardze* guards some 12,000 objects, many of which are of great importance to the state. In distant rural regions, objects are connected to a radio system, and alarms are turned over to the local Home Guard or other officials.

The management of *Apsardze*

Personnel at the central *Apsardze* headquarters respond to alarm calls in an operative way

The *Daugavpils* prison

An aerial view of the *Matisa* prison and the Central prison

The main building of the *Olaine* prison

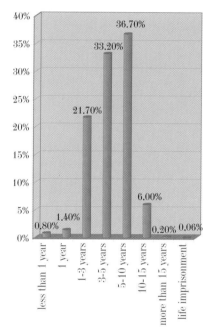

The distribution of prisoners in Latvia according to the duration of their sentence

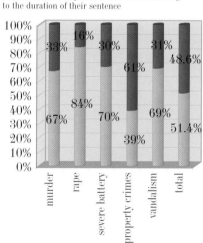

solved not solved

The solve rate for various crimes

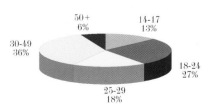

The age of people convicted of crimes

The director of the Department of Incarceration, Vitolds Zahars

The administration of the *Olaine* prison

On September 3, 1998, Queen Sonia of Norway visited the *Valmiera* prison. During her visit, there was a discussion with the commander of the prison, S. Čepjolkins, about living conditions in the prison and the implementation of the Nord-Balt projects. The queen also inspected the athletics facilities of the prison and the places where prisoners work

The chapel of the *Jelgava* prison

Latvia's system of prisons consists of 15 deprivation of liberty institutions and a Training Methods Centre. There are seven closed prisons, three partly closed prisons, two open prisons, two pre-trial investigation prisons and a penal institution for juveniles. In six of the closed and partly closed prisons, there are also pre-trial investigation divisions.

Latvia's prisons house up to an average of 9,000 people – 5,500 who have been sentenced and 3,500 who have been detained. The prison system employs 2,344 people.

Latvia has been reconstructing its prisons since 1994, and the living conditions for prisoners, as well as the safety of the prisons, have been significantly improved. It used to be that each residential room in a prison housed between 50 and 100 people. After reconstruction, there will be cells for 4-8 prisoners. At the time of writing, 4,000 prisoners were already housed in safe and civilised conditions. The number of prisoners contracting tuberculosis is increasing in Latvia. In 1999, work began on reconstructing the *Olaine* prison in order to establish a tuberculosis prison hospital with 450 beds. The Latvian prisons system is involved in the Nord-Balt Prisons Project, which provides for ongoing co-operation with prisons in the Scandinavian countries. The *Jelgava* and *Iļģuciems* prisons and the *Cēsis* penal institution for juveniles work with three prisons in Sweden, while the Training Methods Centre works with a similar centre in *Norrkjöping*, Sweden. The *Griva*, *Jēkabpils* and *Valmiera* prisons, as well as the Latvian Central Prison, have close co-operation with four prisons in Norway.

A newly built recreational field for prisoners at the *Jelgava* prison

Supervision of prisoners at the *Jelgava* prison

The library of the *Olaine* prison

In many prisons, including the *Jelgava* prison, inmates have an opportunity to work out

Each prison has an impatient medical facility and a dental office

The *Babīte* Social Rehabilitation Center houses people who are released from prison

Prisoners at the *Griva* prison make furniture and other items of carpentry

Georgs Rudzitis (1870-1934) was chairman of the Board of the Latvian Fire Fighters Association from 1928 until 1934.

This fire fighter has sprinklers installed in his helmet to reduce temperatures. The photo was taken in *Liepāja* in 1912

A steam pump, known as *Merry Weather*, at a Riga City Fire Fighting Team depot at *Hanzas iela* 5 in 1924

Organised efforts to fight fires in Latvia began in the middle of the 19th century, when volunteer fire fighting societies were founded. In 1865, such societies were founded in Riga and *Jelgava*.

Communal fire fighting teams were set up in several cities – in *Daugavpils* in 1845, in *Liepāja* in 1871 and in Riga in 1907.

After World War II, fire-fighting teams were militarised, and they were placed under the control of the Ministry of the Interior.

In March 1992, Latvia adopted a law *On Fire Safety*, and a unified State Fire Fighting and Rescue Service (*Valsts Ugunsdzēsības un glāb-šanas dienests* – VUGD) was established, which performs preventive work (it has the right to levy administrative fines) and puts out fires. The Service also works to control emergencies and to rescue victims of various accidents. Since 1998, the tasks of the civil defence system have also been placed under the control of the State Fire Fighting and Rescue Service.

In 1999, there were 3,500 specialists working at the State Fire Fighting and Rescue Service, which is under the supervision of the Ministry of the Interior, while another 500 fire fighters were employed by the 59 fire fighting stations of the State Forestry Service. Major companies such as SC *Latvijas dzelzceļš* (Latvian Railways) and SC *Ventspils nafta* have their own fire fighting ser-vices. Voluntary fire fighting societies bring together members of city and parish teams. Latvian law provides that fire fighters may not go on strike, join trade unions or political parties. In 1998, the State Fire Fighting and Rescue Service saved 199 people from fires and another 125 people from accidents on water and ice, from road traffic and other accidents.

Managed by the Service are the Fire Safety Technical School, the Scientific Research Admi-nistration and the Fire Fighters Museum.

The Latvian State Fire Fighting and Rescue Service is a member in the international CTIF organisation, and it has preserved the long-standing traditions of athletic activities among fire fighters.

Horse-drawn fire fighting carts at *Akmeņu iela* 17 depot in Riga in 1922

A Riga city fire fighting team in a *Daag* automobile in 1922

The Latvian Fire Fighters Museum features a steam pump from *Shand Mason & Co.* that was produced in 1899

Practical exercises in saving victims with hook ladders and tarpaulins in 1910

A display of old fire fighting equipment at the Latvian Fire Fighters Museum in 1999

A hand pump from the *C. Metz* company that was produced in 1865 can be viewed at the Latvian Fire Fighters Museum

Another exhibit at the Latvian Fire Fighters Museum is a reproduction of the office of a fire chief

A fire in the attic of a multi-story building is put out with the assis-tance of an automated lifter

The fire station at *Daugavpils*

Emergency aid automobiles which were provided to the fire fight-ing service by the Riga City Council in 1999

The *Bronto Sky Lift* automated lifter extends to a distance of 42 meters and can be moved both horizontally and vertically. The aerial ladder truck has complex fire fighting and rescue equipment

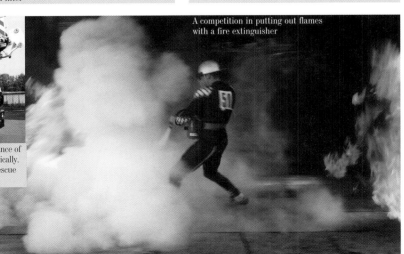

A competition in putting out flames with a fire extinguisher

Chimneysweeps Ivars Grube and Jānis Birnbaums
on the roofs of Rīga

CHIMNEYSWEEPS

Chimneysweeps clean chimneys, of course, but in Rīga they are also responsible for ensuring that heating systems meet fire safety requirements.

Chimneysweeps received professional recognition in Rīga in 1738, according to a document registered at St. John's Guild. The Coat of Arms of the Rīga Brotherhood of Chimneysweeps can be seen at the Rīga Culture and Folk Arts Centre *Mazā Ģilde*, in the ceiling decorations of the small hall.

There are some 100 chimneysweeps who are active in Latvia today. Some 28 of them work in Rīga. 80% of chimneysweeps are associated with the Volunteer Fire Fighting Society, while the remainder are private contractors.

Fire safety regulations in Latvia specify that building owners must entrust their chimneys only to certified specialists. Chimneysweeps have always been thought to bring good luck.

The site of a railroad accident near *Vecumnieki* after a "hellish" night on 11 November 1998. Fourteen tank cars with fuel ran off the tracks, and nine of them caught fire. Fire fighters from *Bauska*, *Jelgava* and Rīga, as well as from Latvian Railways, helped to put out the resulting conflagration

Washing of fire fighting garments after work in a chemically polluted environment (here you see a training session)

Ladder climbing is one of exercises for fire fighting sport

Fire fighters in the Central district of Rīga have access to powerful fire fighting and rescue equipment

Putting out a fire at a petroleum products reservoir in *Ventspils*

The rescue service of *Ventamonjaks* can manage the most complicated fire and chemical accidents

Saving a person from the water (a training session on the *Daugava* River)

Everyday requirements for a fire fighter – dynamism, professionalism, strength and responsibility

THE CENTRE OF DISASTER MEDICINE

Officials from Latvian Centre of Disaster Medicine are engaging in an extensive training program with NATO. Here you see the director of the Centre's Qualifications Division, Dainis Krieviņš, during a training session in the United States

A mock chemical disaster run for training purposes in Rīga in 1998

Pēteris Oss giving a course on heart and lung resuscitation at the Centre of Disaster Medicine

The State Fire Fighting and Rescue Service works in close co-operation with the Centre of Disaster Medicine

To co-ordinate the work of doctors, rescue workers and the police at medical catastrophes, the Centre of Disaster Medicine organises training sessions each year. Here you see rescue work at a mock drill in *Ķemeri* in 1997

Estonia (EST)
343 km

Russia (RUS)
276 km

Belarus (BYS)
161 km

Lithuania (LTU)
571 km

The land border of the Republic of Latvia – 1,351 km

Since 17 September 1996, the Border Guard has been commanded by Colonel and later General Gunars Daboliņš, who is now commander of the State Border Guard. The Border Guard is an individual State structural unit, supervised by the Ministry of the Interior. The Border Guard is an armed civilian authority, which employs professional border guards with special service ranks

Examination of documents at the Riga International Airport is conducted by personnel from the Riga Border Guard administration

Estonian Prime Minister Tiit Vehi and Latvian Prime Minister Andris Šķele sign maps attesting to the maritime frontier between Latvia and Estonia, thus putting an end to what was known as the "Sprat war" – a dispute over fishing rights in the northern part of the Bay of Riga

One of Latvia's largest border control points is the *Terehova* facility on the Latvian-Russian frontier, which was opened in 1999

During Latvia's War of Independence in 1919, the Latvian Army withdrew to the historical frontiers of Latvia, and from the participants of this War the country's first border guard units were formed. The post of Commander of the Border Guard was established on 15 November 1919. On 15 March 1922, the function of guarding the country's frontiers was transferred to the Ministry of the Interior, and it set up the Border Guard Division under the auspices of its Administrative Department. On 26 March 1935, a Border Guard Brigade was established. The Brigade was run with military discipline, and there were very strict personnel selection criteria.

On the night of 14 June 1940, there was an instigated attack on the headquarters of the 1st company, 2nd Guard unit, No. 3 *Abrene* Battalion of the Border Guard in the village of *Masļenki* in *Abrene* District. In the uneven battle, three border guards and two civilians who were family members of the guards lost their lives. The Red Army took 11 other border guards and 32 civilians hostage and transported them across the border into Russia. The commander of the Border Guard Brigade, General Ludvigs Bolšteins, refused to surrender to the KGB, and after Latvia was occupied, on 21 June 1940, he committed suicide by shooting himself in his office at the Ministry of the Interior.

In December 1990, the Supreme Council of the Republic of Latvia adopted the law *On the State Border of the Republic of Latvia*. On 13 December 1991, the Latvian Minister for Defence signed an order on the formation of seven Border Guard battalions. This date is seen as the date on which the modern State Border Guard was established.

The "green frontier" that lies between Latvia and Estonia is 343 kilometres long, and it is guarded by four Latvian Border Guard units – from *Ainaži*, *Rūjiena*, *Valka* and *Alūksne*

The border zone is well marked with border posts of a specific type, and on either side of the border there is a zone that is 2.5 to 3 meters wide. People are prohibited from being in this zone, and anyone who is found there is held to have committed a border violation. It is a crime to cross Latvia's border at any place other than at the specified border crossing facilities

Latvia's maritime border and coastline are protected by a special unit from *Liepāja* and *Aizpute*, which protects the maritime frontier from the Lithuanian border to *Užava*, and the *Valmiera* Border region company, which protects the coastline of the Bay of Riga

The "green frontier" between Latvia and Belarus is 161 kilometres long, and it is guarded by four Latvian Border Guard units – from *Šķaune*, *Robežnieki*, *Kaplava* and *Silene*

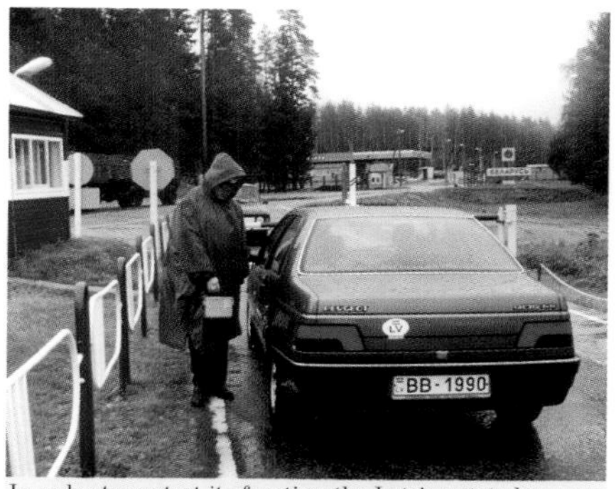

In order to protect its frontier, the Latvian state has passed laws that apply to everyone who crosses the Latvian border. When someone crosses the border in a car, the driver must present to the Border Guards, in addition to personal travel documents, the registration document for the motor vehicle, a civil liability insurance policy (the green card is valid in Latvia), and a license card or a single-use border crossing permit (for vehicles that are engaged in the commercial carriage of passengers or freight). In cases when the border control procedure is conducted with vehicles that are registered in Latvia without the presence of the owner of the vehicle, the driver must also present the original notarially certified authorisation, which gives the bearer the right to use the motor vehicle and to cross the State border in it

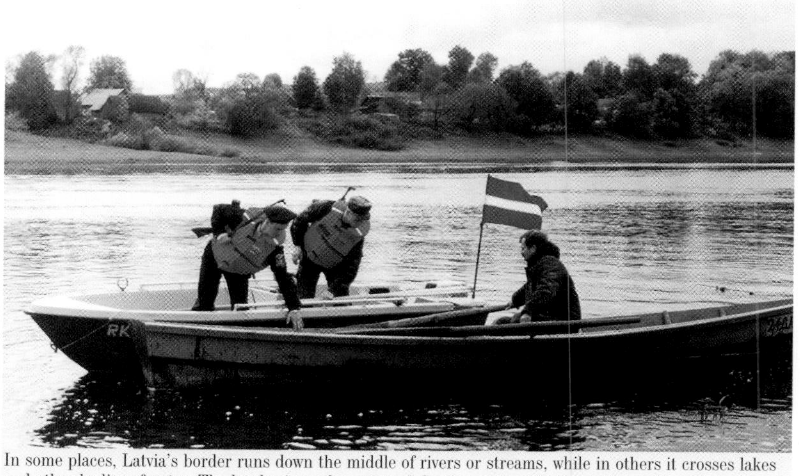

In some places, Latvia's border runs down the middle of rivers or streams, while in others it crosses lakes and other bodies of water. The border in such cases is defined as a straight line between the points where the country's frontier touches the shores of the relevant body of water. The use of motor boats and other floating vessels, including vessels used to travel on ice, fishing, swimming and other activities in these areas are permitted only by the light of day. All vessels and ice-travelling devices that are used in bodies of water through which the country's border passes must be registered with the local territorial office of the Border Guard. When floating vessels are used in these bodies of water to transport tourists on one-time excursions, each trip must be approved by the local office of the Border Guard

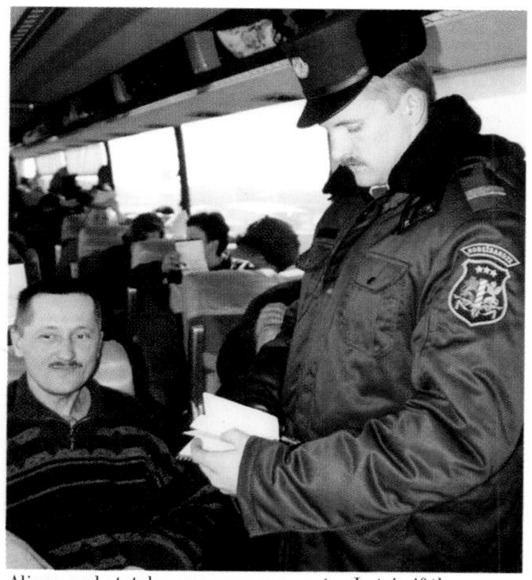

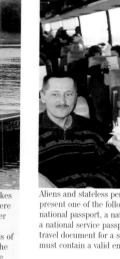

Aliens and stateless persons may enter Latvia if they can present one of the following to verify their identity: a national passport, a national diplomatic passport, a national service passport, a national seaman's book, or a travel document for a stateless person. Each document must contain a valid entry visa or residence permit

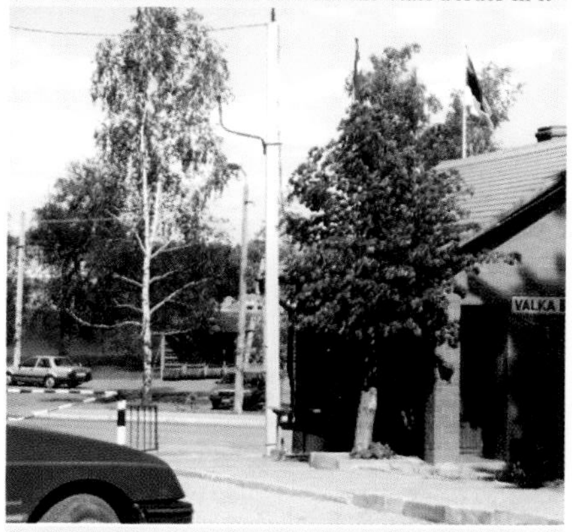

Border crossing points in Latvia are located in places that are provided for in international agreements and operate at specified times. Their purpose is to organise the lawful movement of citizens and residents from neighbouring countries in those cases when customs formalities are not required

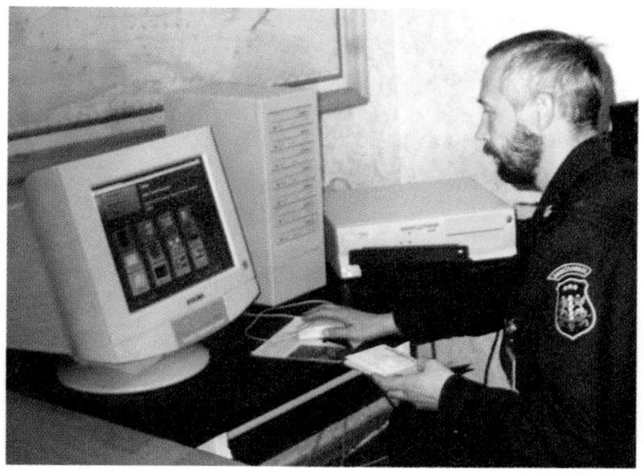

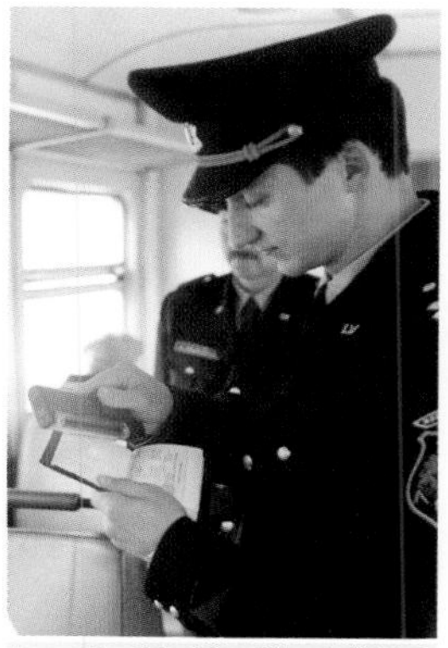

Approximately 7.4 million individuals, 2 million automobiles and 19,000 aeroplanes cross the Latvian State border each year. The Border Guard uses a second-generation information system that was developed by Border Guard specialists and that is based on the Windows 95/98/NT platform. Each year the Latvian Border Guard uncovers more than 100 instances of document forgeries, arrests more than 100 people who are being sought by law enforcement agencies, uncovers between 100 and 150 stolen automobiles, arrests some 200 people who are trying to smuggle goods, and arrests some 80 people who are trying to bring weapons across the border illegally

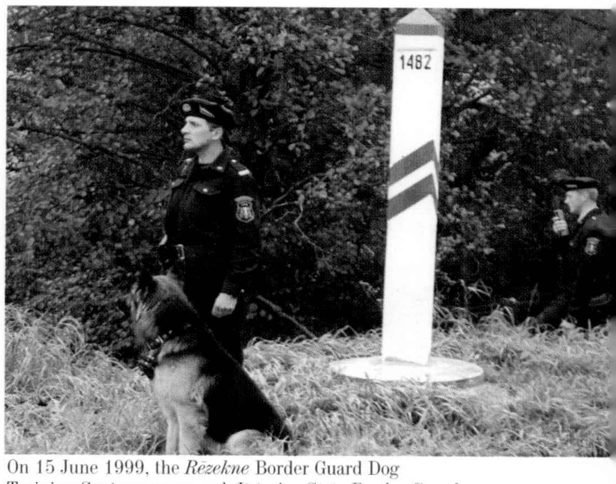

On 15 June 1999, the *Rēzekne* Border Guard Dog Training Centre was opened. It trains State Border Guard dogs and their handlers for work on the State borders

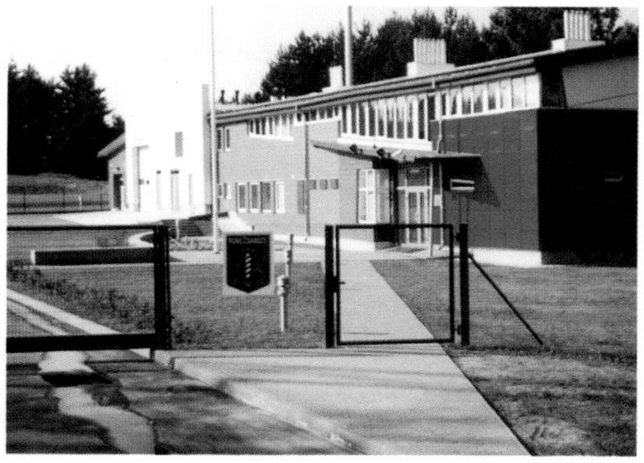

The *Silene* Border Guard headquarters building in *Daugavpils* District

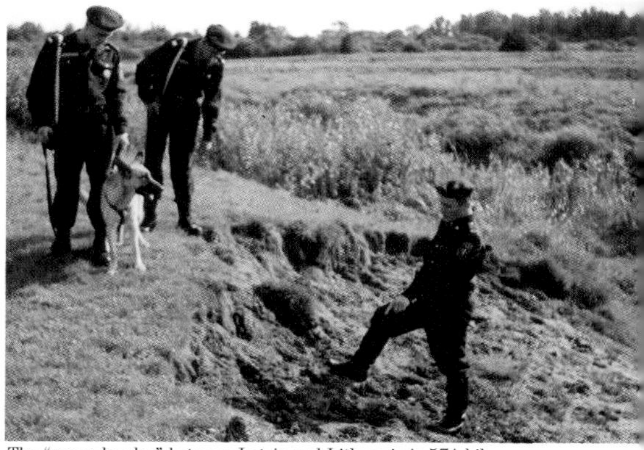

The "green border" between Latvia and Lithuania is 571 kilometres long, and it is guarded by ten Latvian Border Guard units – from *Mēdumi*, *Akniste*, *Pilskalne*, *Mēmele*, *Eleja*, *Dobele*, *Vadakste*, *Piķeļi*, *Aizviķi*, *Lankuti* and *Bauska*

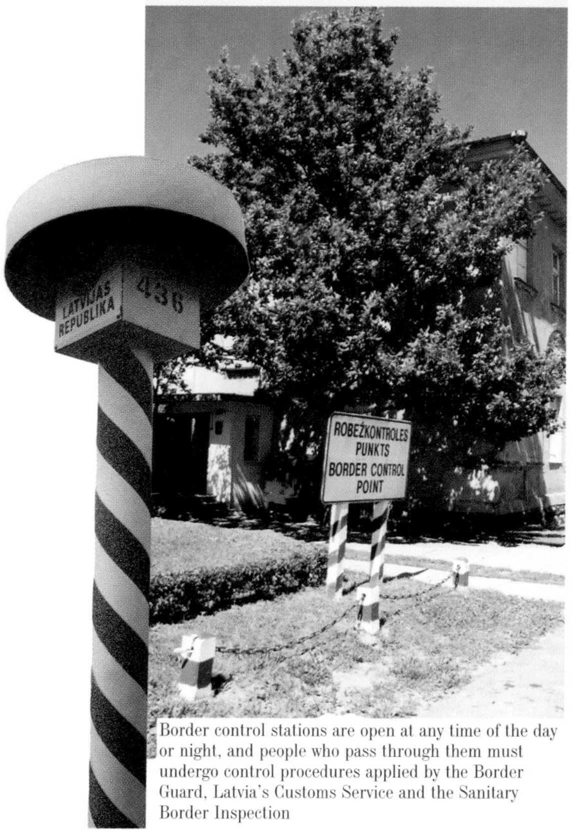

Border control stations are open at any time of the day or night, and people who pass through them must undergo control procedures applied by the Border Guard, Latvia's Customs Service and the Sanitary Border Inspection

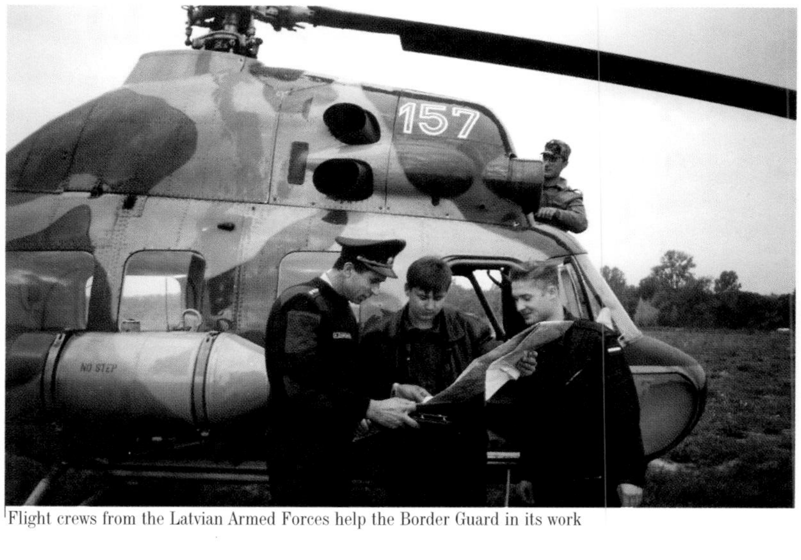

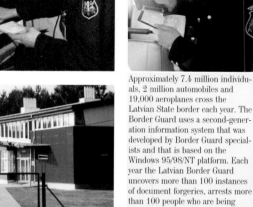

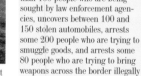

Flight crews from the Latvian Armed Forces help the Border Guard in its work

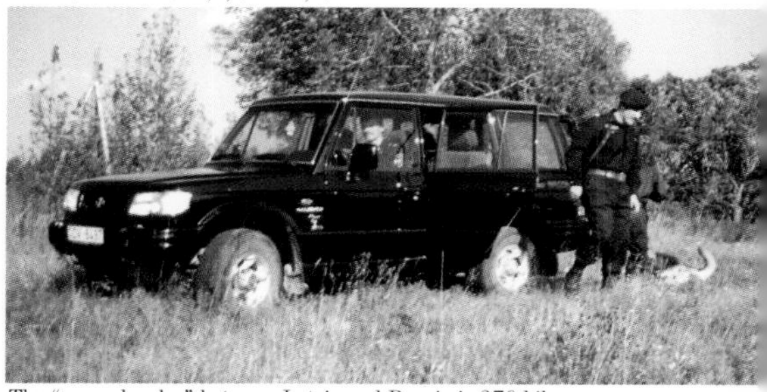

The "green border" between Latvia and Russia is 276 kilometres long, and it is guarded by nine Latvian Border Guard units – from *Pededze*, *Bērziņi*, *Vecumi*, *Punduri*, *Grebņeva*, *Goliševa*, *Krivande*, *Opuļi* and *Pasiene*

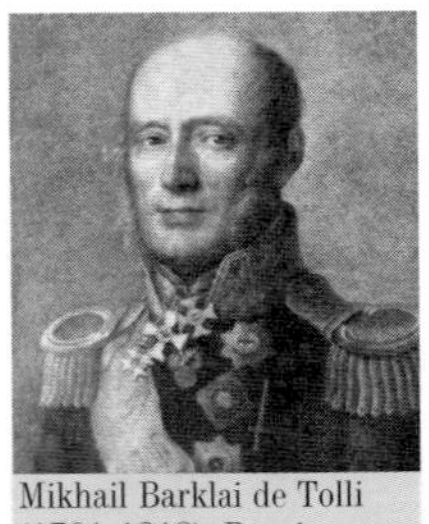
Mikhail Barklai de Tolli (1761-1818), Russian military leader

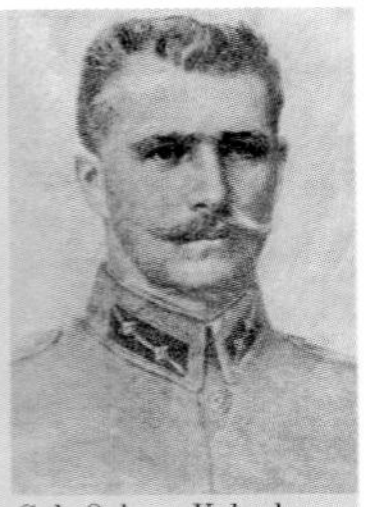
Col. Oskars Kalpaks (1882-1919)

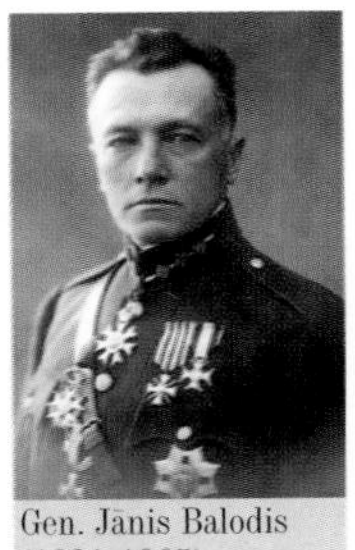
Gen. Jānis Balodis (1881-1965)

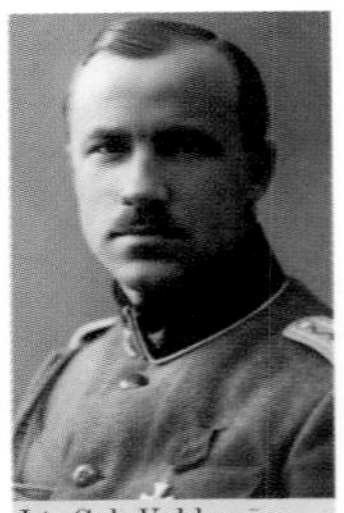
Lt. Col. Voldemārs Ozols (1884-1949)

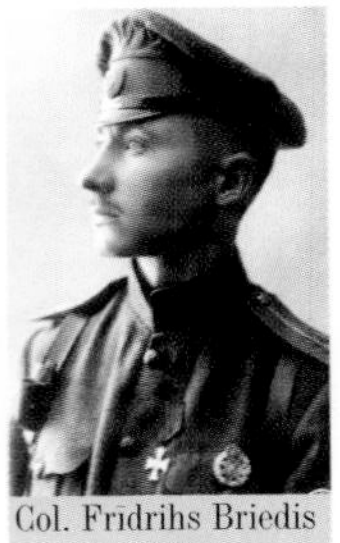
Col. Fridrihs Briedis (1882-1918)

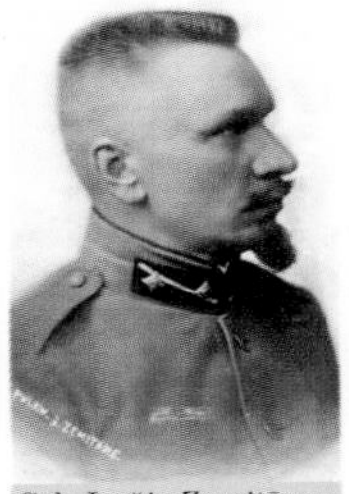
Col. Jorģis Zemitāns (1873-1928)

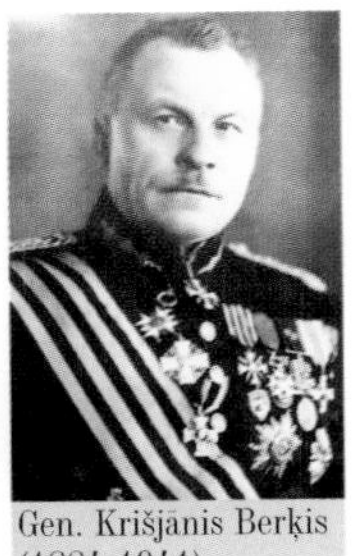
Gen. Krišjānis Berķis (1884-1941)

The history of military formations in Latvia dates back to antiquity, but no major accomplishments have been noted until the early 20th century. Latvians and Lithuanians won a fabled battle against the German Crusaders at *Saule* in 1236, where Lithuanian and Semigallian soldiers slaughtered a German force to the point that the Order of the Brethren of the Sword ceased to exist.

For centuries Latvians participated in military pursuits as nothing more than servants, and only free farmers and Courlandian nobles were allowed to fight as vassals. The first national army units were established in the Swedish armed forces in the 17th century. Latvians who fought in the Swedish army could be exempted from indentured servitude if they served the king of Sweden well. Battalions of men from Vidzeme fought bravely against the Russians and the Poles.

The most distinguished military leader in the Baltic region was Ernst Godeon von Laudon (1717-1790), who was born in the *Ļaudona* Parish and served in the Austrian army in Vienna from 1743. In 1758 he was made lieutenant field marshal, and in 1789 he became the commander of the Austrian armed forces. He was at the helm of the army when it took Belgrade from the Turks. In 1790 von Laudon was made generalissimo and head of the military council of the Austrian crown. Marshal Laudons' name is still remembered with awe in Ļaudona Parish (*Madona* District).

Another distinguished figure in Latvian military history is Moritz of Saxony (1696-1750), a bastard child of Polish King August II the Strong who was duke of Kurzeme and Zemgale and a marshal of France. In 1726 Moritz was chosen as the successor to the duke of Kurzeme and Zemgale by the city council of *Jelgava*. Duchess Anna, who had cast her eyes on Moritz as a possible husband, won the conditional support of Empress Catherine I for his candidacy for the dukedom. Immediately Moritz began to deal with the duchy's affairs, among other things seeking to regain the colony in Tobago.

The rulers of Poland and Lithuania refused to recognize Moritz's appointment and announced it to be void. Moritz lost the trust of duchess Anna, and in August 1726 a Russian army of 20,000 men entered Kurzeme. Moritz sought refuge on what is now known as *Moritz* Island in the *Usma* lake. The Russians were within cannonball distance. The military, headed by de Lasus, called on Moritz to surrender. The would-be duke was supported by some 300 hired soldiers, among whom there were reportedly quite a few Latvians. Moritz disguised himself as a carriage driver and escaped from the besieged island. Soon enough he arrived in France and launched a stellar career, becoming a general in 1733, a marshal in 1734, and a general marshal in 1747. Moritz was a leading military theorist in the 18th century, and his publications on military strategy have not lost their importance even today.

The third distinguished military leader whose life was associated with Latvia was Mikhail Andreas Barklai de Tolli, a Baltic German field marshal in the tsar's army in Russia. Born in *Lugaži* in 1799, Barklai de Tolli rose to the rank of general major. In 1809 and 1810 he was governor general of Finland, from 1810 until 1813 he was Russia's minister for war and a member of the Senate. During this period he did much to reorganize the Russian army. In March 1811 Barklai de Tolli was given command of the 1st Army in its fight against Napoleon. In 1813 he commanded the 3rd army, later becoming the commander in chief of the Russian-Prussian army. In December 1813 the tsar made him an earl, and in 1814 he took Paris and was made a field marshal. In 1815 Barklai de Tolli became a prince in the tsar's court and commander of the entire Russian army. He retired in 1818 and lived in Latvia until his death.

Latvians began to study at Russia's military universities in the mid-19th century, and by the end of the century there were numerous Latvian generals and colonels. In the tsar's armies, military units were often assembled from men of one region, and Latvian units fought against the Turks, the Japanese and the Germans. In 1914, Russia lost a major battle in Eastern Prussia, and some 20,000 Latvian soldiers lost their lives. The front lines moved into Latvia in 1915. Two members of the Russian National Duma, Jānis Goldmanis and Jānis Zālītis, published a call to arms: "Gather under the flags of Latvians!" The Latvian Riflemen were the first truly Latvian army. They fought on their land and for their land, they were closely linked to the nation and deeply loved and respected. The military commanders in Russia, however, neither loved nor respected the riflemen, and legendary battles at "Death Island", *Smārde*, *Ložmetējkalns* (Machine Gun Hill) and *Mazā Jugla* cost many men their lives. Still, the riflemen became true legends not only in the Russian Empire, but also in Western Europe.

World War I divided Latvians into several camps. Many Latvians identified capitalism with foreign enslavement, and they became members of the "Red Riflemen's" brigades. Lenin promised them an independent country, and the truth is that Soviet Russia in 1920 was the only major power which did not try to keep Latvia from becoming independent. The Red Riflemen, in defending Lenin's ideas, gave Latvia its opportunity to be an independent state for 20 years. The first commander in chief of the army of the Soviet Union was Jukums Vācietis, the air force was commanded by Jēkabs Alksnis, and other Latvians were commanders and commissioners in the various military units. All Latvian riflemen were freely conversant in Russian and German – this at a time when only 4% of the soldiers in the entire Russian army were even literate.

The Latvian riflemen demonstrated immense heroism in their fight for their native land during Latvia's liberation battle. The only time in the history of Latvia when the Latvians fought to recover their own land was in 1919, when the forces of Pavel Bermont-Avalov were defeated to the West and Soviet military units were routed to the East.

During the independence of Latvia, the armed forces were at a size that was appropriate for a small country. Soldiers were well trained and discipline was strictly observed. The Baltic States with their small military forces, however, could not stand against the military machine of the Soviet Union when World War II came around. During the war Latvians fought on both sides, and there were national units in both the Soviet and the German armies. Both major powers forced Latvians to go to war, drafting them into Russian divisions and German divisions in complete violation of international conventions which prohibit the drafting of people from occupied territories.

From 1945 until 1990, Latvians served in the Red Army. They were sent to Afghanistan, Czechoslovakia, Vietnam – everywhere where the aggressive armies of the Soviet Union engaged in their inhuman operations. The Soviet army was based on the principle that men from one country or region must not be put together, so Latvian men spent two or three years with military units that were scattered all over the vast Soviet empire. The war in Afghanistan in the late 1970s and early 1980s was merciless – hundreds of Latvian men lost their lives.

Among senior military officers during Soviet times there were Nikolajs Berzzariņš, who was the first commander of Berlin in 1945, Pols Armāns Tiltiņš, who commanded a tank division during World War II, Jānis Čaša, who was the commander of the Baltic Military District and created conditions which allowed Latvian athletes and musicians to serve in Latvia during their mandatory military duty, and Dainis Turlais, who organized and led the withdrawal of the Soviet armed forces from Afghanistan.

Latvians who fled into exile during and after World War II and their descendants have fought in the armies of many of the countries of the world, often in places where Communism was being fought – Vietnam and Korea, in particular. Latvians participated in the Desert Storm operation of the Gulf War, in peacekeeping operations in Albania and in other military operations.

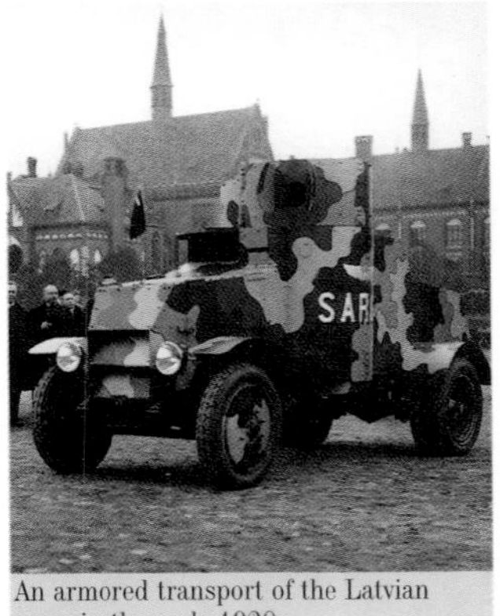
An armored transport of the Latvian army in the early 1920s

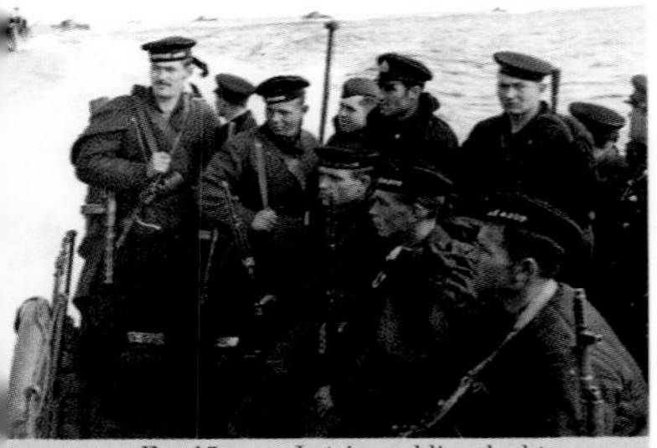
For 45 years Latvian soldiers had to serve in the Soviet armed forces. Latvian men were scattered all across the enormous territory of the soviet Union for two or three years. Service in the Navy was even longer

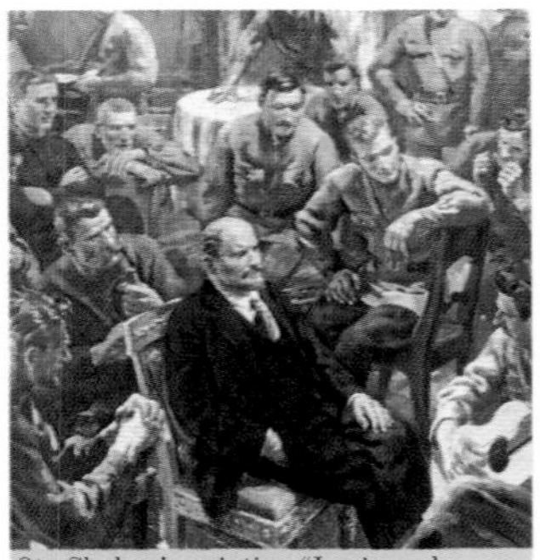
Oto Skulme's painting "Lenin and Latvian riflemen at the Kremlin, May 1, 1918"

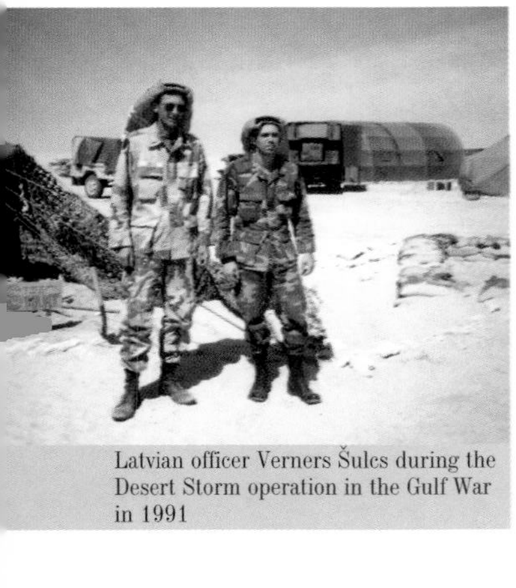
Latvian officer Verners Šules during the Desert Storm operation in the Gulf War in 1991

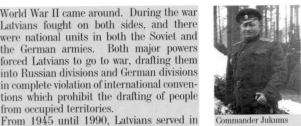

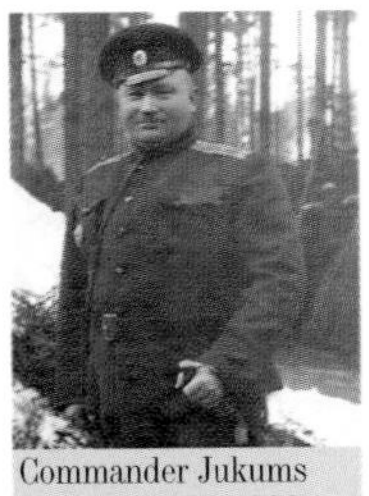
Commander Jukums Vācietis (1873-1938), who served as commander of Latvian Riflemen and as commander in chief of the Eastern front during the Latvian liberation battles. For a very brief period he was also commander of the Soviet armed forces

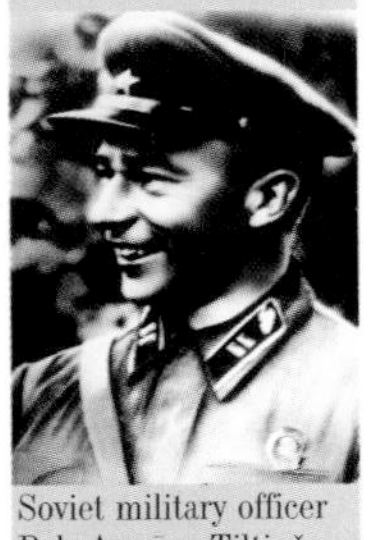
Soviet military officer Pols Armans Tiltiņš (1897-1942)

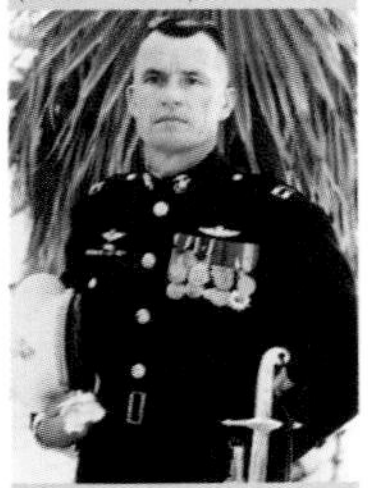
US Marine Capt. Alfons Mednis

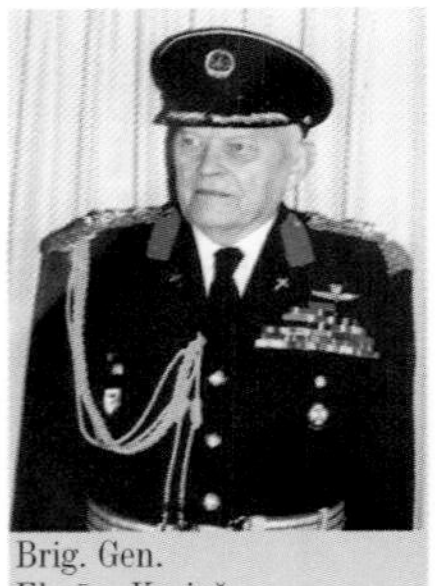
Brig. Gen. Elmārs Kociņš

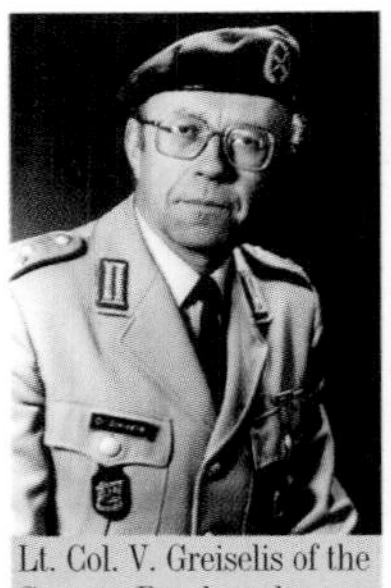
Lt. Col. V. Greiselis of the German Bundeswehr

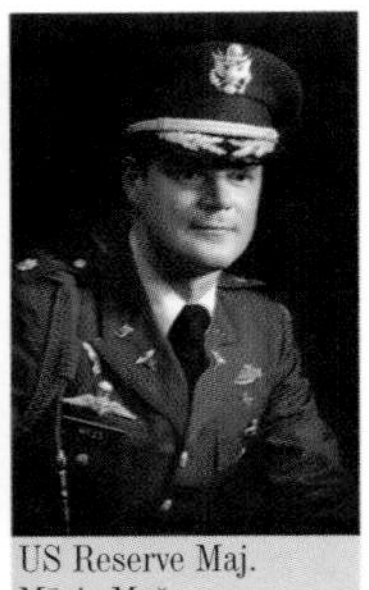
US Reserve Maj. Māris Mežs

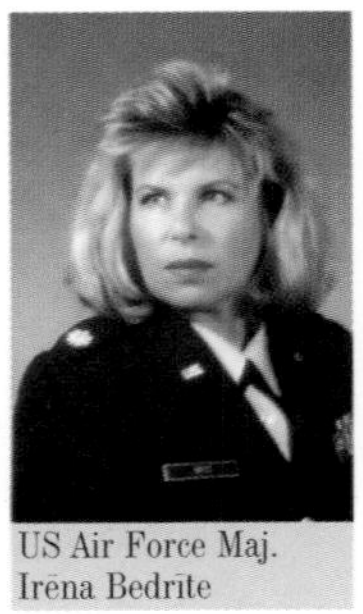
US Air Force Maj. Irēna Bedrīte

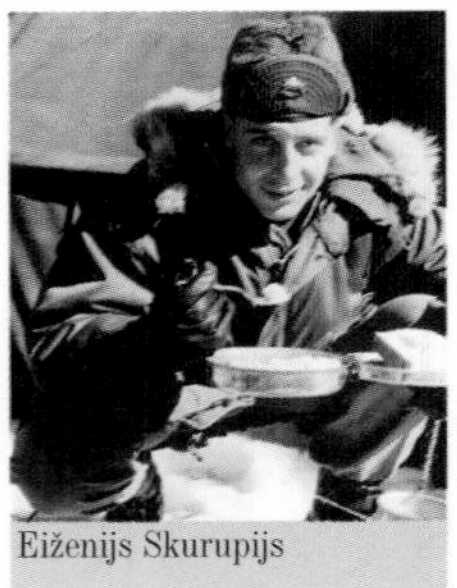
Eiženijs Skurupijs

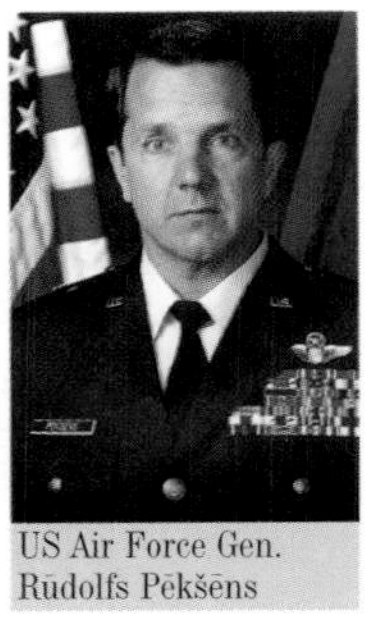
US Air Force Gen. Rudolfs Pēkšēns

The founder of the National Guard, its first commander, Minister for Defence Ģirts Valdis Kristovskis

The Commander of the National Armed Forces, Col. Raimonds Graube

Col. Juris Dalbiņš, a former Commander of the National Armed Forces and a member of the 7th *Saeima*, and National Armed Forces chief-of-staff of the NAF Col. Gundars Abols

The first commander of the Defence Forces was retired Col. Dainis Turlais, who served in the Soviet army and commanded the withdrawal of the Red Army from Afghanistan

Voldemars Veldre graduated from the Latvian Military College on 27 July 1940. On 14 June 1941, he was deported to the Norilsk region of Siberia. He returned to Latvia 15 years later and now lives in *Jelgava*

During World War I, Latvian soldiers first had an opportunity to join together in Latvian military units – rifleman regiments. This occurred in the summer of 1915, when the Tsarist Russian government first permitted the formation of Latvian battalions. After the independence of Latvia was proclaimed on 18 November 1918, the first national military units were formed. The first commander of the National Armed Forces was Col. Oskars Kalpaks.

The first commander of the independent Latvian Army was Gen. Davids Simansons. Colonel (later General) Janis Balodis held the post from 16 October 1919, until 1st April 1921.

The security of Latvia, Estonia and Lithuania is closely linked to the stability of countries around the Baltic Sea, as well as of all Europe. Before 1940, no stable union among the three Baltic republics was ever formed, which was unfortunate. Had a Baltic entente been formed, its military forces could have stood up against the invading Russian occupants for at least two weeks. Encouragement from Latvia's first foreign minister, Zigfrīds Anna Meierovics, to form a Baltic entente was ignored, however.

The occupants mercilessly destroyed the Latvian state and its army. More than 1,000 Baltic military officers were deported to Siberia on 14 June 1941. During what has become known as the Year of Terror, Latvia lost 1,086 officers and 3,579 soldiers and instructors in the Soviet repression. Although Latvia was an occupied country, Latvian men were forcibly inducted into the military of Nazi Germany and, after 1944, the occupying forces of the USSR.

On 21 August 1991, Latvia renewed its independence, and Latvian men immediately organised the National Guard and the Border Guard. On 13 November 1991, the Ministry of Defence was established, and the first minister was Talavs Jundzis. At the time of this writing, the

Minister for Defence is Ģirts Valdis Kristovskis. The first Commander of the Defence Forces was Dainis Turlais. Under his leadership, the National Armed Forces (NAF) (*Nacionālie Bruņotie spēki*) were officially established in October 1994, bringing together the National Guard, the Navy, the Air Force and other military units. The first commander of the NAF was National Guard Col. Juris Dalbiņš. Since 1998, the commander of the National Armed Forces has been National Guard Col. Raimonds Graube. The NAF has continued to upgrade itself, and strong co-operation has been established with the armed forces of other countries. Latvian officers have been trained at foreign military institutions, and Latvian personnel have participated in military training in Latvia and beyond its frontiers. The primary missions of the NAF are development of state self-defence capability and integration in NATO.

The rebirth of Latvia's armed forces may dated from the so-called "Barricade Days" in 1990, when the people of Latvia came from all over the country to protect Parliament and the government. On 20 January of each year, representatives of the NAF lay down flowers in memory of those who fell during that period

American Defence Secretary William Perry visits the *Baltbat* battalion in the fall of 1995

Talavs Jundzis, Minister for Defence in Latvia from 1991-1993 and again from 1997-1998

The senior staff officer of the US National Guard, Lt. Gen. Edward D. Baca, with Latvian President Guntis Ulmanis in *Ādaži*

On 15 September 1999, during the British Bulldogs training session in Latvia, British Ambassador Steven Nash, National Guard Lt. Col. Ildefons Jasens, British Maj. Jeremy Hughes and British commander Col. Kilberns

The head of an American military co-operation group, Col. Roger Allen, the commander of the Michigan unit of the American National Guard, Maj. Gen. Gordon E. Stamp, and former Latvian National Guard commander Col. Juris Eihmanis

The National Armed Forces are targeted toward NATO membership. Here President Guntis Ulmanis of Latvia (far left) is seen with American President Bill Clinton, NATO General Secretary Javier Solana and other Eastern European leaders after a meeting where NATO enlargement was discussed

Manfred Werner at the Latvian Liberty Monument

NATO General Secretary Javier Solana with Latvian Foreign Minister Valdis Birkavs in Riga

The 5th Zemgale Region Brigade of the Latvian National Guard, commanded by Lt. Col. Ildefons Jasens, at a ceremony at Latvia's eternal flame memorial

A competition for reconnaissance units from the National Guard on 20 May 1999, in *Pļaviņas*

Colonel Jānis Kononovs Commander of the *Zemessardze* of the Republic of Latvia

Soldiers from the three Baltic States with the *Baltbat* flag

The Latvian National Guard was established on 23 August 1991, and the law *On the National Guard of the Republic of Latvia* was adopted on the same day. The law specifies that the National Guard is a voluntary militarised formation aimed at involving the citizens of Latvia in the protection of the State and its population.

The National Guard is the largest structure in Latvia's Armed Forces. There are some 16,000 men and women in the National Guard, and another 14,500 are reserve staff who participate on a part-time basis. The National Guard has five infantry brigades and 35 infantry battalions that are distributed in accordance to the administrative-territorial division in Latvia. The National Guard enlists citizens of the Republic of Latvia who are at least 18 years old. Since 1994, Latvia's young men have been able to do their national service in the National Guard.

The National Guard provides critical assistance to State and Local Government institutions in securing public order, in dealing with accidents and natural disasters, etc. Military skills are honed by National Guard personnel in foreign military schools and at various courses.

A youth organisation for the National Guard, known as the *Jaunsardze*, was established in 1992. Its members are young people aged 12 to 18.

In 1998, after a reorganisation of the Latvian armed forces, the National Guard was merged into Latvia's Land Forces. These now include both the territorial units of the National Guard and the regular units of the Latvian Army.

Among the most important regular army units in the Latvian land-based military forces are the *Alūksne* Mobile Rifleman Battalion, the *Sigulda* Communications Training Centre, the *Ādaži* Mobile Rifleman Training Centre, and the *Suži* Airborne Reconaissance Battalion – Latvian Peacekeeping force Battalion. Troops in the latter unit are trained based on a special program, which includes instruction in parachuting, and in various types of commando activities.

Under the auspices of NATO's Partnership for Peace program, Latvian soldiers have an opportunity to participate in military training all around the world, as well as to engage in peacekeeping efforts in the former Yugoslavia.

The Baltic Battalion (*Baltbat*) was established on 19 November 1993, and it brings together infantry companies, a unified battalion headquarters, and support and procurement companies, drawn from all three Baltic States armed forces. The implementation of the *Baltbat* project is co-ordinated by military officers and instructors from Western countries under the auspices of the *Baltbat* training group.

Since 1996, soldiers from the battalion have participated in UN and NATO operations in the former Yugoslavia, as well as in Lebanon.

The National Guard at a memorial ceremony for victims of Communist terror at the Latvian Liberty Monument in Riga in 1996

National Guardsman Guntis Ulmanis and land-based troops participate in international training

US Ambassador Larry Napper wears a Latvian National Guard uniform while watching the Baltic Challenge training session organised by the United States and the three Baltic countries in 1996

Troops from Latvia's Armed Forces have participated in peacekeeping forces in Croatia and Bosnia

Saying good-bye to a soldier on his way to Bosnia

Latvian troops arrive on leave from Bosnia on 20 June 1996 – just before the Latvian summer solstice festival of *Jāņi*, when one has to have a crown of oak tree. Wives, children and fiancées are meeting them

The Presidents of the three Baltic States (from left: Lithuania's Alģirdas Brazauskas, Latvia's Guntis Ulmanis and Estonia's Lennart Meri) visit *Baltbat* in *Ādaži* in 1995

A unit from the *Suži* Airborne Reconaissance Battalion participates in the Baltic Triangle training mission in Germany on 7 September 1999

HRH Prince Andrew, Duke of York, with a Kalashnikov rifle while visiting *Baltbat* soldiers in *Ādaži*

The *Baltbat* camp at the international *Baltic Challenge '97* exercise in Estonia

A unit from the *Suži* Airborne Reconaissance Battalion participates in the Baltic Triangle training mission in Swartzenborn (Germany) in 1999

The commander of the Latvian National Armed Forces, Juris Dalbiņš, reviews troops from the partnership states

Senior representatives of Latvia's major religious denominations visited the *Baltbat*

Baltbat held an open house at its *Ādaži* facility in 1st September 1998. Here a soldier demonstrates the use of a walkie-talkie to schoolchildren

Basic training for new recruits to the *Alūksne* Mobile Rifleman Battalion in 1998

At the 80th anniversary commemoration of the Battle of *Cēsis* in the Latvian War of Independence when the Latvian forces were assisted by the Estonian Army, Estonian Armed Forces Commander Lt. Gen. Johannes Kert and Latvian National Armed Forces Commander Col. Raimonds Graube

An honour guard at the Liberty Monument in Rīga

The Headquarters of the Supreme commander of the Latvian Army was established on 10 July 1919, and a staff commandant's office with an attached commandant's company were also established. The main duty of the company was to protect the Ministry of Defence and the Headquarters, as well as the residence of the President of Latvia and the building which housed Latvia's Constitutional Assembly. The commanders of the battalion and company were all recipients of the Military Order of *Lāčplēsis*.

On 31 January 1992, the structure was re-established as the Headquarters Battalion of the Latvian Armed Forces. Its duties have not changed. An Honour Guard was put in place at the Latvian Liberty Monument on 11 November 1992 (11 November is Latvia's military memorial day). One of the companies from the battalion takes care of this duty, and the battalion has represented the Latvian Armed Forces in greeting Pope John Paul II, US President Bill Clinton, Queen Margarethe of Denmark, and many other foreign dignitaries.

The battalion serves the Headquarters of the National Armed Forces, represents the Latvian state in greeting foreign delegations, organises the accreditation ceremony for foreign ambassadors, provides an honour guard at Parliament and the Liberty Monument, and protects the Ministry of Defence and the Armed Forces facilities that are part of the Rīga garrison.

A parade at the 80th anniversary commemoration of the Battle of *Cēsis*

Soldiers at the Latvian Liberty Monument, honouring the co-operation of Latvians and Estonians soldiers during the independence battles of 1919

At the 80th anniversary commemoration of the Battle of *Cēsis*, Latvian National Armed Forces Commander Col. Raimonds Graube, Estonian Armed Forces Commander Johannes Kert, Latvian Minister for Defence Ģirts Kristovskis, Estonian Prime Minister Marts Laar, Latvian Prime Minister Vilis Krištopans and Mrs. Krištopans, Latvian Foreign Minister Valdis Birkavs, Estonian Foreign Minister Heinrich Ilves, and *Cēsis* City Council Mayor Jānis Beikmanis

Soldiers from the Headquarters Battalion of the National Armed Forces at *Krusta* barracks on 18 November 1997

The Honour Guard Company of the Headquarters Battalion on 14 June 1998

An honour guard at the grave of the first Latvian Foreign Minister, Zigfrīds Anna Meierovics

An honour guard at the Latvian War Cemetery (*Brāļu kapi*) during a commemoration ceremony for Latvian troops who fell during Latvia's War of Independence (1918 – 1920)

The Honour Guard Company of the Headquarters Battalion at Rīga airport

Admiral Gaidis
Andrejs Zeibots

A ship received from the German armed forces is given a new name – *Namejs*

The installation of the new commander of the Latvian Navy in September 1999. Admiral Gaidis Zeibots is at the left and the new commander of the Latvian Navy, Ilmārs Lešinskis, is in the centre

THE LATVIAN NAVY

The Latvian Navy was reborn on April 11, 1991, when the Latvian flag was raised on the first ship of the renewed fleet called the *Sams*.

There are five sub-units in the Latvian Navy – the Navy headquarters, a Naval support base in *Liepāja* with branches in Riga and *Ventspils*, the Radio and Technology Battalion in *Ventspils* with information centres in Riga and *Liepāja*, the Training Centre in *Liepāja*, the Navy flotilla at *Liepāja* and the Coast Guard flotilla in Riga. The Training Centre is used for ongoing training for officers and instructors, as well as for other training purposes.

Latvia's Navy has obtained several ships from Sweden, Germany, Poland and Norway. On 11 April 1995, the Navy was proud to receive the original flag of the Latvian Navy Fleet, which had been thought lost in 1940 but had miraculously been preserved.

Latvia's Navy ships have frequently sailed to other countries on friendship visits, and naval ships and officers from other countries have often been welcomed in Latvia. Latvia's Navy has participated in various international training missions and exercises (*US Baltops, Co-operative Jaguar, Baltic Challenge*, etc.). All of these have been fully in accordance with NATO standards. The Navy has been successful in carrying out its missions in these sessions, and its skills have been praised by international military specialists.

One of the most important steps in establishing Baltic co-operation in military affairs was the establishment of the *Baltron* fleet of ships from Estonia, Latvia and Lithuania in 1998. The first commander of the fleet was Captain Ilmars Lešinskis. Since 17 September 1999, he has also been the commander of Latvia's Navy.

Coast Guard ships take part in international search and rescue training sessions in the Bay of Riga and the Baltic Sea.

Prince Andrew, the Duke of York, places flowers at a monument to fallen British and French sailors at the Latvian town of *Bolderāja*

On the 80th anniversary of the Latvian Navy Fleet, Latvia was visited by naval ships from many countries. Here you see guest ships anchored at the Riga passenger port

French sailors visiting the Latvian Navy in Riga

THE LATVIAN AIR FORCE

The Latvian Air Force was initially stationed at the *Spilve* airport in Riga, but now the Air Squadron and its support facility are located in the town of *Lielvārde*.

The Air Force is responsible for monitoring and protecting Latvia's airspace. It takes part in search and rescue operations, emergency transportation services, and natural disaster response work.

Air Force personnel have received military and professional training in the United States, Germany, the Czech Republic, Italy, Denmark, Sweden and other countries. The commander of the Air Force, Ojārs Ivanovs, has trained at the Air Force College in the United States.

The men and women of the Latvian Air Force have a very active flight training schedule, and they often train with troops from special mission units and the pan-Baltic *Baltbat* battalion. This allows them to participate successfully in international training programs run by NATO. The Air Force has distinguished itself in such training programs as *Co-operative Bear, Co-operative Zenith* and *Baltic Eye*.

On 15 April 1998, the three Baltic States signed a treaty on establishing a joint airspace monitoring system for the three countries. The Air Force has been charged with implementing the project in Latvia. A regional airspace monitoring system is being established under the auspices of the *Baltnet* project. The national information centre for Latvia will be housed at the Riga International Airport, and radar stations are to be set up in the *Ventspils*, *Gulbene* and *Rēzekne* districts. A computer network will be used to exchange data in the system.

The Air Force Information Centre is staffed by 36 officers and senior instructors, all of whom are graduates of the Latvian National Defence Academy, the Riga Aviation University or special training courses in Norway and Denmark.

The President of Latvia, Guntis Ulmanis,
Col. Juris Vectirāns review a military parade,
18 November 1997

Soldiers of the Security Service
protecting the *Saeima* building

The Military Police unit of the National Armed Forces after
the blessing of the unit's official flag on 5 August 1999

THE SECURITY SERVICE OF THE REPUBLIC OF LATVIA

The Security Service of the *Saeima* and the President of the Republic of Latvia is a separate military unit of the Latvian National Armed Forces. The Service provides protection to members of the *Saeima* and the Presidium of the *Saeima*, the President of Latvia and his or her family members, the Chancellery of the President, and the official residence of the President. On 26 November 1990, the Council of Ministers ordered the establishment of what was then known as the Separate Militia Patrol Service Battalion under the auspices of the Ministry of the Interior. The battalion had 300 men, and its first commander was Militia Maj. Juris Vectirāns. The unit was given the name of the Security Service of the Republic of Latvia on 22 January 1992.

Troops from the Security Service have provided protection for such dignitaries as French President Francois Mitterand, Pope John Paul II, Polish President Lech Walensa and US President Bill Clinton.

Four career officers from the Security Service of the Republic of Latvia were awarded the Badge of Honour of the Order of Three Stars in 1998.

Pope John Paul II blesses the flag
of the Security Service

THE MILITARY POLICE

The Military Police (MP) of the Latvian National Armed Forces is one of the most mobile units in the armed forces, and it has been structured in accordance to NATO standards. Soldiers and officers from the Military Police have participated in various MP courses in Latvia and abroad. In addition to its direct duties, the MP provides escorts for military cargo and personnel. It ensures order and conducts patrols. The MP performs investigations into violations committed in units of the Latvian Armed Forces.

On 25 March 1999, in memory of the victims of Communist terrorism, a memorial wreath with a "path of flowers" was placed at the Latvian Liberty Monument
by cadets from the National Defence Academy

The first graduation ceremony of the National Defence Academy on 26 August 1995

The Rector of the National
Defence Academy, Lt.
colonel Ilmārs Viksne

The first Rector of the
National Defence Academy,
Valdis Matiss

Guest lecturers are often invited to train officers

THE NATIONAL DEFENCE ACADEMY

The Latvian National Defence Academy was established on 13 February 1992, and its first Rector was Col. Valdis Matiss. The current Rector of the Academy is Lt. Col. Ilmars Viksne. The Academy is located at *Ezermalas iela* 6/8 in Riga. At the first graduation ceremony, on 2 October 1992, 73 lieutenants received certificates attesting to their completion of officer training courses. On 25 August 1995, the Academy graduated its first group of four-year graduates, each of whom received a bachelor degree in pedagogy and jurisprudence and qualification of mobile infantry platoon commander. Officers in Latvia are trained at two levels – platoon commander and company commander. Senior Latvian officers are trained at the Joint Baltic States Military Academy at Tartu in Estonia. The National Defence Academy has established solid co-operation with analogous units in Great Britain, Denmark, the United States, Canada and Finland. These have assisted in implementing various training programs and in providing training for cadets. At the time of this writing, 13 cadets were studying in Germany, while another 20 had already received certification in artillery, communications and field engineering. The Academy also has developed close co-operation with the military training academies of the other two Baltic States.

Cadets learn military skills

President Guntis Ulmanis visits the barracks of the Academy

SPECIAL TASK UNIT OF THE LATVIAN NATIONAL ARMED FORCES

The Latvian Special Task Unit was established on 19 September 1991. The unit is trained to handle anti-terrorism operations, special military operations requested by the Latvian National Armed Forces, as well as search and rescue operations on land and on water.

Reserve Officers Association of Latvia. In the centre is Benita Feldmane, to her right, the president of the Association, Juris Dalbiņš

Poet Māra Zālīte visits with the soldiers

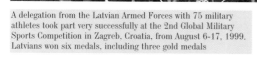

A summer sports competition for National Guard troops in *Aizpute*

The Headquarters Brass Band at a monument to Col. Fridrihs Briedis

A delegation from the Latvian Armed Forces with 75 military athletes took part very successfully at the 2nd Global Military Sports Competition in Zagreb, Croatia, from August 6-17, 1999. Latvians won six medals, including three gold medals

Aigars Fadejevs took gold in the 20-kilometer walk

Staņislavs Olijars won a gold medal in the 110-meter hurdles

Inese Motmillere took gold in Tae Kwan Do

Alla Popova won bronze in Tae Kwan Do

The Officers Ball at the building of the Riga Latvian Society

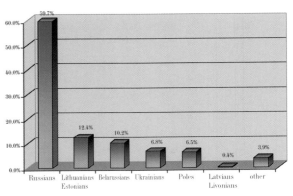

The distribution by nationality of applicants for citizenship

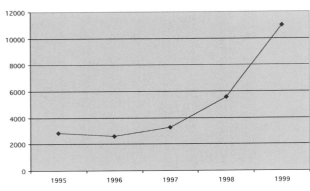

The intensity of the naturalization process

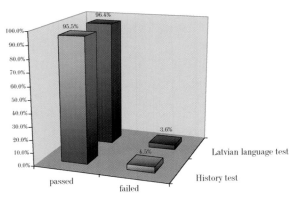

Results of the tests which are taken by applicants for naturalization

In a competition organised by the Naturalization Board for schoolchildren, young people answered questions about citizenship and social integration in Latvia and in foreign countries

The Information Centre of the Naturalization Board provides information regarding citizenship and integration of society issues

One of the most important tasks for Latvia after the restoration of independence was the settling of the issue of citizenship. On 2 July 1994, the *Saeima* [Parliament] adopted a citizenship law, which set out the procedures whereby non-citizens in Latvia could apply for Latvian citizenship. The law was harmonised with international experts, and in order to implement it, the Latvian Naturalization Board (*Latvijas Republikas Naturalizācijas pārvalde* – NP) was established on 18 October 1994.

Since 1 February 1995, more than 26,000 applications for naturalization have been received, and more than 19,000 people have become Latvian citizens. Beginning in 1999, children of non-citizens and stateless persons who were born in Latvia after 21 August 1991 were recognised as Latvian citizens. The NP also performs registration of Latvian citizens, as well as the annulment and renewal of citizenship.

The citizenship issue is just one of the issues, that must be resolved if Latvia is to establish a unified and well-developed society. In 1997 and 1998, a research and action program called *On the Road to a Civil Society* was implemented on the initiative of the Naturalization Board. Information that was obtained from the research project served as a basis for the formulation of the national program *Integration of Society in Latvia*.

Over the course of five years of operation, the NP has not received any serious complaints from the residents of Latvia, or any reproaches from the representatives of international authorities.

The chairperson of the *Daugavpils* City Council, Aleksejs Vidavskis, and the director of the Naturalization Board, Eiženija Aldermane, discussing citizenship issues in *Daugavpils*

An applicant for citizenship signs a promise to be loyal to the Republic of Latvia

The High Commissioner on human rights issues of the Organisation for Security and Co-operation in Europe, Max van der Stoel, is a frequent guest in Riga. He supports the work of the Naturalization Board and provides selfless consultations

The director of the Latvian enterprise *Aldaris*, Vitalijs Gavrilovs, and the director of the Naturalization Board, Eiženija Aldermane, congratulating employees of the company after they received Latvian citizenship

The Naturalization Board is housed in this building at *Smilšu iela* 1/3 in Riga

The Polish ambassador to Latvia, Jaroslav Bratkiewicz, and the head of the European Union's delegation to Latvia, Günther Weiss, talking with employees of the Naturalization Board

The Russian ambassador to Latvia, Aleksandr Udalcov, taking an interest in the work of the Naturalization Board

Representatives of the United States attend an official ceremony granting Latvian citizenship to people in the city of *Jelgava*. US Ambassador James Holmes is at the far right. Others include USAID representatives Howard Handler and Richard Presley

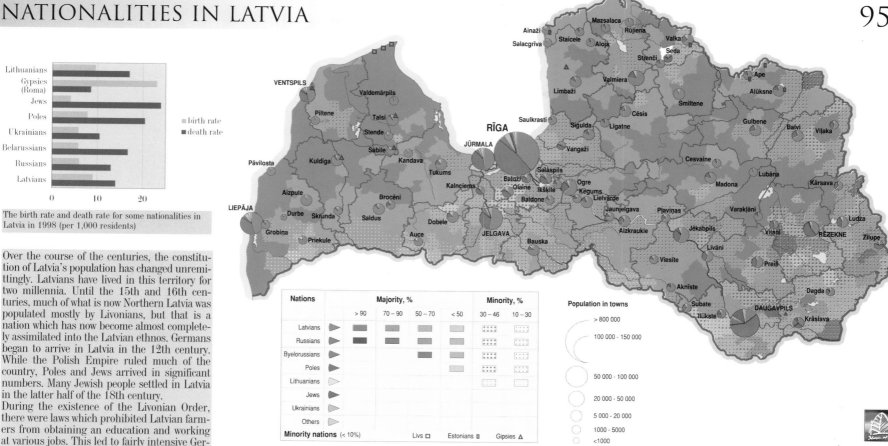

The birth rate and death rate for some nationalities in Latvia in 1998 (per 1,000 residents)

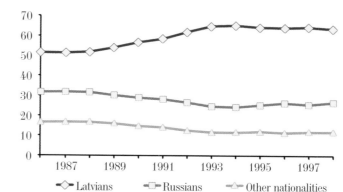

Nations	Majority, %				Minority, %	
	> 90	70–90	50–70	< 50	30–46	10–30
Latvians	▶					
Russians	▶					
Byelorussians	▶					
Poles	▶					
Lithuanians	▷					
Jews	▶					
Ukrainians	▶					
Others	▷					
Minority nations (< 10%)			Livs □	Estonians △	Gipsies △	

Population in towns
> 800 000
100 000 – 150 000
50 000 – 100 000
20 000 – 50 000
5 000 – 20 000
1000 – 5000
<1000

Over the course of the centuries, the constitution of Latvia's population has changed unremittingly. Latvians have lived in this territory for two millennia. Until the 15th and 16th centuries, much of what is now Northern Latvia was populated mostly by Livonians, but that is a nation which has now become completely assimilated into the Latvian ethnos. Germans began to arrive in Latvia in the 12th century. While the Polish Empire ruled much of the country, Poles and Jews arrived in significant numbers. Many Jewish people settled in Latvia in the latter half of the 18th century.

During the existence of the Livonian Order, there were laws which prohibited Latvian farmers from obtaining an education and working at various jobs. This led to fairly intensive Germanization, especially in the 19th century. Latvian surnames were *Germanized*, and children in mixed marriages were usually declared to be Germans.

Another specific group which settled in Latvia was made up of Russian Old Believers who fled repression in Central Russia in the 18th century. Large communities of Old Believers were established in Latgale and in the so-called *Moscow suburb* region of Riga.

Throughout the 19th century the tsar's government pursued active policies of Russification, and many Russian bureaucrats arrived in Latvia. As Riga was industrialized, large numbers of Russian, Polish and Lithuanian workers, civil servants and soldiers arrived in the city, especially between 1897 and 1915. During World War I, the country's population numbers plummeted. Most of the Russians who remained behind were the Old Believers, many of whom saw Latvia as their fatherland. Members of the Russian intelligentsia who also stayed in Latvia. The number of ethnic Latvians has grown more slowly than has been the case among other nations in Europe. In 1720 there were 200,000 Latvians in Latvia, in 1820 the number was 695,000, in 1881 it was 1.23 million, and the maximum was reached in 1914 – 1.8 million Latvians.

Both world wars had a significant effect on the population in Latvia. The number of Germans in the country declined from 120,000 to 58,000 between 1897 and 1920. The German minority departed completely during Hitler's repatriation program in 1939. The Molotov-Ribbentrop Pact contained clauses which addressed the emigration of Germans from territories which the

Soviet Union was planning to occupy. Some 70,000 Germans emigrated from Latvia. Those who remained behind either left in 1940 or were deported to Siberia in 1941. Ethnic Germans who live in Latvia today are people who arrived in Latvia after World War II from the communities of the so-called *Volga Germans*.

Both in World War I and World War II Latvia's influential Jewish minority was decimated. In 1897 there were nearly 150,000 Jews in Latvia, but after the first world war their numbers were estimated at between 80,000 and 100,000. The Nazi occupation of 1941-1945 and its Holocaust murdered almost all of them. During the Soviet occupation Jews who had managed to flee into Russia ahead of the German army returned to Latvia. Jews from Ukraine and Russia also arrived, although many emigrated to Israel and the United States during the relaxation period of the Soviet emigration policy in the 1970s and 1980s, and especially after the restoration of Latvia's independence in the 1990s.

The Soviet occupation completely changed the constitution of Latvia's population. The terror of 1940 and 1941, when civilians were murdered or deported, cost Latvia 35,000 lives. Another 60,000 people were drafted into the Red Army or fled to Russia with the army when the Germans invaded. Another 90,000 people – mostly Jews and Gypsies – died during the German occupation, while another 35,000 people were sent to Germany as laborers. In 1944 an estimated 120,000 Latvian residents fled as refugees to the west. Another 120,000 people fell or disappeared in various military pursuits during the war.

The terror and deportations of the Soviet Union's repressive machine cost another 70,000 people's

chart: Live births in Latvia between 1986 and 1998 (percentage of all live births, referring to the nationality of the mother) — ◇ Latvians ▢ Russians △ Other nationalities

lives, and another 100,000 were killed or deported between 1945 and 1953. Beginning in 1959, there was a massive inflow of Russian, Ukrainian and Belarussian workers into Latvia. The institutions of the Soviet Union gave money and Socialist advantages to people who moved form other parts of the USSR to Latvia to work in factories that had been built. Between 1959 and 1990, more than 575,000 non-Latvians moved into the country. The Geneva Conventions prohibit the settling of immigrants in occupied territories, but Russia did so, and very intensively. There was considerable migration in both directions throughout the occupation – more than 80,000 people moved in one direction or the other each year. The settling of retired Russian military officers in Riga was a particularly sore point. These were people with families, and their presence served to worsen Latvia's demographic situation. The share of pensioners in the population increased significantly. These are people who to this very day in many instances refuse to learn the Latvian language and to join Latvia's society.

In short, Latvia has been a multi-ethnic country since the 13th century. At the end of the 20th century there were 1.39 million Latvians, 719,000 Russians, 100,000 Belarussians, 66,000 Ukrainians, 62,000 Poles, 35,000 Lithuanians, 12,000 Jews, 8,000 Gypsies (Roma), 4,000 Germans, 3,500 Tatars, 3,000 Estonians and representatives of 136 other ethnic groups in the country.

THE IMMIGRATION POLICE

A working meeting with the commander of the Immigration Police, Aivars Kurpnieks

Inspection of passports on Latvia's border

Forged passports confiscated from illegal immigrants from various countries. Some 1,500 people are detained on Latvia's borders each year for passport-related violations

Latvia has acceded to the 1951 Geneva Convention and other international instruments on refugees. The Immigration Police Department is charged with battling against illegal migration. The Immigration Police was established in 1994. There are two kinds of illegal immigrants who arrive in Latvia in most instances – people from Southern Europe, the Middle East and Africa who are seeking for economic or (more rarely) political reasons to get to the Scandinavian countries, and people from the various countries of the CIS who still think of the entire territory of the Soviet Union as their land and who wish to live in the comparatively better economic situation which prevails in the Baltic States. Illegal immigrants are housed at a facility in *Olaine*.

The Estonian choir *Leelo* from Latvia always participates in Estonian Song and Folk Dance festivals in Tallinn. Estonians have close links with their ethnic fatherland, but they are actively involved in the Latvian culture events. All Estonians have a good command of Latvian and are integrated in the localeconomical community

Members of the Latvian Estonian *Leelo* choir in Tallinn

After services at the *Mazirbe* church

Estonian President Jiri Jaakson, who helped to found the Riga Estonian Education and Aid Society, with the first President of Latvia, Jānis Čakste

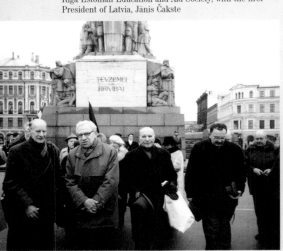

Members of the Latvian Estonian Association at the Latvian Liberty Monument in Riga to mark Estonia's national day

A half-hour broadcast in the Estonian language is aired on the first Monday of every month on Latvian Radio

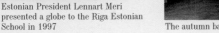

Estonian President Lennart Meri presented a globe to the Riga Estonian School in 1997

The autumn ball at the Riga Estonian Association

Estonians are one of Latvia's oldest ethnic minorities. Contact between Latvians and Estonians particularly developed in the 17th century, when both Estonia and the Latvian region of Vidzeme were part of the Swedish empire, and in the 18th century, after the Great Northern War, when both lands fell under the control of the Russian Tsars. As late as the 19th century, there were parts of Vidzeme in which Estonians formed a majority of the local population. A few colonies of Estonians were found in areas further from the border between Latvia and Estonia. They emerged during the period of serfdom, when members of the aristocracy moved people back and forth among their estates in Estonia and Latvia. Eventually most of these Estonians assimilated into the Latvian nation.

At the end of the 19th century there were still 18,000 Estonians living in Latvia. Contacts between the two nations have also been promoted over the years by the University of Tartu and what is now the Riga Technical University, where both Estonians and Latvians have studied.

The Riga Abstinence Association, which was formed in 1900, turned into the Riga Estonian Education and Aid Society in 1908. At that time, there were some 27,000 Estonian residents in Latvia. In 1911, the Society bought a piece of land and a building in *Nometņu* street in Riga, and in 1913, a six-story building was built for the Society's needs. It was designed by the distinguished architect Eižens Laube. One of the early chairpersons of the Society was Jiri Jaakson, who later became the President of Estonia. He laid the cornerstone for the building on 28 April 1912. An Estonian language school was organised in the building.

The Riga Estonian Association was liquidated after the Soviet occupation in September 1940. The Soviets took over the building, and later Latvian Television was housed there. The Association regained control over its building only in 1997.

Latvia's Estonians have their own choir, *Leelo*, which regularly participates in Estonian Song festivals. Estonian artists exhibit their works in Riga from time to time. Most of Latvia's Estonians are descendants of families that have deep roots in Latvia, so more than one-half of them are citizens of Latvia. Latvia's Estonians tend to have good Latvian language skills, and they are integrated into Latvia's society as active participants in political and social affairs. Members of the Association often travel to Estonia to visit museums or theatres, and to participate in Song and Folk Dance festivals. In 1996, the Latvian Estonian Association was admitted to the Estonian Central Council, which was formed in the 1950s in New York, USA.

The Estonian primary school that began work in Riga in 1908 was also closed down by the Soviet occupation. The school resumed its work in 1989. The primary aim of the institution is to ensure that Estonian children in Latvia learn at least the rudiments of the Estonian language, as well as to provide them with an opportunity to learn about Estonian literature, history and ethnography.

Estonia's pre-war leader and President, Konstantin Päts, and the commander of the Estonian Army, Johan Laidoner, also had links to Latvia. In 1919, the Estonian army helped Latvian forces to free Latvian territory. The Estonians suffered large losses during this time, but their enormous contribution to ensuring the independence of the Latvian Republic was not forgotten. Laidoner was awarded the highest rank of the Latvian Order of Three Stars.

Today, there are approximately 3,000 Estonians in Latvia, concentrated mostly in Riga, as well as the towns of *Alūksne* and *Valka* close to the Estonian border.

Livonians, also known as Livs, are a Finno-Ugric nation which has lived for centuries in Vidzeme and Kurzeme. The ancestors of the Livonians are Finnish tribes which lived in what is now Latvia some 3,300 years BC. The Livonian language emerged during the 1st millennium BC. Archaeologists feel that a distinct Livonian culture emerged in the 10th century AD. The first written report about Livonians and their language which has survived to this day is a report by a monk from Kiev called Sylvester, who wrote a chronicle in the 11th century in which he used the ethnic designation *ļibj*. The first information about Livonians in Latvian historical sources is found in the Chronicle of Indriķis from the 12th century. During this period there were four different groups of Livonians – the so-called *Daugava* Livonians, the *Gauja* or *Turaida* Livonians, the Metsepole Livonians and the Kurzeme Livonians. Between the 10th and 13th centuries, Livonians were an active ethnos, maintaining economic and cultural links with their neighboring Balts and Estonians, as well as with Slavic tribes and Scandinavians.

The Vidzeme Livonians were the first tribe in Latvia to fall victim to the German Crusaders, and they were drafted to fight against Estonians, Latgallians and other ethnic groups. Livonians suffered great losses during the feudal wars of the 16th to the 18th centuries, as well as in the epidemic of the Black Plague which struck Latvia in 1710 and 1711. The Livonian language disappeared from Riga and its environs in the 16th century and from Vidzeme in the 19th century.

In the early 20th century Livonians lived on the Kurzeme seashore, in the *Auce* and *Dundaga* parishes, opposite *Sāmsala* island along a stretch of fishing villages some 60 kilometers long and a few kilometers wide. This band of territory was set apart from the rest of Latvia by uninhabitable forests, swamps and meadows. This was a natural boundary between seashore Livonians and dry land Latvians, and it protected the Livonians from assimilation into the Latvian ethnos. Contacts with Latvians were upheld always, however, and Livonians have always spoken the Latvian language very well. Livonians were fishermen and depended on that industry for their living. The life of a fisherman was more dangerous than that of a farmer. While the men went out to sea, their wives grew potatoes and grain in the sandy soil of the seaside.

Livonian national constumes in northern Kurzeme

The *Ovišbāka* lighthouse, built in 1814. It is an enormous brick building of a height of 38.1 meters. The light itself is 33 meters above the building. *Oviši* is a Livonian fishing village. Among its natives is the former director of the Riga Museum of Nature, the prolific author Karlis Princis

The sea at *Jūrkalne*

A monument to Livonian fishermen on the shore near *Mazirbe*

The number of Livonians in Kurzeme in 1915 was around 3,000, but World War I was fateful for the community. In 1915 the German army occupied the seashore, and people were given 24 hours to move out of the Livonian villages and at least 10 kilometers inland. People were allowed to take along only what they could carry or load into horse-drawn carriages. The land 10 kilometers in from the sea was swampy and forested. The refugees were forced to go even further into Latvian territory and seek refuge in Latvian villages. Many could not find their place and went into exile. Some got into fishing boats and tried to cross the Bay of Riga to Estonia. When three years later the refugees were allowed to return to their former homes, the fields were gone, there were no livestock, and most buildings were ruined. People had lost their boats, their nets and their fishing tools. There were only some 1,000 Livonians left after World War I, and children no longer spoke the Livonian language.

In the 1920s there were people who spoke the Livonian language in the villages of *Lūžņa*, *Miķeļtornis*, *Lielirbe*, *Jaunciems*, *Sīkrags*, *Mazirbe*, *Košrags*, *Pitrags*, *Saunags*, *Vaide*, *Kolka* and *Melnsils*.

Finnish linguist Andress Sogren in 1846 and 1852 studied the Livonian language well enough to be able to publish a German-Livonian dictionary. From 1882 until 1912, another Finnish linguist, Emil Setele, studied the language, and later he became a noted Finnish statesman. In London in 1863, St. Matthew's Gospel was published in Livonian in 250 copies. The gospel had been translated by a Livonian teacher, Nika Polmans.

Professor Lauri Ketunen published a Livonian dictionary in Helsinki in 1938. A period that can be seen as the Livonian national awakening occurred from 1920 until 1930. Activists including Kārlis Stalte and Didriķis Volganskis established the Livonian Association. The national hymn of the Livonians used the same music as the national anthems of Finland and Estonian. The words were written by Kārlis Stalte. A Livonian flag was consecrated on November 18, 1923.

In 1938 a Livonian called Mārtiņš Lepste attended a Finno-Ugric Cultural Congress in Budapest. Delegates to the congress decided to support the construction of a public building for Livonians in Latvia. People and groups from Finland, Estonia and Hungary sent money, and the Latvian government contributed its share. A piece of land was bought in the center of the town of *Mazirbe*, and a Livonian People's Building was put up after a design by the Finnish architect Erkki Hutonen. The building was consecrated on August 6, 1939.

Livonians had two Lutheran congregations, one in *Irbe* and the other in *Kolka*. Beginning in 1923, a teacher called M. Lepste taught the Livonian language for one hour each week to Livonian children at five elementary schools in the region. There were small notebooks in the Livonian language with brief readings from folklore materials – those were the only teaching materials that were available. During Latvia's independence, there was a Livonian administrative center in *Dundaga*, while major support came from the city of *Ventspils*, which the Livonians know as *Lembikila*.

A Livonian man called Edgars Volganskis, who later changed his surname to the more Livonian Vaalgamaa, was a student at Helsinki University when Latvia was occupied by the Soviet Union. He remained in Finland, where he became a clergyman and, later, a dean in the Finnish Evangelic Lutheran Church.

Many of the few Livonians who were alive in Latvia at the start of World War II perished as a result of Soviet activities. A large number in 1944 and 1945 got into boats to flee to Sweden. During the Cold War the Kurzeme seashore was a frontier zone, and access to it was possible only with military permits. Fishermen in seaside villages were banned from going out to sea, and the historical source of employment for the Livonians was lost. Children were banned from learning Livonian in school, and Livonian could not be listed as a nationality in Soviet passports. During the 50 years of Soviet occupation, the Livonians became largely assimilated, and today there are just a few elderly people left who can still speak Livonian.

In the 1970s the Livonian intelligentsia, receiving support from cultural workers in Estonia and Latvia, began to legalize the cultural life of Livonians, establishing the ensembles *Līvlist* in Riga and *Kāndla* in *Ventspils*. In 1988 the Livonian Association, which had been shut down in 1940, was reopened. In 1991 the Council of Ministers of Latvia declared much of the ancestral territory of Livonians along the Kurzeme seashore to be a specially protected zone known as the *Livonian Shore*. A Livonian Cultural Center opened its doors in the zone in 1994. The monthly journal *Līvli* and annual almanacs are published regularly, and Livonians and their descendants enjoy an active cultural life. Toward the end of 1999 the Latvian Cabinet of Ministers accepted a long-term targeted program, *Livonians in Latvia*.

A totem to commemorate the 75th anniversary of the public organization *Līvõd Īt* (Livonian Association)

The first Saturday of every August is Livonian Festival Day. Here Valda Šuvcāne discusses the history of the Livonian People's Building in *Mazirbe*

Song Festival senior conductor Jānis Erenštreits and parliamentary deputy Ilmars Geige are both Livonians

A memorial ceremony to remember Livonians who perished during World War II. Livonian national flag is green-white-green at the same proportions as the flag of Latvia

Edgars Vaalgamaa, son of Didriķis Volganskis, studied in Finland, where he continues to live. He is active in maintaining cultural contacts between Latvia and Finland

Didriķis Volganskis-Vaalgamaa (1884-1968), one of the founders of the Livonian Association

The Livonian People's Building in *Mazirbe*

At the Livonian festival in *Mazirbe*

Professor Saulvedis Cimmermanis is an expert on the traditions, ethnography and history of the Livonians

Icons from the Grebenshchikov Old Orthodox Church in Riga

Yuri Samarin (1819-1876), a public figure and theorist on Slavic philosophy, lived in Riga from 1846 to 1848

Yuri Tinanov (1894-1943), a writer and educator, born in Riga

Vasili Sinaiski (1876-1948), professor at the University of Latvia, Faculty of Economics and Law

Vladimir Bukovski (1867-1937), professor, University of Latvia, Faculty of Economics and Law

Ivan Zavoloko (1897-1984), scientist, researcher of the culture of the Old Believers

Religious literature at the Grebenshchikov Old Believers' Church

Leonid Arbuzov (1882-1951), professor, University of Latvia, Faculty of Philology and Philosophy

Nikolai Zadornov (1904-1993), writer, resident in Riga after 1946

Boris Popov (1871-1947), professor, University of Latvia, Faculty of Chemistry

Nikolai Bogdanov-Belski (1868-1945), artist and instructor, resident in Latvia after 1921

Tsar Nicholas II on the waters of the *Daugava* in 1910

Russian tsars visited Riga on an annual basis, and they were always interested in the construction of the *Daugavgriva* pier and the Riga harbour. Stones embedded in the pier attest to the presence of the emperors

Boriss Vipers (1888 – 1967), historian of art

Roberts Vipers (1859-1954), professor, University of Latvia, Faculty of Philology and Philosophy, historian

The first references to the presence of Russians in Latvia can be found in the 13th-century Chronicle of Indriķis of Livonia. Russian traders lived in the city of Riga, and Russians owned several buildings; they had their own cemetery, the St. Nicholas Church and a convent that was used as a hotel and shelter. The part of Riga's Old City in which Russian residential buildings, public buildings and warehouses were found was known as the *Russian homestead*. It is possible that the first stone Orthodox church, in

Jersika, was built with the help of Russian labourers.

Russia's national specifics were seen most vividly in the lives of Old Orthodox and Orthodox Christians in Latgale. Throughout the 19th century and into the 20th century, various ethnographic elements of Russian life – houses, specifics of clothing, food typical of Northwestern Russia – were common there.

At the end of the 18th century and in the beginning of the 19th century, the first Russian organisations and associations were established. A shelter for handicapped individuals was set up by the Riga Old Orthodoxals in 1750, and in 1818, the cornerstone for a Russian Trade Building was laid. In 1816 the first issue of a Russian newspaper – *Rossijskoje Jezhenedelnoje Izdanije* – was published with the support of Lutheran clergyman August Albanuss.

A new phase in the social life of Latvia's Russian community began around 1860, when liberal forces in Russia achieved significant reforms. The Russians established several associations, the newspaper *Rizhskij Vestnik* (1869-1917), and the Russian Theatre (1883).

The vast majority of Russians supported Latvia's independence in 1918. During the Latvian War of Independence (1918-1920), 30 Russians received the Order of *Lāčplēsis*, the highest military award in Latvia. A specific aspect of Russian culture in Latvia in the 1920s and 1930s was its extensive heterogeneity. Concerts by Fjodor Shalapin and Alexander Vertinski were enormously popular. Mikhail Chekhov brought theatrical performances to Riga. Poets Igor Severjanin and Ivan Bunin organised literary evenings, philosophers Nikolai Berdy and Ivan Ylyin addressed rapt audiences. Among the

Mikhail Chekhov (1891-1955), actor, director, studio director at the Russian Drama Theatre in the early 1930s

Mstislav Keldish (1911-1978), educator, president of the Soviet Academy of Sciences (1861-1975), born in Riga

Yuri Abizov (b. 1921), the writer who translated much of Latvian literature

Marina Kostenecka (b. 1945), writer and active participant of the Latvian Awakening

Ivan Safonov, artist, at a presentation of his paintings at the Russian *RAU Lyceum*

The St. Boris Gleb Church in *Daugavpils*, built in 1907

Services at the St. Boris Gleb Church

The first Old Orthodox prayer house in *Daugavpils* was built in several phases between 1908 and 1928

The St. Nicholas Orthodox Cathedral in *Liepāja*, built between 1900 and 1903. Russian Tsar Nicholas II attended its dedication

Studies at an Old Believers' school

An Old Orthodox church

A Russian home at the Latvian Ethnographic Open Air Museum

The architecture of a Russian farmhouse

Russian newspapers in Riga was one of the largest and most literary publications by Russian émigrés anywhere in Europe – *Segodnja*, which was first published in 1919 and, after 1924, was accompanied by a daily supplement, *Segodnja Vecherom*.

In the late 1990s, there were nearly 750,000 Russians resident in Latvia – more than 30% of the population. The number of Russians exceeds that of all other non-titular nationalities by 2.5 times.

The village of *Židina* in *Daugavpils* district, populated by many Russian Old Orthodox

The graveyard of the *Kiši* cloister church

A cloister church at *Kiši*

The Old Orthodox church in *Panteliški*

During the renewal of Latvia's independence – the period known as the National Awakening – noted representatives of the Russian intelligentsia supported the process – the writers Yuri Abizov, Ludmila Azarova, Roalds Dobrovenskis, Vladlen Dozortsev and Marina Kostenecka and others. Dozorcev, who was also the editor of the popular magazine *Daugava*, became a member of the board of the Latvian Popular Front (LPF). With the participation of the LPF, a Latvian Association of Russians was set up in 1989 to develop Russian national culture, to expand on traditional Russian and Latvian contacts, and to co-operate with representatives of all of the nations resident in the republic.

Much of Latvian public life takes place in Russian. There are Russian language educational institutions at all levels – pre-schools, schools and universities. The largest non-Latvian periodicals in Latvia are all in Russian – the newspapers *Novij Denj*, *Vesti*, *Chas*, *Panorama Latvii*, *Bizness & Baltija*, *Subbota*, *Russkaja Gazeta*, *Obrazovanjije iz Karjera*, and others. The literary and arts journal *Daugava* is published. There are also Russian-language radio and television stations.

Several Russian newspapers in Latvia

A program from a performance a the Riga Russian Drama Theatre

Leo Dribins

UKRAIŅI
LATVIJĀ

Ēriks Jēkabsons

Ilga Apine

POĻI
LATVIJĀ

BALTKRIEVI
LATVIJĀ

Latvian scientists have done research on the history of Ukrainians, Poles and Belorussians in Latvia and gained substantial insight into their cultural and economic activities and their level of integration among Latvians. Books about Ukrainian, Polish and Belarussian ethnic minorities have been published in Latvia in 90's

CZAS ŁATGALII

The masthead of the Polish newspaper in Latvia, *Czas Latgalii*

Ita Kozakiewicz (1955–1990)

Riga Polish high school student ensemble

A celebration at the Ita Kozakiewicz Polish School

Polak na Łotwie

The masthead of the Polish magazine *Polak na Łotwie*

First communion at the St. Christ the King Church on 16 May 1999

Pupils at the Polish school

POĻU TAUTAS
MĀKSLAS UN TRADĪCIJU MĒNESIS

MIESIĄC POLSKIEJ SZTUKI
LUDOWEJ I TRADYCJI

The program of a Latvian Polish festival

Voluntary workers from Latvia's Polish community

BELARUSSIANS

Belarussians, who also used the *Daugava* River as a route for trade and traffic, established contacts with Balts in ancient times. Since the Middle Ages, Belarussian farmers, tradesmen, craftsmen and clergymen have lived in Latgale, Zemgale and Riga. The number of Belarussians in Latvia increased significantly in the second half of the 19th century, when capitalistic modernisation began in the Baltic States, as well as after World War II. The ethnic group reached its apogee in the late 1980s, when some 120,000 Belarussians lived in Latvia.

An extensive Belarussian cultural life began to appear during the first period of Latvian independence. In the 1920s, there were some 50 Belarussian schools in Latvia, two high schools, as well as national associations. The Belarussian scientists and public figures, Sergei Sakharov and Kastus Yezavitav, conducted research regarding Belarussians in Latvia.

In the renewed Latvia, Belarussian cultural development has occurred around a nucleus of two national societies – *Svitanak* and *Pramen* – and the Riga Belarussian Elementary School. The Belarussian Cultural Fund has been in operation in Latvia since 1995, and the *Svitanak* society is a member of the World Association of Belarussians.

POLES

The Polish community began to form in Latvia in the late 16th and early 17th century, during what came to be known as *the Polish times*. Data from an 1897 census show that there were approximately 60,000 Poles in Latvia – one-half of them in Latgale and one-fifth in Riga. This number remained virtually unchanged during the 20th century. In the late 1990s, there were some 62,000 Poles in Latvia.

Polish culture was brought to Latvia by Catholic monks, clergymen, aristocrats and members of the intelligentsia. They maintained the presence of the Polish language in schools, research into the folklore and history of Latgale, the architecture of churches and baronial estate buildings, the establishment of libraries and the foundation of national associations. Even before the declaration of the independence of Latvia in 1918, Poles had theatre groups, newspapers, etc. Poles were actively involved in the political life of the Republic of Latvia.

One of the leaders of the Latvian national renaissance at the end of the 1980s and early 1990s was the president of the Latvian Polish Union, Ita Kozakiewicz. She was, among other things, a member of the executive of the Latvian Popular Front and one of the most active and passionate defenders of the idea of a renewal of the independence of Latvia. Ita Kozakiewicz was proclaimed *Latvia's Woman of the Year* in 1993.

After the restoration of independence in Latvia, several Polish organisations emerged, including the Latvian Polish Union with 13 territorial divisions, *Promien*, and others. The magazine *Polak na Łotwie*, the newspaper *Czas Latgalii* and six Polish ethnic schools were established. Six Polish people were elected to the 7th Latvian *Saeima*, including the chairman of the Latvian Polish Union, Tadeusz Ketler.

UKRAINIANS

The number of Ukrainians in Latvia at the beginning of the 20th century was very small – some 300 people. Still, they managed to establish a national organisation, *Gromada*, in Riga. A much larger Ukrainian community emerged in Latvia after World War II. In 1989, there were 92,100 Ukrainians in Latvia (at the end of the 1990s – 68,000).

During the Latvian national renaissance, the Ukrainians established a national organisation, *Dnipro*. In 1991, the Latvian Centre for Ukrainian Culture and Economy was founded, and in 1996, the Latvian Ukrainian Union emerged. A Ukrainian high school began work in Riga in 1991, and nearly 300 students attended the school at the time of writing. The Ukrainian minority in Latvia actively supported Latvia's efforts to regain independence, and many Ukrainians are enthusiastic about learning the Latvian language and obtaining Latvian citizenship.

The masthead of the Belarussian newspaper *Golas Belarusa* in Latvia

The masthead of the Belarussian magazine *Svitanak*

The Belarussian national flag flew above the Riga Castle during the national renaissance in Latvia

An album of ancient postcards from Riga produced by Viacheslav Telesh

A folklore festival at the Riga Ukrainian school

A meeting between Latvian President Guntis Ulmanis and Ukrainian President Leonid Kuchma

Ukrainian school children at a sports festival

A theatre performance at the Ukrainian school

Mikola Bilosicki

Young participants at an athletic festival organised by the Belarussian society *Svitanak*

The head of by the Belarussian society *Svitanak*, Viacheslav Telesh

ДЖЕРЕЛЬЦЕ 1997

A poetry journal produced by pupils at the Riga Ukrainian High School

Several artistic groups are active under the auspices of the Latvian Ukrainian society *Dnipro*

Pupils and teachers at the Riga Belarussian school

Konstantin Ronczewski (1875-1935) was a sculptor and architect

A bust of the Latvian artist Vilhelms Purvitis by Konstantin Ronczewski

A bust of the collector of Latvian folklore Krišjanis Barons by Konstantin Ronczewski

A meeting at the Lithuanian embassy in Riga. From the left: Lithuanian schoolchildren, Lithuanian parliamentary deputy Rimantas Smetona, Lithuanian Ambassador to Latvia Petras Vaitiekunas, Riga Lithuanian Elementary School principal Aldona Treija, and Latvian parliamentary deputy Romualds Ražuks

Dr. Romualds Ražuks is a neurosurgeon who is also a member of Parliament. He was formerly chairman of the Latvian Popular Front and was known as an outstanding participant in the events of the Latvian national awakening. At this writing, he was head of the Latvian delegation to the Baltic Assembly

Paulus Baltakis, who is the representative of Pope John Paul II among the Lithuanian diaspora, at the Lithuanian Elementary School in Riga. The principal of the school, Aldona Treija, is at the right

A calendar for Latvia's Lithuanians in 1938

A member of the board of the Educational and Cultural Center, Jons Rudoks

Eduardes Vilkelis, executive director of the Lithuanian Association of Commercial Banks, and Teodors Tverijons, president of the Latvian Association of Commercial Banks – both men are ethnic Lithuanians

The Lithuanian delegation at Latvia's Minority Sports Festival

Celebrating the New Year

The dramatic theater troupe from the Riga Lithuanian Elementary School

Lithuanians from Latvia visit a spa town in Druskininkai in Lithuania

Lithuanians and Latvians come from one and the same linguistic group – the Baltic languages – and they are related nations. Lithuanian tradesmen settled in Riga as early as the 14th century. By the second half of the 16th century Lithuanians were establishing villages in Southern Latvia and Latgale, where the community continued to maintain its ethnic identity all the way through the 20th century. Latvians, in return, lived in the *Žemaitija* region of Lithuania, especially around the towns of *Klaipėda* and *Palanga*.

An increase in the number of Lithuanians in Latvia was stimulated by the rapid development of Latvia's industrial sector and the country's cities in the latter half of the 19th century and the early part of the 20th century. At the start of World War I, there were some 50,000 Lithuanian residents in Latvia. During the initial years of Latvia's independence, many Lithuanians went to Lithuania, which had also become free. Some 25,800 remained in Latvia. The number of Lithuanians increased again in the late 1950s, when people who had been deported to Siberia began to return to the region. Many were prohibited from settling in Lithuania, so they instead moved to towns in Latvia that were close to the Lithuanian frontier. Today there are approximately 34,000 Lithuanians in Latvia.

Contacts between the Latvian and Lithuanian nations have promoted close links between the cultures of the two nations. The cultural association *Aušra* opened its doors in Riga in 1881, while in 1894 Lithuanians in Latvia set up a self-help organization which served economic and cultural functions alike. A choir and a theatrical troupe were established. In the early 20th century, a Lithuanian school was opened in Riga. In 1904 Lithuanians in the capital city established a singing and musical association called *Kankles*. It had its own choir, theatrical troupe and library. Beginning in 1909, Lithuanian journalists in Latvia produced the newspapers *Rygos Garsas* and *Rygos Naujienos*, as well as a humor monthly called *Juokdari*.

Lithuanians in Latvia supported Latvia's independence efforts, and some 500 Lithuanians fought with the Latvian armed forces during the war of liberation. Eight were awarded the Order of *Lāčplēsis* – Latvia's highest military honor. Latvia's laws between the two world wars and a high level of tolerance in society allowed the Lithuanian community to flourish. A private Lithuanian elementary school opened its doors in Riga in the 1918 school year. Three other elementary schools were established in Riga and one each in *Liepāja* and *Jelgava* in subsequent years. In 1923 a Lithuanian high school was opened, and it had a choir, a library and a youth club. New cultural organizations, including the youth group *Šviesa* with branches all over Latvia, *Rūta*, a University of Latvia student association called *Viltis* and others were established.

A new phase in the life of Latvia's Lithuanians began in 1931, when the community organized a major congress in Riga at which an umbrella organization, the Association of Lithuanians in Latvia, was founded. Its chairman was Daniels Jasinskis (1866-1939). Several Lithuanian newspapers – *Rygos Balsas*, *Lietuviu Balsas* and *Naujas Žodis* – published news about politics and life in Latvia and abroad.

The restoration of Lithuanian cultural life in Latvia coincided with the period of liberalization and democratization that took place in the Soviet Union in the late 1980s and when Latvia restored its independence in 1991. In 1998 approximately 600 local Lithuanians came together to found the Latvian Lithuanian Cultural Association, chaired by Romualds

Ražuks. After 1989 Lithuanian organizations were also established in other parts of Latvia. 1989 was an important year for Lithuanian journalists in Latvia, who began publication of the newspaper *Latvijos Lietuvis*. The Latvian Lithuanian Community – another umbrella group – was established in 1991, and it, too, was chaired by Ražuks, who was simultaneously chairman of the Latvian Popular Front. The Community engages in a wide variety of cultural activities, and it has set up choirs, folk dance ensembles, folklore groups and athletic teams. A folklore ensemble from the Community participated in the global Lithuanian Song Festival in 1994 in Vilnius, and sports teams participated successfully at the Fifth Global Lithuanian Games. Lithuanians in Latvia have also established an elementary school in Riga, which is directed by principal Aldona Treija.

The President of Lithuania Valdas Adamkus at the Riga Lithuanian elementary School

The song ensemble *Rūta*

The theatrical troupe of the Riga Lithuanian Elementary School on stage

Lithuanian schoolchildren participate in a competition called *Guess what!*

The *Gypsy Friends* ensemble in 1933

Gypsies class in the town of Ventspils. A specialized Roma prime has been published in Latvia

Цыганка.
Я буду пѣть, пока поется,
Пока волненья позабыла,
Пока горячо сердце бьется,
Пока я жизни не пережила.

Kārlis Rudēvičs and a painting he produced of his son, Normunds Rudēvičs, who at the writing of this book was a member of Latvia's parliament

Member of the 7th *Saeima* Normunds Rudēvičs

A Roma-Latvian-English and Latvian-Roma dictionary has been published in Latvia

A volume of poetry, *Gipsy Heart*, by Kārlis Rudēvičs in Latvian and Roma

Justice Minister Valdis Birkavs together with father and son Rudēvičs at the billiard table

The Roma people originally emerged in ancient times from Northern India. In the 15th and 16th century they arrived in Latvia from Germany and Poland, continuing to live in their clans, preserving their traditional way of life, and working as musicians, soothsayers, horse trainers and blacksmiths.

The number of Gypsies in Latvia in 1935 was 3,800, and the population was growing, but during the Nazi occupation the Roma were one of the nations against which genocide was waged. Some 2,000 people were put to death. In post-war years the number of Gypsies increased consistently to some 8,000 at this time. The largest Roma populations are found in Riga, *Ventspils*, *Jelgava* and (especially) *Kuldīga*, *Sabile*, *Kandava* and *Tukums*.

The Roma people in Latvia have a wealth of unique folklore – songs, stories and anecdotes. The cultural heritage of the Gypsies in Latvia has been studied by Jānis Leimanis, who is himself Roma, as well as the Baltic linguist Pauls Ariste. Leksa Manush collected and systematized Gypsy folklore and studied the influence of Baltic languages on the Roma language used in Latvia, as well as the religious life of the Roma and other issues.

The Roma language has split up over the centuries as the Gypsies have moved all across the world. Modern Roma speak in varying dialects, depending on where they live. In Latvia there are four major dialects, but the language of Gypsies in Kurzeme dominates. The cultural association *Roma* was established in *Talsi* in 1990. There are two Gypsy ensembles in *Sabile*. A residential school for Roma children with three classes has been opened in *Ventspils*. Lessons are taught in Latvian, but Roma is taught as a separate subject, using a Roma reader and a Roma-Latvian dictionary.

The Roma minority in Latvia has become well-integrated into Latvia's life. Modern Gypsies live in homes instead of living the wanderer's life. More than 90% of Latvia's Gypsies are citizens of Latvia, and they speak Latvian. They have preserved their own rituals and holidays, but they have also accepted Latvian holidays and traditions – Christmas and the summer solstice. Gypsies do not become assimilated, and some 6,000 people in Latvia consider Roma to be their native language. Families strictly observe tradition, and mixed marriages are very uncommon.

Gypsies in Latvia are currently worried about a lack of educational and professional training opportunities. The Roma poet and cultural worker Normunds Rudēvičs is a member of Latvia's parliament. Indeed, he is the only Roma parliamentarian anywhere in Europe.

JEWS IN LATVIA

The Israeli ambassador to Latvia, Oded Ben Hur

The chairman of the Latvian Jewish Communities, Grigorijs Krupņikovs

At the gates of the Riga ghetto, 1941

Jewish people have lived in Latvia for hundreds of years. In the late 19th century, Jews were the largest ethnic minority in Latvia – 142,000 people, or 7.4% of the total population. In many cities, especially in the Latgale towns of *Rēzekne*, *Ludza* and *Daugavpils*, they were in the majority.

Jews in Latvia worked in various professions, including crafts and trades, as merchants, and many were representatives of the intelligentsia. In the latter half of the 19th century, Latvia's Jews established a strong community with a wide-ranging social and cultural life. The democratic system, which existed in the Republic of Latvia from 1918 until 1934, was particularly favourable for the development of the Jewish community. Jews had their own political parties, including *Ceire Cion* and *Bund* on the left and *Agudat Israel* and *Mizrahi* on the right of the political spectrum.

World War II was a catastrophe for Jews in Latvia, as in the other countries of Europe that were occupied by the Nazis. Most of Latvia's Jews were murdered in the Holocaust. The Germans brought Jews to Latvia from all over Eastern Europe, initially as workers, and then as victims of the slaughter. Assisting the Germans in their barbaric behaviour were some mentally ill and sadistic Latvians who came together in the infamous group known as the *Viktors Arājs group*.

The tragedy of the Jews in World War II is typified by the fate of two brothers, Professor Pauls Mincs and Professor Vladimirs Mincs.

Pauls Mincs (1868-1941) was a lawyer and a professor at the Faculty of Law of the University of Latvia. He had been an elected deputy to the Constitutional Assembly, the Auditor-General, a member of the Cabinet, an official at the Office of the Prosecutor and at the Ministry of Justice. In 1940, when the Soviet Union occupied Latvia, the authorities arrested Mincs with his wife and son. Professor Mincs died in a concentration camp in Siberia.

Vladimirs Mincs (1872-1945) was a physician and surgeon at the Riga Jewish Hospital, and he also lectured at the University of Latvia, heading the Department of Medicine for a while. In 1918,

he was among the surgeons who operated on Lenin after an assassination attempt. When Hitler's forces arrived in Riga in 1941, Vladimirs Mincs was imprisoned in the Riga ghetto, and later he perished in Buchenwald.

There are fewer than 15,000 Jews in Latvia today.

The contribution that Jews have made in Latvian culture has been very significant. Jews have developed their national traditions in art, science, literature and journalism. Jews in Latvia are of critical importance in terms of the development of culture in Europe and the world.

One of the most distinguished Latvian Jews was the historian Shimon Dubnov (1861-1941), who wrote a 10-volume history of world Jewry. Jeshayahu Leibovic (1903-1994) was a biochemist, philosopher and physician who taught organic chemistry and neuro-physiology, and modern-day Israel has recognised him as one of the world's leading religious thinkers. His most important books include *In the footsteps of the Maimonedes* and *Conversations with God and the world*.

Another distinguished scientist and organiser of scientific activities was Solomon Hiller (1915-1975), who organised the Organic Synthesis Institute of the Latvian Academy of Sciences and served as its director after 1957. He was a professor at the Riga Technical Institute and studied a wide range of medications and agricultural medicines, looking for ways for them to be utilised and produced. He personally designed a number of innovations in the development of medications, as well as new ways of synthesis in chemistry. Hiller was the author of more than 400 academic and popular articles. While he was the director of the Organic Synthesis Institute, an experimental medications factory was created which later became the major Latvian pharmaceutical firm *Grindex*.

A major figure in the Jewish theatre, Solomon Mihoel (1890-1948) was born in *Daugavpils*, and the European-renowned singer Herman Jadlovker (1877-1953) was a cantor at the Riga synagogue.

Rabbis became active in Latvia in the 18th century, and especially of note was the Stuls dynasty of rabbis in *Bauska*, Rabbi Lihtenšteins of *Tukums* and others. These were men who produced more than 50 books of importance to the world's culture and literature. The most important contributor was Rabbi Josif Rosin (1858-1936).

Latvian-born Jews were of considerable importance in the development of culture in Latvia and elsewhere in Europe. Among them were the world-famous philosopher Isaiah Berlin (1909-1997), who was a professor at Oxford, and Jurijs Fajers (1890-1971), who was the concert master of the orchestra of the Riga German Theatre and, later, the conductor of the Bolshoi Theatre in Moscow. Fajers staged a performance of Tschaikovsky's *Eugene Onegin* in Riga in 1912

Dentist and teacher Vladimirs Vigdorčiks (1909-1997)

Writer and publicist Marks Razumnijs (1896-1988)

Professor Shimon Dubnov (1861-1941), the 20th century's leading Jewish historian

Professor Makss Šacs-Aņins (1885-1975), an attorney and sociologist

Abraham Isaac Kuks (1865-1935), a rabbi in *Bauska* and chief rabbi of Palestine

Marks Lavri (1903-1967), a conductor at the Latvian National Opera and the composer of the first Jewish opera

Professor Mečislavs Centneršvers (1874-1944), a chemist who was head of the *Ahdut* association of the Jewish intelligentsia

Professor Solomon Hiller (1915-1975), a chemist and an organizer of scientific work

Professor Adolfs Mecss (1885-1944), a violinist

Professor Pauls Mincs (1868-1941), a lawyer who served as the national auditor of Latvia and as a Senator of the Supreme Court

Professor Vladimirs Mincs (1872-1945), a surgeon

Actor and director Arkādijs Raikins (1911-1987)

Philosopher Marks Vaintrobs (1895-1941)

Sculptor Naum Aaronson (1872-1943)

Composer Oskars Stroks (1892-1975)

A monument to Žanis and Johanna Lipke, two Latvians who during the German occupation (1941-1944) hid 55 Jews in their home, thus saving them from certain death

The chief rabbi of Riga and Latvia, Natāns Barkāns at the Riga synagogue

Rabbi Barkāns presents a candlestick as a gift to President Guntis Ulmanis

Israeli Prime Minister Binyamin Netanyahu and President Ulmanis

Rabbi Barkāns, President Vaira Viķe Freiberga and Zālamans Joffe, the head of the Jewish religious community

which did a lot to promote the formation of a Latvian opera troupe at the theatre. Opera star Leonid Zahodnik (1912-1988) was an instructor who taught many of Latvia's prominent stage artists. Romualds Grīnblats (1930-1995) composed a ballet, *Rigonda*, based on Vilis Lācis' novel *Pazudusī dzimtene* (*Fatherland Lost*). Professor Vladimirija Muzaļevskis (1894-1964) organised the Department of Musical Science at the Latvian Conservatory of Music, and hundreds of theorists and instructors were educated there. Professor Lija Krasinska (b. 1911) wrote a number of monographs about Latvian and Russian composers. The violinist Tovijs Lifšics (b. 1928) established a chamber orchestra with an extensive repertoire of some 600 pieces of music. The orchestra became known all over Europe. Oskars Stroks (1892-1975) is known as a composer of tango music.

Among artists, distinguished accomplishments belong to Aleksandrs Dembo (1931-1999), who was a leading graphic artist in Latvia throughout his life, bringing modern reality together with folklore and historical conscience in his work. Chaim Risin (1911-1998) worked with metal in his art, but he was also the designer of a number of underground subway stations and palace interiors.

One of the world's leading sculptors, Naum Aaronson (1872-1943), was born in *Krāslava*, Latvia, and later worked in Paris. Aaronson's work focused on children and famous people. His sculptures of children are gentle and light and imbued with an incomparable sense of joy. He depicted Dante, Moses, Socrates, Washington, Bolivar, Chopin, Wagner, Berlioz and Pasteur. He set up an image of Lev Tolstoy in the town of the great writer's birth, Jasnaja Polana, and he participated in exhibitions all over the world. French critics dubbed him "today's classical artist". In *Krāslava* the artist built a shelter for poor orphans, and his sister, Anna Aaronson, ran it for many years.

The Art Nouveau architect Mikhail Eisenstein (1867-1921) was responsible for one of Riga's most unforgettable thoroughfares – *Alberta iela*. Pauls Mandelštams (1872-1941) built more than 60 buildings in the school of National Romanticism, as well as Art Nouveau.

Jewish people have played a very important role in the development of the theatre in Latvia. Pavels Homskis (b. 1925), a director at the Riga Youth Theatre, established one of the best children's theatres in all of the Soviet Union. He also worked at the Riga Russian Drama Theatre, where he staged the plays of Latvian playwrights in order to introduce Russian audiences to Latvian art. Adolfs Šapiro (b. 1939) was the senior director at the Youth Theatre, and he, too, staged a number of Latvian plays. Šapiro wrote: "He who has lived a long life in Latvia but has not tasted the poetry of Latvian life has spent his days in this country in vain". Arkadijs Kacs (b. 1931) led the Riga Russian Drama Theatre for 25 years, moulding it into one of the best theatres in the entire Soviet Union. He also worked at the *Daile* Theatre with Latvian actors, staging classic Russian plays.

A film by Pavels Armands (1902-1964), *Salna pavasari* (*Frost in the Spring*), was based on several short stories by Rudolfs Blaumanis, demonstrates that the director had a deep sense of the Latvian mentality. Hercs Franks (b. 1926) wrote the screenplay for the film *Gada reportāža* (*Commentry on the Year*, 1965), which demonstrates the approach of a talented artist in analysing complex social problems.

Jozefs Hiršhorns (b. 1899 in Jelgava, d. 1981 in Washington) was a Latvian-born Jewish multimillionaire and art collector who became a millionaire on Wall Street before he reached the age of 30. Shortly before the stock market crash and bank collapse of 1929, he invested $4 million in uranium mines in Canada, where gold was found, too, in 1936. His investments were recouped many times over when the nuclear age began. Hiršhorns was a notable collector of modern art, and in 1974 he presented his entire collection to the American government. Worth $50 million at the time, it featured several paintings by Latvian artists. Hiršhorns never forgot the Latvian language.

Riga also contributed two world-class chess players to the world. Ārons Nimcovičs (1886-1935) was a leading player and world-renowned theorist. Born into the family of a wood salesman in Riga, he was only 10 years old when he began to publish original chess moves in the local press. Mihails Tals (1936-1992) was the world champion in chess in 1960 and 1961, and he won the world chess Olympics eight times as a member of the Soviet team. He won the Soviet championship six times. Tals has been the subject of a great many books and newspaper and magazine articles, but he himself was also a very talented journalist, who wrote: "If chess were clearly seen as a sport, science or art, then I don't believe it would be as possible. Chess is a wonderful cocktail, which every man can mix according to his own recipe. The three components cannot be separated easily. Initially, of course, it is a game for competition and leisure, a game with excellent rules that allow one to forget oneself. It is also a sport, albeit a very specific one, because the battle is over wins and points. Without good physical readiness, you cannot survive modern chess marathons, that's also true. A science? It is no surprise that cybernetics specialists are so interested in chess. Logic, the large volume of knowledge that you have to have – all of that brings chess closer to science – a science which never has a solution that is 100% correct. The scientific and technological revolution has affected chess. The volume of information has increased, the average level of preparedness among chess players has increased immeasurably, and total chess dominates. Everyone has to be a bit of an athlete, a bit of a scientist, a bit of an artist. Each of these properties comes to the fore at its own time."

A delegation of Israeli parliamentarians at a monument to the victims of Fascism at *Rumbula*

The Riga synagogue

The opening of the second international conference *Jews in a Changing World*, August 1997, Riga

Professor Leo Dribins, a historian

Professor Hermans Branovers

The *Purim* festival

Children are being taught the traditions of Sabbath, including the lighting of the candles

A vase produced by artist Haims Risins (1989)

The *Purim* festival, with Israeli ambassador Oded Ben Hur in the center

A Jewish wedding

Porcelain artwork from members of the Studio of Applied Arts

Students from the Riga Jewish High School and the Riga Jewish dance group *Maagaļ*

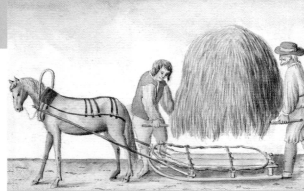
Gathering of hay, a drawing by J.K. Brotze

Threshing of grain in the early 20th century

A farmer mows his hay in the 1950s

People used to harvest grain by hand, tying it into sheaves and drying it out on racks before threshing

The horse was always a good assistant when it came time to gather potatoes

In earlier times, farmers who were sowing their fields had to shoulder a basket and walk across the territory, step by step

In the 18th century, the French ambassador to Stockholm wrote to his government: "The grain that is obtained in Vidzeme is better than grain from any other place, because grain is usually dried out in ovens (in threshing barns) before it is threshed, and so it can be stored for 8-10 years, when needed, without fearing that it will become spoiled, as is the case with Polish and Prussian grain that must be stirred at least once a week so that it does not dry out and rot. The grain in Vidzeme must be stirred just once or twice a year, and there is no risk in that case. The grains are small and even tiny, but the skin of the grain is very thin, and when ground up, it provides much more flour than is the case with grain that comes from warmer countries with larger grains. It is also important that despite the fact that grains are dried, the grain sown in more easterly regions provides an even greater harvest. No area of the world is more useful for storing up grain than Vidzeme." France was also interested in the flaxseed that was grown in Latvia and sold in Riga, in hemp grown in Kurzeme, and in the mast trees of Vidzeme.

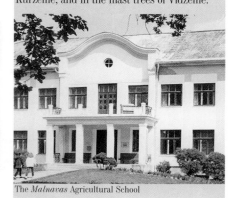
The *Malnavas* Agricultural School

The Latvian schools of agriculture have a long tradition. The first of them was opened in *Veczvārde* in June 12, 1853. The studies lasted for 3 years and comprised teaching of agriculture, vegetable-growing, beekeeping, hop-growing as well as skills for construction, blacksmith, barrel making and roofering.
For training needs the school had cow from Eland and Holstein, Sawdon sheep and Essex and Yorkshire pigs, and farming equipment. Melioration was tought for the first time there. Because of the costly foreign teaching facilities the fee for studies was quite high and the school was closed down after some years due to the lack of students.

AGRICULTURE

The management of the Ministry of Agriculture – Juris Kuzme, Jānis Lapše and Marģers Krams

The hay season is over, and the racks stand empty

Latvia produces wheat, rye, barley and other grains

The photographer Valdis Semjonovs and editor Ilze Bumane of the newspaper *Lauku Avize* have travelled over all of Latvia

Peteris Pikše, a grower of flower bulbs from *Mārupe*, one of the most professional in Latvia

The chairperson of the share society *Uzvara-lauks* Maris Purmalis from the *Bauskas* district in a sugar-beet field

Preparing the land for sowing

The Erdmaņi farming family of *Ezergaiļu* farm, *Vārmes* parish, *Kuldigas* district

The Vinters brothers and their father farm
400 hectares of land in a parish, enjoying good harvests

Janis and Anna Griboniks, who live in *Sama* parish,
Preiļi district, farm 200 hectares of land with the help
of their children

Sowing peas at the
Priekuļi grain-breeding
station

Over the centuries, Latvia has been a country of enormous agricultural wealth. In all times, Latvia has exported grain, vegetables, meat and especially dairy products – butter and cheese. The greatest volume of dairy products and bacon was exported from Latvia when it was independent between the two world wars, and the exports went to Western Europe.

During Soviet times, Latvia was a significant supplier of meat and dairy products to Moscow and Leningrad (now St. Petersburg). Latvia built enormous facilities to raise pigs and cattle, because livestock feed was imported through the Riga port, and it was most advantageous to raise livestock in Latvia, exporting meat to the centre of Russia. When the Russian rouble was devalued in 1991, the import of feed was cut off, and meat and milk production in Latvia declined. Latvian exports of dairy products to Russia declined at the beginning of the 1990s. Since 1990, the volume of added value in the agricultural sector, when measured in fixed prices, has declined from year to year – by 55% between 1990 and the time when this book was written. The proportion represented by agriculture in overall added value declined from 21% to 3.6%. Within agriculture, the proportion of hunting and forestry declined from 10.4% in 1995 to 4.5% in 1998. The decline in agricultural production in the 1990s occurred largely because of a serious narrowing in domestic and external sales markets, as well as unfavourable changes in the price of agricultural products. Latvia's agriculture, generally speaking, has rather low productivity today.

Approximately 15% of all the people who are employed in the Latvian economy work in agriculture. When the added value per employee in Latvia is calculated, the sum is much lower than the EU average. This is mostly because farms are small, equipment is worn out and technologies are out-of-date. Most of the production buildings in Latvia (60-65%) were built 50 or 60 years ago. Latvian agriculture in 1990 was dominated by livestock farming, but now most of the output comes from crop farming products. The volume of meat produced in Latvia reaches only about one-half of consumption volumes, and nearly one-half of meat production involves the processing of pork. Latvia's pig breeders produce far too little pork, however, to meet domestic demand. The main reason is that Latvian farmers cannot compete with cheaper imported pork. Our products also cannot compete in the international market, because other countries subsidise their farmers.

Latvia produces enough milk to satisfy domestic demand for milk and dairy products. Latvia's climate is very appropriate to ensure highly productive and economically effective meadows, pastureland and perennial pasture grasses, and this makes it possible to develop livestock breeding, and especially dairy farming. The productivity of Latvian cows, however, is comparatively low, because unspecialised farms dominate in the industry. In 1999, two-thirds of milk cows in Latvia lived on farms that had between one and five animals. Small farms use less-than-nutritious and otherwise poor-quality feed. The producers themselves consume a lot of the milk that is obtained, or else it is sold

Zeltite and Janis Kavieris, who own the *Silkalni* farm in *Vaidava* parish, medicinal plants and are happy to share in their grow

Janis Rukšans is well known throughout Latvia as a developer of new flower varieties

Martiņš Augstkalnietis from the *Malupe* parish in *Alūksne* district farms 200 hectares of land, mostly growing grains

The Krieviņu family from *Cesvaine* in the *Madona* district at their market garden

Janis Silagailis owns the largest planting of medicinal plants in *Klintaines* parish, *Aizkraukles* district

Inese and Andris Fogeļi from *Vaidava* parish, *Valmiera* district in their potato field

Harvesting of potatoes at *Vārpas* in the *Lēdurgas* parish, *Limbaži* district

Sugar-beet harvesting at the *Uzvara-lauks* in the *Bauskas* district

A shop in *Pūre*, where the villagers and the Riga - Ventspils highway drivers can buy the extremely tasty local goods

Gatis Karlovskis grows rapeseed on his farm, *Veģi*, in the *Sēja* parish of Rīga district

Ruta and Imants Norkarkli from *Salinieki* in the *Rožkalni* parish, *Preiļi* district

- At the *Piebalga* farm in *Jaunpiebalga*, Jānis Duklavs brews beer from Latvian barley, hops and honey.

Barley has been grown in Latvia since about 2000 BC.
The name *alus* (beer) is from the German *alo* or the Estonian *olu*. Latvian names were *miestiņš* or *medalus*, which was very typical in Latvia and sweetened with honey, and *tāpiņš*. Beer was brewed in Latvia not only with barley, but also from wheat, oats and buckwheat. To the beer was added oak bark, milfoil, marsh tea and hops. In ancient times, beer was prepared also from heather. Such beer was also known to the ancient Celts. In the 18th century, beer was prepared from small-reeds, pine and fir branches, but the folksongs also mention a beer made from birch buds.
Prior to the utilisation of oak barrels, beer was fermented in open containers and it was drunk while still fermenting. It is considered that beer began to be brewed in barrels in Latvia already in the 13th century. In Latvia beer is most often prepared from barley malt, hops, water and yeast, with caramel malt and burnt malt added. The basic components are 90% water and food additives: dextrin, sugar, pentazone and various caramelisation products. A light beer with a relatively small content of food additives is most typical in Latvia. Beers brewed in Latvia usually have an alcohol content of 4 to 5.5%.

The potato (*kartupelis*) which are also called *tupeniši* and *rāceniši* in Latvian, is for Latvians another form of bread. They were first introduced into Latvia during the time of Duke Jēkabs (middle 17th century)

Kaspars Brunovskis and his sister Kristine own one of the largest plots of vegetables in Latvia. They farm the *Ezerkalniņi*-4 farm in Rīga district

The only piece of machinery in the Baltic area which, at the same time, ploughs the land, cultivates, sows grain and spreads fertiliser

Farmers Voldemars and Anna Kotāns from *Ilzeskalns* parish, *Rēzekne* district, and their grand-children

Jānis Ieviņš manages *Melba Ltd.* in *Degole* parish, *Tukums* district

One of the largest fields of flax in Latvia is owned by Edgars Mazalevskis, who runs the *Vitoli-2* farm in *Pušmucova* parish, *Ludza* district

Imants Lepsis, chairperson of the *Kurzemes dārza oga* (Kurzeme garden berry) farm, stands among raspberry plants

Flowering plum trees at the *Dobele* Horticultural selection and testing Station

unprocessed. In 1998 and 1999 there was a rapid improvement in the quality of dairy products, however, and processing companies have provided financial stimuli for this.

Along with dairy farming and pig breeding, a priority sector in Latvian agriculture is grain farming. This process must satisfy domestic demand for grain, as well as the demand for high-energy feed milk in cattle breeding, pig breeding and poultry farming. Latvia could produce a high volume of grain for export. Taking into account the development in livestock farming in Latvia, the demand for grain may double over the present-day level. The amount of land and other resources available in Latvia should permit development that is much more rapid. At time of this writing, Latvia was preparing an investment project that would finance the building of the largest plant in the Baltic States to produce grain alcohol, and this would use up all of the surplus grain in the Baltic region.

Good grain harvests and stable grain quality is easier to ensure in large farms. A small farm lacks resources, and in many of them grain is raised in a way that does not conform to agricultural and technical requirements. The harvests on small farms are comparatively low and of poor quality. The smallest farms also have problems in selling their grain, because export and processing require large-volume supplies of grain that is of an even quality.

The production of sugar beets involves a specialisation and concentration in cultures, and agricultural technologies are being modernised. Output is on the rise. There are two sugar factories in Latvia – one at *Liepāja* and the other in *Jelgava*. A third, in *Jēkabpils*, had to be closed because it was not making a profit.

Potatoes are mostly grown for self-consumption in Latvia. Since 1990, the proportion of agricultural products produced on individual farms and household plots in Latvia has increased from 28 to 80% in the overall agricultural sector. Unfortunately, at the time of this writing the trade balance in agriculture and food products in Latvia was negative. A deterioration in the situation in 1998 was caused in large part by a reduction in agricultural and food product exports to Russia, which was suffering a financial crisis. In 1998, exports to the countries of the CIS were nearly one-half lower than in the previous year. The trade balance in food products with Lithuania and Estonia has also been negative.

As it often happens farm owners find untraditional occupations. Arturs Dukulis is a co-owner of *Grūbes* hydroelectric station in the *Ape* rural territory

Galiņi farm was formed by buying an empty wood workers' house in 1989. Now this farm grows potatoes (20 hectares), vegetables (30 hectares) and strawberries (4 hectares). Vegetables and strawberries get into markets of the neighboring Baltic countries as well as to the Latvian market. The farm run by Juris and Kārlis Strazdiņi owns a fruit and vegetable store in Riga.

Strawberries from the *Galiņi* fields

Juris Strazdiņš holding vegetables grown in his farm and the other co-owner of the *Galiņi* farm Kārlis Strazdiņš in the strawberry garden

This 1688 map of the *Vainiši* castle manor in *Limbaži* district was drawn with a goose-feather quill

A hoe that was used to crumble earth

The most ancient evidence of land reclamation in Latvia is a fragment from a building in the *Araiši* lake castle, which features a pile of stones used for drainage purposes in the 9th century. The archaeologist who worked at this site was Janis Apals

A wood board land reclamation box that was used in the 19th century

Clay drainage pipes came into use in Latvia in 1850

This kind of drainage pipe, which was made in *Lode*, was particularly popular in the 1970s and 1980s

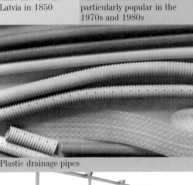

Plastic drainage pipes

A floodgate system controls the water level in the *Pape* lake

Omuļu „Jaun-Viķu" melioracijas projekts 1927.9.

A detailed land reclamation map prepared by the Land Culture Bureau of the Latvian Central Agricultural Association in 1927

Peteris Nomals (1876-1949) was a distinguished researcher of swamps who described swampy areas in all of Latvia's regions

Janis Mednis (1904-1996) established the *Malpils* Land Reclamation Museum in 1967

Antons Kursišs (1883-1968) researched Lake *Lubāna* in Latvia and was instrumental in work that was done to regulate the water level of the lake

Spēkonis

A steam excavator, *Spēkonis*, was bought in 1927 from the American Steel Dredge Company. Its fuel was wood

Pauls Brunavs (1910-1998), who was a high-ranking official in the Canadian Hydrographic Service and directed land measuring work in that country

The main building of the *Mālpils* manor, built in 1760, now houses the Latvian Land Reclamation and Agricultural Museum. It is an architectural monument of national importance

A group of land reclamation veterans who helped to collect the valuable and unique items that are on exhibition at the Reclamation Museum

The history of land reclamation in Latvia began back in 1850, when reclamation of land at the *Puņi* manor began. The fact that Latvia gets quite a bit of precipitation each year means that land becomes swampy on those occasions when there is insufficient drainage. Over the last 100 years, therefore, land reclamation has been an important part of everyday life in the country. During the Soviet occupation, land reclamation was part of the State plan of the USSR, and what was important back then was not whether the swampy land was drained, but rather how many kilometres of drainage pipes were laid. Thousands of kilometres of pipes were also placed in locations, which were too dry. The land reclamation ditches that were dug were usually not tended properly, and they often grew over. Drainage pipes clogged up. What is more, the land reclamation process, was used by the Soviets to destroy the culture of countryside. In the name of land reclamation, unique single-family homesteads were torn down, ancient trees were destroyed, and majestic alleys of trees disappeared forever. Because of this, many people in Latvia think of land reclamation as an evil process, and during the first years after the renewal of independence, no land reclamation was done at all. It was only in 1998 that work to drain swamplands began once more.

Draining of agricultural fields with fascines in Latvia in the 1920s

Drainage work with an ETN 142 excavator

Tree growth after draining

VEGETABLE AND GRAIN SELECTION

Timothy *"Priekuļu 2"*

Potato blossom, times ago used a decoration in royal courts

Potatoes *"Bete"* are good for salad

"Laimdota" is suited for different kinds of toil

Early potatoes *"Madara"*

"Agrie Dzeltenie" — the most demanded sort from *Priekuļi* Selection Station

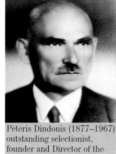

Dr. Uldis Miglavs, Director of the *Priekuļi* Selection Station

Onions *"Kapiņa"*

Kurzemes sēklas Ltd. at an exhibition

The origin of evidence based vegetable selection in Latvia was the beginning of the XX century, when seeds camo from abroad. It gave start to the efforts of local gardeners, who began to estimate, adopt and improve imported seeds, to select new sorts and grow seeds. This work is still carried on in a much more modern way at present.

The most distinguished Latvian vegetable-growing specialists are Pēteris Dindonis (cucumbers *"Dindoņa zaļie ķekari"*, several sorts of tomatoes), Pēteris Veisteris (field tomatoes *"Pūres konservu"*), Vasilijs Taranovs (tomatoes *"Jūrmala"*), Larisa Bite (field cucumbers *Pūres 70*, hot-house cucumbers *"Sprīdītis"*), Lidija Švalkovska (rhubarb *"Tukuma 5"*, *"Ogrese 13"*), Ernests Kapiņš (onions *"Kapiņa"*) etc.

Latvian gardeners have selected also the lettuce sort *"Rīga"*, winter garlicks *"Ķente"*, caraway *"Kamarde"*, sweet peas *"Latvian Red"*, *"Pēcis"*, *"Dzintra"*, and the Swedish turnips *"Dzeltenie ābolu vietējie"*.

The production of seeds of these and other sorts takes place in the seed growing company *Kurzemes Sēklas Ltd*. This company also demonstrates new foreign sorts and estimate their appropriatness for Latvia.

The first Latvian agriculture specialists were trained in the Department of Agricultuire by the Riga Politechnical School, established in 1863. The first teaching institution for gardening was the National Gardening School *Bulduri* (1910). Today the young specialists are trained in the Latvian University of Agriculture and in *Bulduri*.

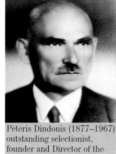

Pēteris Dindonis (1877–1967) outstanding selectionist, founder and Director of the *Bulduri* Gardening School

Cucumbers *"Pūre 70 F1"*, by Larisa Bite

The red clover *"Priekuļu 66"* in blossom

"Griva" cucumbers

Kurzemes sēklas Ltd. demonstrating seeds

Harvesting *"Griva"* cucumbers

Consultants in vegetable growing and agronomy Māris Gailītis and Jan Langerkok from the Netherlands giving advice to farmers

Internationally recognized selectionists Valdis Dubovskis and Mārtiņš Maltenieks by their sweet peas *"Pēcis"*

Seed cabbage *"Amager 611"* in field

Kurzemes sēklas Ltd. in *Talsi* – the biggest seed producing company in the Baltic states

Kurzemes sēklas Ltd. offers seeds of vegetables, flowers and grain. They are in use in Latvia as well as in Lithuania, Estonia, Poland, Ukraine and recently are available in Western Europe

The name of the old master Peteris Upitis is closely tied with the *Dobele* Horticultural Development and Experimentation station

"Forele" apples

"Atro" apples

"Jumurda" pears

Quince

"Iedzēni" apples and the developer of the variety, Rūdolfs Dumbravs

"Suvenirs" pears

"Stars" apples

"Atmoda" apples

Pears at the *Dobele* Horticultural Station

Evalds Pupols has cultivated the largest grape field in Latvia at *Rudziši* farm near *Viesīte* in *Jēkabpils* district

The Hungarian Andrašs Fazekašs cultivates grapes and produces tasty Latvian wine in *Gulbene* district

Apricots in *Dobele*. Rich yields of apricots are gathered farthest to the north

The development of new varieties of fruits and vegetables in Latvia is associated with the names of horticulturists Roberts Aboliņš, Aleksandrs Maizitis and Rudolfs Dumbravs from *Iedzēni*. We must also mention the late director of the *Dobele* Horticultural Development and Experimentation Station, Pēteris Upītis. The work of these masters today is being continued by Professor Mara Skrivele and the current director of the *Dobele* Horticultural Station, Edite Kaufmane. Kārlis Lapiņš, who lives in the United States, has become famous throughout the world with the apple varieties that he has developed. Latvia's fruit horticulturists have moved the natural growth area for peaches, apricots and grapes considerably to the North. Latvian varieties of apples, pears, grapes, plums and other fruits and berries, as well as their taste and quality characteristics, are often not only equivalent to, but actually surpass the world's best varieties.

"Daiga" apricots

A *"Lāsma"* apricot

"Lāse" plums

"Alvis" plums

"Dīta" raspberries

"Ivars" raspberries

Horticulturists Roberts Aboliņš and Aleksandrs Maizitis from *Iedzēni*

Professor Mara Skrivele

"Minjona" plums

Edite Kaufmane, director of the *Dobele* Horticultural Station

"Kuršu dzintars" gooseberries

"Koknese" gooseberries

"Zilga" grapes. The first grapes in Latvia were introduced already by Duke Jekabs

"Supaga" grapes. Good dry red wine is made in Latvia, however it is just for local consumption for now

"Spulga" grapes

Horticulturist Karlis Lapiņš

"Viksnes" currants

"Lapiņš" cherries

FLOWER SELECTION

Viktors Orehovs created Latvia's flower selection school, and his lily, "*Saule*", is still well known today

Horticulturist Jānis Rukšāns spent many years as editor of the magazine *Dārzs un Drava*, and flowers selected by him are famed throughout the world – the Siberian eutronium, the crocus "*Michael Hoog's Memory*", the tulip "*Girlfriend*", the narcissus "*Aivita*", the crocus "*Carpathian Wonder*", and the wormwood "*Snowstorm*"

Between 1965 and 1990 there was a flower *boom* in Latvia. The Latvian Gardening and Bee-keeping Association had some 65,000 members. Latvia's flower-growers had a large ready market – Russia, which bought 15 million flowers every year. On International Women's Day, which was celebrated in the Soviet Union on March 8, Latvian flower-growers set out across the entire former Soviet Union to sell tulips – from Yuzhno-Sakhalinsk in the East to Kaliningrad in the West, from Murmansk in the North to Tashkent in the South. On Victory Day on May 9 and 10, Latvians sold field grown tulips all over Russia. Everyone grew flowers – members of the intelligentsia, blue-collar workers, doctors and teachers. It gave Latvians an opportunity to survive financially, and it taught them the basic principles of a free economy. Most flower-growers sold their own blooms and bulbs, but there were also wholesalers who bought flowers from Latvian growers and transported them for sale in Russia. These were people who gained their first rudimentary business skills early, and later many became important businessmen and politicians in post-Soviet Latvia. The *boom* in flowers promoted a growth in the cultivation of new varieties of flowers. People understood that only those who moved with the times and utilised the very latest varieties of flowers would have success in business. Very soon, Latvians discovered that this was an area in which they could compete with the rest of the world. Today the work of Latvian flower horticulturists has set new standards for bulbous plants and other selected flowers throughout the world.

Jānis Vasarietis
and his selected day lilies

V. Skuja with his tulips that are popular throughout Western Europe – "*Flaming Baltic*", "*Burtnieks' Rose*", "*Green King*", "*Fame of Sigulda*", "*S-680*" and "*S-547*"

Peteris Upitis, who is known as the father of flower selection in Latvia, and his lilacs - *"Zilaiskalns"*, *"Jaunkalsnavas nakts"*, *"Gaiziņkalns"*, *"Imants Ziedonis"* and *"Mother Ede Upitis"*

Professor Rihards Kondratovičs is a distinguished horticulturist, seen here with his son, Associate professor Uldis Kondratovičs. They introduced rhododendrons to Latvia, moving the growing range for this beautiful flower considerably to the North. The two men created excellent varieties of rhododendrons and acacias, including *"Austra"*, *"Liesma"* and *"Polārzvaigzne"*, which are seen here. To the right: A garden of rhododendrons in *Babite*, Latvia.

Aldonis Veriņš is the world's most prominent gladiola selectionist at this time. He has created more than 300 varieties of gladiolas, and of these, 113 varieties are registered in international registers; 25 of which, in the course of time, have been acknowledged as the best. No. 258, *"Dave's Memory"*, was at the top of the North American Gladiolus Council's (NAGC) list for 15 years and has received acknowledgement as the best fine-blossom gladiola of all time. No. 377, *"Janus Song"*, was recognised as the top gladiola variety of 1999 by a NAGC symposium. Aldonis Veriņš' selected gladiolas are grown throughout the world. Here we see *"Janus Song"*, *"Lavender Queen"*, *"Queen"*, *"Zelta dieviete"*, *"Dave's Memory"*, *"Salmon Moon"* and *"Pretty Woman"*

A windmill at Latvia's Open Air Ethnographic Museum

A shelter for mill horses

The *Araiši* windmill and an adjacent sauna

Another windmill at the Open Air Ethnographic Museum

The *Aizpute* water mill

A mill is a machine used to grind grain into flour, pearl barley, groats, etc. Mills are powered by water, steam or the force of wind, with electricity or even with horses and hand power. There are different grades of milling. One produces flour for simple, rough bread and stock feed, while the other grinds rye, wheat and corn into finer and cleaner flour without husks – flour that is used for white bread and other purposes. Individual fine grinding processes include cleansing of grain, the milling itself and sifting.

DOBELES DZIRNAVNIEKS

The stock company SC *Dobeles Dzirnavnieks*, which owns one of the largest mills in Latvia, was established based on the former *Dobele* Grain Products integrated enterprise. The history of the facility dates back to 1976, when the first grain elevator at the site was completed. The production and administrative buildings of SC *Dobeles Dzirnavnieks* are located at *Spodribas iela* 4 in the city of *Dobele*.

The company purchases, stores and processes grain, producing wheat flour, mixed flours, various kinds of groats, macaroni and mixed livestock feed. The company also is always seeking to develop its sales system.

The quality of SC *Dobeles Dzirnavnieks* products is guaranteed by the technical level of its equipment, the highly qualified specialists who work at the company, the high quality of raw materials that are used, and the supervision of the entire process with modern laboratory equipment.

Production director Andris Dancis, commercial director Valdis Muižnieks, technical director Vadims Pavlovičs, general director Broņislavs Skrebs, finance director Lauma Liepa, council chairman Vitauts Paškausks

The central laboratory

The mill of the *SC Dobeles Dzirnavnieks*

SC Dobeles Dzirnavnieks

Grain storage facility at *Bauskas Klēts*

The mills at *Bauskas Klēts*

Bread baked by *Bauskas Klēts*

BAUSKAS KLĒTS

The Latvian region of Zemgale is well known as the breadbasket of the country, and that is how the enterprise *Bauskas Klēts* got its name – the word *klēts* in Latvian refers to a granary. Investments by four founding members and the availability of bank credits allowed the establishment of a modern mill in 1992. Today *Bauskas Klēts* employ 140 persons and boast a net annual turnover of 1.15 million lats.

The word *klēts* in its traditional sense is expanded when it comes to the operations of the enterprise. *Bauskas Klēts* not only processes and stores grain, but also grinds it in its own mills and then with the flour that results produces bread and pastry products.

With the help of German specialists, *Bauskas Klēts* from the very beginning chose equipment that is used in EU countries and that guarantees high-quality products which are certified and fully in conformity with the growing needs of modern consumers. The company produces 21 kinds of bread and more than 50 kinds of pastry products.

The operational policies of *Bauskas Klēts* are aimed at ensuring that the profits of the enterprise are ploughed back into development. A new investment project is put in place every year. In the first year, the enterprise built a grain receiving and storage complex with a drying room. In the following year the enterprise bought equipment, built a white bread baking facility, later a pastry department and shop was opened, along with a mill, the second phase of the baking facility, and a flour storage facility.

Bauskas Klēts was founded by Rolands Vinogradovs, Kaspars Greiselis and Viktors Skrebels, who continue to run the enterprise today.

The *Smiltene* mill

The *Lobe* mill

The dam of the *Ate* mill in the *Alūksne* district

A song by Eduards Rozenštrauhs about an old windmill and a miller was very popular in Latvia during the 1960s and 1970s. To Latvians, a miller is a symbol of honest work and prosperity

THE STABURADZE BAKERY

The president of SC *Staburadze* is Ivars Rudzitis

SC *Staburadze* produces a wide range of bakery products

The Vilhelms Ķuze bakery in the 1930s

The fantastic pies produced by *Staburadze*

In 1910, a man called Vilhelms Ķuze established a bakery in Rīga. Its output was exported to Europe, North America, Australia and several countries in Asia. During Soviet times, the factory was known as the June 17th Factory, but in 1992, it was given the name of *Staburadze*. Today the stock company SC *Staburadze* is one of the leading bakeries in the Baltic States, producing a wide range of sugar cookies, rolled cakes, crackers, butter cookies, butter cakes, waffles, waffle pies, fruit pies and marzipan.

THE JAUNPAGASTS SPIRITS FACTORY

Aivars Podnieks, director of the *Jaunpagasts* Spirits Factory in *Talsi* district

A recently built boiler house produces the steam that is used in the factory's technological processes

A vodka line, *Avoti*, which was opened in 1999 and which uses modern technologies to ensure high-quality output

The executive board chairperson of the factory, Dainis Peimanis, seen here in the brewing room of the facility. Each day the factory processes between 34 and 35 tons of Latvian-grown wheat and rye, obtaining 1,500 decilitres of alcohol in every 24-hour period. The alcohol is used for medical purposes and in the production of vodka

This farm in *Virbu* parish uses products, which have been used in the process of alcohol production as livestock feed

This facility dates back to 1937, when the company *Spirta Kopdedzinātava* was established to produce spirits. Later it also began to produce potato starch. In 1979, the company was transformed into the *Aloja* Starch Factory, and after the Soviet Union collapsed, it became a co-operative enterprise known simply as *Aloja*.

In June 1991, *Aloja* merged with the Swedish starch company *Sveriges Starkelseproducenter* to become the first joint venture in Latvia's food processing sector. *Aloja Starkelsen* produced potato starch and dried fruit products.

In 1994, the *Aloja Starkelsen* company opened a subsidiary, *Lyckeby-Aloja*, which produces glucose syrup, selling it in Latvia, Lithuania, Estonia, Russia, Belarus, Ukraine and other CIS countries.

This machine produces starch

THE LYCKEBY-ALOJA STARCH FACTORY

Packaging of starch at the *Aloja* Starch Factory

Products produced at the *Aloja* Starch Factory

THE LIEPĀJA SUGAR FACTORY

The *Liepāja* Sugar Factory was established in 1933 in a building, which previously had housed a company that built military boats. The factory began to export sugar in 1935. At a food product exhibition in Paris in 1937, the *Liepāja* factory won a *Grand Prix* diploma for the highest level of sugar extraction in the processing of sugar beets. In the late 1990s, after the production technologies at the factory were reconstructed and after co-operation with sugar beet growers was developed, the company reached the highest level of productivity in its entire history.

In 1972, the *Liepāja* Sugar Factory also began to produce instant coffee. The range of coffees produced at the company has expanded since then, and quality has improved considerably. In March 1999, the factory also began to produce coffee for brewing.

Sacks of sugar at the *Liepāja* Sugar Factory

Products produced by the *Liepāja* Sugar Factory

A cafe run by the *Liepāja* Sugar Factory

Packaging of sugar at the *Liepāja* Sugar Factory

Production of the *Liepāja* brand of instant coffee

The stock company *Hanzas Maiznīca* is a Latvian-Finnish joint venture that was established in 1994 and today is Latvia's leading producer of bread. Modern technologies help to ensure high product quality. In order to improve product quality and production efficiency, in 1999 the amount of 1.2 million lats was invested in various upgrades. Each day SC *Hanzas Maiznīca* produces approximately 90 tons of products. The enterprise has 850 employees.

SC *Hanzas Maiznīca* produces more than 100 different kinds of bread and pastry products – rye bread, wheat bread, sourdough bread, cakes, pastries and cookies, which can be purchased at more than 1,500 stores all around Latvia. SC *Hanzas Maiznīca* offers traditional kinds of bread, as well as such types which are characteristic only of this enterprise: *Brokastu grauzdiņu maize*, *Rīta rika*, *Rudzu rika*, *Līgo maize*, *Hanzas saldskābmaize*, and others.

SC *Hanzas Maiznīca* has also opened bakeries at *Rimi* food stores in Riga. They produce pastries from frozen dough – something that is a novelty in Latvia's market and is highly promising for the future.

In 1999, SC *Hanzas Maiznīca* was named the healthiest food producer in Latvia in recognition of its investment in promoting the health of the Latvian nation.

Normunds Bomis works at the limited liability company *Lielezers Ltd.* in *Limbaži* parish. He learned his bread-baking skills from the master baker and technologist Alberts Blumbergs. *Lielezers Ltd.* is one of the largest rural bakeries in Latvia

One of the largest bread producers in rural Latvia is the company *Turība*, which has 24 bakeries and controls 22% of the Latvian bread market

A facility to cool freshly baked bread

The ancestors of Latvians always held bread in great reverence, as they knew how much hard work was put into it before it came to the table. The widespread folk traditions were expressed as unwritten laws, which were obeyed without protest. Folk beliefs contain many instructions, also contradictory ones, as to what needs to be done so that the bread dough would rise well, because from a well risen dough, a delicious bread will be baked. In order for dough to rise well, it must be well kneaded

The General Director of SC *Hanzas Maiznīca*, Andris Sedmalis, at the frozen dough pastry bakery in the *Rimi-Mols* store

Artūrs   *Zvaigznīte*

Magonīte

The *Lāči* bakery has been in operation for more than six years. The director of the company is master baker Normunds Skauģis, who produces the Latvian traditional rye bread known as *Lāču maize* (*Bear Bread*). It contains no yeast and no wheat flour, and is produced instead from roughly milled rye flour raised with natural leaveners in wooden troughs, shaped into loaves by hand and baked in wood-fired ovens

Full-grain bread – *Sveiks un vesels*

Līgo bread

Tīruma bread

Sliced bread for toasting - *Brokastu grauzdiņu baltmaize* by SC *Hanzas Maiznīca* - has quickly become popular among Latvia's consumers

Klēts bread

Rīta rika

Rīgas maize bread is popular in Australia, while the leading bakers of bread in Brazil are Latvians

AGRICULTURAL EXHIBITION AT THE EXHIBITIONS COMPLEX RĀMAVA

Cucumbers from the *Mārupe Ltd.* greenhouses

A tomato blossom

Janis Zvaigzne has been chairperson of the executive board at *Mārupe Ltd.* since 1984

Janis Berziņš has been responsible for running *Mārupe's Ltd.* greenhouses since 1989, and he has been awarded the Latvian state's highest civilian honour – the Order of Three Stars

Lumber-mill at *Mārupe*

A number of large farms in Latvia have emerged based upon the former *kolhozes* and *sovhozes*. After privatisation, they have either preserved a collective form of management, or they have been fully taken over by a specific legal or natural person.

A typical large-scale farm with very extensive operations is *Mārupe Ltd.*, which is located near the city of Rīga and farms 2,800 hectares of agricultural land. *Mārupe Ltd.* produces vegetables, potatoes, grains and grasses for seeding, dairy and meat cattle and fur-bearing animals. Between the early spring and the late fall, the company grows cucumbers and tomatoes in greenhouses that cover 7 hectares. *Mārupe Ltd.* has a herd of 500 dairy cows and 2,500 pigs, and the company is raising 40,000 minks for the production of furs. The company also produces wooden furniture.

Wooden furniture manufactured at *Mārupe Ltd.*

Consumers often prefer *Mārupe Ltd.* tomatoes

Vegetables from the fields of *Mārupe Ltd.*

Harvesting the tomatoes

The "*Favourite*" brand of tomatoes

Mārupe Ltd. piglets having their lunch

Mārupe's greenhouses

Mink breeding is traditional in Latvia. The fur-coats go for export

The *Spring '99* exhibition

A sowing machine is being demonstrated at the exhibition *Agricultural Technologies '99*

Inside the *Agricultural Technologies '99* exhibition

The *Rāmava* exhibition hall since 1993 has been the venue for three international exhibitions organized by A.M.L. Ltd. – *Spring* in April, for farmers, livestock breeders, fish breeders, specialists in agricultural chemicals and construction; *Transport for the Countryside* (August) with various vehicles for farms, forestry companies, road construction and maintenance; and *Agricultural Technologies* (October) – agriculture, forestry, wood processing and food processing. The exhibitions attract some 200 participants each to produce products that have been manufactured in Latvia, Lithuania, Estonia, Sweden, Norway, Finland, Denmark, Germany, Belarus, Russia, Poland and other countries.

The *Transport for the Countryside '99* exhibition featured this machine which cuts up branches and other wood

Latvian bees

Visvaldis Auzukalns with equipment used to grow queen bees

The Coat of Arms of the stock company
Latvijas bite

Hives hewn of logs

Various types of hives

BEEKEEPING

The earliest known information about beekeeping in Latvia is found in the Chronicle of Nestor, which informs us that the Baltic peoples traded with honey as early as 969 AD. The Chronicle of Henricus from the 13th century, for its part, says that Livs drank a honey-based beverage during meetings of their councils.

A natural habitat for bees is a rotted and hollow tree. Early beekeepers found such trees in the forest and took out the honey, thus destroying the bees. Beginning in the 12th century, Latvian beekeepers chopped hollows in trees that were appropriate for bee habitats called *dores*, and these were considered inviolate private property. At the beginning of the 13th century, however, German crusaders arrived in Latvia, and they paid no heed to that principle. In 1212, there was a bloody battle between Livs and the crusaders from *Cēsis* over the fact that the crusaders had destroyed Liv bee trees. Angered at this theft, the Livs and Latvians turned their backs on the Christian religion, which the crusaders were promoting.

Latvians have always held respectful attitudes toward bees, calling them *golden wings*, *honey carriers*, etc. Bee *dores* in trees were often presented to new members of families, and in autumn households gathered to honour the bee, taking honey from the hives and drinking a special honey beverage called *miestiņš*.

As bee *dores* were usually placed high up in trees there was a saying *climbing to the bees*. Even today, when beehives are on the ground, the phrase is still used by beekeepers when going to the hives.

In forested areas, beekeepers had to compete with bears, which are good at climbing trees and which, of course, love their honey. In order to protect their bee *dores* from the greedy bears, beekeepers hung blocks of wood from ropes so that they hung near the trunk of the tree. When the bear swatted the block aside, it swung back and hit the bear in return.

Early portable beehives were similar in appearance to bee *dores* in trees, and some hives of this type survive to this very day. The first book on beekeeping was published in the Latvian language in 1803.

At the Riga agricultural fair in 1851, beekeeping equipment was also on display. Beekeepers organised their first specialised exhibition in 1868. The first beekeeper society was established in 1867 in *Jelgava*, and three years later it published its *Bišu kalenderi* (*Bee Calendars*). In 1874, a handbook called *A Short Course on Tending and Raising Bees* was published by Ansis Leitans. The first congress of Baltic beekeepers assembled in *Jelgava* in 1895.

There were 164,000 hives of bees in Latvia in 1935 in 42,000 apiaries. Just before World War II, the number of hives had increased to 222,890.

Today there are some 6,000 beekeepers in Latvia tending to 50,000 hives. Approximately 20,000 of these belong to professionals. The largest apiary, *Kamenīte Ltd.*, has 1,700 hives, and it is owned by Visvaldis Auzukalns, who has received the Latvian Order of Three Stars for his work.

Latvian beekeepers produce all kinds of products from bees, not just honey. The raw materials from bees lead to food products, health care products and medications. In the 1960s, the *Cēsis* branch of the Latvian Society of Gardening and Beekeeping, acting under the leadership of Evalds Bergs, began to produce beekeeping products, and this work has been recognised not only in Latvia, but also in foreign countries.

The foundations of the science of beekeeping were laid by Professor Pēteris Rizga, Dr. Kira Balode, Dr. Arvīds Kornets, Dr. Silvija Palmbaha and Dr. Monika Mize. Students of agronomy and veterinary medicine learn about beekeeping at the Latvian University of Agriculture, which is Latvia's leading institution for the study of beekeeping. The University has a research apiary, and its main function is to ensure the survival and propagation of *Apis belifera melifera* – the bee species that is native to Latvia. Beekeepers are also trained at the *Vecbebri* Agricultural Technical College.

Latvian beekeepers mostly use standing hives, although multi-part hives have become popular since 1995. Multi-part hives are handier for transportation and for tending to the bees.

The stock company SC *Latvijas bite* sells beekeeping products and equipment. It exports beekeeping products and imports the equipment which beekeepers need. The company has its own stores and a wide network of suppliers. SC *Latvijas bite* also has its own facility for processing beekeeping products. Every month the magazine *Dārzs un Drava* is published while a professional magazine for beekeepers is published once each quarter called *Biškopis*. The Latvian Beekeeping Society, which has branches in all of Latvia's districts, as well as in Riga, works to protect the interests of its members and to promote the development of the sector.

More detailed information regarding the history of beekeeping in Latvia can be found at the *Vecbebri* Agricultural Technical College and in the village of *Priekuļi* in *Cēsis* district, both of which house beekeeping museums.

A Nukleusa hive

A Dadana-Blota hive

Hives built by Visvaldis Auzukalns

Andrejs Mizis is chairperson of the Latvian Beekeeping Society

A swarm of bees outside of a portable hive

Peteris Rizga (1883-1955) researched methods for building better beehives and for improving the process of beekeeping

Beekeeper Jānis Sietiņsons in a field of scorpion-weed flowers

A fumigator for beekeeping

Various beekeeping products produced in Latvia

The Latvian Brown cow

A Blue cow and her calf

Farmer Aivars Tiesnesis, the member of LR *Saeima*

18-year-old Guntars Lutinskis, who farms in the *Aizkraukle* district town of *Nereta*, was the youngest farm-owner in all of Latvia at this writing

Milk was first produced in Latvia in the 1st millennium BC, according to archaeological finds that include the bones of milking cows and clay vessels used to handle milk. In Latvian folklore and in the eyes of Latvians over the centuries, milk and dairy products have been symbols of success and a wealthy life. Folklore talks about rivers of milk and mountains of butter. When a job proceeded quickly, it was, said the Latvians, "moving as if through butter". Diary products were also donated to the ancient gods Māra, the Lord of the Home, and the Mother of the Earth.

Butter was long considered to be one of the most valuable stores that a household could have, and beginning in the 14th century it was used to pay feudal taxes. According to information recorded during Swedish rule in what is now Latvia, milk cows at that time were not particularly bountiful.

A dictionary from the 17th century lists the following dairy products: sweet milk, sour milk, fermented milk, cream, butter, steamed milk (or cottage cheese) and cheese. In 1810 Karl Gotthard Elverfeld produced the first instructional manual on livestock breeding for Latvian farmers.

In the 18th century people began to bring dairy products to market in Latvia's towns and cities. Foreign-bred varieties of cattle were brought in to create herds, feed procedures were improved, the main achievements of livestock farming elsewhere in the world were studied, and interest was displayed in the economies of agriculture. Rational dairy farming procedures began to appear mostly in the baronial estates that were located near cities, but large individual farms appeared soon thereafter.

In the second half of the 19th century Latvia's farmers became increasingly international in their operations. Farmers from Vidzeme trav-elled to Paris to participate in a world dairy exhibitions in 1866, and to Vienna to attend a similar event in 1872. At the end of the 19th century the Baltic region was an important territory for dairy farming, and colleagues from Denmark, Germany and Ireland came on tours to see how they worked.

Collective dairy farms started to appear in Latvia in the late 19th century. The first major collective dairy was the *Spāre* Dairy in *Drabeši* parish near Cēsis. It opened in 1909, and soon thereafter similar operations were started up in *Rauna*, *Matiši*, *Grundzāle*, *Smiltene* and *Džūkste*. When World War I broke out, Latvia boasted 88 dairy collectives.

At approximately the same time, farmers began to set up supervisory organizations to monitor the work of dairies, obtaining precise data about the financial income of dairies, as well as about the amount of milk or butter that could be obtained from each cow. People started to think about developing herds in a rational way, thinking about production issues, feeding and tending of animals. The supervisory network expanded very quickly. The first associations of the kind appeared in Europe in 1895, and in Latvia more than 280 supervisory organizations sprang up between 1903 and 1913, becoming a very significant part of the Latvian dairy industry.

In the 1930s, dairy farming in Latvia was a most profitable enterprise, indeed, and most of the products were shipped to other markets. Exports of butter increased from 10,000 tons in 1926 to 23,500 tons in 1938. The total value of Latvian exports between 1924 and 1938 was 2,694 million lats, and butter accounted for nearly one-fifth of that sum. In terms of the amount of exported butter, Latvia was sixth in the world in 1938. In the prewar period, however, production levels in the dairy industry differed from region to region. Thus, for example, the Ludza, Rēzekne and Daugavpils districts produced less than 900 kilograms of milk on a per capita basis, while the Riga, *Madona*, *Jelgava* and *Tukums* districts produced more than 2,000 kilograms.

If at the beginning of the 20th century dairy products were very popular on the menus of Latvia's residents, then around 1936 and 1937 the situation had changed in favor of plant-based food products – 40.8% of the rations consumed by Latvia's residents were plant-based, while only 23.1% were dairy products and 21.4% were meat products. Still, Latvia was far ahead of other countries in Europe in dairy product consumption.

Around the mid-1930s, information about the dairy industry began to appear in the press. Propaganda trips to the countryside were organized, and lectures were read. In 1935 the government began to run "milk propaganda" weeks, and there were dairy product exhibitions in Riga's *Vērmanes* Garden.

In the postwar years Latvia's dairy industry was based on a continual increase in the number of animals, but feed processes were poor, and milkmaids were forced into socialist competi-tions. The dairy industry was closely linked to the Latvian Brown breed of cow, known for its relatively good productivity.

A milkmaid called Marta Semule was declared all-Soviet hero of labor twice, and when Nikita Khrushchev visited Latvia in the 1960s, he met the director of the *Rauna* cultural building, who was also known as an honored milkmaid. The legend was circulated that the woman harvested no less than 6,000 kilograms of milk from the cows of an enormous herd. This myth, along with a photograph of the pretty milkmaid and a smiling Khrushchev made it into all of the major Soviet papers. Latvia was soon assigned the task of becoming the main producer of milk for Moscow and Leningrad.

After the collapse of the Soviet Union the Latvian dairy industry returned its attention to qualitative growth. Careful work is being done to improve the quality of livestock feed and to introduce new and highly productive varieties of cows, especially in the dairy industry. Latvian dairy exports to Western Europe are once again on the rise.

Pēteris Vaičulis, who runs the *Zundi* farm in *Andrupene* parish, *Krāslava* district, had 10 cows imported from the Netherlands when the authors visited him

Black and white cows

Modris and Sarmīte Vilsons live at the *Ausekļi* homestead in *Augstkalne* parish, *Dobele* district, and they had recently obtained modern milking equipment

THE DAIRY INDUSTRY

Built in the 1930s – the *Trikāta* dairy

Elita Šnepste chairs the SC *Preiļu siers* executive board, and here she is seen inspecting a new machine that will be used to produce *Čedars* cheese

The city of *Preiļi*, with the SC *Preiļu siers* dairy product factory in the foreground

At the unveiling of a new milk processing machine – Arvids Ušča, general director of SC *Rīgas Piensaimnieks*, is joined by TetraPak Baltija general director Pär Söderlund

The *Čedars* cheese plant

This equipment produces the *Jungle Pop* fruit juice based ice lollies

The stock company *Rīgas Piensaimnieks* is one of the largest dairy product enterprises in Latvia. It was established in 1993, and since the very first day, the basic principle of operations has been to ensure the quality of its production. Profits earned by the company are re-invested into the introduction of new milk processing technologies and the improvement of conditions under which the dairy products are produced.

The company produces some 60 different products in all, and it is working successfully both in Latvian and foreign markets. Among the most popular products in Latvia are the chocolate coated curd snack *Kārums*, the processed cheese *Dzintars*, the yogurt *Zilonītis*, the ice lollies *Jungle Pop*, and the margarine *Divi gaiļi*.

In November 1999, SC *Rīgas Piensaimnieks* was awarded the HACCP quality certificate, which attests to the conformity of the enterprise's products to the highest international food quality standards.

SC *Rīgas Piensaimnieks* is one of those enterprises for whom the growth of the country is important, not only the profitable operations of the enterprise. This can be attained by an increase in the prosperity of the inhabitants of Latvia. The SC *Rīgas Piensaimnieks* has always endeavoured to support various charities, donating to the Latvian Children's Fund, as well as to many other public organisations and projects.

The Eastern Latvian town of *Preiļi*, is associated by many Latvians with *Čedars* (Cheddar) cheese, because the stock company *Preiļu siers* is located there. Its flagship product is the *Čedars* brand – a hard cheese with 40% or 50% fat content and a piquant taste. *Čedars* is excellent in salads, on bread and in various savoury dishes. *Čedars* is perfect for grilled cheese sandwiches and pizza, because it melts well, providing a great appearance and aroma. Approximately 90% of the company's cheese is exported to other parts of Europe.

In 1998, SC *Preiļu siers* introduced a cheese spread version of the *Čedars* brand – *Čedariņš*. The cheese spread comes in three varieties – plain, with garlic, and with dill. The product is sold is 200-gram cartons. The cheese spread has a comparatively low fat content, and it is good for 30 days after opening.

SC *Preiļu siers* also produces a diet cheese with 20% fat content and a mild and pleasant taste. The diet cheese is also available in a number of varieties – with mushrooms, greens or paprika, or plain.

Another product from SC *Preiļu siers* is the diet milk beverage *Tīrkultūra*, which is produced from lactic acid bacteria. The drink promotes digestion, is useful after the use of antibiotics, helps to protect people from intestinal disorders and helps people to recover after infectious diseases. The product has a fat content of only 0.05%.

SC *Preiļu siers* produces more than 20 different products in all.

Valentīna and Yuri Lazovskis run a farm called *Apsītes* in *Pušmucova* parish, *Ludza* district. With 1,000 hectares of land, it is the largest farm in Latvia

Leonards Puduls runs the *Latgale* farm, which is the largest producer of bred cattle in Latgale

Anna Svaģere works a farm in *Jaunpils*, and she is in 2nd or 3rd place in all of Latvia in terms of the amount of milk that she gets from her cows

SC *Rīgas Piensaimnieks* products

The Chairperson of the Dairy Industry Association and Minister for Agriculture, Aigars Kalvītis

Mudite Dzelve has 60 goats at her *Apiņi* farm in *Jelgava* district, and milk from the goats is used to produce a very popular cheese in Latvia

Viesturs and Sandra Liepiņš have built a new farm with modern equipment in *Krimulda* parish

CATTLE BREADING

Horses at pasture

Moufflons in the meadows of the *Viesaka* farm in *Madona* district

Latvia's dark-headed sheep

Agris Klimanovs and Gunta Cunska from *Viesakas*, district of *Madona* own a farm of wild animals

Stags and deer on the *Birzgaļi* farm in *Ogre* district and their owner, Andris Vucans

A horse breeding museum at the *Briede* Saloon in *Burtnieki*

POULTRY BREEDING

Janis Gabrusans is the only farmer in the Baltic States to breed ostriches, and he does so in *Robežnieki* parish, which is in the *Krāslava* district

SC *Ķekavas putnu fabrika*

Quails bred in *Mārupe* parish and their eggs

A hen from "*Araukāni*"

White turkeys from the *Lauk-gaļi* farm in the *Dobele* district

The share company *Ainava*, in *Dubna* parish, *Daugavpils* district, is the only farm in Latvia to breed water fowl

Farmer Merija Viļuna raises pearl hens at the *Laukgaļi* farm in the *Dobele* district

BALTICOVO

The general director of the stock company *Balticovo*, Valdis Grimze

The *Iecava* Poultry Plant was established in 1973, and in the early 1990s it was transformed into a Latvian-Swedish joint venture. In 1994 it served as the cornerstone of what became the stock company *Balticovo* – a company with Latvian capital.

Balticovo produces eggs, powdered eggs and poultry products. People can buy 24-hour-old chicks for breeding purposes, as well as birds that are 60-120 days old, laying hens that are 15-18 months old, meat and bone flour, as well as eggs for incubation.

Balticovo is one of the largest companies of its kind in Europe. It covers 140 hectares of land and employs 450 employees. The company's products are of a high quality, and there is considerable output of products. Over the course of just a few years the company has become the unquestioned leader in the poultry industry in the Baltic States. Approximately 65% of all of the eggs sold in Latvia come from *Balticovo*.

The company's products are in great demand all over Latvia, and there are exports to Austria, Ukraine, Russia, Azerbaijan, Lithuania and Estonia.

The company's production cycle is complete and self-enclosed, beginning with breeding hens and production flocks and ending with the production and supply of eggs. The production cycle is completed with the production of poultry meat and powdered eggs.

Farmer Elza Kraukle runs the *Oškalni* pig-breeding farm in *Ranka*, which is in *Gulbene* district, and here she is seen with her family

Tukums Meatprocessing Company

Latvian Ex-president Guntis Ulmanis on a visit to a farm in the *Dobele* district

Uzvara-Strauti Ltd. runs a meat processing plant in *Bauska* parish

A family of pigs

The production of *Tukums* Meatprocessing Company is sold in a cafe

Ligita Jevdokimova of *Ogre* district with one of the rabbits that she breeds

Aigo Gutmanis runs a large grain producing operation in *Ventspils* district, but he also has 1,000 pigs

Inta Māliņa has set up an intensive pig fattening operation in *Launkalne* parish, *Valka* district

Production of the *Tukums* Meatprocessing Company

The stock company *Ruks*, also known as the *Cēsis* Meat Complex, was established in 1928, and to this very day it has preserved ancient Latvian traditions in producing meat products, merging these with the most modern of technologies. Over the course of many years, much in the way of work and resources has been invested in the reconstruction of the company and in the modernization of equipment and technologies. Many kinds of meat processing equipment have been developed at the complex itself. Professional specialists and technologists work to guarantee the highest quality of the company's products. The *Cēsis* Meat Complex has a livestock slaughterhouse, a sausage plant and a plant to produce packaged meat products. There is a network of retail stores in *Cēsis*, Riga and other places in Latvia. *Ruks* offers more than 40 different kinds of sausage and 17 kinds of packaged meat products.

The complex, in fact, is just one part of a larger chain of companies, which includes *Cirmas Bekons* and *Skaunes Bekons* – pig-breeding farms that raise and fatten the animals. Each of the two companies can handle 30,000 fatted pigs each year. By introducing new genetic materials and progressive feeding technologies, the companies are producing valuable pork with a high content of lean meat.

Another company Ltd., *Jaunpūpoli*, provides balanced fodder for the companies. Using computerized production lines, the company produces six kinds of fodder for different kinds of pigs.

The sausage-making plant of the *Cēsis* Meat Complex

Students of the first graduating class at the Tartu Veterinary Institute – Jānis Neimanis, Estonian A. Moss, Alfrēds Bertušs, Kristaps Helmanis, Eižens Bergs and Oto Kalniņš

Alfrēds Bertušs (1849-1890), veterinarian

Oto Kalniņš (1856-1891), veterinarian

Professor Ludvigs Kundziņš (1855-1940), veterinarian

Professor Pēteris Apinis (1904-1960), founder of the Veterinary Institute of Academy of Sciences

Docent Arturs Garančs and the Dean of the Veterinary Medicine Faculty of the Latvian University of Agriculture, Associate Professor Pēteris Keidans, in conversation with students

Professor Zigmunds Brūveris, veterinarian

Professor Igor Afanasyev outside the Veterinary Medicine Faculty of the Latvian University of Agriculture

Everyday work at the Zālītis and Juitinovičs veterinary service – Andris Zālītis conducting surgery

Veterinarian Ģirts Drabče in surgery at his private veterinary clinic

Associate Professor Lev Iemelyanov examines a sick cow

Veterinarian Egils Juitinovičs provides consultations

Veterinarian Juris Tolpežņikovs

The director of the State Veterinary Service, Vinets Veldre

The staff of the Centre for Education in Veterinary Medicine. Director Ivars Lūsis is at centre in the front row

The journal of the Latvian Society of Veterinarians Veterinārais Žurnāls and the newspaper Vēstule Latvijas Veterinārārstiem are both edited by Anna Joffe

A meeting of teaching staff of veterinary medicine from the Baltic States

The director of the State Veterinary Medicine Diagnostics Centre, Rafael Ioffe

At the Veterinary Medicine Diagnostics Centre

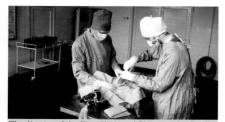

The director of the Riga Clinic and Pharmacy for Small Animals, veterinarian Gunārs Innuss (left)

Latvia's Veterinary Medicine Service was formed during the years of the Russian Empire, when Latvian veterinarians mostly studied at the Tartu School of Veterinary Medicine (1823-1873) and the Tartu Veterinary Institute (TVI) (1873-1919). Many of the students later became directors or professors at these institutions. When Latvia gained its independence, the Veterinary Service retained the organisational structure of the Tsarist Russian veterinary service in that it was subordinated to the medical service. The first director of the Veterinary Board, Vilis Frišmanis, however, reorganised the Service and achieved its being placed under the supervision of the Ministry of Agriculture.

The first veterinary law in Latvia was written by Eduards Cirulis in 1938. Local education of veterinarians began in 1919, when the newly founded University of Latvia established a Veterinary Medicine Faculty (VMF). Methodological and academic traditions at the VMF came directly from the TVI and were brought over by Professors Ludvigs Kundziņš, Ernests Pakuls, Rudolfs Grapmanis and Augusts Kirhenšteins, as well as docents Kārlis Kangro, Voldemars Brencens and Augusts Pētersons. Some graduates of the VMF themselves became professors in the 1930s – Pēteris Apinis, Jānis Dzelde and Miķelis Rolle, among them. Rolle wrote a textbook on physiology that was used by veterinary students around the world from the 1950s until the 1970s.

During the Soviet occupation, the VMF became the Veterinary faculty of the Latvian Academy of Agriculture. Veterinary medicine in the State was managed by the Veterinary Board of the Ministry of Agriculture. It had structures in all of Latvia's districts, and veterinary services existed at State and other collective farms.

After Latvia regained its independence, Docent Jāzeps Rimeicans was appointed director of the State Veterinary Department, and in 1990 he began to reform the work of the institution, beginning the establishment of a network of private veterinary medical practices in the country and laying the foundations for licensing of professional work in Latvia. In 1992, Latvia became a member of the International Epizootic Office.

A Centre for Education in Veterinary Medicine has been set up at the VMF with the support of the Latvian Association of Veterinarians, the State Veterinary Service and the University Veterinary Fund.

The State Centre for Veterinary Diagnostics conducts laboratory diagnosis of diseases and disorders in animals. The Centre tests animal-based food products, as well as animal feed, and it does research on the external environment, as well as regarding the conformity of veterinary medicines and pharmaceutical products to State standards. The Centre also co-ordinates the work of the various veterinary laboratories in Latvia. The director of the Diagnostics Centre is Rafael Ioffe.

The Latvian Society of Veterinarians brings together professional veterinarians in Latvia. The Society defends the interests of its members, provides post-graduate training opportunities, arranges for the licensing of veterinarians, and publicises the latest ideas and achievements in the field. The Society publishes its own professional journal, and it co-operates with veterinary organisations in other countries.

The Latvian Society of Veterinarians was founded in 1921, and today it has 1,200 members. The Society was not active during the Soviet era, and most of the credit for the renewal of its work after the occupation goes to the association's first post-Soviet president, Juris Tolpežņikovs. At the end of the century, the work of the Society was managed by a board headed by its chairperson, Juris Zemzars.

Modris Goba, chairperson of the *Tērvete* stud-farm in *Dobele* district, which is the largest horse-breeding facility in Latvia

The stallion Querides

Maira Balode, publisher of the magazine *Latvijas Zirgi* (Latvian horses) presents the *Sigulda* Prize to Lilita Freivalde

Seoul Olympics participant Sergei Schakurov with the horse *Fināls*

The Latvian breed of horses was officially recognised in 1952. It was formed by improving local horses with German breeds such as the Hanover, Oldenburg and Trakehner varieties, as well as with pure-bred Arabian and British horses. This is a universal breed of horse – the animals are appropriate for sports, for barrier jumping, for show riding and for tourist horseback riding. The horses can also be hitched to wagons and used for various farming functions.

There are four major horse-breeding facilities in Latvia – the *Tērvete* stud-farm in *Dobele* district, the *Burtnieki* stud-farm in *Valmiera* district, the *Turība* stud-farm in *Preiļi* district and the *Okte* stud-farm in *Talsi* district. There are also 29 other stud-farms for horses that are owned by private breeders. There are some 19,200 horses in Latvia. They are raised and trained for sports and then exported to Germany, Denmark, Sweden, the Netherlands, Italy, Estonia, Poland and Russia. Breeding stallions are brought to Latvia from Germany, Denmark and Sweden.

Each year from February until October there are show-jumping competitions in Latvia. The best riders in the 1999 season were Guntars Siliņš with the horse *Salane-Radiants* (owned by Edgars Treibergs) and Sergei Schakurovs with the horse *Ikars*. During the 1999 season Siliņš qualified for the finals of the World Cup in show-jumping to be held in Las Vegas in 2000. In 1988, Schakurov took the horse *Fināls* to the finals of the barrier-jumping competition at the Seoul Olympic Games.

There are also show riding competitions each year. Facilities for this purpose are found at *Līgatne* (*Cēsis* district), *Turaida* (*Rīga* district) and elsewhere. At horse-breeding farms, there are leisure riding activities in addition to horseback sports. In 1992, the Latvian Association of Horse Breeders was re-established, and the Latvian Federation of Riders was founded. It is responsible for popularising the riding sports and organising competitions. In the *Kleisti* area of Riga there is a National School of Applied Sports, and young people learn riding skills under the watchful eye of trainers.

In Latvia horses are also used for medical purposes. At the *Vaivari* Rehabilitation Centre, the *Līgatne* sanatorium in *Cēsis* district, and the *Kleisti* facility in Riga, there are specialists who use horse-related therapy to help people.

Before 1989 there were competitions for heavy work horses, which tested the working abilities of the animals.

A show riding trainer at the Latvian School of Applied Sports, Astrida Belovzorova, riding the horse *Sapnis*

At the Latvian National School of Applied Sports at *Kleisti*

Horse stud-farms also offer rides in sleighs

Sintija Orlova with the horse Quido

Kristine Rozite from the *Mušķi* training centre of the Latvian Agricultural University riding the horse *Lagoss*

Mairis Penelis and the horse *Lirika*

Guntars Siliņš with the horse *Salane-Radiants*, owned by Edgars Treibergs; the rider has qualified for the finals of the 2000 World Cup in Las Vegas

Up to 1989, competitions for draft horses in weight-pulling and endurance were held in Latvia

A herd of breeding horses

At the horse breeding stud-farm *Burtnieki* in *Valmiera* district

ANGLING

A kingfisher

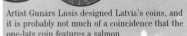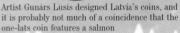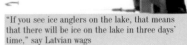

Artist Gunārs Lūsis designed Latvia's coins, and it is probably not much of a coincidence that the one-lats coin features a salmon

Inara Koha and a bream that she caught at a competition

Alexei Gadervec and a salmon

An angler with a pike...

Ruduļu Juris, journalist

"If you see ice anglers on the lake, that means that there will be ice on the lake in three days' time," say Latvian wags

Doctor Janis Ķisis caught a perch and his son, Mārtiņš Ķisis, pulled out a pike, using a spoon bait in the colours of the Latvian flag

They are showing how big the one that got away really was...

Member of the *Saeima* Kārlis Leiškalns and his children, Jēkabs and Dārta, attend an annual fishing event in *Staicele*

Viktors Koroļovs and a salmon trout

A tench

A stream trout

The largest salmon caught in 1999

The largest catfish caught with a fishing pole in 1999

People in Latvia fish both for leisure and for sport, using the tools of an angler to catch fish. Latvian law specifies areas of dry land along the shores of bodies of water where fishing is permitted. The zone is four meters wide along privately owned waterways (and the law requires there to be a sign saying *Private* on the property), while in the case of other waterways the zone measures 10 or 20 meters in width. Anglers require a license.

It is estimated that there are some 150,000 anglers in Latvia – a bit more than 5% of the population. In the 1980s, some 40,000 anglers came together in the Latvian Association of Hunters and Anglers. This was an unwieldy organisation when the Soviet way of doing things collapsed, and members did not really know how to cope. Members began to leave in order to form smaller organisations and clubs, which focus on specific bodies of water. Today the oldest angling club in Latvia is called *Salmo*. Its members specialise in catching trout and salmon.

Fly anglers have their own club, and each October they organise an international fly fishing competition on the *Gauja* River. The *Pacere* organisation, which specialises in trout, is also active in working on programs, which aim to protect fish populations.

During the spring, summer and autumn anglers use various kinds of fishing poles and spinning gear, while during the winter ice fishing is popular.

The most popular lakes in Latvia for fishing are the *Burtnieks*, the *Lubāna* and the *Rāzna*, all of which have ample supplies of pike, perch, carp, eels and other fish. Shallow lakes near the sea – the *Babīte*, the *Kaņieris*, the *Engure* and the *Liepāja* Lakes – have good populations of pike, carp and perch. Anglers often go to the *Venta*, *Salaca*, *Gauja* and *Lielupe* rivers to catch a wide variety of fish. The *Daugava* and its tributary, the *Aiviekste*, are home to Latvia's largest fish – catfish that weigh an average of 50 kilograms. Anglers with nets have caught catfish of up to 100 kilograms in weight.

A number of fish are specially protected during the summer, including trout, pike, perch and salmon, among others. Anglers during a 24-hour period are allowed to catch (with permitted equipment, of course) no more than three catfish and no more than five of a variety of other fish, including stream trout, pike, tench, chub, blue char, burbot, and pike-perch. There are no limits on other kinds of fish.

Unauthorised and unlicensed anglers cause all kinds of problems in terms of the available populations of fish. There are 40 fish inspectors in the country who battle against these people, and the police and Latvian National Guard also help.

Closed private ponds and small lakes are becoming increasingly popular in Latvia. These are known as *anglers' paradise*, because for a fee anglers are allowed to pull out large carps or rainbow trout and keep them.

Executive Gunars Ķirsons each year organises a competition, *The Large Fish of Latgale* on Lake *Lubana*. Anglers, by invitation, catch fish – usually large pike – mark them and then release them back into the water. The Gunars Kirke Memorial Tournament, which is now organised by Gunars Lusis, is also popular.

What are some of the weight records that have been set in the last couple of years? How about a 19.56 kilogram pike? There was a 56.2-kilogram catfish, a 3.05-kilogram stream trout, a 6.66-kilogram rainbow trout, a 10.3-kilogram pikeperch, a 19.7-kilogram carp, and a 5-kilogram bream. Latvia's waters are not lacking for a angler's trophy dream!

They weigh the catch carefully at a tournament that is held each year in memory of the artist Gunars Kirke

Poet Egils Zirnis: "... The waters get around your feet, full of unsensed fish. Ask me not about them, I'll tell you lies."

Actor Harijs Liepiņš gains inspiration on the waterways

The *Large Fish of Latgale* competition run by businessman Gunars Ķirsons involves catching a pike, marking it with a ring, and then letting it back into the water of Lake *Lubāna*

Huge pike have been caught in Lake *Babīte*

Members of the *Salmo* Club – professors, civil servants, business people and politicians – with their flag

There are some 34,000 hunters in Latvia, and they have come together in no fewer than 974 clubs and organisations. The Hunting Law determines the basic principles of the economic organisation of hunting in the Republic of Latvia. Issues concerning how hunts are held and what kinds of animals can be hunted are determined by Cabinet regulations. Hunters must also observe regulations concerning the purchase, registration, storage and sale of hunting firearms.

Animals that can be hunted in Latvia are moose, stags, does, wild pigs, wolves, foxes, lynxes, badgers, racoons, American mink, beavers, rabbits, bean geese, white-fronted geese, ducks, coots, woodcocks, common snipes, wood pigeons, hazel grouses, capercaillie and black grouse cockerels, ravens, crows and magpies.

Hunting in Latvia is associated with ancient cultural and economic traditions. The hunting animals that are found in Latvia make good trophies, and regular exhibitions are held to evaluate these trophies.

Hunters in Latvia take a keen interest in the number of animals that are hunted and the population of hunted animals, as well as the quality of trophies. Various kinds of biological and technical work are done by hunters in hunting areas. Animals are fed, their habitats are improved, and measures are taken to avoid damage to agriculture and forestry. Together with the State Forestry Service, hunters count animal populations in order to make judgments about dynamics of the numbers of the populations.

Regulations in Latvia permit several kinds of hunting, including work with dogs, use of hunting devices (traps), from boats and with beaters. The latter kind of hunting is most popular in Latvia, because it allows many hunters to come together, spend a nice day out hunting, and then gather around the supper table to tell hunter's stories. Especially popular are hunts during the mating season of deer in September. The horns of a stag are a particularly prized trophy. The hunting of water fowl and swamp fowl has increased in popularity in recent times.

What do Latvian hunters wish each other? "No down, no feathers!"

A hunted fox

First work on a hunted animal

A duck hunt

The horns resound!

An exhibition of trophies

A mallard

The forestry museum at Viļani

Hunting trophies

A hunters' carnival – economist Ojars Kehris and military specialist Girts Kristovskis

Hunters receiving instructions before starting the beating of game

Beating of the game …

A hunting tower

The prominent Latvian businessman Uldis Kokins with his hunting trophy

Hunting with a beater in the wintertime

A hunting guard tower

Hunting water fowl

The hunt has been successful!

Hunters heading out to beat the game

A drawing by Johann Brotze, *At the Podrags Dam* (1795). The drawing shows men using large nets to fish for salmon in the *Daugava*.

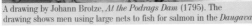

Vecdaugava fishermen fish for pilchard in the Bay of Riga

The fishing port at *Roja*

A fisherman in *Jūrmala*

This shed for fishing nets on a Livonian homestead in *Mazirbe* is built of old boats

The *Vecdaugava* fishing port in Riga

The catch in the Bay of Riga

Fishing for sprat in the Baltic Sea

Latvia has some 500 kilometers of seashore, and there are some 3,200 large and small lakes, as well as many rivers and streams, in the country. Fishing is one of the most widely developed and expansive areas of the food processing sector in Latvia, and traditions in this area are ancient indeed. Early settlers in Latvia fished 4,000 years ago – long before farming was developed. Fishermen are mentioned in the Chronicle of Indriķis. Fishermen formed their first organization in 1220, and its statutes were approved in 1403.

Until the 15th century only fresh fish was sold at the markets of Riga, while later smoked and salted fish went on sale, too. Fishermen could sell their catch during the operating hours of the market, and everything that was left over at the end of the day was confiscated and donated to the St. George shelter in town.

In 1700 the Riga local government allowed members of the Brotherhood of Fishermen to fish without any limitations and also to brew beer for home use and recreational activities.

In tsarist Russia fishing was a backward business, but fish processing developed quite rapidly. In 1884 canning of fish began in Riga, and in 1891 entrepreneurs released a product called *Sprats in oil*. This product won international favor and is still sold in many places around the world today.

When Latvia gained its independence, in 1919, fishermen set up the Latvian Central Association of Fishing. Deep sea fishing began as a process in the 1930s, and in 1938 there were 18 associations of seagoing fishermen and 12 associations of freshwater fishermen. In 1939 there were three canning factories in Riga, which produced canned fish for the domestic market and for export. Exports went all over the world.

During the war fishing deteriorated, because boats off the shore were seen as potential aggressors or traitors by the Soviet and German occupants.

Latvians have always loved to fish close to the shore in the Bay of Riga and in the Baltic Sea, and this was particularly true in the 1920s and 1930s, when some 150 fishing villages along the country's shoreline gave work to some 3,000 men who made their living entirely from the sea. Between 1945 and the early 1990s fishing, like everything else, was a collectivized process, and only 500-700 people were employed. Fishing in many parts of the Baltic Sea and the Bay of Riga – around *Liepāja*, *Lielirbe*, *Ventspils*, *Užava*, etc. – was limited by the activities of the Soviet military.

Deep sea fishing was developed as an industry in the Baltic Sea during Soviet times. Fishing kolhozes were subsidized, and Latvian fishermen worked hard and productively and lived well as a result. After the restoration of independence, small fishing companies emerged from the former collective operations.

After 1993 fishing in the Bay of Riga was very intensive for a while – between 2,500 and 4,000 tons per year. Because of this uncontrolled processes, stocks declined, and in 1996 and 1997 larger companies began to push one-man and other small operations out of the market.

The intensity of fishing along the shores of the Baltic Sea is not as intensive, but there are prospects for the further development of the industry, particularly around *Jūrmalciems*, *Liepāja*, *Pāvilosta*, *Ventspils*, *Staldzene*, *Oviši* and *Kolka*.

The government provided subsidies to the industry since 1998, particularly to fishing companies on the shores of the Baltic Sea. The aim is to modernize production and processing and to support educational efforts in the industry. The total subsidies in 1998 amounted to 150,000 lats, while in 1999 the figure was 41,000 lats.

In several shoreline villages vacation fishing is becoming a lucrative part of the tourism business.

The most common fishing tools in the Baltic Sea are standing traps for pilchard, as well as creels, nets and towlines. Standing traps for pilchard began to be used in the 1960s and are still used extensively from *Ainaži* to *Pape*. Creels are used all along the shoreline, and 12 different species of fish are caught with them.

In shore waters nets are more commonly used. Nets are used for all kinds of fish, except for benthic eelpout and eels. Tow lines are used in the *Irbe* narrows and along the shoreline to fish for flounder.

Creels for benthic eelpout were developed in the 1960s specifically for this species of fish. Today the shoreline of the Bay of Riga is the only place in the Baltic Sea where specialized fishing of benthic eelpout is so active.

Ugis Roze grows rainbow trout in basins that used to hold water purification systems in Riga

Rainbow trout

Fish ponds

A fish growing facility in *Dole*

Fishing for sprat in the Baltic Sea

Dried fish for domestic use and for export

Crabs live in lakes and rivers in Latvia and are a popular treat

A salmon trout heads for spawning grounds on the *Venta* River

Eel fishing in Lake *Usma*

Specialists measure salmon at *Vecdaugava* from which roe has been collected

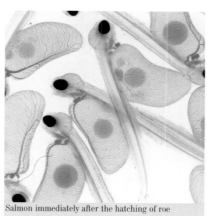
Salmon immediately after the hatching of roe

Young tench at a hatchery in *Tome*

Latvia is justifiably proud not only with developed fishing, fish processing and export of fish products all around the world, but also of the fact that the country has managed to restore depleted stocks of fish. Each year fishing companies in Latvia catch salmon, remove their roe and then hatch young salmon. The young salmon are kept for two years and then released into the open waters at night. Latvia grows more salmon, trout and rainbow trout than any other country on the Baltic Sea. The salmon grown by fishing companies do not suffer from salmon virus that is a problem for fishermen in Finland and Norway. What's more, Latvia is one of the few countries in Europe where salmon and salmon trout spawn in natural habitats – small and rapid rivers in Vidzeme and Kurzeme.

Salmon prepared for the removal of roe at *Vecdaugava*

Removing roe from a salmon

Rainbow trout young at a fish farm in *Tome*

The No. 2 thermoelectric plant in Riga

Director of the Energy
Department, Aleksandrs Ošs

Construction of the *Ķegums* hydroelectric station in 1937. The *Ķegums* hydroelectric station; upper right – reconstruction of one of the main
pieces of equipment at the station

The Riga hydroelectric station, the newest of the large hydroelectric power
plants the Riga hydroelectric station is situated close to the very border of Riga
city. *Daugava* does not have steep banks near to its mouth and thus the water
has covered a large area – nowadays often referred to as the Riga HES sea

A small hydroelectric station *Sprukti*. The energy policy of Latvia
stimulates building of small hydroelectric stations. Some 5 – 10 new
hydroelectric stations are built every year

The *Pļaviņas* hydroelectric station was built during 19-sixties. Its
water reservoir flooded one of the most picturesque sites in Latvia
including the famous symbol of Latvia – the *Staburags* rock. A new
city was built close to the HES named *Stučka* by communists. Today
its name is *Aizkraukle*

The outfall at the *Pļaviņas* hydroelectric station

Latvia imports its fuel, mostly natural and liquid gas, oil products and coal. The country also uses local sources of energy, including wood and peat. Hydroelectric and thermoelectric plants in Latvia produce electricity, and they use 20-25% of the fuel that is imported. Latvia is also an importer of energy supplies. Heat is mostly produced via imported fuel – heavy oil and natural gas. Low-capacity boiler houses are still fired with coal and various local products.

In the structure of the country's energy resources, petroleum products – heavy oil and light oil products – represent approximately 40%, natural and liquid gas represent among 23%. Hard fuel includes coal, wood and peat, and these represent approximately one-quarter of the energy resources. The output of hydroelectric stations – including imported electricity – amounts to approximately 10%.

Natural and liquid gas in Latvia is supplied to residents and companies by the stock company *Latvijas Gāze* and its branches, as well as by other companies. The natural gas supply system consists of 1,216 kilometres of trunk pipelines and 3,500 kilometres of distribution pipelines that are use to supply natural gas to industry, heat suppliers and residents in nearly all of the country's major cities. Natural gas is imported from the Russian Federation during the summer and pumped into the *Inčukalns* underground gas storage facility, which can handle up to four million cubic meters of gas. SC *Latvijas Gāze* provides natural gas during the winter to consumers in Latvia, Russia, Estonia and Lithuania. Two-thirds of the gas goes to various heat suppliers, while one-quarter goes to industry. The consumption of natural gas is rising very rapidly.

Latvia does not have any petroleum drilling locations, or any petroleum processing facilities. Petroleum products are supplied and sold in Latvia by private companies. Heat suppliers (70%) mostly consume heavy oil. The proportions which heating fuel represents in Latvia's energy structure are declining in accordance to European ecological positions. Legislators are particularly focusing on ensuring that the heating fuel used is with a low sulphur content. In the future Latvia is planning to replace heavy oil with fuels that are less harmful to the environment. The excise tax on heavy fuel is being raised from year to year, and it is expected that the consumption of this product in the future will be proportionally inverse to the consumption of natural gas.

Latvia also obtains energy from wood and peat. Most of the coal that is burned in the country comes from the CIS and Poland. Hard fuels are supplied to consumers in Latvia by private structures. Wood is burned by households (60%) and heat suppliers (25%).

Peat is mostly used in those places where it is obtained and processed.

Latvia's basic economic goals include a reorientation from overly extensive use of fuel wood to a more rational use of the product.

The first electricity plant in Riga, built in
the *Andrejsala* neighbourhood in 1905

The president of the
Wind Energy Association, Dr. Sc. Paulis
Barons

Wind generating
electricity plant at *Ainaži*

Today construction of low and medium volume power plants has become actual – small hydroelectric stations, wind rotors and co-generators have been erected in many places. Small and medium energy volume projects are supported by the National Energy Efficiency foundation that issues low interest credits. Latvia's Development agency is responsible for the foundation's daily operation. The financial resources of the foundation come from the PHARE program of EU amounting to 3,6 million euro, from Latvia's Land and Mortgage bank whose input with each loan should be no less than 20% of the money that is contributed by PHARE and from the Latvia's State budget

Earlier, a low-voltage switch
board, 1923. Now a 100.4 kV
transformer sub-station

LATVENERGO

Checking to ensure that a 20 kV line is not operational before repairs can begin

The white storks are often seen on the lines. They are able to build their nests there

A helicopter is used to clear branches along the route of a 110 kV electricity line

Bypass reactors at a 330 kV sub-station in *Valmiera*

This is how electricity lines were put up in earlier times. This pole was put up in 1935

Consumption is stabilising, and wood represents approximately 30% of the fuel that is used in Latvia.

98% of the electricity that is used in Latvia comes from the State-owned stock company *Latvenergo*. Electricity is produced by three hydroelectric stations on the *Daugava* River, as well as two thermoelectric facilities. Over the course of the last few years a number of independent producers have appeared on the scene, especially thermoelectric stations at industrial companies (2.8% of all supplies) and small hydroelectric stations (0.1%). In years when water supplies in the rivers are low, there is not enough electricity for domestic needs. Through effective use of the principles of competition, electricity is bought from Lithuania, Estonia and Russia.

The amount of electricity that Latvia can produce itself is completely dependent on the throughput of the *Daugava* River, as well as the average air temperature in the country. In 1998, the country's hydroelectric stations met 95% of need, while in 1999 the figure was considerably lower.

The State sets electricity purchase prices for the country, and small hydroelectric stations are paid a rate that is twice average

The electricity lines that cross the fields of Latvia in various directions – a heritage from the Soviet Union can still be seen today

Electricity lines these days are built with the help of helicopters. Radio relays are used to ensure communications during the process

A 110 kV line, with the turbine hall of the Riga No.2 Thermoelectric Station at the upper left

Line repair and clearing of trees are done with modern equipment

Transforming substation in *Baltezers*

110 kV line from the Riga 2nd Thermoelectrostation

A 110 kV sub-station at *Tukums*

Assembly of a 110 kV cable in *Ventspils*

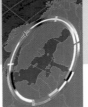

Participants at the founding meeting of the BALTREL project. SSC *Latvenergo* president Valdis Ginters is third from the left in the first row, while the director of the Latvian Ministry of Economics Energy Department, Aleksandrs Ošs, is second from the left in the second row

The SSC *Latvenergo* board of directors: executive director Aigars Meļko, president Kārlis Miķelsons, vice-president, economics director Ivars Liuziniks

A prize from the Baltic Chamber of Industry and Commerce was presented to the best company in the Baltic States – SSC *Latvenergo*. The prize is received by Valdis Ginters

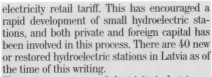

The SSC *Latvenergo* stand at the *Energy '99* exhibition

SSC *Latvenergo* president Valdis Ginters addresses a gathering at the opening phase of reconstruction of the *Pļaviņas* hydroelectric station

An international conference, *Investments in Energy in the Baltic Sea Region*

electricity retail tariff. This has encouraged a rapid development of small hydroelectric stations, and both private and foreign capital has been involved in this process. There are 40 new or restored hydroelectric stations in Latvia as of the time of this writing.

The main consumers of electricity in Latvia are industries (40%) and residents (25%).

Electricity in Latvia is supplied via a highly developed network of lines that exceed 100,000 kilometres in length. SSC *Latvenergo* has launched an ambitious program to restore and modernise its electrical plants and networks. Over the course of 10 years this will take Ls 963 million in investments, and 60% of the money will come from the company itself. The program is being implemented with the use of the most modern technologies and equipment.

The 1939 *Ķegums* hydroelectric station, as well as the *Pļaviņas* hydroelectric station is being reconstructed. Development of electricity grids is occurring most quickly in Riga and *Ventspils*. Among the 500 largest companies in the Baltic States in 1998, SSC *Latvenergo* was deemed the best, and it is also Latvia's largest taxpayer. According to the analysis by the *Datamonitor Group*, *Latvenergo's* economic indicators place it among the world's best electricity producers. The operations of the company are largely in line with European Union directives and other requirements, and SSC *Latvenergo* is actively involved in the establishment of a joint electricity market in the Baltic region and among the Baltic Sea States. The company has helped in the preparation, analysis and implementation of the Baltic Ring and BALTREL projects. Dispatch Centre for the power transmission systems of the three Baltic States is located in Riga, and it also provides co-ordinated operation of the grid with Russians integrated power system.

Heat in Latvia is provided through centralised heating systems, as well as local systems. The advantage of local heating systems in Latvia's Northern climate is the ability to reduce or even to avoid losses of heat during distribution. The

The *Baltija* dispatcher centre

advantage of centralised systems, by contrast, is the opportunity to reduce production costs, as well as harm to the surrounding environment.

The process of supplying heat is becoming increasingly decentralised in Latvia. The extent to which consumers are provided with heat is largely dependent on the type of heating supplies that are used, the region in which companies are located, the availability of natural gas pipelines in the area, as well as the purchasing power of consumers. The production capacity of heat-producing systems is also of importance.

Heat producers mostly use heavy oil and natural gas. In local systems, use is made of natural gas, fuel wood (firewood and wood chips) and peat. In the centralised heating system, natural gas represents 40% of the fuel that is burned, and heavy oil represents another 40%.

Latvia has an Energy Regulatory Council which licenses electricity companies, develops methodologies for calculating tariffs and approves the tariffs that are proposed by energy suppliers. Tariffs in Latvia are set on the basis of principles that are aimed at protecting the interests of electricity consumers, promoting the effective and rational work of energy suppliers, and ensuring that the process of approving tariffs is an open and transparent one. The Energy Regulatory Council approves tariffs on electricity, heat and gas.

The average retail tariff for electricity for residents at the time of this writing is Ls 0.033051 per kWh for those who use a unified tariff, while those who have a tariff differentiated by time of day pay Ls 0.03678 during the day and Ls 0.02574 at night.

A street light in Riga in 1901

Latvenergo and *Latvijas Gāze* are not only the foundation of the economy and energy of Latvia. They are friendly competitors in energy field and social life of Latvia as well. Particularly their basketball teams

Rigas electrical distribution network

LATVIAN GAS

Natural gas is not found in Latvia, and it is imported via pipeline from gas fields in the Russian regions of *Yamala* and *Urengoya*. In Latvia the process is maintained and organised by the stock company *Latvijas Gāze*.

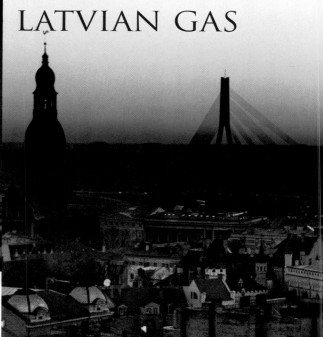

Adrians Davis is the executive board chairperson of the stock company *Latvijas Gāze*. He has worked in the provision of gas system since 1965. He became the head of the company in 1988

Latvia is connected to Siberia's vast natural gas fields via pipelines that are surrounded by broad firebreaks

The network of gas pipelines that covers the entire territory of Latvia was established in the 1960s and 1970s

Riga's first gas factory was built in 1862 in *Vingrotāju iela*. It marked the beginning of the use of gas in the Latvian economy

Natural gas arrived in Latvia 100 years later. A trunk pipeline from *Valdaja* to Riga was built in 1962, and Riga's first gas regulation facility was opened in *Biķernieku iela*

A gas reservoir at *Vagonu iela* 20 was built based on a design by the architect Kārlis Felsko in 1901. It was next to Riga's second gas factory, which was opened in 1874. Since 1997 SC *Latvijas Gāze* has renovated the reservoir, and it has become a symbol for the company. The building is listed on the country's register of protected monuments

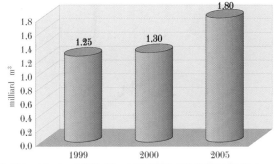

The quantity of gas that is used in Latvia is increasing steadily, by 5-10% each year. Specialists expect this trend to continue

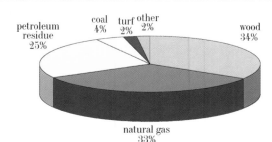

The proportions of various kinds of fuel that are used in Latvia – gas and wood are being used more and more each year, while the use of heavy oil, which is harmful to the environment, is on the decline

petroleum residue 25%
coal 4%
turf 2%
other 2%
wood 34%
natural gas 33%

Quantity and quality measurements are conducted on gas that is received from Russia here, at the international gas measurement station *Korneti*, which was built in 1997 on the Latvian frontier in *Alūksne* district

The stock company *Latvijas Gāze* is the only company in Latvia which imports, transports and sells natural gas, which is environmentally friendly and, when compared to other kinds of fuel, causes very little pollution. SC *Latvijas Gāze* and its clients alike are for a Latvia which is clean and green. A caring attitude toward the surrounding environment is at the root of SC *Latvijas Gāze*'s motto: "For a clean and green Latvia!"

The network of gas pipelines in the Baltic States. The red unbroken lines represent trunk lines that are in operation; purple lines represent planned gas pipelines in the future. The map also shows potential sites of underground gas storage facilities (marked UGSF on the map)

What was once a simple network of pipelines has now become a highly computerised system in which specialised software is used to provide for safety and other important processes. The *Inčukalns* underground control center ensures uninterrupted and precise delivery of gas to all of the Baltic Countries and to Northwest Russia

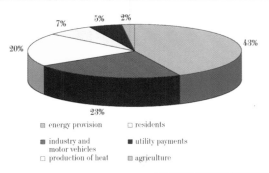

Consumption of natural gas in Latvia. The majority of natural gas is consumed by power industry. Currently individuals are starting to consume a larger proportion of gas

THE INČUKALNS UNDERGROUND GAS STORAGE FACILITY

The *Inčukalns* underground gas storage facility is located in three parishes – the *Sēja*, *Krimulda* and *Inčukalns* parishes. It has been in operation since 1968. The facility can store up to 4 billion cubic meters of gas, including 2.15 billion cubic meters of buffer gas and 1.85 billion cubic meters of active gas.

Natural gas is pumped from Russia to Latvia during the summer and early autumn. Most of the gas is placed into the underground storage facility. Enormous compressors are used to pump the gas into porous sandstone rock that is 700 meters under the ground and is surrounded on all sides by clay and dolomite through which the gas cannot pass. During the winter, the storage facility provides gas to consumers in Latvia, Estonia, Lithuania and Western Russia. The *Inčukalns* facility is completely safe and ecological research has shown that it has no deleterious effect on the surrounding air or groundwater. Underground storage facilities of this kind are very uncommon in the world, but Latvia has several more – at *Snēpele* (with a capacity of 17.5 million cubic meters), *Aizpute* (16 million), *Dobele* (10 million) and *Ziemeļblī- dene* (9 million), among others. Latvia's underground gas storage facilities could theoretically provide gas to most of the continent of Europe for an entire winter.

Compressors pumping gas to the depth of 700 m

A graphic illustration of a cross-section of the Earth's crust at the *Inčukalns* underground gas storage facility

Europe's most significant underground gas storage from a bird's perspective

Latvijas Gāze executive board member Janis Kalvans

Latvijas Gāze executive board member Gints Freibergs

Latvijas Gāze executive board member Berthold Martin Flick

SC *Latvijas Gāze* was one of the first major State-owned companies in the country to be completely privatised. In 1997, a purchase agreement was signed by the Latvian Privatisation Agency, SC *Latvijas Gāze*, the Russian stock company *Gazprom* and a German energy consortium called *Ruhrgas/Preusen Elektra*. The Latvian state retained ownership of 39% of the company, while *Gazprom* bought 16%, *Ruhrgas/Preusen Elektra* purchased 27.5%, and a company called *Itera Latvija* bought 8.9%. In the photo above, the purchase is sealed with the signatures of SC *Latvijas Gāze* executive board chairman Adrians Davis, *Gazprom* president Rem Jahirev and Privatisation Agency general director Janis Naglis.

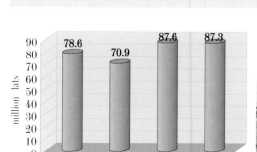

SC *Latvijas Gāze*'s net turnover, in millions of lats

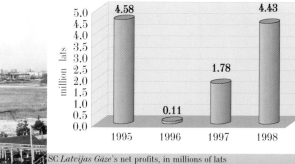

SC *Latvijas Gāze*'s net profits, in millions of lats

Latvijas Gāze executive board member Anda Ulpe

Latvijas Gāze executive board member Aleksandrs Mihejevs

The distribution of shares in SC *Latvijas Gāze*

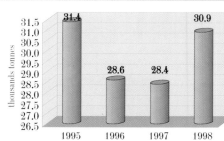

The volume of liquid gas sold to consumers

Liquid gas in gas cylinders is produced by oil processing plants. Latvia imports such gas, mostly from Russia. The gas is pumped from railway cisterns and then filled into cylinders at a liquid gas export facility in Riga

434,000 housing units in Latvia use gas that is pumped from cylinders

The Riga liquid gas export facility has port facilities which allow a/s *Latvijas Gāze* to provide stevedore services, reloading gas which comes by rail from Russia into ships which take the gas to Western Europe

SC *Latvijas Gāze* has always held safety to be a critically important priority. Because the process in which SC *Latvijas Gāze* is engaged always presents potential fire hazards, the company has its own well-equipped fire-fighting service. Professional skills competitions are held each year, and these are attended not only by the company's own specialists, but also by other teams from Latvia and abroad

In places where the natural gas pipeline network is not nearby, SC *Latvijas Gāze* provides opportunities to use liquid gas to produce heat. Aboveground or underground gas reservoirs are used for this purpose

Each year SC *Latvijas Gāze* invests approximately Ls 1 million in installing new gas pipelines and in providing gas to new towns, villages and industrial facilities

SC *Latvijas Gāze* has nearly 900,000 clients in Latvia. More than 400,000 housing units in the country use natural gas, while another 434,000 use liquid gas from cylinders. The largest number of housing units with gas services is found in Riga, *Daugavpils*, *Liepāja*, *Jelgava*, *Jūrmala* and *Ventspils*. For ecological and economic reasons, cities large and small are demonstrating increased interest in using natural gas

SC *Latvijas Gāze* has always supported the use of modern technologies. Virtually every Latvian city at one time had a huge and unsightly boiler heating facility, but now many have been replaced by much smaller facilities that have the same capacity. Gas in these facilities is burned very economically, without harming the environment and without causing a blot on the landscape

People are increasingly using gas to heat private houses, as well as to set up internal heating systems in apartment buildings

Gas is used extensively in Latvia by industrial facilities, especially those that produce metal and glass

Nearly 900,000 housing units in Latvia use gas stoves for cooking

SC *Latvijas Gāze* attends various exhibitions in Latvia and in other countries, demonstrating products and technologies, including ways of using natural and liquid gas in motor vehicles. There are a number of petrol stations in Riga which also provide liquid and natural gas

The president and board chairman of *Ventspils Nafta*, Igors Skoks

Ventspils Nafta is one of the most technologically powerful terminals in the Baltic Sea region. The company sits on less than 100 hectares of land, but the tank park can handle more than 1 million m³ of products

The operations and development of *Ventspils Nafta* are of interest to companies outside of Latvia, too. Here we see *Ventspils Nafta* officials making a presentation in Moscow. From the left: *Ventspils Nafta* vice president Olafs Berkis, president Igors Skoks, the president of the Latvian Transit Business Association and Ventspils Mayor Aivars Lembergs, the first deputy chairman of the *Ventspils Nafta* council, Janis Blaževičs, and the chairman of the council, Mamerts Vaivads

Of great importance in the Latvian fuel and energy market is the transit of oil and oil products through Latvia. Gasoline and oil products from Russia are transported to many countries in the world through Ventspils. The transit corridor of the company *Ventspils Nafta* is the most advantageous and safest route to transport oil and oil products from Russia and other countries of the CIS to Northern Europe and the rest of the world. *Ventspils Nafta* is the largest oil and oil products terminal in the Baltic Sea region, and its shares are floated on the official list of the Riga Stock Exchange. After 40 years of successful operations in the Soviet Union, the company in the 1990s developed very rapidly to become the most modern and promising company in the Baltic States. The main advantages of *Ventspils Nafta* are its geographic location, its ice-free deepwater port, its well developed infrastructure, its free operational capacity, and its long years of experience.

Oil is shipped to Ventspils by pipeline and oil products come by rail from Russia, while diesel fuel is piped in from Russia, Lithuania and Belarus. The company also unloads gasoline from tankers and loads it into railroad cisterns and tanker trucks. Oil and oil products from Ventspils are mostly exported to Western Europe and North America.

Ventspils Nafta sits on a bit less than 100 hectares of land, while its tank park can handle more than 1 million cubic meters of oil and oil products. The tank park and the equipment used therein are the most modern in the Baltic Sea region. The tank park has two rail trestles for the loading and unloading of oil products from railroad cars, technological pumping stations and other important ancillary services.

The loading of oil products onto tankers takes place at three piers. The maximum depth of the Ventspils port channel is 17.5 meters. After a reconstruction of the port and a deepening of the shipping channel, *Ventspils Nafta* can now service ships of a weight of up to 120,000 tons – the largest ships that can enter the Baltic Sea. Today it is common to see two or three ships at a time at *Ventspils Nafta* which carry 100,000 tons and more. This has increased the competitiveness of *Ventspils Nafta* very considerably, allowing freight owners to reduce shipping costs and to reach North America and Eastern Asia without having to reload in Western Europe. The transit corridor of *Ventspils Nafta* has become cheaper by approximately USD 15 million per year thanks to the deepening of the port. As competition in the Baltic Sea region increases in the area of Russian oil exports, the company has made enormous investments and capital investments The reconstruction and modernization of *Ventspils Nafta* in the first five years of the new century will take up investments of USD 380 million – between USD 50 and 80 million each year. *Ventspils Nafta* is expanding and modernizing its operations in line with international standards, both in terms of client services and in terms of environmental protection. The company's environmental and quality management system has been certified on the basis of the ISO-900s and ISO-14001 standards.

A new railroad trestle to unload rail-delivered oil products

Oil is supplied from Russia by pipeline, and *Ventspils Nafta* handles 13% of Russia's oil exports

The restored administrative building

The management center of *Ventspils Nafta* is fully automated, and operators constantly monitor the reloading of oil products

Ventspils Nafta is located in a geographically advantageous place in the world, and it boasts an ice free and deepwater port. The maximum depth of the port channel is 17.5 meters, so *Ventspils Nafta* can handle the largest tankers. Ships with a load capacity of more than 100,000 tons are a common sight at the port

The president of the stock company *Komforts*, Atis Zirdziņš, standing in a boiler house that his company installed in *Bolderāja*

The director of *Saldus siltums*, Leons Žutants, is the president of the Latvian Association of Heating Companies

The director of a new boiler house in *Limbaži*, which was reconstructed with financing from the Swedish SIDA agency – Valentins Tarakanovs

Ivars Morozs, chairman of the Small Hydro-Energy Association, which was founded by 16 owners and designers of hydroelectric stations, as well as equipment manufacturers and others who are involved in the field of hydroelectricity. The Association and its executive board have members from all over Latvia, and the goal of the organisation is to promote the development of small hydroelectric plants in the country. In 2000, there were 56 such plants in Latvia

The executive director of the Latvian Association of Heating Companies, Andris Akermanis, the organisation's president, Leons Žutants, and the vice president, Jānis Mičulis

Aivars Natre, executive director of the Latvian Small Energy Fund

Dainis Reiters, chairman of the Energy Activity Fund's supervisory board

The *Orions* company is a leading producer of boilers and related systems in Latvia. In the foreground – one of the components for a boiler that burns wood chips and peat

Atis Zviedris, the director of the sustainable energy information office *Spars*. The office is a member of the Coalition for a Clean Baltic. It is a non-governmental organisation, which collects, translates and distributes information in the field of sustainable energy, the use of renewable energy resources, and energy efficiency. It publishes a newsletter, *Spars*

Energy is the driving force and development cornerstone of any economy. Latvia does not have many energy resources, and its wealth is found in its forests, its peat, its water and its wind. Local oil deposits and geothermal waters are gradually being discovered, but the fact is that local resources at this time provide for only one-fifth of the country's energy needs. The rest is imported in the form of polluting energy sources such as coal, gas and oil products.

The structure of Latvia's energy use is dictated by the country's climate, as well as the quality of buildings. Approximately 40% of energy consumption goes toward heating, 27% – toward industrial needs, 20% for transport and 11% for electricity.

Heating companies are the leading consumer of natural gas – 60% of total consumption. The vast majority of the natural gas (82%) is used in Riga district. Furthermore, 75% of liquefied gas is used in households. Fuel oil is used throughout the country, mostly for heat. It is extensively used in centralised heating systems because its supply does not involve the expensive construction and maintenance of gas pipelines. Peat is burned by the Riga Thermoelectric Station and a few local boiler houses.

The consumption of coal has dropped to just 2% of the overall sector, because coal is expensive and environmentally harmful. Wood and wood scraps are increasingly being used for heat, especially in individual households. This is a local and environmentally friendly fuel, which already accounts for more than 25% of the fuel used for heating in Latvia.

Any organic fuel, when burning, produces oxygen and emissions such as ash, dust, soot and smoke with CO, CO_2, NO_x, MeO_x, etc. These emissions accumulate in Latvia and contribute to pollution. The country's energy supply policies include principles for sustainable development – fuels which are less harmful and which can be absorbed by nature must be imported and used. Much remains to be done to prevent the illegal importation of low-quality and harmful fuels, which poison the air, the water and all living beings.

Latvia's government policy in the energy sector is also aimed at a more efficient use of energy uses and the wider use of local and environmentally friendly fuels. Particular attention is being devoted to the building of co-generation plants, the heating of buildings, and the thrifty use of resources. Latvia, in accordance with the requirements of the Kyoto Conference, has been reducing consumption of fossil fuels in a targeted way. Since the renewal of Latvia's independence, 56 small hydroelectric plants have been restored, and four high-capacity wind turbines have been installed. The construction of locally significant co-generation plants is on the rise.

The work of major energy suppliers throughout Latvia is supplemented with the work of little energy – a part of the overall energy infrastructure in Latvia which promotes the use of local and natural energy resources, implements

The Riga No.2 Thermoelectric Station

The heavy oil tanks of the Riga No.2 Thermoelectric Station

An experimental co-generation motor facility and related equipment

Professor Vilnis Gulbis of the Latvian Agricultural University gives instructions to the builders of a piece of heating equipment

Equipment that is used for the emulsion of heavy oil so as to make it easier to burn and to reduce harmful emissions of SO_2 and NO_x

The boiler house in *Limbaži*

The executive board chairman of the Association of Energy Resource Suppliers, Vladimirs Barinovs

methods aimed at the efficient and thrifty use of energy resources by end consumers, and promotes the introduction of technologies which are appropriate for environmental protection. *Little energy* is a sector of the economy, which is made up of final consumers, as well as small and medium businesses. Thus the Latvian Association of Heating Companies brings together heating companies, as well as enterprises which produce the necessary equipment. Members of the Association represent fully four-fifths of the heat that is produced in Latvia. The Association works to resolve various problems in this area, focusing on the development of centralised heating as the most efficient and environmentally friendly form of heating. Progressive knowledge is being introduced, modern, energy-saving technologies are being installed, local heating equipment manufacturing is being promoted, and the maximum use of local fuels is being encouraged.

The Association regularly makes proposals concerning legislation, financing and technological considerations. It has participated in the formulation of heating development concepts, programs and plans. It also trains specialists and organises seminars for the exchange of experience.

Members of the Association include enormous companies such as *Latvenergo* and *Rīgas siltums*, as well as smaller heating companies in cities like *Liepāja*, *Ventspils*, *Jelgava*, *Saldus*, *Jēkabpils*, *Ogre*, *Cēsis*, *Madona*, etc. Also represented are the local government heating divisions of *Valmiera*, *Valka* and other towns. Companies which have worked with the association include *Komforts*, *Orions* and *Latura*, which produce boilers and related systems and install modern boiler houses; *Poliurs* and *Elk*, which specialise in the production of insulated industrial pipelines; *REMUS*, *Verta*, *Marine*, *ABB Alstrom Power* and others, which are specialised in the maintenance and servicing of heating; *EFE*, *Strasa Konsultanti*, *Lafipa* and *BEK-Konsult*, which provide energy consultations and design heating systems; and *Fan*, *Onninen LAT*, *Danfoss* Ltd., *Vaks Serviss*, *Rubate*, *Vattenfall Latvia* Ltd. and *Wilo Baltic* Ltd., which supply systems and equipment.

The Association and its members have joined together with the Ministry of Environmental Protection and Regional Development, the Department of Energy of the Ministry of Economics, the Energy Department of the Latvian Development Agency, and various professional organisations in order to prepare proposals for the government in the area of state and local government policy in the area of heating supplies, policies concerning the structure of various kinds of fuel that are used, and the prevention of crisis situations.

The Association is a member of *Euroheat & Power – unichal*, which is an association of heating and energy companies in Europe. It also maintains excellent contacts with similar associations in the Scandinavian countries.

The executive board of SC *Rigas siltums* (from the left): Andrejs Beņķis, Voldemārs Ilguns, Edgars Licis, Aris Žigurs, Hugo Pāvuls, Juris Zeiza, Andris Bože

The administrative building of SC *Rigas siltums*, *Cēsu iela* 3a

An automated boiler house

The *Vecmilgrāvis* heat plant

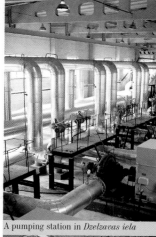

A pumping station in *Dzelzavas iela*

The boiler of a heat plant

The *Zasulauks* heat plant

The Riga district heating supply system rehabilitation project is being discussed together with Swedish experts and representatives of the World Bank

In 1956, the *Andrejsala* transmission pipeline (known then as the Riga *VRES*) began to supply heat to residential buildings in the area of the Riga Trade Port. In 1959, there were 2.3 kilometres of heating networks in Riga, and they provided heat to 89 clients. The amount of thermal energy supplied each year was 47,500 Gcal.

As the district heating system in Riga expanded, there was a need to find new heating sources. Several new heat plant were constructed – *Ķengarags*, *Daugavgrīva*, *Imanta* and *Ziepniekkalns*. Since 1974, the Riga No.2 combined heat and power plant (*TEC-2*) has also supplied thermal energy to Riga.

Up to 1996, the district heating system in Riga were serviced by various enterprises, while the sources of heat and the transmission pipeline belonged to several owners. In order to put the system into order, to make it safer, and to administer it more effectively, a unified heat supply enterprise had to be established. Thus, on 14th March 1996, the stock company *Rigas siltums* was founded. It began work on 1st May of the same year. The shareholders are the Riga City Council (49.73%), the Latvian Privatisation Agency (49.72%), the Baltic Transit Bank (0.54%) and SSC *Latvenergo* (0.01%).

SC *Rigas siltums* is the largest district heating enterprise in Latvia and in the Baltic States. The enterprise owns 747 km of district heating networks, 5 heat plants and 81 boiler houses, the total installed capacity of which is 1,489 MW. SC *Rigas siltums* provides 76% of the total thermal energy consumed in Riga (a city of 796,800 inhabitants at time of writing). Approximately 72% of the thermal energy that is supplied is purchased from the combined heat and power plants of SSC *Latvenergo*, while 28% is produced by SC *Rigas siltums* in its own facilities. Most of the heat that SC *Rigas siltums* produces itself comes from the burning of gas (94%), which is the cheapest and ecologically cleanest fuel available at this time. Taking into account the great potential of the wood processing industry in Latvia, the *Daugavgrīva* heat plant utilises wood chips as a fuel.

The turnover for SC *Rigas siltums* in the 1998/1999 fiscal year was 64 million lats and the volume of thermal energy sold was 3.981 million MWh. In terms of net turnover, SC *Rigas siltums* is the eighth largest enterprise in Latvia, and the 13th largest contributor of social security and income tax.

The infrastructure development strategy accepted by the Riga City Council states that district heating will also in the future be the dominant form of heat supply in Riga. However, given that the basic system is 30-40 years old, it must be updated and modernised. Through cooperation with Swedish experts and with the financial support of the Swedish government, a project to rehabilitate Riga's district heating system has been prepared. The aim is to provide for a system that is safer and economically and ecologically more effective. The total cost of the project is 140 million USD. The enterprise will invest 30 million USD, while the rest of the money will come from the World Bank, the Nordic Investment Bank, the Swedish International Development Agency and the Riga City Council. The rehabilitation of the heating supply system will avert rapid price increases, increase the safety of exploiting the system, and will better satisfy the comfort-related demands of the population.

Up to World War II, the heating supply of most buildings in Riga was ensured mainly by utilising stove heating. Only a few buildings had built-in individual boiler rooms. In some cases gas water heaters were used, but most often water was heated with wood-burning boilers.

The basis for a district heating system in Riga was laid in 1952, when design on the first transmission pipeline began. The construction works was performed at the same time as the Riga No.1 combined heat and power plant (*TEC-1*) was constructed, and in November 1958, this transmission pipeline went on line. The first clients of the district heating system were the *VEF* factory and the Riga Wagon Factory. In 1959, the transmission pipeline was expanded to *Matisa* Street in Riga, and a year later – to the Central Railway Station.

The *Daugavgrīva* heat plant, which utilises also wood chips as fuel

Automated individual heating stations in buildings allow inhabitants to select the most comfortable level of heating for the building

The thermal energy supplied is registered on thermal energy meters installed in Riga's buildings

PEAT

Swamps cover 10.7% of Latvia's territory, and there is a reserve of more than 1.5 billion tons of peat in those swamps – approximately 0.5% of the world's supply.

There are many different kinds of peat in Latvia. Anything that can be made of peat can be made in Latvia – and at a very high quality, too.

Peat is used in full compliance with environmental protection regulations, including international ones. Latvia licenses entities that want to use peat. Industrial peat has been harvested in Latvia for many decades. Approximately 0.6 million tons of peat are harvested each year, and that does not exceed sustainability levels in the swamps. The main ways in which peat is used in Latvia is as a heating fuel, mostly used by the No.1 Thermoelectric Station in Riga. There are also various kinds of high-quality and low-decomposition peat, and most of these are exported. Export volumes have increased from year to year. Latvia exports peat to 36 countries, especially Germany, the Netherlands and Great Britain. Work with foreign companies has expanded, and modern technologies and systems are being introduced in this process.

Since 1996 Latvia's major peat producers have joined together in the Latvian Association of Peat Producers. Companies in the association produce the more complicated forms of products – substrata and briquettes, for example. The goal of the association is to ensure the effective and rational use of peat resources and production potential, devoting particular attention to various extraction and regeneration projects. The use of peat resources is also a subject of attention in the Latvian government. The National Program on Energy Resources plans to increase the proportion which peat represents in the country's overall energy resource structure to 4-5% of the total. Peat boilers are to be used for co-generation, and this will help to improve heating systems in Latvia's small towns.

Extracting cut peat

Milled peat

Cut peat ready for sale

Drying of cut peat

Peat fields

A regenerated swamp after extraction of peat

Zigfrids Jurešs (left), president of the stock company *Seda*, reviews product quality

Loading of crumbled peat

Peat aboard a ship for export

Packed peat before loading aboard a ship

The executive board of the Latvian Fuel Traders Association. In the front: executive board chairperson Kārlis Miķelsons (*Latvija Statoil*), Ziedonis Jansons (*Gulbenes degviela*), Alla Moroza (*Viada*) and Jevgeņijs Kisiels (*Latvijas Nafta*). In the second row: Ojārs Karčevskis (*Astarte Nafta*), Māris Jānis Oga (*Hydro Texaco Latvija*), Edgars Zālītis (*Shell Latvia*), Haims Kogans (*Lukoil Baltija R*), executive director Uldis Sakne, and Argots Lusiņš (*Kurzemes degviela*)

«LATVIJA STATOIL» «SHELL LATVIA» «LATVIJAS NAFTA»
«NESTE LATVIJA» «HYDRO TEXACO LATVIJA» «GULBENES DEGVIELA»
«VIADA» «LUKOIL BALTIJA R» «ASTARTE NAFTA»

The *Kaņepa* petrol station in *Ieriķi*

A *Neste* petrol station

A *Gulbenes degviela* petrol station   A *Latvijas Nafta* petrol station

An *Astarte Nafta* petrol station

A *Statoil* petrol station

Viada supplies fuel to one of its petrol stations

A *Shell* petrol station

The number of motor vehicles in Latvia has been increasing by 10-20% annually since 1990. In the early 1990s, most of the automobiles that appeared on the roads were used cars imported from Germany, Holland and Sweden. At the end of the decade, however, there were increasing numbers of brand new cars. All of the world's major automobile manufacturers operate in Latvia, while banks offer attractive leasing terms. All of this means that consumption of petrol is on the rise in Latvia, and the demand for high-quality petrol is also increasing. People are also seeking good quality repair and technical maintenance services.

Until 1992, the State held a monopoly on the petrol and diesel fuel market. Prices were regulated, and there were often shortages. Latvians took empty barrels and cans to Lithuania, where there was a facility, which produced petrol, just in order to keep their cars running. In 1992, the State began to privatise petrol stations in the country, and private companies began to sell petrol from cisterns along the country's roadsides. Finland's *Neste* and Norway's *Statoil* entered the market in the same year.

Since 1995, the State has allowed petrol sales only at petrol stations that are specifically intended for that purpose. Requirements concerning safety and ecological concerns are much stricter than in many other parts of Europe, and the petrol stations that have been built over the last 10 years are among the most modern in all of Eastern Europe. Petrol stations in Latvia feature convenient and inexpensive stores at which people can buy motor oil, accessories, household goods, magazines and newspapers, food and beverages.

At the turn of the millennium, Latvia's petrol stations were selling approximately 1 million tons of fuel each year. Most of this fuel was being sold by companies that are part of the Latvian Fuel Traders Association – Latvian companies such as *Astarte Nafta*, *Gulbenes degviela*, *Kurzemes degviela*, *Latvijas Nafta* and *Viada*, as well as transnationals such as *Hydro Texaco Latvija*, *Shell Latvia*, *Neste Latvija*, *Latvija Statoil*, *Lukoil Baltija R* and others. The Association was set up to promote honest competition, to defend the common interests of fuel retailers, and to promote growth in the oil products market in the Republic of Latvia. The Association co-operates with the European Fuel Traders Association, and it works to promote the harmonisation of Latvian legislation with the requirements of the EU.

A *Hydro Texaco* petrol station

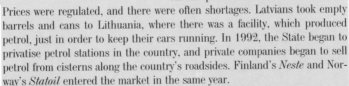

A *Lukoil* petrol station

The dolomite processing complex *Saulkalne S Ltd.*

Dolomite from *Kanciems* is the material, which *Saulkalne S* Ltd. uses in its work

The limited liability company *Saulkalne S* Ltd. was founded in 1995, and today it is the leading producer of dolomite products in Latvia. Dolomite is extracted at *Kanciems* and processed at the *Saulkalne* facility. *Saulkalne S* Ltd. provides supplies to companies that are engaged in construction, road building and agriculture. The main types of products are agricultural and construction lime, dolomite fragments and ground dolomite, mineral powder for bituminous concrete mixtures, and dolomite and quartz sand for dry construction mixtures.

Extracting dolomite at *Kanciems*

Dolomite and quartz sand that is produced at *Saulkalne* is used in construction

Lugaži Ltd. provides grout to construction sites all over Latvia

Lugaži Ltd. produced these reinforced concrete constructions

Lugaži Ltd. was founded in 1994 based on one of the largest reinforced concrete construction factories in the former Latvian SSR. *Lugaži* Ltd. produces cement, grout, reinforced concrete constructions and reinforcement nets. The company mostly uses local raw materials and employs 70 people. Among the construction projects that have made use of *Lugaži* Ltd. products are the building of the Latvian National Opera, *Shell*, *Neste* and *Statoil* petrol stations, the *Akvalandija* construction materials store, as well as private residential buildings all around Latvia.

The stock company *Lode*'s brick and ceramics line

The restoration of Riga's Blackheads House involved the use of bricks from SC *Lode*

Ceramic products from SC *Lode*

The stock company *Lode* is the leading producer of building materials in Latvia, and it is sited on a Devonian era clay deposit. The large amount of iron oxide in the clay is why SC *Lode* products are distinctly red in hue. The factory produces bricks and roof tiles, and it also extracts and processes clay. There are 260 employees at the firm. SC *Lode* also extracts quartz sand from a quarry at *Bale*, which is used for glassmaking. SC *Lode* exports its products to Poland, Finland, Russia and Ukraine.

A house built from bricks that were produced at SC *Lode*

The factory at SC *Lode*

Bloks M1 Ltd. produced these aerated concrete objects

The stock company *Broceņu šiferis* was established in 1997, when it split off from an older cement and slate company that dated back to 1938

The president of SC *Broceņu šiferis*, Martiņš Bumanis

The cement and slate factory *Broceni*

A dolomite quarry at *Kanciems*

Decorative dolomite at the *Birži* quarry

A dolomite cliff near *Cēsis*

Dolomite from *Kanciems* was used for the exterior of the Riga Congress Hall

Dolomite from *Saulkalne* used in an Art Nouveau building on *Alberta iela*

The exterior of the *Rauna* Society's building is covered with travertine that came from a site near *Rauna*

Saulkalne dolomite at the Latvian Botanical Gardens

Travertine was utilised in the Brethren Cemetery ensemble

Sandstone from *Rembate* was used on the exterior of the Ministry of Finance building

Latvian sandstone contains dolomite, quartz and calcite

Travertine in the walls of the *Sigulda* Palace

Dolomite from *Saulkalne* in the exterior of St. Peter's Cathedral in Riga

RESTORATION

Melngalvju nams (the Blackheads House) is the most remarkable building on the *Rātslaukums* square. It is mentioned in writing as early as in 1334. Reconstructed for several times during 1619 - 1625, it was finally blown up in the beginning of World War II. The rebuilding was done by SC *Restaurators* during 1996 – 1999. The Celebration hall has new crystal lustres and oak tree panels. The front wall with sculptural groups and decorations from stone and metal is also new

The house of the Latvian Society was built in 1869 and designed by Janis G.Baumanis. It burned down in 1908 and was rebuilt in 1909 from the design of Eižens Laube and E. Pole. In the Soviet period it was used as the Officers House, what was the reason for decorations of a special military style. In 1999 the SC *Restaurators* managed by Valisa Uzuleņs restored the building. A modern ventilation system and heating was installed. The new copper roof will serve for a century. The front wall and the coat of arms was repainted. Also inside floors, walls and ceiling are renovated and the lustres restored

The restored hall of the Riga Latvian Society House is an appropriate place for important international events. It is chosen to host the annual conference of the European Bank of Reconstruction and Development. The hall is restored by SC *Restaurators*. Left: board members Baiba Slise, Ieva Dobelniece and Zigurds Menole, Board Chairman Valdis Uzuleņš, project manager Ivars Riciks

Building is one of the most important economic sectors for Latvia. It not only attracts one-half of the country's capital investments, but also provides a basis for all kinds of other economic sectors in the form buildings and other structures. The building sector offers a good reflection of the country's culture and its level of economic development.

The building sector employs approximately 6% of all workers in Latvia, accounting for 5-6% of GDP each year. Since Latvia has renewed its independence, the building sphere has been restructured in institutional and legal terms. The *Saeima* adopted a Building Law in 1995, which specifies the mutual relationships among participants in the building process, their rights, obligations and responsibilities, as well as the competence of State and local government administrative institutions in the building area. The Building Department of the Ministry of Environmental Protection and Regional Development performs the overall supervision of building in the country. The building process as such is controlled by the State Building Inspection and city and parish building boards.

The building industry is regulated by the *General Regulations on Building* issued by the Cabinet, other Cabinet regulations, as well as Latvian building standards. Since 1998, regulatory enactments in the building field have been harmonised with the relevant legislation of the European Union. A conformity assessment system is in place – building methods are certified, companies are licensed, as well as building objects are assessed as to their conformity to existing regulations.

In 1996, the Cabinet, seeking to develop the building industry further, accepted a strategic concept in respect of the building sector. In addition to government policy, this document also sets out the tasks, which are part of developing the construction industry, and because the subterranean depths of Latvia are rich with useful raw materials, locally produced construction materials can easily become competitive at the European level.

A national program on the building sector has also been prepared. There are several active NGOs in the field, including the Latvian Union of Civil Engineers and the Latvian Association of Building Workers.

Since 1994, the Ministry of Environmental Protection and Regional Development has been active in the work of the UN's *Habitat* program, which seeks to provide appropriate housing for everybody. Renovation and modernisation of housing has been particularly emphasised.

A multi-story parking garage

The oil terminals of the *Neste* company

THE STATE BUILDING INSPECTION

A power station on the *Ziemeļsuseja* River in *Sala* parish, *Jēkabpils* district

The chairman of the State Building Inspection, L. Jākobsons, and his deputy, H. Endriksone

Employees of the State Building Inspection

The State Building Inspection supervises building processes in Latvia, ensuring that these processes conform to laws and other regulatory enactments with respect to the quality of the procedures and the finished products.

The renewal of Latvia's independence occurred at a time when the laws in the area of building were incomplete. The old laws of the USSR had to be replaced with new laws that were in line with the renewed Latvian Civil Law, as well as with EU law. The task for the State Building Inspection is to ensure that the laws are implemented and followed properly. A full explanation of the relevant laws allows the participants in this process – supervisors, local government building boards and building inspectors – to rationalise the various norms, which are applied. In order to improve professional knowledge, the inspection organises seminars and meetings for building inspectors and the directors of building boards. Over the course of each year the inspection monitors more than 1,200 buildings in Latvia, prepares approximately 700 opinions regarding draft building projects, reviews some 170 complaints, prepares some 500 inspection acts, and participates in the work of commissions which approve buildings and other structures for use.

Since July 1st, 1998, Latvia has prohibited the sale of building materials that are not quality-certified. Criteria have been set out for 20 groups of materials, and assessment of quality is mandatory. The evaluation of building materials in the mandatory sector is done by two certification centres, 14 building materials testing laboratories and the State Building Inspection. The testing system is being shaped so as to be in line with the requirements of the EU.

Along with the hydroelectric stations on the *Daugava* River, smaller stations are being opened throughout Latvia. The first of these began work on the *Malta* River in *Viļāni* in 1994. In October 1999, there were 52 such power stations. These are buildings with heightened risk, and the State Building Inspection monitors the extent to which they conform to safety requirements.

The ice hall in *Liepāja*

SKONTO BŪVE LTD.

The *Skonto* Olympic Hall, which was built by the *Skonto Būve* Ltd. building company, is a closed, multifunctional athletic facility with a total area of 9,491 square meters. The hall has a football field that satisfies all international standards, there is room for 2,000 people in the stands, and there is a fully functional rehabilitation complex, as well

The monumental shopping complex *MOLS* was built in 1993 and 1994, and reconstruction was done in 1998. The shopping complex has a total area of 12,249.5 square meters, while the retail space amounts to 7,787.42 square meters

Skonto Būve Ltd. put up this four-story office building with rounded corners and a prominent column in the main facade. There is an open gallery around the perimeter of the fourth floor. This building fits in beautifully with the architecture of the surrounding city, and in functional terms, it provides excellent working conditions. The building is constructed of a steel and concrete carcass that is set on reinforced concrete piles. All of the materials in the wide-open and light interior spaces are certified, ecologically clean and modern

The executive board of the Latvian Association of Civil Engineers

The staff of the Building Department

RE & RE LTD.

Skonto Būve Ltd. and the stock company *Venceb* built an oil and petroleum products reservoir park for the stock company *Ventspils Nafta*. The reservoirs were assembled, safety walls and foundations were cemented, various pipelines and a pumping station were assembled, the manifold was built, a network for managing the valves in the system was constructed, technological systems were assembled, the cable dock and fire-fighting pumps were reconstructed, the latest technological systems were installed, and the entire system was automated with a computer network. For environmental protection purposes, the entire territory of the facility is covered with a geo-membrane – a high-density polyethylene film that is durable against oil products. This film is placed under all of the reservoirs, as well as under the cement foundations, which surround them

RE & RE Ltd. was entrusted with the reconstruction and renovation and interior design of the German embassy and the apartments of the embassy's employees. Specific work included restoration of decorative interior elements, as well as restoration of windows

The building company *RE & RE* Ltd. reconstructed the *Centrs* department store, as well as its facade, and the company also replaced the engineering network in the building

The *RE & RE* Ltd. building company was founded in 1993, and it does reconstruction, restoration and construction work, as well as preparing and gaining approvals for draft projects. The company has wood processing workshops that fully ensure *RE & RE* Ltd. objects with all necessary woodwork materials. Antique furniture is restored and packet-type wooden windows are built.
The company employs more than 250 people.

For the stock company *Invest Riga*, *RE & RE* Ltd. reconstructed the administration building, doing various restoration and interior design work, as well as fully replacing engineering communications and repairing the facade and the roof of the building

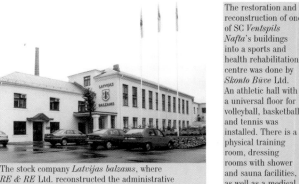

The stock company *Latvijas balzams*, where *RE & RE* Ltd. reconstructed the administrative building and its facade. The company also partly reconstructed the building's engineering network

The restoration and reconstruction of one of SC *Ventspils Nafta*'s buildings into a sports and health rehabilitation centre was done by *Skonto Būve* Ltd. An athletic hall with a universal floor for volleyball, basketball and tennis was installed. There is a physical training room, dressing rooms with shower and sauna facilities, as well as a medical treatment centre

The *Valdemārs* Center at *Valdemāra iela* 21 is the first top-of-the-line office building in Latvia. The total floor space in the building is 12,800 m². The building is constructed of concrete, granite and glass and cost USD 19 million. Work on the building was completed in one year's time. The initiator of the project was the SKANSKA construction company

KALNOZOLS LTD.

Valdis Kalnozols is one of the most successful businessmen in the Latvia, according to a 1999 survey in the financial magazine *Kapitāls*. He is the board chairman and co-owner of *Kalnozols un Partneri* Ltd.

One of the first multi-story automobile garages in Latvia, with room for 517 cars in a total area of 13,634 m². The design was by architect A. Gertmanis

The Volkswagen Center in *Krasta iela* in Riga was the largest Volkswagen showroom in Europe when it was completed in December 1998. It was built in conjunction with the Construction Consultation Entrepreneurship stock company

Kalnozols Celtniecība Ltd. employs 450 specialists of an average age of 31.5 years. It is one of the youngest and most dynamically growing construction companies in Latvia

Lido at *Krasta iela* 76 is Latvia's largest leisure complex – a restaurant with 700 seats (in the first phase of the project), a brewery, a wine cellar and an underground parking lot. The building merges massive horizontal logs with concrete, glass and modern and light metal constructions. This is the largest log building in Europe at this time

SC VENCEB

The stock company *Venceb* was founded in *Ventspils* in 1993 and today is one of the largest construction companies in Latvia. It provides design, construction and reconstruction services. Here we see the company's administrative building

One of the leading clients of SC *Venceb* is the SC *Ventspils Nafta*. SC *Venceb* expanded five of the company's tank parks (each tank holds 20,000 m³ of products) and designed and built a new one

Assembly of a new tank at the stock company *Ventspils Nafta*

SC *Venceb* beat a number of other companies to win a bid for tenders announced by the *Ventspils* Port Board to deepen the shipping channel and the outer part of the port in *Ventspils*

For the first time in the Baltic Sea region, a port was deepened to 17.5 meters so that Aframax type tankers can be received and handled at the port

Pavels Abramovs is the board chairman of SC *Venceb*

A breakwater and the shoreline were strengthened during the project

In 1997 SC *Venceb*, in cooperation with foreign partners, designed the largest mineral fertilizer reloading terminal in the world for the stock company *Kālija Parks*. The first phase of the project involved the construction of four warehouses with cupola-shaped roofs

SC *Venceb* is building engineering networks and access roads for *Noord-Natie Ventspils Terminals*

Latvia's geographic location opens up wide opportunities for the country to be an important phase in trade development between the East and the West. Latvia's transportation system is based on well-developed maritime transport, railroads, roads, pipelines and aviation. The transport infrastructure ensures the ability of the national economy to compete in the world and sets up a foundation for economic growth. Approximately 85% of overall cargo in Latvia is made up of transit freight. Transport, communications and related logistical services account for approximately 15% of Latvia's GDP. Latvia's integration into the European economic process will promote economic and trade development, but it will also increase demands on transport infrastructure and service quality. Latvia's strategic mission is to develop its automobile transport corridor to join in then European transportation system in the North-South and the East-West direction. Because the European Union feels that a route from Finland to Poland is a foregone conclusion, then in 1999, under the leadership of the European Commission, a Transport Infrastructure Needs Assessment was developed which included Latvia's East-West route and its rail connections, ports, combined transport terminals and airports in the European TINA network. The transit industry is concentrated around the three major ports of *Ventspils*, Riga and *Liepāja*. Ports are serviced by an extensive rail network that connects Latvia to the countries of the CIS. *Ventspils*, which is the largest oil export port on the Baltic sea, is connected to Russia with two pipelines – one which carries crude oil and one which carries oil products. In 1998 Latvia's ports handled 52.3 million tons of freight. Small ports are used for export of wood materials, fishing and leisure sailing. Successful work of the small ports provides jobs to local residents, tax payments to the state, and lower unemployment figures.

In 1995, the Cabinet of Ministers approved a national program on transportation development for the period between 1995 and 2010. In 1999 the program was updated with a transport development program for 2000-2006.

The government's policy goals in the area of transportation are to promote privatization and commercialization so as to create competition among various kinds of transportation, as well as within the individual sectors of the system, thus developing more effective and efficient transportation services.

Latvia's road network is well branched and extensive, and of the total length of roads, 1,617 kilometers are major roads. The total length of roads of national importance in Latvia is 20,329 kilometers, of which 7,842 kilometers are paved. There are some 40,000 kilometers of local government and local roads. Since 1996 the excise tax on fuel has been increased on a yearly basis, and part of the income from the tax is used to build and repair roads. Rural roads are a priority so that the needs of residents in the countryside can be met.

The number of automobile drivers in Latvia is

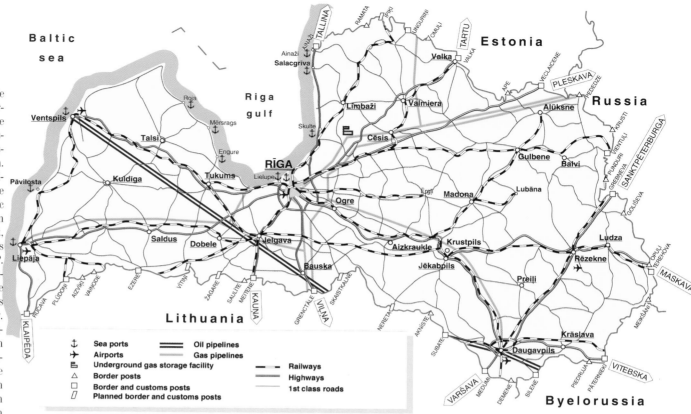

© Satiksmes ministrijas
Informātikas departaments

Latvia is connected to the other countries of the Baltic Sea with passenger and freight ships and ferries. This is a freight ferry which runs from *Liepāja* to Germany and back

Carriage over the river between *Jaunjelgava* and *Skrīveri*

on the rise, as is freight transportation on the country's roads. Latvia's rail system competes successfully with the systems of neighboring countries in the area of transit operations, and it is still competitive against road transportation, too.

The largest airport in the Baltic region is the Riga International Airport, and there are smaller airports in *Daugavpils*, *Liepāja* and *Ventspils*. Since the collapse of the Soviet Union, the structure of Latvia's air transportation market has changed. The number of flights to the East has declined, while the number of flights to the West has increased. Investment projects at the Riga airport have been focused on reconstructing runways and marking lights so that the safety of flights can be improved in line with ICAO standards. Steps have also been taken to allow the airport to receive larger airplanes. USD 10 million of the investment money needed for these projects has been contributed by the EBRD. Modernization of the passenger terminal began in 1997, and the work is to be completed in 2001. A new arrivals terminal was completed in 1999.

In 2000 and 2001 the airport is planning to

reconstruct the areas where airplanes are stored, as well as access routes. A new departure terminal is to be built with a state-guaranteed credit from the European Investment Bank, as well as with financing from departure fees that the airport collects.

International bus transportation to Tallinn, Vilnius, Moscow, Cologne and other cities, as well as between cities in Latvia, is provided by the company *Nordeka*

Rural bus traffic is subsidized from Latvia's roads fund. The former state-owned bus system has completely been privatized, and companies now provide transport with modern buses

On 23 August 1989, the residents of Latvia, Estonia and Lithuania joined hands to form a living chain through all three Baltic countries, thus demonstrating their unity and their opposition to the Molotov-Ribbentrop Pact of 23 August 1939 – a document which represented Nazi Germany's and Communist Russia's criminal intent and served as the basis for the launching of World War II and the occupation of the Baltic States

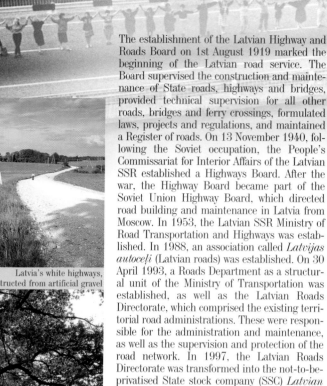

Latvia's white highways, constructed from artificial gravel

Beautiful avenues of trees are a feature of roads that lead to Latvia's farms

Farming road

The establishment of the Latvian Highway and Roads Board on 1st August 1919 marked the beginning of the Latvian road service. The Board supervised the construction and maintenance of State roads, highways and bridges, provided technical supervision for all other roads, bridges and ferry crossings, formulated laws, projects and regulations, and maintained a Register of roads. On 13 November 1940, following the Soviet occupation, the People's Commissariat for Interior Affairs of the Latvian SSR established a Highways Board. After the war, the Highway Board became part of the Soviet Union Highway Board, which directed road building and maintenance in Latvia from Moscow. In 1953, the Latvian SSR Ministry of Road Transportation and Highways was established. In 1988, an association called *Latvijas autoceļi* (Latvian roads) was established. On 30 April 1993, a Roads Department as a structural unit of the Ministry of Transportation was established, as well as the Latvian Roads Directorate, which comprised the existing territorial road administrations. These were responsible for the administration and maintenance, as well as the supervision and protection of the road network. In 1997, the Latvian Roads Directorate was transformed into the not-to-be-privatised State stock company (SSC) *Latvian Roads Directorate* under the supervision of the Ministry of Transport, while the existing district road administrations, also under the supervision of the Ministry of Transport, were merged into four State stock companies – SSC *Central District Roads*, SSC *Kurzeme Roads*, SSC *Vidzeme Roads* and SSC *Latgale Roads*.

Before World War I, there were 702 km of highways and paved roads in Latvia – just 1.23 km per 100 km² of territory. In England at the same time, the proportions were 100 km per 100 km². This is evidence of how little attention was paid by the government of Tsarist Russia, toward the building of roads in Latvia. During the period of independence, the Latvian government tried to create as extensive a roads network as possible, in order that people could move around easily, to ensure the exchange of information, that agricultural products could be brought to markets and railway stations to be exchanged for city goods. In the last year of independence – 1940 – the total length of highways in the country had increased to 11 483 km. In order to finance road building and maintenance, a special financing system was established, which comprised State budget funds and income from the Road Fund. Income for the Road Fund consisted of a 3% surcharge on tariffs that were charged for the carriage of goods, baggage and passengers on Latvia's railroads, as well as a 3% tax on alcoholic beverages.

Agrarian reform in independent Latvia led to the creation of more than 100 000 new farms. In order to connect the farms to the existing roads network, 35 384 km of access roads were built during the period of independence. Road builders at this time started to use the so-called artificial gravel, which was made by crushing granite and dolomite pebbles and stones that had earlier been screened out of gravel. This mass was then used to provide a cover for roads that was between 5 and 8 cm deep. The screened dolomite in the mixture promoted the hardening of the road surface, and this led to a durable road surface, which was appropriate for heavy traffic even during rainy seasons.

Asphalt was first used for road cover on the Riga-*Jelgava* highway in 1925. On those roads

where traffic was particularly heavy, a cement concrete cover was used, as all of the necessary building materials could be obtained in Latvia.

Earth-moving work in road building was usually done by hand, using wheelbarrows, wagons, traction systems and horse-drawn wagons. Horses were used to drag planers, scrapers, road rippers, two stone crushing machines and five steam steamrollers. Latvia's road builders bought their first trucks only in 1930. Two factories – *Stars* and *Tasmāre* – produced motorised graders. On the eve of the Soviet occupation in 1940, Latvia's road-builders were well supplied with more than 600 units of very good technical equipment. During the war this equipment was damaged or destroyed. At the beginning of the post-war period, the system had only a few graders and steamrollers, as well as a few war trophy automobiles.

World War II caused endless losses to Latvia's road system. As the German army retreated, it destroyed some 1000 km of crushed stone macadam highway and blew up or burned down 660 bridges. In the front-line areas, the roads were completely destroyed.

In the 1950s, the main task involved renewing that which had been destroyed during the war. Wooden bridges were built by the district road-building units themselves. Within a period of one year the largest monolithic reinforced concrete bridge in Latvia was renewed– the bridge across the *Gauja* River at *Sigulda*.

The Road Design Institute was established in 1956.

When most of the wartime damage had been eliminated, work began on road reconstruction and new road construction. Major roads were straightened, and in the 1960s, the building of first-category highways was started – the Riga-*Ogre* dual carriageway among them. The highway between Riga and *Jūrmala* was completed in 1972. The first appearance of blacktop highways occurred in 1951, when workers began to mix the blacktop on site as they worked on

A gravel road

A rural road leading to a picturesque windmill

A crushed stone road

The *Rauna-Smiltene* road at *Branti*

At present the international class motorway VIA Baltica – the straightest way from Warsaw to Tallinn and then further to Helsinki is being built on its place

A rural road in winter

The road construction museum in the *Slokenbeka* castle

At this place near *Priekuļi*, where the *Cēsis-Vecpiebalga* and the *Cēsis-Rauna* roads meet, in 1918, the Latvian and Estonian armies came together for joint military operations. The President of Latvia Kārlis Ulmanis and the President of Estonia Konstantin Pets, together with schoolchildren from the two countries, planted a memorial grove of trees there in 1938

roads. In 1957, asphalt-concrete factories were built in *Jelgava* and *Vangaži*.

In the 1960s, facilities for crushed stone fragmentation were opened in *Limbaži* and *Kaltene*, and crushed stone was brought in also from Karelia in Russia. Over the last several years, with the help of specialists from Sweden, Latvia has been preserving many gravel covers through the use of emulsions; this also helps to keep dust levels down. In parallel to the treatment of the surface and the placement of the upper layer, deep recycling of the cover is performed in which it is strengthened with emulsions and cement.

In the 1950s and 1960s, in order to overcome the chronic shortages of spare parts and various types of technical equipment, the building of road equipment in their own workshops and facilities was widespread in the roads sector. These workshops produced trailer-type and self-propelled steamrollers, pneumatic wheels, screens, combined asphalt transports and stone fragmentation equipment. In the 1970s, a factory to produce non-standard equipment and road technical equipment was built in *Daugavpils*, and today it is able to provide just about anything that road builders might need.

Warning and information signs in the post-war years were hand-painted wooden signs that road workers put up themselves. Today the road signs and information signs along Latvia's main highways and also along many of its first-class roads are fully in line with global standards. In 1962, there was an attempt in *Jelgava* to produce light-reflecting beads for use in road signs. Today the *Signum* factory produces road signs and other equipment not only for Latvia, but also for export. Roadway markings are in place on all main and first-class roads. In the 1960s, roadway markings were still painted with brushes, but in 1975, a thermoplastics factory was

opened to provide materials. Today wooden, metal and plastic protective posts along Latvia's roads have all been replaced with plastic signal posts with reflectors. Road barriers to protect careless drivers are also popular.

Latvian road workers have built roads in the Tjumen oil fields of Western Siberia. A more than 600 person strong task force arrived in the Siberian tundra in 1980. Led by Task force director Vasilijs Zaharovs and senior engineer Olafs Kronlaks, they built more than 300 km of high standard roads, as well as 40 major artificial structures and two well-appointed construction towns.

In 1992, Latvia's road workers were the first in the world to open a road construction museum. It is managed by the former head of the Latvian Trest of Road Construction Hamilkars Sviķis. Road machine-operators are trained at the trade high school in *Smiltene*, and the town is known among road workers as their capital.

The maintenance and development of international contacts have made it easier for decisions to be taken at all levels of the roads sector administration. It has promoted a better understanding of development trends in this sector elsewhere in the world, as well as providing engineers and other specialists opportunities to improve their skills and upgrade their qualifications. Latvia has benefited from information about the latest work methods and technologies. The system for managing and financing Latvia's road network today has been recognised as one of the most progressive and promising in all of Europe.

The Latvian Roads Directorate is continuing to actively co-operate with five international roads organisations – the Baltic Road Workers Council, the World Roads Association, the International Roads Federation, the International Association of Bridge Constructors and Engineers, and the Nordic Roads Association. Since the restoration of Latvia's independence, the Latvian Roads Directorate has concluded co-operation agreements with road administrations in Finland, Sweden, Norway, Denmark, Poland, Hungary and the Netherlands. These agreements provide for joint undertakings, projects and consultations regarding issues of road maintenance, construction, planning and development. In 1998, the three Baltic States and Finland launched a joint project to develop a Baltic region roads and meteorological stations information system. Work on the *Via Baltica* highway, which will run from Helsinki to Warsaw, and its associated infrastructure development is also continuing.

Just like in Poland and Lithuania, Latvia's Traffic Police rarely work in the open. Usually they hide with radar in their hands and always fine the careless drivers

For centuries Latvian travellers have stopped at roadside taverns to quench their thirst. In the photo – the *Jaunpiebalga* tavern. Today they are more likely to stop at modern petrol stations instead

The Riga-*Jūrmala* dual carriage-way (above) and the Riga-*Sigulda* dual carriage-way (below) are modern highways with proper access roads, viaducts and information. Road traffic safety is an important concern for road builders and Latvia's road police alike

Road signs on the Latvian roads meet the European standards

The Vidzemes highway near *Sigulda*

The consecration of flag during the celebration of 80th anniversary of Latvian road construction in *Šlokenbeka*. Hamilkārs Svīķis and Jānis Dauksts holding the flag

Reconstruction of a bridge in *Iecava* started works for . *VIA Baltica*

Pedestrian road in *Iecava* within the project *Via Baltica* safety – *Iecava road safety*

Thermoplastic markers on the *Jūrmala* highway

Jānis Klismets, Tālis Straume and Olafs Kronlaks from the Road Department, Ministry of Transportation and the state share company *Latvijas Autoceļu direkcija* planning a road to Europe

A simple facility for dispersion of crushed stone

Construction of a blacktop square

Renovation of a asphalt-concrete road

Laying asphalt-concrete

Building a bridge across the channel of *Baltezers*

Rolling asphalt-concrete

The Latvian Road Traffic Safety Directorate is engaged in the registration of vehicles, the improvement of driver qualifications, the technical control of vehicles, maintains registers of vehicles and drivers, as well as the exchange of information with other European countries within the scope of the EUCARIS program.

In September 1999, the Republic of Latvia and the Republic of Estonia signed a memorandum on the exchange of information between the State registers of vehicles of the two countries, and so establishing a new Baltic States information exchange system, BALTCAR

The Road Traffic Safety Directorate conducts examinations to determine the qualifications of drivers. It also registers driver preparation teaching institutions and supervises the teaching process. Cars in which new drivers are being trained are easy to recognise on the road, because they have a triangular sign with the letter "M"

The Road Traffic Safety Directorate has set limits for maximum speed of driving at the level of 90 km/h and 50 km/h in urban territories

Driver's license of the Republic of Latvia

The license plates of the Republic of Latvia – two letters and four numbers, a small national flag and the Latvian state symbol LV

Road Traffic Safety Directorate building in *Miera iela* 25

The vehicle and driver registers of the Road Traffic Safety Directorate became the first in Latvia to be granted the status of computer systems of State significance. The Directorate utilises the State Significance Data Transmission Network, ensuring that State administration and law enforcement authorities have access to information regarding vehicles and drivers in an on-line regime

In Latvia much attention is devoted to teaching children and teenagers the road traffic regulations and proper behaviour on the road. Children are taught road traffic regulations in school, and lots of teaching materials have been published

In Latvia each vehicle must undergo a technical inspection once a year. Because vehicles in Latvia are frequently rebuilt or adapted for concrete functions, the Road Traffic Safety Directorate conducts expert examination and certification of all rebuilt vehicles. In Latvia specific attention is paid to the composition of exhaust fumes

Not only is the quality of road repairs but also the equipment of reparation sites rapidly approaching the level in European Union

Information about whether or not a vehicle has undergone the technical inspection can be obtained from a holographic sticker on the front windshield of the car. Next to it is a sticker which provides information about whether mandatory third party insurance has been taken out for the vehicle

Riga Railroad Bridge, renewed in 1951

Riga Pontoon Bridge, unveiled in May 27, 1896

The chronicler Indriķis wrote in the 13th century that wooden bridges were built across small rivers and streams in what is now Latvia. The first bridge across the *Daugava* River was the Raft Bridge that was built in 1701. A pontoon bridge replaced it in the late 19th century. Riga's Iron Bridge was opened for railroad needs in 1872, while another rail bridge went on line in 1914. During World War I the so-called Lubeck Bridge was put up, but it was destroyed during floods in the spring of 1924 and 1926. In the latter periods of World War II and for a while thereafter, traffic across the *Daugava* moved across the Valdemārs Bridge. The October Bridge was opened in 1957, followed by the *Salu* (Island) Bridge in 1976 and the *Vanšu* (Shroud) Bridge in 1981. The Riga City Council has recently approved the construction of a traffic tunnel under the *Daugava* in the Northern District of the city.

The country does not have any massive and grandiose bridges, but what bridges there are were all built with the hands of the nation itself. Each bridge represents a certain phase in the history of the Latvian nation. Latvian designers and engineers throughout history sought to build bridges that corresponded to the latest technological principles of the European continent.

An arched bridge was built across the *Abava* river in *Kandava* in the XIX century. In the mansion *Kazdanga* a stone bridge was built in the beginning of XIX century. A brick and stone bridge across the river *Venta* in *Kuldīga* was built in the 70ies of that century.

Wood has always been a popular local building material, because it is easy to handle. Wooden bridges in this century were most often built after world War I and World War II. This was a quick way to replace damaged or lost bridges, and the process didn't cost very much. All of the wooden bridges which cross Latvia's larger rivers are supported by permanent brick or concrete abutments.

The largest pre-war wooden bridge crosses the *Gauja* River at *Strēlnieki*. The largest post-war nailed wooden bridge was put across the *Bārta* River in *Nīca* in 1960. In 1977 a glued wood beam bridge was put up across the *Vaive* River near *Priekuļi*.

Metal bridges were never very popular in the Russian Empire. In 1938 the metal *Zemgale* Bridge was put up in Riga, but the retreating German army destroyed it in 1944. Metal shroud-system bridges were built for infantry troops – across the *Gauja* River at *Sigulda* and *Valmiera*, and across the Ogre River in *Ogresgals* parish. A unique example of bridge architecture is the bridge across the *Gauja* River at *Jāņmuiža*. Ambitious residents of *Cēsis* bought a collapsible bridge in parts from a departing Russian military unit, paying an unknown sum in money and vodka for the privilege. Later they put the bridge up, supporting it on concrete abutments. All railroad bridges have traditionally been made of metal.

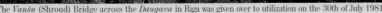

The *Vanšu* (Shroud) Bridge across the *Daugava* in Riga was given over to utilization on the 30th of July 1981

The Raft Bridge in Riga in the late 18th century

A bridge across the *Lielupe* River at *Sloka* was built in 1993

Reinforced concrete has been the most popular and commonly used material for bridge-building in this century, and the same has been true in Latvia. A concretebridge went up across the *Salaca* River near *Salacgrīva* in 1908, followed a year later by a bridge across the *Gauja* at *Strenči*. The largest monolith concretebridge in Latvia was built across the *Gauja* at *Sigulda* before World War II. The 153-meter bridge included three tripled archs on the scheme 36+37+36. The designer of the superstructure of the bridge was a senior engineer from the Latvian Road and Highway Department, Kārlis Gailis, who later became a professor at the University of Latvia. The bridge was unveiled on July 23, 1937, but it was bombed by the Red Army when it retreated from Latvia in 1941. The *Sigulda* Bridge was restored under the leadership of G. Janovskis in the late 1940s.

In the 1950s, bridges which corresponded to a wide variety of generally accepted designs and monolith constructions were put across the *Venta* at *Nigrande* and the *Gauja* at *Vireši*. Then came the period of centralized planning in the Soviet Union, however, and the "national plan" had a role to play in the process. The Central Committee of the CPSU decided that Soviet people would never need personal automobiles and that public transportation – especially the railroad – would be most convenient for them. The development of motor vehicles and related transportation needs, therefore, was ignored. Moscow developed bridge designs, known as N10/11 and N56, which were mandatory for everyone. They were not very good bridges. Many bridges were built according to this design in Latvia, and they're all having to be rebuilt these days. The quality of bridge-building projects improved again beginning in the 1960s. A bridge across the *Gauja* River was put up at *Murjāņi* in 1960, and it features horizontal split beams. In 1968 a 200-meter viaduct across the *Lorupe* ravine near *Valmiera* was unveiled. In terms of its construction technology, it was an important piece of work, and not just at the Latvian level, but for the Soviet Union at whole. In order to protect the unique *Lorupe* ravine from being filled in and to build the very special bridge, road engineers in Latvia had to convince ministry bureaucrats in Moscow that it would be cheaper to build the bridge than to fill in the ravine. Today one of the most important problems facing bridge builders in Latvia is repair of existing cement bridges. It turns out that Soviet-made cement beams have a shelf life of just 40-60 years.

A bridge across the *Lielupe* River at *Kalnciems*

A bridge across the *Gauja* River at *Valmiera* at the beginning of the 20th century

A bridge across the *Lorupe* at *Sigulda*

A stone bridge in the *Kazdanga* palace park

The new bridge across the *Gauja* River at *Valmiera*

The railroad bridge across the *Rauna* River near *Liepa*

A cultural monument of European status – the bridge across the *Abava* River in *Kandava*

A viaduct across the rail tracks at *Torņakalns*

The oldest cement bridge in Latvia – across the *Gauja* River at *Strenči* with a cover of paving stones

The longest brick and stone bridge in Europe – the *Kuldīga* Bridge across the *Venta* River (1874)

A pedestrian bridge in the *Bastejkalns* park in Riga – the longest one-piece stone bridge without any pylons in Europe

A pedestrian bridge and a rebuilt Russian tank bridge across the *Gauja* River at *Jaņmuiža*

A turning bridge at the military port canal in *Liepāja*

A railroad bridge across the *Gauja* River at *Strenči*

95% of passengers on Latvia's trains travel on suburban routes. The railroad is an important part of the Riga transportation system, and electric trains from Riga go to *Jūrmala*, *Jelgava*, *Lielvārde* and the Vidzeme shoreline

A narrow-gauge railroad continues to operate between *Gulbene* and *Alūksne* in far Northeastern Latvia. It is a monument to local technologies

In 1997 the Riga Wagon Factory produced this train car with 76 seats which runs between *Jelgava* and *Krustpils*

This train, the *Latvija*, is seen here at the Riga station, preparing to depart for Moscow. Latvia has direct connections to the largest cities in the CIS – Moscow, St. Petersburg, Odessa, Simferopol and Lvov

In thanks to God for the fact that Tsar Alexander III and his family were not killed in a train wreck in Ukraine, chapels were built at all of the major train stations in Russia. Here we see the chapel at the old Riga train station. The chapel was torn down in 1925

The first rail line in the world was built in England in 1825, connecting Stockton and Darlington – a distance of 21 kilometers. Latvia's railroad initially simply crossed the country's territory, connecting St. Petersburg and Warsaw through *Rēzekne* and *Daugavpils*. This part of the railroad was built between 1857 and 1860, and the oldest railroad station in Latvia is located in *Bozova*, three kilometers away from the train station in *Kārsava*.

In the 1860s rail transportation began to develop very rapidly in Latvia, becoming a main form of support for Latvia's ports and other sectors of the economy. The greatest enthusiasts with respect to the building of the railroad in Latvia were tradesmen in Riga. In 1863 a stock company in Riga and *Dinaburg* (*Daugavpils*) attracted foreign capital to begin the construction of a rail line. The first main line was between Riga and *Daugavpils* (1863), which was soon extended to Vitebsk (1868) and then to Tsaritsina (Volgograd) in 1871. The railroad linked Baltic ports to the inner Russian market. In 1867 work began on a line from Riga to *Jelgava*.

In the 1890s the Russian state awarded concessions for the building of rail lines and also invested money in the process. Private rail lines were bought up. Between the beginning of the 20th century and until World War I the rail network in Latvia expanded to 1,491 kilometers, of which 49 kilometers were 1,000 mm in width, 365 kilometers were 750 mm in width, and the remaining kilometers were 1,524 mm in width – the so-called "Russian gauge".

The construction of railroads in Latvia also promoted the development of transportation, machinery manufacturing and other forms of production. A wagon and mechanical factory, *Fēnikss*, was established in 1895, and before World War I it produced 25% of all of the wagons that were manufactured in Russia. During World War I, the German occupying force rapidly built narrow-gauge rail lines in Kurzeme to bring wood and peat out of Latvia's forests as quickly as possible. During the first period of Latvian independence a wide rail network was established, and it was of key significance in passenger and freight transportation.

Today the railroad remains an important form of transportation in Latvia. Transit cargo represents most of what is carried by rail today – three-quarters of total cargo. 62.2% of the cargo comes from Russia, 15.4% from Belarus and 11.4% from Lithuania. The stock company *Latvijas dzelzceļš* (Latvian Railways) today can carry 45 million tons of freight each year to *Liepāja*, Riga and *Ventspils*, and it is expected that in the next few years the capacity will increase to 60 million tons. Freight is carried with 2TE10M and 2TE10 diesel locomotives that were built in Russia between 1989 and 1991 and have 6,000 horsepower.

The effectiveness of the company's operations is evidenced by the fact that for every 100 lats earned from freight transport, losses for lost cargo amount to less than 2.5 *santims*.

Domestic freight transportation in Latvia is on the decline. Motor vehicles are more flexible and mobile in delivering low volumes of freight for short distances within the country. Passenger numbers are also declining – some 25 million passengers per year are transported at this time.

Latvijas dzelzceļš transports few passengers on international routes – just 3% of the total. Other passengers travel along domestic routes – 95% along suburban routes around Riga and other cities. The railroad is an important part of the transportation system in the capital city. Passengers in suburban Riga are carried by electric trains, while local and suburban traffic in other cities is handled by diesel trains. International trains are pulled by TEP70 diesel locomotives. Today *Latvijas dzelzceļš* has 37 electric trains that were manufactured between 1962 and 1989.

In 1997 the company launched a project to modernize its diesel trains. This is being done at the RRA factory in cooperation with the Austrian company *Voith* and the German firm *MTU*. Each day more than 10 international trains cross Latvia's borders. Passengers can buy tickets for travel to any country in Europe. The passenger transportation information system has a connection to the *KURS 90* rail passenger transportation system of Germany, which allows ticket clerks in Latvia to study train schedules in Western Europe and to reserve seats on Western European trains.

Passenger transportation in Latvia is a loss maker for the railroad, and losses have to be covered with profits from freight transportation. Several very unprofitable rail lines are closed down each year.

Latvijas dzelzceļš, which is state owned, is one of the largest companies in the Baltic States, employing more than 18,000 people. It is the leading payer of the social tax in Latvia. Latvia is in 6th place in Europe in terms of passenger transport by rail.

A restructuring of the state stock company

Latvijas dzelzceļš is supervised by the Ministry of Transportation. Here we see the director of the Technical Railroad Inspectorate, Andris Dunskis, and the director of the National Railroad Administration, Juris Iesalnieks

An electric train approaches the *Riga* station. Suburban rail transport in Riga uses electric trains

The development of Latvia's ports and the country's rail system are very closely linked, and rail transport is an important part of cargo transit through Latvia

The oldest rail station in Latvia – in *Bozova*, near *Kārsava*

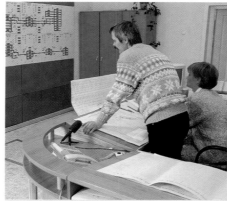

The dispatch service of *Latvijas dzelzceļš* is fully automated and conforms to European Union standards

Freight transport technologies in Latvia are becoming more and more modern and more in line with the requirements of a market economy. Freight containers are carried on special trains, and transport in refrigerated cars is becoming more common

This car is used to fixate and de-bug tracks.

The chairman of the board and executive director of *Latvijas dzelzceļš*, Andris Zorgevics (seated, center) and Finance Minister Ivars Godmanis discuss the financial operations of the railroad. In the background is the headquarters building of *Latvijas dzelzceļš* in Riga

The railroad bridge across the *Daugava* River at Riga

155

Latvijas dzelzceļš led to the establishment of five independent business units – Infrastructure, Rolling Stock, Cargo Transportation, Passenger Transportation and Real Estate.

The Infrastructure Department manages rail lines of 2,412.7 kilometers in length, of which 270 kilometers are electric lines and 33.4 kilometers are a narrow-gauge line. Total track length in Latvia is 4,065 kilometers, with 4,082 switches, 2,295 kilometers of specialized telecommunications networks, 57 automated telephone centrals, 108 stationery electricity plants, 2,980 kilometers of electricity lines, 687.8 kilometers of contact networks, and 702 transformer substations. The Infrastructure Division runs three track divisions – Riga, *Jelgava* and *Daugavpils*, three signal and communications divisions – Riga, *Jelgava* and *Daugavpils*, two track machine stations, a rail welding train, a track repair company in *Daugavpils*, an electro-technical laboratory and an engineering and technical track group. The track division has a fault detection laboratory, a track dimension station, and railroad measuring wagons. A five-year investment program has been developed, with plans to invest 150 million lats in the development of the company. 90% of the investments will go toward the development of the East-West transit corridor.

When the collapse of the Soviet Union began in 1988, an economic crisis ensued, and capital repair of railroad tracks slowed down significantly. Since 1997, however, increasing resources have been invested in these expensive processes. With the support of the *PHARE* program, several new and modern technologies have been purchased, and two-thirds of the company's specialized telecommunications network have been modernized. The infrastructure of the Latvian railroad is financed from the National Railroad Fund. Rail transporters pay fees into the fund in return for use of the infrastructure, and the state repays a share of the excise tax on diesel fuel used in rail transportation. There are also direct contributions from the national budget, as well as payments for use of the railroad's land zones.

Locomotives and wagons are being managed under the auspices of a long-term development concept which addresses the modernization of the railroad and the updating of the rolling stock. There are some 4,050 employees in the division which manages and uses the rolling stock of the company. A new system for technical maintenance and repair of the rolling stock has been introduced, and this allows the company to reduce repair expenditures and to upgrade traffic safety. In 1997 a diesel locomotive maintenance and repair facility was opened at the Riga locomotive yard.

The Riga wagon yard since the restoration of Latvia's independence has been reconstructing its repair and wheel division. In 1996 a unit to manage refrigerated cars was established here.

The department which oversees the company's rolling stock has chemical and technical laboratories which ensure that oil products used in the work are in line with technical standards, monitor the quality of drainage water and other technical water, analyzes air pollution at boilers and on diesel trains, evaluates the effectiveness of existing purification systems, evaluates new foreign materials, and establishes a unified measurement system for Latvia's railroad.

The international train station in Riga

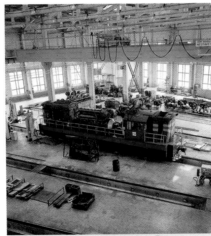

The locomotives' depot of *Zasulauks* in Riga

The board of the stock company *Latvijas dzelzceļš*: (from the left, front row), the director of the Infrastructure Department, M Jagodkins, the secretary of the board, Aija Markote, the deputy general director, Staņislavs Baiko, the general director and boa chairman, Andris Zorgevics, the deputy general director, Rihards Peders, the director of the Technical Inspectorate, Arijs Sina director of the Real Estate Department, Andris Burtnieks, (second row from the left), the director of the Legal Department, Va Vismanis, the director for strategic development, Vladimirs Grjaznovs, the director of the Passenger Transportation Departme Vasilijs Hristins, the director of the Cargo Transportation Department, Ēriks Šmuksts, the chairman of the Latvian Rail Work Labor Union, Savelijs Semjonovs, the finance director, Igors Nikolajevs, and the director of the Rolling Stock Department, Jar Petersons

THE SC BALTIJAS EKSPRESIS

The stock company *Baltijas Ekspresis* is the first private and licensed rail transportation in Latvia. The shareholders in the company are the major transit companies in *Ventspils* – the stock company *Ventbunkers*, the stock company *Kālija parks*, the stock company *Ventspils tirdzniecības osta*, and *Ventplac* Ltd. In 1999 the company handled 80% of the transit freight incoming at the *Ventspils* station. The main goal of SC *Baltijas Ekspresis* is to handle all of the rail cargo that is headed for the *Ventspils* port. The stock company is directed by Ivars Sormulis. At the right we see the rail network in the city of *Ventspils*.

Glider pilot Alfreds Rozentals flew a self-built glider in 1909 over the fields on the shore of the *Ķīśu* lake

General Jēzups Baško
(1889-1946)

General Jānis Indans
(1895-1941)

Alfreds Rozentals in his own aeroplane in 1911

Alfreds Valleika – founder of
Latvia's military aviation in 1919

It is said that in 1684 a blacksmith at the *Priekule* baronial estate called Johansons who fashioned himself two wings and proceeded on a flight that began at the top of the tower of the *Priekule* church. Johansons reportedly flew a distance of two versts (approximately 7,000 feet), to the village of *Knuipji*, where he fell and broke his leg. When the leg was healed, the blacksmith expressed sorrow that it had not occurred to him to construct a tail for his artificial flying machine before his heroic flight. However, he never attempted to fly again.

Johansons' wings were made of split pinewood and stripped elm, held together by copper bands that were wrapped around the wood from both sides and riveted together. The wings were fastened around the flyer's chest and hips with leather straps, and there were smaller leather hooks into which he inserted his hands. The back of the wings was covered with cloth, fastened to the ribs of the wings with flaxen thread and strips of leather. The wings could be bent forward, but they were strengthened at the back so that the air pressure wouldn't bend them back, breaking the hands of the aviator.

For about a year after his flight, the blacksmith from the foundry at *Eda* was under the protection of Baron Korff of *Priekule*. Then he was taken to Vilnius to be introduced to the Polish king. Alas, on the frontier with Lithuania the group was attacked by horsemen from *Grobiņa*. The men who were escorting the blacksmith were scattered, and he himself was taken to *Grobiņa* and burned at the stake as a heretic. Apparently, the blacksmith, due to his mechanical knowledge, was so well known that he was considered a wizard.

Latvian army-navy pilots

Latvian pilots in World War I

The first flights of the Wright Brothers in America in 1903, the rapid development of aviation in France, the successful flight across the English Channel by Louis Bleroit in 1909, as well as the *Aviation Week* that was held in Rheims, France in August 1909 – all these events also found an echo in the society of Riga, especially among students at the Riga Technical Institute. On 8 April 1909, a student called Fridrihs Canders established the *Riga*

Latvian pilots in the early 1930s in *Krustpils*

A Latvian naval aeroplane

Students Air Ship and Flight Technical Association. The members of this association were active in promoting aviation and in the manufacture of a Delone type balanced glider.

The first public demonstrations of aircraft flights in Latvia were held in 1910 and 1911 at the *Zolitūde* racecourse. In 1910 the *Motors* factory of Riga, as well as the Baltic Russian Wagon Factory, began construction of aeroplanes and aviation motors, at the same time also constructing aeroplanes designed in Riga.

When World War I began, the pioneers of Latvian aviation volunteered for service in the air forces of Russia's army and navy, fighting the Germans at Riga and *Daugavpils*, as well as on the Western front in France. More than 100 Latvian pilots fought in the Russian civil war – on both sides.

When the independent State of Latvia was established, most of the flyers returned home, both flying over the border in Bolshevik aeroplanes and returning legally.

The most important aviation unit in the Republic of Latvia was the Latvian Army Aviation Squadron, which was established in 1926 by a group of former Russian army Latvian aviators led by Jēzups Baško.

Sports aviation appeared on the scene in Latvia toward the end of 1920, and in 1926, a law on air traffic was passed. The military aviation services began to replace their older aircraft in 1923, purchasing new aeroplanes from abroad. Several factories in Latvia, including *Arsenāls*, VEF and the workshops of the military port, produced a total of 22 aeroplanes, utilising foreign-made aviation engines. The Latvian Aeroclub was renewed in 1934, and the Latvian Home Guard set up its own aviation squadron in 1932. From 1937, the *Spilve* airport in Riga had become a crossroads for aviation in Northern Europe. In the same year, the Latvian State Airline Company was established with its own passenger aeroplanes.

After the Soviet occupation in 1940, the Home Guard Aviation Squadron and the Military Aviation Squadron were both disbanded. Some of the pilots were assigned to the No. 24 special Latvian reconnaissance squadron, which was evacuated to Russia in 1941, when the German invasion began.

During World War II, Latvian pilots, in special national aviation units, fought on both sides.

By the time of the second Soviet occupation in 1944, nothing was left of the old pre-war Latvian aviation. The two occupying powers, as well as the war had destroyed everything. The air traffic system of Soviet Latvia began work in 1944. The Latvian Civil Aviation Board was formed, and K. Kiršs became the first head of the *Riga* airport. Regular flights to Moscow began in 1945. The chairman of the Latvian Aviation Board was V. Petersons. Over the course of time, the number of aeroplanes and routes increased to encompass the various regions of the Soviet Union. Riga had the third largest civil aviation base in the Soviet Union. A sub-unit for agricultural aviation began work in 1952, as did a sanitary aviation unit under the auspices of the Latvian Aviation Board.

BALLOONING

Oļģerts Teteris

The last commander of the Aviation Squadron, Rudolfs Kandis (1907-1964)

Latvian aeroplane builder, Jānis Rudolfs Akermanis (1897-1972)

The most prominent Latvian aeroplane designer, Kārlis Irbitis (1904-1997)

On 21 November and 1 December 1783, the French brothers Jacques and Joseph Montgolfier became the first people in history to rise above the earth in a balloon. In January 1784, the German magazine *Mittausche Monatschrift* carried an article by the founder of the *Jelgava* observatory and professor of mathematics, Professor Wilhelm Gottlieb Friedrich Bettler, on aerostatic balloons. The first person to develop an aerial balloon in Latvia was a student of Professor Bettler, Ernests Johans Binemanis (1753-1806). Binemanis was a mechanic at the Peter Academy of *Jelgava* and the son of a family of serfs at the Blankenfeld baronial estate. While studying in London, he read several articles about air flight, as well as books by the British chemist Joseph Priestley on the properties of gasses. Binemanis filled his balloons with hydrogen. He demonstrated his first balloon in *Jelgava* on June 26, 1785. The balloon was only 0.54 meters in diameter, and it was produced from the outer skin of cow appendixes. The balloon rose slowly into the sky, and after 15 minutes was out of sight. The next demonstrations occurred in October 1785. On 26 June 1786, the size of the demonstrated balloon was 5.20 m in diameter. The balloon slowly rose into the sky, and after an hour and fifteen minutes could no longer be seen. Latvian enthusiasts have not spent too much time in balloons. Significant flights included those by Margarita and Ernests Vitols and Kārlis Skaubitis in the late 19th and early 20th century.

Since 1992, balloons have once again graced Latvia's skies. One of the most prominent pilots is Gunārs Dukšte, who made it all the way to the North Pole in a balloon in 1999.

Latvian military aeroplanes *Gloucester Gladiators*, in 1938

The I-11, designed by Kārlis Irbitis

Latvian military pilots in 1943, serving in the Soviet army

The I-15 by Irbitis

Nikolajs Pūliņš (1901-1979) and the aeroplane *Ikars 1*

Latvian glider pilots have achieved many successes in international competitions. Daina Vilne from *Liepāja* has been world champion several times

Parachuting is a popular sport in Latvia. Picture: taking her 3000th jump is physician Ruta Jakušenoka accompanied by her husband

An I-12 aeroplane of the Latvian Home Guard, with pilots Kārlis Bandenieks and Jānis Rudzitis

Nikolajs Pūliņš' aeroplane *Sprīditis*, the first sports aeroplane in Latvia, in 1924

Pilots Launics and Blauss – recipients of a major international aviation prize

Pilots Haralds Klints and a technical employee of the airport before a flight

A Latvian State Airline aeroplane which flew the Riga-*Liepāja* route, in 1938

RĪGA INTERNATIONAL AIRPORT

In 1994, flights were performed by the airline "Baltic International Airlines"

Riga has flight connections with nearly all European countries. *British Airlines*, *Lufthansa*, *SAS*, *LOT* and other large international companies have flights to Riga

President of the State Joint Stock Company *Riga* International Airport, Dzintars Pomers, speaking at the 4th European forum of the Airports Council International (ACI)

ACI General Director Philippe G.E. Hamon

The 4th European forum of the ACI took place in Riga in November, 1996

Former Latvian President Guntis Ulmanis at the Riga International Airport

Civil Aviation Administration General director Andris Zalmanis receiving an award from a senior administrator of the US Federal Aviation Administration, Donald D. Engen

Italian Prime Minister Romano Prodi and Latvian Prime Minister Guntars Krasts at the *Rīga* International Airport on 2 February, 1998

Until the restoration of Latvia's independence in 1991, civil aviation in Latvia was completely subordinated to the needs of the USSR airline company *Aeroflot* and all significant documents were approved in Moscow.

After the restoration of independence, the Latvian Aviation Department was established under the auspices of the Ministry of Transportation, and it took over all management and inspection functions in terms of Latvia's civil aviation system. In 1993, it was decided to set up the Latvian Civil Aviation Administration, and the functions were divided up as follows: economic and political issues such as international agreements and the like remained the competence of the Aviation Department (Director: Arnis Muižnieks), while all aspects of flight safety were put under the control of the Civil Aviation Administration (General Director: Andris Zalmanis).

Latvia's activities in the field of civil aviation have yielded notable results quite quickly. One of the first projects completed was the reconstruction of the *Rīga* International Airport's main runway and taxiways. Latvia also continued to develop its air traffic control system, and today Riga can boast of one of the world's most modern air traffic control centres.

Latvian airline companies provide both scheduled and charter services. In 1999, there were 14 Latvian airlines offering their services – two providing scheduled flights, the remaining 12 providing charter services. Passenger transportation is the main area in which all of the companies work. There is no demand at this time for domestic air travel, so all flights are international.

Of all the passengers transported in Latvia, 85% travel on scheduled flights. On average, however, the charter flights cover longer distances per passenger.

Riga International Airport has serviced an increasing number of passengers from year to year. In 1998, nearly 600,000 passengers passed through the airport. Increasing numbers of passengers are being transported by Latvia's flag carrier, *AirBaltic* – 48% of all passengers at this time. *AirBaltic* is rapidly developing into a highly professional and competent company. Initially the company was run by officials from the Scandinavian airline *SAS*, but later Latvian directors gradually began to take over the reins. At the time of writing, *AirBaltic* flew three AVRO RJ70 four-engine aeroplanes and three Fokker 50 two-engine planes.

Latvia ratified the International Civil Aviation Convention in 1992, thus becoming a full member of the International Civil Aviation Organisation (ICAO). Since 1993, Latvia has also been a member of the European Civil Aviation Conference (ECAC). In 1998, Latvia became a candidate member of the European Joint Aviation Association (JAA), and in the near future Latvia will join the European Air Navigation Safety Organisation known as Eurocontrol. Latvia has already participated in some of Eurocontrol's projects with considerable success.

Integrating gradually into the Western European system, Latvia has become a European regional leader in civil aviation.

The new building at *Riga* International Airport stands out with its modern architectural and functional solutions. It provides maximum comfort for passengers and airport employees. Opened in 1999.

For short and medium-distance flights *AirBaltic* uses Dutch-produced Fokker 50 aeroplanes, which can seat 50 passengers

In 1990, the first direct Riga – Washington, USA flight took place without flying through Moscow. On that historical flight were the then Prime Minister Ivars Godmanis and the then Foreign Minister Jānis Jurkāns

AirBaltic's senior vice president for flight management, Pauls Calitis (left) and senior pilot Kārlis Ceplītis in the cockpit of an AVRO RJ70

Juris Miķelsons, president of the American TransAir company, which in the summer of 1993 provided New York – Riga – New York flight services twice weekly

The backbone of *AirBaltic*'s fleet is provided by the British-manufactured AVRO RJ70, which in every respect conforms to European standards

In Sigulda Hofmaņi sen. and jun. have constructed an airplane by themselves

The speaker of Finland's parliament, Rita Osukainen, arrived at the *Riga* International Airport on the *SAS* flight on 20 February, 1995

There are a number of small companies in Latvia's aviation sector, most of them provide charter services, engage in sports aviation, and transporting cargo

The *Mērsrags* port

The *Liepāja* port

There are three major ports in Latvia – at *Ventspils*, Riga and *Liepāja*. There are also eight smaller ports. The ports are an important part of the country's transit system.

Major ports in Latvia engage mostly in the reloading of transit cargoes. The main direction for such freight is from the countries of the former Soviet Union to the West. Latvia's ports are mostly shippers of goods, and the proportion of outgoing cargo is nearly 93%. The figure at the *Ventspils* port for outgoing cargo is nearly 99%, while in the Riga and *Liepāja* ports, there is also a somewhat significant receipt of cargoes.

In order to increase the competitiveness of the Latvia's ports, the Rīga Trade Port and the *Ventspils* port have been given the right to operate as free ports. The *Liepāja* port is part of the city's Special Economic zone.

The eight small ports are of local significance. They handle approximately 1.5% of Latvia's overall cargo turnover, but they are continuing successful development. The main areas of activity are shipment of timber, as well as handling incoming fish and fish products. The small ports also have good prospects of becoming harbours for yacht tourism.

Lighthouse Miķeļtornis

The *Liepāja* port was a closed army port until 1992. It was never intended for freight handling, so most of the wharves need major reconstruction. Much of the cargo that passes through *Liepāja* at this time is general cargo – mostly wood and metals.

Liepāja has set up a Special economic Zone to develop and promote trade, industry, shipping and air traffic, as well as the exchange of international goods through Latvia. The zone covers 65% of the city's territory. It is 3739 hectares in size, including the port (1197 ha), industrial territories (542.7 ha) and the *Liepāja* international airport (251.1 ha).

Tax relief in the Special Economic Zone is available to businesses if they import no more than 20% of the total value of goods, which they sell in the rest of the country during a taxation period. Those companies which meet this standard receive an 80% discount on property tax and land tax, as well as discounts on VAT, customs duty, excise duty and, if necessary, an 80% discount on the income tax.

There are 19 enterprises in the *Liepāja* Special Economic Zone, the largest taxpayer of which is *Liepājas metalurgs* – a metals company that pays 71% of the total taxes paid in the zone. Priority infrastructure projects in the zone include the deepening shipping lanes and sea bed, elimination of pollution in the channel of the former military port, construction of a trunk highway and access roads, and installation of a full complex of water purification systems.

The *Pāvilosta* port

The *Salacgrīva* port

The *Engure* port

The *Skulte* port

The *Kuiviži* port

The *Kolka* port

The *Roja* port

The old lighthouse of Ainaži is the farthest lighthouse in Latvia in the northern direction, but Pape's lighthouse is located farthest to the south

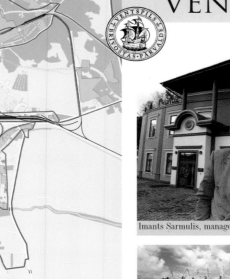

Ventspils free port on a map

Imants Sarmulis, manager of the *Ventspils* free port

The cruise vessel of the *Ventspils* free port is named after Duke Jekabs

The Latvian ex-President Guntis Ulmanis and the Mayor of *Ventspils* Aivars Lembergs opening the excavated port

A station of stock company *Kālija parks*

The section of liquid cargoes in the *Ventspils* free port

Tugboats from *Ostas flote* Ltd.

Ventspils free port from a birds eye

Loading general cargoes

Fishermen's vessels in *Ventspils* free port

A ship on raid

Stick company *Kālija parks* – the world's biggest one

Ventspils port has the biggest turnover of cargoes in Latvia. In this relation it is the first among Baltic ports and in the first twenty of Europe. 69% of all Latvian cargoes are reloaded there. *Ventspils* port has specialised for transfer of oil and oil-related products, which make 72-74% from it's turnover and more than a half from the Whole Latvian amount. The Law on *Ventspils* free port was passed in 1996. The free port covers the whole territory of *Ventspils* port, what makes altogether 2026,45 ha, out of that being 1727,9 ha land and 298,55 ha – water. General cargoes like potassium, liquid chemicals, metal and timber are also reloaded there. It has the biggest terminal for potassium in the world and the biggest facilities for reload of oil and liquid chemicals in Baltics. The main advantages of *Ventspils* are that it does not freeze during winter and the aquatory can serve boats at any weather conditions. The technologies are meant for loading and unloading high tonnage boats. Also the infrastructure is well developed and provide deep water stations, cargo terminals, oil pipe, oil-related product pipe line, railway and roads. The port has well established traditions and practical experience, qualified staff and a good technical support. A democratic management and trading environment and a developed infrastructure, linked to Russia and other CIS states by pipelines and railway are also useful assets for business activities. As there still are free spots available, more terminals and stations may be developed.

Import and export within a territory of a licensed business company or the Managerial Board of the free port are exempted from VAT, custom and excise tax. Eleven business companies are working in the custom free mode, the biggest of them being stock companies *Ventspils nafta, Kālija parks, Ventbunkers, Ventspils Tirdzniecības ostas, Ventamonjaks* and *Ventplac* Ltd.

During 1998 the Managerial Board invested more than 18 million lats for development. It is spent for excavating the shipping channal, reconstruction of stations and building of a terminal for containers.

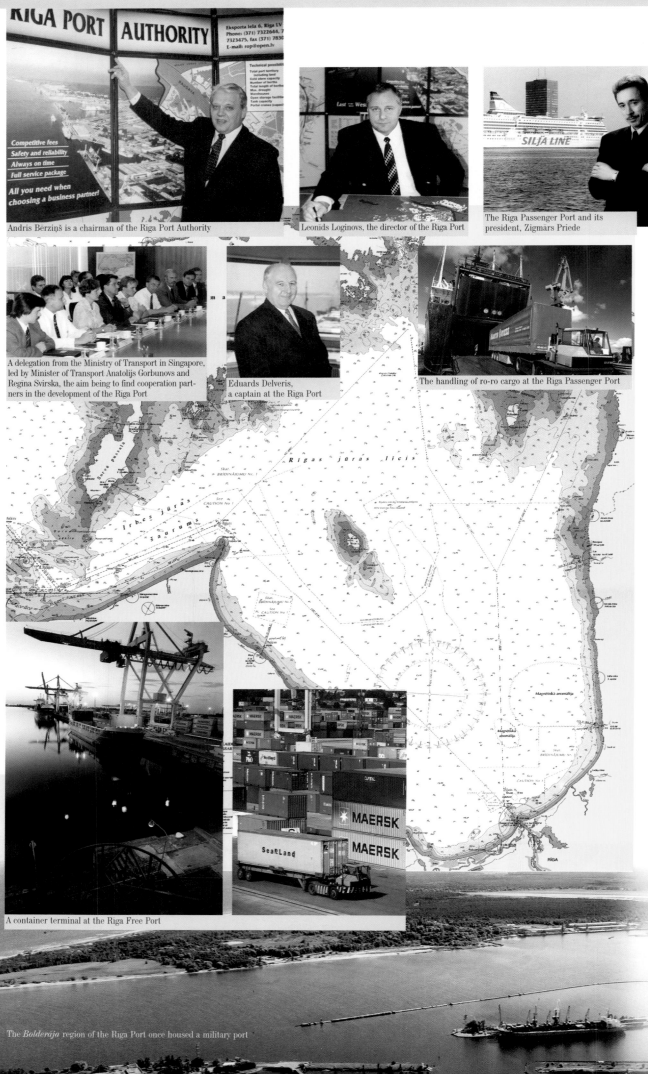

Andris Bērziņš is a chairman of the Riga Port Authority

Leonīds Loginovs, the director of the Riga Port

The Riga Passenger Port and its president, Zigmars Priede

A delegation from the Ministry of Transport in Singapore, led by Minister of Transport Anatolijs Gorbunovs and Regīna Svirska, the aim being to find cooperation partners in the development of the Riga Port

Eduards Delveris, a captain at the Riga Port

The handling of ro-ro cargo at the Riga Passenger Port

A container terminal at the Riga Free Port

The *Bolderāja* region of the Riga Port once housed a military port

The Riga Port is Latvia's largest, both in terms of territory (2,531.5 hectares) and in terms of the cargo that is transported through Latvia (three-quarters of the national total). The Riga Port can handle a variety of freight, and in fact it is used for the transportation of all cargoes except for crude oil. The majority of exported cargo at this time consists of wood products, mineral fertilizers, metals, containers and oil products.

Since 1996 the port's annual turnover has increased by an average of 7% per year. The main advantage of the port is its fine geographic location in relation to Russia and Belarus, as well as the highly developed network of road and rail transport that accesses the port. This saves time in sending freight to and from Western Europe and Russia. 80% of the cargo that is loaded at the Riga Port is transit cargo.

The law on the Riga Free Port provides a variety of benefits to companies that work in the territory of the port, including customs, excise and value added tax relief, which helps to reduce capital construction costs when new terminals or piers are built.

Design of an underwater communications tunnel has been completed as part of a project to deepen the shipping channel to 14 meters in most of the port's aquatorium. By 2010 investments in the Riga Port will be made at a sum of more than 100 million lats, and the money will be used to deepen the port, to rebuild existing piers and to build new piers.

The *Irbe* Straits and the Riga Port can currently handle *Panamax-type* ships with a loaded weight of 50,000 tons and above.

The Riga Port is open for shipping around the year. On the relatively rare occasions when it is needed, an icebreaker is available at any time.

There are some 40 private stevedore companies at the Riga Port at this time, among them BLB, *Rīgas Centrālais Terminals* Ltd., *Strek* Ltd., *LACON* Ltd., *Alfa Osta* Ltd., *VSK Rinūži, Neste Latvija* Ltd., *Statoil* Ltd. and *MAN-TESS* Ltd., among many others.

The Riga Port Authority is a member of the IAPH, ESPO and BPO. Given the fact that sea transportation is of increasing importance around the world, and taking into account the geographic placement of the Riga Port in the Baltic region, many international experts have recognized the port's enormous development potential. Adjoining territories can be used to optimize the port's work, setting up new cargo distribution and handling areas and expanding the port's competitiveness to a considerable degree. Distances speak to the advantage of the Riga Port in terms of transit operations – 992 kilometers from Riga to Moscow, but 1,052 from Tallinn; 1,007 km from Riga to Kiev, but 1,304 from Tallinn. The difference with Hamburg is 640 kilometers for Riga, 700 for Tallinn and 868 for St. Petersburg, while the numbers for Rotterdam are 1,077, 1,139 and 1,209 km respectively. From any port in Europe, the Riga Port is the closest and most convenient port for dry cargo transit in the East-West and West-East direction.

President Guntis Ulmanis visits *MAN-TESS*

The board of the Latvian Association of Stevedores – Aldis Zieds, Aivars Borovkovs and Georgi Shevchuk (first row); Uldis Papāns, Uldis Veispals, Julijs Krumiņš and Imants Cibulis (second row)

The fuel terminals of *Neste* and *Statoil*

The SD3 pier of *MAN-TESS* Ltd.

MAN-TESS Ltd. was founded in 1991 and is one of the largest private companies in Latvia. Its president and sole founder is the well-known businessman Julijs Krumiņš. *MAN-TESS* Ltd. provides port services through four piers at *Sarkandaugava* and *Mangaļsala*. It provides for the reloading of oil products with a reservoir park that can handle 60,000 cubic meters of products. *MAN-TESS* also has 30,000 square meters of customs warehouses for the handling of wood materials, peat moss, containers and other cargoes.

Oil product reservoirs owned by *MAN-TESS* Ltd.

A new satellite center for ship management

The SD 4 and 5 piers of *MAN-TESS* Ltd.

The *MAN-TESS* Ltd. customs warehouse

The equity capital of *Speja* Ltd. is 100% Latvian-owned. The company is one of the leading wood processing and export companies in the world. Its president (right) is Alexander Mežirickis

The Rīga Ship Building Factory builds several ships each year

The *MAN-TESS* Ltd. container precinct

The *Rinuži* territory of the Rīga Port, where *Alfa-Osta* Ltd. runs a terminal for the reloading of chemical cargoes

LATVIAN SHIPPING COMPANY

Refrigerator ships *Pērle* and *Akadēmiķis Bočvars*

Tanker *Rundāle*

LPG tanker *Kurzeme*

A naming ceremony for the *Kurzeme* at the South Korean Hyundai shipyard. *Latvian Shipping Company* President is at the centre, and the company's Council chairman, Druvis Skulte, is at the right

Chemical tanker *Indra* onloading cargo in port

The headquarters of *Latvian Shipping Company*, at *Basteja bulvāris* 2 in Riga.
The building was constructed in 1878 on the basis of a design by the architect Jānis Baumanis

The Latvian Shipping Company (*LSC*) was established in September 1991, when Latvia again became independent and took over its share of the Soviet trade fleet. Latvia received 87 ships from the USSR. Today the State Joint stock company *Latvian Shipping Company* is an international shipping firm which, in circumstances of intense competition, successfully ensures tanker, refrigerator, LPG and general cargo shipments throughout the world. At the present time, the LSC is represented on the world's waters by 60 ships, and they employ some 2,600 sailors.

Despite a shipping crisis in the world that was occurring at the time of this writing, LSC managed to maintain its positions in several sectors of the maritime transportation market. Financial indicators have improved steadily in the late 1990s. LSC has a good reputation throughout the world as a highly experienced company, which maintains its ships in good technical condition. The company's sailors are in high demand on the international job market.

The professional work of the LSC and its conformity to the high demands of international shipping are both evidenced by the fact that the company's management structure and its fleet of tankers have been awarded the International Safety Management certificate which is a recognised equivalent to the ISO 9002 certificate, adapted specifically for the requirements of the shipping industry. LSC received the certificate in September 1997 – a year before most other ship owners in the world.

LSC is an active member of several international shipping organisations, representing the Latvian state. In April 1999, LSC was accepted as a full member of the World Association of Independent Tanker Owners, *Intertanko*. Since 1995, the company has also been a member of the International Mobile Satellite Communications Organisation known as *Inmarsat*.

LSC plays an important role in the Latvian economy, because it is the main company in Latvia to work successfully in the international marketplace. It is also the second largest company in the country in terms of turnover. The LSC provides work not only for its own sailors, but also to several thousand people who work in areas that support the shipping industry. LSC also provides ongoing support to the education of sailors in Latvia, as well as to other shipping-related activities in the country.

The majority of LSC fleet are tankers. There are 39 oil and chemical transport tankers in the fleet. In terms of transportation volumes, LSC is among top five in the world in the product tanker market (first in Northern Europe and fifth in the American region). LSC tanker fleet is preserved in good technical condition, conforming not only to all existing international conventions in this area, but also to the requirements of the world's leading oil companies. Clients of LSC include such prominent names as Shell, Navion, Exxon and British Petroleum. Several of the company's ships have been modernised to improve competitiveness and to expand the spectrum of products that can be transported. The company's most modern chemical transport ships can handle up to 400 different chemical substances, including some very harsh products.

Chemical tanker *Dzintari* in Lisbon

The management of the *Latvian Shipping Company*

Several of the cargo ships of *Latvian Shipping Company* are covered with the polymer paint *Siloxirane Marine Line*, which is the equivalent of non-rusting steel

Chemical tanker *Indra* leaving Lisnave shipyard in Lissabon after modernisation

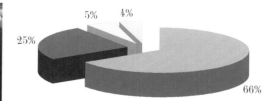
5%   4%
25%
66%

■ tankers ■ reefers   LPG   dry cargo vessels
The fleet of *Latvian Shipping Company* and its turnover, in millions of USD (in 1998)

RĪGA TIME

A view of the highest electric clock in Latvia – the clock of the Riga railway station

Rigensians love to arrange rendezvous at the so-called *Laima* clock in the city center

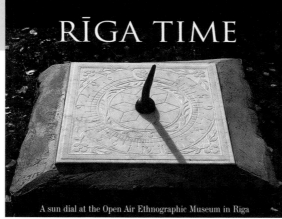

A sun dial at the Open Air Ethnographic Museum in Riga

A sun dial in *Ventspils*

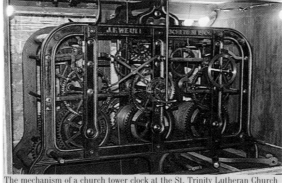

The mechanism of a church tower clock at the St. Trinity Lutheran Church in *Liepāja*

Time zones

Standard time zones

Non-standard time zones

The map shows the time all over the world when it is 12 a.m. in Riga

| Greenwich mean time (GMT) | Middle Europe time | Riga time | Moscow time |

The clock of the *Parex Bank* in Riga

A clock at the corner of *Krišjāṇa Valdemāra iela* and *Ata Kronvalda bulvāris* shows the time in Riga, as well as in Kobe, Japan, which is one of Riga's friendship cities

A building at *Tērbatas iela* 14 (1909-1912), architects Konstantīns Pēkšēns and Arturs Medlingers

Latvia runs on what is known as *Riga time* or *Eastern European time* – two hours ahead of Greenwich Mean Time.

The culture of clocks is an ancient one in Latvia. In every Latvian city one can see several interesting and architecturally appropriate clocks in public places.

"I take the paving stones into my hand, and read the story of the centuries in tiny script." (Jānis Plotnieks)

The restored *Berg's Bazaar* in Riga

"The stones of Sweden sleep and doze along the sides of the road and can never get away …" (Aleksandrs Čaks)

A clock manufactured by a blacksmith, now housed at the *Ventspils* Region Museum of History and Art

A clock in *Ventspils*

The Philharmonic Square in Riga

RĪGA

The Riga skyline, as seen from *Ķīpsala* Island in the middle of the *Daugava* River. The main elements of the skyline are seven church towers. The largest – that of the Dome Cathedral and that of St. Peter's Church – are at the right of this photograph

A map of Riga and its surroundings from 1622. A folk song about the city says: "Long had Riga been praised, Now I saw the city. Sand hills all around, Riga itself in the water."

A popular form of entertainment for Medieval Rigensians was the festival known as *umurku-murs*, where one of the activities was a competition to see who could clamber up a fat-greased pole the quickest and grab the prize at the top

The Riga Rathaus (City Hall) at the end of the 19th century. The building was blown up by the Soviet KGB when the USSR withdrew from Latvia in 1941. Restoration of the building began in 1999

Riga is the capital city of Latvia, located at the place where the *Daugava* River flows into the Bay of Riga. Human settlements in the area appeared at least two millennia ago, when Courlandians and Livonians populated the region. They were craftsmen, fishermen, livestock farmers and traders. Near the village of Riga in 1198, a Livonian called Imauts stabbed the German Bishop Berthold to death.

Both of the significant Livonian villages in the area were located in what is now the center of Riga – one around the place where *13. Janvāra iela* is now located, and the second where *Esplanāde* Park is. The Chronicle of Indriķis reports on the building of Riga in 1201, although the first builders from Gotland arrived only in 1202. In 1201, however, Bishop Albert moved his residence from *Ikšķile* to Riga. Riga won the rights of a city in 1225, and in 1226 a city Rat (council) was set up. Initially there were 12 members of the Rat, later 20. Members were representatives of Riga's governing classes, and an appointment to the Rat was a lifetime appointment.

Riga became one of Europe's leading trade cities in the 17th century, when exports from the port included flax, wood, leathers, fats, hemp, linseed, ashes, grain and wax. There were 42 different business guilds in Riga at the end of the 18th century.

In 1710 Riga fell to Tsar Peter the Great and became the administrative center of the Riga District of the Russian Empire. The first governor general sent by the Russians was called Anikita Repnin.

In 1772 the wooden buildings that surrounded the city's fortifications were torn down and *Esplanāde* Park was installed. The first elected mayor of Riga, Heinrich Strauh, took office in 1786.

When Napoleon advanced on Russia in 1812 defenders of the city burned down all of the suburbs that were outside of the city walls. This was a serious blow to one of the Russian Empire's more important economic cities, and the central government sent blueprints on the basis of which many wooden and brick buildings were put up in Inner Riga.

The architecture of 17th century Riga was influenced by architecture in the Netherlands and Poland. This influence could be seen in the construction that was done around the Rathaus (city hall), as well as during the rebuilding of the ornate House of the Blackheads. Elements of decoration at that time included stone masks, vases, obelisks and portals. Several large Baroque residential buildings with facades that were decorated with stone sculptures were put up in the late 17th century. All of these buildings had vast halls inside. Among them are the Reitern House (1688) and the Dannenstern House (1696).

The first implementation of the principles of Classicism arrived along with the architect Johann Friedrich Ettinger, who in 1765 began work on the Riga Rathaus. Other important monuments in the style of Classicism were Alexander's Gate and the Arsenal building, which was constructed in 1830.

The foundations for the first museum in Riga were laid in 1773, and today the building houses the Riga Museum of History and Shipping – the main repository for exhibits that testify to the cultural and historical heritage of the city. Important reforms in the city were introduced in 1877, when for the first time the City Council became an elected body, along with a city board and the mayor. The first mayor under the new system was called Robert Bingner, but the most distinguished Riga mayor at the end of the 19th century was a Briton called James Armitsted. The first ethnic Latvian to hold the mayor's seat in Riga was Andrejs Krastkalns, who took office in 1916.

Riga in 1572, as depicted in a book called *Civitates orbis terrarum R.P.B.*

| 13th century | 14th century | 15th century | 16th century | 17th century | 18th century | 19th century | 20th century |

In 1999 the Bank of Latvia released 10-lats anniversary coins to commemorate the 800th anniversary of the city of Riga. Each coin shows the great herald of the city from the respective period of time on one side and an image typical of the relevant century on the other

St. George's Church was originally a chapel attached to the first castle of the Order of the Brotherhood of the Sword (early 13th century). In the 16th century the building was renovated for commercial use. After a restoration in 1981 it became the home of Latvia's Museum of the Decorative and Applied Arts

The personal museum of Riga physician Nicolaus Himzel in 1791 was moved to the eastern wing of the Dome Cathedral ensemble, which was rebuilt to house a museum. Today it is home to the Riga Museum of History and Shipping

THE RĪGA CITY HERALD

The present-day herald of the City of Riga was approved on October 31, 1925, during the first period of Latvian independence. The herald was designed by graphic designer Rihards Zariņš. The herald is based on three elements from the city's first, 13th century herald. There is a brick wall with gates and two towers which represents the sovereignty of the city; there are two crossed keys of St. Peter which represent the protection of the *Pope*; and there is a cross which represents subordination to the bishop. In 1347 the image of a lion's head under a gate was added to the herald to depict the courage of the people of Riga. During Swedish rule Riga was given the king's privilege, and this appeared on the herald in the form of a crown above the cross.

In the late 16th century, in keeping with European principles of heraldic design, the herald of Riga was updated with two figures on either side of the seal – golden lions. During Soviet times Communist Party boss and city mayor Alfreds Rubiks came up with an "improved" version in which the cross and crown were replaced with a five-pointed star.

The great herald today shows a silver seal above an open red brick gate with two towers. Below the gate is a golden lion's head. Above are two black, crossed keys, above which there is a golden cross and crown. The seal is held by two lions with red tongues standing on a grey socle and glaring behind their backs

The message from XVI century inside the orb at the pike of St. Peter's Church

In 1876 architects Hermanis Ende and Vilhelms Bekmanis built this residential building which for years was the home of the Benjamiņš dynasty of newspaper publishers. After World War II it was used as the headquarters of Latvia's various creative associations, but in 1998 it was returned to the heirs of the Benjamiņš family

The building of stock exchange in Dome Square, built by the architect Harold Bose in the style of neo-Renaissance in 1855

During the 19th century Riga was absorbed more and more deeply into the Russian Empire, and it was the main export port for the state. The first factory in Riga – a sugar factory – was established in 1784. The first companies in Russia to introduce steam engines into their work were a wood mill and iron foundry, as well as a wool-spinning operation in Riga. Major stock companies included the Russian Baltic Wagon Factory (1869) and a porcelain factory owned by one Sidor Kuznetsov (1841).

In the latter half of the 19th century, Eclecticism was the governing style in Rigensian architecture. The first major buildings in this style were the building of the Riga Stock Exchange (1855), the building of the Great Guild (1857), the building which today houses Parliament (1867), constructed by Latvian architects Jānis Fridrihs Baumanis and Roberts Pflugs, and the National Opera (1863). Baumanis was also responsible for Riga's gorgeous ring of boulevards, which were installed in the 1870s and 1880s. The National Theater was constructed between 1899 and 1902 by Latvian architect Augusts Reinbergs, while the building that today is the Latvian Academy of Arts but initially was the Riga Commercial School was the work, in 1905, of the distinguished architect Wilhelm Bockslaff. The Old St. Gertrude's Church was built by Johann Daniel Felsko in 1858, while the enormous Russian Orthodox Cathedral in downtown Riga was designed by Roberts Pflugs and built in 1884.

There was a global economic boom in the late 19th century, and it did not miss Riga. Factories, transportation, machinery construction, production of electrical and technological systems, the rolling of steel, the production of cellulose and cement – all of these were activities in Riga at that time. Production of rubber, wire and nails expanded. The first bicycle factory in Russia, *Rossia*, was opened in 1886. A major electrical factory was also opened in 1886, which later became known as *Unions* but, in 1928, was turned into the internationally known *VEF* (which stands for State Electro-technical Factory in the Latvian acronym) company. A Russian-French joint venture to produce rubber, *Provodņik*, began operations in 1888.

1899 began with a series of riots in Riga. The Latvian working class was fairly well organized and began to show resistance to Russian oppression. The government of the tsar at that time was relatively reformist, but the timid steps which were taken were not enough.

The largest demonstrations, however, arrived with the Revolution of 1905, when Riga was the site of demonstrations, meetings, strikes and an attack on the Central Prison. The major accomplishment of workers and the intelligentsia in Riga was that they forced the Russian state to become more democratic. The absolute monarchy was liquidated, a national Duma (to which six Latvians were delegated) was established, etc. Despite the revolution, Riga continued to develop into a very important center for the military industry before World War I.

The early 20th century brought along with it the new architectural style of Art Nouveau, and this was decisive for the appearance of Riga. The legendary Mikhail Eisenstein used Art Nouveau in residential buildings which he put up in *Alberta iela* between 1903 and 1906, while architects such as Eižens Laube and Konstantīns Pēkšēns developed a local strain of Art Nouveau that became known as National Romanticism.

When World War I began and the front lines drew close to Riga, many of the city's factories were evacuated and moved lock, stock and

The roofs of Old Riga

The ruins of Riga after the withdrawal of the Red Army in 1941

Old Riga, 1941

The construction of apartment buildings in the *Pines of Agenskalns* neighborhood

Construction of a mass of apartment buildings in *Jugla*

The day on which trolley buses first ran in Riga

barrel to inner Russia. Some 200,000 qualified workers and their family members went to Russia along with the workshops, industries, factories and other companies. During the war, Andrejs Krastkalns became Riga's first ethnic Latvian mayor, and in February 1917 he was appointed governor of Vidzeme and Southern Estonia by the Russian administration. His successor in the mayor's seat was Gustavs Zemgals, who later rose to become President of Latvia.

In 1917 the first elections to the Riga City Council were held, and Social Democrats won the largest number of seats. On November 18, 1918, in the building which now houses the Latvian National Theater, the Latvian People's Council proclaimed the Republic of Latvia's independence. The first leader of the post-independence City Council was Gustavs Zemgals, who remained in office until 1920. During the period of independence other mayors included Andrejs Fridenbergs (1920-1921), Alfreds Andersons (1921-1928), Adams Krieviņš (1928-1931), Hugo Celmiņš (1931-1935), R. Gerselis (1935-1936) and Roberts Liepiņš (from 1936 until the Soviet occupation). In the latter half of the 1930s, a number of buildings in Old Riga were torn down.

The Soviet armed forces occupied Riga on June 17, 1940. Mayor Liepiņš was replaced with one Jānis Pupurs. In November 1940 a temporary Executive Committee was set up under the leadership of Arnolds Deglavs. In January 1941 Riga was divided up into six districts – the Lenin, Kirov, Moscow, Proletarian, Red Army and Stalin districts. After Latvia's annexation into the Soviet Union, Riga was forced to implemented construction and architectural principles that were alien to it. The previous orientation toward Western Europe was deemed inappropriate for the new Socialist system.

Nazi Germany took Riga in June 1941. Even though this happened without much in the way of an attack, Riga suffered great damage as the withdrawing Russian forces burned down or blew up a number of important buildings. The wooden tower of St. Peter's Church burned, and the Rathaus and House of the Blackheads were both destroyed.

The Germans set up a temporary board for the city, led by Pavils Dreimanis. The first Burgermeister of the city was a German called Windgassen.

When the Germans retreated, they blew up all of the city's bridges, electrical plants, warehouses and water pipelines. In 1944, when the Russian occupants were firmly in place, the Executive Committee was reestablished and Arnolds Deglavs was put back into office. The City Council was dubbed the Council of Deputies of the Working People, and elections took place every two-and-a-half years. These "elections" involved a race between one Communist Party candidate and one candidate from the "non-party bloc", both of them carefully vetted by the KGB and the Central Committee of the LCP. In fact the elections were a sham, and the resulting council was a formal institution which rubber-stamped decisions taken by the city's Communist Party and then the executive committee.

In 1947 the Kirov District was renamed the Molotov District, in 1956 the Red Army District was merged with the Lenin District, and the Molotov District was divided up among the Kirov, Moscow and Proletarian districts. After Stalin died, his region was renamed the October District. In 1969 a separate district was split off from the Lenin District and called the Leningrad District.

The elaboration of Riga's general plan was entrusted to a Russian architect from Vladivostok called Yuri Vasilyew, who knew nothing about the history and politics of Riga and who "forgot" to plan territories for housing. Factories were put in all kinds of places, and for 50 years architecture in Riga represented nothing

more than pathetic attempts to copy the architectural and stylistic look of the central cities of the Soviet Union. Albeit with a few half-hearted attempts to include something of the Latvian heritage, architecture in Soviet Latvia was Russian and eclectic in style.

German war prisoners were used to rebuild the shoreline of Riga, which was promptly named Komsomol Embankment. The *Riga* Hotel was built, as were a Song Festival stage in *Mežaparks*, the *Cultural Palace* of the *VEF* factory, and the skyscraper which houses the Latvian Academy of Sciences. The latter building was put up by Latvian architects Osvalds Tīlmanis, Vaidelotis Apsītis and Kārlis Plūksne, who desperately tried to give at least something of a Latvian appearance to the monumental structure, which was inspired by the architecture of Chicago in the 1930s and a copy of which was found in every major city in the Soviet bloc so that locals never could forget Moscow's presence.

In the late 1950s and early 1960s the Soviet Union began to install enormous new industrial facilities in Latvia, focusing on machinery manufacturing and metals processing. Major companies included *VEF*, *Radiotehnika*, *Komutators* and *Alfa*. Companies in the fields of energy, chemicals and oil-based chemicals also emerged – *Sarkanais Kvadrāts* and the clumsily named Association to Produce Chemical Consumer Goods for the People of Latvia. The building of all of these factories involved the inflow of enormous numbers of Russians, Belarussians and Ukrainians into Riga, and this, in turn, led to the need to build large apartment buildings. The blueprints were always the same, and residential districts began to emerge. The first was put in the *Pines of Agenskalns* neighborhood, in 1958. This was a time when the governing principle of the Soviet Union was that Communism was just around the corner, so architects figured that they didn't have to worry much about the quality of their buildings – Communism would arrive no matter what. The buildings in *Agenskalns* were built with the idea that they would serve for 20 years and then be torn down. Of course, the buildings stand today and are a reminder of what a folly that was. Other neighborhoods which received these unattractive apartment buildings included *Jugla*, *Ķengarags*, *Imanta* and *Purvciems*. Buildings were placed in close proximity to one another with large, regular or irregular internal yards in which groups of lower buildings were sometimes placed.

A bird's eye view of Riga

The Riga castle of the Order of the Brotherhood of the Sword, which today houses the offices of the Latvian president

This statue of Rolands was put in City Hall Square in Riga in 1896. It was sculpted by Augusts Foles, the architect was Wilhelm Neumann. The statue was severely damaged during World War II, when Riga was subjected to artillery attacks

169

Ludwig Wilhelm Kerkovius, mayor of Rīga (1890-1901)

George Armitsted, mayor of Riga (1901-1912)

Gustavs Zemgals, mayor of Rīga (1917-1920)

Andrejs Frīdenbergs, mayor of Rīga (1920-1921)

Alfreds Andersons, mayor of Riga (1921-1928)

Ādams Krieviņš, mayor of Riga (1928-1931)

Hugo Celmiņš, mayor of Riga (1931-1935)

Roberts Liepiņš, mayor of Riga (1936-1940)

Andris Teikmanis, chairman of the Riga City Council (1990-1994)

Māris Purgailis, chairman of the Rīga City Council (1994-1997)

Andris Bērziņš, chairman of the Riga City Council (1997)

RĪGA'S FLAG

The flag of the city of Rīga is a rectangular fabric with two equal, horizontal girdles: the top one is in blue, the bottom one – white. Its proportion, height against width, is 1:2. A colored coat of arms of Riga is in the center on both sides of the flag, which is 2/5 of the width of the flag. The citizens of Riga are familiar with the basic colors of the flag, blue and white since 1673, when the articles of Riga demanded a flag with equal girdles in blue and white to be raised on all the ships of the city. The light blue color is assumed to symbolize honesty, loyalty, and generosity, while the white color is assumed to be a symbol of water and good thoughts in heraldry. The combination of blue and white is the Christian symbol of St. Peter's, the patron of Riga since the XIII century.

The flag of Riga is always raised at the building of the City Council in *Krišjāņa Valdemāra iela* 3

From the left: Andris Grīnbergs, executive director of Riga; Aivars Draudiņš, chairman of the Environmental Protection Committee; Maija Rubīna, chairwoman of the Utility and Housing Committee; Andris Argalis, deputy chairman of the City Council; Andris Bērziņš, chairman of the City Council; Juris Ritiņš, deputy chairman of the City Council; Linda Baltiņa, chairwoman of the Traffic and Transportation Committee; Heinrihs Lācis, chairman of the Social Affairs Committee

The Riga Dome is the most important architectural monument from the 13th and 14th centuries in the entire Baltic region. Construction of the church and an adjoining cloister began in 1211, and the first phase of construction ended in the late 13th century. The church has from the very beginning been divided into three areas of equal height. During the period of the Livonian Order, the Dome was the ideological center for the expansion of Catholicism in Livonia, and the church was headquartered there. The cloister ran a school and trained clergymen. After the Reformation the school was taken over by the City of Riga and became the first non-religious institution of higher learning in the city. Over the course of the centuries the Dome has been built and rebuilt in strata of various architectural styles – everything from the Roman style to the Gothic, Baroque and Classicist styles. Initially the building was made of limestone, but later field stones and bricks were brought in for Gothic elements. Inside the church fragments of 14th century grave markers are can still be seen, along with works of Mannerist and Baroque works of art from the 16th and 17th century, grave epitaphs, the organ loft designed by a master builder from Gdansk in 1601, the pulpit built in 1641, pews from the 17th century and stained glass windows from the 19th century.

The magnificent pipe organ of the Dome was installed in the 1880s and was the largest in the world at that time. During Soviet times a concert hall was installed in the church to take advantage of the wonderful instrument. The church was restored as the cathedral of the Lutheran archbishop in 1991.

The Riga Dome Cathedral

Pope John Paul II celebrated mass in *Mežaparks* in Riga on September 8, 1993

The St. Albert's Catholic Church (late 19th century) is a Neo-Baroque building designed by architect Johann Koch

St. Jacob's Catholic Church was mentioned in documents as early as in 1226, and it is a monument of Early Gothic architecture. The tower was put up in its present form in 1756

The building of the Latvian Baptist Church (1900), designed by architects Harijs Mēlbarts and Oskars Bars

The Riga Orthodox Cathedral (1876-1884) is Neo-Byzantine in style and was designed by the architect Roberts Pflugs

The Boris Grebenshchikov prayer house of Russian Old Orthodox in Riga (1814). The building contains a unique treasury of icons from the 16th to the 19th century

The Church of St. Peter and St. Paul (1785) – a Classicist building by architects Siegmund Seege von Laurenberg and Christopher Haberland. After reconstruction in 1987, a concert hall was installed in the church

The construction of so-called "panel buildings" developed particularly quickly. In the early 1960s most apartment buildings had five stories, but later the system began to put up buildings of nine and even 12 stories. These buildings were put up in regions which formerly had been the site of single-family homes, the aim being to eliminate the stratum of Latvians who had inherited private homes from their parents. The homes were torn down, and owners were assigned to impersonal apartment buildings all over town. The Central Committee of the communist Party had a rule that on each floor of an apartment building on which there were three or four flats, one was to be given to Latvians, while the rest must go to "guest workers" from other parts of the Soviet Union or to retired Soviet military officers. The hope was that Latvians would become integrated into Russian society. The new arrivals seldom bothered to learn Latvian, and Russian lessons were an unfailing part of the schooling of every Latvian child.

The construction of cultural facilities and stores ground pretty much to a halt, but schools and kindergartens were built in all of the new neighborhoods.

The residential neighborhoods of *Zolitūde*, *Pleskodāle*, *Mežciems*, *Pļavnieki* and *Ziepniekkalns* went up in the 1970s and 1980s, not only with the identical and completely boring five- and nine-story buildings, but also with equally uninteresting 14- and 18-story buildings. Buildings in *Purvciems* and *Ziepniekkalns* were 300 meters high or higher, and among the people they were known as *The Great Wall of China*, or by names which mocked the leaders of the Soviet Union. Architecture stopped being an art form in the soviet Union in the 1950s, and all buildings in the USSR were simple, ugly and functionalist. Among them are the central railroad station, the main children's department store, and the Riga bus station. Cement and glass were the main construction materials, sometimes combined with unsuccessfully adapted decorative motifs borrowed from the East or copied (inadequately) from the national style. In order to drive home the point about what architecture should *not* look like the system put up the first high-rise buildings in the city center in the mid-1960s. The building which now houses the Ministry of Agriculture was built between 1965 and 1985, and the Hotel *Latvia*, which also took nearly 20 years to build, was completed in 1979. Another example of the functionalist approach to architecture is the Press House on *Ķīpsala* Island. The Hotel *Latvia*, which is the severest example of bad taste in all of central Riga, deserves special mention.

The level of architecture improved just a bit in the 1970s, when public buildings finally became more individual in appearance. The decoration of facades was differentiated, and architects finally remembered that cement is not the only available construction material in the world. Relatively attractive buildings such as the *Daile* Theater, the headquarters of the Communist Party (now the World Trade center, 1974), the

The great stage at *Mežaparks* (1955), architect Arturs Reinfelds. The national Song Festival takes place here with choirs from all over Latvia once every five years

The deputy chairman of the Riga City Council, Andris Argalis, against the background of the Riga canal, which separates Old Riga from the city's ring of boulevards

The tropical building of the Botanical Gardens of the University of Latvia. The gardens were established in 1922 on 16 hectares of land. Today the facility has some 8,550 different species of plants

Riga Sports Palace (1970) and the *Riga* airport (1974) were built. Only in the late 1980s, however, did buildings begin to appear on the Riga skyline which did not cripple the view. Among them are the building of Latvian State Television (1986) and its tower, the Hall of Congresses (1982), and the former *Ridzene* Hotel (1984). The *Gaiļezers* medical complex, which includes a cancer hospital, was built after 1970 in concert with globally recognized principles for planning medical institutions. The same is true of the building of the Latvian Academy of Medicine in *Dzirciema iela* (1987).

After the restoration of Latvia's independence, in 1994, the Riga City Council approved a development plan for the period through the year 2005. The plan assumes that the population of the city will remain stable at approximately 800,000 residents, that existing buildings will be preserved and reconstructed, and that efforts will be made to protect the city's natural environment.

The first herald of the Latvian national awakening was a process of public protests against the construction of an underground metro in Riga in 1987 and 1988 – many of the city's residents participated in this process. The Executive Committee of the city became a place in which the defenders and opponents of Latvia's independence grappled with one another. The national efforts of the Latvian people were opposed by the orthodox wing of the Riga Communist Party, headed up by the city's boss, Alfreds Rubiks, and a senior leader of the party, Arnolds Klaucens. They tried to use armed force to oppose Latvians. Alfreds Rubiks, it must be said, was among the very few Latvian Communist leaders who never changed his principles. He opposed a change in the Soviet system and proclaimed the teachings of Lenin. During the Soviet putsch in 1991 he tried to send military units to destroy Latvia's quasi-independent government. When the putsch collapsed and Boris Yeltsin rose to power, Latvia declared its independence, and Rubiks spent four years in prison for his attempt to force the issue through terrorism. The first democratic City Council elections in post-war Riga took place in 1989. A law on the local government of the capital city was adopted by Parliament in 1992, and the City Council was named as the highest decision-making institution in the city. Andris Teikmanis was elected as the first chairman of the council. He was followed in 1994 by Maris Purgailis and in 1997 – by Andris Bērziņš.

Since the 12th century Riga has been an important port city. During the rule of the Russian Empire in the 19th century, Riga was

Janis Aventiņš, executive director of the Central District of the City of Riga

the largest port on the Baltic sea. Today, too, Riga is among the top 20 ports of the world in terms of size. In 1282 Riga joined the Hanseatic League, which for centuries brought together European cities in what can now be seen as a predecessor of the European Union. Between the 14th and 16th centuries Riga was one of the most influential cities in the league – it could be said that it was once the capital of the Medieval European Union.

Riga was the most important transport node on the line from Paris to St. Petersbourg after the 17th century. Today it remains an important railroad hub, with tracks that lead off into six directions.

The *Daugava* River runs through 31 kilometers of the city of Riga, and at Old Riga it is approximately 700 meters wide and between 8 and 15 meters deep. The *Daugava* has many tributaries and canals, and it used to have others which have disappeared. At the edges of the city there are two major lakes – *Juglas* Lake (5.7 square kilometers) and *Ķīšezers* Lake (17.4 square kilometers) – as well as the smaller *Bābelītis*, *Gaiļezers*, *Linezers* and *Velnezers* lakes, and the artificial *Māra* Pond. In fact bodies of water of various kinds take up 13% of the city's territory. Another 18% of the city is forested with stands of pine, birch and other trees and bushes. In the *Vecdaugava* and *Daugavgrīva* regions, as well as on the shores of *Jugla* Lake, natural meadows still grow. There are many kinds of introduced plants in the city's public green areas, gardens, parks and squares. Some 600 different species of trees and bushes can be found in Riga's parks.

The population of Riga has changed greatly over the centuries. From the 13th to the 18th century especially and to a somewhat lesser extent also in the 19th century, most of the city's residents were Germans and Latvians. Latvians became the dominant ethnic group in Riga in the late 19th century, and at the beginning of the 20th century 63% of the city's residents were Latvians. During the Soviet occupation Riga became much more multi-national. Germans and Jews were replaced in post-war years by Russians, Belarussians and Ukrainians who came from other parts of the Soviet Union. Most of them were factory workers, and rapid and unbalanced development in the 1950s created national, economic and social problems that have not been resolved to a certain extent even today. The architectural wars of the last 60 years drew to a close in 1999 when a modern office building known as the *Valdemārs* Center was built at the corner of *Valdemāra* and *Elizabetes iela*. Riga finally had a new building that was traditional in its six floors but also modern, with a typical emphasis on small towers at the corners of the building and with traditional colors on its outer facade. As Riga entered the 21st century, moreover, the rebuilt House of the Blackheads was opening its doors

Romelds Podskočijs, executive director of the Northern District of Riga; Raimonds Lomikovskis, acting executive director of the Central District; Guntis Grinbergs, executive director of the Latgale District; Jānis Kositis, executive director of the Zemgale District; Ita Zariņa, deputy executive director of the Riga City Council; Uldis Šmits, executive director of the Vidzeme District

A building put up by Rudolfs Cirkvics at *Vilandes iela* 1. The center of Riga is dominated by six-story buildings, typically with small towers at their corners

Andris Grinbergs, executive director of the City of Riga, with the restored House of the Blackheads behind him

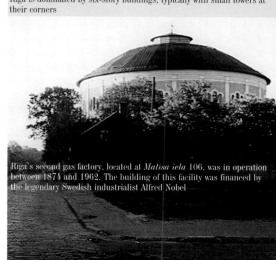

Riga's second gas factory, located at *Matīsa iela* 106, was in operation between 1874 and 1962. The building of this facility was financed by the legendary Swedish industrialist Alfred Nobel

One of the dominant scenes in the center of Riga is the cohabitation of old wooden buildings and Art Nouveau buildings

A reconstructed part of the Medieval fortifications of Old Riga, standing in *Jāņa* Yard and rebuilt in 1960

Trokšņu iela – the old fortifications and the Rahmer Tower, restored in 1987

Meistaru iela – residential buildings along the place where the city wall stood between the 13th and the 18th centuries

In the winter of 1998 German Chancellor Helmut Kohl spent several hours on a stroll through Old Riga

Audēju iela, featuring the first purely Art Nouveau building in Riga's center (1899)

The Latvian State Cultural Monuments Protection Inspectorate works in one of the most unique objects in Old Riga – the three houses known as the *Three Brothers*, which were put up between the 15th and the 18th centuries. The presence of the inspectorate in the buildings serves as testimony to the efforts of Riga to preserve its historical center as an important element of the world's cultural and natural heritage. One of 506 objects on UNESCO's global list, the old city in Riga ranks alongside the pyramids of Egypt, the Taj Mahal and the Grand Canyon in the United States

Warehouses in *Vecpilsētas iela*. Buildings of this kind were common in the 17th century. People lived on the first and second floors of the buildings on the street side, while the remaining parts of the building were used for warehousing. This building is Baroque in style

St. John's Church in Riga was a Dominican chapel when it was established in 1234. The church was built in the 13th century, destroyed in the 15th century and rebuilt afterward

The Jacob's Barracks of the 18th century were reconstructed in 1997, and now they house offices, stores and apartments. The architects for the project were Visvaldis Sarma and Janis Norde

The Mentzendorf's House at *Grēcinieku iela* 18. The building was put up in 1605 and has been reconstructed several times

The old city in Riga sits along the right bank of the *Daugava*, in a place where a Livonian village was located in the 12th century. Old Riga is typical of fortified Medieval cities in that its planning is irregular, and buildings are packed together quite densely. The Chronicle of Indriķis, issued in 1198, mentions a village called Riga around which a city was being built. The fortifications which surrounded the city started to go up in 1201, and they were approximately 2.5 meters thick and 10 meters high. One could gain access to the city only through gates. Over the course of the centuries the fortifications were rebuilt several times, and towers were occasionally added. Some of the ancient wall and one of the towers has now been restored in what is now called *Trokšņu iela* in Old Riga. There were also several major squares, including the one in front of the Rathaus (in the 14th century a public market was organized there) which was fronted not only by the City Hall, but also by the House of the Blackheads and St. Peter's Church. Also in the old city were Castle Square, Dome Square and Parade Square. The latter was located between the old walls of the city and newly built ramparts next to which the so-called Jacob's Barracks were built in the 18th century. There were also several enclosed yards – that of the Livonian Order (now known as Convent Garden), that of the Riga bishop, that of the headquarters of the church in Riga, and that of the city's tradesmen. The latter enclosure was surrounded by the first brick buildings in the city. Tradesmen and craftsmen built their homes in the center of the city, and many of the streets in Old Riga are named after the various trades.

In the 13th and 14th centuries, most of the buildings that went up in Riga were Roman in style, and this can still be seen in the most ancient parts of the city. Because many buildings were built over the course of a longer period of time and restored and rebuilt many times, frequently we see houses with a mixture of architectural styles. Most of the buildings that are now standing in Old Riga were built between the 17th and the 20th century, and virtually all of the historical styles of architecture can be seen there. Thus, for example, the Dome Cathedral is a distinguished monument to Gothic Architecture, as are St. Peter's and St. John's Churches. The architecture of the Northern Renaissance is seen most vividly in the three buildings that are known as the *Three Brothers* and in the now-restored facade of the House of the Blackheads. In the latter half of the 17th century, even warehouses were decorated with portals in which the elements of Mannerism could be seen. The Baroque style appeared in full in the 18th century, but even in the late 17th century the facade and tower of St. Peter's Church, as well as the Reitern House in Old Riga, were built on the basis of Baroque architectural principles. The Church of the Reformation, built between 1727 and 1733, is also Baroque in style. The Church of St. Peter and St. Paul was built in the style of Classicism, as were the old customs warehouses which now house the *Arsenāls* art museum. A mixture of Art Nouveau and Baroque can be seen in several buildings in *Teātra iela*.

Old Riga is a unique complex of historical building. Over the course of many centuries, Riga developed inside its fortifications. Wooden buildings were prohibited for fire safety reasons, although buildings outside of the city walls were usually built of wood – so that they could be burned down in case of war, thus averting the ability of enemies to sneak up on the town. The territory which was surrounded by the fortifications today is known as Old Riga, and here we can see buildings that went up in the days of the Hanseatic League, as well as in the period between the 18th and 20th centuries. Of course, not everything has survived. In the 1930s a series of government buildings went up in Old Riga, including the fairly expressionless building of the Finance Ministry. During World War II Old Riga suffered great damage at the hands of the Russian secret services which went to work as the Red Army withdrew.

During Soviet times there was no overall concept for the rebuilding of Riga, and a number of large buildings which do not fit in with the historical appearance were put up – the Riga Technical University and its laboratory building, residential buildings in *Kungu* and *Kaļķu* streets, the No. 3 High School and the building which now houses the Occupation Museum.

It was only 1967 that Old Riga was put under official state protection which created a legal foundation to put an end to thoughtless construction projects. Between 1977 and 1983 a regeneration project was worked out for Old Riga, setting out the main principles for the restoration of buildings, the development of functional zoning, the classification of streets and the improvement of open territories. The most important objects to be restored during this time were the tower and interior of St. Peter's Church. The 123.5 meter tower was restored in 1968. Between 1983 and 1993 extensive restoration work in Old Riga was done by a Polish enterprise which specialized in cultural monuments.

Since the restoration of Latvia's independence, building and reconstruction work in Old Riga have been financed by private companies, banks and foreign investors. Dozens of stores, cafes, restaurants and other objects have been opened on the first floors and in the cellars of buildings. The most important accomplishments in Old Riga include the restored Rome Hotel, a new bank building in *Vaļņu iela*, the fully reconstructed complex at Convent Garden, and the restoration of the Jacob's Barracks to house offices, stores and apartments.

Reconstruction of Rathaus Square has been begun, and the House of Blackheads, which was blown up in 1941, has been rebuilt. On December 4, 1997, Old Riga was included on UNESCO's list of the world's elements of cultural heritage.

ART NOUVEAU IN RĪGA

The interior of a residential building (1902) at *Smilšu iela* 8, built by architects Heinrich Scheel and Friedrich Scheffel

Interiors at the turn of the century represented a variety of tastes

A. Boguslovskis' tenement house from 1906 in *Alberta iela* 2a by the architect Mikhail Eisenstein

This building at *Skuņu iela* 10/12 (1902) had apartments and retail space. The architects were Scheel and Scheffel

The image of downtown Rīga is in large part dictated by the architectural style of the late 19th and early 20th century that is now known as Art Nouveau. The main impulse for the development of Art Nouveau was an exhibition of industry, trade and art that was staged in Rīga to mark its 700th anniversary in 1901.

In the early 20th century, the decorative aspects of Art Nouveau appeared first in Rīga, especially in the buildings that were constructed by architect Mikhail Eisenstein in *Alberta*, *Elizabetes* and *Strēlnieku* streets. At the front of these buildings we see figures of lions and sphinxes, carved and stylized depictions of plants and masks, and ornate arrangements of bricks and ceramic tiles. The facades away from the street are all bare.

Many decorative Art Nouveau buildings were constructed in *Elizabetes*, *Blaumaņa*, *Tērbatas*, *Rūpniecības* and other streets by such architects as Heinrich Scheel, Kārlis Felsko, Edmund von Trompovski and others. The rationalist version of Art Nouveau, also known as Verticalism, was represented by such architects as Reinhold Schmeling and Wilhelm Bockslaff. These buildings make wide use of bay windows, pilasters that pass through several floors, vertical and ornamental bands of decoration, etc. These can be seen in *Brīvības*, *Marijas* and *Ģertrūdes* streets. The rationalist direction was used by some of the most prolific architects of the early 20th century – Konstantīns Pēkšens, Jānis Alksnis, Eižens Laube, Pauls Mandelšteins, etc. Konstantīns Pēkšens employed a number of young Latvian architects who were graduates of the Rīga Politechnical School and were trying to develop a national style of architecture. This came to be known as National Romanticism and merged the latest concepts of architecture with elements of the decorative and applied arts. Folklore contributed a great deal of inspiration to this process. The first buildings done in the style of National Romanticism are those at *Marijas iela* 26 and *Tērbatas iela* 15/17, and both were the work of architects Konstantīns Pēkšens and Eižens Laube in 1905. Both buildings have blank facades and tilted window apertures that are reminiscent of the tilted roofs of Latvian farmhouses. Eižens Laube was one of the most dedicated fans of National Romanticism. He called on architects to use construction materials in natural ways, to study the applies arts of the Latvian nation and to reject all attempts at imitation. Architect Aleksandrs Vanags, too, designed buildings (in *Brīvības*, *Čaka*, *Lāčplēša* and other streets) in which natural construction materials were used, and national ornaments are active parts of the facades. After 1912, Art Nouveau began to disappear in Rīga, as in all of Europe, and National Romanticism went with it.

A rental building at *Teātra iela* 9 (1903), built by Scheel

The stairwell of a residential building (1933) at *Alberta iela* 12, designed by Konstantīns Pēkšens and Eižens Laube

The building at *Alberta iela* 11 (1908), built by architect Eižens Laube, is a good example of the style of National Romanticism

A building at *Alberta iela* 4 (1904), designed by architect Mikhail Eisenstein. It is a good example of an eclectic and decorative approach to Art Nouveau

A statue of St. George on the facade of the building at *Baznīcas iela* 31 (1908), architect Pauls Ribenzams

The building at *Tērbatas iela* 15/17 (1905), built by Konstantīns Pēkšens and Eižens Laube in the style of National Romanticism.

A building at *Smilšu iela* 8 (1902-1903), designed by Scheel and Scheffel in the style of eclectic and decorative Art Nouveau with detailed ornamentation on the facade

An allegorical figure on the facade of the building of the Rīga Stock Exchange (1855) on Dome Square. The architect was Haralds Bose

The building at *Vilandes iela* 1 (1899), designed and built by Rudolfs Heinrich Cirkvics

The Golgotha Baptist Church in *Hospitāļu iela*

Along with its Art Nouveau heritage, Riga boasts an historical centre that contains many wooden buildings, and on 4 December 1997, Riga's Old City was placed on the World cultural and natural heritage list. This indicates the special and universal nature of the wood buildings of Riga. Latvia has joined in an international project in which it, together with Finland, Sweden, Norway, Lithuania, Estonia and Russia, is maintaining, preserving and restoring wooden architectural monuments.

The Church of Jesus, built in 1822, is one of the largest wooden churches in Europe today. Its architect was Christian Friedrich Breitkreitz

The Alexander Nevsky Orthodox Church, 1822, designed by Christian Friedrich Breitkreitz

The Epiphany of Christ Orthodox Church in the *Sarkandaugava* area of Riga

The building at *Tallinas iela* 49, the architect – Jānis Alksnis

A building at the corner of *Tērbatas* and *Akas ielas*

A building at *Krišjāṇa Barona iela* 59/61, built in 1895 by architect Appolonius Edelson

A residential building in *Ropažu iela*, built in 1911 by architect Jānis Alksnis

A trading building built in 1878 at the corner of *Krišjāṇa Barona* and *Stabu ielas*, the architect – Viktors Grabbe

Wooden buildings at the corner of *Pērnavas* and *Asara ielas* in the *Griziņkalns* neighbourhood of Riga

The building at *Slokas iela* 23

This building, which is at the corner of *Zeļļu* and *Eduarda Smilģa ielas* in Riga, is typical of the wooden buildings that were put up in working class districts in the 1890s and thereafter. This building was designed by Jānis Alksnis in 1909

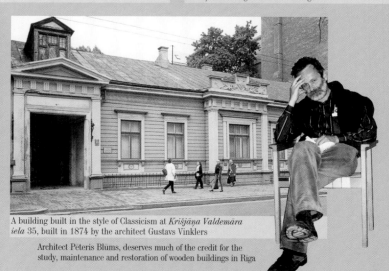
A building built in the style of Classicism at *Krišjāṇa Valdemāra iela* 35, built in 1874 by the architect Gustavs Vinklers

Architect Pēteris Blūms, deserves much of the credit for the study, maintenance and restoration of wooden buildings in Riga

A small pathway alongside the *Mārtiņa* Church in the *Pārdaugava* area of Riga

The architectonic environment of the *Ķīpsala* neighbourhood in Riga is typified by this Swiss-style balcony on the building at *Balasta Dambis* 38/40. The building was designed by Jānis Alksnis

Alksnis was also the designer of this *Ķīpsala* building, at *Ogļu iela* 28

Architect Edmund von Trompovski designed this 1899 building in *Azenes iela* in *Ķīpsala*

A suburban villa built in *Zvanu iela* in 1897 by architect Harijs Melbarts

Wooden buildings in the *Iļģuciems* neighbourhood are typified by this building in *Buļļu iela*

An 1897 building in *Kapseļu iela*, designed by architect Alfrēds Pilemanis

A 1911 building at the corner of *Ormaņu* and *Lapu ielas*, designed by the architect Eižens Laube

Ludviķa iela in *Torņakalns*

The decorations on this 1898 building in *Meteora iela* features a motif based on acorns. The architect was Indriķis Devendruss

Eižens Laube designed this pearl of National Romanticism at *Enkuru iela* 5a, built in 1909

Private house in *Lavīzes iela*, 1896, architect Rudolfs Cirkvics

A 19th-century fisherman's house at *Gundegas iela* 1 in the *Bolderāja* area of Riga

A project of appartment block designed by Juris Poga and built in a row in *Ķīpsala*

The cafe at the Riga Zoo, built in the early 20th century

The kangaroo house at the Riga Zoo, built in 1999

A new wood building, put up in *Stokholmas iela* in the *Mežaparks* neighbourhood of Riga in the 1990s

In 1813, the widow of a prominent industrialist in Riga, Anna Ģertrude Vērmane, and her son, Consul-General H. K. Vērmanis, presented to Rīga as a gift a piece of land and a sum of money for the establishment of a park. Today the park is known as *Vērmaņdārzs* (Vērmanes Garden), and it is one of the most beautiful parks in the City – located right in the City centre

Tourists are carried along *Bastejs* Boulevard and the shore of the City canal in a tram that was built in 1901

Riga's canal with a floating fountain – an element of significance in terms of appearance and the ecology.

In 1710, after Latvia had been conquered by the armies of Tsar Peter I, the park, *Ķeizardārzs*, in the Tsar's residence in Riga, was established in the Holland regular style. In 1813, the Governor-general, Philipp Paulucci, founded a committee for the establishment of green areas in the Riga's suburbs. *Vērmaņdārzs*, as well as a number of lanes and paths, were established. In 1857, the establishment of green areas in place of the former city walls, which had been torn down, began. The Riga Gardens Administration was established in 1879, and the German garden architect Georg Kupfaldt was invited to come to Riga and to turn it into a city of parks and gardens. When World War I began, Kupfaldt departed Riga, and a new director of

The first greenery of *Esplanāde* was started in 1902 in G. F. Kupfaldt's design. The monument of Rainis by the sculptor Kārlis Zemdega was unveiled on the 11th of September 1965

After Riga's fortress walls were torn down in 1857, extensive opportunities were presented for the development of the City centre and its parks and gardens. The building, which now houses the Latvian National Opera was built in 1863. A fountain featuring a nymph with a seashell was set up outside the building in 1887. Terraced flowerbeds were installed on the lower terrace of the territory in 1982. In the photographs you see the Opera square in the summer and under the cover of snow

Riga's gardens, Andrejs Zeidaks, was appointed. His artistic garden style was rooted in Latvia's nature and in the traditions of Latvian farms. Zeidaks was the first garden architect in Europe to use extensive beds of perennial plants in parks. Each of Zeidaks' parks is a true work of art – united in form and content, with functional planning and convincing spatial construction. Riga's parks and gardens make the City one of the greenest and cared for cities in all of Europe.

 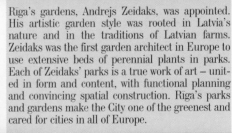

The Riga canal is often used for sports and leisure. Here you see preparations for the start of a regatta

Georg Kupfaldt (1853-1938), the first director of Riga's gardens and author of the book *The Practice of Applied Dendrology*

Andrejs Zeidaks (1874-1964), director of Riga's gardens from 1914 until 1944. He designed and established the Riga War Cemetery and reconstructed many of Riga's parks

Kārlis Barons (1912-1996), Riga's gardens architect from 1945 to 1967

Agnis Kalnkaziņš, director of Riga's parks and gardens

Professor Gundega Samoviča, a leading gardens architect in the 1990s

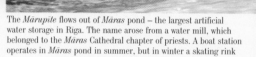

The *Mārupīte* flows out of *Māras* pond – the largest artificial water storage in Riga. The name arose from a water mill, which belonged to the *Māras* Cathedral chapter of priests. A boat station operates in *Māras* pond in summer, but in winter a skating rink

Arkādijas Park was designed by Kupfaldt, who re-routed the *Mārupīte* and created several ponds. In 1910, the restaurant was renewed, and its owner called the park *Arkādijas* Park. In 1927, under the direction of architect Pauls Kundziņš, a stage was built in the park. The sounds of the *Mārupīte* waterfall produce a special mood in the park

A monument to Latvian composers and choral directors in Song Festival Park

The green area along the canal in wintertime

The green area along the canal in the summertime

In the Soviet-era multi-apartment building suburbs, many places have been planted with colourful parks and green areas by the residents

The stage at *Dzegužkalns*

After World War II, a territory near Riga, which had previously been the site of small private gardens, was gradually transformed into a park. Architect Kārlis Barons proposed the planting of large stands of trees.

Valdis Garoza, the president of SC *Mežaparks*. Mežaparks, the favorite place of recreation of Riga people was opened in 1950, it covers a territory of 365 ha of pine forest on the coasts of *Ķīšezers*

The *Tatra* company from the Czech Republic built Riga's city trams, which were renovated in Hungary after a loan was received for this purpose from the World Bank. Now the trams are in conformity with EU standards

Trolley buses built by the Czech company *Škoda* are used in Riga

The Riga City Council has ruled that vehicles which are used for taxicab services must be no more than seven years old

Trolley buses and ordinary buses in Riga are usually painted blue and white – the official colors of the city. Expanded *Škoda* trolley buses service Riga's "bedroom districts", providing convenient connections to the city center

In 1998 the Riga City Council organized a bid for tenders for the purpose of finding a company to renovate Riga's city buses. Financing was provided by a World Bank loan. Today Riga uses Turkish-produced *Mercedes Benz* buses, and services are provided by two companies – *Tālava* and *Imanta*

Many parts of Riga's Old City are closed to car traffic. On either side of the Liberty Monument, Riga's main thoroughfare – *Brīvības bulvāris* – is open only to pedestrian traffic

Suburban electrical trains are of key importance in the city's transportation system in Riga. This electric train was produced by the Riga Wagon Factory

There are 32 companies in Riga which provide taxicab services

In 1998 the Riga City Council purchased *Mercedes Benz* ambulances which can reach a patient or victim in 15 minutes or less

Small numbers of passengers can travel in comfort in so-called *route taxis*. The vans which are used for this service are produced by the *Ford* motor company

Ferry boats on the *Daugava* River are used for tourism purposes, not for scheduled traffic

The chairwoman of the Riga City Council's Transportation Commission, Linda Baltiņa, is proud of the fact that in 1999 the city's Stone Bridge (built in 1957) was repaired and modernized

The "odds and ends" market on the shore of the *Daugava* River in 1880

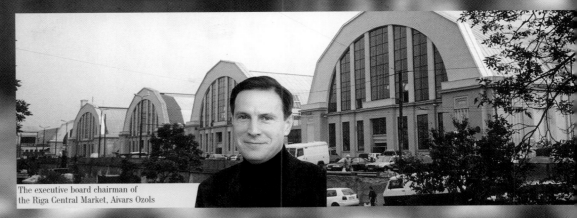

The executive board chairman of the Riga Central Market, Aivars Ozols

Riga before Christmas. A postcard from early XXth century

The fish market in 1905

The distinguished Spanish tenor Jose Carreras visiting at the fish pavilion

The veterinary service laboratory of the Central Market conducts thousands of analyses to ensure that the food that is sold at the market conforms to quality standards

A market on the shores of the *Daugava* River first appeared in written records in 1571. The market was located outside of the castle walls on the shores of the river. It was a place where food was sold – fish, poultry, vegetables, wild game, etc.

After Riga was incorporated into the Russian Empire in the late 18th century, market goods – salt fish, melted butter, watermelon, melons, grapes, etc. – were also brought in by Russian traders. Russian gardeners travelled to Riga from Moscow each spring and they leased land for vegetable gardens, providing the Riga market with cabbage, beets, onions, lettuce and other vegetables.

For several centuries, the market on the shores of the *Daugava* was the largest food market in Riga. Improvements were made to the market after the Riga city walls were torn down. In 1863, a series of open sheds and lean-tos were erected, and two wells were dug. Until 1910 people at the market sold not only food, but also various small industrial goods and used property. In the early 1920s, the market covered 20,000 square meters.

Between 1924 and 1930, based on a design by architects Pavils Dreimanis and Pavils Pavlovs, engineers Vasilijs Isajevs and Georgs Tolstojs built a new central market. Brickwork on the market was done by Old Orthodox bricklayers from Latgale. The pavilions have reinforced concrete foundations, brick walls, and arched metal roofs, which were built utilising constructions from zeppelin hangars raised during World War I in the town of *Vainode*. Initially the largest pavilion - where meat is now sold - with a floor space of 5,000 square meters was intended for wholesale trading. There are basements under all of the pavilions. These basements are connected by tunnels, while other tunnels lead to the shore of the nearby Riga canal. From there, goods can be readily transferred to warehouses and freezers. The pavilions are well ventilated, illuminated and heated. Since 1987, the market has been connected to the city's central heating system.

The Riga Central Market, which began operations in 1930, is the largest market of its kind in Europe. Within the complex there are meat, dairy products, fruit and vegetables, fish, as well as dry goods sales pavilions. The total floor space of the pavilions is 14,000 square meters, and there are also two lean-tos with a total area of 4,700 square meters. The market has installed 94 stalls for the sale of industrial goods, as well as a large open-air area. The aboveground area of the market is 87,800 square meters, and there is approximately 5,000 trading places.

The market complex also includes a hotel, an automobile repair shop and a covered parking lot. Every day some 100,000 customers shop at the market. Nearly all foreigners who visit Riga want to take a look at this unique institution. The Riga Central Market has been visited by princes and kings, as well as by the distinguished tenor Jose Carreras.

VENTSPILS

Ventspils from the 18th century. The old city has been cleaned up, and the streets have been covered with paving stones

The reconstructed *Ventspils* castle – a monument to 13th century architecture

The *Ventspils* Orthodox church (1901) – an architectural monument of national significance

An old water pump in the center of the city

The *Ventspils* University

City Hall Square

Ventspils was first mentioned in historical documents in 1263 under the name of the port of *Vinda*. In 1290 a brick castle was built, and between the 14th and 16th centuries the city was part of the Hanseatic trade league. In the 17th century it was an important port for the Duchy of Courland – a center for ship building and craftsmanship, with shops that produced metal, wood and amber products. In the mid-19th century a new phase in the city's economic activities began. a new ship building facility was opened, breakwaters were restored. A winter port was put into operation in 1891. The strongest impulse in the development of the city came when a rail line between *Ventspils* and Ribinsk was opened. Industry developed. During the first period of Latvian independence, the city's residents worked at ports and sawmills, others earned their living through fishing or trade. After World War II Ventspils became a Soviet export port for oil and oil products.

Today *Ventspils* is a modern, European-level city. the ice free port has become the largest oil and oil products export port in the Baltic Sea region – an important transportation node and a fundamentally important element in the West-East transit route. Since 1997 *Ventspils* has had free port status. There are some 50,000 residents in the city, and it has the highest level of employment, as well as the highest average wage, in all of Latvia. Most residents work in companies that deal with the reloading, storage and transit of cargo, as well as in companies which service and underpin the work of the *Ventspils* port.

The city is continuing its economic development today. Several profitable stock companies have emerged on the basis of the port, and they are continuing their development. New oil product terminals have been built, and construction work at the port is continuing. Under the leadership of Mayor Aivars Lembergs, the City Council has done a great deal to ensure that conditions are right for the launch and successful development of businesses in the city. More than 1,700 companies and enterprises are registered in the city. Money from the city's privatization fund is used only for business support. *Ventspils* has the highest per capita level of investment in all of Latvia, so the city's infrastructure is very well developed. *Ventspils* has long-standing traditions in fishing and wood processing. Serious thought is being given to the installation of a new oil pipeline to *Ventspils* with a throughput capacity of 18 million tons of products each year. A project to renovate the *Ventspils* airport is on the drawing boards, and an oil processing plant is being designed.

Over the last 10 years there have been significant changes in *Ventspils* in many areas of life. The old part of the city has been restored, parks and the seashore have been brought into order, streets have been repaved. The local government has created favorable conditions for improving and restoring privately owned buildings, too.

Ventspils City Council chairman Aivars Lembergs: "The *Ventspils* City Council each year spends a lot of money on improving the standard of living for the poor. Cultural life in the city has become much more active, there are various local and international events quite frequently, including guest performances by the opera, concerts and art exhibitions. *Ventspils* has branches of the Nordic Information Bureau and the British Council. The city has nine schools, as well as several professional and secondary specialized educational institutions. A higher education is available at the *Ventspils* University, the *Ventspils* branch of the Riga Technical University, the local affiliate of the Baltic Russian Institute, and at the *Ventspils* branch of the Riga University of Pedagogy and Educational Management. Residents and guests of *Ventspils* have every opportunity to participate in athletic activities at modern sports facilities in town."

The stock company *Ventbunkers* reloads various types of oil products, forwards cargoes, loads ships and provides other port services. *Ventbunkers* handles two million tons of cargo each year, and the throughput capacity of the terminal is 4 million tons. The company has 43 storage tanks with a total capacity of 130,000 cubic meters. In 1999 the company installed four new tanks with a capacity of 80,000 cubic meters

A monument to fishermen and sailors who have not returned from the sea

The new sports facility in *Ventspils*

The small train at the *Ventspils* Open Air Museum

The *Ventspils* Open Air Museum displays sailing and fishing equipment from various eras

The president of the transnational stock company *Lukoil*, Vagit Alikperov, and *Ventspils* Mayor Aivars Lembergs in a friendly conversation of the transit of oil products through the *Ventspils* port

The finance director of *Ventamonjaks*, Laimonis Strujevičs, and the president of the company, Krists Skuja, outside the *Ventspils* Port Business Center

Ventspils Major Aivars Lembergs and the board chairman and general director of the stock company *Kālija parks*, Nikolajs Baštavojs

The stock company *Ventamonjaks* is one of the largest chemical reloading terminals on the Baltic Sea. The terminal handles ammonia and 12 other liquid chemicals and oil chemistry products. The company handles 1.8 million tons of products each year. *Ventamonjaks* has three deepwater piers and storage tanks with a capacity of 200,000 cubic meters

Ventspils is a major railroad hub

The project *Ventspils Linear Center Games* was a new complex of avant garde principles in designing and establishing the urban environment. 13 architects from the Baltic States took part

The president of the stock company *Ventspils Tirdzniecības Osta* (*Ventspils* Trade Port), Oļegs Stepanovs: *Ventspils tirdzniecības osta* is a leader in the reloading of dry cargo among all Latvian companies. The company reloads steel in rolls or slabs (one unit can weigh up to 32 tons), cast iron, ferrous metals, alloys, refrigerated cargoes, cotton, food, packaged chemical cargoes, etc. The company has a specialized cotton warehouse with a capacity of 16,000 tons, a unique warehouse for ferrous silicate that can handle 8,000 tons of products, a 4,400 square meter warehouse for rolled steel and other general cargo that can handle up to 40,000 tons of products, warehouses for frozen fish and meat products, etc. The piers can handle ships with a draught of 15.5 meters, which allows us to handle the largest refrigerated ships. The company handles ships with a loaded weight of up to 75,000 tons, and we can handle up to 15,000 tons of products every 24 hour period. We have a factory which cuts up, sorts and packages alloys."

The old *Ventspils* fishing port is a popular place for yachts to dock

The stock company *Kālija parks* is the world's largest terminal for reloading of potassium salt. There is no other facility of its kind on the shores of the Baltic Sea. In 1998 the company handled 4.35 million tons of potassium chloride – a record for terminals. Four new sphere-shaped warehouses with a capacity of 40,000 tons have recently been installed, and this has increased the warehouse space of *Kālija parks* to 115,000 tons. This allows it to increase cargo turnover at the terminal considerably. In addition to the three kinds of potassium chloride which the terminal handles, it will now be able to store and reload new types of fertilizer, including nitrogen and phosphorous fertilizer and combined fertilizers. The terminal can handle up to 250 wagons in a 24-hour period. Pier No. 4 was deepened at the end of 1998 and Panamax-type ships are handled there. In the latter half of 1999 a new 280-meter pier with a depth of 15.5 meters was installed. It has a ship loading machine that can handle 3,000 tons per hour. Now *Kālija parks* can service two Panamax-type ships at once, with a loading intensity of 20,000 tons per 24 hours period at each pier. The locked warehouses, which have a capacity of 115,000 tons, can handle up to six different kinds of fertilizer

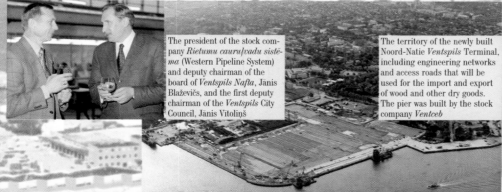

The president of the stock company *Rietumu cauruļvadu sistēma* (Western Pipeline System) and deputy chairman of the board of *Ventspils Nafta*, Janis Blaževičs, and the first deputy chairman of the *Ventspils* City Council, Janis Vitoliņš

The territory of the newly built Noord-Natie *Ventspils* Terminal, including engineering networks and access roads that will be used for the import and export of wood and other dry goods. The pier was built by the stock company *Ventceb*

The *Liepāja* port

The *Liepāja* lighthouse on the southern shore of the city's port channel was constructed in 1868, and it has survived to the present day without any significant changes

Fishing trawlers in the *Liepāja* port

Liepāja has been known as a place for bathing and spa treatments since the 18th century. In the photo: An old spa house

Liepāja in 1867 (drawing by Wilhelm Stavenhagen)

A historical image from *Liepāja*

The dry dock at *Tosmāre*

Liepāja is Latvia's third largest city. It obtained the rights of a city in 1625. In the 13th century, the site that is now occupied by *Liepāja* was the location of a Liv fishing port and a village, which was first mentioned in historical documents in 1253. The *Liepāja* port was built between 1697 and 1703 and then extended between 1860 and 1904. During the latter period there were 70-80 ships registered at the port, and there was regular steamship traffic with all the Baltic Sea ports in Russia and Germany, as well as Scandinavia.

Liepāja's development has always been dictated entirely by economic considerations – first the port, then expanded industrial activity. In 1825, the first savings bank was founded in *Liepāja* – City Savings Bank. It was one of the first such institutions in the former Russian Empire. In 1899, *Liepāja* became the first city in Eastern Europe to boast an electric tram. The "Green Pharmacy" in *Liepāja* served as an example for Tsarist Russia's first 100 pharmacies – each of which was a precise, inch-by-inch copy of the pharmacy in *Liepāja*.

The St. Trinity Evangelical Lutheran Church in *Liepāja* is the most distinguished example of Prussian sacral architecture in the Baltic region.

There are 47 educational institutions in *Liepāja*, including 17 general education schools, the Maritime College, the Music College, the Applied Arts College and the Nursing School, as well as the *Liepāja* Pedagogical University and a branch of the Riga Technical University. Latvia's oldest symphony orchestra is located in *Liepāja*, conducted by maestro Imants Resnis. *Liepāja* is also the site of Latvia's largest rock festival, *Liepājas Dzintars* ("*Liepāja* Amber"), and the city boasts two theatres and an ice hall where Latvia's national hockey team – one of the top 10 teams in the world – holds its training sessions.

St. Anne's Church was mentioned for the first time in historical documents in 1509, when it was located in *Liepāja*'s Old Cemetery. The church was built at its present location in 1587. It was restored several times before in 1893 an entirely new Gothic building was put up after a design by architect Paul B. Bertschy.

A water tower in *Liepāja*

The St. Nicholas Cathedral, built in 1903 by architect Vasily Kosjakov

The St. Trinity Church in *Liepāja* was designed by architect Johann Dorn. Construction work began in 1742, and the church was blessed for the first time in 1758. The interior is a magnificent example of Rococo design. The altar, the pews and the organ loft were all designed by sculptor Joszef Slavichek.

Nicholas Sefrens jun. made the altar at St. Anne's church

On 13 February 1918, St. Anne's was the site of a flag blessing ceremony at which Finnish soldiers swore fealty to Finland's lawful government before heading home for their country's battle of independence

The *Liepāja* Theatre has been under the *Liepāja* City Council since 1998

The *Liepāja* City Council in 1928

The Hoijere Hotel where Tsar Peter I lived in 1697 while waiting for a ship to take him to Western Europe

Liepāja as seen on old-time postcards

After the illegal government of Andrievs Niedra fell, Prime Minister Karlis Ulmanis and members of the legitimate Latvian government disembarked from the ship *Saratov* in *Liepāja* on 27 June 1919.

On 7 January 1919, Karlis Ulmanis and his government arrived in *Liepāja* and did their work for a while at a private clinic run by Professor Jēkabs Alksnis

A pigeon post station was once located here

The first electric tram in the Baltic region was opened in *Liepāja* in 1899

The *Liepāja* Symphony Orchestra is conducted by maestro Imants Resnis

A mid-summer holiday

Amber jewellery

Liepāja's fire fighting tower

The concert stage "*Pūt Vējiņi*" was reconstructed in 1989. In this photo - the traditional *Liepājas dzintars* rock festival

One of the newest buildings in *Liepāja* is the ice hall designed by architect Uldis Pilēns

A view of *Liepāja* from the tower of the St. Trinity Church

Liepāja Mayor Uldis Sesks is an automobile racer in his spare time

The *Dinaburg* fort

The St. Boris and Gleb Orthodox Cathedral

The St. Peter and St. Paul Catholic Church

The Virgin Mary Catholic Church

A view of downtown *Daugavpils*

Daugavpils Mayor Aleksejs Vidavskis

An ensemble of local government buildings

The post office

Rīgas iela

An international dance festival, *Sudmaliņas*, gathered in front of the *Daugavpils* Unity Hall, built in 1936 and 1937

The *Daugavpils* Pedagogical University

Celebration of a traditional winter festival in Unity Square

The *Zeltkalns* department store in the neighborhood known as *Jaunā forštate*

Daugavpils residents in Parliament – deputies Helena Soldatjonoka, the former and long-serving executive director of the *Daugavpils* City Council, Jānis Lāčplesis, and Vanda Kezika

Daugavpils is the second largest city in Latvia and the center of the Latgale region. Most of the city is located on the right bank of the *Daugava* River, between the river and *Stropi* Lake. On the left bank of the river is the *Grīva* neighborhood which was once a suburb of *Daugavpils* in what used to be Selonia. It was attached to *Daugavpils* only in 1956.

Daugavpils is an important transportation hub for Eastern Latvia. Rail lines connect the city to Rīga, Vilnius, St. Petersbourg, Kaunas and Šiauliai. There are nine lakes within the city, the largest of which is the aforementioned *Stropu* Lake.

Daugavpils has a very varied population. In the 18th century many non-Latvians settled in the region. In 1897, in fact, only 1.8% of the city's populations were Latvians – the remainder were Jews, Russians, Poles and Germans. In 1925 Latvians represented 27% of the *Daugavpils* population, and Poles (19%) were the second largest ethnic group. After World War II, many people arrived from Russia and Belarus.

Daugavpils was mentioned for the first time as a settled area in the 5th century, when people from the island of Gotland sailed up the *Daugava* River to Russia, later traveling to Greece. In the 10th and 11th century people from Gotland and Denmark had fortified themselves along the *Daugava* River. In 1275 the Livonian Order began to build a brick castle in the area, which was at that time known as Dinaburg. Between the 12th and 14th centuries it was an important trade location, and the city of Riga had a trade office there. In 1481 Tsar Ivan III of Russia attacked Livonia and sacked Dinaburg, but it was restored and fortified to an even greater extent. In 1559 the master of the Livonian Order, Gotthard Kettler, gave the Dinaburg castle to the kind of Poland and Lithuania, Sigismund II Augustus the Strong. In 1566 Dinaburg became the center of Poland's Vidzeme region. In 1577 Tsar Ivan the Terrible conquered the castle and destroyed it completely. King Stefan Batorius of Poland refused to restore the castle, choosing instead to build a new one where the *Daugavpils* fort stands now. Building started in 1582. A settlement emerged around the new castle, and it was soon awarded the rights of a city.

In 1656 the city was once again taken over by the Russian armed forces, and Tsar Aleksi Mikhailovich dubbed the town Borisoglebsk. The city regained the name of Dinaburg in 1667. In 1893

Tsar Alexander III named the town Dvinsk, and on July 27, 1914, the *Daugavpils* fort was announced as the center of the Dvinsk war region. The German army entered the city in February 1918, but in December of the same year it turned *Daugavpils* over to the Bolsheviks without a fight. On January 3, 1920, Latvian military units liberated *Daugavpils* from the Bolsheviks, working together with the Polish army to do so.

Daugavpils does not have what would be called an old city. The oldest part of the city is found around the *Daugavpils* fort, built in the 19th century. When work on the fort began in 1810, many old buildings were torn down or moved. The iron bridge across the *Daugava* River was built in 1853. The first school in Latgale was opened in 1630 in *Daugavpils* by Jesuit priests. In 1761 the Jesuit school was transformed into a gymnasium.

Daugavpils is the only city in the world in which you can stand in one place and see the churches of all four of Latvia's major Christian confessions – the Lutherans, the Roman Catholics, the Orthodox and the Old Orthodox. St. Peter's Church, which is owned by the Catholics, as well as the Lutheran church in town, were built by the architect Wilhelm Neumann. The Lutheran church suffered heavy damage during World War II. After the war the church was confiscated by the Soviet government, and a warehouse was installed in it. The largest Orthodox church in town is the St. Boris Gleb Orthodox Cathedral. The St. Neva Alexander Cathedral, which was built in the mid-19th century, was torn down in a single night in the 1950s.

Daugavpils is an important center for education and culture. There are more than 20 general education schools, several elementary schools and pre-schools, four trade high schools, several technical schools, the *Daugavpils* Pedagogical University, and a branch of the Rīga Technical University. Many important people have lived and worked in *Daugavpils*. The distinguished poet Rainis grew up not far from the city. Mark Rothko, the legendary modernist painter, is from *Daugavpils*. His real name was Mark Rotkovich. Composer Oskars Stroks is also from the city.

Daugavpils has a locomotive repair factory at which locomotives from all over the ex-Soviet Union are repaired, and spare parts are manufactured. *Daugavpils* has other important factories, too, including several which produce chemicals, and several which produce textiles for domestic use and export.

RĒZEKNE

The *Latgales Māra* monument, sculpted by Kārlis Jansons. The monument was restored in 1992 by sculptor Andrejs Jansons

Liberation alley

The ruins of the *Rēzekne* castle

The roofs of *Rēzekne*

Bishop Jānis Bulis

A museum of cultural history and art

Mayor Jānis Jukna outside the City Council building

The *Adamova* baronial estate

The Roman Catholic Church of the Mother of God (1937), designed by architect Pāvils Pavlovs

The long-time director of the *Rēzekne* Arts College, Osvalds Zvejsalnieks, who is an artist and has been a member of Parliament

The home of cultural worker and teacher Valērija Seile

The residents of *Rēzekne* call it the capital of Latgale. *Rēzekne* is indeed located in the center of the Latgale region and received the rights of a city in 1773.

There was a Latgallian castle in the region in the 10th and 11th century. After the German invasion, in 1285, the Livonian Order built a brick castle in *Rēzekne*, and a settlement emerged around it. Over the course of the centuries, the population of *Rēzekne* changed considerably, especially in the late 17th and early 18th century, when a large number of Old Orthodox arrived in *Rēzekne*. Tsar Nicholas I visited the city in 1846.

The first public school in *Rēzekne* opened in 1826, and the district school from *Krāslava* was moved to *Rēzekne* in 1831.

Rēzekne's Medieval castle and its ancient cemetery are national archaeological monuments. *Rēzekne* also is home to the *Latgales Māra* monument which commemorates the liberators of Latvia. The monument was unveiled in 1939 and was destroyed on a number of times,

only to be restored each time – most recently in 1992.

The *Ērgļi* Pharmacy, which was founded in 1836, is one of the oldest in Latgale.

Rēzekne is an important transport center. There are major roads from *Gulbene* and *Krāslava*, and the international routes Riga-Moscow and Kaunas-St. Petersbourg pass through here. So does the rail line Warsaw-Riga-Moscow-St. Petersbourg.

14% of the city's territory is taken up by industrial factories – the largest are the stock company *Rebir*, the stock company *Rēzeknes piena konservu kombināts*, *Rēzeknes būvmateriāli* Ltd., the stock company *Rēzeknes dzirnavnieks*, *Rēzeknes mežrūpniecības saimniecība*, Ltd., and others. Most of the companies produce goods both for the domestic market and for export.

Rēzekne has a university, an important regional hospital, art and music colleges and other educational institutions.

A monument of wooden architecture at *18. Novembra iela* 26, restored by students from the art college

The *Rēvis* nightclub

The *Rēzekne* River

The *Latgale* Hotel

New residential buildings

The *Latgale TV* Music Festival, 1997

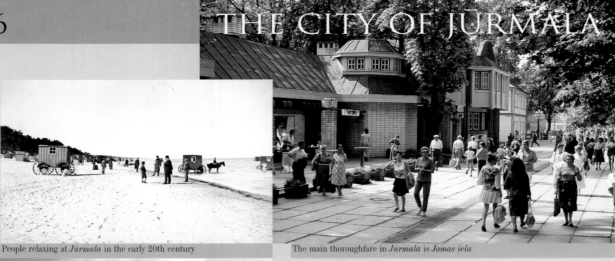

People relaxing at *Jūrmala* in the early 20th century

The main thoroughfare in *Jūrmala* is *Jomas iela*

The *Dubulti* Lutheran Church (1909) at *Baznīcas iela* 13. Its architect was Wilhelm Bockslaff

The *Priedaine* railroad station (1938), designed by architects A. Grundmanis and J. Šarlovs. The building is well proportioned and elegant in its details

The *Jūras pērle* (the Sea Pearl) restaurant in 1964. It was built by architect Josif Goldenberg

The *Dzintari* Concert Hall (1936, expanded in 1960). It was built by architects Aleksandrs Birzenieks, Viktors Mellenbergs and Modris Ģelzis and is located at *Turaidas iela 1*

A hotel at *Turaidas iela* 13 in *Dzintari* which was one of the earliest works of the architect Teodors Hermanovskis

A local architectural monument is this 1910 residential building that is located at *Meža prospekts* 28, *Bulduri*

A summer house in *Bulduru prospekts* 10, early 20th century

Archaeological sites indicate that the territory around *Jūrmala* was first populated between the 6th and the 4th millennium BC. Between the 9th and 12th century AD, there was a Semigallian port on the *Lielupe* River. After the invasion of the German Crusaders, trade through this port was banned. There was also a trade route from Kurzeme to Riga that ran along the seashore – thus through what is now *Jūrmala*. The territory was long populated exclusively by fishermen. The situation changed when in the 19th century the governing authorities began to distribute State-owned land in the area for the construction of summer homes. The area that is now in the town of *Dubulti* became the centre of *Jūrmala*. In 1877, a rail line from Riga to *Tukums* was opened, and *Jūrmala* quickly blossomed as a leisure centre. In the early 20th century, more than 50,000 people visited the region each year. The areas was damaged very severely in World War II, but in the post-war area, several populated areas – *Lielupe* (*Buļļi*), *Bulduri* (*Bilderliņi*), *Dzintari* (*Edinburga*), *Majori*, *Vecdubulti*, *Jaundubulti*, *Melluži* (*Karlsbāde*), *Asari* and *Valtermuiža* – were merged into the city of *Jūrmala*. In 1946, *Jūrmala* was declared part of the city of Riga, but in 1959, through a merger of *Ķemeri*, *Sloka* and *Jūrmala*, it was once again split apart as a resort area. During the Soviet occupation *Jūrmala* was the best known resort in the entire Soviet Union, and some 2.5 million people from all over the USSR visited it annually. For a city that had only 60,000 permanent residents, this posed a very serious social and ecological burden. Closed health care facilities were opened for government officials and high-ranking military officers.

Jūrmala is still Latvia's leading resort, and its best-known medical institution is the rehabilitation centre *Vaivari*. There are several other health resorts in *Jūrmala*, and all kinds of relaxation and entertainment opportunities are on offer. The food industry is another part of the *Jūrmala* economy, and there are many clothing and consumer goods stores.

The national rehabilitation centre *Vaivari* initially was built for the Soviet Space Centre. For a bird's eye it has the shape of *a sputnick*

A residential building at *Bulduru prospekts* 1 built in 1903

The *Villa Marta* was built in the 1920s and restored in the 1990s, when designers *updated* it with inappropriate details. The building is located at *Bulduru prospekts* 16, and its original architect is not known

A wax statue of Duke Jēkabs at the *Jelgava* History Museum

Old wooden buildings in *Jelgava*

The *Jelgava* shore, depicted on a postcard in 1902

Uldis Ivans, chairman of the *Jelgava* City Council

The region where *Jelgava* is now located was populated in the 2nd millennium BC. During the 1st millennium AD, the region was populated by Semigallians. The city of *Jelgava* was mentioned in documents for the first time in 1265, when the Livonian Order started to construct a wooden castle there. A brick castle was put in its place in the 14th century, and a settlement of craftsmen and tradesmen emerged around it. *Jelgava* gained the rights of a city in 1573, and five years later the duke of Courland moved there. After the Polish-Swedish war the city grew very quickly, but it was sacked by Sweden in 1658. Economic life was restored after the Northern War, and *Jelgava* turned into an important center for trade and crafts. In 1738 Duke Ernst Johann Biron began to build the Jelgava castle, which today is the most important architectural monument in the city. In the late 18th century and throughout the 19th century *Jelgava* was a significance center for culture and education. The Latvian Agricultural University was opened there in 1939.

The city suffered extensive damage during World War II, with Russian aviation bombing the city as intensely as the Allies bombed Dresden. After the war *Jelgava* was the site of various factories working in light industry, food processing, the manufacturing of construction materials, machinery and metal processing, and it was the fourth largest industrial center in Latvia. A factory to produce 10-seat passenger vans and ambulances for the entire Soviet Union was also opened. The city is a railroad node.

Today *Jelgava* is a student city. The Latvian Agricultural University, a People's University, the Zemgale Business School, an affiliate of the *Daugavpils* Pedagogical University and the Adult Education Center are all located here.

A monument to the liberators of Jelgava, sculptor Andrejs Jansons, restored in 1992

The Roman Catholic church

The sarcophagi of the dukes of Courland and Zemgale at the *Jelgava* castle

A pre-war wooden building freshened up for a contemporary appearance

The *Jelgava* History Museum, also known as *Academia Petrina*

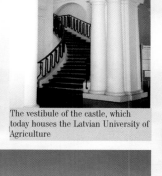

The vestibule of the castle, which today houses the Latvian University of Agriculture

The *Jelgava* castle as seen from a bridge across the *Lielupe* river

The St. Anne church was originally a wooden building that was put up in 1574. The present-day brick building (1638-1641) is the oldest church in the city. It has been rebuilt several times. In the garden of the church is an oak tree that was planted in 1883 to mark the 400th anniversary of the birth of Martin Luther and to honor his Reformation

A form of "small architecture" – the white goat at the entry to *Jelgava*. The white goat has long been a symbol of *Jelgava*. The poet Aleksandrs Čaks wrote: "A small, small city, its symbol a white goat."

The *Valdeka* castle, built by dukes for hunting purposes in the 17th century. The facade was redesigned in the Gothic style of Great Britain in the mid-19th century, when the castle was purchased by a different Baltic German family. Today the building is used by the Agricultural University

A school which was burned down when the forces of Bermont-Avalov withdrew from *Jelgava* during World War I. During the first period of Latvia's independence there was a teachers institute there. The building was destroyed once again in the summer of 1944. Today it houses the Faculty of Economics of the Agricultural University.

The *Villa Medem*, which was designed as an adaptation of a design for the *Eleja* castle, built in 1818 and rebuilt in 1843. At the turn of the 19th century it was the summer residence of a local aristocrat

A fragment of the monument *Lāčplēsis and the Black Knight*, sculpted by Kārlis Jansons and unveiled in 1932. It was destroyed in 1950, but a fragment was preserved and has been standing outside the Ģederts Eliass *Jelgava* Museum of History and Art since 1988

A monument to the artist Ģederts Eliass (1987), sculpted by J. Zariņš. The *Jelgava* museum has a permanent exhibition of Eliass' paintings, as well as a memorial exhibit

A copy of a monumental urn installed in 1897 in what was known as the *Mīlestības aleja* of the Duchy of Courland and Zemgale

An ice sculpture festival, December 1999

A popular leisure complex, *Brize*, in *Atmodas iela*

The tower of the St. Trinity Church, lit up at the turn of the millennium

PĀVILOSTA

CITIES

The stone castle of *Pāvilosta* was built in 1290. There was also a lighthouse at the site, and a small town sprang up. The place was not called *Pāvilosta* at that time. It was known as *Akagals*. Economic activity was particularly intensive during the rule of Duke Jacob of Kurzeme. Between 1642 and 1682 ships entered the local port flying the flag of the Duke of Kurzeme and forging links between the shores of Kurzeme and the distant reaches of the world. In 1878, a man called Pauls Lilienfelds laid the foundations for the first breakwater on the coast at *Pāvilosta*, although the first real port was opened only on 22 May 1879. A village was built for construction workers, builders, bakers, salespersons and sailors. The village was named after its founder – *Pāvilosta*. In 1890, the port was deepened, and 100-meter breakwaters were installed. There were three shipbuilding yards along the shores of the local river, and in the late 19th century, they built 15 two-mast sailing ships. *Pāvilosta* presents a textbook example of urban construction in the late 19th century. The Lutheran Church does not have a tower because laws at that time prohibited the construction of churches or other buildings with towers, lest sailors at sea be confused. Today local residents are developing the wood processing industry and individual fishing operations, and the life of the city is once again subject to the rhythm of the sea and the port that is nearby.

KANDAVA

The Kurs had a castle at what is now *Kandava* between the 10th and the 12th centuries. The name of the city appeared in historical documents for the first time in 1230. The Livonian Order took over *Kandava* in 1253 and built a castle there. The city blossomed in the 17th century to become a major trade centre for the surrounding region. A city council was established in 1893, although the full rights of a city were awarded to *Kandava* only in 1917. *Kandava* is interesting because of its early-20th century architecture. The oldest buildings are found mostly at the market square and along *Lielā iela*. The most important building monument is a four-arch bridge across the *Abava* River, which was initially built at the suggestion of Baron von Fircks on an open field, after which the flow of the river was diverted. The site of the former castle still has a square tower with walls that are two meters thick. During Duke Jacob's reign, gunpowder was stored in the tower, and it is known as Powder Tower to this very day. There are two important schools in *Kandava* – the Kārlis Milenbahs High School and the Agricultural Technical College. The city is known for its cleanliness and order. The long-time mayor is Dainis Rozenfelds.

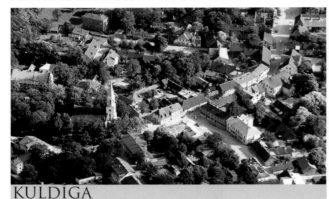

KULDĪGA

The name of *Kuldīga* first appeared in historical documents in 1245, when Bishop Wilhelm decreed that Kurzeme would be part of Prussia. A region populated by Kurish tribes along the *Venta* and *Abava* rivers was an important object of international interest in the 13th century. In 1378 *Kuldīga* was granted the right of a city, and in 1398 it joined the Hanseatic League. *Kuldīga* experienced its true golden age between 1642 and 1682. *Kuldīga* has an urban environment, which was built up by artisans, traders and bureaucrats. This is the only city in Latvia where large and unchanged areas of wooden buildings from the 18th and 19th century have survived *en masse*.
Kuldīga is home to the St. Catherine's Lutheran Church, where the altar and pulpit, produced by wood sculptor Sefrenss the Elder, date back to the 1660-1663, while the pipe organ, produced by K. Rāneuss, dates back to 1712-1715. Both are architectural monuments of global importance. The foundations of the St. Anne Evangelical Lutheran Church were laid in 1899. Employers in the city today include automobile repair, food processing, transportation and service companies. There are affiliates of the Riga College of Education and Educational Management and the *Liepāja* Pedagogic Academy in city.

SKRUNDA

Skrunda is the youngest (77th) city in Latvia, and it obtained the right of a city only in 1996. The local residents do not feel that this is right, because a German feudal castle was built on the site of the present-day city in 1368, right at the shore of the *Venta* River. The name of *Skrunda* echoed around the world on 4 May 1995, when a Soviet-era radar detection station, which was being built when the USSR collapsed, was dismantled with a targeted explosion. The radar station at *Skrunda* was to be part of the Soviet Union's defence against the American *Star Wars* policy. When Latvia regained independence, Russia wanted to keep a military base here. An agreement was signed on the operations of the radar station until 1998, after which the last active duty military personnel from the Russian armed forces withdrew from the country. The fact that the city is in good shape is largely because Russia paid rent on the land, which was used for the radar station. The *Skrunda* railroad station has a monument: a memorial railway wagon-museum in commemoration of the people who were deported to Siberia in 1941 and 1949.

TALSI

The *Talsi* castle hill was once one of the most important fortifications of the Kurs. *Talsi* was first mentioned in known written sources in 1231. In 1253, the city fell to the Livonian Order. The construction of a brick castle began forthwith, but it was not completed until 1354. In 1894, *Talsi* was given limited rights to self-government. The city suffered great damage in various revolutions and during the time of the Bolsheviks and the forces of Pavel Bermont-Avalov. In October 1939, after the first wave of the Soviet military arrived before World War II, an airport was built at *Talsi*, and an air defence radar system was installed.
The historical centre of *Talsi* is located on the shores of the *Talsu* lake. Following a fire in 1733, among the old wooden buildings people started to build two or three-story brick buildings with gabled roofs of a type that are found only in *Talsi*.
The local baron, von Fircks, built a summer manor for himself between 1883 and 1885, and today it houses the local museum. The mansion is an outstanding architectural monument. *Talsi* is also the site of a pharmacy that first opened its doors in 1787 and is still working today.
The food processing industry is a key part of the local economy in *Talsi*. Mr. Harijs Poļevskis runs a printing house, and there are also companies that produce construction materials and build roads.

AIZPUTE

Aizpute is one of the oldest cities in Latvia. Archaeologists date the earliest settlements in the area to the 2nd to the 4th century AD. A fortified Kurish castle was located on the right shore of the *Tebra* River, along the Riga-Prussia trade and military route, in the 13th century. This castle was known locally as the *Beida* Castle, but in some documents, it is referred to as *Asenpute*. At a short distance from the castle, German Crusaders built a castle for the Bishop of Kurzeme in 1248. Later it became the administrative centre for the *Piltene* region. *Aizpute* gained the rights of a city in 1378. After Kurzeme was annexed by Russia in 1795 *Aizpute* remained the administrative centre for the local region. *Aizpute* is an important centre of art, cultural history and architecture. The city was built up between the 13th and the 19th centuries, and many old wooden buildings remain standing today. The most important architectural monuments in city are the ruins of the *Aizpute* Castle of the Livonian Order, as well as the local Lutheran church.
The industrial company *Kurzemes Atslēga 1*, which produces some 100 different kinds of locks, is a major local employer. Road repair, food processing and other companies are also developing.

DOBELE

The 10th-century *Dobele* castle hill was once the site of one of the most important castles of the ancient Semigalians. Between 1279 and 1289 the Livonian Order attacked the castle six times, but they could not take it. In 1289 the Semigallians themselves burned down their castle and departed for Lithuania. In 1335 the Livonian Order began to put up a brick castle in place of the former Semigallian castle. The *Dobele* Castle was the seat of the local governor.
A clergyman in Dobele called Johann Rivius prepared the first Lutheran Catechism published in the Latvian language (in 1586). Another man who spent a long time in *Dobele* was the distinguished composer of spiritual songs and hymns, Christofor Füreccerus.
Dobele had a unique history after World War II, when the Russian occupation force installed enormous military units in the city in case Western Europe had to be attacked. Several military bases for soldiers were built a few kilometres from the city, and they were called *Dobele 1*, *Dobele 2*, etc. *Dobele* is home to well-known Latvian companies such as the stock company *Spodriba*, the stock company *Dobele*, the company *Tenax*, the stock company *Dobeles dzirnavnieks*, etc.

SALDUS

The *Kurish Treaty* of 1253 says that the region of *Saldus* was turned over to the governance of the Livonian Order. In the 14th century the Germans built a brick castle for themselves in *Saldus*, but it was destroyed in the 18th century. On the site of the former castle, the *Saldus* manor was established, and the mansion of the manor was later turned into a hospital.
Buildings in *Saldus* were mostly built in the 19th and 20th century. The city centre is gathered around the Rīga-*Liepāja*, *Kuldīga-Dobele* and *Saldus-Ezere-Mažeiķi* roads.
In 1972 a Soviet *kolhoze* called *Druva* was established in *Saldus*, and its administrative building, sports facility, school and water tower can be seen as a monument to the architecture of the 1970s and 1980s in the Soviet Union. During the Soviet occupation, the *Zvārde* parish which is to the South of *Saldus* was liquidated, and an aviation base was installed over most of its territory. Aviation bombs fell on the city of *Saldus* on several occasions during practice runs at the facility. Now some of the former air base is part of a nature reserve.
Today there are several food processing, wood processing, carpentry, building, transportation and other companies in *Saldus*.

Bauska was first mentioned in historical sources in 1443, when the *Bauska* Castle was built along the Lithuanian transit road. At the place where the *Mūsa* and *Mēmele* rivers come together a settlement for craftsmen and fishermen gradually sprang up, and in 1518 it was named *Bauska*, although others called it *Vairogmiests*. In 1561, *Bauska* became part of the Duchy of Kurzeme. In 1706, Russian forces blew up the castle. The *Bauska* Castle today is an archaeological monument of national importance because it was the last brick castle that the Livonian Order built in the southern reaches of its lands. It is also one of the biggest castles of the Livonian Order, and the Landtag of the Duchy of Kurzeme met there. The Church of the Holy Spirit is an outstanding example of church architecture in the region, and it was built between 1591 and 1594. The tower was built in 1623. At the corner of *Kalēju* and *Rūpniecības* streets is the so-called *Peter's stone*, so named because according to legend Tsar Peter the Great and Polish King Augustus II the Strong had lunch on the rock in 1701.

Bauska has been a crossroads since time eternal. The *Via Baltica* highway which runs from Tallinn to Vilnius is an important part of the city's life.

BAUSKA

The German Crusaders sacked Selish and Latgallian castles on both sides of the *Daugava* River in the early 13th century and built the *Krustpils*, *Sēlpils* and *Dignāja* castles instead. After the Livonian War the land on the right bank of the *Daugava* belonged to Poland, while the left bank was part of the Duchy of Kurzeme. When Duke Jacob was in power (1642-1682), refugees from Russia and Poland established a settlement at a local domain manor, and in 1670 the settlement was given the right of a city. It was named *Jakobstadt* or *Jēkabmiests*. The economy of what later was called *Jēkabpils* began to change in 1861, when the Riga-*Daugavpils* railroad was opened and passed through the town. During Latvia's first period of independence industry blossomed. In 1936 a bridge across the *Daugava* River was built. The town on the opposite shore, *Krustpils*, was given the rights of a city in 1920.

During World War II the city suffered great damage, and the bridge across the *Daugava* was blown up. A new bridge was built only in 1960. After the war *Krustpils* was a centre for the manufacture of construction materials and for the food processing industry. *Krustpils* was incorporated into *Jēkabpils* in 1962.

JĒKABPILS

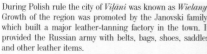

A Selish castle was located at the site where *Jaunjelgava* now stands in the 13th century, but the German Crusaders sacked it. Later a settlement emerged at the site, first known as *Sērene*, then later as *Jaunpilsētiņa*, *Jaunpilsēta*, *Jelgaviņa*, *Jaunā Jelgaviņa*, *Lubu Jelgava* and, finally, *Jaunjelgava*. It was given the right of a village in 1590 and of a city in 1647. Trade in Riga was heavily dependent on the waterway of the *Daugava* River, and *Jaunjelgava* was a place for the reloading of products. Between 1795 and 1924 *Jaunjelgava* was a district city. The historical centre of the city is a nationally important monument of urban architecture, dating back to the 17th and 18th centuries. The ancient street plan has been preserved between *Jelgavas* and *Rātūža ielas*. The oldest house in the city is a 19th-century pharmaceutical warehouse at the corner of *Jelgavas* and *Uzvaras ielas*. The Latvian-Swedish forestry joint venture *Latsin* Ltd. operates in town, as does a sawmill called *Laura*, and a carpentry company called *Larsa*. In 1997 the city was granted the status of a region deserving of special support. A project was set up on the maintenance of the natural, cultural and historical heritage of the region.

JAUNJELGAVA

KRASLAVA

In the 13th century *Krāslava* fell to the Livonian Order. The city is mentioned for the first time in documents, which date back to the 14th century. There was a manor in *Krāslava* from the mid-16th century, and in 1729 it was given the rights of a village. *Krāslava* subsequently was under the control of both Russia and Poland. In 1923, when Latvia was independent, *Krāslava* was given the rights of a city. After World War II *Priedaine* was incorporated into *Krāslava*, and since 1950 it has been the district centre. The historical centre of the city itself, including the *Krāslava* Castle and St. Ludwig's Church, are national architectural and historical monuments.

The city's economy is based on wood processing and retail sales. There is a sewing factory called *Nemo* which produces goods both for the domestic market and for export. There is also the food processing company *Krāslavas piens*. In 1997 the city was declared a region deserving of special support by the government.

During Polish rule the city of *Viļāni* was known as *Wielany*. Growth of the region was promoted by the Janovski family, which built a major leather-tanning factory in the town. It provided the Russian army with belts, bags, shoes, saddles and other leather items.

The city was sacked during World War II. In 1950 a hydroelectric station went on line on the *Malta* River in town, and in 1994 the facility was reconstructed. The *Viļāni* Selection and Experimentation Station does scientific work on the growing and development of long-fibre flax.

The most important areas of industry in *Viļāni* are wood processing, textiles, charcoal manufacturing and bakeries. Large agricultural exhibitions are organised in town, and on the second Sunday of each month there is artisans' fair. Once a year the artisans organise a major exhibition of their wares.

VIĻĀNI

Varakļāni obtained the rights of a city in 1928. The city stands as an unusual testament to the interaction of cultures and to the ethnic and administrative history of Latvia. In 1638 there was a Lutheran congregation in town, but the minister was run out of town in 1696. Since 1819 the city has been part of the largely Roman Catholic *Rēzekne* district.

In the early 20th century more than one-half of the residents of *Varakļāni* were Jewish, and many families perished during World War II at the hands of the Nazis. After World War II *Varakļāni* was the district centre, but in 1956 it was joined to the *Madona* district (unlike nearby *Viļāni*, which was made part of the *Rēzekne* district). The territorial redistribution was done because there was a need to divide up land reclamation and agricultural equipment enterprises. The *Varakļāni* manor and park are one of the most outstanding monuments to the culture of the period of Classicism in the Latgale region of Latvia. An architect from Rome designed the residential building of the manor, as well as its placement in the total ensemble. Another important historical monument is the Catholic Church in *Varakļāni*, with two massive towers that are supported by six brick pillars, as well as an entrance terrace.

The city has wood processing, retail trade and service companies today, and various options for territorial development are being considered.

VARAKĻĀNI

LUDZA

Ludza is one of the oldest cities in Latvia. It was mentioned in several historical chronicles in 1177, although the area had been settled in the 8th millennium BC. The ancient settlement was located near six large lakes. The *Ludza* castle ruins and the Chapel of St. Tadeus are historical monuments of national importance.

There are several major companies in *Ludza* today, including *Ludzas piensaimnieks*, which produces more than 100 tons of pasteurised milk, butter, cream, yogurt and cheese every day. *Lina Eks* Ltd. produces 10 tons of flax fibre a day. Other companies include the stock company *Metālists*, the wood processing company *Ludzas koks* Ltd., and an affiliate of *Linda* Ltd. Lots of people in Latvia know and love the bread which is baked by *Ludzas maiznieks* Ltd.

There are two high schools, and evening high school, a music school, and art school, a children's and youth centre and a sports school in *Ludza*.

In the 12th century *Preiļi* was a part of the Latgallian state of *Jersika*, but in the 13th century, after the German Crusaders attacked, it fell to the Livonian Order. *Preiļi* was first mentioned in a document in 1382. The town was owned by a local dynasty for a while, then was part of the Duchy of *Pārdaugava*, and later was subordinated to the Poles and then to the Russians. *Preiļi* has always been a local trade centre, and in the mid-19th century it was given the rights of a village. The rights of a city were awarded to it during Latvia's first period of independence, in 1928. After World War II several light industry and food processing companies were established in the city. Today the best known companies are the stock company *Preiļu siers*, which supplies its cheese products under the leadership of director Jāzeps Šņepsts both to the domestic and to export markets. There is also a textiles factory called *TEKS* which exports about 95% of its products, and there are other private companies, too. The castle of the *Preiļi* manor is one of the most outstanding examples of Neo-Gothic baronial architecture in Latgale. The *Preiļi* Catholic Church was built between 1878 and 1886.

PREIĻI

PRIVATIZATION OF RESIDENTIAL BUILDINGS

There are approximately 1 million apartments and one-family homes in Latvia, of which approximately one-half (505,000 apartments) were owned by the State and local governments when the process of privatisation began in Latvia. The property conversion principles that were implemented in the early 1990s provided that these State and local government-owned buildings and apartments would be turned into private property. At the end of 1999, more than 350,000 State and local government apartments had already found their owners. People bought their apartments mostly in return for privatisation certificates.

The privatisation of residential buildings in Latvia has created a significant development impulse. The real estate market in Latvia has strengthened and developed, and private initiative has attracted new investments from domestic and foreign companies. There is no longer a monopoly in the management of Latvia's residential buildings, and companies which manage buildings compete among themselves. Residential buildings and parcels of land are being registered in Latvia's Land Register.

Tenants who privatised their apartments became the true owners of the housing. Joining together with their neighbours and taking over management of the building, people have made the process more profitable and effective. Latvian law allows the owners of privatised apartments to sell them, present them as gifts, exchange them for other housing, use them for inheritance or mortgage them. There is no limitation on the benefits which private owners can gain in using and increasing the value of the property in any way which they see fit, as long as they don't violate the law or the rights of other apartment owners. A privatised apartment can also be used for business activities, or they can be rented out on the basis of the relevant agreements.

Privatised apartment buildings are increasingly being run by apartment owner associations. There are companies, which provide management services, as well as renovation and restoration services. People's attitudes toward apartments, apartment buildings and their surrounding environment have changed. People now have the understanding that comes with ownership – that property means responsibility and obligations.

In the photograph, we see the Central Housing Privatisation Commission. Chairman Ziedonis Ziediņš is carrying the large yellow sunflower.

THE STATE REAL ESTATE AGENCY

The state-owned stock company *Valsts nekustamā īpašuma aģentūra* (State Real Estate Agency) is responsible for State-owned real estate, maintaining registers and assessments of properties and registering them in the Land Register. The Agency is responsible for the management and maintenance of State-owned real estate, as well as the repair and restoration of buildings and other constructions. It invests money in State-owned real estate objects, leases the properties to natural persons and legal persons, engages in civil transactions with real estate and represents the State's interests in this area.

The general director of the State Real Estate Agency, Kalvis Bricis

The equity capital of the Agency is 4.1 million lats, but the law requires it to increase its registered equity capital to the sum of 7 million lats by the year 2001. At present the Agency manages 900 real estate objects and leases 300 pieces of real estate and 300 parcels of land.

A computerised and integrated real estate management information system has been introduced in the agency's work with the technical assistance of the Phare Program.

Between the first and eighth centuries AD, this was the site of the best-fortified Livonian castle hills – the *Rati* Hill, as well as the *Turaida, Satezele, Vikmeste* and *Vieši* castle hills. In the early 13th century, however, the German Crusaders cast their eyes on the territory. The right bank of the *Gauja* River fell to the Bishop of Riga, while the left bank went to the Order of Brotherhood of the Sword. In 1207 the master of the Order, a man called Venno, began to build a castle at *Sigulda*. A castle for the Riga bishop in *Turaida* was built beginning in 1214. *Sigulda* was also home to several other officials from the order. The oldest standing building in town is the Lutheran Church, which was built around 1225.

In 1878, the owner of the *Sigulda* manor, Princess Kropotkina, built a new castle in *Sigulda*. The construction was done under the leadership of a construction expert Meņģelis from *Cēsis*. Today the building houses the *Sigulda* City Council. Today *Sigulda* is a city of tourism, the centre of the *Gauja* National Park. The *Gauja* valley is around one kilometre wide and between 70 and 85 meters deep around here. Visitors are attracted by bobsled and luge competitions, six slalom tracks and a hotel. Since 1993, *Sigulda* has been the site of a summer opera music festival each year, and there are also traditional ballooning festivals.

The *Turaida* museum reserve is the main tourist attraction on the opposite side of the *Gauja* River.

SIGULDA

The area that is now *Cēsis* was first populated in the first millennium BC. The name of *Cēsis* appears for the first time in the Chronicle of Indriķis, in a report of events in the year 1206. In that year, the local tribe of Vendians converted to the Christian faith. Next to the Vendian castle, the Order of the Brotherhood of the Sword put up a brick castle, and a town emerged alongside it. *Cēsis* won the rights of a city in 1323. During the Livonian Order, *Cēsis* flourished. Between the 14th and the 16th centuries the city was known far beyond the borders of Livonia. *Cēsis* was a member of the Hanseatic League of Northern German trade cities, and it was as part of this league that the town enjoyed its long moment in the sun.

In 1778, a local count built a new castle in *Cēsis*, and it today houses the local museum. In 1849, a highway from Riga to Pliskau was built, and in 1868, a six-kilometre branch from the road to *Cēsis* was opened for traffic. In 1889, the Riga-Pliskau railroad was opened, and it passed through *Cēsis*.

Several of the buildings in the city are nationally important architectural monuments – the castle of the Order, St. John's Church, the *Rucka* manor and park, the ensemble of the old and the new *Cēsis* castle with its park, etc. The largest and most modern printing house in Eastern Europe is located in *Cēsis*, as is the famous spa *Cīrulīši*.

CĒSIS

The Chronicle of Indriķis mentions a place called *Autine*, which was a Latgallian castle. In the 13th century, the Order of the Brotherhood of the Sword built a brick castle on the site, and a settlement of craftsmen and tradesmen sprung up around it. *Valmiera* gained the rights of a city in 1323. Over the course of the centuries the name of the city has been written very differently – *Wolmaria, Wolmahr, Wolmar, Waldemer*, etc. Between the 14th and 16th centuries, *Valmiera* was a city of the Hanseatic League. After administrative reform in 1783, *Valmiera* became the local district centre. A postal road, which had been constructed during the rule of the Swedish crown, passed through *Valmiera*, and it linked St. Petersbourg to Riga and Western Europe.

The first teachers college in Vidzeme was opened in *Valmiera* in 1741. In 1802, farmers rose up against the feudal system in what became known as the *Kauguri* riot.

The entire centre of the city, featuring buildings from the 13th to the 19th centuries, was destroyed during World War II.

In 1963 a fibre glass factory was established in *Valmiera*, and today it is a public stock company which represents a significant share of Latvia's overall export structure. Another company that is an active exporter is the Latvian-Australian joint venture *Valpro*, which produces fuel cans and boilers. The largest food processors in town are the stock company *Vidzemes piens* and the stock company *Sviesta siera eksports*, as well as the German-Latvian joint venture bakery *Valmieras maiznieks*. The interests of entrepreneurs in the city are represented by one of the most influential business associations in Latvia – *Ozols* (Oak).

Valmiera has the largest hospital in Vidzeme, and the *Valmiera* University opened its doors for the first time in 1996.

VALMIERA

Strenči has been a forestry centre for centuries, home to forestry workers and log rafters from the *Gauja* River. To this very day, a log raft festival is held at the beginning of May each year on the *Gauja*. A national mental hospital was opened in 1907, after three years of construction. Two-story and three-story buildings are placed all around a wide territory, which is actually a park with a harmonic and decorative environment. Even before World War I the *Strenči* facility was one of the best of its kind not only in Russia, but also in all of Europe. In 1943 the Nazis murdered all of the patients of the hospital who had not been taken away by relatives.

In the post-war years, the development of the city was completely halted. *Strenči* is the only city in Latvia in which no buildings at all were constructed after the war – no water purification systems, no water pipelines, no heating system. These are things, which were installed only in 1996, through co-operation between the Ministry of Environmental Protection and Regional Development and the Danish government. The city is home to forestry and food processing companies, and there is also a modern nursery for trees and decorative plants.

STRENČI

The city of *Mazsalaca* is located on the northern shore of *Burtnieku* Lake – at a site where Latvia's oldest known settlement from the Mesolithic period was located. At the place where the *Salaca* River flows out of the lake, there is also a late-Neolithic settlement called *Riņņu* Hill, which provides testimony to the most ancient Baltic tribes that were present in Latvia. The first written information about *Mazsalaca* as a populated place date back to 1228. The town has a pharmacy, which has been open since 1863, and a textile factory, which was opened in 1864. *Mazsalaca* has always been one of the most Latvian cities in the country, both before the war and now, too.

Under the leadership of a teacher called Hincenbergs, a choir from *Mazsalaca* participated at a regional song festival in *Dikļi* in 1864, and in 1873 it competed in a choir competition at the first national song festival and won the top prize of the *Silver Lyre*. *Mazsalaca* has been a city since 1928, and most of its residents are employed as farmers, at the local fish cannery, and in various retail operations.

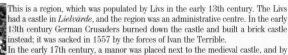
Mayor of *Mazsalaca* Ojars Beķeris and the city council

MAZSALACA

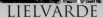

This is a region, which was populated by Livs in the early 13th century. The Livs had a castle in *Lielvārde*, and the region was an administrative centre. In the early 13th century German Crusaders burned down the castle and built a brick castle instead; it was sacked in 1557 by the forces of Ivan the Terrible.

In the early 17th century, a manor was placed next to the medieval castle, and by the end of the century, it was a powerful force in the region.

The poet Andrejs Pumpurs was a student at the *Lielvārde* church school in the 19th century, and another poet, Auseklis, worked for a time as a teacher there.

The ruins of the medieval castle can still be viewed on the old shore of the *Daugava*. The city has a museum dedicated to Andrejs Pumpurs, and in a bend in the *Daugava* there is a wooden castle built by one Agris Liepiņš in memory of a warrior called *Uldevens*.

Lielvārde blossomed during Soviet times because of its local *kolhoze*, *Lāčplēsis* and its long-time director, Edgars Kauliņš. Despite Soviet restrictions, Kauliņš managed to establish a powerful agricultural complex with a good infrastructure and good living conditions for people who worked there. Most of the economic infrastructure of *Lielvārde* today emerged from the *kolhoze*. There are food processing companies, a brewery, a farm for fur-bearing animals and a number of nurseries.

LIELVARDE

Archaeological work at the old *Cesvaine* castle hill suggests that the place was populated early in the Iron Age – between the 2nd and the 4th centuries AD. In the late 14th century, a Catholic archbishop built a castle in *Cesvaine*, and it was one of the most important buildings in Vidzeme. The castle was sacked in 1656. The new castle of *Cesvaine*, which today is home to a high school, is a European-level architectural monument. The castle was built of fieldstones. The same is true of a local Lutheran church, which was built between 1876 and 1879.

For many years, *Cesvaine* was home to the longest building in Latvia. This says something about the nature of the people of the town. They learned that the longest tavern in the country was in *Jaunpiebalga*, so they measured it. They learned that the so-called Jacob's Barracks in Riga was a long building, so they measured it, too. Then they went home and built a tavern six meters longer than the barracks.

Cesvaine is located in a gorgeous place – a restricted nature area *Salājs* with a virtually untouched landscape and the beautiful *Ežezers* lake are nearby. The city is surrounded by no fewer than 24 castle hills. The two major companies in town are the stock company *Cesvaines piens* and the stock company *Cesvaine*.

CESVAINE

The first Latgallian castle and settlement was found at a place that is now known as *Tempļa* Hill. In 1225, the Latgallian castle was burned down by German Crusaders. *Alūksne* was first mentioned in a chronicle in 1285. The city was conquered by Russians, then the Swedes. In 1702, it was besieged by a Russian force, which destroyed the castle and the village. Many people were taken hostage, including Rev. Ernest Glück and his foster child, Marija Varna (Skavronska), who later came to be Russian Empress Catherine I. Glück was the most important person in the history of *Alūksne*. In 1685 he completed a translation of the Old Testament into the Latvian language and in 1689 – the New Testament, as well. In honour of each of the translations, Glück planted an oak tree, and the *Glück oaks* are there today. The oldest residential building in *Alūksne* is located at *Ezeres iela* 6, next to what was once the *Šlosa* tavern. It dates back to the 17th century. The *Alūksne* church was built between 1781 and 1788. A Bible museum honouring Glück was opened next to the church in 1990. One of its collection is a facsimile of the 1689 Glück Bible.

Alūksne today is being developed as an environmentally friendly territory.

ALŪKSNE

THE UNION OF LOCAL AND REGIONAL GOVERNMENTS OF LATVIA

The Union of Local and Regional Governments of Latvia (*Latvijas Pašvaldību savienība* – LPS) was founded on 15 December 1991, and is a volunteer public organisation, which brings together the local governments of parishes, cities and districts. The goals of the LPS are to preparation of local government policies and to defend the interests of local governments. The highest decision-making organ of the LPS is its congress, which meets at least once a year.

Members of the organisation's Council are its chairman, as well as representatives of local governments – seven from the Riga City Council, six from the councils of national cities, 26 from the councils of district cities, 26 from parish councils, and 26 from district councils. The Council nominates representatives of Latvian local governments to the European Congress of Local and Regional governments.

A visit to Latvia by the vice president of the Regional Committee of the European Union, R. Kaliffa (second from the left) on 7 December 1998. This is a press conference. From the right: The president of the Turin Province in Italy, M. Bresso and *LPS* chairman Andris Jaunsleinis

Members of the *LPS* Council

The Latvian Local Government Training Centre provides training for local government employees and politicians, allowing them to learn about the experience of democratic countries in this area. The LPS has also set up a non-profit-making organisation – a family care centre in *Bulduri* which provides social, educational and medical care for children from impoverished families.

The LPS has also established the Local Government Consultation Centre to work with local governments.

In 1998, the LPS joined the International Local Government Association as a fully-fledged member. A very important function for the LPS is to represent local governments in negotiations with the government on such issues as social guarantees, economic reform, state governance and local government reform, target subsidies and other subsidies to the Local Government Equalisation Fund, etc.

Since January 1998, Latvian local governments have been working together to deal with such matters as the collection and storage of waste, road management, and local and regional planning. Associations of local governments have been established in Northern Kurzeme around *Dundaga* and Southern Kurzeme around *Bārtava*. There have been other local governments that have simply merged – the city of *Kandava* with its rural territory, *Salacgrīva* with its rural territory, etc. The LPS helps the EU to implement many of its programs in Latvia, including the transfrontier co-operation program *Credo*, the *Phare* Program, etc.

At the recommendation of the LPS, the European Congress of Local and Regional Governments at a session in May 1998 reviewed the issue of local government democracy in Latvia. The Congress recommended that the principle of local governance be enshrined in the Constitution of Latvia and that local government taxes be instituted, allowing local governments to set the rates. The chairman of the LPS is Andris Jaunsleinis. The organisation publishes its journal, *Logs* (Window).

Kurzeme's amber

A granary in *Padure*

Europe's only acting leprosory is located in the town of *Strazde*, near *Talsi*

This building houses a museum in honor of Oskars Kalpaks, the first commander of the Latvian armed forces during World War I. He fell near the location of the building

The mansion of *Jaunpils*

The old city of *Kandava*, where Mayor Dainis Rozenfelds has done a lot to spruce the city up in nostalgic beauty

The *Dundaga* hospital

Rudbāržu nature park is unique with a wide variety of flora

Kurzeme, more commonly known in the West as Courland, took its name from the ancient Courlandian tribes – famed throughout Europe in their day as sailors and warriors. Kurzeme is bounded by the sea on two sides, with land borders with the territory of the ancient Semigallians (Zemgale) and with what is now Lithuania. The northern part of the region is a natural peninsula. Kurzeme is the region of Latvia which is most distinctly influenced by the sea, both in terms of its climate and in terms of the lives of its residents. Winters are more gentle, with more moderate shifts in temperature, while summers are cooler than is the case in Eastern Latvia. Fishing villages have existed for centuries along the coast, and since time immemorial the sea has provided the people of Kurzeme with sustenance.

The territory was populated mostly by Courlandian and Livonian tribes in the 1st millennium BC. The region lost its political sovereignty in 1267, when it fell under the control of the German crusaders. The Germans built stone castles in *Kuldīga*, *Aizpute*, *Embūte*, *Ventspils*, *Dundaga*, *Kandava*, *Alsunga* and *Grobiņa*. Between 1562 and 1795, Kurzeme and Žemgale were joined into a sovereign duchy which, during the reign of the legendary Duke Jacob, was the site of factories and a ship-building plant in *Ventspils*. The people of the duchy left their mark all around the world, not least on the island of *Tobago*, which the duchy colonized in the 17th century. *Tobago* to this very day has a Kurzeme river, a Kurzeme cape and a Kurzeme bay. The duchy also colonized the Western African country of Gambia for a while, and it is remembered there, too. At its height, the Duchy of Courland had diplomatic and trade representatives in many cities all around the world, selling wood, grain, glass, iron ore, ships and other products that were rated very highly in other countries.

Kurzeme was the site of savage fighting during World War II in what has ever since been known as the Kurzeme Fortress. The Nazis capitulated there after the fall of Berlin, and the seashore of Kurzeme was the place from which countless Latvians went into exile at war's end. Today Kurzeme is made up of the *Liepāja*, *Ventspils*, *Kuldīga* and *Talsi* districts, as well as parts of the *Tukums* and *Saldus* districts. Kurzeme is home to two of Latvia's larger cities – *Liepāja* and *Ventspils*, both of which boast ice-free ports. The most important city in olden days in Kurzeme was *Kuldīga*, which in the 10th century was an important trade center. *Aizpute*, which is on the shore of the *Tebra* River, was located alongside an old military route in days gone by. On the *Talsi* castle hill, there was once a magnificent Courlandian castle, but today it is the site of one of the country's most Latvian cities – *Talsi*, built on nine hills and on the shores of two lakes. *Sabile* is known as a place where wine grapes have been grown. Even in the days of the German Crusaders, grapes were planted, and wine from *Sabile* was sent all over Western Europe. The vines were restored for the first time in modern times in 1937, but they were allowed to wither during Soviet days. *Sabile* was once listed in the Guinness Book of World Records as the most northerly vineyard in the world. Today, it must be said, grapes are grown even farther North in Latvia, and the fruit is just fine.

The gunpowder tower of *Kandava*

The *Roja* port with fishing boats at anchor

The village of *Koniņciems* is located right alongside the sea. Calm, with a rhythm that has not changed very much over the centuries, *Koniņciems* is truly an outdoor ethnographic museum

The *Nogale* castle

The old gate of *Priekule*

The *Valdemārpils* Church (1646). Old Lutheran Churches in Kurzeme are stark on the outside, but beautiful and well kept on the inside

The *Venta* River flows through Kurzeme, and it includes Europe's widest waterfall. There are also several nature reserves in Kurzeme – the *Slītere*, *Griņi* and *Moricsala* reserves.

The old traditions of ancient Kurzeme have best been preserved in the South of the region – in the towns of *Nīca*, *Bārta* and *Rucava*, where folk costumes are unique and vividly colorful and where people still use many uniquely Courlandian words in their speech. The shores of the Baltic Sea in Kurzeme are populated with small villages, in which each homestead is set apart and bordered. There are huge granaries and monumental threshing barns – the farmers of Kurzeme have always been rich, proud, spiteful and ambitious. The women of Kurzeme have long been legendary for their cleverness in thinking up songs to sing about men – songs with long, drawn-out sounds and other specific elements. In 1990, a three-mile zone along the shore, between *Ovīši* and *Ģipka*, was set aside as the *Līvodrānda*, or the Livonian Shore, in honor of the traditional Livonian or Liv residents of the region.

Zemgale is the smallest region of Latvia and is located right in the center of the country. To the North the land is slaked by the waters of the Bay of Riga, while to the South lays Lithuania. The territory of the ancient Semigallians was mentioned in Scandinavian historical sources as early as the 9th century, and the main cities of ancient Zemgale in the 10th and 11th century were *Mežotne* and *Tērvete*, both of which had magnificent castles. The Semigallians stood fast against the German Crusaders longer than other local tribes. The castles of the Semigallian lords Viestarts and Nameisis were located at *Tērvete*. There are castle ruins from the period of the Crusaders in *Bauska* and *Dobele*. On the other hand, the region was very strongly influenced over the centuries by Lithuania.

Zemgale and Kurzeme (Courland) were united for decades in the Duchy of Courland, which at that time was by far the most developed region in Latvia. The mightiest city of the Duchy was *Jelgava*. Zemgale has two masterpieces of architecture – the castles of *Jelgava* and *Rundāle*.

Zemgale was the site of the bloody Christmas Battles of World War I, where Latvian riflemen fought with unprecedented heroism. The battles of *Džūkste* and *Lestene* took place in Zemgale during World War II, when Latvian soldiers fought in two different armies, but with one goal – the liberation of Latvia.

Zemgale is the richest region in Latvia and is known as the granary of the nation. The features of Zemgale people are stability and pride. Four of the six Latvian Presidents come from this region. One of the leading sons of Zemgale was the author Edvards Virza, who expressed his love for his region in the beautiful and poetic novel *Straumēni*. Zemgale also produced the poets Vilis Pludonis and Aspazija, as well as the beloved children's author Anna Brigadere. The characters she created in her books – Spridītis, Annele, Lutausis and others – have been recreated in wooden sculptures by the sculptor Krišjānis Kugra, and they are now on display in a landscape par in the *Tērvete* Forest. Latvia's slowest river, the *Lielupe*, flows through Zemgale.

One part of Zemgale in the olden days was populated by Selonian tribes. This is a narrow strip of territory between the *Daugava* River and the Lithuanian border. The Selonians lived in a much larger territory, but some of it is now in Lithuania. The fact that the Selonians were found in both countries is evidenced by place names – Latvia has *Birži*, Lithuania has *Biržai*; Latvia has *Viesīte*, Lithuania has *Viešbutis*. People on both sides of the border speak a similar language and have a similar mentality. The Selonian dialects spoken in the region are close to Latgallian dialects to the East.

The largest city in Selonia is *Jēkabpils*, which was granted the status of a city by Duke Jacob – who named the city after himself (Jekabs). The ancient center of the region, however, was *Sēlpils*, which today lies in ruins. Selonia provided Latvia with its greatest poet, Rainis, as well as the artists Kārlis Brencēns, the Hermanovskis family, Alfrēds Plīte, the old masters Uga and Oto Skulme, and others. A homestead called *Riekstiņi* is found near the town of *Nereta*. It is known far better by Latvian readers as the *Mūsmājas* (Our home) that was described in vivid detail by the popular writer Jānis Jaunsudrabiņš in his work.

The fields of Zemgale are known as Latvia's granary. The earth is fertile, crops grow well

The *Rundāle* castle was built by Ernst Biron between 1736 and 1768 on the basis of a design by the architect Francesco Bartolomeo Rastrelli. The castle is a masterpiece of Baroque and Rococo design

The town of *Skaistkalne* with a Catholic church and monastery that date back to 1692. The tower of the church was destroyed during World War II

The sauna of the *Lejnieki* homestead of the poet Vilis Pludonis. Thanks to a children's poem which the author produced, the little building will forever be known as "Rabbit's sauna"

The *Via Baltica* highway from Riga to Vilnius passes through the city of *Bauska*

The *Valdeka* castle (late 19th century)

The castle ruins of *Dobele*

A bridge across the *Lielupe* while the ice is breaking up

Sauka

The *Nereta* Lutheran church (1584–1593)

The place where Latvian author Janis Jaunsudrabiņš was born – the *Riekstiņi* homestead near *Nereta*

The Zemgale train station in *Daugavpils* district

The *Subate* Catholic church

A view from Selonia of the *Daugava* River

The granary at the first home of the poet Rainis (b. Janis Pliekšāns) in *Tadenava*

VIDZEME

Mist over the ancient *Gauja* Valley near *Sigulda*

A rail bridge across the *Rauna* river

The *Sigulda* City Council is housed in this castle, which was built between 1878 and 1881

The *Valmiera* City Council's building

Burtnieki park

The *Līgatne* paper factory has been in operation since 1816, and it is an historical monument in Latvia's industrial sector

The *Zvārta* cliff on the *Amata* river

The *Skangaļi* estate near *Liepa*, where the mother of the Swedish statesman Ulov Palme was born

The *Cēsis* city park

The *Vidzeme* seashore near *Ķurmjrags*

A Livonian festival in the *Salaca* river near *Skaņaiskalns*

A rural road in *Augstroze*

The *Saulrieti* home in *Vecpiebalga*, where Latvian poet Kārlis Skalbe lived

The ornate water tower at the *Strenči* mental hospital was designed by architect Augusts Reinbergs

The "sun bridge" in *Alūksne*

The *Smiltene* Red Cross Hospital is run with pedantic precision and order by chief physician Jānis Krūmals

The region of Vidzeme includes the *Cēsis*, *Limbaži*, *Valmiera*, *Valka* and *Gulbene* districts, as well as parts of the *Rīga*, *Ogre*, *Aizkraukle*, *Alūksne* and *Madona* districts. Before the invasion of the German Crusaders in the early part of the 2nd millennium, the largest government structure in Vidzeme was the town of *Tālava*, which was centered around the *Beverīna* castle and ruled by a man called Talivaldis. The Livonians, meanwhile, lived in four larger regions.

Vidzeme was conquered by the Germans in the 13th century, but after the Livonian War it fell under the subordination of Poland. In 1629 the region was taken over by Sweden, and after the Great Northern War it fell to Russia. Vidzeme has always posted the highest educational levels in all of Latvia. The first Latvian schools were established there in the 17th century, and more than 200 years ago, virtually all of the residents of Vidzeme were literate.

There are three major dialects of the Latvian language in Vidzeme – one that is related to the Livonian influence, one that is known as the central dialect, and the third that is called the dialect of the highlanders. The central dialect served as the foundation for literary Latvian. There are many larger and smaller towns in Vidzeme, including *Cēsis*, *Strenči*, *Valmiera*, *Valka*, *Alūksne*, *Gulbene*, *Sigulda*, *Rūjiena*, etc. Vidzeme has beautiful nature, especially around *Cēsis*, *Sigulda* and *Valmiera*. The Vidzeme Central highlands are the highest point in Latvia. There are relatively few large fields in the region, but there are plenty of areas which are appropriate for livestock breeding – a process which was once well developed in Vidzeme and survives today. The Latvian brown cow is particularly well known. The *Gauja National Park* presents the beautiful views of the *Gauja* River and its many caves, entwined in legend. The Vidzeme coastline is rocky, with red cliffs that have been the focus of a great many tourist visits. Legend has it that the Livonian warrior Imanta, who in 1198 killed German Bishop Berthold during a battle over Riga, is buried on *Zilaiskalns* hill. The town of *Blome* is linked in popular memory with the first Latvian poet – a Hernhutian preacher called Ķikuļu Jēkabs. Vidzeme has given Latvia many notable writers, composers and scientists, among them the brothers Kaudzītes, who produced the first full-length novel in Latvia's history and who looked at their friends and neighbors for inspiration in that book. Tartu University student and poet Eduards Veidenbaums was born and raised in *Liepa*, while the man who assembled Latvia's first scientific library, Jānis Misiņš, grew up at the *Krāces* homestead in *Tirza* parish. Poet Ojārs Vācietis has produced countless lines of verse about the area around *Gaujiena*, where he was born.

Today, as throughout history, the Latvian summer solstice festival has been celebrated most ornately in Vidzeme, where a bonfire is lit on every hill and where people go from home to home with solstice songs – more in Vidzeme than in any other region. The people of Vidzeme have a sunny and open nature. They love life, and they are great singers and rejoicers. Economically, Vidzeme has always been open for business. In the 17th century there were trade centers in *Rauna* and *Piebalga*, where textile weaving was the main form of activity, in *Brieži* and *Strīķi*, where furniture was made, and in *Piebalga*, where spinning wheels were the local product. Today towns in Vidzeme are successfully developing the wood industry and food processing companies. More rapidly than in other regions of Latvia, modern technologies and business techniques are being developed here. Latvia's most modern printing houses are in *Cēsis* and *Madona*, computers are assembled and software is designed in *Valmiera*, and the fishing industry is centered in *Salacgrīva*.

The Eastern Latvian region of Latgale covers the *Krāslava*, *Ludza*, *Rēzekne*, *Preiļi* and *Balvi* districts, as well as parts of the Daugavpils, *Jēkabpils* and *Madona* districts. During the Soviet occupation, historical borders among the various regions were eliminated. The Latgale city of *Varakļāni* was attached to the *Madona* district in Vidzeme only because that made it easier to divide up land reclamation and agricultural equipment institutions. Six former regions in the *Jaunlatgale* district, as well as the city of *Abrene*, were absorbed into Russia on October 12, 1945.

Latgallians have lived in this region for millennia. In the 12th century, the kingdoms of *Tālava* and *Jersika* ruled here. History has caused Latgale to become different from the other regions of Latvia. During the Livonian era Latgale was closely linked to Vidzeme, but in 1629 the region known as *Inflantija* was set up as part of the Duchy of *Pārdaugava* that belonged to the Catholic Polish Empire. Vidzeme went to Sweden, which was Lutheran in faith. During the time when in Vidzeme officials were developing parish schools, when farmers were being set free, and when many rural residents learned to read and write, no such opportunities existed in Latgale. The region was known as *Inflantija* in some circles even in the early 20th century.

After Poland was divided up in 1772, Latgale became part of the Vitebsk region of Russia. Latvians in Latgale preserved their culture and style of life, but many elements from Slavic culture gradually seeped in to affect clothing, architecture, and life not on single-family farms, but rather in villages. Latgallian farms differed from those in other parts of Latvia – they were smaller, buildings were decorated with carved wood ornaments, and ridged roofs were the norm. In the late 18th century, Latgale became home to a great many Russian Old Orthodoxes, who brought along their own cultural and living traditions.

Latgale is known as the land of the blue lakes, and it has more lakes than any other region in Latvia – the large *Lubāna* and *Rāzna* lakes, the deep *Drīdzis* and *Garais* lakes, and the *Ežezers* lake with many small islands. Rivers flow out of these lakes, and they are peaceful at their upper reaches.

The beautiful *Sauleskalns* hill was once a holy place to Latgallians. The earth in Latgale is sandy, there are many swamps, and crops require a good deal of work. Flax is the most commonly grown culture. Latgale's residents have long been horse breeders, too. It has been a long, hard road for the people of Latgale to get to the point of wealth, but the region is the most sincere, hospitable and helpful in all of Latvia. Latgallians love to sing at work and at play, and harmony singing is particularly common here. The women of Latgale love the color white – in their head scarves, in their flax tablecloths, towels and sheets – all woven as ornately as if they were woolen blankets. Among men there are many potters, and Latgale has always been home to the most beautiful works of ceramics in Latvia. Many have received prizes and praise throughout the world. The names of ceramic artists Čerņavskis, Voguls and Ušpelis are known to specialists far removed from Latvia.

During a long period when it was illegal to print books in Latvian or Latgallian, a man called Andrivs Jurdžs wrote nearly 200 books by hand. Latgallians who have become famous include the painters Francisks Varslavans and Juris and Nikolajs Soikans, and a number of Catholic clergymen, including Cardinal Julians Vaivods and Bishop Jezups Rancans.

Decades of rule by Poland and Russia left their mark on the economic of Latgale, which remains the poorest of Latvia's regions, with high unemployment and few economically developed farms. Roman Catholicism is of greater importance in Latgale than in other parts of Latvia. God is worshipped, families are stronger, and women have more children than elsewhere in the country. A holy place for Catholics in Latgale and beyond is the basilica at *Aglona*, which has beautiful white towers that can be seen from quite a distance.

Two of Latvia's largest cities – *Daugavpils* and *Rēzekne* – are located in Latgale.

The view from *Grietes* hill in *Ambeļi* parish

The *Ludza* musical stage is in the middle of a forested park

The *Daugava* river near *Slutiški*

The *Vecsaliena* castle (1870) in *Daugavpils* district

An old hospital in *Aglona*

The view from *Mākoņkalns* hill, with *Rāzna* Lake in the distance

The Roman Catholic Church of the Trinity in *Dagda* (latter half of the 18th century)

Ludza

On a clear day, you can see no fewer than 15 small lakes from the *Sauleskalns* hill

A sculpture of St. Michael at the *Kalupe* Catholic Church

A monument to the family of Latgallian cultural worker Piters Migliniks (1850-1883) in *Nautrēni* parish

Easter worship at the Catholic church in *Krāslava*

The village of *Tilti* and *Līksna* parish – a typical Russian-inspired village of a main street with homes on either side

A village of Russian Old Orthodoxes, *Žīdina*

The *Park Hotel Ridzene* is located in what is known as Riga's ring of boulevards. The *Park Hotel Ridzene* features pleasant and cosy facilities that are popular among those who organise conferences and symposia.

The *Radisson SAS Daugava* Hotel boasts views of the Riga skyline

The *Hotel de Rome* is in the heart of Riga, across the street from a popular meeting spot – the *Laima* clock

The Hotel *Viktorija* at the corner of *Čaka* and *Stabu iela* in Riga. One of the city's most popular restaurants – the *Staburags* – is on the lower floors of the building

The *Konventa Sēta* Hotel in Old Riga is housed in buildings that were built in the 14th and 15th centuries. The antiquities live beautifully with modern design and comfort

A room on the 20th floor of the Hotel *Latvija* in Riga. The hotel is in the centre of Riga, across the street from the Cabinet building

The *Rīgas Līcis* Hotel in *Jūrmala* is on the seashore and is up to five-star standards

Hotel *Majoru viesnīca* in *Jomas iela 29, Jūrmala* is in unique premises designed by a Baltic German Arthur Badlinger and built by Jekabs Paeglis

The *Latvija* Hotel in *Daugavpils*

Latvia's hotels became part of world hostelry in 1990. Of course, there were hotels built in the Soviet-era, such as the *Rīga*, the *Latvija*, the *Rīdzene* and the *Daugava* in Riga, the *Tērvete* in *Cēsis*, and the *Latvija* in *Daugavpils*. At this time, Latvia's small-town hotels, however, did not even provide such services as hot water or breakfast. These so-called hotels often offered only a bed in a room with four or eight beds instead of a room or apartment.

Most of Latvia's hotels have now been privatised, and this privatisation has brought with it investments to bring them up to European standards in terms of service quality. The *Daugava* Hotel, for example, was privatised by the *Radisson SAS* group, which added a second floor to the building and modernised it to *Radisson's* five-star level of quality. The *Rīdzene* was turned into the *Park Hotel Rīdzene* by Norwegian investors. Nearly every major city in Latvia now has four or five-star hotels with all of the amenities.

The Latvian Association of Hotels and Restaurants (*Latvijas Viesnīcu un restorānu asociācija* – LVRA) was established in 1993, bringing together more than 40 hotels, guest houses and restaurants, as well as educational specialists who train employees for these facilities.

In Latvia, hotels and guest houses are certified in accordance with European Union requirements. The Latvian Association of Hotels and Restaurants regularly participates in international tourism exhibitions and fairs in Latvia and elsewhere in Europe. Since 1995, LVRA has been a member of its international equivalent. In 1998, a co-operation agreement was signed with the Latvian Association of Tourism Agents. LVRA also publishes an advertising catalogue, *Hotels in Latvia*.

Hotel and restaurant *Vilnis* in *Ventspils*

An excellent hotel in *Jelgava* that is named after the city itself

The *Amrita* Hotel in *Liepāja* was built according to Swedish standards

The Hotel *Oma* is in *Ernestīnes iela*, and it is meant for people who like small, cosy hotels in quiet, tree-lined streets

TOURISM

A cosy motel *VIA* in *Jelgavkrasti* on the Tallinn highway or *Via Baltica*

Verbelnieki cottage in *Pērkone*, *Liepāja* district, beach of Kurzeme

Information about recreation facilities is available from the web *http://www.country.holidays.lv*

Lielkruzes in *Jaunpiebalga* offers hospitality and tasty meals made from natural goods as well as the fascinating landscape of *Piebalga* region

Ate mill – a museum near *Alūksnes*. There are many small, well organised local museums exhibiting traditional craft and habits

Ina and Uldis Kapteinis have established a frequently visited place for recreation

A variety of *Jaņa seta* maps for countries, districts, roads and routes are available in the shop of Aivars Beldavs on *Elizabetes iela* 83/85, Riga

There is definitely a lot of to be seen in Latvia. Elderly Plinius noticed and described Latvia's beautiful nature. The convenient location of Riga has been used by travelers in all times. Peter the Great visited Latvia so often that the first hotels were opened to make his visits more convenient. The hotel buildings can still be seen in Riga and *Liepāja*. The site of the *Jerusaleme* Hotel on *Ojāra Vācieša iela* at that time was in the suburbs of Riga.

The famous health resorts in *Baldone*, *Ķemeri* and *Jūrmala* were founded at the end

Aivars Kalniņš, the Director of Latvian Tourism Agency is convinced that Latvia fits into any cartrip around the Baltic sea

of the 18th and the beginning of the 19th century. The Russian tsars, the Prussian princes, landlords, and traders came here as well as to the sulphur water springs of More for treatment.

The beginning of the 20th century marked a rapid development of tourism in Latvia. The beneficial geographic location, monuments of history and art, picturesque nature, and the developed infrastructure made it attractive for travellers. A moment of spas' zenith was in 1912. 15 thousand guests spent summer in *Ķemeri*, another 60 thousand – in *Jūrmala*. The most common forms of tourism were relaxation on the beach and in Rīga vicinities. The reservation of *Moricsala* was initially open for tourists as a spot of uncivilised nature. Tourism had a considerable impact on the economy of the First Republic of Latvia. The Latvian Central Tourism Society was established in 1920. The Ministry of Public Affairs had the Department of Tourism. Tourism became a profitable business. The income from tourism in 1938 was twice the income from the famous Latvian bacon export. When the construction of hotel in *Ķemeri* was completed, the first public event there was the World Chess Championship. Latvia was one of the most visited countries in Western Europe of that time. In 1931 Latvia hosted 85.7 thousand tourists, compared to 71.2 thousand in Norway, 40 thousand in Lithuania, 37.5 thousand in Finland. Looking forward to the transit flow of tourists going to the Olympic games in Helsinki in 1940, roads were repaired and small hotels were built in nearly all towns. The expectations were shattered, when the Soviet Union started the Winter War with Finland and invaded the Baltic States later on.

For forty five years following the World War II Latvian tourism was a part of the Soviet policy of tourism. *Jūrmala* became a construction site of enormous sanatoriums where people came from all over the USSR. Having only 60 thousand residents, *Jūrmala* hosted 2 million visitors every year.

The independence regained in 1991 stimulated collaboration with tourism centres all over the world. Since 1993 the Ministry of Environmental Protection and Regional Development is the main institution promot-

The Danish Crown Prince Frederick visited Riga and as a tourist admired the *Three Brothers* in *Vecriga*

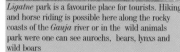

Pilot project *Abavas ieleja* helps the preservation of a unique, unharmed Landscape with assistance of European Commission

ing tourism. Latvia is being integrated in the global tourism network. The Latvian Board of Tourism, which elaborates our strategy of tourism, is a member of World Tourism Organisation.

Latvia has a variety of tourism resources. Recreative resources like the sea, rivers and lakes are the most well known. Ecotourists from Germany and the Scandinavian countries visit Latvia more and more often, attracted by the relatively well preserved nature, interesting animal and plant life and the plenty of opportunities for camping, gathering wild berries and mushrooms, hiking in woods and marshlands. Also the cognitive resources like monuments of architecture, history and art attract tourists to Latvia. Unfortunately there is still too little information and tourists learn about Riga the architectural pearls of Art nouveau, the old manor houses, churches, and homesteads only when they are already in Latvia. Latvia has two National parks were acheological and historical entities can be seen in lovely landscapes.

The impact of scientific and business resources grows year by year. Latvia successfully hosts big international conferences, meetings and exhibitions. The exile Latvians and their friends and acquaintances from Canada, America and Australia visit Latvia in the years of the Song and Dance Festivals. Visiting of friends and relatives becomes a sort of ethnic tourism. Hunters, anglers and sport tourists often choose Latvia as their final destination. They appreciate the small Latvian cottages, surrounded by beautiful landscapes where comfort and good cuisine is available for reasonable prices.

Approximately 2 million tourists visit Latvia every year, staying here for two days on the average. The majority came from Lithuania – more than 600 thousand in 1998 and 1999. The polls inform that people from Denmark, the UK, and Finland are among the most satisfied ones.

The tourists love going to *Jūrmala*, Riga, *Cēsis*, *Tukums* and their vicinities. The number of motels is increasing constantly. Gas stations, restaurants, roadside cafe's, and bars are open 24 hours a day. Grocery stores and pharmacies are open at any time. The nightlife in Old Riga is famous for the small bars, cafes and clubs open until the last guest. The police take care of security. Latvia is long known for its delicious cuisine and fine eating habits.

Līgatne park is a favourite place for tourists. Hiking and horse riding is possible here along the rocky coasts of the *Gauja* river or in the wild animals park were one can see aurochs, bears, lynxs and wild boars

Schoolchildren outdoors. Latvia has plenty picturesque spots of wild nature and untouched ecology, also places for swimming and bonfires

Hotel *Tērcete* was built in *Cēsis* in 1940

Cēsis hotel is well known among Latvians and foreigners

The Latvian Tourism Agency participates in all the main messes

The Riga Congress House. Conferences and congresses are often held in Riga because of the favourable location and effective management. In 2000 the European Bank of Reconstruction and Development will have it's annual meeting here

The only restaurant in Latvia to feature variety shows is the *Grand Cabare Admiral*. The comfortable restaurant has a menu of delicious dishes from the Russian cuisine – pancakes, fish soup, cabbage soup with a dough "cover", meat prepared to the taste of riflemen, and sturgeon cooked according to an old cloister recipe. The restaurant is proud of its exciting show program. A European-level casino is also included in the facility, and it is popular among prominent Latvians. The casino features nine card tables, including a blackjack table and *Golden Oasis Poker*. There are also three roulette wheels and state-of-the-art slot machines featuring the new *American Poker III* program

Latvijas Loto is Latvia's national lottery, and it provides high-class gaming opportunities to players, while accruing benefits for everyone. Some people win prizes, but everyone who participates can be proud in the knowledge that help is being given to very important projects in the country. The national lottery was born on 3 January 1993. In 1996 the company was transformed into a State-owned stock company. The State holds a monopoly in the field of lotteries in Latvia. The company's successful operations have served to develop a lottery which is based on the world's traditions and developmental directions and which represents a significant share of Latvia's gambling market. The annual turnover of *Latvijas Loto* exceeds 2 million lats, which means that each resident of the country, on average, spends about 1 lats on the lottery. More than 1 million lats each year is paid out in cash prizes. A share of income is transferred to Latvia's government special budget for culture and sports. *Latvijas Loto* organises 11 scratch-card lotteries and one lotto game. Lottery tickets are sold at more than 1,100 locations. Since 1996, *Latvijas Loto* has used an on-line lottery system that is widely used throughout the world and is a cornerstone of qualitative ticket sales. *Latvijas Loto* is a member of the World Association of Lotteries, and specialists from the company have been able to improve their professional skills at professional congresses and conferences. *Latvijas Loto*, like lotteries around the world, donates some of its income to charity. A *Good Goals* program was launched in 1997, and most of the contributions from the program go to finance children's health, welfare and educational projects

Bāru spēles Ltd. at the resort town of *Majori*

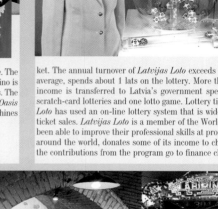

The *Admirāļu klubs* restaurant

The *Labirints* gaming hall. The firm *Post & Nevada* is engaged in leisure business for more than ten years. Its halls are equipped with the gambling machines of i *Sega*, *Namco* and *Konami*. Adults cam play and win a *Jack Pot* of 5000 lats

The *Amugames* gaming hall

BILLIARDS IN LATVIA

The Latvian Billiard Federation was founded in 1994. President Vents Anševics co-ordinates tournaments in *pool*, *snooker*, *Russian billiards* and all other kinds of billiards. The Federation has joined the *International Billiards and Snooker Association*, the *Continental Billiards and Snooker Association* and the *European Billiards and Snooker Association*. In April 1999, the Federation organised its first international snooker tournament – the *Baltic Cup '99* for players from Eastern Europe.

In 2001, the Federation will organise the European championships in snooker. In January 1999 the Federation set up its own billiards school. The *NB* company, which owns Latvia's largest pool halls and is run by president Nikolajs Butvillo, was founded in 1991.

At the opening of the billiards school of the Latvian Billiards Federation on January 15, 1999. From the left – Oto Pāže, Margarita Javiča and (in the back), Vents Anševics and Nikolajs Butvillo

The European snooker championships in Belfast, Northern Ireland, in June and July 1995. From the left: Vladimirs Siņicins, Oļegs Demjanovs, Nikolajs Butvillo, Normunds Kvilis and Vladimirs Grigorjevs

The Latvian snooker championships in 1998. The year's best players included Valdis Ivbulis, Aleksandrs Jermoļajevs, Vilnis Mainulis, Vladimirs Siņicins, Oļegs Demjanovs and Vladimirs Ladins. Seated in front, from the right – international category judge Janis Lukaševskis, LBF president Vents Anševics and *NB* president Nikolajs Butvillo, who is also the chairperson of the Riga Billiard Federation

Nikolajs Butvillo, owner of the *NB* company and president of the Riga Billiard Federation, at the pool table with Riga Mayor Andris Berziņš

One of the pool halls of the *NB* company

LATVIAN CUISINE

Fried salmon

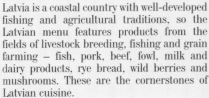

Baked herring with beans, grey pea dumplings and grey peas with bacon

At Christmas time, a baked hog's head with grey peas is a traditional dish

Boiled potatoes are put into a wide variety of salads and meat dishes, including rolled beef

Slot machines at the *Klondaika* gaming hall

The *Klondaika* gaming hall

The bar of the *Klondaika* gaming hall

The *Mirage* nightclub, which is owned by *GAO* Ltd.

Latvia is a coastal country with well-developed fishing and agricultural traditions, so the Latvian menu features products from the fields of livestock breeding, fishing and grain farming – fish, pork, beef, fowl, milk and dairy products, rye bread, wild berries and mushrooms. These are the cornerstones of Latvian cuisine.

Since ancient times, Latvians have eaten rough-ground rye bread, as well as wheat and sourdough bread. Modern Latvians love rye bread toast with garlic, which is often served with beer.

Fine wheat flour is used to bake various flat cakes with cottage cheese, apples, rhubarb or crumbs, the stuffed bacon rolls known as *pirāgi*, and various pastries, cookies and cakes.

The most classic Latvian dishes include various pea and bean dishes, sausage, and porridges made from a variety of grains. Sometimes barley groats are boiled together with potatoes or peas. Porridges are eaten with bacon and onions or butter. Fermented milk or buttermilk are popular drinks to go along with porridges. Some kinds of porridge – manna, rice porridge, oatmeal – are sometimes eaten with sweetened fruit or berries. Sometimes porridge is used to make baked goods, puddings or dumplings.

By far the most popular legume is the grey pea, which is cooked with bacon or bacon sauce and served with lots of salt and sour cream. Sometimes dumplings are made from the boiled peas. Rough rye flour is used to produce *sklandu rauši* – a roll filled with boiled potatoes and carrots.

Approximately three-quarters of Latvian cuisine consists of cold dishes – various kinds of salads, baked or smoked pork, rolled beef, pork, game or fowl, stuffed or smoked chickens, as well as all kinds of fish. Mustard and horseradish have an unfailing presence on the Latvian table.

Guests in Latvia usually start with fish-based appetisers – salmon or smoked eel, baked lamprey, sprats, hard-boiled eggs with anchovy, or rolled herring. Cold pork roast or smoked chicken follows along with various salads. Latvians are fond of both hot and cold soups, and sour cream is always added. Fish soups are sometimes prepared with milk.

Hot dishes include various kinds of pork, as well as ground beef dishes, often with sour cream sauce and salted onions. Beef rolls stuffed with smoked pork, onions and rye bread are popular. When these rolls are sautéd in cream sauce, caraway seed is sometimes added for a more piquant taste.

Caraway seed tea and other herb and spice teas are very popular, and sometimes black currant leaves are added.

Potatoes are a staple in Latvia – boiled or baked potatoes are served in one way or another every day. Beets, cabbage and carrots are also popular.

People in Kurzeme have traditionally eaten *sour porridge* which is a barley porridge with fermented milk. It provides refreshment in the heat of summer. Birch sap juice and a drink produced from quinces are also common.

Latvians have always known about beer, and in

Garden-grown strawberries are popular

Antoņina Masiļune, author of a number of Latvian cookbooks

Dr. Lolita Neimane is Latvia's leading dietologist and has done a lot to promote healthy eating habits in the country

Small individual cheeses and *Jāņu siers* – eaten during the Summer Solstice festival and at other times of the year, too

The rolls *Sklandu rauši*

ancient times, beer-making was a woman's work. Beer was produced with hops, without hops or with honey. Nearly every ethnic region in Latvia has its own beer recipe.

Latvians produce a variety of special homemade cheeses, and this, too, is a matter of ethnic taste. There is one universal cheese, however – *Jāņu siers*, which is prepared throughout the year, but especially during the Summer Solstice festival. There it becomes a ritual food that is consumed together with beer.

Latvians love their dessert. At a wedding in Kurzeme, there had better be at least two desserts on the table, including a fruit compote known as *buberts*. It is possible that the taste of sweets was developed in ancient times, because beekeeping has always been a staple activity on every Latvian farm. Latvian chefs also have developed a variety of interesting ways to use rye bread in desserts.

Desserts are prepared from fresh, dried or conserved fruits and berries, as well as flour, groats, milk, eggs, vegetables (pumpkin cream, pumpkin compote, pumpkin mousse, carrot cream, carrot compote and baked carrot). Sweetened fruit and berry soups are also popular.

Blood sausage with sauerkraut

Baked lamprey

A goose prepared for the festival known as *Mārtiņdiena*

Bacon *pirāgi* and a fruit compote with whipped cream

One of the leading supporters of beer-making traditions in Latvia is the director of the *Aldaris* brewery, Vitalijs Gavrilovs

Rigas Melnais balzams (Riga Black Balsam) has been known for centuries as a healing tonic, and it is produced in Latvia

An illustration of the Jerusalem hotel in Riga, which is the oldest of its kind in Latvia and now houses the Ojars Vacietis Museum

The inn was a cherished institution in Latvia over the centuries – a place where farmers could meet each other, feed their horses and themselves, stay the night if necessary, and shelter their wagons. In tsarist Russia, it must be added, saloons were also a source of alcoholism-related misery

The *Grivaiši* inn in *Saldus* district. The building is a national architectural monument, built of adobe, but it is fairly run down

Inns, of course, were usually built alongside major roads, and on roads which were traversed by postal routes there was a saloon every 5 or 10 kilometers. The saloon in *Lizespasts* was located right across the street from the post office so that tired postmen on their way to St. Petersburg did not need to go thirsty

In the 19th century a number of ambitious people opened up inns, later becoming the first Latvians to send their sons to university. The *Silakrogs* inn in *Vecpiebalga* was built by the great grandfather of the president of Latvia's largest bank, *Unibanka*

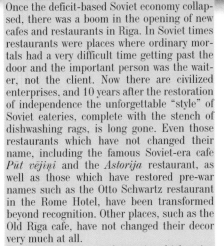

Once the deficit-based Soviet economy collapsed, there was a boom in the opening of new cafes and restaurants in Riga. In Soviet times restaurants were places where ordinary mortals had a very difficult time getting past the door and the important person was the waiter, not the client. Now there are civilized enterprises, and 10 years after the restoration of independence the unforgettable "style" of Soviet eateries, complete with the stench of dishwashing rags, is long gone. Even those restaurants which have not changed their name, including the famous Soviet-era cafe *Pūt vējiņi* and the *Astorija* restaurant, as well as those which have restored pre-war names such as the Otto Schwartz restaurant in the Rome Hotel, have been transformed beyond recognition. Other places, such as the Old Riga cafe, have not changed their decor very much at all.

Food service is an industry in which gains have been made by local residents, as well as by Latvians who returned to Latvia from exile in post-occupation years. the most popular saloons in Latvia today belong to Gunars Ķirsons, head of the *Lido* company. He himself worked as a waiter in the best restaurants of Soviet Latvia. In the early 1990s the only *Lido* restaurant was extremely expensive, but since then Ķirsons has opened

Former *Auciems* Inn

Grundzāle Inn

The *Alus Sēta* in Old Riga

The interior of the *Vērmanītis* restaurant, run by Gunārs Ķirsons

The M6 restaurant

The interior of Gunars Ķirsons' *Alus Sēta*

The Bible says that Jesus fed a multitude with several fish. Latvia's most popular restaurants are those which are run by Gunars Ķirsons, and in his democratic eateries he feeds tens of thousands of people each day

The *Melnie Mūki* restaurant

The *Jaunais restorāns* of Andrejs Žagars

The interior of M6

Aparjods in *Sigulda* – a traditional log building with excellent Latvian cuisine and a hotel for the weary

The ancient Balts were the first to put hops in the world's favorite beverage, beer. Latvians have been brewing beer for thousands of years, and among popular brands today are *Tervete* beer and *Zelta Alus*

Influential politicians Māris Mednis and Kārlis Leiškalns at *McDonald's* – loved by some Latvians, not by others

The *Anšpēteri* eatery, which is supported by a large farm and serves true rural treats – quickly and in enormous portions

Actor Klaus Brandauer likes his beer from the *Aldaris* brewery

As in ancient days, Latvians are building inns along the side of their roads. Perhaps they are known by different names now, perhaps the food is fancier – but they're still saloons. This one is along the Riga-*Liepāja* highway, and it is very traditional in design

Mārtiņš Rītiņš, owner of the *Vincents* restaurant has returned to his fatherland. He hosts a very popular TV cooking show

more democratic cafes and restaurants with Latvian cuisine – *Alus Sēta* in Dome Square, *Dzirnavas* in *Dzirnavu iela*, *Ķēķis* in the *Ķengarags* neighborhood, and *Staburags* in downtown Riga. Early in 2000 Ķirsons unveiled his largest project yet – a *Lido* restaurant and entertainment complex that is the largest log building in Europe, featuring several beer halls, a bistro and a buffet.

The director of the Latvian National Opera, Andrejs Žagars, has opened restaurants of a different quality and price level *Jaunais Restorāns* and *Symposium* offer modern European cuisine, while the cafe *Osiris* and the music club *Dizzy* are also popular. Former Western Latvians who own popular eateries are Mārtiņš Rītiņš, who runs the *Vincents* restaurant, and Elmārs Tannis, who owns Latvia's leading pizza chain, as well as several restaurants such as

Andalūzijas Suns and *Lidojošā Varde*. Other well known restaurants in Riga are the *Skonto* fish restaurant, *Astorija*, and the restaurant of the Park Hotel *Ridzene*.

Young people in the center of Riga often hang out in one of several Irish pubs. Also gaining popularity are eateries which serve *pelmeņi* – a popular Russian dish from Soviet times. There are several *McDonald's* restaurants, as well as a number of Chinese restaurants which, unlike in many parts of the world, are on the expensive side. The capital city of Latvia has Armenian, Japanese, Indian, Thai, Vietnamese, Russian, Jewish and other ethnic-based restaurants and cafes.

Outside of Riga there are relatively few good restaurants, because purchasing power outside the capital city is not high. Among those that are well known are *Aparjods* in *Sigulda* and the Minchausen Saloon on the Vidzeme seashore.

Chef Elmārs Tannis enjoys the food at his own restaurant *Čarlstons*. Elmārs grew up in Canada and brought the secrets of Western cuisine to Riga

The most popular restaurant in the 1980s was *Sēnite* in *Inčukalns*

Tim McShane's, an Irish pub

The banquet hall of *Čarlstons*

The restaurant *Raibais Balodis* (Vivid Pigeon) in Convent Garden

The *Skonto* fish restaurant

The Chinese restaurant *Šaņ Duņ*

Pelmeņi are the national dish of Siberia, and in Soviet times they became popular in Latvia, too. *Pelmeņi* cafes were popular throughout Latvia in Soviet times, and today *pelmeņi* eateries are imbued with a very charming sense of nostalgia

Former Economics Minister Vladimirs Makarovs and the headquarters of the Economics Ministry at *Brīvības iela* 55 in Riga

Former Economics Minister and businessman Atis Sausnitis

An advisor to the president on economic issues, Inese Vaidere

The first Economics Minister in post-Soviet Latvia, Ojārs Kehris

PROTOCOL OF ACCESSION OF LATVIA
TO THE MARRAKESH AGREEMENT ESTABLISHING
THE WORLD TRADE ORGANIZATION

PROTOCOLE D'ACCESSION DE LA LETTONIE
À L'ACCORD DE MARRAKECH INSTITUANT
L'ORGANISATION MONDIALE DU COMMERCE

PROTOCOLO DE ADHESIÓN DE LETONIA
AL ACUERDO DE MARRAKECH POR EL QUE SE ESTABLECE
LA ORGANIZACIÓN MUNDIAL DEL COMERCIO

WORLD TRADE ORGANIZATION
ORGANISATION MONDIALE DU COMMERCE
ORGANIZACIÓN MUNDIAL DEL COMERCIO

Geneva
14 October 1998

On February 10, 1999, Latvia became the first of the Baltic States to join the World Trade Organization. This opened the way for Latvia to develop most favored nation relationships with and to export goods to some 130 countries

A 1928 novel by Pāvils Rozītis, *Ceplis* (Kiln), was made into a film in Soviet Latvia in 1972, and it became a symbol for economic activity. Helga Dancberga and Eduards Pavuls starred, the director was Rolands Kalniņš

The European Integration Bureau (EIB) is a government institution which promotes Latvia's integration into the European Union. On the basis of information from the EU, the integration process in Latvia is planned, and interests in various spheres are coordinated. The EIB also coordinates foreign aid and provides information to society about the EU. The bureau has a Translation and Terminology Center which translates EU and Latvian law and which is elaborating EU-related terminology in Latvian. In cooperation with various ministries the EIB has elaborated a national program for integration into the EU. A series of publications called *Es un ES* (Me and the EU) has been published. The journal *Latvija un Eiropas Savienība* (Latvia and the European Union) has been published for three years. The EIB plays an important role in evaluating and, in some cases, monitoring EU Phare program projects. EIB director Edvards Kušners is at the right in this photograph, speaking to the former French ambassador to Latvia

During the 50 years of the Soviet occupation, Latvia had a planned economy with exaggerated, extensive and centralized industry in which imported workers from other parts of the Soviet Union worked. There was fully centralized supply of goods, trade did not involve anything of the free market, and although Latvia's level of infrastructure was far above that in many other places of the Soviet Union, it was equally far behind the level in Western Europe. Private initiative was squashed, and industry was simply part of the political process.

The first move toward a free economy in Latvia occurred in the early 1980s, when flower growers became active. Latvians brought flowers and bulbs to many places in the Soviet Union and earned quite a bit of money that way. Some successful kolhozes began to engage in true business in producing and processing agricultural products.

The liberalization of the Soviet economy in the late 1980s opened the floodgate in Latvia. People joined in cooperatives first and then developed freer forms of entrepreneurship. When the independence of Latvia was restored in 1991, however, many people were not ready for the free market. There were efforts to preserve centralized industry and agriculture, and privatization and a move toward free market conditions occurred comparatively slowly. It must be said, however, that in comparison to other countries in Eastern Europe, Latvia has managed to liberalize its economy very successfully indeed.

After Latvia shed the Soviet occupation, it based its economic development on the establishment of a Western, market-type economy, involving competition and private property and free trade with other countries. Latvia's strategic goal is to join the European Union, and this is gradually taking place as Latvia has adapted its economic environment to EU requirements. Latvia's government has engaged in various reform programs and has brought stability to economic policy. Macroeconomic stability, indeed, is the government's key economy priority. Monetary and fiscal policies are aimed at ensuring a stable currency exchange rate and at preserving a balanced budget. Inflation in Latvia has been low over the last several years.

With an eye toward joining the European Union, the Latvian government in 1993 defined the need to develop a competitive economic environment, to promote the ability of entrepreneurs to do their work, to foster small and medium business development, to reach new foreign markets and to encourage the flow of foreign investment into high-technology sectors of the Latvian economy. Trade policy was aimed at opening up the Latvian economy, gradually lowering import tariffs on agricultural and other food products. Domestic market liberalization was promoted by privatization, which was nearing completion at the turn of the millennium.

In the 10 years since the restoration of the Latvian state, a system has been established in which resources are divided up through a market economy. The state devotes its attention primarily toward regulation of natural monopolies, environmental protection, education, culture, health care, science, information, defense, public order, law enforcement, improvement of the national infrastructure, water supplies, se-

wage purification and household waste management. The economic environment in Latvia is one which stimulates the private sector. The government must improve the country's infrastructure, strengthen the financial system and take all necessary steps to support the private sector. Throughout the period of independence the government has implemented programs to support those regions in particular which were hardest hit by the restructuring of Latvia's industrial sector.

Between the early 1990s and the end of 1999, foreign direct investment in Latvia amounted to more than 1 billion lats. In 1998 FDI was equal to 4.3% of the country's gross domestic product. Government investments are aimed largely at infrastructural projects. The government investment program, including state-guaranteed credits and other sources of financing, each year is equal to between 2.9% and 5.8% of GDP.

Since 1996 the volume of domestic loans issued to companies and to entities engaging in privatization has grown very rapidly. This has been both because of more active economic pursuits and to reduced risks in the crediting process. The Russian financial crisis in 1998 led to a reduction in overall banking assets, which led to lower deposit volumes and higher interest rates, but when the economy healed the volume of deposits increased again and interest rates fell. Latvia has an open economy. The export of goods and services amounts to approximately 50% of GDP, while imports amount to approximately 60% of GDP. Latvia's largest trade turnover is with Germany (more than 16% of the total volume of foreign trade), Russia (12%), Sweden (9%), and Finland, Great Britain and Lithuania. Industry contributes the largest share of GDP (nearly 25%), followed by trade (17.5%), transport and communications (14%). Because Latvia is a relatively small country, the external economic environment is quite important for its economic development. In 1999 the European Union began to introduce its new currency, the euro, in non-cash settlements, and this marked a new step in the coordination of the economic policies of EU countries. Candidate countries, most of which are from the former Socialist bloc, were far more seriously influenced by the Russian crisis. It hit hardest in the Baltic States and Poland. The entire post-Socialist region was influenced by the Balkan crisis.

Very rapid inflation in Russia, devaluation of the ruble and virtual economic collapse had both a negative and a positive effect on the Latvian economy. Imports from Russia in the first quarter of 1999 were 49% less than imports in the same period in 1998. Exports to Russia from Latvia declined by 68%, while exports from Lithuania to Russia declined by a full 76%. This means that the Latvian and Lithuanian export structure had formerly been dominated by goods which Russia could easily produce itself or buy more cheaply from China or the EU. Overall exports in Latvia and Lithuania, however, have increased, and this has been thanks to greater exports to Western Europe, various developing countries and Eastern Europe. In other words, the Russian financial crisis stimulated business activity in Latvia, forcing people to produce the kinds of goods that can be sold in more developed countries. In 1998, Latvia's exports to the European Union were 27% higher than in 1997. Export to the other Baltic States increased by 10% – food products and chemicals lead the way in the export structure. GDP growth in 1996 was 3.3%, in 1997 – 8.6%, in 1998 – 3.6% and in 1999 – 3.5%. Consumer prices in 1991 increased by 262%, reaching the level of hyperinflation in 1992 – 958.6%. By the end of the 1990s, however, inflation was down to just 1-2% in mid-1999 when compared to the same period in 1998. Inflation in 1999 was not above the single digits in a single one of the Central and Eastern European countries. There has been significant price stabilization, although occasionally this leads to fears that deflation may occur, thus putting the brakes on economic development.

Since 1998 food prices in Latvia have declined, while non-food prices have grown more expensive by approximately 3%. There has been a jump in overall consumer prices in recent years, thanks largely to increases in regulated prices, especially housing rental costs.

Deflation in producer prices occurred in the fourth quarter of 1998, and throughout 1998 and 1999 the construction price index declined. This was related to working wages, as well as the lower cost of construction materials. The export price index is below 2%. Export prices have declined on wood products, machinery and textiles.

Latvia's current accounts deficit in the balance of payments grew in 1998 and 1999, reaching the equivalent of 11% of GDP at one point. This situation, in which the overall payment balance remains positive, ensures sufficient capital inflow into Latvia, not only to cover the current accounts deficit, but also to increase foreign reserve assets.

At the end of the millennium foreign direct investment in Latvia slowed down, largely because the privatization process was coming to an end, but also because of the Russian financial crisis – many foreign investors do not see the Baltic States as a completely separate market from Russia yet. The attitude of investors remains careful. The structure of incoming foreign capital flows has changed. The proportion represented by portfolio investments and debt-creating capital flow has increased in the overall capital flow.

Since 1990 Latvia has suffered a trade deficit each year, but it has declined every year. The situation is improved and indeed dictated by the volume of incoming capital.

The main export product in Latvia in the late 1990s was wood and wood products, including paper and cardboard – these represent 38% of overall exports, and the products are mostly exported to the European Union. 18.2% of overall export is represented by motor vehicles and products from metals processing and machinery construction, 17.5% by light industrial products, 10.8% by agricultural and food products, and 7.1% by chemical products and plastics.

In terms of import products, the import of automobiles has increased very rapidly, as has the import of new equipment and technologies – products that fall into the category of capital products. Consumer goods are imported at unjustifiably high levels, and this is part of the reason for why domestic products are often not competitive to foreign products.

Imports from the CIS, and especially from Russia, plummeted in 1998. Russia used to export mostly mineral products, as well as metals and chemical goods.

Latvia's leading trade partner is Germany. Leading import products include motor vehicles, machinery, equipment and technologies. Latvia's negative trade balance is covered in part by a positive service balance. Two-thirds of the export of services are made up of transit services, which represent approximately 10% of GDP. The transit products which pass through Latvia usually come from Russia and Belarus, loaded into ships in Latvia's ports and sent on to various regions in the world.

The most important elements of this transit process are port services and the Latvian railway system. 60% of transit involves oil and oil products.

Domestic and world-known transnational companies have become far more active in recent years in offering a full cycle of cargo transportation services, and Riga is starting to become a regional hub for the transportation sector.

Latvia's foreign trade policy is aimed at integration into the European Union, expansion of regional cooperation, and better economic relations with countries in which there are the political situation is stable. Latvia's industrial market is liberal and open, and policies are clearly aimed at a higher level of economic integration with the European Union. Latvia is an active member of the World Trade Organization, and it is moving constantly toward the development of free trade relations. Relationships among the Baltic States and the countries of the North American Free Trade Association are developing, as is the development of long-term stable and mutually advantageous trade and economic relations with Russia, Ukraine and Belarus. Latvia is also expanding its MFN relations with countries that are not members of the WTO.

The Russian market will always play a certain role in the Latvian economy. The Latvian Economics Ministry has cooperation agreements with a number of the republics and regions in the Russian Federation, including the Saha, Mari, Chuvashi, Karelia and Bashkiristan republics and the Omsk, Moscow and Kirov regions.

Along with increasing market liberalization, the Latvian government has also sought to protect the domestic market and the interests of local producers in an effective way.

The volume and quality of accumulated capital in Latvia has much to do with the country's competitiveness on world markets, economic growth and increases in the standard of living of the country's residents. Investments, in turn, are resources which are used for capital growth, restoration, maintenance and modernization. There was a significant increase in investment in Latvia in 1996 and 1997, thanks to the successful process of privatization in Latvia, as well as to the high credit rating which Latvia obtained from international credit rating organizations. Also, interest rates were low and the banking sector had recovered from a 1995 crisis. There was overall economic growth, and business had a rosy view of the future.

The Latvian government has always devoted attention to attracting foreign investments.

These are the people who work to develop quality-related policies in Latvia – the director of the Economics Ministry's Quality Structural Policy and Management Department, Anrijs Matiss, deputy state secretary and PRAQ II quality assurance program coordinator Lilija Stelpe, and the state secretary of the Economics Ministry, Kaspars Gerhards

The board of the Latvian Quality Association

The staff of the SC *Aldaris* after receiving a quality award in 1997

The editor of the magazine *Kvalitāte*, Janis Galviņš

Representatives of the SC *Grindeks* after receiving a quality award in 1997

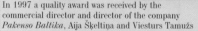

In 1997 a quality award was received by the commercial director and director of the company *Pakenso Baltika*, Aija Šķeltiņa and Viesturs Tamužs

The SC *EF Jauda* and the *Turiba* business university both received diplomas as finalists for the quality award

Latvia's national program on quality assurance is supported by the European Commission's PRAQ 92 and PRAQ III programs. One of the most important elements in ensuring proper quality is the Latvian quality award, which is based on a similar business model in Europe. The award was established by the Latvian Quality Association in cooperation with the Economics Ministry. Since November 1998 the association has published the magazine *Kvalitāte*. Under the auspices of the national quality assurance program, a training system has been set up to teach people to introduce quality control systems in line with the ISO 9000 and ISO 140000 standards. Latvia has begun negotiations with the European Commission on joining the European Common Market as an equal partner.

A meeting of the Latvian Competition Council. Chairman Pēteris Vilks is at the center of the photograph

The main activities of the Consumer Defense Center are to review complaints about the insufficient quality of goods, to provide consultations on quality-related issues, to provide information and consultation on consumer protection laws, to monitor the market, and to engage in obtaining and exchanging information at the international level. Here we see employees of the center at a training course in Belgium which was organized by the European Consumer Policy and Science Center to introduce newcomers to consumer defense laws in the EU

THE LATVIAN DEVELOPMENT AGENCY

The Latvian Development Agency is a state-owned, non-profit stock company which works to speed up and support Latvia's economic development by attracting foreign direct investment and by promoting exports. The agency has eight offices abroad which help to reach this goal. The LDA is the first investment agency in Central Europe.

The agency has set up an active dialogue between foreign entrepreneurs and the Latvian government, so various steps are being taken to improve the climate for business activity, to simplify requirements in the law, and to make it easier to launch a business in Latvia.

The work of the LDA also involves informing business circles throughout the world about the Latvian economy and its development, as well as the comparative advantages and business opportunities which Latvia affords. The agency also helps to prepare investment projects and provides a full spectrum of assistance to foreign businessmen.

Reviews of the LDA's professionally prepared information, publications, video films and other materials – all available at Latvia's embassies abroad, at the LDA's own offices, and during various seminars, conferences and *business days* events which the LDA attends – have been extremely positive.

The LDA also helps Latvian companies to establish business contacts abroad, organizing trade missions and helping companies to participate in international exhibitions. The LDA is also responsible for the country's export promotion programs. Most of the projects of the LDA are financed with money from the EU PHARE program. Latvia's businessmen receive information about the LDA's work and projects through an informational bulletin, *Latvija Pasaulē* (Latvia in the World), which has been published since 1999 in cooperation with a business journal in Latvia. There is an LDA home page on the Internet (http://www.lda.gov.lv), where information is available about the agency and about Latvia as a whole.

THE LATVIAN ASSOCIATION OF BUSINESS CONSULTANTS

The development of business activities is closely linked to improvements in the business of consultancy. Any entrepreneur who is interested in increasing the operational efficiency of his or her company uses advice from professionals on issues of management, information, finances, marketing, security, etc. The spectrum of consultation services which are provided by the Latvian Association of Business Consultants is expanding all the time.

The agency was built up from scratch, because business consultations were not offered by anyone in the early 1990s. Today the value of consulting services in Latvia can be calculated in the millions of lats, while the benefits which accrue to companies that take advantage of these services are worth tens of millions of lats. Latvia's consultants have won international recognition and are involved in a number of very important projects.

At this time the association brings together more than 60 consulting firms, as well as individual consultants. At the beginning of 1999 the LABC was admitted to the Federation of European Management Consulting Associations. Now the association can issue certificates to its members, attesting to the fact that they are LABC members and operate in accordance with the federation's ethics code.

The association represents Latvia's business consultancies and independent consultants, promoting improvements in their professional qualifications, popularizing, explaining and informing society and enterprises about the ways in which consulting can help in business development, and helping new and existing businesses to attract members of the association to help with specific projects.

The LABC is a link between clients and consultants, helping the former group to define problems and needs, providing complex solutions to issues in accordance with client demands, and ensuring fast and high-quality work. The LABC provides free information about consultations on the establishment of new companies, business planning and strategies, attracting investments, project management, company management, personnel selection, operations analysis, business and property evaluation, auditing, finances, bookkeeping, taxes, legal and customs issues, marketing, information services, quality management, business security, patenting, selection of business training programs, organization of seminars and conferences, information technologies and the various sectors of the economy. The LABC certifies its members, thus guaranteeing their conformity to generally accepted European quality standards. Members of the association guarantee absolute confidentiality with respect to information which they receive from their clients.

President Guntis Ulmanis (center, holding award) with a delegation of Latvian companies after receiving an award from the Institute for East-West Studies for his investment in the democratic development of Latvia, June 22, 1996

The Economics Ministry studies the experience of other countries in which economies are in transition, and it works to protect foreign investment, to create an economic environment which foreign investors understand, to provide consultations and to ensure that all necessary information is available to investors. In order to preserve internal and external balance in the economy, to avoid a current accounts deficit in the balance of payments and to avoid threats to the stability of the Latvian national currency, the country's economy is based on the assumption that internal accumulated resources must cover the volume of investment by at least 80%.

The total volume of foreign investment in Latvia amounts to more than 1 billion lats, but overall investments are close to 2.5 billion lats. Approximately 2/3 of foreign investment involves debt obligations, while 1/3 does not create debt – foreign direct investment and capital securities. Government investments in Latvia are invested under the auspices of a National Investment Program, using state budget resources, guaranteed credits, gifts and the resources of those who are implementing projects. Of 198 investment projects in 1998, 56 were local government projects, most often aimed at improving energy supplies and water supply management. 60% of the financing from the national investment program goes toward transport, energy and environmental protection.

The largest volume of foreign investment in recent years has gone into the finance sector (SEB bought 48% of shares in *Unibanka*, *Merita Nordbanken* acquired 100% of the shares of the Latvian Investment Bank). International companies that are active in the economy include *Linstow Warner*, *Coca Cola* and *Scania*. A significant share of the investment made by these companies goes toward real estate.

Investments from the countries of the European Union represent more than 50% of FDI. Latvia's economic stability and its ability to overcome the consequences of the Russian economic crisis are affirmed by the favorable BBB credit rating for loans in foreign currencies that was specified by *Standard & Poor's* in June 1999. The interest rate on euro obligations which Latvia borrows is also comparatively low – 325 points above LIBOR.

Danish capital represents the highest percentage of FDI – 15.5% (but only because a British-Finnish partnership which bought a minority state in Latvia's telecommunications company was registered there), followed by the United States – 10.7%, Russia – 8.7%, Germany – 8.4%, Great Britain – 7.5% and Sweden – 6.9%.

The central bank, the Bank of Latvia, monitors monetary and currency exchange rate policies and supervises commercial banks. The securities market is based on the Riga Stock Exchange, which organizes regular and open trade in public securities, as well as the Latvian Central Depository. The securities market in Latvia remains in its infancy, however, and its influence on the country's macroeconomic condition is insignificant. At the end of March 1999 the capitalization of the Riga Stock Exchange was 492 million lats, and shares in 70 companies were being bought and sold. The Eastern Asian and Russian financial crises had a deleterious effect on the Latvian securities market. The most important problem is the lack of trust among foreign investors in Russia and countries which are near to it. In the medium term there are plans to set up a harmonized and unified Baltic securities market and to integrate into the Northern European financial market.

Since 1996 the volume of credits issued to companies and private individuals has increased very rapidly. Banks are encouraged to issue loans because the profitability of securities is declining, and also because banks are finding it easier to attract foreign capital. Growth in loan portfolios is also promoted by such types of crediting as mortgage of security, factoring, forfeiting and, especially, the wide use of leasing programs.

The Bank of Latvia operates similarly to a currency council, purchasing and selling foreign currency freely. Latvia's currency is fully covered with foreign currencies and gold reserves.

Latvia's fiscal policies have been quite strict for several years, in order to avoid increases in budget expenditures and the fiscal deficit. Government expenditures are carefully monitored and rationalized. In the future information will continue to be devoted to issues which have to do with tax collection, tax debt, capitalization, late fees, punitive sanctions and the "shadow economy".

Latvia has closely monitored the Maastricht Criteria, which provide for internal debt at or below 20% and a fiscal deficit in the budget of no more than 3% of GDP. Latvia is in full compliance with these and other EU and IMF requirements in its economic, financial and fiscal policies.

Latvian Ex...

Textile INDUSTRY of LATVIA

BUSINESS DEVELOPMENT POLICY

The creation of an environment which is favorable for business development is one of the key priorities for Latvia's government. Laws in this area have been harmonized with the requirements of the European Union, the work of small and medium businesses is being stimulated, and quality systems are being introduced.

The main problems in Latvia's business development include the comparatively low competitiveness of Latvian companies, insufficient knowledge to promote the transfer and implementation of the most progressive business ideas and technologies, insufficient financial resources, a fairly burdensome tax system, and the high cost of introducing quality systems and relevant standards. Business development requires not only a favorable legal structure, but also financial support from the state. Without such support, companies – especially small and medium ones – have problems in learning management and marketing skills, accessing new markets, introducing new technologies and quality standards, etc. This, in turn, has a deleterious effect on the competitiveness of companies in the international market. Even in countries with developed market economies there are various programs to support entrepreneurial activity. The goal is to even out disproportions in economic environments, to increase competitiveness, and to support small business or specific regions.

In Latvia, the government provides support for business in specific regions

which have been declared as deserving of special assistance, in free economic zones, and in the area of agricultural production. Latvian law provides tax relief for small businesses and for the restoration of equity resources. In some instances companies are allowed to extend their tax payment terms. State support is also given in the area of exports, allowing companies to attend international exhibitions and markets, financing one-time external market research projects, guaranteeing and providing credits for export operations, supporting regional development, financing the purchase of patents and the introduction of progressive technologies, supporting environmental protection, energy savings and the production of electricity from resources that can be regenerated, helping to improve employment levels and work conditions, and providing support for companies that are facing crisis situation. Small and medium sized companies can receive help in the form of consultation and training, and SMEs can receive support that is 25% or even more extensive than that which is given to large companies.

There is also tax relief specifically for small and medium companies. For example, the law provides for a 20% discount on taxable income if the value of equity assets at the company is not greater than 70,000 lats, if net turnover in the tax year was not greater than 200,000 lats, and if the number of employees at the company over the course of the year has not exceeded 25.

Latvia has a national program for the development of small and medium companies, as well as a program aimed at promoting economic development in those regions which have been chosen for special support. There are also programs to promote exports through export guarantees and specialized crediting institutions. The state stock company Latvian Export Credits provides such services in Latvia.

The main goal of Latvian Export Credits is to ensure the ability of exporters and banks which finance exports the ability to compete on the international market through export insurance, guarantees and financing. The aim is to expand sales markets for goods and services, and to reduce losses caused by commercial and political risk by using export payments, contract or credit insurance, credit guarantees and other services.

Small and medium companies are one of the most important areas of support in Latvia. The main problems which hinder the development of SMEs include insufficient financial resources to launch and develop businesses, limited opportunities to receive credits and credit guarantees, a lack of information about markets and possible partners, and a shortage of knowledge about management and marketing. With the support of the PHARE program, business incubators have been established in *Jelgava*, *Madona* and Riga. The Latvian Center for Business Innovation in the Electronics Industry, as well as nine business support centers, have been set up.

PRIVATIZATION. THE LATVIAN PRIVATIZATION AGENCY

The General Director of the Latvian Privatization Agency, Jānis Naglis (second from the left) and the Minister for Cooperation with International Finance Organizations, Roberts Zīle (far left) meet with representatives of the European Bank for Reconstruction and Development

PA board member Viktors Šadinovs

The General Secretary of the EBRD, Antonio Maria Costa, and Privatization Agency General Director Jānis Naglis at a press conference

PA board member Imants Mantiņš

PA board member Uldis Kriķis

PA board member Didzis Azanda

One of the leading Italian investors in Latvia, Ernesto Preatoni, at a press conference with Jānis Naglis

Approximately 80% of output at the privatized SC *Ogre* is exported to the West

The SC *Valmieras stikla šķiedra*, thanks to privatization, has obtained a powerful investor – the German company *Glasseiden Gmbh Oschatz*. Here we see Inārs Poļaks, the president of the company

In implementing radical economic reforms and in moving the Latvian economy toward market principles, the process of privatization has been undergone in Latvia. Privatization has led to the establishment of efficient and competitive companies, promoted the development of the local capital market, attracted foreign direct investment to balance out the country's balance of payments, and to reduce the negative social effects of the process of transformation.

The Latvian Privatization Agency was established in 1994. By selling majority share holdings in formerly state-owned companies to strategic investors, the agency has helped to establish competitive companies and to ensure the emergence of a Latvian community of entrepreneurs. With the help of the Riga Stock Exchange, shares in the best companies are being sold in return for privatization certificates, thus promoting public support for the reform process and creating a large group of private business owners.

Shares in 83 companies have been sold for privatization certificates, and 110,887 natural and legal persons in Latvia have become shareholders as a result of this. Of the 66 companies which are floated on the Riga Stock Exchange, 60 are privatized enterprises.

The Privatization Agency has created equal opportunities for people to purchase objects that are being privatized, and the process has always been a transparent one.

The process of privatization in Latvia can basically be considered to be completed. The agency has concluded more than 1,200 purchase agreements. In less than six years, 97% of state-owned companies and enterprises were turned over for privatization. As the result of this consistent program of privatization, the proportion of the private sector in GDP was 66%, and the private sector employed 70% of Latvia's working individuals. The share of GDP represented by private enterprises in such areas as industry, agriculture, fishing, construction and trade is above 90%.

The work of the Privatization Agency has covered the entire national economy, starting with the metals industry and ending with cultural and social objects. This has affected all of the residents of the country, as well as the employees of the companies that are being privatized.

Specific attention has been devoted to softening the social consequences of the privatization process. A unified process for compensating the employees of insolvent state-owned companies has been instituted to cover injury claims, as well as claims for unpaid wages and social taxes.

One of the primary missions for the privatization process has been to attract strategic investors so that companies can be run by owners who can make the necessary changes in ensuring that the enterprises are able to operate under the conditions of a market economy. Positive examples of privatization in Latvia include such companies as *Liepājа Metalurgs*, *Ogre*, *Aldaris*, the Riga Ship Repair Factory, *Latvijas Balzams*, *Ventspils nafta*, *Latvijas Gāze*, *Unibanka*, the Valmiera Glass Fiber Factory, *Krāsainie lējumi*, *Lauma* and many others – companies which since privatization have improved the quality of their work, created new jobs, produced products which are competitive at the European level, and ended up at the top of the list when it comes to Latvia's leading taxpayers. As was noted by the credit agency Fitch IBCA in June 1998, "the sale of a majority of shares to a strategic investor, in concert with significant participation by foreign investors, has ensured a high quality of privatization in Latvia, especially with respect to the pace of restructuring at companies, management structures, and access to free capital".

The entry of foreign investments into Latvia is a sign of the country's economic stability, a favorable environment for business operations, and the potential of the state for further development. Privatization is one of the most effective mechanisms for promoting the inflow of foreign investment. In the first four years of its operations, the agency signed 259 purchase agreements with foreign investors and Latvian companies that belong to foreigners, and it attracted foreign investment of LS 197 million. Foreign buyers paid 110 million lats for companies and promised future investments of 86 million lats.

Active privatization in Latvia has basically been completed. At the turn of the millennium the Privatization Agency has been focused on completing the privatization of the remaining large state-owned companies, and on monitoring those firms which have already been privatized.

Gazprom Board Chairman Rem Vjahirev, *Latvijas Gāze* Board Chairman Adrians Dāvis and Privatization Agency General Director Jānis Naglis, Ruhrgas deputy Board Chairman Burkhard Bergmann and Vice President Eberhard Krahtz, PreussenElektra board member Andreas Eiholtz and energy saving department deputy director Reiner Lehmann, after the signing of a purchase-sale agreement on shares in *Latvijas Gāze* in 1997

Representatives of Latvia's leading political parties discuss privatization. From the left: Andrejs Panteļejevs, Jānis Ādamsons, Andris Šķēle, Jānis Naglis and Gundars Krasts

Since its privatization the SC *Preses nams* has become one of the largest printing companies in the Baltic States

The successful post-privatization operations of the SC *Latvijas Balzams* have allowed the company to become Latvia's leader in the production of alcoholic beverages

Not everywhere does the process of transformation occur smoothly or easily. The privatized factory *Toleram Fibers* in *Daugavpils* became insolvent because of the Russian financial crisis, and this was a matter of enormous concern to the employees of the factory. Here the Privatization Agency's General Director Jānis Naglis is explaining the positive and negative aspects of privatization to picketers

Einars Repše, Governor of the Bank of Latvia

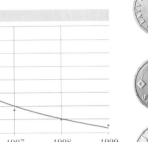

In the Republic of Latvia, the central bank is one of the most important public institutions. The Bank of Latvia operates under the Law *On the Bank of Latvia*. Its main tasks are to implement monetary policy with the aim of maintaining price stability in the country, issue the national currency, ensure the functioning of settlement and payment systems in the country, collect banking statistics and data on the country's macroeconomic environment, manage foreign reserves and act as the Government's financial agent.

The Bank of Latvia has implemented fixed exchange rate policies since 1994, when the Latvian lats was pegged to the SDR basket of currencies (at the rate XDR 1 = LVL 0.7997). Fluctuations in the exchange rates of individual currencies in the SDR basket against the lats are prompted by developments in world foreign exchange markets. The SDR basket of currencies is comprised of major world currencies. Two of these, the US dollar and the German mark, are used by Latvian companies in settlements. In non-cash settlements and in the SDR basket, the German mark and the French franc have been replaced with the euro. Fixing to a basket of currencies instead of a single currency has ensured the stability of the lats. The main priority of Latvian foreign and eco-

ANNUAL INFLATION (%)

THE EXCHANGE RATE OF THE US DOLLAR
AS SET BY THE BANK OF LATVIA (IN LATS)

nomic policies is the accession to the European Union, and in the future, perhaps joining to the European Monetary Union. In the more distant future, the peg could be switched to the euro. In 1997, the share of trade turnover with the EU member states exceeded 50 percent of Latvia's foreign trade turnover, and this figure follows an upward trend.

Since the introduction of the lats in March 1993, its free

The Board of Governors of the Bank of Latvia, January 1998

The Bank of Latvia

The first Minister of Finance of the post-war Republic of Latvia, Elmārs Siliņš (on the right) and the Managing Director of the International Monetary Fund, Michele Camdesi

convertibility has been ensured, and there are no restrictions on current and capital account transactions. The backing of the national currency with gold and foreign currency reserves exceeds 100 percent.

The contribution of Einars Repše, the Governor of the Bank of Latvia since 1991, in the introduction of the national currency and implementation of strict monetary policy has been remarkable. He was one of the members of the Monetary Reform Committee, which took all major decisions with respect to the introduction of the national currency. The transition period began in 1992, when Latvia introduced a temporary currency, the Latvian ruble, replacing the Russian ruble and avoiding the enormously high inflation (nearly 1000 percent in 1992). The Latvian national currency, the lats, was reintroduced in 1993. The monetary reform was completed in 1998 with the issue of the 500-lats note. Due to the consistent monetary policy of the Bank of Latvia, the lats is a stable and valuable currency, trusted in Latvia and abroad. This is reflected in the low inflation and increasing investment stock in Latvia.

Under the guidance of Einars Repše, the Bank of Latvia has become a full-fledged central bank, whose activity is aimed at economic development and growth. In 1997, Einars Repše was awarded with the Order of the Three Stars (Commander's degree) for his contribution to the development of Latvia's financial system. His work has also been acknowledged by international financial institutions, the International Monetary Fund among them. A number of times he has been ranked among the world's most successful and important financiers.

Dr. Ivars Godmanis, the first Prime Minister of the post-war Republic of Latvia and Minister of Finance (1998 – 1999)

Dr. Roberts Zile, Minister of Finance in several governments and Minister for Cooperation with International Financial Institutions

Uldis Osis, Minister of Finance (1992 – 1994), one of the founders of the liberal economy in Latvia

Valentina Andrejeva, State Secretary, the Ministry of Finance

Edmunds Krastiņš, Minister of Finance in several governments

Ilgonis Gaugers, Deputy State Secretary, the Ministry of Finance

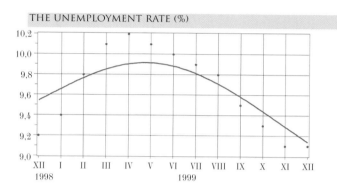

THE GOVERNMENT'S INTERNAL AND EXTERNAL DEBT (% OF GDP)

External debt / Internal debt

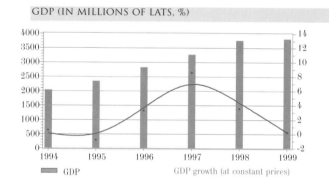

THE UNEMPLOYMENT RATE (%)

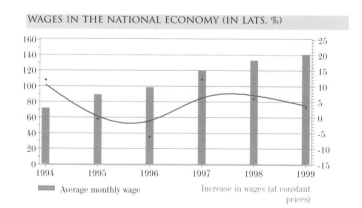

GDP (IN MILLIONS OF LATS, %)

GDP / GDP growth (at constant prices)

WAGES IN THE NATIONAL ECONOMY (IN LATS, %)

Average monthly wage / Increase in wages (at constant prices)

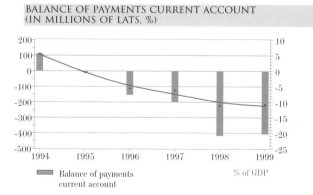

BALANCE OF PAYMENTS CURRENT ACCOUNT (IN MILLIONS OF LATS, %)

Balance of payments current account / % of GDP

The eagles on the Bank's facade symbolize power and wealth. From the very beginning, the facade has featured a parapet for the Bank's logo. True to contemporary custom, the first logo was in stylized Russian letters. After the Bank of Latvia was established in 1922, the logo was changed to read *Latvijas Banka*. At the end of 1996, the logo of the restored Bank of Latvia was once again placed on the parapet

Constructed in the early 20th century, the historical building of the Bank of Latvia is being rebuilt to suit the needs of a modern central bank. In stead of effacing historical traces, the renovations are designed to emphasize them and to support the Bank's image represented by its building – impressive, historical, yet also modern and functional

The early 20th century bank counters with windows for servicing customers are a unique feature not to be found elsewhere in Latvia. The hall is divided into three archways, and the rhythm of arches and vaults is accentuated. Ornamental zones further emphasize the harmony of the lines

THE BANK OF LATVIA BUILDING

The central bank of a country represents safety, stability and continuity. As a symbol of an independent state, an emission bank has a special place in the financial system.

The building that houses the Bank of Latvia was designed by the Latvian architect Augusts Reinbergs (1860–1908) for the purposes of the Riga Branch of the State Bank of Russia.

The building was put into operation in January 1905. In 1922 it became the main building of the newly founded Bank of Latvia. At that time, the building, where reinforced concrete was used for its operational halls, was considered state-of-the art. Sparely yet elegantly decorated, the building's exterior can hardly be considered pretentious. The facade features stylized Renaissance shapes, with decorative pargeting used to accentuate windows. Compatible in style with other buildings situated on the Palace Square, it is one of the last eclectic buildings in Riga and is listed as a monument of national significance.

During its life the building has housed banks, whose special working environment has allowed to maintain both its exterior and interior in a good condition.

The Bank of Latvia is aiming for a uniform interior design, successfully blending historical and modern elements. The large operational halls have been divided into smaller offices. In the spring of 1997, the attic was rebuilt to house modern offices, where unconventional architectural ideas have been executed in contemporary materials. Several departments of the Bank have been relocated to these offices.

The reconstruction and restoration of the building continues. The historical building gradually regains its former splendour, without losing sight of contemporary solutions and functionality.

The walls and arched ceiling in the second floor hall are decorated with plaster ornaments. The counters with their small cash windows evoke other classical banking institutions. The distinguished Latvian architect Gunars Birkerts, photographed here, has participated in the construction of the new building of the Bank's Riga Branch as a consultant

The bank's central staircase with its balustrade cut in dark marble from Belgium and four richly decorated candelabra placed on tall podiums is monumental and imposing. The walls and ceiling of the stairwell are adorned with plaster embellishments. It is one of the most beautiful parts of the Bank's building. Uldis M. Klauss, on bottom right, is advisor to the Governor of the Bank of Latvia

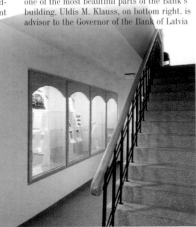

A NEW BUILDING FOR THE LATVIAN CENTRAL BANK

The Deputy Governor of the Bank of Latvia and Chairman of the Executive Board, Ilmārs Rimšēvičs, and the Governor of the Bank of Latvia, Einars Repše.
On July 23, 1999 the cornerstone for the new branch was laid. In the foundations of the building there is a capsule that someday will provide information to future generations. It also contains samples of the money that is in circulation today. The facility is expected to open for business in August 2001.

The Governor of the Bank of Latvia, Einars Repše, places a capsule in the foundations of the new building

The Governor of the Bank of Latvia Einars Repše

Since 1992, the Bank of Latvia's note and coin reserves are stored in the vaults of the *Deutsche Bundesbank*. That bank, however, is now reclaiming its storage facilities as a result of the introduction of the single European currency in preparation for 2001 when the euro will become the currency used in cash settlements from January 1, 2001. During the period of transition, two currencies will be in circulation in each of the member states.

The lats has a high nominal value, and it is likely that in the not too distant future there will be a need for far more euro notes in circulation than there are lats notes today. The new vault will, for a time, have to house both currencies. The building of a secure vault is very expensive, but it is important to build it sufficiently large to cope with any possible volume of notes and coins. In the absence of such a vault, Latvia would not be likely to become a member of the European Monetary Union. Also politically, it would not be right for Latvia to hold its reserves in another country's territory, because this would suggest that Latvia is unable to protect its own money.

Growth of the Latvian economy is another reason why the central bank needs a new vault. Currency in circulation has grown since 1991, and the volume of notes and coins handled by the Bank of Latvia Riga Branch has increased accordingly. The amount of notes and coins to be destroyed has also increased.

Notes and coins need to be processed effectively. Likewise, they need to be stored in a secure and modern vault. The Bank of Latvia has considered various solutions, including the possibility of constructing a modern vault in the Bank's main building. A few years ago, in consultation with foreign specialists, the necessary security measures were taken. Much has been done to adapt the Bank of Latvia's building at 2a *K. Valdemāra iela* in Riga, which is listed as a monument of national significance, to the specific needs of a modern central bank and to

ensure its security. It would not, however, be possible to reconstruct the central building without interrupting the work of the Bank as it would have to be deconstructed completely, down to its ancient foundations. Building requirements in the territory of Old Riga are a further constraint. Designing a draft project for a new branch building was finally found to be the cheaper, simpler and safer alternative. The concept was created in co-operation with specialists from the *Deutsche Bundesbank*, and the development of the project commenced.

The secure, high-capacity vault will provide for the needs of an emitting bank. Money will be received from banks, processed and issued to banks. Residents needing to replace damaged currency, purchase anniversary and souvenir coins, or to buy US dollars will also be served. Through an accounting centre, the Bank will provide effective interbank settlements. The vault will be the central node for accounting within Latvia, as well as for accounting with EU member countries. The new branch will house the Bank of Latvia's central computer, and it will secure both the internal information systems of the Bank, and the safe and stable working of the electronic interbank accounting system. There will be a unified, mutually duplicating information systems infrastructure at the central building of the Bank and at the new branch. The system will be designed to ensure uninterrupted operations even during accidents or emergencies.

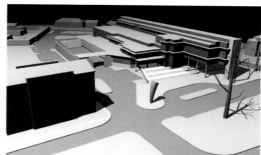

A sketch of the new Bank of Latvia branch produced by the architectural firm *Kronbergs, Kārkliņš and Partners*.
The building will be approximately 113 meters long and 45 meters wide, with a total height of 22.4 meters (including 5.20 meters underground). With security as top priority, it will be a very specific building. In 1994, an invitation to tender was held in Latvia to find a designer for the structure. Two design offices were selected, and they merged to establish the office of *Kronbergs, Kārkliņš and Partners*. Together with the Latvian specialists, the Bank also selected two experienced German companies – the architectural office *Held & Partner* and the engineering company *Alhauser+Konig*.
The leading building contractors for the building, also selected by an invitation to tender, will be the partnership *E. Heitkamp Lettland* and *Rigas Būvapvieniba*, which comprises three Latvian construction companies – Latvia's *Kalnozols and Partners*, BKD and *Velve*, and Germany's *E. Heitkamp GmbH*.

The new building in the winter of 2000. The new building will have three floors above ground and a basement. Within the building, there will be a two-floor vault. The main functions of the branch – receiving money from and issuing it to banks, handling non-cash transactions and providing services to individual clients – will be carried out on the second floor. The architects have provided for maximum convenience for visitors and employees alike.

UNIBANKA

Andris Bērziņš, president of *Latvijas Unibanka*

The *Latvijas Unibanka* bank was founded in 1993 as a state-owned stock company, *Latvijas Universālā Komercbanka*. It represented the merger of 21 former branches of the Bank of Latvia which had engaged in commercial activity and which were separated from the original system by the Latvian Bank Privatization Fund. Over the ensuing years Unibanka has become an important commercial bank with a wide range of clients in Latvia and stable cooperation partners in other countries.

Since January 1996 shares in *Unibanka* have been sold on the official list of the Riga Stock Exchange. In 1997 the shares were also floated on the London Stock Exchange, and under the auspices of the *Global Depository Receipt* (GDR) program, shares in the bank which

belonged to the Latvian Privatization Agency were successfully sold.

The major shareholder in *Unibanka* at this time is Sweden's *Skandinaviska Enskilda Banka*.

Unibanka offers its clients a variety of services which can be accessed without personally visiting the bank – telephone banking and Internet banking. Clients of the Internet banking system have 24-hour access to information about billing and payment card accounts, and they can handle the money which they have in the bank from any computer in the world which is connected to the Internet.

Latvijas Unibanka has been rated by the internationally recognized agency Fitch-IBCA. *Unibanka*'s short-term and long-term ratings coincide with those awarded to the Latvian state, and they are the highest that are presently available to commercial banks in Latvia. *Unibanka* has a BBB long-term credit rating, an F3 short-term credit rating, and the bank-specific individual rating C/D and a support rating of 3.

The board of *Latvijas Unibanka*

RIETUMU BANKA

The president of *Rietumu* Banka, Michael J. Bork

Rietumu Banka was established in 1992, the first bank in Latvia which was developed in the spirit of Western banking and the management principles of American banks. The bank is run by specialists with extensive experience in the United States, the EU and in international finance institutions. The bank services corporate clients – large, small and medium-sized enterprises and companies – as well as private individuals. *Rietumu Banka* offers clients a wide range of services, seeking to ensure that each client

has access to the very best in terms of financial and banking service and providing high-quality payment and cash-related services.

Rietumu Banka offers the most extensive opportunities in the area of currency exchange and securities operations, using flexible deposit programs, high-class investment consultations, and help in attracting capital and strategic partners. *Rietumu Banka* is one of the most dynamically growing banks in Latvia, and in terms of assets and equity capital, it is the third largest bank in Latvia and in the top 10 among all banks in the Baltic States.

MONEY

A 20-kopeck banknote issued by the WWI German occupation regime. Printed in Poznan on 17 April 1916. The note bore text in several languages

A silver shilling, minted in 1533 in Riga

The Albert thaler. Albert (1582-1621) was the governor of the Netherlands at the time when these thalers were first minted. His monetary system existed between the 16th and 18th centuries and was the most widely used system of currency in trade among the countries of the Baltic Sea

A coin of the *Suži* manor from the 19th century, which could be used only on the estate itself

A 1000-mark banknote issued by the WWI German occupation regime in Kaunas on 4 April 1918. The note bore text in several languages

A silver dreipolcher of the Polish King Sigismund III, minted in 1620 in Riga

A note of exchange worth 10 kopecks printed in Riga in 1920. The designer was Rihards Zariņš

A 3-kopeck iron coin produced by the WWI German occupation institutions and minted in Berlin in 1916

A 5 rouble banknote of the Riga Workers Deputies Council. Printed in Riga in 1919. The designer was L. Liberts. It was a means of payment in Riga and Riga county

A temporary note of exchange of the volunteer Western army known as the Bermont-Avalov force, printed in *Jelgava* in 1919. The note bore text in German and Russian

Money printed for military needs (1919-1920) – the so-called Council Money, stamped with the seal of the Latvian partisan regiment of Latgale. The money was used only in the areas where the partisans were active, and it was popularly known as Skujiņš money, named for the commander of the regiment

The Bank of Latvia's 25-lats banknote, printed in 1928 in England. The Latvian currency at that time was fully covered by gold reserves

A 5-ruble loan coupon produced by the executive committee of the *Cēsis* Region Workers Deputies Council in 1919. Each banknote was hand-signed by officials, sealed and numbered. There is a warning on the banknote that forgers of the coupons will be shot. Printed in *Cēsis* based on a design by Jānis Skundrikis (the 5-ruble coupon) and Jānis Vitiņš (a 10-ruble coupon)

The Latvian rouble of 1919, known as Niedre money

The Latvian rouble, which was used between 1919 and 1922. The provisional Latvian government issued it from April 1919 until September 1922, and it was printed in *Liepāja*, Riga and Helsinki. The author of the design was Julijs Madernieks

A 10-lats note from the Latvian Treasury, printed in 1933 on the basis of a design by Rihards Zariņš and Kārlis Krauze

A 25-lats banknote from the Bank of Latvia, printed in 1938 in England

A 20-lats note from the Latvian Treasury, printed in 1936 in Riga on the basis of a design by Rihards Zariņš and Kārlis Krauze

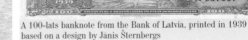

A 100-lats banknote from the Bank of Latvia, printed in 1939 based on a design by Jānis Šternbergs

A Latvian 100-rouble note (1919-1922), printed in *Liepāja*, Riga and Helsinki, and designed by Hermanis Grinbergs

Riga City one rouble bond (1919) was a legal means of payment in Riga and its vicinity. Printed in Riga

A note of exchange from the Latvian Treasury issued in Riga in 1940 and worth 5 lats. The notes of exchange were produced beginning in 1939 thanks to the fact that 5-lats coins began to disappear after the start of World War II. These notes of exchange, designed by Harijs Gricēvičs, were meant to replace the coins

A Bank of Latvia 500-lats banknote, printed in 1934 in England and covered by gold reserves

A 10-santims coin, produced in 1922 in Switzerland and designed by Rihards Zariņš

A 1-santims coin, minted in 1938 in Riga and designed by Ludolfs Liberts and Arturs Apinis

A 2-santims coin, minted in Riga in 1939 and designed by Liberts and Apinis

A 20-santims coin, 1922, Switzerland, Rihards Zariņš
A 50-santims coin, 1922, Switzerland, Rihards Zariņš
A 1-lats coin (silver), 1924, England, Janis Roberts Tilbergs
A 2-lats coin (silver), 1926, England, Rihards Zariņš
A 5-lats coin (silver), 1931, England, Rihards Zariņš

The long history of money in Latvia owes much to Latvia's link to important trade routes, among which the so-called Amber Route, the Route from the Varangians to the Greeks, and the Silk Route were the most popular. Coins are the most traditional form of money. Until the 18th century, when paper money began to spread, coins were the main means of payment throughout the world. The oldest Roman coins date back to the reign of Marcus Agrippa (31–12 B.C.). Between the 5th century and the 8th century, silver was used as a means of payment in the territory of present day Latvia. In the 9th century the Middle Eastern silver coins, Arab dirhams (drachmas), appeared. German, Danish, Czech, Hungarian and other silver coins reached Latvia in the last quarter of the 10th century. In the 13th century, bracteates and half bracteates from Gotland, as well as German denars struck in the towns of Westphalia reached the territory of Latvia along with crusaders, missionaries and knights. There was also an attempt to mint coins in the Bishopric of Riga in accordance with Bishop Albert's privilege of 1211, which required coins made in Riga to be of the same weight and standard as those of Gotland.

The first coins reliably dated as manufactured in Riga, artigs, were struck in Johann VI Ambundi's time (1418–1424). Since the Livonian money reform in 1426, shillings, pfennigs and sherfs were minted exclusively by the archbishops of Riga, and after an agreement signed in *Salaspils* in 1452, also by the masters of the Livonian Order.

The minting of marks and *vērdiņš* (1/4 mark) began in Riga in 1515. The word *dālderis* (a thaler) was first applied to silver coins, which the Count Schlick family began to produce in their mints in the Bohemian town of Joachimstal in 1518. Gold coins were known as *dukāts* (ducats). Wolter von Plettenberg was the first in Livonia to mint silver thalers and gold ducats (from 1523 to 1525). The Polish monetary system was introduced in 1581. Its basis was the silver thaler, which had smaller denominations of three groats, groats, dreipolchers and shillings.

With the annexation of Riga and Vidzeme by Russia in 1710, Russian money came to be used as legal tender. The Empress Elizabeth of Russia ordered the mintage of special coins, the so-called livoneses, for Estonia and the province of Vidzeme in Moscow in 1756 and 1757.

At the beginning of the 20th century, Russian gold and silver rubles, copper and silver kopecks, and notes were the only legal tender in the territory of Latvia. In 1915, the local governments in *Liepāja*, *Jelgava* and *Ventspils* began to issue their own money in notes of different denominations. The local government in Riga began to issue its own money on August 15, 1919, local government promissory notes with a face value of one and three rubles.

At the end of 1918, "tsar" rubles, "money of Duma", "kerenkas", German marks, ostrubles, ostmarks, and local government notes were all common. Estonian banknotes appeared in northern Latvia. In *Jelgava*, Colonel Pavel Bermont-Avalov issued provisional exchange notes of the Western Army of Volunteers.

In 1919, under the power of the Bolsheviks, the Riga City Council of Working People's Deputies issued 1-, 3-, 5-, and 10-ruble notes, declaring them as legal tender in the whole territory of Soviet Latvia. The Council of Workers' Deputies of the province of *Cēsis* issued their own money called "loan coupons" (in denominations of 5 and 10 rubles). On March 22, 1919 In *Liepāja*, the Provisional Government of the Republic of Latvia authorized the Minister of Finance to issue Latvia's Treasury notes, Latvian rubles, backed by all state assets. These notes were the first national currency of sovereign Latvia.

The lats was introduced in the Republic of Latvia on August 3, 1922 by the Law "Regulations for Money". The lats was based on gold (1 lats = 0.2903254 g of gold). On September 28, 1936, the lats was devalued to a level of GBP 1 = LVL 25.22. On November 25, 1940, the USSR currency was introduced as a parallel legal tender in Latvia at the exchange rate of one lats for one ruble. On March 25, 1941, the lats was withdrawn from circulation without any prior warning.

During World War II, there were two foreign currencies in circulation in Latvia: the reichsmark, the German occupation money, and the USSR ruble at the exchange rate of 10 rubles = 1 reichsmark. After World War II, and until 1992, USSR rubles and kopecks were in circulation in Latvia. Until the first post-war monetary reform in 1947, all denominations of pre-war notes and coins remained in circulation. During the reform, only banknotes of the earlier issues were withdrawn from circulation and exchanged for ruble notes issued in 1947 at the rate of ten to one. The notes of chervonetz were replaced with banknotes issued by the State Bank of the USSR and Treasury notes. The second post-war money reform took place at the beginning of 1961. USSR coins and notes of the new issue were used in Latvia until the restoration of independence.

The collapse of the Soviet Empire provided for the transition to a market economy and gave rise to the need to counteract inflation. The final goal of the monetary reform in Latvia was to reintroduce the lats and to stabilise the economy. In 1991, the Parliament entrusted the Government and the Bank of Latvia with the task of creating a national monetary system. On May 7, 1992, the Bank of Latvia introduced a temporary currency, the Latvian ruble, in parallel to the Russian ruble. The next step was the adoption of a floating exchange rate policy. On July 20, 1992, the circulation of the Russian ruble was discontinued and the Latvian ruble became the only legal tender. On March 5, 1993, after stability of the Latvian ruble was reached, the first lats banknote was put into circulation: the 5-lats note of the Bank of Latvia, which was in circulation simultaneously with the Latvian ruble at the rate of 1 lats = 200 Latvian rubles. Twenty days later, the 1-lats coin was put in circulation. On April 15 the Bank of Latvia introduced the 2-lats coin, on April 22 the 50-santims coin, and on June 28 10- and 20-lats notes and the 1-, 2-, 5- and 10-santims coins. With the introduction of the 500-lats note on July 20, 1998, the monetary reform was completed.

THE COMPONENTS OF LATVIA'S BUDGET INCOME

Value added tax 21%

Social insurance contributions 29%

Personal income tax 16%

Customs duties 1%

Foreign financial aid 2%

Property-related income 2%

Self-earned revenue 5%

Corporate income tax 6%

Non-tax revenue 7%

Excise tax 11%

THE COMPONENTS OF THE LATVIAN NATIONAL BUDGET

million lats

revenue   expenditure

■ General Government budget
■ Central Government budget
☐ Local Government budget

A deputy state secretary of the Finance Ministry, Inguna Sudraba

Prime Minister Andris Šķele and advisor Uģis Salna explain the 2000 budget. The Finance Minister must prepare the next year's budget by October 1 of the current year, and Parliament must, by law, adopt or reject the budget before Christmas. The budget is usually defended in Parliament by the Prime Minister and the Finance Minister

The director of the State Treasury, Aivars Veiss

ELEMENTS IN THE EXPENDITURE PORTION OF THE LATVIAN NATIONAL BUDGET

General government services
Defence
Public order and safety, law enforcement
Education
Health care
Social insurance and social welfare
Environmental protection, housing and utility services
Culture, sports, recreation
Heat and energy services and related programs
Agriculture, forestry and fishing
Industry and construction
Transportation and communications
Other economic activity and services
Other expenditures, not classified otherwise

0   100 000   200 000   300 000   400 000   500 000

The Minister for Cooperation with International Financial Organizations, Roberts Zīle, reports to the annual conference of the International Monetary Fund

The management of the Finance Ministry. Seated, from the left: the Director of the Lottery and Gambling Supervisory Inspectorate, Signe Birne; the director of the Budget Department, Solvita Zvidriņa; a deputy state secretary, Inta Vasaraudze; the State Secretary, Valentīna Andrejeva; the Director of the Tax Policy Department, Gunta Kauliņa; the Director of the Economic Analysis and Fiscal Policy Department, Daiga Gulbe. Standing: the board chairman of the Transportation Bureau, Gvido Janēvičs; the General Director of the State Revenue Service, Andrejs Sončiks; the General Director of the State Real Estate Agency, Kalvis Bricis; the chairman of the Insurance Supervision Inspectorate, Gvido Romeiko; the governor of the State Treasury, Aivars Veiss; the Director of the Customs Law Department, Guntis Kozinda; the Director of the Central Finance and Contract Unit, Armands Eberhards; the Director of the State and Local Government Procurement Supervision Department, Edvīns Pārups; a deputy state secretary, Ilgonis Gaugers, and Ivars Tiltiņš, Chairman of the State Hallmark Supervision Inspection

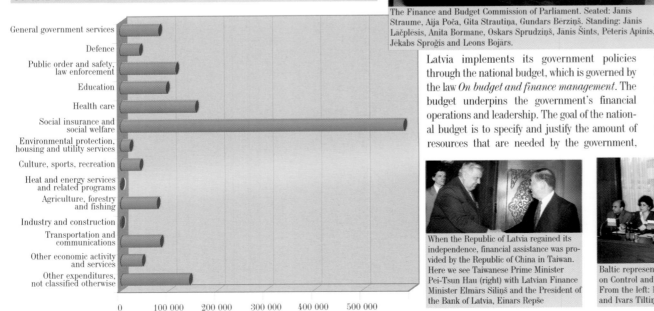

The Finance and Budget Commission of Parliament. Seated: Jānis Straume, Aija Počа, Gita Strautiņa, Gundars Bērziņš. Standing: Jānis Lāčplēsis, Anita Bormane, Oskars Sprudziņš, Jānis Šints, Pēteris Apinis, Jēkabs Sproģis and Leons Bojārs.

Latvia implements its government policies through the national budget, which is governed by the law *On budget and finance management*. The budget underpins the government's financial operations and leadership. The goal of the national budget is to specify and justify the amount of resources that are needed by the government,

other state institutions and local governments in order to perform the functions which are assigned to them by law. The budget also specifies income levels which cover these expenditures in the relevant time frame.

State and local government income is based on taxes. The share of GDP which is redistributed through the budget is specified by tax laws and by the way in which the clauses of these laws are carried out. Only Parliament is allowed to adopt tax laws and set tax rates. In 2000 Latvia has both indirect taxes (the value added tax, the excise tax on non-alcoholic beverages, precious metals, coffee, motorcycles, automobiles, alcoholic beverages, beer, oil products and tobacco products, the customs tax, the natural resources tax, and the lottery and gambling tax) and direct taxes (the company income tax, the personal income tax, social insurance contributions and the real estate tax).

Over the last several years, the objective of government tax policy has been to increase the proportion of indirect taxes in overall budget income. In 1993 indirect tax income was equal to 9% of GDP, in 1995 the figure was 12.3%, and in 1998 it was 13.4%. Since then the proportion has increased very slowly. This is in line with European Union requirements. In the interests of promoting economic development, the share of social insurance contributions that is made by employers is being reduced, staging in 2000.

The income part of the national budget is based on a maximum austerity regime, ensuring that the fiscal deficit in the national budget does not exceed the equivalent of 2% of GDP. This is in line with an agreement between the Latvian government and the International Monetary Fund. In 1998 the requirement posed no problem, but in 1999, when the Russian financial crisis hit Latvia hard, the requirement was not met. The government also sets out specific financing priorities (education and defence in 2000) on a program-based principle.

Along with the national budget proposal, Parliament also receives draft laws on budget expenditures and revenue each year. The law on the budget cannot be adopted until all of the related laws are passed. The acceptance of the budget represents a vote of confidence in the government. If the budget is rejected, this is a vote of no confidence.

The implementation of the budget law depends in large part on the State Treasury, which makes payments as set out in laws and Cabinet of Ministers regulations, registers all tax and non-tax income in the budget, registers expenditures and payments of the national debt, and monitors all other budget obligations of the state, thus ensuring the rational and effective management of budget resources. The Treasury is subordinated to the Ministry of Finance.

When the Republic of Latvia regained its independence, financial assistance was provided by the Republic of China in Taiwan. Here we see Taiwanese Prime Minister Pei-Tsun Hau (right) with Latvian Finance Minister Elmārs Siliņš and the President of the Bank of Latvia, Einars Repše

Baltic representatives at the signing ceremony of a Convention on Control and Stamping of Precious Metals in Geneva in 1996. From the left: Emantas Mitkus (Lithuania), Tina Touiste (Estonia) and Ivars Tiltiņš (Latvia).

A meeting of former revenue officials and the General Director of the State Revenue Service, Andrejs Sončiks – (from the left) Jurijs Pupčenoks, the director of the Latgale Department of the State Revenue Service, Vanda Gurkovska, former Prime Minister Vilis Krištopans, Andrejs Sončiks, and Imants Griķis

The leadership of the State Revenue Service in early 2000: first deputy general director and Customs Board director Aivars Krastiņš, general director Andrejs Sončiks, first deputy general director and Tax Board director Vaira Gromule, and deputy general director and Informatics Board director Andris Anspoks

At the signing of an agreement between Latvia and the United Kingdom on cooperation in the field of customs services. Seated: the General Director of the British Customs and Excise, Dame Valery Strakhan and Latvia's minister for national revenue, Aija Poča. Behind them (from the right): Juris Bone, Aivars Krastiņš, Andrejs Sončiks, Normunds Penke and two representatives of the British customs service

Andrejs Sončiks and the director of the Lithuanian Tax Department, Nijole Pitriniene

Income in the national budget is supervised by the State Revenue Service. It is a unified tax administration institution which was established in 1993 through a merger of the Latvian National Customs Board and the National Finance Inspectorate. Several new support structures were established, too. The State Revenue Service provides for the inflow of money into the national treasury, among other things administrating the payment of the social insurance contributions. Only a few taxes, including the real estate tax, are received and used by local governments. The fact that the sum collected by the state through taxes grows from year to year suggests that the process of collection is modern and appropriate, and the country's economic frontiers are protected with maximally little in the way of costs. The State Revenue Service has earned the trust of society in terms of the honesty, competence and justice of the way in which it administrates its work. A very important role in the agency's work is played by the Finance Police, which operates under its auspices. There is also an important Anti-Corruption Supervisory Division and an Excise Goods Board. In order to allow law enforcement institutions to battle smuggling more effectively, the State Revenue Service has established an Anti-Smuggling Center which coordinates all of the

work related to this issue and collects all of the necessary information.

When Latvia regained its independence and moved to a market economy, the State Revenue Service operated in a repressive manner, learning from its mistakes on many occasions. As the amount of experience accumulated by the agency increased, it came to understand that its service functions are a priority. In accordance to the experience of the European Union, the agency is restructuring some of its areas of operations in accordance with the requirements of taxpayers, making it more convenient for residents to settle their affairs with the state. One of the elements of this change has been a shift in the way in which taxpayers are served at the agency's territorial institutions. Previously people met with revenue agents in small offices, which was a fertile environment for corruption, but now there are large and comfortable client service halls.

In 1998 the State Revenue Service adopted a long-term development, operations and modernization program for the period between 1998 and 2002. This was done in accordance with the relevant EU charter of 1985 and in cooperation with the International Bank for Reconstruction and Development. The program has been financed in part by the World Bank. The installation of the aforementioned client service halls is one of the processes which is occurring under the auspices of the program.

Representatives of the State Revenue Service regularly participate in conferences, seminars, working groups and other events organized by the United Nations, global customs organizations, Interpol, and European tax administration organizations, the point being to study foreign experience and to develop contacts for ongoing cooperation.

The tax system is the only known method for implementing the principles of social justice in a society. The paying of taxes is one of the main stabilizing factors in the relationship between the state and society, and for that reason the State Revenue Service has set for itself the goal of becoming a modern institution which is respected by taxpayers for its justice, honesty and professionalism.

Employees of the department of the State Revenue Service which battles corruption – senior inspector Milda Nedeļa, deputy director Skaidrīte Jaungaile-Gaile, senior tax inspector Ilona Kukare, chief tax inspector Valentīna Dzalbe and chief tax inspector Anita Locāne

Signing an agreement between Latvia and the Netherlands on cooperation in the area of customs services

The Zemgale district office of the State Revenue Service in Riga

The deputy directors of the National Tax Board, Jānis Nesaule, and Gundars Zaķis talk about delicate aspects of administering tax payments

Raimonds Cers, Head of Audit Division SRS Zemgale district office in Riga

The Excise Goods Board coordinates and organizes supervisory programs to oversee the registration, storage, transportation and sale of excise-related goods which are manufactured in Latvia or imported into or exported from the country. The board collects and analyzes information about the situation in the market for these goods, and about the economic and financial activities of relevant legal persons – the taxes which they pay, etc. The board also engages in strategic planning when it comes to marking and supervising excise goods and increasing income in the national budget.

The Excise Goods board also evaluates customs warehouses which are be used for the storage and marking of imported excise goods, ascertaining that these facilities are in conformity with all requirements in the law.

Ludmila Resečkina, Deputy Head of SRS Zemgale district office in Riga

Each year the State Revenue Service organizes a ceremony to honor Latvia's leading taxpayers. Here representatives of Latvia's leading companies and taxpayers are seen with Finance Minister Edmunds Krastiņš (fourth from the left in the front row) and State Revenue Service General Director Andrejs Sončiks (to the right of the minister)

Large companies from *Ventspils* – exporters of oil and chemical products – are always among the country's leading taxpayers. Here we see officials from the companies in *Ventspils* which paid the most in terms of taxes in Latvia

The client service hall at the State Revenue Service in *Bauska*. The establishment of these halls represents a fundamental shift from the previous system, where people met with customs officials in small offices – a good environment for corruption

7323438

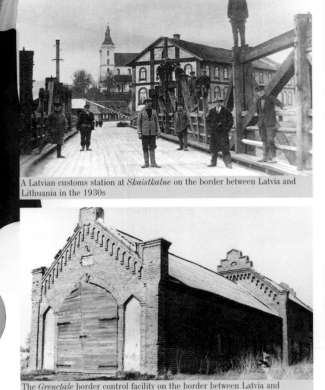

A Latvian customs station at *Skaistkalne* on the border between Latvia and Lithuania in the 1930s

The *Grenctāle* border control facility on the border between Latvia and Lithuania in the 1920s

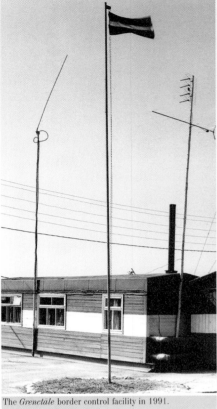

The *Grenctāle* border control facility in 1991.

The *Grenctāle* border control facility in 1999

The *Grebņeva* border control facility on the border between Latvia and Russia in the early 1990s

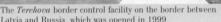

The *Terehova* border control facility on the border between Latvia and Russia, which was opened in 1999

The *Veclaicene* border control facility on the border between Latvia and Estonia

The director of the State Revenue Service, Andrejs Sončiks (left) opens the *Terehova* border control facility

The Latvian delegation at the 90th session of the Customs Co-operation Council in Budapest

In 1918, a Customs Division was established at the Ministry of Trade and Industry, and almost immediately thereafter, a customs station in *Liepāja* was opened. In 1921, a Customs department was established in the Ministry of Finance and the basic principles of the department's operations were defined.

The department had four divisions and employed 60 customs clerks. There were eleven customs stations in the country.

The Latvian Customs Service was renewed on 3 July 1990, by the Council of Ministers of what was then still the Latvian SSR. The first independent Latvian customs station was opened in the town of *Vientuļi* in the *Balvi* District on the Eastern border on 1 October 1990. Between 23 May and 12 August 1991, Latvian border control and customs control facilities were attacked no fewer than 23 times by soldiers from the Soviet Interior Ministry's special forces, known as the OMON forces. Even though no Latvian customs officials were killed (which was not the case in Lithuania) many were injured.

The Latvian Customs Code was adopted on 25 September 1991. On 2 June 1992, Latvia became the 114th country in the world to join the Customs Co-operation Council, which is the existing global customs organisation. In the same year, the European Union's PHARE program provided financing for equipment for several of the country's customs stations.

In 1993, the Law "On the State Revenue Service" created a unified tax administration authority in Latvia, bringing together Latvian Customs and the Finance Inspection.

The installation of a LAN computer network in some customs facilities began in 1995.

On 1 July 1997, a new customs law came into force in Latvia. It is fully in line with European Union standards. Co-operation agreements on mutual assistance on customs issues have already been signed with Finland, Lithuania, Estonia, Ukraine, Denmark, Sweden, Norway, Uzbekistan, the Netherlands, the United States, Belarus and Great Britain.

The duties of the Customs Authority are to protect the economic sovereignty and domestic market of the country, to protect society by monitoring the import of conventionally prohibited goods into Latvia, to collect customs duties, and to work with foreign customs administrations in revealing and preventing violations of customs regulations. The modernisation of Customs is aimed at establishing an organisation that can implement truly effective control over the customs procedure, promoting trade by simplifying customs procedures and introducing computerisation into the process. Systems must be improved, and skills in averting and preventing violations of customs regulations must be upgraded.

There are free trade zones at Latvia's three major ports. An infrastructure for border crossing points is being put into place, and there are three joint border crossing facilities. Automated data processing systems have been installed in some customs facilities on an experimental basis, and a computerised risk aversion system is also in place. Systems for financial guarantees and security deposit payments have been introduced. A council established to provide mutual consultations between the Customs Service and businesspersons is working effectively. It is chaired by the director of the Central Customs Administration. Members include various associations, chambers of trade and other organisations that are interested in customs issues.

The director of the Central Customs Board of the State Revenue Service, Aivars Krastiņš

Since 1998, all customs officials have been required to take an oath

Customs control at the Riga Free Port

Customs control at the Riga international airport, where modern X-ray equipment is used to inspect baggage

In 1998, PHARE funding allowed the Latvian Customs Authority to purchase state-of-the art laboratory equipment for the analysis of oil products, metals, alcohol and other products

The *Ainaži-Ikla* border control facility which is run jointly by Latvia and Estonia

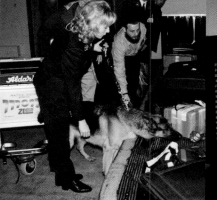
Passenger baggage at the Riga international airport is inspected by dogs that are trained to sniff out narcotics

Officers of Sanitary Border Inspection always work with customs officials

THE SANITARY BORDER INSPECTION

The Latvian Sanitary Border Inspection was set up in 1997 to protect Latvia's interests. It conducts veterinary, phytosanitary and hygienic monitoring of goods that arrive at the frontier of the country or that are in customs warehouses. By monitoring import, export and transit cargo, the inspection stops the entry of poor-quality products into the State.

The Sanitary Border Inspection inspects cargo that crosses the country's border at 26 control points along highways and railways, as well as at ports and 80 customs warehouses. Each year the inspectors look at some 340 000 loads of cargo. Particular attention is devoted to improving the process so that it can meet European Union requirements. Close co-operation is being developed with the other border-related services in Latvia – the Customs Authority and the Border Guard.

Laboratory tests in corresponding with European Union quality standards are carried out in *Rīnuži* Sanitary Border Inspection labs

Sanitary Border Inspection does goods' document, identity and physical control on highways, ports, airports, and railroads, in order to promote circulation of goods of quality within the state

THE RĪGA STOCK EXCHANGE
THE LATVIAN SECURITIES MARKET

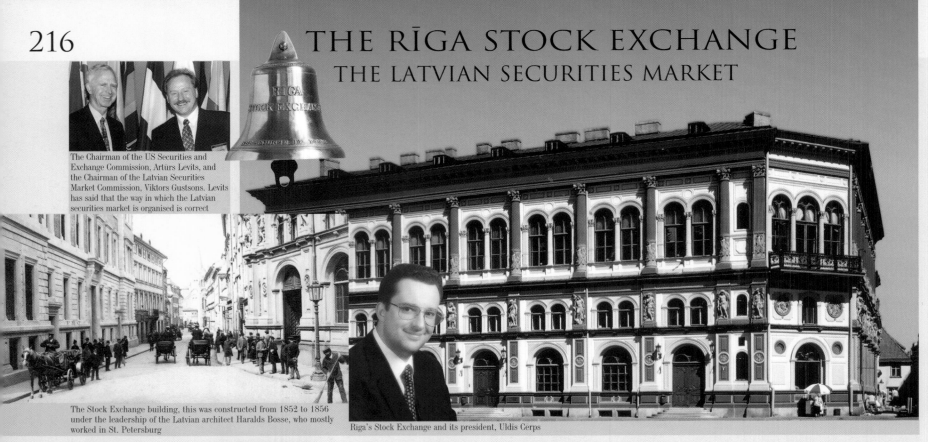

The Chairman of the US Securities and Exchange Commission, Arturs Levits, and the Chairman of the Latvian Securities Market Commission, Viktors Gustsons. Levits has said that the way in which the Latvian securities market is organised is correct

The Stock Exchange building, this was constructed from 1852 to 1856 under the leadership of the Latvian architect Haralds Bosse, who mostly worked in St. Petersburg

Riga's Stock Exchange and its president, Uldis Cerps

Members of the Securities Market Commission

Exhibitions at the Riga Stock Exchange allow people to become acquainted with the companies, which have securities on public offer

US President Bill Clinton visited the Riga Stock Exchange in 1994

A group from the United States Agency for International Development who worked at the Securities Market Commission in 1998

A gold memorial medallion for the Riga Stock Exchange

In September 1994, the Cabinet of the Republic of Latvia approved a Securities Market Development Concept, the aim of which was to ensure the pre-conditions necessary for the development of the Latvian securities market as an international financial market. The Government sought to introduce investor protection mechanisms that were in conformity with European Union requirements and to promote the development of a national capital market. In August 1995, the *Saeima* (the Parliament) adopted a law on securities.

The Latvian Securities Market Commission is a State authority, which promotes the development and stability of the securities market, protects investor interests and ensures that proper competitive conditions exist in the securities market. The *Saeima* adopted the law *On the Securities Market Commission* on 24 August 1995, and the Commission commenced opera-

tions in 1996. The decision-making institution of the Commission is its Council, the members of which are appointed for seven-year terms by the *Saeima*.

In 1997, the Securities Market Commission undertook co-operation with the International Organisation Securities Market Commissions, or IOSCO. At the 23rd annual meeting of the IOSCO in Nairobi, Kenya, on 15 September 1998, the Latvian Securities Market Commission was admitted as a full member of the organisation.

The Riga Stock Exchange (*Rīgas Fondu birža* – RBF) was established in December of 1993, and it held its first trading session in July 1995. The RBF has three securities lists – the Official List, the Secondary List, and the Free List, in which are quoted the securities of enterprises in accordance with the regulations of the RBF. In order to trade in the RBF, an intermediary company must become a member of the Exchange. In June 1997, in co-operation with the *Dow Jones* company, the RBF commenced calculation of the *Dow Jones* Riga Stock Exchange Index. The Index reflects the capitalisation of the market in lats and in US dollars. In 1998 the RICI index, which reflects changes in the market price of securities, was implemented.

The Latvian Central Depository (*Latvijas centrālais depozitārijs* – LCD) was established in January 1995. The activities of the LCD are based on the law *On Securities*, the LCD regulations and instructions, as well as other associated regulatory enactments.

Corresponding accounts at the depository are opened for those banks and brokerages, which

have obtained licenses to provide intermediary services in the public circulation of securities. The depository also opens special securities accounts for the emitters of securities - the Bank of Latvia (the Central bank), the Riga Stock Exchange, and the Latvian Privatisation Agency. It is also a task of the LCD to organise settlements among the holders of accounts.

The leaders of securities market supervision authorities from all three Baltic States sign a protocol of intent regarding co-operation between them

A meeting of the Council of the Securities Market Commission

Securities from the first period of Latvian independence, 1918-1940

The bull is a symbol of a growing market, and on the back of the bull is Viktors Gustsons

The Latvian Mortgage and Land Bank is located on Dom Square in Old Riga. Executive Board members are Jēkabs Krieviņš, Aija Laicane, Inesis Feiferis, Rolands Pānko and Juris Lujans.

The new offices of the Mortgage Bank's branch in *Valmiera* were opened in November 1999. Economics Minister Vladimirs Makarovs (center) was among those to attend

Bank president Inesis Feiferis at a map of Latvia: "The bank has branches in all of Latvia's districts. It provides credits to Latvian farmers and fishermen, as well as to small and medium enterprises."

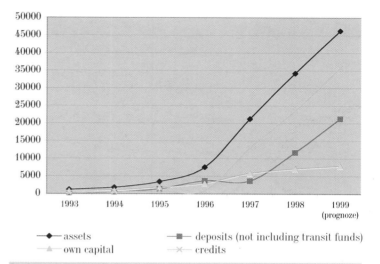

Development of the Mortgage Bank(estimate)

The Latvian Mortgage and Land Bank is the only State-owned bank in Latvia. Despite an assumption that in transition economies business activities by the State cannot be effective, the experience and activities of the Mortgage Bank proves quite the opposite. The bank supports small and medium business and provides mortgage loans – a process, which, thanks to Latvia's liberal land market – is a very promising area of activity. The Mortgage Bank is also involved in the process of the privatisation of housing by privatisation certificates. The rapid development of the bank is ensured by professional specialists who regularly undergo additional training in Latvia and in foreign countries.

The bank highly values the achievements of its clients. Each year some clients are selected on a competitive basis to go on information exchange trips. Here we see the winners of the competition in 1998 in Great Britain, at the Case International factory

The bank financed a project to build a new pier at the *Skulte* port, from which timber is exported. Among those attending the ceremonial opening of the pier in the summer of 1998, were President Guntis Ulmanis (right) and Transportation Minister Vilis Krištopans (second from left)

There are Mortgage Bank branches in every district centre in Latvia

INVESTMENTS AND SUPPORT FOR BUSINESS ACTIVITIES

INVEST-RĪGA

The *Invest-Rīga* auditing company was founded in 1991 as the first private auditing company in Latvia. *Invest-Rīga* is a member of the global association of independent auditing companies that is called BDO. It is the sixth largest association in the world. *Invest-Rīga* provides sworn auditing services, including servicing of bookkeeping accounts, evaluation of property values, preparation and evaluation of business plans, and consultations on tax, finance and other issues. *Invest-Rīga*'s clients include many State and local government institutions, as well as leading Latvian and foreign companies. *Invest-Rīga* helps to ensure a favourable environment for business activity, and it helps its clients to enter the Latvian economic process.

The deputy director of *Invest-Rīga, Dr. oec.* Dainis Tunsts, and the director, Professor *Dr. oec.* Andris Deniņš

Until 1991, insurance in Latvia, as throughout the Soviet Union, was a State monopoly. Latvia began to license insurance companies in 1991, when the State Insurance Division of the Finance Ministry had two employees. The first private companies began to emerge in 1991, but it was not until 1995 that the Insurance Supervision Inspectorate was established. By 1996, an accounting and book-keeping system that is in full conformity with European Union requirements was introduced in the insurance industry. In 1997 a law was adopted On Mandatory Civil Liability Insurance for Owners of Means of Transport, while in 1999 - the Insurance Companies and their Supervision Law, the Establishment of Private Pension Funds Law, and the law On Insurance Contracts. There were 29 insurance companies in the market (at the time of writing), eight of them life insurance companies and 21 – risk insurers.

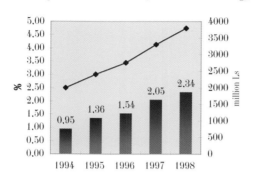

insurance premiums
as a percentage of GDP   GDP, million Ls

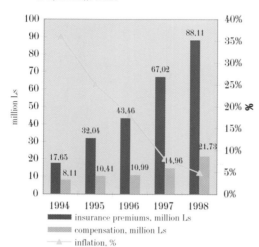

insurance premiums, million Ls
compensation, million Ls
inflation, %

The development of the insurance process in Latvia goes hand in hand with the economic situation and monetary policy. As can be seen in the graphs, the volume of insurance premiums grows in a geometric progression to the growth of GDP and in inverse proportion to inflation

The Latvian Insurance Supervision Inspectorate has issued 15 licenses to a/s Balta for various kinds of insurance operations that are appropriate both for private persons and for legal persons

The largest insurance company in Latvia is the insurance stock company *Balta*, which was founded in 1992 and was the first joint venture in the insurance sphere in Latvia. The company is a member of the Latvian Association of Insurers, and it has some 450,000 clients in Latvia and outside its borders. According to data from the Insurance Supervision Inspectorate, *a/s Balta* in 1998 controlled 19% of the non-life insurance market in Latvia according to gross premiums and 25% of the market according to paid compensation.

SC *Balta's* management restructured the enterprise as a public share company. In 1997, the first SC *Balta* public shares were issued, and on 3 September of the same year, the company's shares were quoted on the Riga Stock Exchange.

The central office of SC *Balta* is located in *Vaļņu iela*, where insurance companies have operated since the beginning of this century

Employees of the Insurance Supervision Inspectorate

The Insurance Supervision Inspectorate is an independent government administration authority that operates under the supervision of the Ministry of Finance and in accordance with the Insurance Companies and their Supervision Law. The director of the Inspectorate is appointed by the Cabinet, and at the time of writing, it was Gvido Romeiko. There are five people on the Council of the Inspectorate. There are 22 people employed in the Insurance Supervision Inspectorate in 1999, all of them graduates of a training course at the Chartered Insurance Institute. The Inspectorate issues licenses to insurance companies for the performance of insurance operations and private pension fund activities, it controls the activities of insurers and private pension funds, issues licenses to insurance broker companies, certifies insurance brokers, and registers insurance agencies and agents. Since 1998, the work of the Inspectorate has been fully computerised. The examination of complaints and claims from insured persons is a very laborious process.

The president of the SC *Balta*, Andris Laizans, with executive board chairman Ivars Muzikants and Council chairman Janis Medens

Services of ISC *Balta* are used by the largest companies in Latvia, Gunars Ķirsons has insured his construction operations, while one of the most beautiful women in the world, *Mis Globe* Ieva Bondare is a user of a health insurance card

Complex insurance for families has become very popular in Latvia

SC *Balta's* own capital (at the time of writing) is nearly 8 million lats. The main shareholders are the American investment firm *Vista Capitals Corporation, LLC & Development Capital Corporation Latvia, SC Bastions* and *Sampo Enterprises, Ltd*

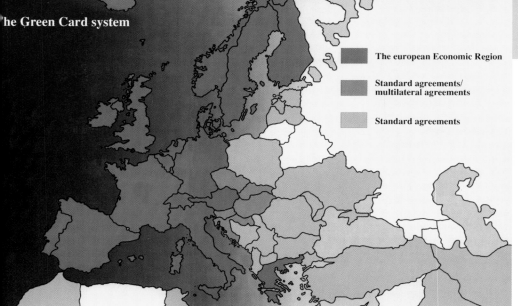

Pēteris Sliede, president of the Latvian Association of Insurers, and Ilmārs Veide, vice-president of the Association, at the 3rd International Conference *Insurance in the Baltic Region '99*

The Traffic Bureau of the Republic of Latvia was established in 1995. Its task is to establish a unified system of mandatory civil liability insurance in Latvia so as to protect the interests of people who have suffered injury as the result of traffic accidents and to ensure compensation for the losses occurred by them.

Latvia adopted a law on mandatory civil liability insurance for motor vehicle owners of land means of transport in 1997. With the coming into force of this law, the Traffic Bureau began to co-ordinate the activities of the mandatory civil liability insurance system throughout Latvia. At the same time, the Traffic bureau also organised Latvia's accession to the International Mandatory Civil Liability Insurance for Owners of Means of Transport System - also known as the Green Card system.

Latvia has established a unified database, which is still unique in Europe, based upon full information regarding all insured persons, and which mutually links several government authorities.

In 1998, the 32nd General Assembly of the Green Card system admitted the Latvian Traffic Bureau into the Green Card Bureau Council, thus making Latvia the 43rd country in the world to join the Green Card system. The Traffic Bureau now has the ability to defend the rights and interests of Latvian insured persons in other Green Card system member countries, and Latvian inhabitant interests in compensation for losses to those people who have been injured by other Green Card state drivers of means of transport in the territory of Latvia. It can also perform mutual billing procedures with other Green Card state national offices, and to conclude international agreements that serve the interests of drivers of means of transport.

Latvian Traffic Bureau(from left) Solvita Skore, Dzintra Isajeva, Oļegs Vovčenko, Baiba Gribuste, Gvido Janevičs, Guntis Pommers, Ieva Ziediņa, Igors Kiršbaums, Sanita Miezīte and Juris Stengrevics

The Latvian Association of Insurers is a public organisation that was established in 1993 and unites 19 Latvian insurance stock companies that control 95% of the total insurance market of Latvia. The purpose of the Association is to represent the collective interests of Latvian working insurers, to promote and protect free entrepreneurial activity in insurance, and to improve the insurance of natural persons and legal persons.

The main tasks of the Association are to participate in the drafting of laws that regulate the insurance industry in Latvia, to provide information to the public about various aspects of insurance in Latvia and abroad, and to co-operate with legislative, executive and local government authorities in Latvia, as well as with international insurance organisations. Since 1996, the Latvian Association of Insurers has been an associate member of the European Committee of Insurers.

Since 1997, the Latvian Association of Insurers has organised annual international conferences, *Insurance in the Baltic Region*, which bring together insurers, re-insurers, brokers and representatives of supervisory institutions from all over Europe.

Insurance Supervisionary Inspection

Participants at a meeting of Green Card Bureau representatives from the Nordic and Baltic countries in Riga on 26 October 1998. From the left: Tomass Köhler (Sweden), Jens Peter Tranberg (Denmark), Kai Doring Larsen (Denmark), Thorstein Iversen (Denmark), Roger Stenseth (Norway), Triin Sikemäe (Estonia), Yrjö Mäkikärki (Finland), Dzintra Isajeva (Latvia), Pentti Ajo (Finland), Gvido Janevičs (Latvia), Ulf Blomgren (Sweden), Leena Tervonen (Finland), Per Käre Herredsvela (Norway), Aurika Peleckaite (Lithuania), Vladimiras Žukovskis (Lithuania), Juris Stengrevics (Latvia) and Eugenijus Bulavas (Lithuania)

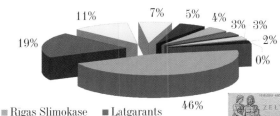

ISC *Rigas Slimokase* has four levels of voluntary health insurance policies: *Zaļā polise*, *Sarkanā polise*, *Sudraba polise*, and *Zelta polise* (Green, Red, Silver and Gold policies)

- Rigas Slimokase
- Latgarants
- BTA
- Rigas AS
- Rigas Fenikss
- Ezerzeme
- Balta
- Salamandra Baltic
- Balva
- others

The division of the health insurance market in Latvia. Almost half of the Latvian health insurance cases were insured by ISC *Rigas Slimokase*

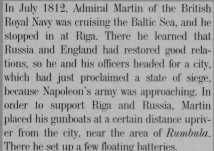

Post Office Branch No. 51 in Riga

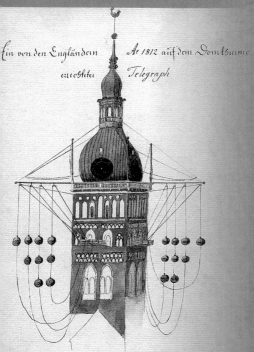

Ein von den Engländern At 1812 auf dem Domtourme erreichtet Telegraph

The telegraph on the Dom Cathedral tower that was installed in 1812. The drawing is by Johann Christoph Brotze

Postmen in Dom Square in the 1920s

Latvijas pasts' colour is yellow – which is the colour of postal vans, mailboxes, etc.

In July 1812, Admiral Martin of the British Royal Navy was cruising the Baltic Sea, and he stopped in at Riga. There he learned that Russia and England had restored good relations, so he and his officers headed for a city, which had just proclaimed a state of siege, because Napoleon's army was approaching. In order to support Riga and Russia, Martin placed his gunboats at a certain distance upriver from the city, near the area of *Rumbula*. There he set up a few floating batteries.

In order to provide for communications between his ships and the city, Martin ordered that a semaphore telegraph system be installed on the tower of the Riga Dom Cathedral (see illustration). Two horizontal poles were installed, from which four wires hung down. Large, black metal balls could be raised or lowered along the wires, and these were used for signalling purposes. Two platforms were built alongside the tower, and they were strong enough to carry several sailors who operated the telegraph. The black balls were made of ordinary woven baskets, covered with sail material and painted black. There were also four upright poles upon which flags could be raised.

The first semaphore telegraph was invented in 1791 by a French engineer, and high towers were built between Paris and Lille – a distance of more than 200 kilometres. Each tower was built so that the next tower would be visible from it. The towers carried high poles with three movable wings that were the actual semaphore. The wings were moved around to represent letters, numbers and other signs. Russia began to use the system in 1820, and what was then the longest semaphore telegraph line in the world was installed from St. Petersburg to Warsaw. It was 1,200 kilometres long and had 149 20-meter towers, each at a distance of approximately eight kilometres from the next. The telegraph line ran alongside the St. Petersburg-Warsaw highway, which had been built in 1836, and it crossed Latvia's territory, too. The foundations of one of the telegraph towers can still be seen on *Cauna* hill near the *Aglona* railway station in Latgale. The St. Petersburg-Warsaw telegraph line was used until 1874, after which it was replaced with an electric telegraph system.

The speed at which messages were transmitted along the semaphore telegraph was not very fast. A 100-character telegram took approximately half an hour to get from St. Petersburg to Warsaw. When it was dark outside or the weather was poor, the system could not be used at all. What's more, the text could be read by just about anyone who knew the system, because coding was not used.

What was then the first electric telegraph line in all of the Russian Empire went on line between Riga and *Bolderāja* on 1 November 1852.

The first organised postal services in what is now Latvia were established more than 360 years ago, during the reign of the Russian empress Catherine the Great. She established a line of messengers from her summer residence

Latvians usually send Christmas, New Year's and Independence Day cards, as well as birthday cards and cards marking other events

The *Smiltene* Post Office

A rural Post Office at *Branti*

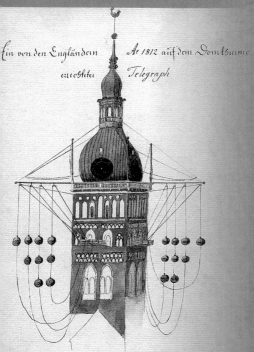

Training of electric telegraph operators

The horseback mail station at *Lizespasts*

Horse-mail post office of *Straupe* – the oldest post building in Latvia

A Mail railway wagon in 1924

in *Anniņmuiža* to St. Petersburg. All of the authorities that have ruled Latvia over the course of time have tried to set up a postal communications network. The Swedes, for example, had an extensive horseback mail network.

Between World War I and World War II, independent Latvia had its own postal system. Latvia joined the International Postal Union.

After the Second World War, the system was merged with telecommunications services, and Latvia became part of the Soviet system of communications. After the restoration of independence, postal and telecommunications services in Latvia were reorganised and split apart. In 1992, what is now known as *Latvijas pasts* (*Latvian Post*) was established.

BLS-Latvija Ltd. is a joint venture with the Swedish Post Office

The Latvijas pasts service network provides an information system that works throughout Latvia

The data processing centre

The placing of correspondence into envelopes (8,000 envelopes per hour)

Help was provided in early years by the Finnish postal service, which donated to Latvijas pasts several used Mercedes Benz trucks. Over the course of time, Latvijas pasts bought Mercedes Benz light cargo trucks, as well as Renault cars and trucks.

Postal services in Latvia are provided by the stock company Latvijas pasts, which has branches throughout the country – 30 or 40 Post Offices in each of the country's administrative districts. Some postal services are handled by companies licensed specifically for that purpose. The courier market, for example, is largely in the hands of such firms. Private firms have also become involved in the delivery of press publications. Because of the rapid increase in the number of press publications in Latvia, the number of magazines and newspapers delivered by Post Offices has also increased.

Latvijas pasts has paid a lot of attention to the development of information technologies and related services. In 1995, through co-operation with IBM and SWH-Riga, a Postal Accounting System was established. Latvijas pasts has established its own computer network and the stock company Latvijas pasta pakalpojumu tīkls. Joint ventures have been established: Latvijas elektroniskais pasts - a Latvian-Finnish joint venture that provides high-volume electronic data printing, placing in envelopes and sending services; BLS-Latvia – a joint venture with the Swedish Post Office, offers clients door-to-door package delivery services within Latvia and to foreign states. In 1992, the International Postal Union was one of the first international organisations to recognise the restoration of Latvia's independence, and admitted Latvia to the organisation as a full member. The Baltic Postal Union was established in 1994.

The first stamp after the regaining of independence was produced in 1991, and it featured an image of the Coat of Arms of Latvia. Since then Latvijas pasts has released more than 200 different stamps.

Latvijas pasts is gradually becoming a modern postal communications enterprise, which colleagues from other countries have visited to gain experience.

Packaging of letters on a KERN 2500 machine (12,000 envelopes per hour)

In the Post Office Branch No. 51 in Riga

Latvijas pasts representatives at an international philately exhibition in Stuttgart in 1997

Jonas Šalovejus (Lithuania), Tarmo Jaans Tieleids (Estonia) and Aivars Droiskis (Latvia) at the headquarters building of the International Postal Union

Aivars Droiskis (Latvia), Vassos Vasiliuss (Cyprus), Tarmo Jaans Tieleid (Estonia) and Jonas Šalovejus (Lithuania) at a meeting of postal administrators from Central and Eastern Europe

Postal workers learn about the computerised postal accounting system

The post office branch No. 50 in Riga

Krister Blumkvist, a vice president of the Finnish postal service, Mosibahu Mazu, deputy general director of the international bureau of the International Postal Union, and Latvijas pasts general director Aivars Droiskis in negotiations about the establishment of the Latvian-Finnish joint venture Latvijas Elektroniskais pasts

Latvijas Elektroniskais pasts is a joint venture with the Finnish post office. Here you see an electronic printer that prints out data entered by electronic means.

The accounting and bookkeeping staff

UPS has brought an invitation to the Sydney Olympic Games to the President of the Latvian Olympic Committee, Vilnis Baltiņš

Ilja Štolcers, head of the UPS Latvian office

UPS clients are found at the Ventspils port, too

United Parcel Service (UPS) is the world's leading transportation company, established in 1907 and with clients in more than 200 countries. The company handles more than 12 million shipments each day, and its turnover each year is at around 23 billion dollars. There are 52 UPS staffers in Latvia, complete with 20 trucks, a daily charter flight, and annual turnover of approximately USD 1 million. Latvia's UPS since 1992 has provided services that are fully in line with UPS's express services.

A UPS truck in the streets of Riga

A Commission chooses a location for the radio station at *Kuldīga* in 1933

The Latvian State Radio and Television Centre broadcasts radio and television programs, transmitting them from studios to transmitters, and also designing, organising and operating broadcasting systems.

A radio central was first set up under the auspices of the Transportation Ministry's Postal and Telegraph Department in 1924. Jānis Linters was appointed its first director. By 1940, the system had built broadcasting stations in Riga, *Madona*, *Kuldīga* and *Liepāja*. During World War II, when the Soviet army was forced to retreat from Latvia in front of the advancing German army, it tried to blow up the broadcasting station in *Madona*, but due to the actions of the staff at the station this failed. By 1945, however, only the station in *Kuldīga* remained intact; the Germans had destroyed all the rest.

In 1944, a Communications administration answerable to Moscow began the process of restoring the destroyed communications systems. Later the Latvian SSR set up a Communications Ministry, which supervised radio and television broadcasting and the operation and development of related technical systems.

Since 1996, the enterprise has been known as the non-profit State stock company *Latvijas Valsts radio un televizijas centrs* – LVRTC (*Latvian State Radio and Television Centre*). The Centre is wholly owned by the State, and it is supervised by the Ministry of Transport. At the end of 1999, the LVRTC employed 370 people. In accordance with its articles of association the basic areas of activity for the enterprise are the broadcasting of radio and television programs, maintenance of radio communications, installation of engineering systems, construction, design of radio systems, etc. The equity capital of the LVRTC at the time of this writing was 4.3 million lats. The economic activities of the Centre are based on income that is received in return for services provided on a contractual basis. The main clients of the Centre are *Latvian State Television*, *Latvian State Radio*, *Latvian*

The construction of the *Kuldīga* radio station's tower in 1934

The AM antenna-feeder system of the *Kuldīga* radio station

Independent Television and the commercial radio station *SWH Radio*. All of the enterprise's income is ploughed back into development and modernisation. At the time of this writing, 70% of the employees had a higher qualification in radio, television and communications. Since 1996, the general director of the LVRTC has been Maris Pauders. Stability of both work and personnel together with long-term development is characteristic of the LVRTC.

The LVRTC also manages Latvia's specialised telecommunications network, which contains 11 complex radio and television transmitters, three of which require no individual servicing. The Riga Radio and Television Station (RRTS) is connected to the others via microwave radio relay lines (RRL). The RRL consists of 23 relay stations with a total length of some 900 kilometres. Television programs in Latvia are broadcast via 46 transmitters of various capacities, in both the VHF and the UHF range. In 1999, four new TV transmitters were built with 20 kW exit capacity, as well as four smaller TV transmitters.

Radio broadcasts in the FM-2 band are transmitted via 42 FM transmitters, while AM programs are broadcast on six transmitters. There is also one short-wave transmitter. Between 1997 and 1999 the system was completely moved from the FM-1 band to the FM-2 band, which is used elsewhere in Europe. Many modern transmitters were acquired.

The LVRTC uses 28 TV antenna-feeder systems, 16 FM antenna-feeder systems and more than ten AM and short-wave antenna-feeder systems. More than 40 towers and masts support the antenna system, of which six towers and one mast are more than 200 meters in height, while 27 others are between 50 and 200 meters high. The modernisation of the system of TV transmitters and antennae is continuing. At the time of this writing, a DVB transmitter was soon to be installed in Riga, thus launching the age of digital television in Latvia.

LVRTC general director Maris Pauders

LVRTC technical director Maris Rutks

Zoja Ivaščenko, finance director of the LVRTC

The tower of the *Liepāja* radio and television station

A radio relay line tower in *Sigulda*

The *Rēzekne* radio and television tower

Uldis Rutks is the LVRTC consultant on business strategy and planning issues. He is an Officer of the Latvian Order of Three Stars.

Management and control systems at the Riga radio and television station

Management and control systems at the *Kuldīga* radio and television station

A short-wave antenna at *Ulbroka*

Television tower in *Zaķusala*, Riga (1986)

Satellite antennae at the Riga radio and television station on *Zaķusala* Island

The old pre-war radio tower of Riga

TV tower in *Cesvaines* RTS

Tower of radio-relay in *Sabile*

There are nine user service centers of modern standards in Riga and other cities in Latvia

TELECOMMUNICATIONS

Investment in telecommunications

Valmiera 4,0
Valka 3,2
Limbaži 0,9
Aluksne 0,6
Ventspils 16,2
Talsi 3,2
Cesis 10,3
Gulbene 1,7
Balvi 2,2
Kuldiga 10,0
Tukums 2,2
Riga 162,1
Ogre 4,6
Madona 1,0
Rezekne 5,6
Ludza 1,8
Saldus 5,5
Dobele 2,3
Jelgava 16,5
Aizkraukle 3,7
Preili 3,2
Jekabpils 4,3
Liepaja 22,4
Bauska 2,4
Kraslava 5,7
Daugavpils 12,5

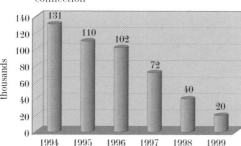

Employees of a network control center control the digital network of the entire country with the help of a special computer system, operating in Riga since 1997

Number of people waiting for telephone connection

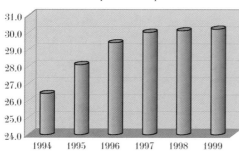

thousands

- 1994: 131
- 1995: 110
- 1996: 102
- 1997: 72
- 1998: 40
- 1999: 20

Number of telephone lines per 100 inhabitants

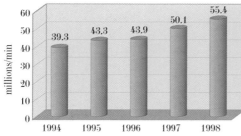

(scale 24.0 to 31.0)
1994, 1995, 1996, 1997, 1998, 1999

Outgoing international traffic

millions/min

- 1994: 39.3
- 1995: 43.3
- 1996: 43.9
- 1997: 50.1
- 1998: 55.4

Although Latvian telecoms network was the best in the Soviet Union, until 1993 it was developed along classical soviet model – a rapid increase in number of telephone sets regardless of quality. The structure of the national network was shaped according to the radial principle without bypass links or alternative channels. Only 0.8% of cables were glass fiber, while connection of international calls was arranged through an exchange in Moscow with intermediation of an operator. More than 146,226 people were waiting waiting for their telephone connections. After the reclaim of independence the development of infrastructure was recognised by the government of Latvia as the most important step toward securing of state independence and promotion of national economy.

Development of telecoms was given a preference. Telecoms in Latvia are handled by several operators. The operator of fixed-line, public telecoms network is the enterprise *Lattelekom*, which has monopoly rights to provide telecoms service in the net. In the field of mobile telecoms, there is a cell-type network operator – *Latvijas Mobilais Telefons* of NMT 450i and GSM mobile telecoms as well as *Baltcom*, providing service only in GSM system. Latvian fixed-line telecoms network is being transferred to digital lines, and there is an increase both in the total number of users and the users of digital system lines year after year. There is an increase of long distance calls in the public telecoms network every year. Inland long distance calls increase by 21.4% on average annually, while international calls by 5.7%. The increase is chiefly due to mobile telecoms. During the last few years, the number of cell-phone users has doubled every year. Cell-phone users against the users of fixed-line telephones have reached the proportion of 1 : 2.5. According to calculations done by international telecoms companies, Latvia will be in number one position in number of mobile telephones per 1000 inhabitants by 2006. Leader – the largest and oldest mobile telecoms operator in Latvia – is a Latvian, Finish, and Swedish joint-venture enterprise *Latvijas Mobilais Telefons*. The enterprise was founded on 2nd of January 1992, but the first mobile telecoms exchange was operational on 7th of October same year in Riga. The first established communications network in Latvia was a NMT-450 network. Since January 1995, a GSM-900 network is operational, a GSM-900/1800 network since December 1999. Years of dynamic development and evolving are characteristic to LMT

during the period in brief. A little more than 1000 users were registered in the first year of operation of the enterprise. At the present moment, that is an average of one week, while the total number of users exceeded 210000 at the beginning of March 2000. Thanks to roaming agreements, LMT users are able to use their cell-phones in

For more than two years new and up-to-date TELEcard phone-booths are found in the streets of Latvian cities. Their numbers reached 3200 by the end of 1999

182 networks in 76 countries around the world. Fixed-line telecoms operator *Lattelekom* is a monopolist in Latvia. As a result of an international competition, the government of the Republic of Latvia and *Lattelekom* Ltd. signed a contract in January 1994 with SC TILTS *Communications*, committed to invest USD 160 million in three years to upgrade the telecoms network in exchange for a 49% ownership of *Lattelekom* fixed capital. 90% stock of consortium TILTS *Communication* are held by a Finnish enterprise *Sonera Holdings B.V.* and 10% stock by an international financial corporation. In order to create a modern telecoms network, a secure network structure had to be created. Two international exchanges have been taken into service, a loop embracing whole of Latvia with optical fiber cables and cable lines joining Latvia, Lithuania, Estonia, Belarus, and Sweden have been built. 13 digital exchanges have been installed with a total capacity of 340400 numbers. *Lattelekom* provides service for 739049 telephone lines. *Lattelekom* has made enormous investments exceeding USD 485 million. *Lattelekom* provides telecoms services, teletext service, data transmission, lines for rent, and other telecoms services for individuals and companies.

Latvian telecoms market is expecting a liberalization in 2003.

The enterprise *Lattelekom* has drawn up a voluminous project of development, which contains technical solutions of network structure according with perspective technologies, quality, and other important directions. Far-sighted actions, emphasizing innovative solutions in developing customers service and new telecoms services will guarantee, that the enterprise evolves into a leading telecoms operator, able to provide telecoms solutions stimulating the development of business environment in Latvia.

An information hotline service 118 has gained a great deal of popularity during the three years since *Lattelekom* founded it in 1996. Operators of the hotline provide information on private and company telephone numbers, railroad and buss timetables, and other objects of social interest. 140 people are employed in the service.

The board of directors of *Lattelekom* in 1999. 1st row from left: Kristers Nikops, Indra Sāmīte, Gundars Strautmanis, Guntis Bērziņš, Tapani Holopainen; 2nd row from left: Arvo Kuko, Duglass Gustafsons, Ivars Biļinskis, Valdis Lokenbahs, Viktors Kulbergs un Kari Oitinen

This average size house in *Unijas iela*, Riga, once provided all the necessary office space for LMT employees. Now the enterprise has eight filial branches, not just in the capital, but also in *Ventspils, Liepāja, Daugavpils*

Latvijas Mobilais Telefons – at the very heart of telecoms – the international exhibition *Telecom'99* in Geneva, from left: marketing director Maija Ozola, commercial project manager Sandis Stibe, head of the department of commercial and public relations Ilze Rupkus, consultant in public relations Davids Dane, and chief executive Juris Binde

On LMT initiative and support, teams of hot-air balloon navigators from all over the world gathered for the fifth annual festival. Many festivities in Latvia have been brightened by the LMT balloon

The colorful arrangements of LMT stands have often received much attention in different exhibitions. The international telecoms exhibition *Baltic IT & T* spring 1999 was not an exception

The flag of *Latvijas Mobilais Telefons* waves in pride even in racing tracks. That is taken care by racers of LMT sponsored *Broceḗnu* motorclub and brothers Uģis and Ivo Traubergs in both local and international races

Eižens Ariņš, the first director of the Computing Center of Latvian University for many years

The Computing Center of Latvian University at the beginning of the *Age of information technology*

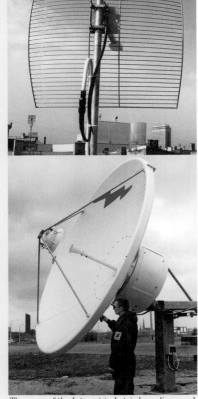

Internet in Riga via radio-antenna connection. The antennas is a common sigh in *Vecrīga* and the new sections of Riga by now

Internet cafe

Guntis Bārzdiņš, known as the father of Internet in Latvia, during a speech in *INET* conference in San Hose

An index of Latvian *www* resources

The users of the Internet in Latvia have discovered a convenient method of connection via satellite suited to the circumstances of Latvia. The method is now used to help Internet pioneers with their connection in Moldavia, Ukraine, and several African states

Latvian Internet companies compete with one another in quality and design in exhibitions of computer technology

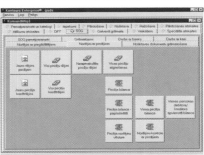

Kentaurs Enterprise home page

Research in the science of information technology in Latvia began with establishment of the Computing Center of Latvian University in 1959. Six month later, the Institute of Electronics and Computing of *LZA* (Latvian Science Academy) and the Faculty of Automatics and Computing Technology of Politechnical Institute of Riga were established. These institutions grew rapidly, many talented graduates of Latvian universities got involved with information technology, also the members of *LZA*, Janis Barzdiņš, Ivars Biļinskis, and Rusiņš Freivalds.

The Computing Center of Latvian University, founded and headed by Eižens Ariņš for many years (1959 - 1978), was the first of the kind in the Soviet Union. Later the center was turned into Institute of Mathematics and Information technology of LU. It is the most significant institution of research in the field in Latvia. Internet made its way into Latvia with the help of the institute in 1991, immediately after the reclaim of independence. Intensive research in the areas theories of algorithms, inductive synthesis, language and tool specification is being conducted (J. Barzdiņš, R. Freivalds, Andris Kalniņš, and others). The well known system modelling tool *GRADE* was also developed mainly in this institute.

The Institute of Electronics and Computing of *LZA* was one of the best research institutes in Latvia. The main direction of research was computer networks. The research previously done on the reception of discrete signals has proved to be valuable (Ivars Biļinskis and others). The research is now successfully being continued in cooperation with western universities.

The Faculty of Automatics and Computing Technology of Technical University of Riga is doing research in modelling of large systems, theory of system development, and artificial intelligence (Janis Osis, Arkādijs Borisovs, J. Grundspeņķis, and others).

A large share of the talented scientists got involved in fast-growing software development companies at the end of 90's. They explain most of the success of these companies in competing in western software markets. Information technology is a field of science, in which great achievements have been attained by Latvians in exile: Juris Hartmanis is a winner of *Tiuring Award* (an equivalent of *Nobel Prix*), the founder and the head of the Department of Computer Science of Cornela University (USA); Janis Bubenko, professor of Stockholm's University, one of the founders of the science of information technology in Sweden.

Internet is now spreading to every country town village. A satellite antenna for Internet connection attached to a water-tower of a small village

The developers of Latvian Internet network are helping with Internet connection in the Republic of Ghana, Africa

Commercials of the largest Latvian Internet companies is a part of the face of Riga by now. The largest operator *Latnet* is now in Central Station Square, *Apollo* by sponsorship of sports and cultural events, while *Delfi* made a confident entrance in the market in 1999

Latvia has had the prerequisites, which promote the development of information technology. Radio-technology and computers were developed in Latvia during the soviet times. A large amount of important research in electronics and physics was conducted in the Soviet Latvian Science Academy. Several industries of war and space technologies were placed in the Republic by the Soviet Union. The highly qualified labor to support this part of the infrastructure was trained mostly in Rīga, however the education was often continued in Moscow and other large centers of education in the Soviet Union. After the collapse of the union, there was a great potential of highly skilled and qualified researchers of electronics.

There were several large computing centers in Latvia at the end of the Soviet era, the main objectives of which was to carry out state orders of statistical analysis for the large industrial enterprises (calculations of salaries, for e.g.) and conduct scientific research. Personal calculators with an increasing capacity were used more and more frequently in the everyday life, making the calculation in the large centers a relatively ineffective and an expensive process, thus decreasing the amount and importance of their work. Around 1994, many companies had computers based on good i486 and the first *Intel Pentium* processors. Internet had already found its way to Latvia at the time. Both of these circumstances encouraged an explosive increase of interest in computers, Internet, and programming.

Larger software companies, e.g., *SWH Rīga*, *Tilde*, *IT Alise*, *Lursoft* – one of the first in Latvia to provide business information from data base, as well as companies specialized in accounting software suited for Latvia, were founded and developed. Manufacturers of computers were rapidly developing as well – *ELVA*, *ELKO*, *Capital Datoru Serviss*, *Fortech*, *VAR*, *Soft-Tronic*, providing training for network specialists in courses authorized by *Novell* and *Microsoft*. *Sylvan Prometric*, the first to provide authorized services of testing and certification in the Baltics. Considering *Lattelekom* monopoly on telecoms, the development of companies providing Internet services is very successful, and will probably be even more so after the period of this monopoly. The changes in the system of education are slower and the demand for qualified specialists considerably exceeds the supply at the moment. Besides, young and talented programmers often look for and find better paid jobs abroad. Companies of other countries like the good skills, the will to work intensively, and the low level of salaries of our labor.

Information on information-related topics can be obtained from the Internet on sites: *http://www.latnet.lv/* in the section *Internet* and *Computers*. All the companies mentioned can be found in this location. The best insight in Latvian art connected with the Internet and computer technologies are found on server *http://re-lab.net*. *DT Media group*, which organizes annual IT exhibition

and publish the respectable magazine *Datoru Pasaule*, site *http://www.dtmedia.lv* provides a good review of computer news. The slightly alternative site *http://search.lv* is also commendable.

Moscow was ruled by a slogan – *cybernetics is a fake science* – while computer science was started in Latvia in 60's

Instead, the SU made a slogan: the largest computer in the world – in the Soviet Union

Tilde – the largest software-producing company in Latvian, the creator of the Latvian Computer Dictionary – a dictionary of computer terminology

The largest exhibition of computer science and information technology in the Baltics takes place in Riga every year. *Canon* stand in the exhibition

Dzintars Zariņš, the chief executive of the Association of Latvian Computer-manufacturers

Inna Gudele – the director of *Appolo* Internet service

Dr. habit. mat. Agnis Andžans

The director of *ELKO Vecrīga*, Jānis Kaģis

The director of *IBM Latvija*, Aivars Traidass

The head executive of *Fortech* Ltd., Jānis Bergs

The head of the board of director of SC *VAR*, Aldis Puisitis

SC *Dati* is the largest private consortium in Eastern Europe, developing information systems. The companies of *Dati* provide services for clients: analysis of company management and computer modelling, software development, administration and maintenance of information systems, purchase of computers, data transmission, data-network design, set-up and utilization, computer training and consulting. 450 employees are engaged in *Dati* group, of which, 5 professors, 31 doctors of science. *Dati* quality is granted by the international certificate ISO 9001. The enterprise was given the *Trade Leader Club* awarded of *European Technology* in 1998. From the right: the commerce director of SC *Dati*, Ojars Krumbergs, the president of SC *Dati*, Valdis Lokenbahs

Different competitions in computer science of children and youths have become regular in Latvia, the young students will probably be teaching their parents in computers soon

The board of directors of the Association of Latvian Computer-manufacturers: Sergejs Simonovs (*Latinsoft*), Dace Vetra (*Microlink*), Dzintars Zariņš (chief executive of *LDRA*), Stella Ankrava (the vice-chief executive of *LDRA*), Jānis Bikše (*EET*), second row: Andris Patans (*ELKO*), Jānis Lelis (*Association of Latvian Telecoms*), Viesturs Zeldiņš (*Elva-1*), Egils Ginters (*LIS*)

The leaders in Latvia, like the rest of the world are PC system computers, which are used by almost all public institutions as well as the largest companies

The opening of *Microsoft* office in Riga – the ribbon is cut by Bo Cruse, the director of *Microsoft Baltija* and the president of *Microsoft Europe*, Michael Lacombe

The *Macintosh* system computers are used in Latvia more often that in the rest of Europe

The vice-general director of VID, Andris Anspoks, created the information system of the institution and customs

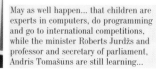

May as well happen... that children are experts in computers, do programming and go to international competitions, while the minister Roberts Jurdžs and professor and secretary of parliament, Andris Tomašuns are still learning...

THE LATVIAN EDUCATION INFORMATIZATION SYSTEM

The CD which describes the Latvian Education Informatization System (2nd edition)

The Latvian Education Informatization System is featured at the electronic addresses *http://www.liis.lv* and *ftp://ftp.liis.lv/macmat*. Many samples of teaching materials can be found there

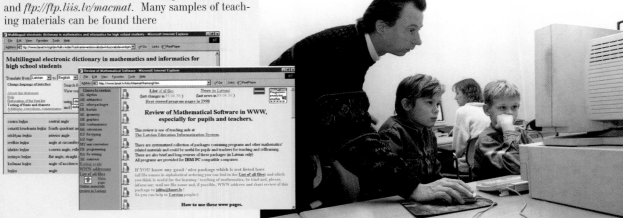

In the rational information field of mathematics, there are 56 different materials

Training of schoolchildren takes place in the computerclasses of the Latvian University. Uldis Straujums, the head of Information service LIIS provides his advice

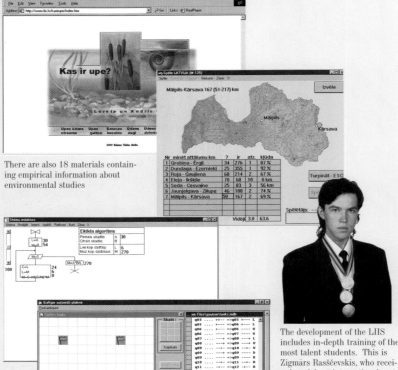

There are also 18 materials containing empirical information about environmental studies

Modelling information in informatics is contained in 34 materials

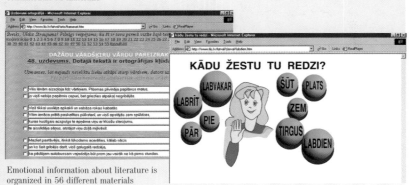

Emotional information about literature is organized in 56 different materials

The development of the LIIS includes in-depth training of the most talent students. This is Zigmārs Rasščevskis, who received medals at international mathematics Olympiads in 1997, 1998 and 1999. At this writing, Zigmārs is studying at the University of Latvia and working with schoolchildren to train them for their own Olympiads

Since the early 1980s, Software Designers Day has been observed in Latvia.
Here we see recipients of the Ada Lovelace and Charles Babbidge Prizes which are awarded on that day – Santa Sproģe, Atis Straujums and Līga Ramana

At the 9th international informatics Olympiad in Cape-town,
Renārs Gailis (left) won a silver medal, Jānis Sermuliņš took gold, and Krists Bitmanis received a silver medal

The 5th Baltic Informatics Olympiad in Riga in April 1999, which attracted competitors from Latvia, Lithuania, Estonia, Sweden, Finland, Poland and the United States

The Latvian Education Informatization System (LIIS in the Latvian acronym) is a national project which has been implemented since 1997. The aim is to improve Latvia's educational system with the help of the latest achievements in information technologies. The informatization process covers the infrastructure of the Latvian educational system, as well as all of the functions of the system – management, education, information services and – especially – the teaching of children who are handicapped. A network of pilots schools and regional centers has been developed to test various aspects of the LIIS structure – teaching materials and software. Teachers and course leaders have been trained.

Since 1999 Latvia has been providing for the informatization of the country's schools. Computer technologies are being purchased, teachers are being trained, curricula are being developed and the necessary management structures are being set up. Each school has at least one computer. Various aspects of the LIIS program can be found on the Internet (*http://www.liis.lv*), as well as in CD form. The implementation of the LIIS is coordinated by the University of Latvia, bringing together professors, instructors, teachers, students, schoolchildren and foreign specialists.

Since 1992, Latvia's schoolchildren have participated in global informatics Olympiads, and they have brought home two gold, five silver and 15 bronze medals.

A NETWORK OF PILOT SCHOOLS AND REGIONAL CENTERS IN LATVIA

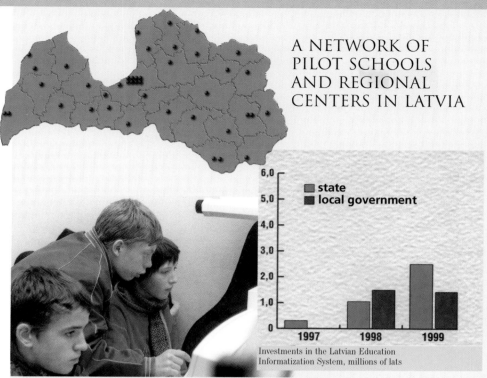

state
local government

Investments in the Latvian Education Informatization System, millions of lats

Children in Latvia learn computer skills for the earliest primary classes – often starting while they are still in pre-school. UNESCO research has shown that Latvia's children in the 7-10 age group are best in the world when it comes to using the Internet

Latvia's intellectual potential has been developed through activity groups led by scientists and academics at exclusive schools. This photo is of a mathematics and informatics study group at the Riga No. 1 high school in 1984, and its members have achieved a great deal. In the first row, from the left – Kārlis Čerāns, a docent at the University of Latvia who is a former member of Parliament; Daina Čodare, a docent at the Riga Technical University and leader of the group; and Agnis Andžāns, a professor at the University of Latvia. In the rear – Vilnis Sjomkāns, a senior programmer at Computerland; Jānis Liepiņš, director of the LETA news agency; Jānis Britāls, general director of the Latvian State Information Network; and Māris Detlavs, project director at Computerland

Institute of Mathematics and Computer Science
University of Latvia
Rainis boulevard 29, Riga, LV1459, L atvia   http://www.latnet.lv/LU/MII/

GRADE Modeler

GRADE web-site at http://www.latnet.lv/LU/MII/Grade is visited 20-30 times every day. Read more about GRADE, download and try a free **demo version**. If you are already using GRADE, you can download the most recent software update free of charge.

GRADE Modeler is a toolset for
- **Enterprise** modeling and simulation
- Business process engineering and **reengineering**
- Creating of extra **large blueprints**

GRADE Modeler is ideal as a toolset for business and management **consulting companies**.

GRADE Modeler covers all phases of system development life cycle before programming.

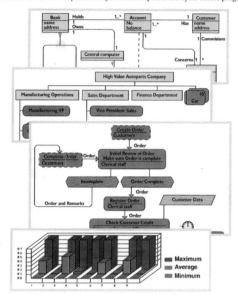

The GRADE system-modelling tool was developed in Latvia and is used around the world. Here we see the first page of an advertisement for the GRADE modeler

Latvia's team in the 11th global informatics Olympiad in Turkey.
From the left: Dr. Māris Vītiņš, head of the team; Arturs Žogla (bronze medal), Pēteris Paikens (bronze), Jānis Sermuliņš (gold), Dmitrijs Rutko (Bronze); and Mārtiņš Opmanis, deputy head of the team

More than 3,000 students from all over Latvia take part in Latvia's Open Mathematics Olympiad, which is held each spring at the University of Latvia

Dr. Andris Ambainis, who won many mathematics and informatics Olympiads in Latvia and who defended his doctoral dissertation in computer science at the age of 22 – on the day after he was graduated from the university. The dissertation has been published internationally and is often quoted as a reference

Two informatics experts: Latvian Academic Library director,
Prof. Edvins Karnitis, and Bill Gates shake hands, 1999

Venta Kocere is the Director of the
Latvian Academic Library since
January 2000

The director of the *Misiņš*
Library, Anna Šmite

The collection of rarities

Ex-libris by Rihards
Zariņš for Janis Misiņš

Librarian and bibliog-
rapher Janis Misiņš
(1862š– 1945)

In the reading room of the Manuscripts and
Rare Books Department of the *Misiņš* Library

The *Misiņš* library has a large and
comfortable exhibitions room

Johann Christoph
Brotze's "*Sammlung
verschiedener
lieflandischer
Monumente*"

There are nearly 2,000 libraries in Latvia, and among the academic libraries of the country the most distinguished one in terms of its history and collection is the Latvian Academic Library with the *Misiņš* Library as a separate structural unit, while among public libraries the most significant is clearly the National Library of Latvia.

In the 13th and 15th century, the first cloister and church libraries were established in Latvia. During the Reformation, in 1524, the first public library opened its doors in Riga. It is now the Latvian Academic Library. At first the library had just five religious books (four of which have survived) which the Riga City Council turned over for "general use". Today the library is one of Europe's oldest, and from 1524 until 1945, it was known throughout the world as the Riga City Library ("*Bibliotheca Rigensis*"). Most of its holdings were religious books, and most of those were in Latin. There were also books by medieval philosophers and ancient authors, as well as books about medicine and history. Initially the collection of the library was regularly supplemented through gifts. In the 17th century, for example, it regularly received dissertations from instructors at the Dom School and Gymnasium, as well as publications issued by Riga publishers and books bought from foreign traders. In 1941, the library, then housed in what used to be the Riga City Council, burned down. Of 400,000 printed works, only 46,000 were saved, and only because they were in safes. Today the collection of the Latvian Academic Library holds 3.1 million works, including 14,000 manuscripts and 32,000 rare books dating back to the 13th century – "*Psalterium Davidi*" (13th century), "*Missale Rigense* (14th century) and others. The library has several originals of the work of Martin Luther, as well as a unique collection of the work of J.K. Brotze, including the 10 volumes of "*Sammlung verschiedener lieflandischer Monumente*". The library also has Latvia's most extensive collection of incunabula (210 works).

The collection of the library is listed in bibliographic databases and electronic catalogues. In the new Information Technologies Department, users can work with the STN International Online databases and several specialised Internet databases to find the latest information.

The *Misiņš* Library has been a branch of the Latvian Academic Library since 1954. The *Misiņš* Library was Latvia's first scientific library, and it was founded in 1885 by a bibliographer and bibliophile called Janis Misiņš. He set himself the goal to collect everything that was published in Latvia, as well as publications from other countries, which had something to do with Latvia and the Latvians. In 1906, his library was moved from the *Tirza* Parish to Riga, and in 1925, it was turned over to the City of Riga. The library houses an astonishing wealth of national literature – books, periodicals, miniature printed works, photographs, audio materials, manuscripts – nearly 1 million items from all around the world. The distinguished poet Edvarts Virza put it best: "What is the Misiņš Library? It is the nation, turned into books and put upon the shelves."

The collection of the *Misiņš* Library of the
Latvian Academic Library

George Mancel's dictionary *"Lettus"* (1638)

The Latvian National Library, for its part, was established in 1919. Thanks to support from the State and the professionalism of the staff of the library, the collection of the library grew very rapidly, and international co-operation was soon developed. In 1922, the Latvian National Library concluded its first agreement on the exchange of books with the Prussian State Library. In the 1930s, a similar agreement was concluded with the Library of Congress in the United States, as well as the national libraries of Belgium, Portugal and other countries. During World War II, many of the valuable parts of the collection of the library were evacuated to Germany.

The collection of the Latvian National Library today contains 4.9 million documents in 60 languages, including 47,000 titles of ancient works and manuscripts. The library's holdings actually represent several different collections that were first acquired in 1918 – from the Royal Lyceum, the Riga Seminary, and the Alexander I Gymnasium. The centrepiece of the collection of the library is national Latvian literature. The *Lettonica* Fund contains 57,000 volumes, and it is the second largest collection of national literature in Latvia. Extensive bibliographic work has been done on the collection – establishment of bibliographic indexes, catalogues, a card catalogue and databases.

Among the most ancient and unique volumes in the library's collection are the Martin Luther Catechism (1586), and a church handbook from 1615 that was the first book in the Latvian language to be published in Riga. The library has a fine collection of incunabula (61 books) and 287 paleotypes.

In 1958, the library took over control of the Central Sheet Music Library, and now it has the largest and best collection of scores and musical literature in the Baltic States. In 1995, the Baltic Central Library, which was presented to Latvia as a gift by the Baltic German Otto Bong, was turned over to the Latvian National Library. At the time of writing the National library is scattered over nine buildings, and the need for a new library building has become actual. The Latvian architect Gunārs Birkerts from the United States has designed a new building, and plans are being made to build it on the Left Bank of the *Daugava*, opposite Old Riga.

The director of the Latvian National Library, Andris Vilks

Symbolorum et emblematum... centuria collecta by Joachim Camerarius (1534–1598)

The Scientific Medical Library was established in 1945, and it has nine branches all around Latvia. The collection of the library is used by more than 9,000 subscribers. Here, deputy director Velta Pozņaka, and physician and member of the *Saeima*, Andrejs Požarnovs, examine a part of the collection

The smallest book at the Latvian National Library

Reading rooms at the Latvian National Library

The card catalogue of the Latvian National Library

The library of the Riga Stradiņa University was established in 1951 on the basis of what had once been the library of the Medical Faculty of the Latvian State University. Today the library holds 351,594 volumes. Computerisation at the library began in 1991, and since 1995, readers have had access to the Internet. Here you see the main reading room of the library

Architect Gunārs Birkerts talks about his design for a new library building

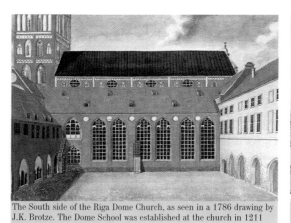
The South side of the Riga Dome Church, as seen in a 1786 drawing by J.K. Brotze. The Dome School was established at the church in 1211

The front of the Riga Imperial Lyceum (drawn in 1791 by Brotze). The building was built in 1787 after the old lyceum at St. Jacob's Church could no longer be used

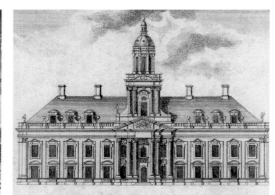
A draft of the building which housed the Academia Petrina in *Jelgava*, as designed by the architect Severine Jensen

The Riga State Gymnasium No. 1 is a direct successor to the congregational school at St. Peter's Church, and today it is with good reason considered to be one of the most prestigious schools in Riga. It specialized in the teaching of informatics and mathematics

Jānis Greste (1876-1951) was a very distinguished Latvian educator. It was he who in 1923 launched a movement against the old method of teaching and learning by rote in Latvia's schools

Ludvigs Ernests Bērziņš (1870-1965), an outstanding Latvian educator, folklorist, literary specialist, poet and author of children's books. He worked tirelessly to bring Latvian content into the educational process and to tend to the Latvian language

Judging from Scandinavian Rune stones, archeological findings and folklore, Baltic tribes in the 10th and 11th century already knew about reading and writing. There is no doubt that some Latvians could read Latin, Scandinavian or Slavic texts. There is indirect evidence that youngsters from noble families in the tribes of *Tālava* and *Jersika* had opportunities to go to school.

The first true school in the European sense of the word was founded by the Riga Dome Church in 1211. Lessons were taught in Latin, and the school trained clergymen. In 1631, when Sweden ruled Riga, a general high school was opened, and today's Riga No. 1 High School is the direct successor to that venture. The School of Mauritius was opened at St. Peter's Church in 1353, and it devoted more attention to secular lessons than did the Dome Church's school.

After the Reformation, schools where lessons were taught in Latvian were opened by St. Jacob's Church and St. John's Church in Riga. Schools were opened for children of all nationalities in several cities in Kurzeme (Courland).

Congregation-based schools began to emerge throughout Latvia during the rule of Sweden. Ernst Glück opened several schools for the children of farmers in 1683. Teachers and lay employees for churches were trained in *Alūksne*.

In the early 1730s, under the influence of a Hernhutian congregation, a noblewoman in *Valmiera* called Magdalena Hallart (1683-1750) opened a school at her baronial estate. In 1738 she also opened an institution to train teachers. The most distinguished achievements in education in the 18th century can be attributed to a Kurzeme clergyman known as Old Stenders. He published the first secular readers for children. Also of key importance was the Academia Petrina, which was opened in 1775 in *Jelgava*. One student from that university, Ernests Binemanis, went on to be the first person to fly in a balloon in *Jelgava*. In 1800 Tsar Pavel of Russia ordered that the academy be turned into a

university, and his son, Alexander I, moved the school to Tartu, Estonia, in 1802.

In the 18th century in Latgale there were several schools at which lessons were taught exclusively in Polish. A nobleman in the town of *Dagda* organized a school where the children of farmers could be taught, and they were instructed by a missionary.

School laws passed by the Russian Empire in the 19th century mandated that in any parish with more than 500 male residents there must be a school. A teacher training institute was opened in Kurzeme in 1833 and run by a Latvian called Andrejs Bergmanis. A second teacher training institution was opened in *Irlava* in 1840. Probably the most famous teacher training school, however, was the one which Janis Cimze opened in 1839 and ran for many years. Lessons there were taught in German. The Baltic Teachers Seminar was established in 1870, and there people studied in Russian. Teachers were also trained in *Valka* and *Ilūkste*. In the 1850s, increasing numbers of Latvians began to study at Tartu University. Around the 1860s Germanization was a key process in the development of Latvians, but in the 1880s the Russian tsar ordered that lessons in all schools must be taught exclusively in Russian. After the Revolution of 1905, these strictures were eased to a certain extent.

On the eve of World War I, there were 2,034 educational institutions in Latvia of various kinds, with 170,239 students and schoolchildren in attendance.

When Latvia's independence was proclaimed on November 18, 1918, Professor Kārlis Kasparsons was named the country's first Education Minister. At the same time in Latvia there was the Communist government of Pēteris Stučka, where the Education Ministry was run by a Latvian called Jānis Bērziņš-Ziemelis, and lessons were taught in the native language of the children who were present. Both the Ulmanis and the Stučka governments established the University of Latvia.

The first education law in independent Latvia was adopted on December 8, 1919. Six years of primary education and four years of high school were mandatory for everyone; minority nationalities enjoyed cultural autonomy at their schools. A system for the training of teachers was established in the early years of the new republic. Teachers institutes were located in Riga, *Jelgava*, *Daugavpils* and *Rēzekne*. The National Pedagogical Institute was located in *Jelgava*.

In the first year of Soviet rule, Russian became a mandatory subject in all schools, as did the history of the Soviet Communist Party and the constitution of the USSR. The teacher training institutes were closed down and many teachers were deported. Two pedagogical institutes were set up – one in *Jelgava* and the other in *Rēzekne*.

During the German occupation, the Nazis dictated the teaching of all subjects, but history and biology in particular. The point was to *demonstrate* the superiority of Aryans over other nations.

After World War II, Sovietization of Latvia's schools began in earnest. Russian language lessons became the most important subjects of study in Latvian schools, while the Latvian language in Russian schools was taught perfunctorily or not at all. The teaching of English and

Professor Janis Mencis wrote many textbooks in mathematics. Math is taught on the basis of a method elaborated by Professor Mencis in Latvia

Aivars Žogla (right), a physics and informatics teacher at the *Ugāle* High School in Latvia. His students have won awards in informatics Olympiads in Latvia and the rest of the world, and they have been successful in an Internet-based informatics Olympiad that originated in the United States – a true informatics superpower

Organizers of education in Latvia – Silva Golde and Oskars Spurdziņš

The outstanding educational organizer, Jānis Gaigals (right), served as Education minister in several governments in Latvia, and here he is seen with teachers at the trade school which he himself established

A meeting of the Education Ministers of the Baltic States in *Cēsis*, Latvia, on November 5, 1999. They signed an agreement on cooperation in the institution of a common educational space in the Baltic States

German all but disappeared.

At the end of the 20th century, the content and principles of Latvia's educational system are set out in a basic education standard which was issued in 1998 and a general education standard that was approved in 1999. Since 1999 specific programs have been instituted at various levels of the educational system.

Children can obtain a general secondary education in a variety of specializations – general education, the humanities, the exact sciences and professional studies.

In addition to high schools there are also state and local government gymnasiums which specialize in one or more subjects of study. Since September 1, 1999, they have offered a choice in educational programs.

Since the 1999/2000 school year, basic education programs for minority students have been introduced. Basic education can be obtained in the child's native language, in a bilingual system, or entirely in Latvian. The program ensures the ability of minority students to continue their education later in the national language, to be competitive in educational and professional processes, to be able to integrate into Latvia's society, but also to be able to preserve their national identity. There are also special educational institutions in Latvia for children

This elementary school in *Vecpiebalga*, named for the Kaudzīte brothers who were prominent 19th century writers, was open for more than 100 years but has now been shut down as the Latvian educational system moves toward larger schools

The *Valmiera* Gymnasium

The Brīvzemnieki High School in *Limbaži* District

The *Bauska* High School No.1 was built on the basis of a design by architect Jānis Neijs in 1930. During World War II the building was heavily damaged, and restoration began in 1949.. There used to be a small tower above the building for astronomical observations; it was not restored

The *Ieriķi* Elementary School. Schools built in the 1960s were completely identical all over the soviet Union

Instructors at the Pedagogy and Psychology Institute of the University of Latvia

The *Nīkrāce* Elementary School is modern in design, but functional in use. It features an energy savings system

The *Krāslava* Gymnasium. During the first period of Latvian independence, and especially in the 1930s, the government put an emphasis on the education of people in Latgale, and several gymnasiums were built

The *Iecava* High School is being reconstructed, and the process is being financed through a targeted loan from the World Bank

Nurses are taught at this Red Cross school in Riga

The St. Gregor School for Serving Christ in *Saldus*

The *Nigrande* High School. In the 1980s, the most beautiful and functionally comfortable schools in Latvia were built in those towns which had the richest kolhozes

The *Jaunsaule* School is being rebuilt with financing from a World Bank targeted loan

Professors A. Kruze and L. Žukovs study the history of pedagogy so that future generations can learn about it

Culture Minister Ramona Umblija presents an award to *Valmiera* Gymnasium student Rolands Puhovs for his creative work in photography

Teachers who are recipients of the Atis Kronvalds Prize at the Latvian presidential palace

Each year students are surveyed to find the most popular teacher of the year, and the winner receives the *Golden Pen* as a prize. Biology teacher Indra Vevere received the prize in 1999

Physics teacher Inese Lapiņa won the *Golden Pen* in 1996 and 1998

Geography teachers from Vidzeme have a change to visit the Alps in France during a summer internship. Here they are seen at the foot of Mont Blanc

Educational programs are designed at the Educational Content and Examination Center in cooperation with scientists and teachers from all over Latvia

Educational reform issues are discussed by Education Ministry employees, school directors and teachers

An international conference on mathematics teaching in the 21st century, organized by the Association of Mathematics Teachers

The Forum of Latvian Educational Leaders brings together active and erudite educational leaders from various levels of the system. In this image we see Latvian Educational Fund President Aldis Havinskis, Mārīte Grebzde and Zigfrīds Grinpauks

Geography teachers from Vidzeme on a tour of the ancient valley of the *Daugava* River

A market for methodological ideas in *Liepāja* in 1998

The Riga High School No.3 in Old Riga

German is taught at the *Agenskalns* Gymnasium in Riga by the principal of the school Sandra Sile. There are several schools in Riga where students can learn in-depth English, German and French, and the language skills of these students are often sufficient to allow them to study abroad after they are graduated from high school

Riga No. 1 Gymnasium teacher Maija Balode has received the *Golden Pen* award several times, and she has successfully trained students for international mathematics Olympiads. Here we see her with students on an excursion in *Mežotne*

Latvian students at an international biology Olympiad in 1997

Latvian students at the opening of an international chemistry Olympiad in 1999

Latvia's best mathematics students after the awards ceremony at a mathematics Olympiad in Bucharest in 1999

The best students at the *Valmiera* Gymnasium after an awards ceremony

with physical or mental handicaps. Such children can also go to general schools, where they receive the specific assistance which they need. In 1999/2000, there were 63 special schools and special education classes for disabled children in Latvia, and there were 10,077 children with special needs. 58 schools have special classes for handicapped children.

After the restoration of Latvia's independence, reform schools aimed at social and pedagogical instruction were also opened in the country. A reformatory for boys was opened in the village of *Strautiņi* in the *Alūksne* District.

Beginning in 1991, private schools began to emerge in Latvia. In the 1999/2000 school year there were 48 private schools, of which 39 had been accredited by the state.

Teachers have joined into 30 professional organizations. In the country's districts and in major cities, there are also organizations of teachers in various subject areas who meet to discuss methodological issues.

The work of educational institutions in districts and cities is supervised by local government school boards or education boards.

A conceptual document on education and a national program on education and science were adopted in Latvia in 1995, and the country's education law was updated in 1998. In 1999 Parliament adopted a law on general and professional education.

Until 1998 primary education in Latvia lasted for eight years, but since then it has been for nine years. Education is mandatory for children to the age of 18.

In 1997 the World Bank awarded Latvia a grant from the Japanese government for the preparation of an educational investment project. 1,150 educational institutions were studied, and on August 19, 1999, a loan agreement to finance the project was signed. The World Bank loaned the sum of US $31.1 million.

Since 1990 Latvia has participated in the EU's TEMPUS program. Between 1994 and 1999 Latvia has received approximately ECU 15 million, and 51 European joint projects have been financed, along with 19 compact event projects, 391 individual travel projects, and 13 youth exchange projects. Since the end of 1998 Latvia has also been an active participant in the EU's Socrates and Leonardo da Vinci educational programs.

Schools in Latvia are financed from the national and local government budgets. The state pays teacher salaries and covers some of the expenses of purchasing educational literature, while local governments are responsible for the remaining expenditures. Schools in Latvia lack money, teachers are poorly paid, and the process of educational reform which has continued for 10 years is still difficult to judge in terms of its directions and its developmental prospects. Even though reforms have taken places, teachers are continuing to leave schools in favor of other, more lucrative jobs. Still, the educational level of children in Latvia remains high. High school graduates have proven that they are competitive at universities around the world.

The educational level in Latvia is illustrated very well by the participation of children in international educational Olympiads. Latvia is a small country with just 2.5 million residents, but it very often brings home just as many medals from the events as do major Western European countries. Over the last 10 years, international educational Olympiads have been attended by 161 students, and they have brought home four gold medals, 15 silver medals, 55 bronze medals and 10 certificates of recognition. The winners of these Olympiads and their teachers also receive awards from the Latvian Cabinet of Ministers. The best teachers in Riga each year are awarded the "Golden Pen" award. There are similar awards in other districts and cities, too.

Schoolchildren traditionally work at the blackboard in Latvian schools, and the computer has not managed to take away the blackboard's role in the educational process

School directors

Chemistry lessons are usually based on lab experiments. The Riga High School No.3 features in-depth chemistry teaching

The Riga Gymnasium of the Humanities teaches the relevant subjects in great depth, and both because of this and because of the good foreign language skills of graduates, the school is seen as very prestigious

Parliamentary deputy Jakovs Pliners with first grade students on September 1 at Latvia's largest private school, *Evrika*

A poetry festival at the *Valmiera* Gymnasium

A textbook exhibition at the Ludis Berziņš Memorial Museum

President Guntis Ulmanis visits the Hansa High School on September 1. Schools in Latvia always open on September 1, and ceremonies are held to mark the fact. During the summer schools are renovated and cleaned up, and on September 1 various schools are visited by the president of Latvia and other important officials

Graduation at the *Lizums* Elementary School. Students graduate after the 9th and the 12th grade, and these are usually very beautiful ceremonies. Students receive their diplomas in the presence of teachers and parents. Afterward there is usually a party that continues until the sun comes up

Physical education is becoming more and more popular in Latvia. The Riga High School No.58 specialized in basketball. Students engage in athletic activities not only during physical education classes, but also on extracurricular teams

Latvia's educational program provides for the mandatory teaching of swimming skills. This is the pool of the Hansa High School

Teacher's Day at the *Valmiera* Gymnasium on October 1, 1999. Questions are being posed by a 12th-grade student, Aigars Berzs, and answers are being given by the deputy principal of the school, Janis Reinvalds

A 2nd-grade Christmas carnival. Latvian school traditions involve various *class evenings* where younger children play games and older students dance

An exhibition to mark the *Miķeļis Day* festival, which is a traditional autumn festival during which rural people look back at what they have accomplished during the summer. They evaluate their harvest, go visiting and have a good time. At schools in the countryside, students display vegetables which they have grown or arts and crafts that they have produced

A display of the work of an arts and crafts group at the *Valmiera* Gymnasium. Teacher Janina Gravere is at the right

A weaving group at the *Valmiera* Gymnasium

Work done by a group focusing on the applied arts at the *Valmiera* Gymnasium

Young people at the Riga Schoolchildren's Palace have fun with model automobiles

Students from the Riga Schoolchildren's Palace attended the European championships for remote control boats in Croatia in May 1997

International cooperation is developing, and Latvian children have an opportunity to go to other countries. Here we see students form the *Olaine* High School in Germany

Two times a year all schools organize excursions – once in the spring and once in the fall. The slogan for these events is usually *Travel Your Native Land*

Children demonstrate their ballroom dancing skills

A *fashion theater* at the *Valmiera* Gymnasium

A vocal ensemble from a children's and youth center, *Altona*

Girls from the Riga Schoolchildren's Palace play the traditional Latvian instrument, the *kokle*

In the 1990s beauty contests have become very popular in schools. Virtually all of the competitors in the Mr. and Miss *Gulbene*, for example, are high school students. Here we see the finalists at their school

The *Superboy* competition allows boys to compete in strength, agility, knowledge, organizational skills and computer skills

The dance and music club *Liesma* has a children's and youth dance ensemble, *Dzirkstelite*, and they are seen here on stage

Jānis Marcinkēvičs is the director of the folk dance group *Dzirkstelite*

An aerobics lesson at the Hansa High School. Competitions among aerobics teams are very popular

The *Olaine* College basketball team. Every school in Latvia has a basketball team, and basketball is the most popular sport in Latvia

A friendly game in volleyball between teachers and students at *Valmiera* High School

At the beginning of each year at the Hansa High School, new 10th graders undergo an initiation ceremony that is very much reminiscent of a carnival

A traditional form of entertainment for schoolchildren is streetball. Here we see a game behind the *Daugava* Stadium in Riga

Students in *Sigulda* learn to ski. Skiing is becoming increasingly popular in Latvia as the years go by

A school dance festival in *Alūksne* district, with young dancers parading through the town. Students from the Anna School are in the foreground. The school has singing and dancing traditions which are nearly two centuries old

The distinguished chamber choir *Kamēr* is made up of students from the Riga State Gymnasium No. 1. Conducted by Maris Sirmais, it has won a number of international prizes

A gathering of boy's choirs in *Cēsis*

Another winner of international recognition is the *Tonika* choir of the Riga Schoolchildren's Palace

Non-governmental organizations are very important in the area of children's rights. The National Children's Rights Defense Center, in cooperation with the Latvian national committee of UNICEF, organized a children's drawing exhibition and competition called *My Rights*

On January 1, 1999, there were 545,071 children in Latvia, or 24.5% of the Latvian population

On November 20, 1989, the General Assembly of the United Nations approved a Convention on the Rights of the Child, and on September 4, 1991, Latvia acceded to this convention. This document states that a child is any person until the age of 18. Children must grow up in families and in an atmosphere of joy, love and understanding if they are to develop fully and in a balanced way. As people who are physically and intellectually immature, children require particular protection and care. Any institution, including government institutions, local governments, companies, non-governmental organizations and individuals must focus on the needs of children in their work and everyday lives so as to ensure that the rights of children are observed.

When Eastern Europe began to rid itself of the burden of Communist ideology, it soon became bitterly clear that the transformation process, among other things, involved the exploitation of children, including sexual abuse and the involvement of children in pornography. Children were sold into these processes, and this happened in Latvia, too. Organized criminals from Russia and Belarus, and probably also in Latvia, sold boys and girls to Western Europe for prostitution. Initial attention was focused on this problem by a television program called *Nedēļa*, and law enforcement agencies have successfully sought to find those who are responsible. A parliamentary investigations commission was set up to investigate claims that high-ranking government officials were involved in pedophilia.

Latvia has taken all of the legislative, administrative and other steps which are needed to create a proper foundation for the protection of children's rights and the provision of a proper standard of living for them. A law on the rights of children was adopted in 1998. There are many institutions in Latvia which are involved in the protection of children's rights – the Subcommittee on the Protection of Children's Rights of Parliament's Human Rights Commission, the Cabinet of Ministers, the Welfare Ministry, the Interior Ministry, the Education and Science Ministry and the Justice Ministry. There are children's rights defense centers in Latvia's districts and cities, as well as custody and parish courts, district, city and parish social aid services, local government police institutions, health care institutions and educational and cultural institution. The first institution to deal with issues of children's rights is the appropriate local government institution at the place where the child lives. At the public level, however, the focus is on families, on non-governmental organizations and on all members of society.

Since 1999 the National Children's Rights Defense Center, which operates under the supervision of the Ministry of Education and Science, has been coordinating work in this area. The center monitors the extent to which laws and regulations in this area are fulfilled, and it also coordinates and manages various other aspects of protecting the rights of children.

The largest and most important children's rights organizations in the NGO sector are the Save the Children Foundation, headed in Latvia by Dr. Inguna Ebela, and the Latvian Children's Fund, which is chaired by parliamentary deputy Andris Bērziņš.

In 1999, for the first time, every schoolchild in Latvia received a pocket-format card, drawn by other children, containing information about where help can be obtained

The staff of the National Children's Rights Defense Center. In cooperation with NGOs and experts, the center has elaborated a national program to avert sexual violence against children. Latvia is the first of the three Baltic States to have such a program

Dr. Inguna Ebela, president of the Save the Children Foundation in Latvia

Andris Bērziņš, member of Parliament and president of the Latvian Children's Fund

"Baltais zvirbulis" (White Sparrow) is a public organization which works successfully with children and adolescents who are facing problems in their lives, including those who have come to the attention of the police

On September 4, 1999, the National Children's Rights Defense Center gathered children in Old Riga to focus national attention on the protection of children's rights. An interactive project allowed children to express their views about these issues on cardboard cutouts, to organize presentations, and to involve parents and grandparents in the process

The director of the National Children's Rights Defense Center since March 30, 1999, has been Ineta Ielīte

In 1999 there were 3,639 children who lived outside of families. The National Children's Rights Defense Center, in collaboration with the "Mrs. '97" club, launched a charity program called "You can do it" in 1999. Children learn to take care of themselves and to recognize their rights

PRE-SCHOOL EDUCATION

Children at the Riga kindergarten No. 91

The *Zilīte* pre-school in *Aizkraukle*

Pre-school education began to develop as a system in Latvia around 1910. The number of kindergartens in Latvia expanded particularly rapidly in the 1930s.

After 1990, there were 527 pre-school education institutions in Latvia, but today there are already more than 800 such institutions, reaching some 41% of children in the respective age group.

Pre-school education in Latvia is obtained both in these educational institutions and in families. During the Soviet years, the institutions were known as kindergartens, but after the restoration of independence people felt a need to change everything and to seek new ideals. General pre-school educational institutions, specialized pre-school educational institutions, pre-school education consultation centers, game groups and preparatory groups attached to schools all appeared in place of the old kindergartens. It must be said, in truth, that the general institutions may have changed their name, but nothing much has changed in their content. They are open to children from the age of 1 until the age when they begin school (but not past the age of 7). The 800 or so pre-school education institutions in Latvia today are attended by some 65,000 children.

The Education Ministry's pre-school education program is based on the idea that children must learn social skills and undergo other kinds of development. The institutions differ from one another in terms of the level and quality of education that is provided, but the ministry claims that there are various types of activities and 15 different teaching subjects at the schools. The true mission for pre-school educational institutions is to foster the individual development of children and to prepare them for school.

The content of learning has to do with the surrounding world. Children are given an opportunity to reflect their world through color, sound and movement. The Soviet approach was to prepare children for membership in the Communist children's organizations, but that approach has been changed. Today pre-school institutions are more focused on helping chil-

dren to learn about themselves, to express themselves through various creative activities, and to develop contact skills, tolerance and compassion for others. Children are taught both individually and in small or larger groups.

Lessons in pre-school institutions in Latvia are available both in Latvian and in Russian, and since 1990 there have also been pre-schools where children learn in Polish, Lithuanian and other minority languages. Children in non-Latvian schools are taught the Latvian language. In the late 1990s Russian and other minority parents very often demonstrated a desire to send their children to Latvian pre-schools so that children might learn the national language from the very beginning.

Dance lessons for pre-school children

At the Riga kindergarten No. 91

A folk dance ensemble, *Uguntiņa* (Little flame), hosted by the Riga Schoolchildren's Palace

Pre-school children often enjoy physical activities, and some pre-schools even have miniature swimming pools

For 30 years the popular children's musical ensemble *Dzeguzīte*, run by Daila Martinsone, has been a joy to young and old alike. Many former participants of *Dzeguzīte* go on to become professional musicians. In the center of this photograph is the distinguished Latvian composer Raimonds Pauls, who has always been faithful to the boys and girls of *Dzeguzīte*

Children from the *Zilīte* pre-school in performance

Lego games are a good way to encourage the imagination of children through exciting and interesting practical activities

Children from the Riga kindergarten No. 91 spend all day playing interesting games and engaging in fun activities

ZELTA KAMOLĪTIS (THE GOLDEN BALL OF YARN)

Children in Latvia go to schools where lessons are taught not only in Latvian, but also in many minority languages. The *Zelta kamolītis* competition is meant for national folk dance groups from the various schools. Children learn about the traditions, songs, dances, cuisine and festivals of other nations at the event.

THE JANIS ROZENTĀLS COLLEGE OF ART

The Janis Rozentals College of Art is a high school in which students receive an in-depth education in various areas of the arts. Children from all over Latvia attend the school, and many continue their studies at the Latvian Academy of Art

Talented children at the Janis Rozentals College of Art study drawing and painting.

Young people at the Janis Rozentals Colege of Art also learn about computer design

Latvia's system of professional education is based on the UNESCO-approved international standardized education classifier (ISCED) and the European Union's system for evaluating professional qualifications (CEDEFOP). The mandatory content of professional education programs is specified in the state's professional education standards, as well as in standards which are issued by the relevant professional organizations. Professional mastery competitions are one of the ways in which students demonstrate the quality of their skills, and these are very common events in Latvia, always attracting a great deal of interest and recognition.

THE EMĪLS DĀRZIŅŠ SPECIALIZED MUSIC HIGH SCHOOL

There is a network of music schools in Latvia, and the achievements of students from these schools in international competitions attest to the high professional level which prevails at the school. The Emils Darziņš school was attended in their time by such prominent musicians as Valdis Zariņš, Ieva Graubiņa, Ilze Urbane and Baiba Skride, as well as the globally known Gideons Krēmers and Mikhail Maiski. The flute player who is shown above is the scion of a dynasty of musicians, Ieva Rutentale, who has studied at the Dārziņš school and has done very well in international competitions

THE JĀNIS MEDIŅŠ SCHOOL OF MUSIC

Students demonstrate their skills in concert at the end of a school year

THE TRADE SCHOOL

Students here learn to use the tools and techniques of days gone by, learning about the traditions of woodwork and making copies of antique furniture

The *Krēsls* (Chair) competition at the Riga Trade High School gathers together young men with skills in furniture making. Logically, competitors are asked to make a chair

Students in the Textiles Department of the school have access to four workshops where they learn weaving, handicrafts, knitting, sewing and fashion design

In the Wood Processing Department students learn to produce and restore furniture in various styles of woodworking

The orchestra of the Mediņš School of Music in Riga has sent many outstanding musicians to symphony orchestras in Latvia and the rest of the world

SCHOOL OF CHOREOGRAPHY

Students at the Riga Trade High School learn their skills by working with very modern equipment

The winners of the "Chair" competition in 1998.

GLOBE

The non-governmental organization known as the Environmental Protection School is popular in Latvia. Students who are interested in ecology and environmental protection are brought together at the global level by the GLOBE organization. In Latvia students worry about the cleanliness of the Baltic Sea

Students at the Riga School of Choreography study under the leadership of Juris Kapralis, who has taught such legendary ballet stars as Mikhail Baryshnikov, Maris Liepa and Alexander Godunov

THE OLAINE COLLEGE OF MECHANICS AND TECHNOLOGY

The student government of the college participates actively in organizing various activities at the school

Young bakers learn their skills with joy

Food product inspectors of the future learn how to determine the content and quality of good. Here a student is testing the quality of chocolate

Students at the college often work in the yard of the school

THE BULDURI GARDENING HIGH SCHOOL

The Bulduri Gardening High School was established in 1910 by Peteris Dindonis, and it is the only school in Latvia where students can learn about gardening, flower growing, landscape art and plant design. Today the director of the school is Andris Turks.

THE MURJĀŅI RESIDENTIAL SPORTS SCHOOL

The *Murjāņi* Residential Sports School is the place where Latvia's leading athletes are trained. The school has been in operation for 35 years and is located in a beautiful place on the shores of the *Gauja* River. Each year the school hosts between 150 and 180 students who train in track and field, volleyball, handball, bicycling and other sports. The school has an affiliate in *Jūrmala*, where boat racers train.

Teacher Guntars Gailītis with discus throwers Dace Ruskule and Maris Urtans, formerly students at the school, at a school awards ceremony

The *Murjāņi* school as photographed by former student Gunars Dukšte, who was a well known athlete at the Soviet level and who took this picture from his hot air balloon

Teachers Ernests Pūce and Janis Veide, as well as the principal of the school, Ivars Sprancis, have trained bicyclists who have won medals in the Olympic Games, the Goodwill Games, and adult and junior world championships.

INTEREST-BASED EDUCATION

Education in Latvia is provided at state, local government and private educational institutions. There are 70 children's and youth centers with 87,700 participants, 61 sports schools with 41,700 students, and 132 art and music schools with 17,700 students. This means that 42% of the country's children are receiving an interest-based education. Nearly one-half of students in general education schools, moreover, participate in at least one club, activity group, dance collective, choir or orchestra, which means that they make good use of their free time. Language learning groups and groups focused on the applied and visual arts have become particularly popular. The favorite sports of Latvian students are basketball, track, volleyball, orienteering, soccer and technical sports of various kinds.

The National Youth Initiative Center, which operates under the auspices of the Ministry of Education and Science, organizes festivals for brass bands, theaters, choirs and visual and applied arts groups from Latvia's schools, as well as the Latvian School Youth Song and Dance Festival, which each time gathers together some 30,000 participants.

THE PROFESSIONAL CAREER SELECTION CENTER

The Professional Career Selection Center has been in operation for 12 years. People can receive consultations on educational and professional choice issues. In 1999 the center received 16,000 visitors, mostly 9th-grade students and unemployed adults. Among the center's employees are psychologists and professional choice consultants, who help clients to learn more about themselves and the determine their compatibility with various professions. Since the beginning of 2000 the center has also been offering informational seminars on the educational system and educational opportunities in Latvia, as well as a program of professional self-determination. The center also organizes specialized seminars and publishes informational literature about educational opportunities.

THE UNIVERSITY OF LATVIA

The building of the University of Latvia was built in 1869 after a design by the architect Gustav Ferdinand Alexander Hilbing.

Students at the University of Latvia launch each new study year with the *Aristotle Festival*, where new students are initiated

The rector of the University of Latvia, Juris Zaķis

Leaders of the University of Latvia on the steps of the university at a ceremony held to mark the school's 80th university. Ancient traditions hold that everyone must enter and leave the university via the two curved staircases that are alongside the straight-forward one at the building's front entrance. The only exception to this rule is that someone who has just graduated or defended his or her dissertation may go down the straight steps.

Students at the Faculty of Management and Economics of the University of Latvia

The University of Latvia was opened on September 28, 1919, in a building which used to house the Riga Technical Institute. The university was the first place in the world where a higher education could be obtained in the Latvian language. Between 1919 and 1940 the university was Latvia's leading center for education, science and culture. In 1999 there were 30,205 enrolled students at the university.

THE RĪGA TECHNICAL UNIVERSITY

Dorm area of Technical University in *Ķīpsala*

Rector of RTU Ivars Knēts

Assertion of diploma in the Faculty of Architecture by Oskars Redbergs who took part in an international competition on renewal of Sarajevo

Profesor Juris Saulitis and asociate professor Maija Šeinfelde with graduate magisters

The Riga Technical University is the oldest institution of higher learning in Latvia, dating back to the privately run Riga Technicum, which was founded in 1862 and taught engineering, chemistry, agriculture, mechanics, trade, surveying and architecture. In 1896 the school was reorganized and became the state-run Riga Technical Institute. After the establishment of the independent Latvian state, the school was turned into the University of Latvia. The Riga Technical Institute was renewed in 1958, and since 1990 it has been known as the Riga Technical University.

Today the university has 30 institutes which are joined together in eight faculties – Architecture, Automation and Computer Technology, Construction, Energy and Electric Technologies, Engineering Economics, Chemistry Technology, Machinery, and Radio Technology and Communications. The faculties and institutes are divided up into 133 groups of professors. The university has branches in other cities in Latvia – a learning science center in *Daugavpils*, a scientific and technical complex in *Liepāja*, and an engineering department in *Ventspils*.

THE RĪGA SCHOOL OF ECONOMICS

The prestigious Riga School of Economics was founded in 1993 by the Stockholm School of Economics and the Latvian Ministry of Education. The school trains economists, and students from all three Baltic States attend. Lessons are taught in English, and most graduates pursue post-graduate study opportunities in Sweden or the United States. The students are also in high demand in the job market.

VENTSPILS UNIVERSITY

Ventspils University was founded on July 23, 1997, teaching economics, management (which, in turn, allows students to specialize in finance management, marketing management, bookkeeping and auditing, and logistics), and translation (with specialization in Latvian-English-Russian and Latvian-German).

VIDZEME UNIVERSITY

Vidzeme University was established in 1996 in cooperation with a university in Lillehammer, Norway. Students can pursue degrees in political science, economics, tourism and public relations. In the photo we see Queen Sonja of Norway during a visit to the school.

THE LATVIAN ACADEMY OF CULTURE

The Latvian Academy of Culture was founded in 1990 as the first new institution of higher learning in the new state. In 1999/2000, students studied cultural theory, history and management, intercultural communications, the sociology of culture, folklore and traditional culture, and cinematography at the bachelor's level, and cultural theory and cultural management at the master's degree level. There were 650 students. The academy also offers a doctorate in cultural theory and history.

THE LATVIAN AGRICULTURAL UNIVERSITY

The Latvian Agricultural University is located in *Jelgava* and was founded in 1939 on the basis of the Faculty of Agriculture of the University of Latvia. The university has seven faculties – Agriculture, Economics, Technology, Veterinary Medicine, Rural Engineering, Food Technology and Mechanization. The total number of students in 1999/2000 was 7,393. Academic personnel numbered 420, including 46 people with habilitated doctorates and 117 with doctorates.

FRATERNITIES

Fraternities in Latvia date their history to Tartu University in the 19th century. Fraternities were outlawed during the Soviet occupation, but they remained active among Latvians in exile and were renewed in Latvia after 1990. Today there are a number of academic fraternities in Latvia. Here we see the *Fraternitas Lataviensis* fraternity at a ceremony to mark its 70th anniversary.

HIGHER EDUCATION

Today 3.1% of Latvia's residents are students. In the late 1930s Latvia had the highest proportion of students in all of Europe, and in 1939 it had the highest proportion of residents with a higher education. In the late 1990s Latvia tried to renew these traditions. In the last five years of the millennium, the number of students in Latvia increased three times – a faster pace than ha been seen anywhere in Europe in the last 30 years. In 1998/1999, there were 76,620 university students in Latvia, of whom 67,992 (88.7%) were attending state-run institutions of higher learning and 8,628 (11.3%) were at private universities.

The Higher Education Council at *Ventspils* University

The higher education strategy in Latvia is overseen by the Higher Education Council, members of which are appointed for four-year terms by Parliament. The council organizes cooperation among universities, government institutions and the public in pursuit of the further development of higher education in the country.

The network of regional universities in Latvia is expanding. The Riga Technical University has affiliates in *Liepāja* and *Ventspils*, where students can study customs and business issues, among other things. Vidzeme University is located in *Valmiera*, and one of the country's most prominent universities is in *Ventspils*.

The state supervises and accredits universities, and a program of student loans has been launched.

The rector of the Banking University, Baiba Brigmane, the chairwoman of the Higher Education Council, Baiba Rivža, the rector of the Christian Academy, Skaidrīte Gutmane, and the rector of *Rēzekne* University, Irena Siļiņeviča

On April 11, 1997, Latvia and 42 other countries signed the Lisbon Convention on the mutual recognition of qualifications in higher education. In 1999 the director of the Latvian Academic Information Center, Andrejs Rauhvargers, was elected president of the European Network of Information Centers (ENIC).

Since 1999 Latvia has been a participant in the EU's 5th Framework research and technology development program. Since 2000, Latvia and other EU member and associated countries have participated in the EU INTAS program and in several projects of the EUREKA program.

Latvia, Lithuania and Estonia recognize each other's educational diplomas. In the center of this photograph is Andrejs Rauhvargers, president of the European Network of Information Centers

TURĪBA

The *Turība* university helps unemployed people to learn new skills, especially in those professions that have to do with informatics

The leaders of the *Turība* university – Ilvars Forands, Aigars Rostovskis and Juris Birznieks – with Education Minister Silva Golde

Students at *Turība* can learn to become waiters or tour guides

The *Turība* Business University was founded on July 5, 1993, and licensed in 1995. All of the study programs at the university are now accredited. Today the number of students in the Faculty of Business Management, the Faculty of Law and the Faculty of International Tourism is 2,100. Since 1997 the school has worked together with master's degree programs at foreign universities, and 46 master's degree students have obtained an MBA through an international distance education program. Since 1997 the commercial school of the university offers a general secondary education specializing in business, and this is attended by 112 students in the 10th to the 12th grades. The school also cooperates with the National Employment Service, and some 7,000 unemployed people have taken courses in business operations and business management, advertising and trade, restaurant services, etc.

People have been doing scientific research in Latvia since the times of the Reformation. Initially the work was done by individual scientists, but organized science began to emerge in Latvia in the 18th century. The first center for science was the Academia Petrina university which was founded by the duke of Courland in 1775. Many important scientists worked at the university at that time. A professor of natural sciences there, Jakob Ferber was a member of the academies of science of Sweden, St. Petersburg and Berlin. A mathematics professor, Wilhelm Beitler was a member of the academies of St. Petersburg and Berlin, as well as the Swiss Scientific Association. His successor in *Jelgava*, Georg Magnus Paucker, was a correspondent member of the St. Petersburg Academy of Science. Scientists in Latvia had very close relations with that institution, which was founded in 1724 by Tsar Peter the Great and officially opened one year later by Empress Catherine I, who was of Latvian origin. Among the first presidents of the academy were noblemen from Kurzeme – Keiserling, Korff and Brehwern. The cornerstone of the library of the St. Petersburg Academy of Science came from the library of the dukes of Courland. Peter the Great ordered the transfer of that library to St. Petersburg.

Tartu University was opened in 1802 and quickly became a very important center for higher education and science for Latvia and Estonia alike. A Latvian pharmacist who became the rector of the new Tartu University, David Hieronym Grindel, established the Riga Association of Chemists and Pharmacists in 1803. The Kurzeme Association of Literature and Art was established in 1815, followed in 1822 by the Riga Society of Practicing Physicians, in 1834 by the Association of Researchers of History and Antiquity of the Baltic Provinces, and in 1845 by the Riga Association of Natural Researchers.

The Kurzeme Association of Literature and Art had 1,124 members in all between 1815 and 1915, among them the distinguished researcher of Latvian culture, Dr. August Bielenstein (1826-1907), the famous linguist Jakob Grimm, the history professor and adviser to Kaiser Wilhelm V, Theodor Schumann, linguist Ferdinand Wiedemann, and Kiel University history professor Karl Schirren, among others.

Theodor Grothuss (1785-1822) wrote his classic work *On the chemical nature of light and electricity*, which is still recognized as the earliest important work in photochemistry, in Latvia and presented it to the Kurzeme Association of Literature and Art on November 6, 1818.

Later important scientists worked and did significant research at the Riga Technicum, which was established in 1862 and renamed the Riga Technical Institute in 1896, and at the University of Latvia, which was founded in 1919.

Scientists from the St. Petersburg Academy of Sciences did a lot of work in studying Latvia's nature, territory and nation in the 18th and 19th century. Among the members of the academy (which was later the Russian Academy of Sciences), there were some 70 specialists who were born in or studied in Latvia. Particularly important among them were the chemist Pauls Valdens and the linguist Jānis Endzelīns. Krišjānis Barons received support from the academy for the publication for volumes 2-6 of his collection of Latvian folksongs.

Several scientists from Latvia were members of the Leopoldina Academy of nature researchers in Germany – physicians B. Fischer, E. von Bergmann, Z. Amstler, R. Adelcheim, F. Neureiter, V. Ķikuts, natural scientists J. Ferber, K. Panders, E. Eichwald, K. Kupfer, chemists Wilhelm Ostwald and Pauls Valdens, geologist E. Kraus and zoologist E. Strandt. One of the leading lights in the history

of world chemistry was Nobel Prize recipient Ostwald (1853-1932), who was a chemist from Riga. P. Valdens was a member of the scientific academies or equal institutions of St. Petersburg, Germany, Geneva, Goettingen, Paris, Sweden and Finland.

Scientists who were born or worked in the Baltic States enjoyed significant international prestige, and an undeniably important factor in ensuring this was the fact that the Baltic region played a transit role in the transfer of scientific ideas between the Russian and German empires. The Baltic region was an intellectual bridge between the East and West of Europe, allowing new scientific ideas and technical innovations to flow into Russia from the West, and ensuring a concentration of specialists in the three Baltic provinces, especially at Tartu University.

The Knowledge Commission of the Riga Latvian Association (1869-1932) brought together ethnic Latvian teachers, civil servants, members of the free profession and students who were interested in knowledge and who were dedicated to the preservation of Latvian culture. Among the members of the commission there were such scientists as linguists Kārlis Mīlenbahs, Jānis Endzelīns and Pēteris Šmits. The commission was the first center for the humanities in Latvia, and it was an ancestor of the Latvian Academy of Sciences. The importance of the commission in Latvia's academic life is evidenced by the fact that its members collected 40,000 Latvian folk songs that were submitted to Krišjānis Barons, and they also published important collections of folk stories, legends, riddles, traditions and sayings.

The commission published books and helped to organize, under the leadership of Matīss Siliņš, the Latvian Open-Air Ethnographic Museum. A scholarship fund was set up to support Latvian students. The publication of a monumental dictionary by Mīlenbahs and Endzelīns was supported financially (Mīlenbahs published four volumes between 1923 and 1932, and Endzelīns was their editor).

An unquestionably important contribution to Latvian science which was made by the Riga Latvian Association was the encyclopedic *Conversational Dictionary*, which was published in 22 volumes during the first period of independence (war put an end to the project – the last entry in Volume 22 concerns the Italian painter Giovanni Tiepolo). The association also organized an exhibition of Latvian ethnography during the First Professional Latvian Art Exhibition, which the Knowledge Commission organized during a Russian archaeology congress in 1896.

In 1932 the Riga Latvian Association set up a Science Committee and charged it with collecting, systematizing and researching materials about Latvia's nature and the Latvian language, history and culture". Membership was open to professors and senior docents from the University of Latvia, other people with a doctorate or a master's degree, and distinguished scientists and writers.

Andrew Dietrich Loeber, Jānis Graudonis, Elmārs Grēns, KC director, Jānis Stradiņš, SA president, Juris Upatnieks, candidate of Nobel Price, Edmunds Lukevics, Jānis Lielausis, Jānis Krastiņš

Georg Friedrich Parrot (1767 – 1852), naturalist, medic, physicist, TU professor (1827 – 1840) and rector (1831 – 1833)

Pēteris Šmits (1869 – 1938), Latvian linguist, etnographer un folklorist, LU professor (1920 – 1938)

Swante Arrhenius (1859 – 1927), physicist, chemist, astrophysicist, recipiant of the Nobel Price (1903), worked in RPI, since 1912. g. honorary member of RPI

Karl Blacher (1867 – 1939), chemist technologist, professor of RPI and LU

Painted by Auseklis Baušķenieks *Wilhelm Ostwald and Paul Valdens in Riga 1887.* (1987), is now found in Technical University of Riga, Faculty of Chemistry and Technology

Pirss Bols (1865 – 1921), mathematician, professor of RPI and LU

Erchard Bricke (1877 – 1953), technologist of chemistry and metallurgy, associate professor of RPI (1906–1918), academician and vicepresident of SA of the USSR (1936 – 1939)

Karl Adam Bischoff (1855– 1908), chemist, professor of RPI (1887–1908)

August Toepler (1836 – 1912), physicist, RP professor of chemistry

Engelbert Arnold (1856 – 1911), electrotechnologist , associate professor of RP (1880 – 1891), later Rector of Karlsruhe Technical University

Charles Clark (1867 – 1942), ship building specialist, associate professor of RPI and LU (1898 – 1942, professor since 1902)

Theodor Kalep (1866 – 1913), engineer of aviation, associate professor of RPI (1895 – 1913), the founder of the factory *Motors*

Maximillian Glasenapp (1845 – 1923), chemist, associate professor of RPI un LU (1870–1923), professor since 1878)

The period between 1940 and 1945 was a time of fateful changes in Latvia's history, as well as in her sciences, especially insofar as Baltic German scientists were concerned. In 1940 and 1941 the Soviet Union killed or deported many Latvian scientists, among them professors Julijs Auškaps, Ludvigs Adamovičs and the noted statistician Marģers Skujenieks, all three of whom were shot. Professors Juris Plaķis, Ernests Birkhāns, Pauls Mincs, Edgars Rumba, Kārlis Dišlers, Kārlis Ducmanis, Longins Ausejs, Pēteris Stakle and others were deported to Siberia and died while there. Several scientists died during the Nazi occupation, too. In fear of the return of the Soviet terror, no fewer than 60% of the instructors at the University of Latvia and the Academy of Agriculture fled to the West in 1944 and 1945. After World War II, the Soviet Union sought to "re-educate" distinguished scientists in the spirit of Bolshevik criticism and self-criticism. Among those who were affected by this campaign were members of the Academy of Sciences – linguist Jānis Endzelīns, medic Pauls Stradiņš, chemist A. Ķešans, biologist P. Galenieks, agricultural specialists Pēteris Apinis, J. Apsītis, Pēteris Rizga and Paulis Lejiņš, literary specialists J. A. Jansons and A. Birkerts, architects Ernests Štālbergs and P. Bērzkalns, etc. In 1949 and 1950 attention was turned to a number of academicians who initially had supported the Soviet regime, including Augusts Kirhenšteins, Andrejs Upīts, Jānis Peive and Matvejs Kadeks.

On November 4, 1945, the Soviet government decided to establish the Academy of Sciences of the Latvian SSR. The first members of the academy were linguist Jānis Endzelīns (1873-1961), geographer Matvejs Kadeks (1897-1950), forestry chemist Arvīds Kalniņš (1894-1981), microbiologist Augusts Kirhenšteins (1872-1963), architect Arturs Krūmiņš (1879-1969), agriculture specialist Pauls Lejiņš (1883-1959), swamp researcher Pēteris Nomals (1876-1949), agricultural chemist Jānis Peive (1906-1976), medic Pauls Stradiņš (1896-1958), biochemist Aleksandrs Šmits (1892-1978), architect Ernests Štālbergs (1883-1958), writer and literary specialist Andrejs Upīts (1877-1970) and philosopher Pēteris Valeskalns (1899-1987).

Between 1946 and 1951, 16 research institutes were founded, and in 1947 a magazine of the Academy of Sciences was established. In 1951 the academy opened a publishing house. Specialized magazines included one on chemistry which was launched in 1961 and which in 1990 became known as *Latvijas Ķīmijas Žurnāls* (Latvian Chemistry Magazine), and one on physics and technology, which was first published in 1964 and since 1991 has been published in English under the title *Latvijas Journal of Physics and Technical Services*.

In 1965 three of the Soviet Union's central scientific magazines were published in Riga – one on magnetic hydrodynamics, one on chemistry and one on polymer mechanics. After 1967 all three of the magazines were translated and published in English by the Plenum Press and the Consultants Bureau in New York.

Contacts with Latvian scientists in the West were all but completely cut off. It was only in the summer of 1966 that, on his way back from an international congress on crystals in Moscow, the distinguished chemist and professor Mārtiņš Straumanis could meet with

Arfreds Vītols (1878-1945), a specialist in hydraulics and a docent and professor (after 1924) at the University of Latvia (1919-1944)

Alvils Buholcs (1880-1872), a specialist in geodesics and a docent at the Riga Technical University (1904-1919) and a professor at the University of Latvia (1920-1944)

Pauls Lejiņš (1883-1959), an agriculture specialist and professor who was the first president of the Academy of Sciences of the Latvian SSR (1946-1951)

Antons Birkerts (1876-1971), writer and literary specialist

Pēteris Birkerts (1881-1956), folklorist and literary specialist

Gustavs Vanags (1891-1965), an organic chemist who was a professor beginning in 1939

Aleksandr Nikonov (1918-1995), agriculture minister of the Latvian SSR until 1959 and later the president of the Agricultural Academy of Sciences of the USSR and an advisor to Mikhail Gorbachev

Arvīds Kalniņš (1894-1981), forestry specialist and docent and professor at the University of Latvia and the Latvian Academy of Agriculture

Alfreds Ieviņš (1897-1975), chemist, academician of the Academy of Sciences of the Latvian SSR (1960)

Mārtiņš Straumanis (1898-1973), physical chemist and docent and professor (after 1939) at the University of Latvia (1925-1944), later a professor at the University of Missouri in the United States

Arthur Shawlow (1921-1999), an American physicist with Latvian roots who in 1981 received the Nobel Prize for his investment in the development of laser spectrology

Edgars Andersons (1920-1989), a historian who was a professor at San Jose University in the United States beginning in 1957 and in 1988 was named an honorary member of the Latvian Academy of Sciences

Uldis Ģermanis (1915-1997), historian and foreign member of the Latvian Academy of Sciences after 1992 who lived in Sweden after 1945

Tālis Millers, a chemist and member of the Latvian Academy of Sciences (1992) who was president of the academy between 1994 and 1998 and vice president after 1998

Nikolai Vedernikov, chemist and member of the Latvian Academy of Sciences (1992)

Ernests Foldāts, a biologist who lived in Venezuela after 1948 and was an instructor at the Central University of Venezuela. He did research on orchids and became a foreign member of the Latvian Academy of Sciences in 1994.

Dr. Raita Karnīte, an economist and director of the Institute of Economics

Benjamiņš Treijs, an economist and an honorary member of the Latvian Academy of Sciences (1990)

Raimonds Valters, chemist and member of the Latvian Academy of Sciences (1992)

Andrejs Siliņš, a physicist who became a member of the Latvian Academy of Sciences in 1992 and has been the general secretary of the academy

The *Irbene* radio telescope with a diameter of 32 meters

Dr. Andris Buiķis, mathematician and member of the Latvian Academy of Sciences

The nuclear reactor of the Latvian Institute of Physics in *Salaspils*, long the center for nuclear physics research in Latvia but shut down in 1999

242

Andrew Dietrich Loeber, a law professor who has been a foreign member of the Latvian Academy of Sciences since 1990 and received the Grand Medal of the academy in 1995. He lives in Germany

Juris Upatnieks, a physicist who works in America, laid the foundations of holography and is a foreign member of the Latvian Academy of Sciences (1991).

Laureats of the Tiuring Award, mathematicians Rusiņš Freivalds (right), a member of the Latvian Academy of Sciences since 1992, and Professor Juris Hartmanis, a professor at Cornell University and a foreign member of the Latvian Academy of Sciences (1990).

Ivars Kalniņš, a chemist and member of the Latvian Academy of Sciences since 1994 and its Senate since 1998

Mārtiņš Beķers, a biotechnologist and member of the Latvian Academy of Sciences since 1978 and its Senate since 1998

Dr. Elmārs Blūms, physicist, academician of the Latvian Academy of Sciences and director of the laboratory of the University of Latvia's Institute of Physics

colleagues in Rīga and read four lectures to them. He also published an articles in several magazines. In October 1966, at the Institute of History, historian Uldis Ģermanis presented a paper on the way in which the battles of the Latvian Riflemen were presented in the Swedish press of the time. Upon returning to Sweden Ģermanis published an emotional book about Latvia called *Zili stikli, zaļi ledi* (Blue glass, green ice), which so irritated the Soviet authorities that for many years he was prohibited from visiting the country of his birth. Other scientists who were invited by the Academy of Sciences to visit Latvia in the 1970's and 1980's to deliver lectures or to engage in joint research projects included computer scientists Imants Freibergs, psychologist and folklore specialist Vaira Viķe-Freiberga (who spoke about the processing of Latvian folk songs with the help of a computer), historians Eduards Andersons and Andrievs Ezergailis, linguist Velta Ruķe-Draviņa, engineer Andris Palejs, chemist Andrejs Dravnieks, writers Velta Toma and Mārtiņš Ziverts, and a few other of the more notable representatives of Latvian science and culture abroad.

After the restoration of Latvia's independence, the first Western Latvians to be elected as members of the Latvian Academy of Sciences were the historian Edgars Dunsdorfs, Vaira Viķe-Freiberga, Andrievs Ezergailis, Uldis Ģermanis, political scientists Rasma Šilde-Kārkliņa, oncologist Jānis Kļaviņš, Velta Ruķe-Draviņa, religious historian Haralds Biezais, Baltic philologist Valdis Zeps, mechanics specialist Jānis Dundurs, physicist Jānis Melngailis, informatics specialist Juris Hartmanis, biologist Jānis Skujiņš, surgeon Kristaps Zariņš, economist Gundars Ķeniņš-Kings, biotechnology specialist Andrejs Daugulis, astronomer Dainis Draviņš, literature specialist Lalita Muižniece, microbiologist Uldis Streips, chemist Edvīns Vedejs, economist Juris Vīksniņš, and medic Vitauts Kalniņš.

After World War II, scientists in Latvia engaged in a variety of research which gained wide recognition and was extensively quoted abroad. Today scientists in Latvia are working in many more areas, but in Soviet times there were some who were known around the world. Ivars Knēts and Aleksandrs Malmeisters did research on composite materials. Physicists Igors Kirko, Jānis Lielpēters and Jurij Mihailov proposed new ideas and research methods in heat physics and magnetic hydrodynamics. Pjotr Prokofyev worked in nuclear physics and Kurts Švarcs – in solid state physics. Computer network design and measurements in the construction of information transformation systems were developed by Eduards Jakubaitis and Vladimir Popov. Semi-conductors were constructed by Voldemārs Apsitis, Alfons Kroģeris, Vikorija Baumane and Andrejs Valdmanis. Jānis Peive researched ways of increasing agricultural output. The development of microbiology in Latvia was largely in the hands of Mārtiņš Beķeris, Uldis Viesturs and Romāns Kārkliņš. Fundamental work in organic chemistry was done by Marģers Lidaka, Edmunds Lukevics, Jānis Stradiņš and Solomon Hiller, while Elmars Grēns and Gunars Čipens worked in bio-organic chemistry and biotechnology. Arvīds Kalniņš, Pjotr Odincov, Varvara Sergejeva and Valeri Gromov worked with wood chemistry. Histori-

The president of the Latvian Academy of Sciences since 1998, Jānis Stradiņš (right), who has done fundamental research in organic chemistry and the history of science, together with his son, Professor Pauls Stradiņš. The Stradiņš family is one of the rare families in Latvia where the highest level of scientific recognition has been received by three generations of scientists

ans Jānis Zutis, Vasilij Doroshchenko, Henrihs Strods, Jānis Stradiņš, Aivars Stranga, Saulvedis Cimermanis, Boļeslavs Brežgo and others have broadened the understanding of Latvia, and philosopher Maija Kūle has expanded public interest in the humanities.

Today scientific work in Latvia is organized and led by the Latvian Academy of Sciences. Its president at this writing is academician Jānis Stradiņš. Work is also done at the University of Latvia, the Latvian Medical Academy, the Latvian University of Agriculture and other universities.

Professor Jānis Priedkalns, a professor of anatomy and histology and a neuroendocrinologist, has researched the effect of brain centers on the endocrine system and is the author of more than 50 publications

Professor Nikolajs Balabkins, an economist who has been a foreign member of the Latvian Academy of Sciences since 1991 and heads the foreign section of the academy. He lives in the United States

Literature specialist Valters Nollendorfs became a foreign member of the Latvian Academy of Sciences in 1990 but has since returned to live in Latvia

Egons Lavendelis, a mechanics scientist, has been a member of the Latvian Academy of Sciences since 1989 and a member of its Senate. In 1994 he received the Great Medal of the academy. He is a long-term rector of the Riga Technical University

Viktors Hausmanis, literary specialist and a member of the Latvian Academy of Sciences since 1989. He has served as the chairman of the Humanities and Social Sciences Division of the academy

Jānis Kristapsons, informatics specialist, advisor to the president of the Latvian Academy of Sciences and corresponding member of the academy (1995)

Chemist Jānis Freimanis, a member of the Latvian Academy of Sciences since 1992

The foundations for the Latvian Academy of Medical Sciences were laid in 1999. This group of scientists visited the prime minister. From the left: Professor Kārlis Arons, Professor Haralds Jansons, Professor Iveta Ozolanta, Academician Anatolijs Bļugers, Academician Jānis Stradiņš (president of the Latvian Academy of Sciences), the rector of the Latvian Academy of Medicine, Professor Jānis Vētra, Prime Minister Vilis Krištopans, Academician Vija Kluša, Professor Uldis Vikmanis, Professor Ludmila Vīksne, Academician Jānis Volkolakovs, Professor Juris Leja and Professor Jānis Gaujens

Haims Kordonskis, mathematician and a specialist in the theory of probability

Boris Plotkin, mathematician and professor who did research in the algebra theory of automated systems and data bases

Moisejs Finkelšteins, a radio location specialist and professor who did research on the subsurface radio location

Kalvis Torgans, a law specialist and a member of the Latvian Academy of Sciences since 1997. He has served as the chairman of the academy's Supervisory Council

Ivars Knets, rector of the Riga Technical University and member of the Latvian Academy of Sciences who has done research in biomechanics and biomaterials

Oļģerts Krastiņš, academician at the Latvian Academy of Science and professor at the Faculty of Economics and Management. He has also served as the director of the laboratory of the Latvian Statistical Institute

Professor Raisa Deņisova, director of the Anthropology Division of the Institute of Latvian History, University of Latvia, and honorary member of the Latvian Academy of Sciences

Linguist Aina Blinkena, a member of the Latvian Academy of Sciences (1992) and its Senate

Pēteris Zvidriņš, economist, a member of the Latvian Academy of Science (1992) and its Senate. He has researched demographic and labor resource problems in Latvia and the rest of the world.

Biologist Elmārs Grēns, a member of the Latvian Academy of Sciences (1987), who in 1995 received the Great Medal of the academy for his research in molecular biology

Vija Kluša, medical scientists and member of the Latvian Academy of Sciences (1992) and its Senate. She specializes in pharmacological research.

Vera Rudzīte, medical scientist and member of the Latvian Academy of Sciences (1994) who researches the metabolism of triptophane

Chemist Gunārs Duburs, a member of the Latvian Academy of Science (1992), has researched new groups of antioxidants and heart and bloodcirculation medications.

Oļģerts Lielausis, a physicist and member of the Latvian Academy of Sciences (1992) and its Senate

Edmunds Lukevics, chemist, a member of the Latvian Academy of Sciences (1987) who received the Great Medal of the academy in 1996

Abrams Feldhūns, linguist and holder of an honorary doctorate from the Latvian Academy of Sciences. He translates from German, Ancient Greek and Latin.

Vitauts Tamužs, mechanics specialist and member of the Latvian Academy of Sciences (1992) and its Senate

Pēteris Vidinieks, informatics specialist and corresponding member of the Latvian Academy of Sciences (1987)

Juris Ekmanis, physicist, member (1992) and vice president of the Latvian Academy of Sciences, chairman of the academy's Physics and Technical Sciences Division

Jānis Krastiņš (left), architectural specialist and member of the Latvian Academy of Sciences (1994), received the Great Medal in 1998; and Pauls Rumpēns, biologist and member of the Latvian Academy of Sciences (1992)

Rolands Rikards, professor and member of the Latvian Academy of Sciences. He has done research on the mechanics of composite materials, the optimization and identification of properties

Professor Mārtiņš Kalniņš, a member of the Latvian Academy of Sciences and a guest professor in the United States, Sweden, Germany and Spain. He has studied the processes whereby polymer composite materials are formed

Jānis Viba, a habilitated doctor in engineering and a professor in theoretical mechanics, a corresponding member of the Latvian Academy of Sciences. He specializes in theoretical mechanics, collision theory and the optimal management of dynamic systems.

Andris Krūmiņš, a habilitated doctor in physics and a professor at the University of Latvia

Physicist Marcis Auziņš, a member of the Latvian Academy of Sciences (1998) and chairman of the Senate of the University of Latvia

Biologist Jānis Skujiņš (left), who works in the United States and is a foreign member of the Latvian Academy of Sciences (1990), and Pēteris Cimdiņš, an ecology specialist and a member of the academy (1992)

Young scientists and recipients of awards from the Latvian Academy of Sciences together with the academy's leaders and their project directors in 1999. The president of the academy, Jānis Stradiņš, is at the center of the group.

Professor Jānis Grundspeņķis of the Riga Technical University is a specialist in system theory and a corresponding member of the Latvian Academy of Sciences. He has created a new approach in the development of hybrid intellectual systems, as well as a new method for obtaining systematic knowledge rooted in structural models.

Professor Andris Kreslinš, a specialist in heat and gas technologies, is a corresponding member of the Latvian Academy of Sciences who has studied optimization of energy consumption, as well as automated management of heating, ventilation and air conditions systems.

Dr. Kārlis Rocēns, member of the Latvian Academy of Sciences, works in the mechanics of composite materials and construction materials. He has 20 copyrighted projects and patents.

Dr. Juris Jansons, a corresponding member of the Latvian Academy of Sciences, researches the mechanics of composite materials and has published 54 scientific papers.

Dr. Pēteris Eriņš, professor at the Institute of Wood Chemistry of the Republic of Latvia. In 2000 he received the Arvīds Kalniņš Prize in forestry for his research on wood-related chemistry.

The president of Latvia, Vaira Viķe-Freiberga, is a psychologist and folklore specialist who has received the Great Prize of the Latvian Academy of Sciences. Her husband, Imants Freibergs, is a professor of informatics at the University of Toronto and the University of Latvia.

The ruins of the *Ikšķile* Church, which was built in 1185 on an island that is now in the reservoir of the Riga Hydroelectric Station. It is the oldest sacred building in Latvia, as well as the oldest masonry building in he country

The memorial plaque to Bishop Meinhard in the Riga Dom Cathedral

The Rev. Ernest Glück in 1689 published a Latvian language Bible that he had translated from the Ancient Hebrew and the Ancient Greek. A Bible Museum with some 2,000 unique Bibles, is located in the town of *Alūksne*

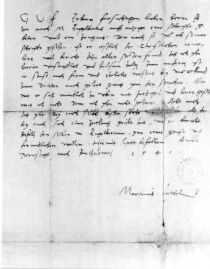

Martin Luther's letter to Riga

The Latvian Evangelical Lutheran Church marks Meinhard's Day every 13 August in the ruins of the *Ikšķile* Church

Lutheran Archbishop Jānis Vanags is seen travelling by boat to a Meinhard's Day event at the *Ikšķile* Church

Christianity arrived in Latvia both from the East and the West. During the first millennium, the Principality of Polock lay to Latvia's East in what today is part of the Russian Federation. The rulers of Polock had accepted christianity in the 9th century AD. To the West of Latvia lay a number of small states and principalities in what today is known as Europe. In the 12th century, the continent could already boast of magnificent cathedrals, as well as cloisters that preserved the knowledge and the traditions of the Christian faith.

The rulers of Polock sought to impose Christianity in Latvia through the sword. Churches were built in Vidzeme and along the *Daugava* River as early as in the 11th century, but all of these efforts to force people to become christians paled in comparison to the achievements which were gained by a middle-aged missionary who arrived along with a group of traders in 1185. This was a monk called Meinhard, who was later made Bishop of Livonia. Meinhard arrived in Latvia armed only with the word of God, and not the sword, and his teachings took hold. Meinhard has been sainted by the Catholic Church as the Apostle of Livonia, and the Latvian Lutheran Church honours the monk on 13 August each year with a church service amid the ruins of the *Ikšķile* Castle, which was the site of Latvia's first cathedral.

Another man who certainly was of key significance in bringing christianity to Latvia was the Liv chieftain of *Turaida* and *Krimulda* called Kaupo. This politician and ruler, who was christened with the name Jēkabs, turned to christianity at a time when the conversion might well have meant rejection by his people or even death. Kaupo was one of the first politicians to bring Latvia's name into the world. In 1203, he and a monk called Teoderich went to Rome to visit the Pope. They arrived in Rome after two years on the road and gained an audience with Pope Innocent III, one of the most distinguished holders of the Throne of St. Peter.

The oldest active church in Latvia today is found in *Krimulda*, and its altar nave was built during Kaupo's time. Some historians claim that Kaupo was also a predecessor of the Lieven dynasty of Baltic barons.

In the early 13th century, Bishop Albert oversaw the transfer of the bishop's seat in Livonia from *Ikšķile* to Riga. Meinhard's remains were reburied in Riga in 1235, when construction began on the Riga Dom Cathedral. His burial site can be found to the left of the main altar of the church.

The Reformation swept across all of Europe in the 16th century, and it did not bypass Latvia either. In the late 1510s, a Catholic priest from St. Peter's Church in Riga, one Andreas Knopken, went to Germany to expand his theological knowledge. When he returned to Riga in 1521, he was a true believer in the Reformation. Around the same time, another dedicated reformist priest, Sylvester Tegetmeier, arrived in Riga from Hamburg. The first Evangelical Lutheran congregation was formed in Riga in 1522 – earlier than in the motherland of the Reformation, Germany itself. The new congregation kept up correspondence with Martin Luther, and originals of several of these letters have been preserved to this very day. Luther dedicated his explanation of Psalm 127 – "If the Lord does not build the house, the work of the builders is useless" – specifically to the Riga church.

Riga was one of the cities in Europe, which adopted the so-called radical direction of the Reformation. Churches were sacked, monks were ejected from the city, etc. One tragedy of this process was that the unique library, which was kept by Franciscan monks at the Cloister of St. Catherine was lost. We can also see the consequences of the radical Reformation today in the Dom Cathedral and in St. Peter's. None of the side altars that were dedicated to the Catholic saints was left standing.

The fact that Riga opened its doors so eagerly to the new ideas may be attributed to the desire of the Riga City Council to get rid of the Livonian Order and the resident Catholic bishop. It is also possible that Riga in the Middle Ages was simply a rebellious city. At the same time, however, even at the very beginning of the Reformation, when the master of the Livonian Order was the legendary Walther von Plettenberg, christianity in Riga was a uniquely ecumenical faith. Never has any blood been shed in the city over religious causes, even though two or three christian denominations have always been present.

An old Hindu saying holds that "when the bulls fight the pain is suffered by the frogs, which get trampled under their hooves". Something similar can be said about small countries that are located among major powers that seek to divide up their spheres of influence and to set up trade routes. Latvia is precisely such a country. In the late 16th and early 17th century, borders were

Pope John Paul II and President Guntis Ulmanis of Latvia at the *Riga* airport on 8 September 1993

Pope John Paul II in Latvia

Pope John Paul II says Mass at the *Mežaparks* open-air stadium in Riga on 8 September 1993

Meinhard's Day in Riga

The Roman Catholic Archbishop in Latvia, Metropolitan Jānis Pujāts

Julians Vaivods (1895-1990) was a Roman Catholic Cardinal from 1983 until his death

A Catholic song festival in *Aglona* in 1991

The Latvian Evangelical Lutheran Church was split between occupied Latvia and the West during the Soviet occupation. Today the church has two archbishops – Jānis Vanags in Latvia (right) and Elmārs Ernsts Rozītis outside of Latvia

One of the most popular clergymen in Latvia is Lutheran Pastor Juris Rubenis

The Latvian town which during Soviet times was known as *Stučka* is now once again *Aizkraukle*, and during the occupation it did not have a church at all. A Lutheran church was built in the city in the late 1990s, and here we see Archbishop Jānis Vanags at the dedication of the church

Dean Maris Ludviks of the *Kandava* district and Archbishop Jānis Vanags dedicate the *Talsi* Deaconry Center

The 10th anniversary of the renewal of the St. Catherine's Evangelical Lutheran Church in *Kuldīga*. From the left: the Rev. Viesturs Pirro, Archbishop Jānis Vanags, and Father Romans Grantovskis of the St. Trinity Catholic Church of *Kuldīga*

Dean Jānis Liepiņš of the Evangelical Lutheran Church

The Rev. Rihards Zariņš of the New York, USA congregation

Father Alexander, Archbishop of Latvia's Orthodox Church

The senior rabbi in Latvia is Natāns Barkāns, and here he (far right) and Professor Hermann Brannover are seen meeting President Guntis Ulmanis in 1999

Andrejs Šterns, bishop of the Latvian Association of Baptist Congregations

Ioan Mirolyubov, chairman of the Council of Latvian Old Believer Churches

Regulation on the *Araiši* parish school, *Cēsis* circuit, January 29, 1766

Graduates of the Department of Theology of the University of Latvia

Archbishop Jānis Vanags ordains a new clergyman

drawn between the Poland of Stefan Batorius, the Russia of Ivan the Terrible, and the Sweden of King Gustav Adolphus. The three great rulers never went to war with one another, but their armies marched across Latvia gain and again, dividing up the country not only territorially, but also in terms of christian denominations. Catholic Poland took the East, Lutheran Sweden took the North and West, including the relatively independent Duchy of Kurland. The principle of *cuius regio, eius religio* (He who holds power sets the religion) was put into effect. Christianity is divided along pretty much the same invisible lines even today, even though the migration of people around the country over the last century has blurred the picture somewhat.

The first Latvian clergyman, physician and philosopher Janis Reiters (1632-1695) was active in the 17th century. Fortunately, the Swedish kings were adherents to a school of Lutheran thought which said that any nation has the right to read the Holy Book in its own language, and so during the so-called *Swedish times*, the Bible was translated into Latvian. This was particularly made possible because Riga was seen along with Stockholm as one of the two capitals of the Swedish Empire. In 1689 a translation produced by the Rev. Ernest Glück from the Ancient Hebrew and Ancient Greek was published, and several of the first editions of this magnificent work survive today.

Dean Linards Rozentals of the *Daugavpils* district has organised a Christian theatre festival in *Daugavpils*

Father Rolands Melkers of *Sigulda* sings *The Passion of Matthew* by Latvian composer Juris Kulakovs

The Christian theatre festival in *Daugavpils* gathers Christian theatres from all of the countries of the Baltic Sea States, as well as countries in Eastern Europe

The premiere of Juris Kulakovs *The Passion of Matthew* at a church in *Talsi*

Lessons at the *Lazdona* Christian Primary School

The *Lazdona* parish Christian primary school and shelter

At the Catholic song festival in *Aglona* in 1991

Worship at the *Usma* Church, which is now housed at the Open-Air Ethnographic Museum in Riga

A Sunday school at *Lielvārde*

The Rev. Valdis Strazdiņš has organised the Christian school

Mara Zaķe directs a senior citizens' home that is run by the Catholic Church

The Gustav Adolphus Church in Riga is named after a Swedish king

The altar at the *Kolka* Evangelical Lutheran Church

The Great Northern War between Russia and Sweden erupted in 1700, and for Latvia, this meant the imposition of tsarist rule from 1710 to 1918. For the country's religious life, it meant the arrival and strengthening of the Russian Orthodox Church. After a major schism in the church in the mid-18th century, opponents of reform who were known as the Old Believers were forced to flee to the more distant reaches of the Russian Empire, and quite a few of them arrived in what is now Latvia, especially in the region of Latgale. The Old Believers built what was then the largest church in the world in Riga, and unlike other churches, it had the right to a tower and a bell - the Grebenschikov Church.

In the 19th century, the Herrnhuter Brotherhood sent missionaries into Vidzeme who brought along with them a new spiritual awakening. The Herrnhuters established traditions, which today are kept alive by Baptists in Latvia. When national schools were established in the Baltic provinces of the Russian Empire, Latvians gained new opportunities to obtain and continue their education. This immediately led to the emergence of Latvian pastors. Previously clergy had all been non-Latvians, especially Germans, who often had very weak skills in the Latvian language. In the late 19th century, many wealthy Latvians were studying theology. The period of Latvian independence between the two world wars was a time when extremely distinguished men of the church were active – Orthodox Archbishop Jānis Pommers; the political activists Jāzeps Rancāns and Francis Trasuns; the first chaplain of the Latvian Armed Forces, Pēteris Apkalns, who was himself a soldier and earned the *Lāčplēsis* and the Order of Three Stars; teacher Roberts Slokenbergs; Aloizs Broks, who translated the New Testament into the Latgallian dialect and founded the *Aglona* Gymnasium; theologians Edgars Rumba, Kārlis Kundziņš and Voldemārs Maldonis; artist Miervaldis Ķemers; Christian publisher and editor Teodors Grīnbergs, who later became the archbishop of the Latvian Lutheran Church; and missionary Anna Irbe, who established a Latvian Christian mission in India that is in operation to this very day.

When the Soviet Union occupied Latvia, persecution of churches was a key element of the repression. Many clergymen and church officials were murdered or deported to Siberia. The church was banned from working with children and adolescents. Many congregations were forced to leave their churches, and the buildings were used for athletic halls, warehouses, etc. The churches of Latvia suffered a particular blow when, at the close of the war, many of their senior and junior clergymen and other officials fled as refugees to the West, thus dividing the churches into two. This was particularly true with respect to the Latvian Lutheran Church. In emigration, Latvians set up Lutheran congrega-

tions in Sweden, Germany, Canada, the United States, Australia and England.

During the Latvian national awakening in 1989 and the renewal of Latvia's independence in 1991, the church gained new life. Nearly all of the pre-war congregations, which had been disbanded during Soviet times, came back together. Church buildings were reclaimed and restoration was begun. Sunday schools were set up and young people formed groups, too. The Department of Theology was reopened at the University of Latvia, and various denominations set up their own educational institutions to train clergymen. The church returned to the areas and institutions of Latvian public life from which the Soviet authorities had ejected it – social work, hospitals, the armed forces, prisons, etc.

St. Paul's Church runs a soup kitchen for the poor in Riga

The *Shola Gregorianum Riga* choir rehearses for a week of Gregorian chanting performances in *Araiši*. The conductor of the choir is Guntars Pranis

A church in Lincoln. The Latvian diaspora was eager to keep their latvianness and links to their native land. The role of religious parishes was to hold them together and strengthen self esteem and the expectations for a free Latvia

Apriķu Church was built in the XVII century. There is a remarkable harmony of baroque and rococo forms in the interior. The author of the sculpture group of apostles in the picture is Curlandian J. Kreinefelds

The St. Trinity *Kuldiga* Catholic Church, built in 1640 during the period of Duchy of Kurzeme

The *Aizkraukle* Evangelical Lutheran Church was opened in 1999. Most new churches that are built in Latvia are built in architectural styles that are traditional in the country, and local building materials are used

Janis Janelsitis from *Gaujiena* is the eldest among clergymen and a Chevalier of the Tree Star Order

A church service during a Liv festival in *Mazirbe*. The Livs are a minority indigenous population in Latvia, and since the 18th century they have had two churches – one in *Kolka*, and the other in *Mazirbe*

Latvia's largest christian denominations are the Lutheran Church, which has 302 congregations, the Roman Catholics (243 congregations), the Orthodox (112 congregations), Baptists (84 congregations) and the Old Believers (65 congregations). There are also 44 congregations of the Church of the Seventh Day Adventists and 57 congregations of the Pentecostal Church, even though these are not traditional denominations in Latvia. Religious pluralism has also led to the emergence of dozens of sects, which do not belong to any of the major denominations and, in many cases, are not registered with the Religious Affairs Department of the Ministry of Justice. The New Generation and Church of the New Apostles congregations are the largest of these.

The basilica of *Aglona*

Pilgrims on their way to *Aglona*

The annual church service at *Aglona* on 15 August

The Alexander Nevsky Church in Riga

Each August, Catholics go on a pilgrimage to *Aglona* from other parts of Latvia, as well as from other countries

Pope John Paul II at *Aglona* on 9 September 1993

The garden of the basilica of *Aglona*

Receiving communion at *Aglona*

The Alexander Nevsky Orthodox Church in Riga

A funeral at a church

Marriages in St. Jazeps catholics church (Christmas)

Marriages in church were prohibited throughout the Soviet occupation, and people got married at civilian institutions instead. In the late 1990s, however, most Latvians marry in church

THE LATVIAN RELIGION OF DIEVTURĪBA

Through the centuries, Latvians have managed to preserve some elements of their ancient, indigenous faith. With the arrival of Latvian nationalism in the early 20th century, a need was felt for an expression of Latvian piety. This piety can be found in the storehouse of the purest values of the Latvian nation – Latvian folksongs. Ernests and Arvids Brastiņš together with some of their contemporaries studied, collected and put in order the folksongs, providing a renewed Latvian faith, which they called *dievturiba* (literally – holding of God).

Arvids Brastiņš (1893-1984) was editor of the magazine *Labietis*, he was been a senior leader of the Latvian *dievturi* commonweal in the US since 1947

The Latvian faith held that there was a single, higher God who could be manifested in many ways. The material expression of God was the (female) deity Mara, who kept track of the material world, as well as Laima (also a female deity), who was responsible for the fates of humankind. *Dievturiba* is not a religion in the traditional sense of the word, because the emphasis is on the discovery of God rather than on God as such. *Dievturiba* is expressed through various processes – praising of God, praying to God, donating to God, and living a godly life.

The ceremonies of the *dievturiba* movement usually take place outdoors, so as to emphasise the links of the movement to the natural world. There are congregations of *dievturi*, who refer to members as *savieši* ("of us"). *Dievturiba* was of some significance in the maintenance of Latvian culture and folklore in emigration. Some Latvians adopted *dievturiba* as a way of maintaining Latvianness in themselves and in their children.

Janis Tupesis at a cemetery in Wisconsin

Dievturi ceremonies of worship

CRUCIFIXES

Crucifixes are most commonly found in Latgale – in the photographs, we see crucifixes from Latgale (*Daugavpils* District), Selonia (*Akniste*) and Zemgale (*Skaistkalne*)

Crucifix-like functions in Latgale are often fulfilled by sculptures. Here we see a statue of Jesus Christ near the *Bērzgale* Church

A crucifix in *Daugavpils* district

The cross at the corner of the *Daugavpils-Rēzekne* and *Preiļi-Aglona* roads. The upper bar, without reason, has been shortened

A Crucifix in Latgale

A six-meter cross in *Daugavpils* (architect V. Bauliņa) at the place of burial of Polish Legionnaires. The graves were levelled during the 1970s by the Communist regime

In the rural areas of the Eastern Latvian region of Latgale, most often at some distance from major roads, we find many roadside or village crosses. Crosses outside of people's homes can also be seen in Bavaria, Austria, Poland and Lithuania, but in Latgale, the tradition is more beautiful, and crosses have been set up in the places of most honour. In Bavaria, crosses were usually fastened to the roof of a barn, a granary or a byre, but in Latgale, roadside crosses are set up at significant places on a road. The crosses are high, made in such a way as to encourage people to raise their eyes upward. For the people of Latgale the cross has traditionally held to be a place to stop, where one must raise their hat, make a cross and pay their respects. Often people sat down for a while.

The crucifix in Latgale was a thing in common that unified the people. There have always been large church congregations in Latgale, but the churches were located at a considerable distance from each other. Because of this, in the late 19th century a tradition was established whereby Catholic worship services in May were organised at the local village cross – without a priest and under the leadership of someone chosen by the worshippers. Most often, it was a woman who was a good organiser and had a beautiful voice. By the end of the 19th century there were an estimated 2,000 crosses in Latgale.

The Reformation had little effect on Latgale, and the only people to convert to the Lutheran faith were the German country nobility, who later came under the rule of Poland and went back to Roman Catholicism. The peasants in Latgale continued to pray to their ancient gods as though nothing had happened. In 1661, the Jesuits set up a collegium in *Daugavpils*. A Dominican order was established in *Pasiene* in 1694. A Dominican cloister at *Aglona* was built in 1699. Although the Jesuits came from abroad, they could speak and write in latgallian – the local dialect, so that they could not only preach the Gospel of Christ, but also teach local people to read and to write. They chopped down the sacred trees which were worshiped by the people of Latgale, but more often than not they placed holy pictures in the sacred places of the people, as well as affixing pictures of Christ on the Cross on their sacred trees. This was the beginning of the building of outdoor crucifixes.

When Poland was divided in 1772 and Latgale fell under the control of Russia, Polish aristocrats and clergymen began to pay reverence to local farmers. They set up small places for prayer in the centre of residential areas, as well as at major crossroads in the region. Usually these were covered gazebos, with a crucifix with the image of the Saviour on the Cross. The depictions of Christ that were produced this time are to a certain extent in personally spiritual, and the anatomy build of human beings is largely ignored. Most of the crucifixes were produced by amateur artisans from local cloisters.

Within the policy of russification of the Tsarist government, in 1863, Catholic Church processions and worship services were banned, and many

Notre Dame of *Ludza*

churches were converted into Orthodox churches. The people, however, closed ranks with the Catholic Church and marshalled all efforts in order to survive. Now the people themselves promoted the building of outside crucifixes. The figure of the Saviour at this time was carved by master artisans.

The repeal of serfdom in Latgale allowed people to move freely and the opportunity to buy land for the purpose of setting up farms. When they put up their buildings, the new farm owners sought the protection of God, and crucifixes were erected near homes, covered by ornately decorated roofs. Crucifixes under small structures with a four-sided or six-sided roof were also built.

Toward the end of the century, the wealthier people of Latgale began to build houses that are more ornate and ordered crucifixes from professional artisans in the capital city.

When the revolution of 1905 began, for the first time the village crucifixes were desecrated, which, during the communist occupation in 1918 and 1919, developed into their being openly demolished.

The most significant wood sculptors are Janis Cibuļskis, Janis Kļavinskis, Peteris Kozuļkaža, "Grandfather" Bogdans, Kazimirs Ruskulis, Antons Gleizds, Antons Kivkucans and Antons Removičs.

From 1932 to 1938, many wooden crucifixes, including those that depicted the Saviour, were dismantled and in their place were erected uniform, three metres high concrete crosses, with small metal cast figures of Christ.

During the years of the Soviet occupation, many of the crosses were desecrated once again, and the occupants sought to get rid of them altogether. The loss of the sacral cultural traditional heritage of Latgale is also evidenced by the trend of replacing the very personal wooden crosses with gigantic metal or concrete ones. Such a naked concrete cross is at the corner of the *Daugavpils* and *Aglona* highways. The upper bar of the cross is two times shorter than the side bars. The people of Latgale more commonly used crosses in which all three bars of the cross were of equal height, which symbolised to them the equilibrium between the aspiration to rise, completeness, and the real abilities of God and Man. When the vertical bar is shortened, the natural aspiration of humankind to completeness is reduced or limited.

A crucifix by Antons Rancāns at *Dekteri*

Artist Antons Rancans

Crucifixes under board or tin roofs are found throughout the region of Latgale. This crucifix is found near the village of *Vabole* in the *Daugavpils* district

The *Alsunga* crucifix – a typical example of crucifixes in Kurzeme region

Crucifixes were often built as copies of nearby churches. Here we see the *Kučinski* crucifix hut, built in the 1920s to resemble the *Rudzāti* Church

Alsunga parish, unlike other, more Lutheran areas of Kurzeme has always had a Catholic church, complete with Catholic traditions such as the *Alsunga* crucifix

On holidays, crucifixes are often decorated. This is the village crucifix of *Sarkaņi*

A crucifix at the village of *Guti* in *Kapiņi* parish, built in 1887 by Odums Leitans

LATVIAN COUNTRY CHURCHES

A church built in a *Libieši* settlement *Kubesele* (*Krimulda* since the XVI century) by preacher *Alobrant* in 1206 in the vicinity of the burned *Kaupo's* castle. The church has been renovated in 1643 and 1699. An extending adjunction built in 1865; a new stone church-tower was built replacing the old wooden one by August Reinberg

Apriķi Lutheran Church, one of the most beautiful late baroque pieces of architecture with rococo elements, built in the XII c., was rebuilt and had the tower upgraded in 1710

A sanctuary of a Baptist Congregation in *Saka*, near *Pāvilosta*, built in 1896. At the beginning of 20's, there was a wave of migration to Brazil by the Catholic population

The St. Catherine's Church in *Kaltene* was first mentioned in records in 1567. In 1689 it was nearly collapsed. A new one was built in 1704, was renovated in 1848

Pūre Lutheran Church, built in 1805, was rebuilt in 1858

Drusti Lutheran Church was built by a Livonian Marcis Sarums 1835-1838. First organ was built in 1838, the new one – in 1901

Christianity started to spread in Latvia in the XI-XII c. and the church had a peculiar role in the process – it served both ceremonial and military purposes. During the centuries, when the Baltics were swept by many armies, church was always a shelter for its congregation, because the warriors usually complied with the chivalry ethics – no weapons and no bloodshed in the sanctuary. In the XIII c. the largest churches were planned and measured out in *Riga* – the *Dome Cathedral* and the *St. Peter's Church*, which were accomplished in the XV c. and became masterpieces of Gothic brickwork. The churches in *Cēsis*, *Valmiera*, and *Krimulda* also built in the XIII c. embody ascetic simplicity and strength of the strange faith which had entered the lands of Livs and Latgallian, preached not just with a cross, but also fire.

During the time of Reformation, artwork was taken away – altars and altar-pieces. They returned home after the passions settled.

The official faith of duchy of Kurzeme selected by Gothard Kettler in 1561 was the one of *Augsbourg*. He ordered construction of 27 churches in Zemgale and 43 churches in Kurzeme. The churches built at the end of the XV c. Kurzeme were of especially fine masonry. The contrast of simple form and rich interior is striking. The interior is decorated with characteristic carvings in wood the most exquisite of which are still preserved in *Subate* Lutheran Church and *Vecpils* Catholic Church. Carvings by Joahim Kreutzfeld are preserved in *Usma* Church (now in the *Ethnographic Open-Air Museum of Latvia*), in churches of *Apriķi*, *Durbe*, and *Piltene*. The ceiling of *Apriķi Church* is ornamented by H. Rode with painted allegories, because of which the church is a part of European cultural heritage.

The first important Lutheran church was built in Riga – the *St. John's Church* and its adjunction built by the Latvian congregation between 1587 and 1589. The superintendent H. Samson, appointed by Sweden in 1611, promoted construction of churches by Lutheran congregations. Churches built in *Limbaži*, *Matiši*, *Mazsalaca*, *Burtnieki*, are still more or less preserved. Many churches were damaged during the Northern War, because the Russians ignored the established customs and slaughtered the folks hiding in the sanctuaries and burned the churches.

At the end of the XVIII c. erect and fine masonry churches were built all over Vidzeme. The churches in *Alūksne*, *Lēdurga*, *Apekalns* show a transition from baroque to classicism. An interesting feature of churches in *Katlakalns*, *Palsmane*, *Gostiņi*, and Riga Jesus Congregation Church, resembling a pantheon, is their chancels. Art Nouveau has also left its features on churches from the shift of the XIX c. and the XX c. especially noticeable in Riga Cross Church and *Dubulti* Church. During the inter-war period new churches were built in all the communities without ones.

More than 100 churches were destroyed during the World War II. After the war, Latvia was set to outlast the flourish of communist ideology, an

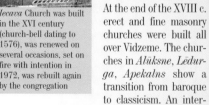

Iecava Church was built in the XVI century (church-bell dating to 1576), was renewed on several occasions, set on fire with intention in 1972, was rebuilt again by the congregation

important part of which was atheism. During the period from 1960 to 1970, the 124 churches of all confessions were closed, 34 of which

The Holy Sacrament by K. Meijers

were fitted up as warehouses, 22 were fitted for cultural purposes, the *Doma Cathedral* became a concert hall, 20 churches were demolished, and 21 were left to desolation.

The return of capitalism at the end of 80's was accompanied by people's desire to sell everything that could be. Until 1992 when borders were not controlled, Latvian churches were plundered by bands of Russian as well as local vandals steeling altar-pieces, tableware, books in order to sell them for pennies to western collectors.

The end of millennium may be characterized by a rebirth. Almost all of the abandoned churches are now gathering congregations. New churches are being built, the old ones are being renovated. Latvia enters the new millennium with a harmonized attitude towards historic and religious values – Latvia can be proud over her sanctuaries as well. The sanctuaries mentioned here are displayed in different pages dealing with related topics describing not just the religious, but also the architectural and the cultural environment.

Tērvete Lutheran Church was built in 1614 according to a carving in one of the logs. The new church-tower was raised in 1721. It was renovated twice, in 1815 and in 1902

Lībagi Catholic Church was built under the supervision of priest Antonijs Springovičs (later an archbishop) from 1909 to 1913. The sound of the church organ has great qualities

Eleonorvile Catholic Chapel was built in 1815 in *Rudzāti*, near *Daugavpils*, it can be found in the Ethnographical Open-Air Museum since 1975

A Lutheran sanctuary in *Renda*, built in 1786, the church-tower was built in 1887

Construction of *Alūksne* Church was financed by the local landlord O.K. von Fitinghof, designed and built by architect K. Haberland from 1781 to 1788

Lode Lutheran Church was dedicated to St. Peter and St. Paul and was a constant landmark in the beginning of the XVII c. New log churches were built in 1670, in 1728, the present one was built in 1780

Jersika Orthodox Church was composed of steal plates in 1866

St. Anna's Church in *Kuldiga* was built from 1899 to 1904 by architect Vilhelms Neimanis

St. John's Lutheran Church in *Saldus* was built between 1718 and 1737 and rebuilt in Vilhelm Neumann's design in 1898 to 1899. The church was repaired in 1997, had its altar, altar-piece, and organ renovated

Roja Lutheran Church, built in 1786 (church-bell record – 1684), was renovated in 1876

Ķekava Lutheran Church (1783) did not have a church-tower until 1900, when the church was rebuilt

Palsmane Church form 1817 – an octagonal building in *Valka* district

Renovation of *Salaspils* Catholic Church was started in 1995 by architects R. Krustopa, V. Ozola, and L. Tikmanis. It was given blessing in 1996

Vecpiebalga Church was damaged in the war and demolished during the soviet atheist assaults after the war. It was rebuilt by Ausma Skujiņa, financially supported by Latvians in exile

The largest of the charismatic sects, which has built its sanctuary is *New Generation*. Latvians have traditionally looked upon religion as intimate and have never showed off in a religious manner, which is why so few Latvians join charismatic congregations. The new confessions obtain more popularity among Russians, separated from their religious roots by 80 years of communism. Besides many have left their ethnic homeland, loosing ties with their land, culture, and religion

LATVIAN BOOKS

Indriķis Alunāns (1835-1904) was a translator and book publisher who in 1873 opened a book store and publishing house in *Jelgava*. In 1892, he also bought a printing press

Eduards Zīslaks (1850-1888), a German publisher who in 1875 opened his own publishing house in *Jelgava*, attaching a printing press to it in 1881

Ansis Gulbis (1873-1936), a writer and book publisher who opened his own publishing house in St. Petersburg in 1903 and in 1918 moved to Riga

Jēkabs Dravnieks (1858-1927), journalist and book publisher. He owned a bookstore, a publishing house and printing press in *Jelgava* from 1887 until 1895

Jānis Ozols (1859-1906), was a book publisher who in 1895 opened a printing press in *Cēsis* and produced some 200 books

Jānis Roze (1870-1942) was one of Latvia's leading book publishers and sellers, working in Riga after 1917

The first book published in Latvian in Riga was a church handbook in 1615

The Glück Bible (1689)

Jānis Rapa (1885-1940), book publisher. In 1912, he and Arturs Valters established the book company *Valters un Rapa*

Arturs Valters (1870-1924), book publisher, worked together with Janis Rapa to establish the *Valters un Rapa* publishing house

Kārlis Rasiņš (1886-1974), book publisher. In 1926, he established the *Literatūra* publishing house. In 1944, he went into exile, and in 1957, he re-launched his publishing house in Canada

The Latvian book publishing industry first emerged in the context of the Reformation in the early 16th century. A Protestant Latvian congregation was established in Riga, and worship services were held in Latvian. This meant that the texts of worship services had to be produced in Latvian. A book that is thought to have contained the Protestant order of worship was published in 1525, but no copies of it have survived. Information about the fact that such a book was published is found in a protocol from a Roman Catholic dean in Lübeck, who wrote in 1525 that the Catholic authorities in the city had confiscated a large barrel full of Lutheran books from a travelling salesman who had been on his way to Riga. Among the books were masses printed in Liv, Latvian and Estonian. The books were burned. Apparently, a Protestant printer in Germany printed the texts. The translator may have been a German clergyman at the Riga Latvian congregation called Nicolaus Ramms. We do not know whether the book contained the texts in all three languages in parallel, or whether three separate books were published. We do know enough, however, to say that the history of Latvian book publishing industry began in 1525.

The first printed text in the Latvian language that has survived to this day is a book on cosmography that was published in 1550 by Sebastian Münster. The next known printed work in Latvia was a 1585 translation of the catechism that was published in Vilnius by Peteris Kanzijs: *Catechismus Catholicorum. Īsige pamācīšen no tiems papriekše galve gabliems hristites mācibas*. It is believed that the translator may have been a German priest, Ertmann Tolgsdorf.

Three volumes of a Lutheran handbook – Martin Luther's catechism, portions of the gospels, and a selection of hymns – were published in 1586 and 1587.

During the so-called Calendar Riots, a printer called Nicolaus Mollinus (1550-1625) arrived in Riga. Among the earliest books that he published were paeans to the forces that had won in the Calendar Riots, and in 1590 he was rewarded by the Riga City Council with a privilege from the Polish king which banned anyone else from printing Mollinus' books in the Polish Empire, or to import any unauthorised copies from abroad (in 1621 Mollinus received a similar privilege from the king of Sweden). Mollinus' first printed work – a collection of hymns produced in 1588 – has not survived. The first book that he published in Latvian in Riga was a church handbook in 1615, which came complete with wood engravings depicting various subjects from the catechism. The engravings were imported from Western Europe, and the book was meant for clergymen. During his 37 years in Riga, Mollinus produced some 170 books, most of them in Latin and German.

We know of eight books that were published in the Latvian language between 1525 and 1625. This was the period when the cornerstone of Latvia's book publishing industry was laid, and the basis for future work in the printing industry was created.

Book publishing in the 17th century in Latvia focused on a wide range of theological literature – books by Georg Mantzel, a Bible (1689) translated by the Rev. Ernst Glück, and various hymnbooks. A printing house run with the support of the government of Sweden by a man called Johann Fischer is also known to have been in operation in Riga during this period.

In the 18th century, there were two notable book publishers in *Jelgava* – Johann Friedrich Hartknoch (1740-1789) and Johann Friedrich Steffenhagen (1743-1812). Both men first began their work in *Jelgava*, although in 1762 Hartknoch moved to Riga. He published early work by Immanuel Kant, Jean Jacques Rousseau, various Baltic participants in the Enlightenment, Mikhail Lomonosov, and others. Steffenhagen, for his part, produced Latvian hymnbooks, textbooks, calendars and newspapers. The quality of his output improved from year to year. In 1801 Steffenhagen' nephew, Johann Martin Peterss-Steffenhagen, became involved in his uncle's printing house, taking it over after the older man's death. In 1822, the printing house began to publish the newspaper *Latviešu Avīzes*. During World War I, in 1919, the forces of Bermont-Avalov burned the old printing house down.

Illustrated primers for Latvian children published by *Vecais Stenders*

A Polish-Latvian dictionary printed in Vilnius in 1683 and produced by Georg Elger

A Latvian annual, *Latviska Gada grāmata*, published in 1797 at the publishing house of Johann Steffenhagen in *Jelgava*

The first history of Latvia, published in 1649 by Paul Einhorn

A German-Latvian dictionary produced by Georg Mantzel and published in Riga in 1638

A Latvian calendar printed in *Jelgava* in 1766

Vecais Stenders wrote this *Book of high wisdom* in 1776, and it was printed by J.F. Hintz in *Jelgava*

Gustav Manteuffel published these dialect between 1862 and 1871. The Russian Empire banned printing in the Latin alphabet, and that put an end to the process

First editions of the work of the poet and playwright Aspazija

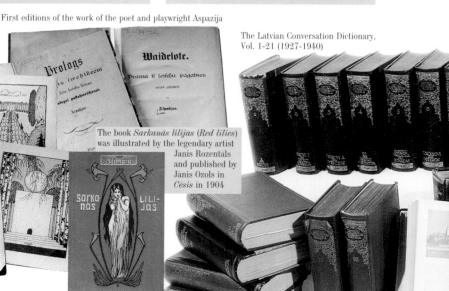
The Latvian Conversation Dictionary, Vol. 1-21 (1927-1940)

The first edition of Krišjānis Barons' *Latvju Dainas*, published in *Jelgava* and St. Petersburg. Barons' life work was published in a series of editions between 1894 and 1915

The first edition of the poet Rainis' *Tālas noskaņas zilā vakarā* (*Distant moods on a blue evening*), published by the *Kalniņš un Deičmanis* publishing house in Riga

Poetry by Rainis published by the *Kronenbergs* and *Gulbis* publishing house and illustrated by the prominent artists Vilhelms Purvītis and Alberts Kronenbergs

The book *Sarkanās lilijas* (*Red lilies*) was illustrated by the legendary artist Janis Rozentāls and published by Janis Ozols in *Cēsis* in 1904

In 1867, the Latvian publisher Kārlis Štālbergs (1837-1895) began publication of a series of books called *Citu tautu rakstnieki* (Writers of other nations). Štālbergs also published original work by Latvian authors. In 1875 and 1876 he and Kaspars Biezbārdis produced a weekly newspaper called *Pasaule un Daba* (The World and Nature).

A tragic page in the history of Latvian book publishing is the life, work and death of Jānis Ozols (1859-1906). Ozols set up a printing house in *Cēsis* in 1895 and published more than 200 books. During the period when the people of Latgale were banned by the Russian Empire from publishing books in the Latin alphabet, he tried to help by doing some of the work for them. He was shot without trial during the counterrevolution in 1906.

The Latvian book publishing industry really began to develop in the early 20th century, when major figures in the industry were Ansis Gulbis, Jānis Rapa, Arturs Valters, Jānis Roze and Helmars Rudzītis.

Gulbis began his work as publisher in 1903 in St. Petersburg, and in 1918 he moved to Riga. His publishing house produced important series under the title *Universālā bibliotēka* (Universal Library), and his crowning achievement was the encyclopaedic *Latvian Conversational Dictionary*, which was published in 21 volumes between 1927 and 1940 (war and occupation stopped the process, and the last entry in Volume 21 is an article on Syria; the letters T through Z remained uncovered).

The *Valters un Rapa* publishing house was established in 1912 by Arturs Valters and Jānis Rapa. The prolific publishers issued more than 3,000 titles, including the second volume of Krišjānis Barons' collection of folk songs, 15 volumes of Latvian folk stories and legends as assembled by Pēteris Šmits, and many other books and textbooks by Latvian authors.

Jānis Roze managed Ozols' publishing house in *Cēsis* after Ozols was murdered in 1906, but in 1915 he moved to Riga and opened a printing house there. Roze published a great many books, including the collected works of Jānis Akuraters and Jānis Poruks, as well as the magazine *Piesaule*.

Helmars Rudzītis (b. 1903) ran a publishing house called *Grāmatu Draugs* (Friend of Books), which was established in 1926. Rudzītis' innovation was that he published books by the most prominent authors of Latvia and the world and sold them for one lats. The very first book went into nine printings. By 1944, the publishing house had managed to published some 1,500 Latvian books. Rudzītis went into exile after World War II. He re-established his publishing house in Germany and then in the United States, where he arrived in 1949. *Grāmatu Draugs* continued its work in exile throughout the Soviet occupation.

Another interesting phenomenon in Latvian book publishing is the *Zelta Ābele* (Golden Apple Tree) publishing house of Miķelis Goppers, which produced small books of outstanding design. The books were published in small print runs, and every copy was autographed and numbered by the author. After the war, Goppers continued to publish books in Sweden.

In 1940, the Soviet authorities nationalised the publishing industry, and all publishing companies were merged into an enterprise known as *VAPP*. All publishing work was subject to strict censorship. Because paper supplies were limited, most of the books that were published in 1940 and 1941 were propaganda materials. The Latvian industry was no less encumbered when the German occupation began in 1941. The Germans, too, dictated what had to be published, and once again, it was mostly propaganda – often celebrating the Aryan peoples and promoting virulent anti-Semitism.

After the war, the communists set up the Latvian State Publishing House with several sub-divisions. In 1965, they merged to become the *Liesma* (Flame) publishing house. The Latvian Academy of Sciences opened its own publishing arm, *Zinātne* (Science) in 1951, while the publishing house *Zvaigzne* (Star) was opened in 1965. The publishing industry was a very active one during the Soviet occupation – in 1985 there were five publishing houses in Latvia, and each year they published the equivalent of seven books for each resident of the country. Fiction and books about technologies and sciences were published less seldom during the Soviet occupation than had been the case before the war, but some books were published with unusual print runs and snatched up by the people. The books of poet Imants Ziedonis, for example, were sometimes published in 200,000 copies – a very large number given that there are only 1.5 million Latvians. Political literature, of course, was not forgotten in the Soviet Union – no amount of money was too great when it came to publishing vast editions of the works of Lenin, Stalin and Brezhnev, both individually and in collections. The shelves of bookshops groaned under the weight of studies about the history of the Communist Party, "scientific Communism" and "scientific atheism". Many of the books were sent directly from the warehouse to the shredder.

Another aspect of book publishing in the Soviet era was the Main Literary Board, universally known as *Glavļit*. This was the Communist Party's censorship arm. Every published work was read and edited very carefully. Poetry and the work of foreign authors were not exempt from these "corrections". In order to avoid problems, the work of foreign authors was translated very seldom, although Latvian readers were fed an endless stream of work by Soviet authors. It must be said, however, that many writers who shunned the lies and hypocrisy of the Soviet era nevertheless managed to produce an extensive body of philosophical and valuable literature.

The system of censorship was one of the first things to go when Latvia renewed its independence, and many independent publishing houses sprang up. *Valters un Rapa* and the *Jānis Roze* publishing house reopened their doors after 50 years of Soviet occupation. In 1989 there were six publishing houses in Latvia; in 1991 there were 60, and in 1998 – 407. The Soviet-era *Zvaigzne* (now known as *Zvaigzne ABC*) is still in operation under the leadership of Vija Ķilbloka. It specialises in the production of textbooks and accessible scientific books. The *Zinātne* publishing house publishes serious scientific books and books about scientists. The *Sprīdītis* (named for a fictional children's hero in Latvian literature) publishing house continues to specialise in books for children and adolescents.

The *Daugava* publishing house focuses on the classics of world and Latvian literature. *Daugava* was established in 1945 in Sweden, and its books are nicely designed and carefully bound. The publishing house has now moved to Latvia. *Atēna* entered the publishing world as the producer of translations of the work of Scandinavian authors, and the books of the publishing house have often received awards for their outstanding design. The *Karogs* (Flag) publishing house specialised in original Latvian literature, as does the publishing arm of the rural newspaper *Lauku Avīze*, which publishes popular novels and sells them for 1 lats a piece.

The largest among the newly established publishing houses are *Jumava* and *Nordik*, both of which aim their work at specific audiences.

It should be added that the book publishing industry has always worked hand-in-hand with the printing and book selling industries in Latvia, and *Jānis Roze*, *Jumava*, *Jāņa Sēta*, *Zvaigzne ABC* and other publishing houses all have their own printing presses and stores.

In 1993, 23 publishers joined together to form the Latvian Book Publishing Association, and by 2000 it had expanded to 47 members. The Association works to improve the professional and artistic level of Latvian book publishing and to publicize good books. Since 1993, a competition on the most beautiful book of the year has been staged, and every April there is a book festival in Latvia. Latvian book publishers have also participated with some success in international book fairs. In 1999, there were 2,168 published titles in Latvia at a total print run of some 6 million copies. The first "best-seller" in the history of Latvian book publishing was Glück's Bible, which retained that honour for 200 years – until Barons published his massive collection of Latvian folk songs. In terms of volume, Barons was replaced during the first period of Latvian independence by Ansis Gulbis and his Latvian Conversational Dictionary. In terms of length and information, that dictionary has not been surpassed to this very day.

Books from the Zinātne publishing house

Zvaigzne ABC publishes school textbooks, dictionaries, and translations of popular encyclopaedias

The Preses nams publishing house publishes encyclopaedias and original literature

Daugava in 1999 published books by Latvian and non-Latvian authors

The output of the Nordik publishing house expands from year to year

The president and director of the Nordik and Tapals publishing houses, Pēteris Zirnītis and Jānis Juška

The president of the Jumava publishing house, Juris Visockis, is also the chairman of the Riga City Council's Cultural Commission. Jumava's books are often among the most beautiful publications of the year, and outstanding management and market sense distinguish the publishing house

The president of the publishing house Elpa, Mairita Solima

Neredzigais Indriķis (1783-1828), poet

Ernests Dinsberģis (1816-1902), author, translator, promoter of the sciences

Reinis Kaudzīte (1839-1920), writer

Matīss Kaudzīte (1848-1926), writer

Tirzmaliete (1876-1942), poet

Rudolfs Blaumanis (1863-1908), playwright, writer

Augusts Deglavs (1862-1922), writer

Eduards Veidenbaums (1867-1892), poet

Rainis (1865-1929) and Aspazija (1865-1943)

Jānis Pliekšāns, more commonly known as Rainis, was the most distinguished poet and playwright in the history of Latvia, as well as a noted public official. He studied Latin and Ancient Greek at school, and he was very much familiar with the classics of world literature. Rainis studied law at St. Petersburg University. Between 1891 and 1895 he was the editor of the newspaper *Dienas Lapa*. In 1894 he met the poet Aspazija, whom he was to marry. In 1895, *Dienas Lapa* published Rainis' first poet, *Cold Soul, Proud Soul*. On May 31, 1897, the poet was arrested and deported (1897-1903) for being a member of the *New Current* movement. While in exile in deep Central Russia, Rainis translated works by Goethe, Lessing and Ibsen, and he also produced his first collection of poems, *Distant Moods on a Blue evening* (1903). Rainis expressed his opinion of the 1905 Revolution in another collection of poems, *The Face of the Storm* (1905). In the following years Rainis produced his most philosophical works – the poetry collection *End and Beginning* (1912), and the tragic play *Joseph and his Brothers* (1919). The dramatic poem *Daugava* (1919) accents spiritual strength as the savior of the nation and promotes the idea of Latvia as an independent nation. Rainis' major plays, including *Fire and Night* (1905), *The Golden Horse* (1909) and *Indulis and Ārija* (1912), have been staged on countless occasions at Latvia's theaters, and motifs from several of the plays have been used by composers such as Arvīds Žilinskis, Jānis Mediņš and Imants Kalniņš to produce operas. From 1905 until 1920 Rainis was in exile in Switzerland, but when he returned to Latvia he was a member of the Latvian Constitutional Convention and of three sessions of Parliament. Rainis also wrote poetry for children, and books like *The Golden Sieve* (1920), *A Window of Flowers* (1924), *The doll Lolīte* (1924) and others have become classics of Latvian literature. Rainis marked a new phase in the development of Latvian literature.

Aspazija (Elza Rozenberga), was Rainis' wife and a distinguished poet and playwright in her own right. Her first published poem, *At the New Year*, was published in a supplement to *Dienas Lapa* in 1887. Her first play, *The Avenger* won a competition organized by the Rīga Latvian Association, but was banned by the tsar's censors for praising the idea of freedom too openly. Aspazija won immense popularity with her plays *Vaidelote* and *Lost Rights*, both of which dealt with issues of women's rights and emancipation. Poetry which she wrote during the period when the New Current movement was active were collected in the book *Red Flowers* (1897). Rainis and Aspazija were married in 1897, and she spent time with him in exile in Switzerland. A play which she wrote in 1905, *The Silver Shroud*, won great public recognition. While in Switzerland she also produced collections of poetry – *The Sunny Corner* (1910) and *A Lapful of Flowers* (1911), the latter book the first of a trilogy of lyrical and autobiographical poems. Upon returning to Latvia in 1920 Aspazija became very active in various public affairs, and she increased her literary output. The collections *Sun of Three Colors* (1926), *At the Time of the Asters* (1928) and *Journey of the Soul* (1933) were published. Her last books were *Under the Evening Star* (1942) and *Moon Garden* (1943). In 1939 she was awarded the Fatherland Prize.

The first Latvian poet was called Neredzīgais (Blind) Indriķis, and his collection of poems, *Songs by Neredzīgais Indriķis*, was published in 1806.

The best known Latvian authors in the first half of the 19th century were poet Ansis Līventāls and the self-taught storyteller and translator Ansis Leitāns, who edited the major Latvian newspaper *Mājas Viesis* and who produced moralizing stories and poetry. He gained great popularity with his localization of literature, including Kristoff Schmied *Genoveva*, *Grand Mother of the Earl* and *Master of war Eistakius*. A very prolific author was teacher Ernests Dinsberģis, who published some 100 books. A revolutionary called Jānis Ruģēns wrote a dramatic poem on the basis of the Book of Job from the Bible, addressing the injustices of the world through parables. The poem was banned by the tsarist government, because Ruģēns was among the first to dare to challenge the lack of rights of ethnic Latvians: "When will the times that other nations see arrive for Latvians, as well?", he asked. All of these authors were not professional writers.

A very specific aspect of the early days of Latvian literature was the hand-written literature that emerged during the Herrnhutian period – texts which farmers themselves created. The first of these texts emerged between 1740 and 1770 – half a century before Neredzīgais Indriķis produced his work. The texts were of speeches made at church meetings, spiritual songs, the life stories of the Herrnhutians and histories of the various congregations that were established. Some of the authors are known. A man called Ķikuļu Jēkabs produced vivid poems which represented the spirit of tradition in those days (1777). There were also translations. Texts were distributed in hand-written and copied form, and they were more lively than was the printed page. This was a massive process which lasted for more than a century. The Herrnhutians were fanatical writers and copiers of documents. Their work led to widespread literacy among Latvian farmers. In the early 19th century in Vidzeme, virtually no one was illiterate. Today we know of approximately 500 of these hand-written manuscripts, but it is clear that only a very small portion has survived.

The early Latvian intelligentsia promoted the idea of Latvians as fully vested people who deserved the right to be known as a civilized nation. A movement known as the *New Latvian* movement emerged. The *New Latvians* used literature as a way of discovering and reestablishing the Latvian identity. Authors began to create the myth of a lost paradise – fabled freedom in the distant past that had to be regained. The *New Latvians* undertook the difficult task of educating the people, publishing popular and scientific articles in the press and collecting folklore. Talented individuals tried their hand at prose and poetry. One of the most educated Latvians of the day, Krišjānis Valdemārs, published a book called *300 stories, funny tales and riddles*. Krišjānis Barons was not only an enormously successful collector of folk songs, but also the author of the first book of geography about the Baltic provinces – *A Description of our Fatherland* (1859). He also authored a number of successful stories (*Grandfather's Marriage*, *The Clever Man*, etc.) and poems.

Juris Alunāns was the first Latvian national poet. He was a biting satirist who produced clever epigrams and many new words in the Latvian language. His book *Songs translated into the Latvian language* (1856) launched a new period in Latvian linguistics. Alunāns not only translated great works of foreign literature into Latvian, but proved that the Latvian language was of equal standing with the languages of Horace, Goethe and Lermontov.

The most vivid representative of national romanticism in Latvian literature was the poet known as Auseklis (Miķelis Krogzemis), who wrote about the battle of the Latvian nation for freedom and celebrated the ancient Latvian gods. Still beloved today are choral songs composed by Jazeps Vītols, *The Singer of Beverina* and *Castle of Light*; Auseklis was the author of both of these poems.

In the body of work that emerged at the beginnings of Latvian literature, the most important opus was a 4,700-line epic poem by Andrejs Pumpurs, *Lāčplēsis* (1888). It was truly a masterpiece of Latvian literature, based on Latvian folk stories and legends. Pumpurs used the mythical hero Lāčplēsis to express the political ideas of 19th-century Latvians, increasing the national self-confidence of Latvians in the process. The epic shows the battle for social freedom as a requirement of history itself in satisfying the needs of the people.

The first important novel in Latvian literature, *The Times of the Surveyors* (1879) was produced by the brothers Reinis and Matīss Kaudzīte. The ethics of their prose were distinctly Christian in nature, even though poets at that time were rejoicing over the gods of antiquity and pursuing the national awakening. Historians of literature are still writing about the brothers Kaudzītes novel today, arguing over the true authorship of the work. Some feel that German nobles ordered up the work in order to make fun of the national romanticism of the Latvians. Be that as it may, the brothers laid the groundwork for Latvian humor with their work. Their humor was neither excessively dark nor clear and resonant. The brothers Kaudzītes created the impression that prose must be light and rhythmical, and that any work of prose first of all requires a successful story.

The Latvian nation produced authors in the mid-19th century whose work went far past national borders and was translated into many different languages all around the world. One of them was Rudolfs Blaumanis, who was the leader in writing stories of psychological realism. Blaumanis proved that Latvians were entirely capable of producing highly valuable literature, and he was the first to formulate the

Janis Poruks (1871–1911), poet and writer

Kārlis Skalbe (1879 –1945), writer and poet

Jānis Medenis (1903 – 1961), poet, translator

Jānis Akurāters (1876 – 1937), writer and poet

Edvarts Virza (1883 – 1940), poet

Jānis Ezeriņš (1891 – 1924), writer

Fricis Bārda
(1880-1919),
poet

Jēkabs Janševskis
(1865-1931),
writer

Andrievs Niedra
(1871-1942),
writer, politician

Teodors Zeiferts
(1865-1929), literature
critic and historian

Jānis Ziemeļnieks
(1897-1930),
poet

Pāvils Rozītis
(1889 – 1937),
writer, journalist

Vilis Plūdons
(1874 – 1940),
poet

Jānis Sudrabkalns
(1894 – 1975),
poet

conclusion that the important thing in literature is not what is being described, but who is doing the describing. Even more, he freed Latvian literature from didactics. Many of his novellas, including *Through the Swamp*, *In the Shadow of Death* and *The Lady of Raudupe*, are among the most classic works of Latvian literature. Several of Blaumanis' plays, including *Indrāni* and *Tailor's Days at Silmači*, are still produced today.

Fully free of the descriptive tendency to celebrate a lost paradise that was very widespread at that time was poet Eduards Veidenbaums, whose main contribution to Latvian literature was irony – beginning with satirical verses aimed against the high and might of this world and ending with the bitter laughter of a philosophically tended intellectual about the harsh paradoxes of existence. Intellectual aggression is a challenge for nearly the entire world, and that is why Veidenbaums' poetry is never out of date. He died young, and we have been left with his legend and with the social solutions which he proposed – ideas that stood above the ages.

Janis Poruks laid the foundations for the romantic branch of Latvia literature. He synthesized classical approaches to writing and broke out of the stereotypical role of Latvian prose writers – describing nothing other than rural life. Poruks produced some 200 stories, the psychological novel *Riga* and more than 300 poems. His work was very clearly influenced by Nietzsche. Poruks was the first to bring a sense of individual experience to Latvian poetry. He wrote verses about the lyricism of love, often grim, full of sadness and heartache. Many of Poruks' poems are masterpieces of classical Latvian poetry, and many have been set to music.

The genre of lyrically epic works of art in the finest classical European tradition was brought into Latvian literature by the poet Vilis Plūdons, born Vilis Lejnieks. His talent at producing ballads and long poems was unsurpassed in Latvian poetry. Plūdons emphasized visual imagery in long poems such as *The Widow's Son* and *Into the Sunny Farness*. His patriotic songs, including *May you Live Forever, Latvia* and *Song for a Free Latvia*, are still popular today. Fricis Bārda bewitched his readers with vividly bright yet simple images. His collection *Son of the Earth* is one of the most distinguished works of Neo-Romantic literature in Latvia.

Andrejs Upīts was an astonishingly prolific and varied author who published for a full 70 years. Among his most popular works are a cycle called *Robežnieki*, as well as books such as *In the Mills of Time*, *The Green Earth*, *Gold*, *Woman*, and others. He produced novels, socio-psychological short and long stories, and historical and critical treatises. Upīts was a convinced Marxist, and eventually his political beliefs turned into dogmas that he tried to impose on everybody's literature. He was a particularly bitter enemy of Romanticism as a direction of literature. Upīts allowed the Soviet government to use his authority as a means of bringing politics into

literature. In 1967 he produced a very slanted look at Latvian literature abroad that was called *Sunset without a Sun*, thus becoming a tool of the Bolshevik rulers of Latvia. Upīts became a true phenomenon in Soviet-era criticism, and his sharp and often bilious pen put fear into writers not only in Latvia, but throughout the Soviet Union.

Latvia's most-read author in the 1930s was Vilis Lācis, a contradictory person who upon the arrival of the Soviet occupation became the head of a collaborating government. During the occupation he became a master of the Socialist Realism school of literature, and various honorary titles were showered upon him. Lācis wrote 20 novels and long stories, 58 short stories, six plays and many articles. His prose was the source material for films such as *The Fisherman's Son*, *Homeward with Victory*, *The Little Hawk*, *The Zitars Dynasty* and others. Marģers Zariņš composed an opera on the basis of motifs from *To the New Shore*. Lācis wrote intriguing plots in which the positive and negative characters were clearly set apart. In modern terms, Lācis was a global master of the *belles lettres*. Lācis is the most widely translated Latvian author, especially into the Russian, and for a while he was the most published writer in all of Eastern Europe. Because of his favor with the Soviet occupants he has often been denied by Latvians, but the fact is that even if he written only *The Little Hawk*, he would ever have secured a place in Latvian literary history.

Janis Ezeriņš was a master of the long story and the most distinguished author in the genre in Latvian literature. He also wrote poetry and translated the works of Western masters such as Oscar Wilde and Boccaccio.

The writer known as Tirzmaliete was born Minna Dzelzkalne, and her poems of love, religion and patriotism were collected in *The Forgotten Heart* (1927). Tirzmaliete's most popular poem is called *I'll Sing of You, My Fatherland*.

The prose of writer and journalist Pāvils Rozītis was collected in 10 volumes. His talent was revealed most vividly in humorous long stores which focused on the bad habits of the proletariat. Rozītis also produced four psychological novels, among which the most popular are *Kiln* (1928) and *The Boys of Valmiera* (1936). He wrote essays, worked as a publicist, and translated the literature of other nations.

A poet and publicist called Andrejs Eglītis was the founder of the Latvian National Fund in Sweden. From 1945 until 1998 he lived in exile before returning home to Latvia. Eglītis' works pulsate with his hatred of the Soviet regime in Latvia. He is most famous for the cantata *God, Your Land is Burning*, which brings together Christian faith and the suffering of a nation. Eglītis brought prophetic pathos, Biblical forms of expression and a synthesis of the poesy of the Latvian folk songs that are known as *dainas* to his work.

The most prolific Latvian author in emigration was Anšlavs Eglītis, who wrote some 50 books

ALEKSANDRS ČAKS (1901-1950), born Aleksandrs Čadarainis, was the first Latvian poet to celebrate the city as a sovereign and poetic work of art. Čaks expressed his literary emotions with urban-based forms of expression, earning the reputation of an expressionistic and pessimistic urban poet-hooligan. Čaks gained enormous popularity with his poems, and many were set to music. His most important work was the heroic epic *Those Touched by Eternity* – an atypically reflective and lyrical work for him. Čaks also produced prose – stories and descriptive works. In post-war years he was forced to subordinate his talent to the dogmas of Socialist Realism, and this broke his spirit and, eventually, his life.

JĀNIS JAUNSUDRABIŅŠ (1877-1962) first became known for a long story called *Blossoms of the Wind*. His most important works include the trilogy *Aija*, *Dance of Death*, *The Farmer and the Devil*, *Don't Look into the Sun*, *Money*, and others. Jaunsudrabiņš' *White Book* is one of the most beautiful reflections on childhood in all of Latvian literature. Jaunsudrabiņš also wrote philosophically thoughtful poems. In 1944 the author moved to Germany, where he published a number of books, including a memoir called *I'm Talking to my Wife*. His long poem *Remember Latvia* strengthened the hope of Latvians both in exile and in Soviet-occupied Latvia that someday the country would be free again. Jaunsudrabiņš illustrated many of his own books. When Latvian regained its independence, his remains were disinterred and reburied in the cemetery of his hometown of *Nereta*, as he had requested in his will.

Andrejs Upīts (1877 – 1970), writer

Vilis Lācis (1904 – 1966), writer

Poet Mirdza Ķempe (1907-1974), Indian philologist Suniti Kumar Chateriji (1890-1977), literature historian Kārlis Egle (1887-1974)

Poet Andrejs Eglītis and artist Juris Soikans

Gunars Janovskis, writer

Veronika Strēlerte (1912 – 1995), poet

Ojars Vacietis (1933 – 1983), poet

Imants Ziedonis, poet

Zigmunds Skujiņš, writer

Harijs Gulbis, writer and playwright

Gunars Priede, playwright

Pauls Putniņš, playwright

Andris Kolbergs, writer

Jānis Peters, poet

Vizma Belševica,
poet and writer

Māris Čaklais, poet, publicist, essayist

Alberts Bels,
writer

Regina Ezera, writer

Māra Zālīte, poet

Janina Kursite, literary
historian, dean of the
Faculty of Philology,
University of Latvia

Nora Ikstena, writer

Anna Rancane, poet

Karlis Vērdiņš, poet

of prose and drama. He was a particular master at short stores and long stories, although he is perhaps best known for his novels, which all contained fast-paced stories, beautifully drawn characters and enormously rich and clever dialogue. Eglītis was extensively translated into English, and he was known worldwide as a successful and popular film critic in Hollywood, California.

Gunārs Janovskis, author of many novels and stories, lives in England. His particular focus has been the tragedy of the Latvian Legionnaires of World War II. His writing is concentrated in expression and deeply felt and even painful in terms of national subject matter.

Among post-war authors in Latvia, the most distinguished are Miervaldis Birze, a doctor and author, and Zigmunds Skujiņš. Birze gained popularity with a long story called *Roses Bloom in Everyone's Garden* (1958), and he also wrote plays, including *That was not the Last Day* (1961) and *Visiting the Black Grouse* (1965). Among his other works were descriptive pieces, reminiscences, satirical novels, travel descriptions, and diaries. Skujiņš' novels, stories and long stories are laconic, imbued with an elegant and clever style, aphoristic dialogues and unusual metaphors.

A popular and much read story teller is Regīna Ezera. The history of late-20th century Latvian literature cannot be written without mentioning Andris Kolbergs, who wrote detective novels and long stories in which he wrote about important social problems in a very precise way despite the watchful eye of Soviet censors. Many of Kolbergs' works were filmed.

Post-war Latvian playwriting has been the field of activity for three very distinguished playwrights – Gunārs Priede, Pauls Putniņš and Harijs Gulbis. Priede has studied the way in which people develop their personalities and deal with ethical problems, as well as the effect of the negations of history on society and overarching human problems. Putniņš is a playwright and publicist whose plays are mostly set in rural areas and small towns. Audiences remember plays such as *Oh World, You Building of People* (1983) and *The Sweet Burden of Trust* (1987) as the work of an author who had a good sense of humor and could put fast-paced stories and clever dialogue on the stage.

Gulbis is best known for a play called *Lullaby, the Child as a Bear* (1973). Unlike many other authors who lost their bearings when Soviet censorship collapsed, Gulbis continued to work in the 1990s, too.

Poetry in the latter half of the 20th century in Latvia is a subject that has not been discussed much, but unquestionably the true leaders of the genre from the literary and social perspective were Ojārs Vācietis and Imants Ziedonis. Vācietis published 13 collections of poems in occupied Latvia, although many other poems remained unpublished, either because of Soviet censorship or Vācietis' own self-censorship. Sometimes he produced poems that were too long to publish in collections. Ojārs Vācietis was a clarion horn and tore down many of the canons of Socialist Realism. His poems were universal in viewpoint, he saw the world as being in perpetual movement and the conscience of humankind as the maintainer of positive values. The collection *Breath* and the poem *Einsteiniana* that was in it caused Vācietis to be banned from publishing until the late 1970s, with the censors

explaining that his work could not be understood. Vācietis was also a masterful translator *The Master and Margarita* to Latvian readers, among other works of literature.

Imants Ziedonis has been at the height of popularity as a poet and publicist for at least four decades. From his first collections of poems, *The Sand of Land and Dreams* (1961), *Dynamite of the Heart* (1963) and *Motorcycle* (1965), he has produced a truly new style which involves conversational language and aggressive intonations. Each new collection of poems has represented a new step forward for Ziedonis. He has published countless articles on important issues of the day. His books of descriptive pieces, *Little Kurzeme* (1970-1974) and *Anyway* (1985), were popular. Ziedonis' children's stories have been published in several books and have been translated extensively into other languages.

Vizma Belševica is a poet and translator with an exquisite feeling for the Latvian language. Her language is rich, precise and melodic, her poetry – expressive and dramatic. After the publishing of her poem *Indriķis Marginalies of the Livonian Chronicle* (1968), she was banned from publishing for many years. Belševica also produced many works of prose – long stories, short stories, children's stories, etc. She has translated Shakespeare, Edgar Alan Poe, Jerome K. Jerome, Dante, Hemingway, Mark Twain and other classics.

A truly Latvian poet is Jānis Peters, who has written about the destiny of his nation. Since the late 1970s he has worked mostly as a publicist, but he has proven himself as a talented writer of song lyrics. He was a leader of the national awakening in the early 1990s and Latvia's first post-occupation ambassador to Russia. He has also worked extensively in translating poems written in other languages.

Latvia's most popular poet-playwright is Māra Zālīte. Her fourth collection of poems, *Sky, Sky* (1988), was published just as the national awakening was starting, and it is the one book in which she discusses the destiny of the Latvian nation most distinctly. In 1988 she wrote the plot for Zigmars Liepiņš rock opera *Lāčplēsis*. Zālīte's work has always involved important elements of Latvian folklore. She has also worked as a journalist and public speaker, and some of her speeches and articles were collected in the book *What Was Sown in Faith* (1997). In 1999 she proved once again her talent at producing outstanding plays, this time the vastly popular musical *Kaupēns, My Dear*.

The most distinguished poet from the Latgale region of Latvia is Anna Rancāne, who has written about farm life and Christianity. Her mainvalues are the home, the mother, and God. Rancāne has also written in the Latgallian language.

Nora Ikstena is a young writer who has been recognized by the critics and the public alike. She has published three books of prose – *Trifles and Joys* (1995), *False Romances* (1997) and *Celebrating Life* (1998).

Among the youngest generation of poets in the late 20th century, attention has been attracted by Karlis Vērdiņš, who was only 19 years old when he was admitted to the Association of Young Writers in 1998. He has also translated poems from English.

Despite the fact that translated works of literature from other countries dominate much of the book selling market in Latvia today, Latvian literature has not died, and it frequently bursts forth to surprise critics and audiences alike with its vitality and quality.

Johan Friedrich Hartknoch (1740 – 1789) has published all the works of Immanuel Kant in Riga

A monument to the German philosopher and writer Johann Gottfried Herder (1744-1903) is located outside the Dom Church in Riga

Issues of the Book of Higher Wisdom by Vecais Stenders

At the conference dedicated to Kant's *The critique of the Pure Reason* 200th anniversary prof. Teodors Celms delivered a study on Kant

PHILOSOPHY

In the development of Latvian mythical consciousness and spiritual culture, a specific and unified ethnic community mentality's world view manifestation was created, in which there was undeniably the presence of a philosophical sense of existence. Philosophy as the history of a particular culture's theoretical self-understanding is, of course, different.

Over the course of the centuries, a number of cultural and historical facts have been enacted in Latvia that are not linked by tradition but are nevertheless quite vivid. For example, some of Immanuel Kant's most important works, including all three of his *Critiques*, were published for the first time in Riga and *Liepaja*. Kant's ideas were critical in the development of Latvian philosophical thinking in the 20th century.

Attempts to produce independently orientated philosophical works first occurred among Latvians during the period of the national awakening in the latter half of the 19th century. Social thought was given a theoretical grounding, although at that time the processes was not in line with the criteria for academic philosophy that existed in Western culture. Western philosophers had a great influence on the philosophical worldview of Latvians in the early 20th century. This could be seen clearly in literature, prose and poetry (the work of Janis Poruks, Fricis Barda and others). The Latvian national poet Rainis helped to lay the foundation for dramatic humanism and philosophical literature in our era.

The academic traditions of philosophy emerged in full bloom in Latvia in the 1920s and 1930s, mostly at the University of Latvia. Professor Teodors Celms, who did much original work in

the area of phenomenology, was the most significant Latvian philosopher at that time. Zenta Maurina produced her first literary and philosophical essays at this time. After World War II Maurina became well known and popular in Germany, Sweden, Italy and Switzerland. Another person who was important in maintaining the traditions of academic philosophy was Pauls Jurevics.

During the Soviet occupation, official Marxist ideology dominated every area of thinking, but many philosophers nonetheless produced work that had elements of freethinking in them. The University of Latvia continued to offer degrees in philosophy. A number of important philosophical works were produced at this time by people like Yuri Vedin (cognition theory) and Peteris Laizans (the history of philosophy).

A new generation of philosophers emerged after the renewal of Latvia's independence in the early 1990s. Research at the University of Latvia is mostly aimed at the philosophy of culture and the arts, the philosophy of society and morality, and the modern aspects of phenomenology. There has been a great deal of international co-operation, and Latvia's philosophers have become active in Western academic circles.

Professor Yuri Vedin (1925-1985) has conducted research in Cognitive theory

German philosophy professor G. Funke

Isaiah Berlin, an outstanding Latvian-Jewish philosopher, who worked in Great Britain and the USA

Author of many essays in philosophy, Zenta Maurina (1897-1978)

The Mexican ambassador to the USSR and his wife attend a conference *The critique of Pure Reason and the Present Day* in Riga in 1981. The conference was dedicated to the 200th anniversary of the publication of Kant's famous work in Riga

Latvian Pauls Jurevics (1891-1981) was a professor of philosophy in Australia

Philosopher, pedagogue Teodors Celms (1893-1989) was in exile in Germany and the USA since 1944

Tamara Zalite at the 1981 Immanuel Kant conference

Associate professor of LU, sociologist Aivars Tabuns

Peteris Lakis, Rector of the Latvian Cultural Academy

The speciality of professor Vilnis Zarins is history of philosophy

Peteris Laizans, Author of numerous disquisitions in history of Latvian philosophy and culture history of Latgale

Associate professor of LU, sociologist Brigita Zepa

SOCIOLOGY

Sociology as a field of study first emerged in Latvia in the late 1960s, mainly in form of specific empirical research projects. The most important project during this period was done by Talivaldis Vilcins, who analysed the prestige of various professions in society. Of course, during the Soviet period the process of sociology was strictly controlled by Marxist precepts.

A system of education in sociology first began to emerge in the late 1980s, when sociologists first had an opportunity to choose their own methodologies and research projects. The experience of sociologists from the West was of much assistance in this process. Today sociology in Latvia is based both on private companies, which collect empirical data (the Baltic Data House, for exam-

Associate professor Rihards Kulis, Translator of works by western philosophers

Maija Kule, director of the Philosophy and Sociology Institute of the University of Latvia

Professor of Art Academy Andris Rubenis, author of many monographs in culture history

The speciality of professor Mara Rubene is contemporary ethics

ple), and on the academic tradition at the University of Latvia, the Latvian Cultural Academy and the Latvian Agricultural University, all of which have relevant research centres. These activities are mostly aimed at political sociology, rural sociology and cultural sociology.

The newspaper *Rigische Novellen* (1680-1710)

The newspaper *Mājas Viesis* (1856-1910)

Ansis Līventals (1803-1878), editor of *Mājas Viesis*

The newspaper *Tas Latviešu Ļaužu Draugs* (1832-1846)

A youth magazine called *Jaunības Tekas* (*The Paths of Youth*, 1910-1930)

Latviešu Avīzes, the first newspaper in latvian (1822-1915)

A publication by the Ministry of Education, *Izglītības Ministrijas Mēnešraksts* (*Monthly of the Education Ministry*, 1920-1939)

The newspaper *Amerikas Vēstnesis* was published by émigré Latvians in Boston (1896-1920)

A newspaper of the Latvian Farmers Union, *Brīvā Zeme* (*Free Land*, 1919-1940)

In 1949 Helmārs Rudzītis began to issue the newspaper *Laiks* (*Time*) in New York. The newspaper is still published today and is read by Latvians around the world

The newspaper *Jaunākās Ziņas* (1911-1940)

The newspaper *Dienas Lapa* (1886-1905, 1913, 1914, 1918)

The first periodical publication in Latvia was the newspaper *Rigische Novellen*, which was published in German during the rule of the Swedish crown. The newspaper was published between 1680 and 1710, and contained information about wars, diplomatic issues and legal matters.

The first periodical in the Latvian language was called *Latviešu Ārste* (*Latvian Doctor*,1768-1769), edited by a Dr. Vilde. An almanac called *Latviskas Gada Grāmatas* was published in 1797 and 1798 by German journalist Matthias Stobe and publisher Johann Friedrich Steffenhagen. The almanac contained information about the natural sciences, farming, gardening, etc., and it was published four times a year.

After indentured service was repealed, the newspaper *Latviešu Avīzes* (1822-1915) became the first Latvian language newspaper in the country. It was initially a weekly that was published in *Jelgava*. After 1901 it became biweekly, in 1911 it began to appear three times a week, and after 1913, it was published every day – always in *Jelgava*. The first editor was a German clergyman called Kārlis Vatsons, and other important editors included Wilhelm Pantenius, Rihards Šulcs, Augusts Bilenšteins, Jānis Veismanis and Nikolajs Puriņš. There were Latvians on the staff, and the newspaper had many supplements – *Church and School News*, *Farming and the Homestead*, *The Story Chapter*, etc.

A newspaper called *Tas Latviešu Ļaužu Draugs* (*That friend of Latvian people*, 1832-1846) was published by a German clergyman in Riga who aimed his writing at farmers in Vidzeme. The German aristocracy viewed the publication with a jaundiced eye, fearing that it would encourage farmers to move to the city since the repeal of indentured service. The clergyman invited Latvians, including Ansis Leitāns and Ansis Līventals, to work on the staff of the paper, and it was *Tas Latviešu Ļaužu Draugs* which first published a very free-thinking poem by Jānis Ruģēns which was called *When will those times arrive for the Latvians?*

Next came a newspaper called *Mājas Viesis* (*Guest at Home*, 1856-1910), which was a political, scientific and literary publication that was edited and published in Riga. Its first editor was Ansis Leitāns, followed in 1887 by Ernests Platess and then later by Pēteris Zālīte and Antons Benjamiņš. Staff members included the prominent writers Rūdolfs Blaumanis and Augusts Deglavs. The newspaper gathered the Latvian intelligentsia around itself, including students from the *Tērbata* (Tartu) University. The censors clamped down after a while, Leitāns grew more cautious, and the paper lost its popularity among the *New Latvians*.

Pēterburgas Avīzes (1862-1865) was a political weekly which launched a new era in the Latvian newspaper business. It was edited and published in St. Petersburg and edited by Juris Alunans and Krišjānis Barons. *New Latvians* on the staff included Alunans, Kaspars Biezbardis and many others. The newspaper reported on foreign affairs, on life in other countries, on various aspects of the sciences (especially the natural sciences), and about eco-nomics and philosophy. The supplements *Dzirkstele* (*Spark*) and *Zobugals* (*Mocking*) were important and aimed at *teaching the Latvian nation to laugh*, as the editors put it.

The Baltic German aristocracy and the Tsar's censors aimed their sights not only at the newspaper, but also at its readers. People shied away, and the paper's publication was suspended in 1865.

Pasaule un Daba (*World and Nature*, 1875-1876) was the first illustrated scientific and literary weekly in Riga, edited and published by Kaspars Biezbardis, who wrote most of the content himself. He talked about various aspects of the exact sciences and philosophy. A four-volume book on *Farm, Nature and World* that had been published by Alunans between 1860 and 1873 can certainly be seen as an indirect progenitor of this publication.

Dienas Lapa (*Daily Page*, 1886-1905, 1913, 1914, 1918) was a political, social, literary and economic daily which was edited and published in Riga. Among its illustrious editors were Fricis Bergmanis, Jānis Pliekšāns (Rainis), Jānis Bisenieks, Pēteris Stučka, Jānis Jansons-Brauns and others. The newspaper gathered around itself members of the *New Current* movement. After the movement was crushed in 1897, the newspaper's leaders were arrested and deported, while others went into exile abroad.

The first Latvian émigrants in the American city of Boston issued a newspaper called *Amerikas Vēstnesis* (*American Herald*, 1896-1920), which was a religious and political newspaper published twice per month. The editors were Hanss Rebane and Jēkabs Zibergs.

In 1904 the Latvian Social Democratic Workers Organisation began to publish an illegal underground newspaper, *Cīņa* (*Struggle*, 1904-1991), which later turned into the official newspaper of the Central Committee of the Latvian Communist Party. *Cīņa* was initially published once a month (in 1905 some 18,000 copies were published each time). Between 1910 and 1914 it was published in Brussels and smuggled into Latvia. *Cīņa* was also published during the chaotic 1910s in London, Boston, St. Petersburg and Moscow. Between 1919 and 1940 it was printed in Riga – legally when the Soviets were in charge and illegally when they were not. When the Soviet Union occupied Latvia in 1940 and 1941, the newspaper once again became an official daily. During the war, the editors moved to Kirov and Moscow. During the post-war occupation, it was the main newspaper of the Communist Party in Latvia. The last editor was a man called Jānis Britans, who in 1990, despite being a member of the Central Committee of the CPSU, cast his lot with the national awakening in Latvia, renamed the paper *Neatkarīgā Cīņa* ("Independent *Cīņa*), and resigned from the editor's post.

Antons Benjamiņš (1860-1939) was a journalist who was a graduate of the Cimze Teachers College in *Valka* and worked as a teacher for a while. In 1904, he went to work at a German newspaper in Riga. From 1907 until 1908 he was employed by *Mājas Viesis* and from 1910 until 1911 – by *Rīta Vēstnesis* (*Morning Herald*). In 1911, he established his own newspaper, *Jaunākās Ziņas* (*The Latest News*), and this marked the beginning of his distinguished career in journalism. Beginning in 1924 he also published an enormously popular magazine called *Atpūta* (*Leisure*). Both publications were very popular among readers both in cities and in rural areas. Benjamiņš attracted the most able journalists, writers and artists to his publications.

Benjamiņš' wife, Emīlija (1881-1941) was listed on the masthead of both *Jaunākās Ziņas* and *Atpūta* as publisher. She worked in journalism from the age of 17 and knew the technical aspects of the business. Sometimes she wrote theatre reviews. Like her husband, she was able to attract the most distinguished people of her time around her. She was an extremely accomplished host and a star of the upper reaches of society in her time. She died after deportation to Russia.

Helmārs Rudzītis (b. 1903 in Riga) was a graduate of the Faculty of Law of the University of Latvia who in 1926 established the publishing house *Grāmatu Draugs* (*Friend of Books*), which became popular by issuing a series of books that were priced at just one lats. Eventually these books reached print runs of 18,000 copies in place of the far more usual 2,000 copies. Later the publishing house put out a series of very important works. In 1928, it had its own printing and binding facilities. By 1944, *Grāmatu Draugs* had published some 1,500 books in Latvian. In 1931, Rudzītis founded a sound recording company called *Bellacord Electro*, which supplied LPs not only to Latvia, but also to Estonia and Finland. In 1944 Rudzītis went into exile and re-established his publishing house in Eslingen, Germany, publishing books and a monthly newspaper, *Laiks*, which Rudzītis himself edited. Eventually Rudzītis moved to New York, where he continued the publication of *Laiks* – a process which is still in operation today. At the height of its readership in the 1960s, *Laiks* was published in 13,000 copies.

Illustrated magazines on literature, the arts, housekeeping and handicrafts – *Zeltene* (*Golden Girl*), 1926-1940), *Sievietes Pasaule* (*Woman's World*), 1932-1940) and *Sieviete* (*Woman*)

The most popular illustrated weekly in Latvia was *Atpūta* (1924-1940), published by Emīlija Benjamiņa

Ilustrēts Žurnāls (*Illustrated Magazine*, 1920-1929) also wrote about literature and the arts

Daugava (1928-1940) was an important journal on literature, science and the arts

In 1910 a literary and scientific magazine for young people – *Jaunības Tekas* (*Paths of Youth*) – appeared in Rīga. It was published and edited by Andrejs Jesens, who printed work by distinguished Latvian authors such as Aspazija and Jānis Jaunsudrabiņš.
Latvian journalism was most active during the country's independence, between 1920 and 1940, when there were nearly 2,000 periodicals in 10 languages, including Latvian, Polish, Lithuanian, Hebrew, Russian, etc.
Jaunākās Ziņas, under the editorship of journalist Antons Benjamiņš, reappeared after a war-induced interruption on 15th November 1918. The newspaper started out as a cheap daily, but later it became a paper that stood close to liberalism in the country and had extensive and very well edited information. In the 1930s, the Sunday edition of the paper was printed in 250,000 copies. The newspaper published installments of popular novels and various theme-based pages with the intention of attracting a broader readership. Benjamiņš hired the country's best and most talented journalists.
Daugava (1928-1940) was a very important magazine on literature, art and science, and it was published once a month by the publishing house *Valters un Rapa* in Rīga. Among staff members were Jānis Grīns and Jānis Kadilis, and the magazine premiered a number of very important pieces of literature, including Edvarts Virza's *Straumēni* (a novel about a homestead of the same name), Anna Brigadere's *Kvēlošā lokā* (*In the Burning Ring*), and work by Anšlavs Eglītis, Aleksandrs Čaks and other writers.
Latvians, like many nations, have always had many women's magazines, which are more or less similar in terms of appearance and content. In Latvia this process began at the beginning of the 20th century and continues today. During the first period of independence in Latvia there were such richly illustrated women's magazines as *Sieviete* (*Woman*), *Zeltene* (*Golden Girl*) and *Sievietes Pasaule* (*Woman's World*).
The Soviet and German occupation authorities placed a great deal of emphasis on journalism. Both Stalin and Goebbels understood that propaganda meant everything in times of conflict. Both the Russians and the Germans decided to subordinate the freedom-loving Latvians with an offensive in the press and with other ideological methods. This was particularly true in the 1960s and 1970s, when Soviet censorship was particularly strict, and someone up above always decided what had to be on the first and second page of the newspapers. When an article about discussions on the new Soviet constitution mistakenly contained not the words *visas tautas apspriešana* (*discussion by the entire nation*) but *visas tautas apspiešana* (*oppression of the entire nation*), many people at the Press House were fired, and several were arrested. People in Latvia still remember those journalists from the 1960s, 1970s and 1980s who wrote more freely, in allegories, speaking not only of the great deeds of the governing regime, but also about the errors of the system, the problems of the oppressed and the level of crime that existed. Latvian journalism reached an apogee of sorts in the late 1980s when, despite the remaining tentacles of censorship, journalists became increasingly able to publish their honest views.

It is believed in Latvia that the national renaissance of the 1980s began with a concerted effort to stop the building of an underground railway in Rīga. The effort was spearheaded by Elita Veidemane, a journalist at the newspaper *Padomju Jaunatne* (*Soviet Youth*) who collected letters to the editor about the subject and wrote very heated articles arguing against the construction project. Later she became editor of the main awakening-period newspaper, *Atmoda* (*Awakening*). Also in this photograph is the distinguished Latvian publicist Visvaldis Lācis

Jānis Britāns for many years edited the newspaper of the Latvian Communist Party, *Cīņa*. In 1990 he renamed the newspaper *Neatkarīgā Cīņa* and quietly resigned his post, thus supporting the Latvian national awakening and supporting the entry of a new style into Latvian journalism. *Cīņa*, so long a mouthpiece for Communist propaganda, eventually turned into an independent paper called *Neatkarīgā Rīta Avīze* (*Independent Morning Newspaper*)

Professor Ābrams Kleckins has trained numerous generations of journalists at the University of Latvia. He is a senior member of the faculty of the Department of Communications and is a great authority among Latvian journalists

Teacher, poet and publicist Felikss Zvaigznons (1950-1989) was the senior editor of *Skolotāju Avīze* (*The Teacher's Newspaper*) and a star of Latvian journalism during the Latvian national awakening. *Skolotāju Avīze*, which had once been a tool of the authorities, turned into the newspaper *Izglītība* (*Education*), which featured interesting content and a large print run. Many people from the Latvian intelligentsia participated in the publishing of the newspaper

Writer and publicist Ēriks Hanbergs has written popular stories about agriculture and farming. He has also edited a number of important publications including, for a while, *Neatkarīgā Rīta Avīze*

Writer, publicist and journalist Andris Jakubāns, who worked at *Cīņa* and then *Neatkarīgā Rīta Avīze* for years, eventually rising to become editor-in-chief

Journalist Juris Kaža worked in Sweden before coming to Latvia as a reporter for Swedish Radio. When the *Baltic Way* protest was organised in the Baltic States in 1991 Kaža filmed the human chain from a helicopter and was ejected from the Soviet Union for his trouble. He returned to Latvia in 1991 along with the restoration of the State's independence and is now a journalist at the business newspaper *Dienas Bizness*

Vladlen Dozorcev was the senior editor of the Russian language edition of the literary journal *Daugava* and the first senior editor in the Soviet Union who was not a member of the Communist Party. Dozorcev stood with the Latvian intelligentsia during the national awakening, received citizenship for his distinguished contributions to the State, and was a member of Parliament in the mid-1990s

Latvia's largest newspaper in terms of print run today is the rural newspaper *Lauku Avīze* (*The Rural Newspaper*), which is published three times a week. The president of the newspaper, Voldemārs Krustiņš (who founded the paper and was its first editor), was formerly a popular editor of *Padomju Jaunatne*. In the picture he is in the centre, between *Lauku Avīze* editor Viesturs Serdāns and the director of the paper's publishing house, Alfrēds Kundziņš

Monika Zīle, once editor-in-chief of *Padomju Jaunatne*, later headed the magazine *Sieviete*. She is also known as the author of many popular books, and she has served in Parliament

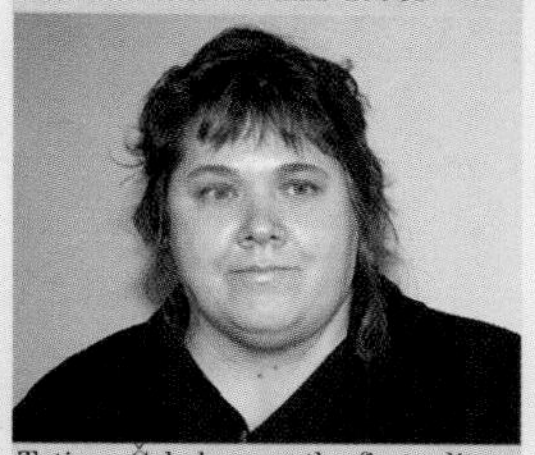

Tatjana Čaladze was the first editor of the Russian edition of the Latvian Popular Front's newspaper *Atmoda*. She is the only journalist in Latvia who has ever been arrested for her political beliefs

The name of Juris Blaumanis in Latvia is closely associated with criminal information – for years he has been writing in newspapers about crimes, their causes, preventive efforts and the complicated work of law enforcement agencies

Viktors Avotiņš was the deputy editor of the newspaper *Literatūra un Māksla* (*Literature and Art*) in the 1980s, when he allowed people to publish criticisms of the governing regime. During the period of *perestroika*, he was a deputy in the Supreme Council of the Soviet Union

Askolds Rodins is known as a commentator at several leading newspapers. He was particularly popular at *Atmoda* and now works at Latvia's leading morning newspaper, *Diena*

Dzintra Krievāne was deputy editor of *Padomju Jaunatne* before the collapse of the Soviet Union and saved from trouble a good many journalists who were too revolutionary in their approach

Andrejs Cīrulis edited *Padomju Jaunatne* when it was transformed into *Latvijas Jaunatne* (*Latvia's Youth*). During the period of the national awakening, the newspaper became a symbol of sorts of popular resistance against the Soviet occupation. Cīrulis was kicked out of the Communist Party and sharply denounced

Dainis Caune, the editor of the magazines *Liesma* (*Flame*) and *Viesis* (*Guest*). He is a certain symbol to the generation, which became active in the mid-1970s, sometimes known in Latvia as the lost generation. He is widely known as a propagandist for sports and as a founding member of the Latvian Olympic Committee

Philosopher Ilmārs Latkovskis was editor of the short-lived newspaper *Nakts* (*Night*) and is better known as the host of a television broadcast called *Tādi esam* (*That's How We Are*). He has written analytical and delicately humorous articles in the press for which he will long be remembered

The children's magazine *Zīlīte* (*Titmouse*) has been published for 60 years.
Today it is dedicated largely to nature, helping children to understand the world around them. The editor of the magazine is poet and biologist Jānis Baltvilks

This is Vija Vāvere, who was the first teacher of many distinguished journalists in Latvia. She worked for years at *Padomju Jaunatne*, *Zinātne un Tehnika* (*Science and Technology*) and *Sestdienas Rīts* (*Sunday Morning*), attracting young people from various specialities to her publications who later left a lasting impression on journalism in Latvia

One of Latvia's best known journalists is Kārlis Streips, who grew up and was educated in the United States and moved to Latvia when it regained its independence. He hosts television and radio broadcasts which attract a significant audience, and he teaches at the Department of Journalism of the University of Latvia

A powerful creative team in 1997 was the editorial group of the *Diena* supplement *SestDiena* (*SaturDay*) – Vita Pētersone, Egils Zirnis, Annija Pelude, Andrejs Kaufmanis, Sarmīte Māliņa and Solvita Smiļģe. Egils Zirnis is a biologist by training, but he is certainly one of the star journalists of the 1990s

A leading high-brow publication in Latvia is the magazine *Rīgas Laiks*, which is alone among magazines in Rīga to offer an intellectual look at life. It does not print cheap jokes, and the principles of the "yellow press" are alien to it. Here we see (back row) photographer Andris Krieviņš, philosopher Uldis Tīrons, philosopher Ilmārs Šlāpins and (front row) writer, poet and journalist Inese Zandere, journalist Ieva Lešinska and Rudīte Šteinere. *Rīgas Laiks* is more a philosophy than an example of journalism

Writer and journalist Aivars Tarvids, who writes in a sharp and critical style reminiscent of the Latvian writer Andrejs Upītis, but could perhaps devote more attention not only to journalism, but also to literature and literary criticism

Another element of journalism during the Soviet period was the fact that all publications were strictly regulated from Moscow. The rule was that one Communist newspaper, one Communist youth newspaper, one evening newspaper and one newspaper for every administrative district could be published in the national language of each Soviet republic. The regional newspapers could be published twice a week – no more. Nobody could publish any other newspapers. The same was the case with magazines – one for women, one on health, one on the arts, one on agriculture, one for schools and families, etc.

The first underground publications began to emerge in the 1987, although most of them were printed in Sweden and smuggled into the country. The first magazine to be published legally in the Soviet Union without official censorship was a publication from the Latvian Medical Association called *Latvijas Ārsts* (*Latvian Physician*). It appeared in June 1989 and opened the floodgates – within a few weeks there were lots of independent publications.

Since the occupation journalism in Latvia has involved three trends. First of all, the Western understanding of journalism has come into the process. An example of this is found in radio and television broadcasts hosted by American-born journalist Kārlis Streips, who has a proper broadcasting voice and is familiar with the issues that are discussed, usually politics, as well as in the

Kaspars Goba – biologist, publicist, photographer and film cameraman. He writes about foreign countries, about Latvians in Russia and about complicated issues such as pedophilia and corruption

Dina Vjatere, editor of the magazine *Doctus*, is one of Latvia's leading professional journalists in the field of medicine and health

Nikolajs Kabanovs

The popular Russian journalist Alla Petropavlovska is known as a publicist and as editor of the women's magazine *Lubļu* (*I Love*)

Māris Krautmanis has become known for anecdotes and funny stories, and he heads a department at *Neatkarīgā Rīta Avīze*

Inta Lehmusa-Briede, presently with the magazine *Una*

Juris Laksovs, an outstanding Latvian publicist with a very sharp pen who has served as an editor of several Latvian newspapers. He has interviewed Mikhail Gorbachev, Boris Yeltsin and other leading political figures

Armands Puče is an outstanding sports journalist, photographer and publicist who has written several books about Latvian athletes and about the Olympic movement. His photographs often grace the pages of the world's leading sports publications

Ainars Vladimirovs is a senior journalist at the leading tabloid newspaper in Latvia, *Vakara Ziņas* (*Evening News*). He not only provides information about things that are happening, but also wraps those things in some intrigue

The editor of Latvia's leading daily, *Diena* – Sarmīte Ēlerte – and the publisher and president of the stock company *Diena* – Arvils Ašerādens

Silvija Radzobe, a leading theatrical critic in Latvia who holds categorical, clever, interesting and lively opinions about the productions which she watches

Atis Klimovičs in Latvia's only war journalist – wherever there is a world hot point, there is Atis Klimovičs, whether it be Bosnia, Kosovo, Chechnya, Tajikistan, Turkmenistan, Afghanistan or any other military zone. He's there with a camera and his pen and paper

Lato Lapsa (right) may be regarded as the father of Latvian current information. The former head of news department in *Diena* and the information agency *Leta*, now a journalist in men's magazine *Klubs*

morning newspaper *Diena*, which operates largely according to Western principles. A second trend is negativism which is based on the idea that "if the dog bites John, that's not news, but if John bites the dog, that is". Newspapers are full of negative materials and journalists seldom seek out alternative viewpoints. Front pages are occupied with stories about low-level scandals among businessmen, politicians or artists. Third, there has been an unjustified commercialization of journalism. Often articles are based on the fact that the company (or, sometimes, government) officials who are described in articles pay something to the journalist, newspaper or publisher. The problem here may be that the publishers of some of Latvia's leading newspapers and magazines live in the West and see Latvia as a newly developing banana republic in which nothing positive is happening. The press reflects the nihilistic views of its owners. All the same, press freedom is the order of the day. If in the Soviet times no new publications were possible, then in the 1990s magazines and newspapers are published by all kinds of public and private organizations, including state and local government structures. In many cases, it must be added, a publication appears only once or twice before financial problems set in.

The Latvian market for magazines and newspapers is not very large, because there are few Latvian residents. Russians and other minority groups do not need many more publications because they have access to the press from Russia and other countries. At the same time, the Russian language newspapers which are published in Latvia are often in high demand in other parts of the ex-Soviet Union.

Because of comparatively low print runs, Latvian publications are relatively dependent on advertisers, and newspapers and magazines often come under the influence of individual political or economic groups.

Today the largest print run of any newspaper is enjoyed by the rural newspaper *Lauku Avize*, which is published three times a week and is aimed at rural residents, farmers and people in the food industry.

The leading morning newspaper is *Diena*, followed by *Neatkarīgā Rīta Avīze*. The two newspapers hold radically different editorial positions when it comes to economic issues.

Magazines in Latvia are still read mostly by women, and women's magazines fall all over each other to be more colorful and elegant – *Sieviete*, *Ieva*, *Una*, *Santa*, *Sievietes Pasaule*, *Aija* and others. There is a men's magazine called *Klubs* and a magazine for intellectual readers, *Rīgas Laiks* (Riga Time). A different audience is served by the magazine *Privātā Dzīve* (Private Life), which looks into the lives of well known individuals.

Dainis Lemešonoks is a very talented journalist who has worked at publications where owners and their specific interests set the tone of coverage

Aivars Ozoliņš is a distinguished Latvian analyst and commentator who writes about domestic and foreign policy issues in the newspaper *Diena*

Anita Kehre for many years published and edited the newspaper *Jūrmala*, and she now heads a journalism training center

Maris Zanders, and outstanding Latvian journalist who writes about economic issues and was at one time the editor and senior writer of the magazine *Laterna*

Andrejs Voroncovs

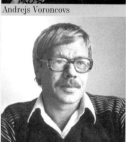

Aleksandrs Bļinovs

Ilma Rugāja, editor of the afternoon newspaper *Rīgas Balss* (*Voice of Riga*)

Inese Lusiņa writes in *Diena* about music

The outstanding publicist Dzintra Šubrovska is the press secretary to the Latvian Prosecutor General's office

A widely known journalist and commentator from *Lauku Avize*, Egils Licitis

Janis Mozulis, editor of the magazine *Mans Ipašums* (*My property*)

Una Meistare, one of Latvia's leading fashion journalists who writes about fashion trends in Latvia and abroad and is published in virtually all of the country's women's magazines

Theater and film critic Normunds Naumanis

Leonids Fedosejevs, a popular journalist in the Russian press

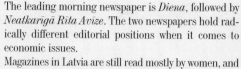

Sandra Zaiceva, chief editor of the gossip magazine *Privātā Dzīve*

The recipient of several journalism awards, Anita Smoļenska-Brauna of *Diena*

Cinema critic and arts journalist Dita Rietuma

Arturs Vaiders, sports journalist at *Diena*

Guntis Keiselis, a popular sports journalist

Inga Gorbunova edits the Latvia's most widely read women's magazine, *Ieva*, which is published weekly

Political commentator Uldis Dreiblats gained fame for being the first journalist to focus on a financial scandal at the Latvian electricity company

The editor of the leading financial magazine *Kapitāls*, Guntis Rozenbergs

The director of the NIP investigative journalism bureau, Janis Domburs. NIP is the only independent investigative journalism organization in Latvia

One of Latvia's most popular music journalists is Klass Vavere, who wrote the Latvian musical encyclopedia and hosts a popular musical program on Radio SWH

PRESS AND PUBLISHING BUSINESS

Preses apvienība, Pluspunkts and some other companies distribute press in Latvia

The evening yellow paper *Vakara Ziņas* is really yellow and dares to publish uncertain news

The paper *Brīvā Latvija* is published since 1946. In 1994 it moved to Latvia. Here the new edition is coming from the typing house *Elpa*

Ivars Zariņš, the Latvian press genius and publisher of nearly all biggest magazines (*Santa, Ieva, Klubs, Privātā dzive, Rigas Laiks*)

Andris Eglītis, photo editor in *Diena*. It is no enough to take a good picture, it must be also placed and published in a right way

Bizness Baltija is the biggest Russian business paper and the most significant Russian press media in Latvia. Chief editor Tatjana Fasta is a star of Rusian journalism in Latvia, here with the publisher Vladimirs Gurovs. The paper has expanded also to the Russian market and is very welcome among Russian readers in all Baltic States and Belorussia

Dienas Bizness is the biggest Latvian business paper. Juris Paiders is its' manager since the establishment

Staff of the magazine *Santa*

Creative staff of the journal *Ieva*

Politicians are careful with the magazine *Privātā Dzive*

A stormy press conference weekly take place in the Cabinet

Aleksejs Šeiņins, manager of the biggest Russian publishers house *Petit*

Authors of *Neatkarīgā Rita Avize* – the second biggest daily paper

Riga city evening paper *Rigas Balss* comes in every afternoon

SC *Preses nams* paper's *Vakara Ziņas* chief editor Ainis Saultis, chief editor of the paper *Rigas Balss* Ilma Rugāja and chief editor of the paper *Neatkarīgā Rita Avize* Aldis Berziņš

People from the advertising agency *Santa* work for distribution of magazines

BNS and LETA are the two Latvian information agencies

The National Radio and Television Council. Seated: Everita Šimanovska, Ojārs Rubenis (chairman), Dace Ķezbere. Standing: Jānis Sīkstulis, Ilmārs Šlāpins, Baldurs Apinis, Oļģerts Dzenītis, Dainis Stalts and Imants Rākins

The general director of Radio Latvia, Dzintris Kolāts

A mobile satellite transmitter – modern technology that allows Radio Latvia to broadcast from virtually any place in Europe

The old days – Radio Latvia's first van

In March 1924, a Latvian engineer called Jānis Linters persuaded Parliament's Budgetary Commission to finance the opening of a radio station in Latvia. On November 1 of the next year, the dream came true with a broadcast of the opera "Madame Butterfly". Initially Latvia's radio station was part of the Postal and Telegraph Department, and for a while it broadcast for only a few hours each day.

The introduction of radio to Latvia has always involved Radio Latvia – for 15 years during the country's independence, and then for 50 years of Soviet occupation. During both periods – paradoxically in the latter instance – Radio Latvia played an invaluable role in maintaining Latvian identity and culture. During the period of the national awakening in the late 1980s, Radio Latvia shifted from serving as a tool for government propaganda to becoming a true public radio operation. In 1991, the country'' radio and television operations were deemed "national radio" and "national television", because they played an inestimable role in the regaining of Latvia's independence. During the August putsch in Moscow, Radio Latvia was the only source of information for the entire country. Radio Latvia is still financed from the national budget, but it works as a public broadcasting organization. The radio serves the needs of the public as an important information bearer and as an element of the national culture. Since 1991, when Radio Latvia shed its propaganda functions, it has gained a very high reputation for trustworthiness. Radio Latvia strengthens national identity, preserves Latvian culture and upholds the Latvian language and spirit. Radio Latvia also helps to promote the integration of non-Latvians into Latvia's society. Many people feel the Radio Latvia is their best and, in some cases, only partner for conversation.

Today Radio Latvia employs 337 people, including the members of one of the best radio choirs in the world. At the turn of the millennium Radio Latvia was broadcasting on four channels, with total airtime of 73 hours a day. Radio Latvia's first and second programs run around the clock, the integration-aimed program

"Dome Square" airs for seven hours each day, while a program devoted to classical music is hear for 18 hours a day. In August 1999 international news broadcasts in English and Russian were moved from short-wave radio to the Internet. All of Radio Latvia's programs can be heard in real time on the Internet.

The studio where musical broadcasts and radio plays are aired has been rebuilt with the latest digital technologies, and today it is one of the best studios in Latvia

Radio Latvia program director Dārija Juškeviča (right) and Imants Rākins, a long-time executive at both Radio Latvia and Latvian TV, presently a member of the National Radio and Television Council

Pop music surveys for many years helped the Latvian nation to stay together and for Latvian music to develop. Here are the hosts of a greatest hits program focusing on traditional stage music known as *šlāgeri* – Karlis Vahšteins and Viola Lazo

Gunārs Jakobsons has served as commentator at many Olympic Games and was the host of an enormously popular broadcast called *Mikrofons*

Newsreader Māra Krontāle

Radio journalist and parliamentary deputy Rišards Labanovskis

Newsreader Māra Eglīte

Newsreader Sandra Glazupa

Newsreader Arita Grinberga

Newsreader Mārtiņš Hofmanis

The Radio Latvian Choir (est. 1940) is one of the most professional choirs in Europe

Radio Latvia's children's ensemble, *Dzeguzīte*, and its long-serving director, Daila Martinsone

A studio from which Radio Latvia's first program is aired

RADIO FREE EUROPE

In 1949 the American Congress approved the establishment of a radio service called Radio Free Europe. The point of the service was to air programs into the countries that had remained behind the Iron Curtain at the conclusion of the second world war. The first 30-minute broadcast, for Czechoslovakia, was aired on July 4, 1950. In 1953, Radio Liberty was established in Munich to broadcast programs into the Soviet Union. The first Latvian-language broadcast of 30 minutes was aired on July 19, 1975. The Latvian department of Radio Liberty was founded and headed for three years by Valdemars Kreicbergs, who had once served as a Latvian diplomat in Sweden. Later he was replaced in turn by Vilis Skultāns, Jānis Trapans, Rolfs

Ekmanis, Uldis Grava and Peteris Zvagulis. In the mid-1980s the Baltic departments were moved from Radio Liberty to Radio Free Europe. Programs aired on short-wave every day for 60 minutes. In 1992 RFE opened an office in Riga, and in 1995 the radio's central headquarters were moved to Prague.

Radio Free Europe remains an important medium for information and education in Central and Eastern Europe. Today the broadcasts of RFE are of greater importance then ever, in supporting the establishment and strengthening of democratic societies.

The Latvian department of RFE: Michelle Du Bach, Jeffrey Trimble (director of broadcasting), Dainis Mjartans, Inese Zinovska, Peteris Zvagulis, Rita Rudusa, Pāvils Bruvers and Maruta Kārkla

Rita and Pāvils Bruvers with US Senator Robert Dole at the Senate in Washington

The studio of the RFE Latvian department

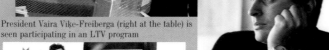

President Vaira Viķe-Freiberga (right at the table) is seen participating in an LTV program

The general director of LTV, Rolands Tjarve

One of the favourite on-air personalities at LTV is Arta Andersone, who anchors the Sunday edition of the news program *Panorāma*

Ija Tamkeviča is the sports anchor on *Panorāma* and also hosts the LTV morning program

Krista Vavere is one of the lead anchors on *Panorāma*

The *Labvakar* production group produced one of the most popular television shows in Latvia in the late 1980s and early 1990s. From the left – Edvīns Inkēns, Jānis Šipkēvics, Martiņš Jurjans, Ojārs Rubenis, Juris Vaičunas, Aldis Neimanis. Centre front – Harijs Beķeris

Ten years later the men of the *Labvakar* production group are successful and popular politicians and entrepreneurs. From the left – Ojārs Rubenis, Haralds Apogs, Edvīns Inkens, Harijs Beķeris, Jānis Šipkevics and (seated in front) Juris Vaičunas and Mārtiņš Jurjans

Daina Bruņiniece hosts a popular show on rural subjects – *Savai zemītei*

Programs produced by independent producers are an important part of the LTV mix. Here we see the Russian-language program "From Positions of Power", which is produced by the Alter A company. Host Vladimir Novodvorski is to the right; Latvia's Prime Minister, Andris Šķele, is at the left

Daira Aboliņa is a film critic who produces two cinema-related programs at LTV – *Aci pret aci* and *Zootrops*.

A new serial, possibly to be called "It Happened in Riga", is being produced at LTV

Journalists Dainis Lemešonoks, Sallija Benfelde and Askolds Rodins discussing political news with the host of a popular political program Kārlis Streips

The first television broadcast in Latvia occurred on 6 November 1952. The studio was located at *Nometņu iela* 62 in Rīga, and the very first program to be aired by a movie from the Rīga Film Studio, *Mājup ar uzvaru* ("Homeward with Victory"). The first made-for-television broadcast, an adaptation of P. Voiniča *Saulgriežu vētra* ("The Solstice Storm"), was also produced in 1956. One year later, a cinema group was established, and it later was transformed into the company *Telefilma Rīga*. The first black-and-white video recording was produced in 1969, and the first colour broadcast – a concert called *Dzintariņš* ("Little Amber") – was shown in 1974. A new television studio was built on *Zaķusala* Island in Rīga, and in 1985, the first broadcast from the new studios was an end-of-the-year music competition. The studio was fully completed only in 1988.

In 1992, the Soviet-era Radio and Television Committee was split up into Latvian State Television and Latvian State Radio. In 1993, LTV joined the European Broadcasting Union. A new law on radio and television was adopted in 1995. A satellite earth station went on line in 1996, and in 1998, LTV began to use the PAL colour coding system.

Latvian State Television is a national public broadcasting organisation, which is charged with providing a variety of balanced programming for all groups in society. Informational, educational and entertainment programs are all broadcast.

LTV broadcasts an average of 21 hours a day on

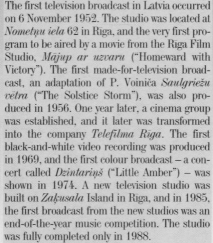

The game show *Mini mani* is an adaptation of the American show "What's My Line", and in 1998 it won top honours among viewers as the most popular show of the year. Here we see secret guest Raits Černajs, who is the Auditor-General, and the host of the program, Sandra Freiberga

The broadcast "The Soul in Everyday Life" is seen here with Latvian Lutheran Archbishop Jānis Vanags and journalist Ojārs Rubenis

two different channels that are seen throughout the country. Surveys show that 80% of Latvia's population watch LTV's channels every day.

A government subsidy, as well as income from business activities and sponsors finances LTV. LTV 1 is the national channel, aimed at the broadest audience and it broadcasts approximately 12 hours of programming per day. Informational and analytical broadcasts, news from Latvia and the rest of the world, cultural programs, television plans, musical, folklore, children's and advice broadcasts make up the bulk of programming. All programs on LTV 1 are broadcast in Latvian.

LTV 2 is a public channel on which 20% of the total broadcasts are aired in languages other than Latvian. There are programs on integration in society, sports programs, including live broadcasts of major domestic and international athletic events that are of importance to Latvia, informational documentaries, educational programs for social minorities, religious shows, and educational programs. Broadcasts produced by independent producers and the EBU are also shown.

LTV airs news broadcasts four times a day, and the evening news show, *Panorāma*, is the main show.

Since 1998, the LTV News Department has posted a permanent correspondent in Brussels, and it has a mobile brigade of correspondents in the Baltic States. The News Department does not have a network of regional correspondents within the country, choosing instead to work with local television stations to get materials as needed. LTV uses the PAL colour broadcasting standard, BETACAM SP and DVC PRO video recordings are used, and coverage is of 95% of Latvia's territory.

There are five studios in the LTV complex. Two are 80 m² in size, while the others are 100 m², 450 m² and 600 m² in size. LTV has a mobile television station called Magnolia, which boasts extensive sound processing equipment and is used for live broadcasts of musical events.

The mobile station Laura, for its part, is used to produce documentaries, athletic broadcasts and serials, as well as to present live broadcasts. The television station's satellite earth station has allowed it to receive and broadcast a wide range of programming. The diameter of the antenna is 9.2 meters. Broadcasts are transmitted on one channel and received on two. The broadcast frequency is $1.0 \div 14.5$ GHz, while the reception frequency is $10.95 \div 11.7$ GHz.

Baiba Strautmane hosts the analytical program *Mūsu cilvēks* "Our Person", Dagnija Neimane is a *Panorāma* journalist who was once the News Department's special correspondent in Moscow, and Ilva Liepiņa is a lead anchor on *Panorāma*

Every resident of Latvia knows the man on the left – Jānis Dimants, who for many years reported on rural life for *Panorāma* and was the head of the News Department in the 1980s. *Panorāma* airs every night at 8:30 PM

Līga Kalnača, Līga Ozola and Līga Krapāne – all present or former employees of LTV

Director Ilze Pētersone and production director Ansis Berziņš

Producer Ilze Strenga is the author of the LTV program "Behind the Scenes", and she produced the LTV's 45th anniversary event at the Latvian National Opera, as well as the millennium program *LTV 2000*

Irina Viņņika is the anchor of LTV's Russian language news program, and she is very popular among Latvian viewers, too

Natalija Abola hosts the popular *Shockshow* in russian

Ansis Bogustovs is a journalist at *Panorāma*

Žaklīna Cinovska hosts the show "Žaklīna's Top Stars"

LTV finance director Edgars Brēmers

The head of the News Department, Gundars Rēders

The LNT news studio. Since September 1999, LNT has broadcast an hour-long news program each day, along with shorter broadcasts throughout the day and later in the evening. Egils Zariņš (photo) is one of the anchors of the news, and he is also popular as the host of the programs *Nedēļa* and *Mikslis* and as the author of two cookbooks

LNT's advertising specialists don't get their face on camera very often, but they are seen each year when the LNT Choir produces its annual "hymn"

LNT used to have just a few cameras, but today it is a technologically modern studio with highly qualified resources and staff

The heart and soul of LNT is its general director, Andrejs Ēķis. He developed the most widely viewed TV channel in Latvia, gathering around himself what he calls crazy and talented people – a very active team indeed

The sports news are becoming more recognised once again, after two of the station's leading sports anchors left for other pastures. Here we see Jānis Traubergs

Kristine Anže is one of the four attractive and energetic hosts of the LNT morning program. The broadcast has been seen every weekday morning since late 1998. It wakes people up with a positive charge, telling them about what has already happened and what is to happen in the future

The brothers Igors and Gvido Linga produce musical shows for LNT. Both are the authors of the broadcast *JAM*, which looks at new elements of foreign music, as well as the daily *Latvijas mūzikas stunda* ("Latvian Musical Hour"). Igors is also an active director at LNT

Ilze Dobele and Egils Zariņš appear on LNT's news programs. Ilze is known for her beautiful and correct smile, as well as her activities in charity programs

In addition to Latvia's State or public television station, there are also several commercial operations, the largest and best known of which is Latvian Independent Television (LNT). The company was formed through the merger, in 1996, of two smaller television stations – NTV-5 and Picca-TV. Founded in 1992, NTV-5 was the first television station in Latvia to offer competition to Latvian State Television, which had previously held a monopoly on television news in the country. Picca TV was established in 1994, and it featured a morning schedule of entertainment and news.

After the merger, LNT in less than two years became the country's leading television channel in terms of viewer audience. LNT has positioned itself as a family-oriented TV channel and its original programs and foreign serials are aimed at audiences of all ages and nationalities. This has allowed the company to take the lead in the television advertising market, too.

LNT has produced a number of original programs that have been extremely popular among viewers, among them the situation comedy *Sirdsmīļā Monika* ("Dear Monica"), which is an adaptation of the famous American sitcom "I Love Lucy". *Sirdsmīļā Monika* has become something of a cult hit in Latvia, thanks to the popular actors who play the roles and the funny situations in which the characters find themselves.

Many viewers are glued to their chairs when the weekly informational program *Nedēļa* ("the Week") goes on the air. The program has focused public attention on such issues as corruption, the pedophilia scandals, narcotics use, etc. The popularity of the program is guaranteed by the sharp look at life which is taken by its producer – the journalist and politician Edvīns Inkēns.

Egils Zariņš, who hosts the popular cooking show *Mikslis*, has published two cookbooks on the basis of the show. The program, which airs on Sunday mornings, features prominent people from Latvian society who demonstrate their favourite recipes. The program is unhurried and presents an interesting discussion of life, work, politics, food, eating cultures and taste. Viewers who are less demanding are fascinated by the program *Savādi gan* ("How peculiar!") which has absolutely no fantasy to it, but does have a courageous parody of things that others would never dare criticise – the country, the nation, news broadcasts, politicians.

LNT is undergoing international growth at this time, cooperating with Estonia's TV1 and Lithuania's Baltijos TV to set up a common advertising market and to purchase programs jointly. This will certainly allow viewers in Latvia to see better and more expensive films and serials. LNT – television that never leaves you bored.

LNT has presented itself as a news and film channel, and much cinema-related advertising is featured. A face that undoubtedly personifies LNT's films is that of announcer Baiba Kranate

Baiba Auzane produces the show *Mājas akadēmija* ("Home academy"), which is seen in the mornings and talks about everyday subjects, problems and solutions. Baiba never loses her femininity or her professionalism. Together with the other "Baibas" at LNT – Kranate and Sipeniece – she sang on the hit song *Tris vientuļas beibes* ("Three lonely babes"), which is heard on the LNT's third-year anniversary album "LNT Choir and Friends"

The weather is seemingly a mundane part of the news every day, but Laila Liduma (photo) and Ieva Bērziņa have helped make weather forecasting one of the ways in which LNT promotes its image

Iveta Balode is the youngest LNT news anchor, but her balanced approach to news and her intelligence have made her the leading anchor, along with Andris Auzāns (above)

Nedēļa is a weekly review with the biggest audience in Latvia. The producers of this program are Signe Reinfelde and Egils Zariņš (sitting), Aija Gramzde, Aivars Erdmanis, Edvīns Inkēns, Aivars Rupkus, Vairis Stašāns

Baiba Sipeniece is one of the most colourful personalities at LNT. She used to report on culture for the news programs, but today she is the host of her own daily talk show – *Zvaigžņu stunda* ("the Star hour") – where she interviews musicians, writers, artists and other creative individuals

The most popular Russian program on LNT is *Rižskij balzam na russkuju dušu* (*Riga balsam for Russian soul*), hosted by Svetlana Ivaņņikova (far left) and Igors Proņins

JAUNUMS

The advertising agency *ADM Group* designed this Internet home page for a company that offers vacation opportunities in Latvia's rural areas

An *Aldaris* beer add by the advertising agency *Divizija*

The Latvian Advertising Association is a member of the International Advertising Association, which is the world's largest professional organisation for marketing specialists. The five main tasks of the Association are: to explain the meaning of advertising, to protect commercial freedom of expression and the right of the consumer to choose, to implement advertising self-regulatory codes in practice, to conduct professional development and training programs, and to provide for the publication and distribution of professional market publications among members of the Association.

The Latvian Advertising Association was established on 25 February 1994. At the time of this writing, it had 39 members from the largest Latvian advertising agencies, mass media outlets and advertisers. An advertising code of behaviour was in effect in Latvia. One of the main projects of the Association has been the annual *Golden Hammer* awards competition for the best and most professional advertising. The awards ceremony is the event of the year each year for the advertising industry in Latvia – both for advertisers and for those who create the advertising, as well as the mass media and, of course, the consumers of advertising.

AVE LAT
G R U P A

The logo of the AVE LAT group by the advertising agency *Balta Communications*

The *Golden Hammer* awards for excellence in advertising have been held every year since 1993, and the awards ceremony is the event of the year for the advertising industry – for those who advertise, for those who create the advertisements, for those that publish or broadcast the advertisements, and for those who are the end consumers of the advertisements

QUOTE OF THE DAY

Vladis Goldbergs, the director of the Marketing Communications Agency

The advertising agency *Divizija* produced this advertisement for women's lingerie for the stock company *Lauma*

Izjūtiet augšācelšanās prieku!

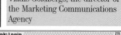
1 ola,
100 svaigas iespējas:

izbaudi vasaras garšu

nemoki maizi,
izvēlies
TUKUMA SVIESTU!

BALTIC OVO
AVE LAT GRUPA

The *Balta Communications* agency was responsible for this egg advertisement for the stock company *Balticovo*.

The *Garāža 4x4* marketing and communications agency designed the exterior appearance of the *Baltcom GSM* client service centre

The *Santa* advertising agency's advertisement for butter for the stock company *Tukuma Piens*

IZVĒLES BRĪVĪBA

NOKIA 5110

NOKIA
CONNECTING PEOPLE

The advertising agency *Rīgas Dizains* put this *Nokia* advertisement on a building wall in Riga

MiniMaks

LIETO UN NEMAKSĀ
Peidžeru pakalpojums bez abonēšanas maksas

1999. gadā būs 574 *Dienas*

abonē uz gadu
6,00
ietaupi Ls
maksā pa daļām

Diena

Advertising agency *Balta Communications* produced this advertisement for the subscription campaign of the daily newspaper *Diena*

Nemainiet partneri, mainiet prezervatīvu!

Lai bagātinātu savu dzīvi, nav nepieciešams meklēt jaunu partneri – labāk izmēģiniet jaunus "COOL GOLD" prezervatīvus ar pumpiņām

Adell Saatchi & Saatchi is an advertising agency that has been working in the Latvian market since 1993. It is the representative of Britain's *Saatchi & Saatchi Advertising Worldwide* (which has 167 offices in 90 countries) in Latvia. Clients in Latvia include *Procter & Gamble*, the *Unibanka* bank, *Merrild*, *Hewlett Packard*, *Toyota* and the agency, which is preparing Riga's 800th anniversary celebrations in 2001 – *Riga 800*. Since 1995, the Agency has regularly won nominations and awards in the Golden Hammers awards. To the right: A *Saatchi & Saatchi* advertisement for the "Cool Gold" brand of condom

Dzīvākais krus-tojums ceļošanai pasaulē.

Sākot no 31. marta British Airways četras reizes nedēļā veic lidojumus no Rīgas uz Getvikas lidostu Londonā. No Londonas British Airways un tās aviopartneri piedāvā lidojumus uz vairāk nekā 500 vietām visā pasaulē.

The *British Airways* campaign known as "Take-Off" was designed by the *Balta Communications* agency

The *Santa Ltd.* advertising agency was established on 3 May 1993, and today it is a powerful full-ser-vice advertising agency. The agency's sales division services the eight publications, which are issued by the *Žurnāls Santa* publishing house. The advertising projects and marketing division provides professional advertising ser-vices to clients. In the photos – adver-tisements for the women's magazine *Ieva* and the men's magazine *Klubs*

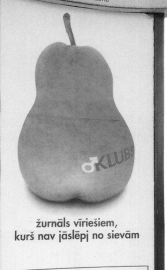

žurnāls vīriešiem, kurš nav jāslēpj no sievām

ŽURNĀLS
KLUBS Ls 12,89

Brand Sellers DDB Baltic is a full-service adver-tising agency, part of the world's second largest international communications network, the *DDB Worldwide Communications Group Inc.* The agency, which was established on 14 September 1994, has extensive experience in marketing communications planning, in the preparation and implementation of creative strategies, and in the development of design concepts, branding, graphic styles and packaging. The agency's part-ners include the *Datum Optimum Media Latvija* media agency, the *Rapp Collins* direct marketing agency, and the *DDB & Co. Hintzy Heymann* public relations agency. The agency *Brand Sell-ers DDB* offers clients advertising in all three Baltic States. In the photo: Advertising produced for the second anniversary of SC *Latvijas Neatkarīga televīzija* ("Latvian Independent Television")

Ivars Strautiņš,
president of Turība

Ivars Kalviškis, general director of Laima,
is known in Latvia as "the chocolate man".

The company *Cido pārtikas grupa* (Cido food group) is the leading producer of non-alcoholic beverages in the Baltic States. The company was founded in 1994, and it gained popularity in the Latvian market with the *Mangaļi* brand of mineral water, extracted from a stream that is 265 meters underground. In 1996 Cido began to offer natural fruit juices in one and two-liter packages. Today the company produces nine juices and nine nectars. Since 1996 it has sold the carbonated beverage *Fantastika* in cola, orange and lemon-lime flavors, as well as tonic water. *Cido* always keeps up with the times and with shifts in consumer taste. New products are offered on a yearly basis. A new brand of juices, *Primavera*, emerged in 1998, and a non-carbonated version of *Mangaļi* was on store shelves in 1999, as were the refreshing beverages *Tarhūns* and *Kvass*. Another new brand name, *Oma*, covers jams, fruit and sunflower oil.

Company *Cido pārtikas grupa* has become the leading producer of food products in the Baltic States by investing ongoing resources in modernization, sales and marketing. *Cido* provides consumers with beverages and other products that are always in demand, both in Latvia and abroad. The director of the company is Andrejs Ceplitis.

An organization called *Turība* (roughly translated as *Wealth*) was established in Latvia in 1937 as a central economic structure which even today remains one of the country's leading taxpayers and rural employers. *Turība* is made up of 33 cooperatives, and it is a member of the International Alliance of Cooperatives. Among the food processing companies in this group are facilities in *Skrīveri*, *Saldus*, *Smiltene* and *Tukums* which use only natural and local produce to offer ecologically pure and healthy products on the market.

Vastly popular Latvian food products include the *penuche*-type candy known as *Gotiņa* (Little Cow). There are 13 different versions of this sweet, including versions with nuts, dried fruit and seeds. Many other kinds of sweets are also produced in Latvia, including sherbets and toffees.

Companies in the *Turība* group also produce more than 50 kinds of vegetable, fruit and berry conserves, vegetable soups and lunch dishes that are quick and easy to prepare, fruit and berry compotes, jams, marmalades, fresh juices, syrups, marinated vegetables, vegetable salads and sauces. The system also has 12 bakeries which control 20% of the bread market in the country. Without preservatives and chemical additives, *Turība* produces the nutritional supplements *Osteonorm 2*, *Gastronorm* and *Puteksnītis*. *Turība* also three farms at which mink, polar fox and silver fox are grown. *Turība* controls the largest wholesale and retail network in rural Latvia, as well as a ceramics factory, a textiles plant and a factory in *Daugavpils* at which pellets are produced.

A company in Latvia which is truly a Latvian treasure is one of Europe's best producers of chocolate, the stock company Laima. The first major sweets factories in Latvia emerged in the mid-19th century. An industrialist called Teodors Rigerts began to produce chocolates in Riga in 1870, and in 1924 his traditions were taken over by the stock company *Laima*. For 130 years the company has been selling its products not only in Latvia, but also in France, England the United States and other countries.

In 1881 a factory called *L.W. Goegginger* opened its doors, producing candy, chocolate, biscuits and various kinds of preserved foods. In 1940 it and *Laima* were both nationalized by the Soviet authorities. *Laima* retained its name, but the Goegginger plant was dubbed *Uzvara* (Victory).

Laima was privatized in 1993 and *Uzvara* followed suit in 1994. Both companies were turned into stock companies. In 1998 they merged, retaining the name *Laima*, but preserving both trademarks. *Laima* offers a wide variety of products — dozens of kinds of chocolates, caramels, marmalades and soufflé sweets. *Laima* brings together high quality, modern production technologies and decades-old traditions to produce new varieties of candy all the time. Today *Laima* provides jobs to more than 800 specialists, and its products have won recognition and praise at international food exhibitions. *Laima* products are on sale in Latvia, Lithuania, Estonia, Germany, the Czech Republic, Sweden, Canada, Israel, the United States and elsewhere.

The exhibition firm *Creatio* is known in Latvia for its commercial exhibitions *Reklāma* (Advertising), *Stils & Mode* (Style and Fashion), *Baltic Industry* and the Riga Book Fair. Each of these events has become the leading event of its kinds in Latvia, and all of them have won international recognition.

In-depth client interest in various sectors of the economy led *Creatio* to organize conferences for specialists. The first international marketing and advertising conference *Reklāma 2000* (Advertising 2000) gained a great deal of recognition in 1999. *Creatio* also has worked hard to increase the level of

quality and the prestige of its exhibitions, as well as to make them more visually interesting. For that reason *Creatio* has launched a subsidiary which produces exhibition stands both for *Creatio*'s own exhibitions and for shows that are organized by other companies.

In 2000 *Creatio* launched two major new projects — organization of Latvia's participation in the *Expo 2000* world fair in Hannover, Germany, and the first international advertising competition *Golden Hammer*, which grew out of Latvia's domestic advertising competition of the same name.

The director of the international exhibitions company *BT 1*, Viesturs Tīle (right)

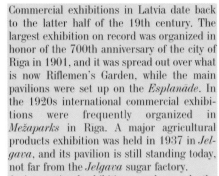

Commercial exhibitions in Latvia date back to the latter half of the 19th century. The largest exhibition on record was organized in honor of the 700th anniversary of the city of Riga in 1901, and it was spread out over what is now Riflemen's Garden, while the main pavilions were set up on the *Esplanāde*. In the 1920s international commercial exhibitions were frequently organized in *Mežaparks* in Riga. A major agricultural products exhibition was held in 1937 in *Jelgava*, and its pavilion is still standing today, not far from the *Jelgava* sugar factory.

An international exhibition complex run by the Riga Technical University was opened on *Ķīpsala* island in Riga in 1997. The *Ķīpsala* complex offers participants and visitors services that conform to international standards and quality levels. The facilities are occupied between 250 and 260 days a year. Approximately one-half of the exhibitions at *Ķīpsala* are the work of the international exhibitions company *BT 1*, which is a member of the Latvian Chamber of Commerce and Industry. *BT 1* was one of the first companies in Latvia to organize international and regional exhibitions at a professional level, and the shows have covered an enormously wide spectrum of subjects with the support of national and local government institutions and various professional groups. The number of participants and visitors has expanded enormously – nearly 400,000 people attended exhibitions at *Ķīpsala* in 1999.

A strategically important exhibition at the Baltic level of the *Māja* (Home) exhibition which has been the largest and most popular exhibition of its kind in the Baltic States for the last three years. The *Māja* exhibition is held twice a year – in the spring and in the fall.

The *Auto* show is the only one of its kind in the Baltic States and Scandinavia. The show is listed on the calendar of the global association of motor vehicle manufacturers, *OICA* – a list which includes only the 18 most prestigious shows in the world once every two years.

An international and annual food show, *Riga Food*, the educational exhibition *Skola* (School) and the tourism market *BALTTOUR* are among other *BT 1* exhibitions that have developed very dynamically over the last several years. In the spring of 2000 a third hall was scheduled to be opened at the *Ķīpsala* complex, thus expanding the floor space of the facility to 23,000 square meters. That will make the complex the largest exhibition facility in the Baltic States.

The *Ķīpsala* facilities are also used for various cultural, athletic and entertainment events. Summer solstice parties, costume balls run by the radio station *SWH*, and performances of the rock opera *Lāčplēsis* have all been held here. In 2001 *Ķīpsala* island and the exhibition center will be leading venues for events held during the celebration of Riga's 800th anniversary.

THE SKONTO OLYMPIC HALL

The Skonto Olympic Hall was opened on 1st April, 1996, on 3.8 hectares of land. The exhibition hall itself has floor space of 8,100 m². The Skonto Olympic Hall is located in the heart of Riga, which is convenient for participants and visitors alike. From December until March each year the hall is used as a soccer training facility, but during the rest of the year it hosts exhibitions, concerts, festivals and other public events.

The level of technologies and services at the Skonto facility is fully in line with European exhibition standards. The hall has a cement floor with steam and hydro-insulation. Communications run underground with connections at every 10-20 meters. The hall has its own boiler house to provide automatic air temperature and hot water control.

Stands in the hall can be hooked up to the water system, and there is a computerized telephone central with 100 numbers.

The exhibitions company *Prima Skonto* is a stable player in the Latvian exhibitions market. It has organized shows on a wide variety of subjects – security, printing, packaging, comfort, energy, health, the construction world, exotic aspects of automobiles, wood processing and instruments. Each year *Prima* helps thousands of people to learn about the very latest in dentistry, fashion, restaurant, bar and hotel supplies, furniture production, food production and heavy industry.

Many of the exhibitions have grown enormous over the years. The *Drošība* (Security) exhibition, for example, has grown from a simple exhibition into an annual weeklong program called *Security Week*. It is organized by the Latvian Interior Ministry.

Employees from the Central Statistical Bureau's International Affairs Division and European Integration Division regularly organise *European statistics days*

At the 80th anniversary celebration of the Central Statistical Bureau, a portrait gallery of former directors was unveiled. Seated in the front row of this photo you see Arvils Sautiņš, who managed the institution from 1993 to 1998, Elerts Aboliņš, who was its director from 1958 to 1970, Aija Žigure, the present director of the Central Statistical Bureau, and Gunars Baltiņš, who was director from 1970 to 1993

Marģeris Skujenieks (1886-1941), a political leader, economist and statistician. He was Prime Minister of Latvia several times

This Statistical Atlas, which was published by Marģeris Skujenieks in 1938, stands in a place of honour at the Central Statistical Bureau. More recent statistical publications are always available

Aija Žigure is the current director of the Central Statistical Bureau. Here you see her at the opening of the international conference *Obtaining Regional Statistical Information*

THE CENTRAL STATISTICAL BUREAU

Soon after the establishment of the independent Latvian state, the country also turned its attention to the issue of statistics. On 1st September 1919, the Latvian Cabinet approved regulations that led to the establishment of the State Statistical Board. The first director of the Board was Marģeris Skujenieks, who had begun collecting systematic information about the territory of Latvia at the beginning of the 20th century. He directed the Board from 1919 until 1939, with interruptions between 1926 and 1928 and then again between 1931 and 1933 – periods that he spent as the Prime Minister or Deputy Prime Minister, a member of the *Saeima*, the Minister for the Interior and the Minister for Finance. During Skujenieks' tenure, the Statistical Board collected information regarding 30 statistical sectors.

There are several distinct periods in the history of Latvian statistics. The first is the independence period (1919-1940), followed by war, the post-war period of the Soviet occupation (1940-1990), as well as the current period of renewed independence.

In the early 1990s, the Latvian State Statistical Committee became independent of Moscow. In 1998, it was renamed and became the Central Statistical Bureau. Since the renewal of independence in Latvia, the main directions for the development of the Bureau have been the selection of new and progressive methods for the collection of data in statistical observations, the widespread utilisation of international standards, new statistical studies and indicators, as well as the implementation of modern information technologies.

Today, the Central Statistical Bureau collects information about all sectors of the national economy. It provides society, government institutions and international organisations with true, objective and all-encompassing statistical information that is available to any user. Each year the Bureau publishes some 70 different titles, mainly in Latvian and English. The Central Statistical Bureau employs some 500 staff – both people who work at headquarters and people who conduct interviews.

LATVIA IN THE STATISTICAL MIRROR

Here are some statistics regarding the Republic of Latvia supplied by the Central Statistical Board:

Latvia is 64,600 square kilometres in area, and its population at the time of this writing was 2,439,000 individuals – 46% men and 54% of women. 69% of Latvia's population lived in cities, 31% in the countryside. The largest cities: Riga (797,000 residents), *Daugavpils* (115,000) and *Liepāja* (95,000). Ethnic Latvians represented 55.7% of the population. The life expectancy of new-borns was 64 years for boys and 76 years for girls.

The average value of a full "basket" of goods and services needed by individuals in Latvia at the time of this writing was USD 139, while the average net wage of individuals employed in the economy was USD 165 – a 10% increase in 1999 over the average wage in 1997. Consumer prices during the same period increased by 5%. Latvia's GDP at the time of this writing at current prices was USD 6.396 billion, or USD 2,612 per resident. GDP growth in one year at comparative prices was 3.6%. The proportion of industry and construction in overall added value was 29%. The figures for other sectors were 5% for agriculture, hunting, forestry and fishing, and 66% for the service sector. Accumulated foreign investment at the end of the year (1999) amounted to USD 4.25 billion, or a per capita rate of USD 1,742. Exports (FOB prices) amounted to USD 1.811 billion, while imports (CIF prices) amounted to USD 3.192 billion. 56% of Latvia's foreign trade turnover was with the countries of the European Union (mainly with Germany, Sweden, Great Britain and Finland), and 17% of trade turnover was with the countries of the CIS (mostly Russia, Ukraine and Belarus). Latvia's most important export goods included wood and wood products, textiles and metals, while the main imports included machinery and mechanisms, electrical systems, motor vehicles, chemicals and chemical products and mineral products.

The currency exchange rate for the Latvian lats, as set by the Bank of Latvia, changed from 0.835 lats per dollar at the end of 1992 to 0.569 lats per dollar at the end of 1998.

A training session at the Central Statistical Bureau. Staff at the Bureau is always updating their knowledge about the computer sciences and statistical standards

The Information Centre at the Central Statistical Bureau, where you can obtain information from the publications which the Bureau and its various divisions publish. You can also access statistical documents published in other countries

The building of the Central Statistical Bureau. A stained glass window from this building is in the background of this page

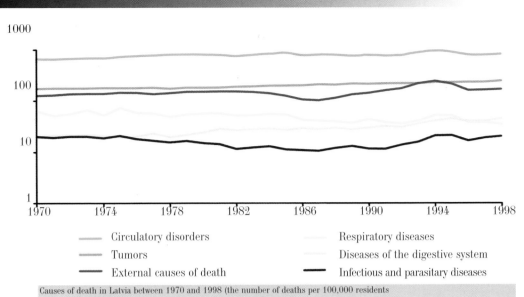

Causes of death in Latvia between 1970 and 1998 (the number of deaths per 100,000 residents

- Circulatory disorders
- Tumors
- External causes of death
- Respiratory diseases
- Diseases of the digestive system
- Infectious and parasitary diseases

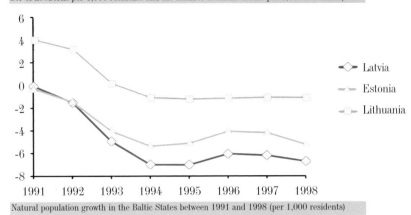

Coefficients concerning fertility and infant mortality in Latvia between 1986 and 1998 (the number of newborns per 1,000 residents and the number of infant deaths per 1,000 live births)

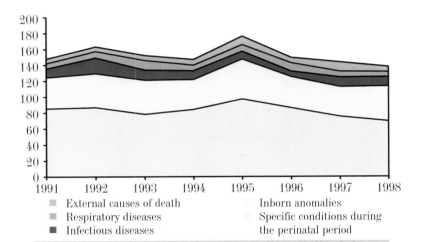

- Latvia
- Estonia
- Lithuania

Natural population growth in the Baltic States between 1991 and 1998 (per 1,000 residents)

Natural growth

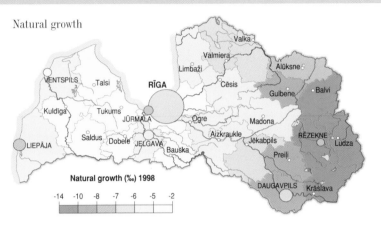

Natural growth (‰) 1998

-14 -10 -8 -7 -6 -5 -2

Each year there are one or two births of triplets per 1,000 births in Latvia. Here you see the triplets who were born in the family of veterinarian Gunars Innuss.

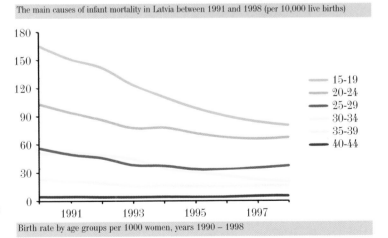

- External causes of death
- Respiratory diseases
- Infectious diseases
- Inborn anomalies
- Specific conditions during the perinatal period

The main causes of infant mortality in Latvia between 1991 and 1998 (per 10,000 live births)

The proportion of pensioners

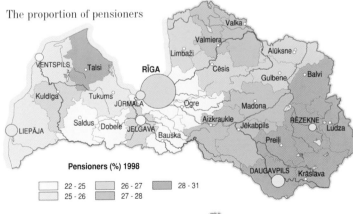

Pensioners (%) 1998

22 - 25   26 - 27   28 - 31
25 - 26   27 - 28

- 15-19
- 20-24
- 25-29
- 30-34
- 35-39
- 40-44

Birth rate by age groups per 1000 women, years 1990 – 1998

Vice-mis Latvia' 97 Diana Dravniece, her husband Maris and their eight children Anna, Marta, Janis, Jēkabs, Elizabete, Toms, Peteris and Matiss. The family has musical talents and education, they often use to play together

Birth rate

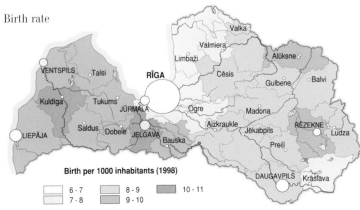

Birth per 1000 inhabitants (1998)

6 - 7   8 - 9   10 - 11
7 - 8   9 - 10

Mortality

Death per 1000 inhabitants (1998)

< 13   14 - 16   > 19
13 - 14   16 - 19

0   50 km

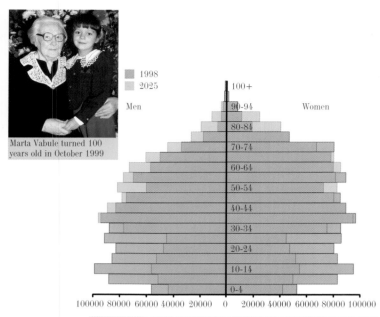

Marta Vabule turned 100 years old in October 1999

1998
2025

Men   100+   Women
             90-94
             80-84
             70-74
             60-64
             50-54
             40-44
             30-34
             20-24
             10-14
             0-4

100000 80000 60000 40000 20000 0 20000 40000 60000 80000 100000

The age structure of Latvia in 1998 and 2025 (forecast)

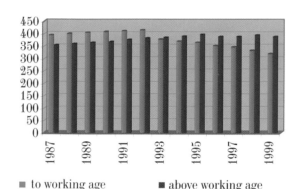

■ to working age   ■ above working age

The level of the demographic burden in Latvia between 1987 and 1997 (at the beginning of the year per 1,000 working age individuals)

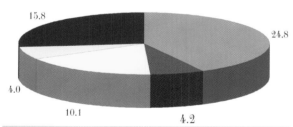

15.8
24.8
4.0
10.1
4.2

The main priorities in terms of household expenditures (monthly average per family member, in lats, 1998). Overall consumption expenditures per month – 58.9 lats

■ food products

■ clothing and footwear

☐ housing and maintenance thereof

☐ transportation

■ other

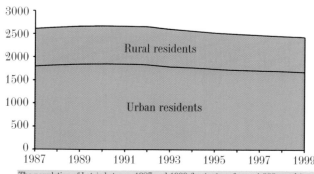

Rural residents

Urban residents

1987 1989 1991 1993 1995 1997 1999

The population of Latvia between 1987 and 1999 (beginning of year, 1,000 people)

The demographic situation in Latvia has not been favorable in recent times. Since 1991 the natural increase in Latvia's population has been negative, which means that the number of deaths exceeds the number of births. In 1997 the number of deaths was greater than the number of births by 14,700, while in 1998 the number was 15,800.

Migration led to a reduction in Latvia's population of 234,000 residents between 1990 and 1998. At the beginning of 1999 there were 2,439,000 people living in Latvia – a decline of 8.5% since the last national census in 1989.

The population of the capital city of Riga declined by 115,000 individuals between 1990 and 1998. At the beginning of 1999 the population was 797,000 people. Since the last census, the number of urban residents in Latvia has declined by 8.8%, while the number of rural residents has declined by 7.9%. Although the number of people representing Latvia's largest nationalities decreased in 1998, the overall proportion of Latvians in the population increased to 55.7% in 1999, as compared to 55.5% at the beginning of the previous year. The proportion of ethnic Latvians in the overall population, however, differs greatly from region to region.

In 1998 there were 18,410 births of children in Latvia – 420 fewer than in 1997, and 23,700 (2.3 times) fewer than in 1987, which was the year that saw the largest number of live births in post-war Latvia. 4,887 children were born in Riga in 1998. The fertility rate in the country at large declined by 1.3% in 1998 (and by 3.8% in 1997). The mortality rate in Latvia has shifted recently. The overall mortality coefficient between 1993 and 1995 (15-16 deaths per 1,000 residents) was the highest since 1947. The mortality rate peaked in 1994 and began to decline in 1995, although in 1998 there was once again an increase – 14.0% in 1998 as compared to 13.6 in 1997.

There have been significant changes in the way in which people marry and divorce over the last several years. The absolute and relative indicators in the area of marriages have declined. 9,641 marriages were registered in Latvia in 1998 – 14,000 or 2.4 times fewer than in 1990.

Latvia's population is aging at an increasing rate. The proportion of children and adolescents (aged 0-14) in the overall population declined from 21.3% in 1987 to 18.5% at the beginning of 1999, while the proportion of people aged 60 or over increased from 16.8% to 20.3% in the same period. Since 1996 the number of people aged 60 and over has exceeded the number of children and adolescents.

The burden on working age people (i.e., the number of children and pensioners per 1,000 working age people) has begun to decline.

A FULL SURVIVAL MINIMUM CONSUMPTION "BASKET" (1999)

■ Food products (Ls 26.2)

■ Clothing (Ls 7.7)

☐ Footwear (Ls 4.4)

☐ Other non-food items (Ls 21.2)

■ Utility payments, electricity, rent (Ls 10.3)

☐ Other services (Ls 9.7)

■ Other payments (Ls 3.2)

Total   (Ls 82.7)

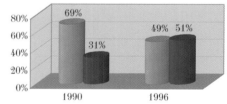

■ state-owned housing
■ privately owned housing

The housing fund in Latvia. In 1997 the average amount of housing space per resident in Latvia was 21.6 cubic meters. For many decades almost all housing in Latvia was owned by the state or local governments, but when the country began its move toward a market economy, people first gained the opportunity to purchase or privatize state or local government-owned apartments

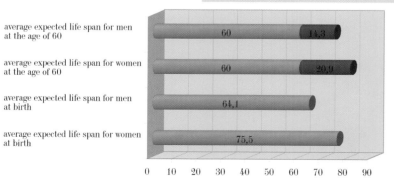

average expected life span for men at the age of 60 — 60 | 14.3

average expected life span for women at the age of 60 — 60 | 20.9

average expected life span for men at birth — 64.1

average expected life span for women at birth — 75.5

0 10 20 30 40 50 60 70 80 90

years

Average expected life span

Valdis Nagobads, Director of the Riga City Welfare Department is in charge of social affairs

Latvian social security system

[Diagram: Latvian social security system — national social ensurance / social assistence]

- vocational training and retraining
- unemployment
- sikness
- maternity
- benefits
- pensions
- service
- loss of provider
- disability
- old age
- social benefits
- state programms
- social care institutions
- vocational trainig and rehabilitation by disabled persons
- state
- municipalities
- social rehabilitation
- social assistance for homeless
- social care institutions
- half-way houses and day care centres
- social assistance for orphans and parentless children
- social benefits

Latvia has a social security system for insurance payments and state benefits. It's share was 15,8% in the budget of 1998. Above: Social security office in *Sarkandaugava*

The leaflets of National Social Insurance Agency provide information on the social reform and the right to benefit from social services

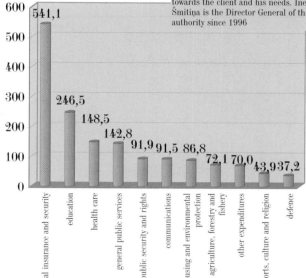

Modern premises for client service in Riga city *Ziemeļu* district Social security office are open since 1997

The reform of social security legislation is a challenge to administration. The Social Insurance Agency is oriented towards the client and his needs. Inese Šmitiņa is the Director General of this authority since 1996

The new social security system started it's development as soon as Latvia regained independence. In January 1, 1991 two laws on social insurance were passed. They were followed by administrative reforms in order to separate national and municipal responsibilities for social assistance.

An overwhelming reform of the social security system took place in 1995, when *Saeima* passed a package of social security laws under the umbrella law On Social Security. It stipulates the basic rights to social security and compensation in case of any internationally recognized risks. The execution of these rights is stipulated in branch laws. According to them, Latvia has four types of social insurance. Approximately 76% of the total financial resources are spent on retirement pension insurance, 16% for sickness, disability and maternity leave , 8% for unemployment insurance and 0,3% – for occupational accidents. The objective of the social security laws is to ensure accessible and on-time support. The basic principles for Latvian social security officers are: guarantee of equal services regardless of one's gender, age, race, nationality or religion in providing social insurance and assistance, prevention, autonomy and individual approach.

The contents of the legal framework is approached to the Western understanding of rights. The reforms, especially the retirement pension reform are appreciated by international experts. Gradually Latvia develops a system, which differs from the classic western insurance schemes. It is organized in three levels: first of them being the national mandatory scheme based on the principle of redistribution; the second the national mandatory funded pension scheme and third – voluntary pension funds.

Although the first level is a scheme of solidarity among generations, it has certain special features. It is a system of fixed payments. The pension is calculated by taking into account life expectancy at the age of retirement. It motivates people to work longer in order to increase their pension. Indexation prevents the loss of value of the pension capital, which is a sum of payments during the period of employment. Valorization of pensions is also planned. The second level scheme will be organized according to the principle of accumulation of individual payments and investments. The Law on State Funded Pensions will come into force in July 1, 2001. Its distinction from the first level, where a relative capital is accumulated is that the second level accumulates a real capital. The scheme of third level enables accumulation of private savings in pension funds. It is a future-oriented system and will show it's impact on the whole welfare system only when implemented *en masse*. In compliance with the EU recommendations the Cabinet passed a decision in February of 2000 that all residents have to be granted a basic income. By this the Latvian social security system became a universal one.

The proportion of the retired population increases. Today one fourth of Latvian residents are retired. For 1000 economically

[Bar chart values, top to bottom on x-axis categories:]

- social insurance and security — 541,1
- education — 246,5
- health care — 148,5
- general public services — 142,8
- public security and rights — 91,9
- communications — 91,5
- housing and environmental protection — 86,8
- agriculture, forestry and fishery — 72,1
- other expenditures — 70,0
- sports, culture and religion — 43,9
- defence — 37,2

The National Expenditure Programs within the consolidated state budget

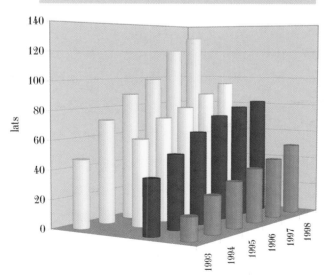

[Chart axis: lats; years 1993, 1994, 1995, 1996, 1997, 1998]

- ▪ average pensions of retirement age
- ▪ value of survival minimum per capita
- ▫ average monthly salary, neto
- ▫ average monthly salary, bruto

Dynamics of salaries and other income (in lats)

Social nursing home in *Lauciena, Talsi* district

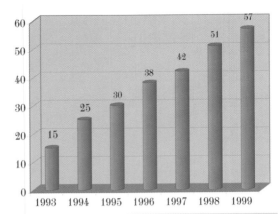

Pension dynamics 1993 – 1999 (in lats)

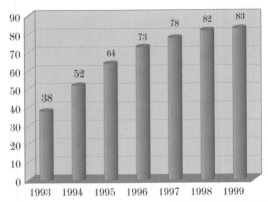

Increase of the survival minimum 1993 – 1999 (in lats)

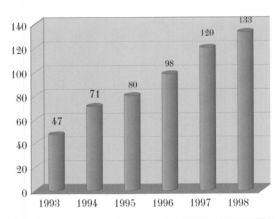

Salary increase 1993 – 1998 (in lats)

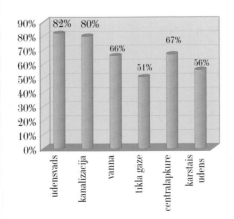

Housing comfort, 1997

Riga social care centre *Mežciems* was established in 1975. It is also a day care facility for the retired and handicapped individuals living nearby

active individuals there are 550 retired ones to support. The demographic burden (proportion of persons below and above the age of retirement to the number of people in economically active age) in Latvia is 695 on 1000 individuals in economically active age (1999). The age of retirement will be gradually increased to 65 years. Every tenth individual in the age of retirement continues to work. The income for one household member on the threshold of a new millenium is 75 lats. A state in transition from one economical system to another is facing rapid economic changes, new values, unexpected failures and social contradictions. It gives rise to psychological stress, uncertainty of future and adaptation problems to the new environment.

Compared to other East-European countries, the share of gross national product spent on social benefits and services is a large one. The personal spendings have reduced considerably because of a 50% decrease in GNP per capita and an increase in consumer prices. The inflation of 1992 resulted in loss of personal savings. Also the bank crisis of 1995 made an impact on savings.

The majority of employed individuals are not able to make any savings as they spend all the earnings on primary needs, rent and services. Retired individuals without additional sources of income and large families with only one or two working members face hardships. According to household surveys by the Sate Statistic Committee, the spendings per family member are too small. Average household income per person in 1998 consisted of 55,8% from salaries, 26,5% from social benefits (pensions etc.) and 6,7% from farming activities. Economic studies from 1998 highlights the increasing social stratification. It has a negative impact on families with many children and unemployed individuals.

Today the labour market is not balanced. Individuals with medium qualification and with secondary or academic humanitarian education have problems in finding jobs. On the other hand, private enterprises are unable to hire qualified staff. The average unemployment rate is 9 – 10%.

In *Mežciems* retired and handicapped persons can engage themselves in activities like weaving, knitting and other according to their wishes

The social care centre *Mežciems* organize different events and celebrations for mental stimulation for the residents

Bauska district *Vecumnieki* parish dance ansamble for elderly

A home for retired persons in *Subate* subsidized by the Catholic church

Several generations tape part in the folk ansambles in the *Vecumnieki* parish

Social care centre *Ezerkrasti*

Residents of the *Vecumnieki* nursing home enjoy helping in the kitchen or watching TV and reading

The sports club for disabled individuals *Optimists* provides opportunities for enjoying different sport activities

During examinations in 1998, 40 000 individuals were recognized as handicapped:

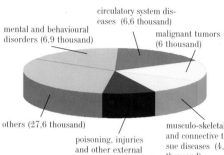

circulatory system diseases (6,6 thousand)

mental and behavioural disorders (6,9 thousand)

malignant tumors (6 thousand)

others (27,6 thousand)

poisoning, injuries and other external causes (3,8 thousand)

musculo-skeletal and connective tissue diseases (4,3 thousand)

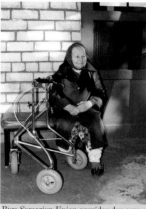

Riga Samarian Union provides day care and full time care for disabled persons

I. Purenkova from the Association of Persons with Vision Impairments is proud of her wickerworks

Disabled Latvians on Mont Blanc. It was not possible to clime it on a wheel chair, but it was carried up by a man with one hand only

The sanatorium for disabled persons was built in 1936, in *Ķemeri, Durbes iela* 2. Today it is a social care facility for elderly, who have returned to their fatherland

A. Grinbergs (Association of Persons with Vision Impairments) is willing to demonstrate his skills

A. Tušinskis (Association of Persons with Vision Impairments) popular ceramics

A traditional sports festival in the Sports club for disabled individuals in *Tukums*

Social care centre of the Riga Samarian Union

The works exhibited in the Art Centre of the Latvian Association of Disabled persons

The first international creativity festival *Solis* (Step) for mentally handicapped individuals took place in August 1999. Above: residents of the social rehabilitation centre *Baldone* performing a puppet show

The Malta Order supports retired and handicapped individuals and children from socially disadvantaged families. Left: Normunds Snarskis, representative of the Order

Day care centre *Cerību ligzda* is a place where handicapped children engage in various activities

A rehabilitation specialist working with a visually impaired child according to Partridge methodology

An asylum for orphans in *Liepāja* was established in the beginning of the XVIII century and is one of the oldest in Europe

Nursing house for children *Imanta*, 1957

Guests and residents of *Imanta* in summer 1999

Composer Arvīds Žilinskis visiting *Imanta* in 1974

Residents of the *Graši* nursing home for children

The present Latvian nursing homes for children is a living proof to all problems of our history. In the 40's and 50's they provided sheltered for children who's families were split during the war and the deportations. In 70's and 80's there was an increase of congenital anomalies due to alcohol abuse in families. It was a period of enforced russification and many Latvian children did not learn their native language being placed in the institution. Since 80's there are more and more mothers leaving their newborns in the delivery units, from were they are transferred to national institutions for infants. In 90's more and more individuals from Western countries were willing to adopt these children, despite the knewledge that not all of them were allowed to adopt children in their home countries due to their psychological or physical peculiarities. From year to year Latvia provides a better care to her children.

Imanta residents and staff in *Aglona* in 1996

The founder of *Graši* children nursing home Alexander Christoph and his fosterchildren

Graši residents by their homestead *Ozoliņi*

Children crisis centre in *Pļavnieki*

A training course for the staff of *Skalbes* in May 1999, two weeks before the opening

Cerību ligzda play room for children on an individual program

Individual sessions in the Family Support centre

Crisis centre for mothers and children in *Talsi*

]Opening of the crisis centre *Skalbes*. Phare Consum project manager Franc Kumpl and the president of the centre Inta Dzelme

REHABILITATION

The premises of Family Support Centre encourage children to creative playing

The National Rehabilitation Centre *Vaivari* was established in 1992. It provides a wide range of medical rehabilitation services for children and adults

The sanatorium *Jaunķemeri* offers modern medical care and a comfortable accommodation

Reittherapy (horse – back riding) is one of recently provided services in NRC *Vaivari*. It is mostly used for children with cerebral palsy

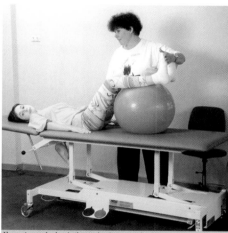

Experienced physiotherapist in a session in NRC *Vaivari*

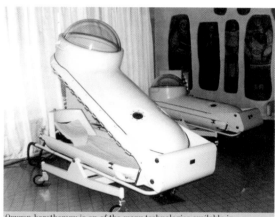

Oxygen barotherapy is on of the many technologies available in *Jaunķemeri*. In Latvia it is used for years. Now the Latvian schemes are applied worldwide

In the fitness hall of *Jaunķemeri* everyone may find an appropriate training device

Rehabilitation centre *Imanta*. The former policlinics offer more modern rehabilitation services for year to year

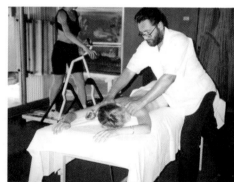

A highly qualified massage is available in NRC *Vaivari*

Both kids and grown-ups enjoy the swimming pool of *Jaunķemeri*

Tērvete sanatorium (1930), architects Ansis Kalniņš and Aleksandrs Klinklāvs

Latvia joined the European Confederation of Employers in 1995. The Minister of Welfare Andris Bērziņš signed the agreement on behalf of Latvia

Andris Siliņš and delegates from US and Puerto Rico during the International Conference of Employment Services in Puerto Rico In 1998

Trilateral meeting of the Employers Confederation, Central Council of Trade Unions, and the Cabinet, represented by Roberts Jurdžs, the Minister of Welfare

Ilmārs Stabrovskis, Director of the training centre *Buts*

A session of the Employers Confederation

A session of the Parliamentarian Commission of Social and Employment Affairs

The 4th Congress of trade unions in November 28, 1998

A trade union march to encourage solution of the pension problems

The number of employed individuals in Latvia was increasing from 1996, but it came to a halt when many Latvian enterprises had to dismiss employees due to the Russia crisis before the end of 1998.

The restructurisation of economy since 1990 has caused major changes in the division of employment in different branches. The number of individuals employed in industries of manufacturing, construction and agriculture has decreased, while the number of employees has increased in state administration, defense, social insurance and financial sectors. In 1998 the number of employees in service industry considerably exceeded any other branch. One fourth of all working individuals were employed in manufacturing and construction, one fifth – in agriculture and fishery. Out of the total number of employed individuals, 83% were employees, 3.3% employers, and 8.4% self-employed.

The number of employers compared to 1997 has mostly reduced in trade, which meant that the small retail sellers could not compete with modern supermarkets and trade centres. The proportion of household members not receiving salary and the self-employed is decreasing by 20 thousand annually. It might mean that small production can not find it's way into the market. In rural areas this kind of employment is responsible for 81% of the total, because it is not easy to find a paid job there.

Many Latvians are looking for additional sources of income. 46,5 thousand or 4,6% of all employed are engaged in at least two jobs. More than 48 thousand or 5% are looking for a position.

THE QUALITY OF LIFE AND EMPLOYMENT

Gross domestic product in Latvia is calculated by purchasing parity in dollars. By the end of 90's it was about 30% of the EU average.

A growing polarization of welfare in Latvia is obvious. Gini index, describing the unequally divided mass of income was 0.32 in 1998.

The mean bruto monthly salary is 140 lats, neto – 100 lats only, which correspond with USD 240 and USD 167 respectively. There are major differences of average salaries among regions, cities and districts. The mean bruto salary in *Ventspils* is 173 lats, 142 lats in

The Conference on Collaboration of the Baltic Trade Unions

A consultant of the Employment Information Service. A. Raibs highlighting recent situation on labour market in Riga

Riga, and 75 lats in *Rēzekne* district. Qualified workers and craftsmen in *Ventspils* make 156 lats, 136 lats in Riga, 130 lats in *Liepāja* and only 66 lats in *Balvi* district.

The Central Statistics Committee has conducted household surveys. In 1998 the monthly income was 62.33 lats per household member. It was 77.51 lats in families of two childless individuals, 58.58 lats in families of two parents and children, while only 48,21 lats in single parent families.

THE STATE EMPLOYMENT SERVICE AND RETRAINING OF UNEMPLOYED INDIVIDU-ALS

The State Employment Service, established in 1992 is responsible for the implementation of national labour policy by providing employment management, registering of unemployed persons, and organizing employment activities. The 28 centres and 34 sections of the State Employment Service are located all over Latvia. According the Law on

Staff of the State Labour Inspection

Dace Bāliņa teaching how to write a good *Curriculum Vitae*

CLS inspector Una Igaune gives her advice

Trainees of the centre *Mācību komercfirma* learning hardware for IBM repair

Training of dressmakers in the training centre *Buts*

Training of welders in the training centre *Buts*

APSD project for developing a park and plant station in *Andrupene* parish

Employment, employers have to report vacancies there. The Service fills in 30-38% of all the reported vacancies.

The main problems today are the growing demands of employers - companies require well educated and skilled people with good knowledge of the State language and foreign languages. Any layman may be informed about the free vacancies in the Employment Information Service in *Jēzusbaznīcas iela* 11, Rīga. The retraining of unemployed persons is oriented towards the requirements of employers and drawn up according with the analysis of demands in the labour market. The State Employment Service has established long term cooperation with the training centre *Turība*, highschool *BUTS*, adult educational centre *Attīstība*, Rīga Professional School No.3, etc.

The quality of retraining has been improved by foreign contributions. In 1997 the Labour Affairs Authority from Germany provided financial support for modern training, premises, and equipment for training of construction electricians and carpenters meeting EU standards.

One solution to the unemployment problem in Latvia is opening of short term public jobs like cleaning and auxiliary services, were the unemployed individuals could earn living by performing unqualified duties. Since 1998 the State Employment Service has stared to organize paid public jobs as permanent employment.

The Club of Labour Seekers works for the stimulation of self - initiative, assistance for adaptation and psychological support in the conditions of a changed labour market. Informative-psychologic training is organized for target groups like long term unemployed in pre-retirement age and mothers after the maternity leave.

The Baltic sea regional labour market policy program has a project for establishment of Employment Information Offices, financed by Danish Ministry of Labour.

The State Employment Service is engaged in collaboration with NGO's. Since 1993 its staff members are in the International Association of Public Employment Services (IAPES).

THE STATE LABOUR INSPECTION

The State Labour Inspection control the compliance of employment, labour protection and supervision of dangerous technologies with the Latvian legislation. There are 7 Regional Labour Inspections. 181 staff members supervise more than 80 000 enterprises.

The State Labour Inspection investigates and analyses the violations of labour relations, labour protection and safety, labour accidents and occupational diseases. It has introduced a training system for the inspectors, and a system of information. The legal acts are constantly being improved. A public relation campaign is conducted with the help of mass media. An emphasis is put on modern administration by *Phare* projects.

Retraining of the unemployed by the German equipment

Valda Hudčenko provides individual consultations in the Employment Information Office

Training of welders

Computer training in Rīga Professional School No.3

A dressmaking facility in *Kalnciems* is established within the APSD project

Welding equipment in the training centre *Buts*

Training of unemployed in the training centre *Buts*

The unemployed develop skills in the training centre *Buts* in using different equipment

Primitive treatment of a head injury in an ancient tribal community, as seen in an exposition at the Pauls *Stradiņš* Museum of Medical History

A physician providing bedside treatment – an exposition at the *Stradiņš* Museum

The Riga Red Cross Hospital in 1914

Kristaps Helmanis (1848-1892), a microbiologist who was instrumental in establishing the Institute of Experimental Medicine in St. Petersburg. His research specialists included malleus, rabies and tuberculosis

The guest book of a leprosy treatment facility in *Talsi* with the signature of Rudolfs Virhovs

The *Baldone* Sanatorium, which offered various kinds of medicinal baths, in the 1920s

A ward at the Riga No. 1 Hospital in the 1920s

Ernest von Bergmann (1836-1907) was a Baltic German surgeon who was born in Riga. A professor at Tartu University, he was a leading specialist in aseptics, and his work in brain surgery laid the foundations for neurosurgery

Marija Vecrumba (1885-1919) was one of the first female physicians in Latvia

Employees of the Children's Hospital in the 1930s. Paediatricians Gedimins Ebels and Gerhards Feders are in the front row

An operating theatre at the Riga No. 1 Hospital in the late 1920s. At the far right, surgeons Pauls Stradiņš and A. Ziediņš, the latter the director of the hospital

Professor Martiņš Zile (1863-1945) was a general practitioner who founded an academic school for general practitioners

Professor Jēkabs Alksnis (1870-1957) was a leading surgeon between the two World Wars

Psychiatry professor Hermanis Buduls (1882-1954)

Professor Gaston Backman (1883-1964), a Swedish anatomist and anthropologist who founded the Department of Anatomy at the University of Latvia

Docent Gerhards Feders (1890-1974), a paediatrician and tuberculosis specialist

Testimony to the fact that Latvia's residents have been practising medicine for several millennia is found through the work of archaeologists, ethnographers and paleopathologists. Professor Vilis Derums, who studied archaeological materials, found evidence that ancient Latvians successfully treated skull injuries. Medicinal plants, sulphured water and the medicinal properties of mud baths were also widely used.

Physicians have worked in Riga since the 13th century, and an official medical administration system for the city was established in 1360. In the late 13th and early 14th century, three hospitals were opened in the city – the Hospital of the Holy Spirit, St. George's Hospital and St. Lazarus' Hospital. The Black Plague ravaged Latvia several times over the successive centuries – first in 1351 and, most devastatingly, in 1710.

Leprosy was also widespread, and the only currently operating leprosory in all Europe is located in the city of *Talsi*, although no new patients have been brought to the centre for a long time.

In the 16th century, there were several physicians in Riga who were famous throughout Europe for their work. A doctor called Oto Huhn in 1800 was one of the first physicians in the world to use smallpox vaccines. Medicinal spas such as *Bārbele*, *More* and *Baldone* were enormously popular in the 18th century, and among those who went there for curative purposes were the tsars of Russia and the emperors of Germany.

Physician Aleksandrs Neibergs (1883-1962) was the director of the Latvian Red Cross Hospital for many years

General Peteris Sniķeris (1875-1944) was a professor of dermatology and participated in the founding of the Department of Medicine at the University of Latvia

The Latvian Red Cross in the 1930s. Third from the left in the front row – Kārlis Goppers, and alongside him Professor Janis Jankovskis, nurse E. Nolle-Sieciniece and nurse Marta Celmiņa. Third from the right in the second row is Professor Kārlis Barons

Professor Jēkabs Primanis (1892-1971), an anatomist and anthropologist

Professor Roberts Krimbergs (1874-1941), a physiologist and biochemist

Inspection of a leprosy patient at *Talsi* in 1958

Surgeon Janis Jegermanis (1895-1968)

Microbiologist Augusts Kirhenšteins (1872-1963), an academician in the Academy of Sciences of the Latvian SSR

Surgeon and professor Janis Bune (1891-1973)

The Riga No. 1 Hospital was established in 1803. By 1900 there were only some 200 ethnic Latvians who were trained physicians. They studied in Tartu, St. Petersburg and Moscow. A school for midwives was opened in Riga in 1826, while a training school for pharmacists was established in 1835.

The first in the Russian Empire to use ether for anaesthesia was Dr. Bernhard Friedrich Berens in Riga in 1847. August Hacken invented the urethroscope in Riga in 1862. Ernsts Bergmanis of *Rūjiena* announced a basic law of aseptics while working in Berlin in 1890 that remains in effect to this very day – anything that touches a wound must be sterilised. The first X-ray image in Russia was taken in 1896 by Hermann Pflaum. Among the most distinguished Latvian scientists of the 19th century were the microbiologists Eižens Zemmers, Kristaps Helmanis and Oto Kalniņš, who did research on tuberculosis and rabies long before Pasteur and Koch. The Latvian specialists, however, were slow to publish the results of their research into the causes of these illnesses and the preventive opportunities that existed. Latvians do, however, hold copyright on several research projects focused on the diagnosis and treatment of malignant malleus, as well as in many other medical areas.

Roberts Krimbergs, working with his teacher, Vladimir Gulevic (1867-1933), discovered carnitine in Moscow in 1905.

Two distinguished Latvian medical specialists met with tragic fates at the beginning of the 20th century. Pharmacist Karlis Pelekzirnis was shot by the tsar's militia during the 1905-1906 revolution, while Dr. Marija Vecrumba was shot by the German *Landeswehr* in 1919 in *Jelgava*. She was found on the street offering aid to the injured, arrested and executed for having fulfilled her duty as a physician.

Early anthropological research in Latvia was done by Gaston Backman and Jekabs Primanis. Caesar Amstler did seminal research in the pharmacology of cocaine and morphine. Martiņš Zīle introduced the concept of active diastole into the medical lexicon, and the tuberculosis symptom, which he discovered is still well known in the world.

Jēkabs Alksnis did important work on the sur-

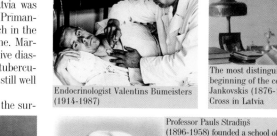

Endocrinologist Valentins Bumeisters (1914-1987)

The most distinguished Latvian surgeon at the beginning of the century, Professor Janis Jankovskis (1876-1925), founded the Red Cross in Latvia

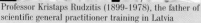

Professor Kristaps Rudzitis (1899-1978), the father of scientific general practitioner training in Latvia

gical treatment of the urethra. Pauls Stradiņš worked on nerve damage and cancer surgery. One of the sons of the legendary folklorist Krišjanis Barons, Karlis Barons, was a distinguished practitioner and teacher of dentistry in the 1930s.

The independent Latvian state that existed between the two World Wars had a mandatory medical insurance scheme in place, and it was adopted virtually without any adjustments by Germany, which uses a very similar system to this very day. In 1938, Latvia accepted a democratic and very modern (by pre-war European standards) law on medicine.

The war devastated the medical profession in Latvia. Many distinguished physicians were shot or deported by the Russian and German occupations. Many others emigrated in 1944, fearing the second occupation by the Soviet Union, which had already, and, as it turned out, would continue to impose great suffering upon the Latvians.

The Soviet system provided State financing based on very strictly defined wage scales. A surgeon received the same salary whether he worked at a clinic in Vladivostok or a hospital in Riga. This led to a certain amount of unification in medicine, but it also caused a very serious deterioration in the quality of care, especially in the 1970s and 1980s. Until the late 1960s medicine in Latvia did not differ very much from German or Swedish standards, but in the late 1980s the one area of activity in the Soviet Union which was farthest behind the times in terms of equipment and technologies was medicine. Doctors achieved amazing results with inadequate and inappropriate resources. The rate of anaesthesia-related death and complications was lower in Latvia than in Sweden, and this was despite the fact that equipment

Professor Pauls Stradiņš (1896-1958) founded a school of surgery in Latvia, was a cancer specialist and medical historian, and served for many years as the director of the Latvian Clinical Hospital. He founded a museum on medical history, which today bears his name.

The office of Professor Pauls Stradiņš, reconstructed at the Museum of Medical History

NURSING

The graduating class from the Latvian Red Cross School of Nursing in Riga in the 1930s. The senior physician of the Red Cross Hospital, Aleksandrs Neibergs, is in the centre

The building which housed the Latvian Red Cross School of Nursing in 1930

The president of the Latvian Association of Nurses, Jolanta Zalite

At the Riga No. 1 School of Medicine – unit director Grieta Meldraja, director Inese Bunga and deputy director for education Ausma Cebere

The Florence Nightingale Medal in Latvia has been received by four nurses – Justone Kuške, Elza Grivane, E. Nolle-Sieciniece and Marta Celmiņa

The nursing journal *Māsa* (*Nurse*) has been published for years, with some interruptions

The *Dagda* Hospital in 1938

The *Kalnamuiža* Sanatorium in the 1920s. A tuberculosis sanatorium was opened there in 1924, and after 1932 it was known as the *Tērcete* Sanatorium

The Riga No. 1 School of Medicine each year prepares secondary medical personnel in six specialties

Prof. Ivars Ebels (1925-1998) was not only an outstanding paediatrician, but also a talented pianist. Above: At the 1968 All-Union amateur artists festival in Russia, Ebels was awarded a prize

Dzidra Kalniņa was the only physician in Latvia to receive the honorary title of People's Doctor of the USSR (in 1979). Here she is pictured working at the *Dzērbenes* clinic

Vilis Kaņeps (1923 – 1993) was the Latvian SSR Minister for Health (1962 – 1989)

Paediatrician Grigorijs Groms (1928 – 1987) was a Latvian SSR Distinguished Merit physician. He researched diabetes in children

Vilis Derums (1899 – 1988) was Latvia's only paleopathologist. He researched the pathologies of the people of the Baltic region from archaeological materials

Aina Damberga (1914 – 1971) was for many years the senior physician at the City of Riga No. 4 Clinical Red Cross Hospital

Prof. Ernests Burtnieks (1898 – 1958) general practitioner, phthisiotherapist. First director of the Riga Medical Institute

Surgeon professors Evalds Ezerietis, Maris Mihelsons, Jānis Volkolakovs, Janis Gaujens and Vladimirs Utkins at a scientific conference in 1986. Prof. Ezerietis, aged over 80 years of age, still works in the Clinical Surgery at the P. Stradiņš Clinical Hospital, giving consultations to patients

Physician and writer Miervaldis Birze survived a German concentration camp during World War II and became a phthisiotherapist and worked in *Cēsis*. His prose works have been translated into more than 20 languages

Gastro-enterologist Prof. Nikolajs Skuja

The City of Riga No. 7 Hospital was built from 1976 – 1982, based on designs by Andris Purviņš, Maija and Atis Biviņi and others. Much credit for the establishment and development of the hospital belongs to its first senior physician Jānis Prombergs. In the photo: the *Gaiļezers* City of Riga No. 7 Hospital complex with the current director Edvins Platkājis

The P. Stradiņš Medical History Museum, and medical historian, docent Karlis Eriks Arons

Janis Kļaviņš, a professor at Cornell University, president of the International Academy of Tumour marker oncology

On 4 may 1990, after the declaration regarding the renewal of Latvian independence, singing the National anthem are the first president of the Latvian Physicians Association Ivars Krastiņš, Professor of Philosophy Pēteris Laķis and Professor of Anaesthesia (later Foreign Minister) Georgs Andrejevs

Vilens Tolpežņikovs, roentgenologist. As a USSR people's deputy, opposed the genocide in Tbilisi in 1989

On 22 June 1989 the journal *Latvijas Arsts* was published – the first independent, but legal journal in the Soviet Union. Editor: Peteris Apinis

The 1st World Latvian Physicians Congress was held in Riga 19 – 28 June 1990, which was the first event in Latvia in which émigré Latvians took part. Most of the credit for the organisation of the congress goes to Prof. Kristaps Keggi (in the photo), Prof. Viktors Kalnberzs, Prof. Bertrams Zariņš, Indulis Ozols, Prof. Juris Leja and Prof. Vilnis Dzerve-Taluts

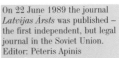
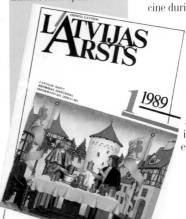

From the right: Prof. Viktors Kalnberzs in Afghanistan in 1987 together with Afghanistan academician Prof. Mohamed Mussa

Traumatologist Eduards Žeidurs (1918 – 1987)

was badly out of date and ether was still being used in many places. Infant and children's mortality rates were also maintained at pan-European levels. When foreign physicians began to visit Riga extensively in the early 1990s, they often expressed astonishment at the fact that such good results could be achieved with such poor technological capabilities. Much of the credit here must go to the level of medical education in Latvia. The Riga Institute of Medicine, now known as the Latvian Academy of Medicine, was the best medical school in the entire Soviet Union.

One of the most complicated problems in medicine during the post-war period was the issue of russification. For 28 years, the Minister for Health of the Latvian SSR was a man called Vilhelms Kaņeps. He was a Russian-born Latvian who had a very poor command of the Latvian language, and so the Ministry mostly hired people whose native language was Russian. Medical diagnoses and charts had to be prepared in Russian, and Latvian professors at the academy were forced to deliver lectures to

Latvian students in Russian. Kaņeps and his deputy, Edvins Platkājis (who later became Minister), did a lot of work in building new medical institutions, including the *Gaiļezers* Hospital and the Oncological Hospital which was one of the most modern facilities of its type in Europe in the 1970s.

One of the specifics of the Soviet medical system was that it was heavily hospital-based, because while one was in the hospital, medications were financed by the State, but as soon as one became an outpatient, that stopped, and the patient had to buy medications himself. That is why Latvia had more hospital beds per 1,000 people in the late 1980s than any country in Europe.

In the 1980s, the Latvian SSR launched a relatively successful attempt to conduct outpatient screening of the health of all of the Republic's residents through a system called KOSMON, which was an early application of information technologies in Latvia. Hatred for Minister

The director of the National Mandatory Health Insurance Agency, Ināra Bluķe, can be described as a woman through whose hands most of Latvia's health care money passes. She is a professional economist who runs Latvia's health care organisation and its financing system, and she was responsible for setting up the relevant billing and registration system

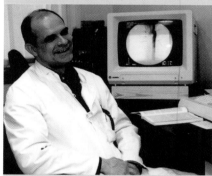

Aigars Migals came up with the idea of founding the Latvian Physicians Association, and so he did. He is the director of the Invasive Radiology Division of the P. Stradiņš University Clinical Hospital

Henriks Runds, a long-time director of the P. Stradiņš University Clinical Hospital, was a distinguished Latvian health care manager. He fell out of favour among incompetent bureaucrats at the Ministry of Welfare and was replaced

Surgeon Jānis Ozols, the director of the Riga No. 1 Hospital, has also served as a member of the Riga City Council. A well known member of the Board of Latvian Physicians Association, head of different commissions and critical opponent for any authority.

The rector of the Latvian Academy Medicine, Jānis Vetra, with an assistant to the Auditor-General of Latvia, Indira Ozola

The most distinguished health care manager after the restoration of Latvia's independence was Director of Health Department Zigmunds Kovaļčuks

Ludmīla Viksna, a professor of infectious diseases, has for many years been the director of the Latvian Infectology Centre and the chairperson of the Certification Commission of the Latvian Physicians Association

An international agreement between the United States and Latvia on co-operation in health care was signed at the White House in Washington in 1995. The next day First Lady Hillary Clinton organised a reception for the Latvian delegation, which included Latvia's First Lady, Aina Ulmane (to the right of Mrs. Clinton), as well as Uldis Ivars Lamsters, Pēteris Apinis and Arkadijs Gandzs

Pēteris Alberts is a neurophysiologist who works at Uppsala University

Three distinguished Latvian surgeons outside the building of the Latvian Physicians Association in Riga – Viesturs Boka, who is president of the Association and director of the *Linezers* Hospital, Gunārs Purmalis, who is the president of the Latvian Association of Surgeons and the head of the surgical division at *Gaiļezers* Hospital, and Professor Jānis Gardovskis, who is prorector of the Latvian Academy of Medicine and heads the academy's Department of Surgery

Juris Jakovins, director of the *Valmiera* Hospital – one of the largest and most modern among Latvia's rural district hospitals. The pride of the hospital in *Valmiera* is its children's ward, its division for intensive paediatric therapy, and its maternity ward

Stanford University Professor Kristaps Zariņš, who is the director of the university's surgical clinic, and his brother, Bertrams Zariņš, a professor of orthopaedics who for many years was the president of the Association of American Latvian Physicians and Dentists. He is also a member of the board of the World Association of Orthopaedists

The dispatch centre of Riga's emergency medical aid facility is equipped to supervise first aid procedures in all of Latvia

Renate Helda, who specialises in endocrinology, is the editor and publisher of the medical journal *Jums, Koleģi* ("For you, colleagues")

Semjons Štrihs, an outstanding health care manager, served for many years as the director of the Riga emergency medical aid facility. For many years, ambulances in Latvia were RAF vans made in the city of *Jelgava*, but today the emergency aid workers can use modern *Mercedes* vans for their work

Modern technologies and medical equipment are appearing in Latvia. Here we see Agris Švarcbergs, president of the *Amerilat* company, which developed a technology for the treatment of prostate disorders

Anaesthesiology and intensive therapy in Latvia were for two decades based on the *iron lung* in the Soviet Union – the artificial ventilator RO-5, which made it all but impossible to monitor the flow of gases during procedures. Still, anaesthesia-related complications in Latvia were always less common than in other parts of the world. Here we see anaesthesiologist Einars Piekuss administering anaesthesia to a patient

When people think of the most outstanding urban doctors in Latvia, they inevitably think of the director of the surgical clinic of the *Liepāja* Central Hospital, Viesturs Rozitis

Dainis Kalns is not only the chief surgeon at the *Sigulda* Hospital, but also the organiser of the annual *Sigulda* Opera Festival in Latvia – an outstanding cultural event which attracts the world's most distinguished opera performers, as well as music lovers from Scandinavia and Western Europe

The chief physician of the *Ventspils* Hospital is the nationally known anaesthesiologist Gundars Daudze

Anaesthesiologist Juris Svaže works at the Latvian Dentistry Centre

Three of the most outstanding Latvian professors in cardiac surgery – Romans Lacis, Janis Volkolakovs and Aris Lacis – work in two different clinics, but they often come together to discuss the results of their work

Two neurosurgeons at the Riga No. 7 Clinical Hospital – Janis Ozoliņš (right) and Ingus Gārša – in the neurosurgery operating theatre

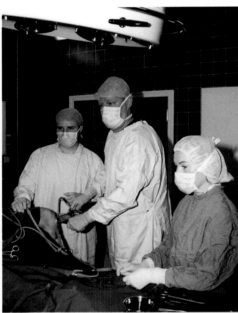

The director of Riga's Hospital of Traumatology and Orthopaedics, Valdis Zatlers (centre) is seen here engaging in an arthroscopic operation on a patient's knee joint. The clinic has been praised at the European level for these operations, and today 17 physicians from Eastern and Central Europe are studying the speciality at the clinic

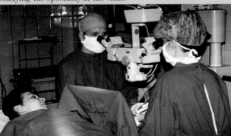

Since 1983, Latvian doctors have been performing microsurgical operations, mostly in the area of plastic surgery, beauty surgery and hand surgery. The operations are done with the use of modern microscopes and modern stitching materials, and good co-operation has been developed with the Toronto University Clinic in Canada and the Mayo Clinic in the United States

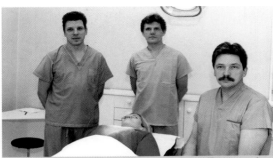

Dynasties of doctors are not at all uncommon in Latvia. Here we see three brothers who are all outstanding surgeons – micro-surgeon and plastic surgery specialist Janis Ģilis, urologist Dainis Ģilis, and micro, plastic and trauma surgery specialist Valdis Ģilis – at their plastic surgery centre in Riga. Valdis Ģilis is also a Parliamentarian of the 7th *Saeima*

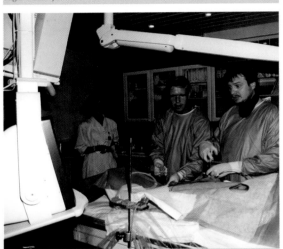

Doctors Andrejs Erglis and Indulis Kumsars conduct a procedure at the digital angiography division of the Cardiology Centre of the P. Stradiņš University Clinical Hospital

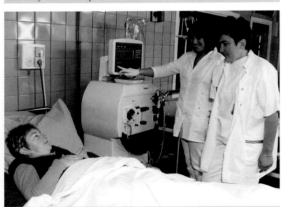

The director of the hemodialysis ward at the Riga No. 7 Clinical Hospital, Anda Grigane, works with people from all over Latvia who suffer from kidney disease

At the University Children's Clinic Hospital's intensive care ward, the director of the hospital, Dzintars Mozgis, professor Aigars Petersons, and paediatric surgeon and professor Janis Gaujens, who studied with the patriarch of paediatric surgery in Latvia, Professor Aleksandrs Bieziņš

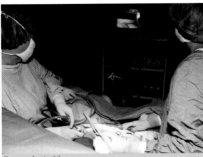

Gynaecological laparoscopy at the Riga No. 1 Hospital

Use of a cardioscope at the Riga No. 1 Hospital

Kaņeps, however, was vast, and everything that he did was automatically considered to be a mistake. Health screening disappeared from the field of preventive care in Latvia for an entire decade.

It seems that there is no area of life in Latvia, which has suffered such great pain in the movement from the Soviet system to a market economy system as has the field of medicine. Ministers and other senior officials have replaced one another at a dizzying speed. In 1988 Aigars Migals, Professor Ilmars Lazovskis, Ivars Krastiņš, Janis and Aivars Vetra, Valdis Zatlers, Vladimirs Strazdiņš, Janis Meikšans and a few other courageous physicians established the Latvian Physicians Association as the first truly free professional organisation in the Soviet Union. The Association basically stopped functioning in 1994, and it became nothing more than a facility for the business and self-expression of a small group of individuals.

Since the restoration of the independent Latvian state, the government has no longer provided guaranteed financing for medicine. Health insurance facilities were set up in the various regions of Latvia, and the principle of payment for services rendered were put into place. At this time, one of the most important missions for reform is the development of primary health care based on the family doctor model. An entire structure of primary health care services is being developed in the country. Each resident of the country is supposed to register with a family doctor who then undertakes leadership over the patient's health care, including preventive care and treatment. A new payment system has been put in place to correlate with this new model of medical care.

A certain form of mandatory health insurance is also in effect in Latvia. The State guarantees payment for certain medical services, and financing for this process comes from general budget subsidies, as well as a dedicated part of the income from individual income tax. Approximately 20% of the cost is covered by patients themselves, but optional insurance is available to cover this cost. Government money is placed into a special health care budget. The resources in this health insurance system are administered by the Latvian Mandatory Health Insurance Agency. It concludes agreements with health insurance and medical institutions

The faculty and staff of the Latvian Medical Academy (also known as the Riga Stradiņš University) in 1998/1999. First row, from the right: Associate Professor Ieva Ranka, director of the Paediatric Division; Docent Vija Eniņa, dean of the Department of Pharmacy; Associate Professor Juta Kroiča, director of the Foreign Students Division; Docent Anita Villeruša, dean of the Department of Public Health (she has since been made an associate professor); Docent Biruta Geidane, dean of the Department of Nursing; Docent Maija Kučinska, deputy dean of the Department of Dentistry; Dr. Ilva Duļevska, deputy dean of the Department of Medicine; Smuidra Žermanos, dean of the Foreign Students Division. In the second row, from the right, Dr. Aivars Vetra, dean of the Department of Rehabilitation, Associate Professor Viktorija Linaberga, deputy dean of the Department of Rehabilitation; docent Ilze Ostrovska, dean of the Department of Social Sciences (she has since become the director of the European Integration Institute); Professor Dace Gardovska, dean of the Department of Post-Graduate Education; Professor Janis Zaļkalns, prorector for education; Marina Gulmane, prorector for economics and administration; Professor Janis Vetra, rector; Professor Janis Gardovskis, prorector for clinical studies; Docent Vitālijs Zirdziņš, dean of the Department of Medicine (he has since been made an associate professor); Professor Indulis Purviņš, deputy dean of the Department of Medicine. Background: The building of Anatomicum (1877), by the architect Heinrihs Šels

Latvia is the only country in Eastern Europe where there is a hospital owned by the local Jewish community. Against the background of the *Bicur Holim* Hospital we see Dr. Arkadijs Gandzs, the director of the hospital; Professor Julijs Anšeļevičs, who is a leading cardiologist in Latvia and head of the Department of General Practice at the Latvian Academy of Medicine; chief physician Rašela Šaca; and infectious disease specialist Anatolijs Bļugers

The Latvian Academy of Medicine is located at *Dzirciema iela* 16 in Riga

Post-graduate studies in Latvia are organised by the University of Latvia Institute of Post-Graduate Education in Medicine, headed by Viesturs Šiliņš (left), as well as the Department of Post-Graduate Training of the Latvian Academy of Medicine, headed by Professor Dace Gardovska (centre in the right-hand photo)

The director of clinic *Linezers* Aivars Lejnieks and Sandra Lejniece, Director of the Latvian Haematology Centre. The Centre is preparing to begin bone marrow transplant operations in 2001. The Latvian Haematology Centre has laboratory and treatment facilities, which rival any that can be found in Eastern Europe

Professor Ilmars Lazovskis is one of the leading minds in the field of medicine in Latvia. He is the highest authority on medical education in Latvia and has written a great many books and scientific papers. Professor Lazovskis has also worked in the area of updating medical terminology in Latvia

Associate Professor Janis Jirgensons is the director of the Cardiology Clinic of the P. Stradiņš University Clinical Hospital

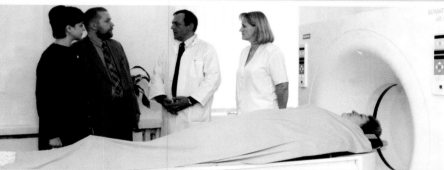

Modern diagnostic and treatment technologies are becoming increasingly common in Latvia. Since 1990, several nuclear magnetic resonance tomographs and computer tomographs have been installed at virtually all of Latvia's leading hospitals. A computer tomograph from the *Siemens* company was installed at the *Jūrmala* Hospital. Here we see the commercial director of the *Siemens* office in Latvia, Viktorija Zefirova, and the head of the medical service, Juris Zvigulis, in conversation with the chief physician of the hospital, Juris Tračums

Professor Gunta Lazdāne heads the Department of Gynaecology and Obstetrics at the Latvian Academy of Medicine

Marija Zvaigznīte, is the senior intern at the Gynaecology Division of the National Oncology Centre

Professor Ģertrūde Eniņa is the director of the Neurology Clinic at the Riga No. 7 Clinical Hospital and president of the Latvian Association of Neurologists

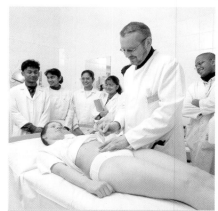

Youth from the Arab Emirates, Kuwait, India, Bangladesh and other countries are studying in the Latvian Medical Academy. Docent Roberts Ribenieks during surgery classes

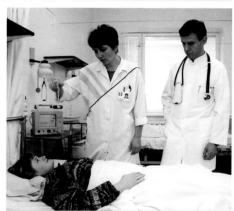

A patient on the intensive care ward of the *Jūrmala* Hospital is consulted by the director of the Neurology Division, Anita Djačenko, and the director of the General Practice Division, Juris Leitans

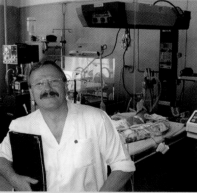

The founder of the Latvian Perinatal Care Centre, Docent Marcis Cirulis, is seen in a neonatology ward in *Daugavpils* which he assembled himself. Neonatology wards in Latvia were established thorough a grant from the Swiss government

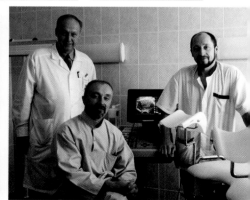

Since 1997 the *Linezers* Hospital in Riga has featured the *Embrions* Centre for Reproductive Medicine, and families which have trouble in conceiving a child receive qualified help from embryologist Uldis Banders and gynaecologists Juris Vitols and Gints Treijs

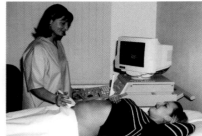

Managers of Latvia's main centres for out-patient medicine, Māris Revalds of the *Veselības centrs 4*, and Māris Andersons, director of the *ARS* medical company

Two cousins – Dace Matule uses an ultrasonograph to examine pregnant women in Riga, while Professor Elvira Lange is the director of the Vascular Angiography Centre at Harvard University's School of Medicine

For the diagnosis of osteoporosis, the medical company *ARS* utilises modern equipment – an osteodensiometer

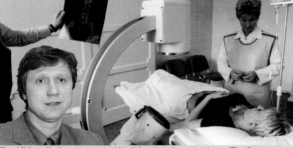

The *ARS* medical company provides lithotripsy for outpatients. The first lithotripsy equipment in the world was designed by an engineer at the Latvian VEF company, Leo Roze, in 1959. To the left, we see the head of the lithotripsy programme at *ARS*, Egils Vjaters

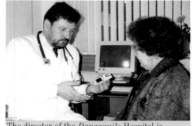

The director of the *Daugavpils* Hospital is endocrinologist Arvīds Krompans, seen here examining a diabetes patient

Family doctors provide the foundations for outpatient medical care in Latvia. A very popular physician in Latvia is Guntis Ķilkuts, seen here with a patient in Riga

Dentist Līga Apine treats patients at the *ARS* medical company

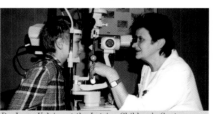

Dr. Inese Valaine at the Latvian Children's Centre provides consultations to a young patient.

Use of a Doppler graph at the *ARS* medical company

The largest private laboratory in Latvia is the *E.Gulbja laboratorija*, and here we see director Egils Gulbis, deputy director Didzis Gavars and laboratory director Biruta Bandere

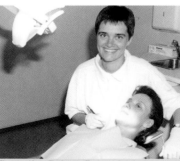

Dentist Alēna Butkeviča-Zvaigzne is in private practice. Indeed, Latvian dentistry is almost entirely based on the principles of private practice today

The insurance stock company *Rīgas slimokase* is the leader in personal health insurance in Latvia

First aid health case center *Ziepniekkalns* was started in 1997 as a pilotproject of development and improvement of first aid conception of Riga. A teamwork of family doctors, nurses of first aid center, and Social workers is achieved. Daiga Pētersone, the director of the center

Fathers are present for the birth of their children at the Latvian Family Centre. Director Anita Plume is seen at the right

Dr. Edite Vītola and the *Vidriži* medical centre, which is 70 years old. The building was built specifically for this purpose before World War II, and today, fully renovated, it is in full conformity with global standards

regarding payment for health care services provided to residents, it develops methodologies for setting the price of medical services and for paying for them, and it informs residents about the way in which these health care services are received. The director of the Latvian Mandatory Health Insurance Agency is Inara Bluķe.

Health insurance institutions in Latvia are local government enterprises which plans and organises the way in which people receive medical services in the respective territories. Agreements are concluded with the Mandatory Health Insurance Agency and with service providers.

There are several nationally important medical programs, including the Disaster Medicine Program and the Mental Care Program, which are financed with subsidies from the State budget with the direct involvement of the Mandatory Health Insurance Agency.

The Agency also finances such centralised processes as the purchase of medications for specific disorders, the provision of highly specialised medical services, and the provision of medical information. In 1998, the Latvian government signed an agreement with the World Bank regarding a 15-year credit line aimed at reform of the Latvian health care system.

Not everything has proceeded smoothly since the restoration of Latvia's independence. Between 1996 and 1999 the competent organisational structure of health care which had existed in Latvia was completely destroyed. Preventive care was ignored and all resources were put into primary care without a sufficient material and technological basis and retraining. The incidence of serious diseases and complications increased.

The health insurance stock company *Rīgas Slimokase* was established in 1994 with the aim of launching a program of voluntary health insurance in Latvia. In 1999, it was among the largest health insurance companies in Latvia, with an extensive network of branches and representatives. The company has some 160,000 clients throughout Latvia. Various levels of insurance policies have earned the trust of Latvia's residents – everybody knows the Red Policy, the Green Policy, the Silver Policy and the Gold Policy.

THE NATIONAL ENVIRONMENTAL HEALTH CENTER

Latweeschu Ahrste

Weselibas grahmata, Latweeschu Behrnem par wahiibu sarakftita.

There are long-standing traditions in Latvia in the area of hygiene and public health. The journal *Latviešu Ārste* (*Latvian doctor*), which was published in 1768 and 1769 was aimed at helping hard-working farmers to avoid diseases. 25 issues of the journal were published by the German doctor Peteris Vilde after a translation into Latvian by *Smiltene* clergyman Jekabs Lange. The journal contained advice about what today would be known as holistic medicine. The first book on hygiene aimed at children was published in Latvia in 1795

The incidence of tick-borne encephalitis in 1998 (incidents per 100,000 residents)

<20   40-59   80 un >
20-39   60-79   Occurrences – 1029

The director of the *NVVC*, Imants Rezebergs

Latvia's *Nacionālais vides veselības centrs – NVVC* (National Environmental Health Centre) is a preventive medicine facility with more than 50 years of experience. It was initially established as a sanitary and epidemiological centre. The *NVVC* conducts various kinds of laboratory investigations – physical, chemical, radiological, microbiological and virological. The work of the laboratory is accredited by the *LATAK* and Russian accreditation systems, and the virology lab is certified by the World Health Organisation. The everyday work of the Centre involves efforts to limit the spread of infectious diseases, to provide advice to international travellers, and to handle documentation concerning international vaccination programs. It is possible to avoid many infectious diseases only by getting timely vaccinations, and the *NVVC* has its own vaccination office. Immunisation is available there not only for those diseases that are common in Latvia, but also for rare or exotic diseases. The Centre is also working to develop a preventive system of vaccination.

Another very important function for the Centre is monitoring and analysis of such environmental health risks as radiation, electromagnetic fields, noise, and water, air and food pollution. The Centre trains people who work in the manufacturing, processing and sale of food, in the health care system and in the provision of hygienic services in Latvia.

The Service was very unpopular and often scorned in Soviet times and for a while thereafter. The situation changed only after a new and energetic health care worker, Imants Rezebergs, took over the reins at the facility.

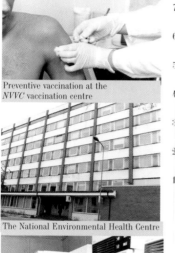

Preventive vaccination at the *NVVC* vaccination centre

The National Environmental Health Centre

A storage facility for immunology and disinfecting products

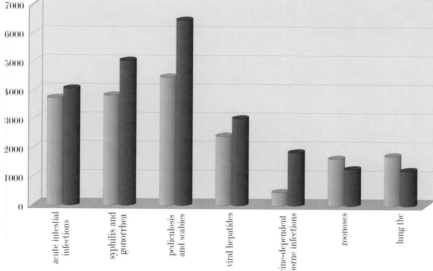

The spread of infectious diseases in Latvia

7000
6000
5000
4000
3000
2000
1000
0

acute intestinal infections
syphilis and gonorrhea
pediculosis and scabies
viral hepatides
vaccine-dependent air-borne infections
zoonoses
lung tbc

■ 1998 ■ average (1993-1997)

The *NVVC* stand at the *Health '99* exhibition in Latvia

The Centre's virology lab has been certified by the World Health Organisation

Viktors Voļskis heads the Research Laboratory Centre, and is seen here in the hygienic research laboratory

Vaira Kalniņa runs the Virology Laboratory

Measurements of electromagnetic fields and noise levels

THE HEALTH PROMOTION CENTER

VESELĪBAS VEICINĀŠANAS CENTRS & B

In 1996 the Ministry of Welfare set up the Health Promotion Centre, which is charged with developing various health promotion programs in line with existing international programs, researching public health risk factors, and formulating recommendations for the prevention of public health problems that are based on the latest scientific discoveries. The Centre also works to provide general education to the public on factors that have an impact on health. *Health Week* has become a positive tradition in Latvia, and the Centre's activities during that week take place in all of Latvia's regions, involving local governments, school boards and NGOs in the work.

Davids Hieronims Grindelis (1776-1836) was a Latvian-born chemist, pharmacist, natural scientists and physician. He was the founder of the Riga Chemical and Pharmaceutical Society

Professor and pharmaceutical specialist Caesar Amstler (1881-1965) conducted world class research in pharmacology of morphine and other narcotic analgesics

Professor Janis Maizite (1883-1950). Long term head professor at the Faculty of Pharmacology of the University of Latvia

A pharmacy in the Old City of Riga in the 19th century

The Nikolajs pharmacy in 1900

Work at the pharmacy of the University of Latvia in the early 20th century

A collector of medicinal plants (an exposition at the Pauls Stradiņš Museum of Medical History)

The world's first known pharmacy was established in 754 AD in Baghdad. Around the turn of the first millennium, pharmacies or apothecaries began to appear in Europe, as well.

In the 13th century, there were pharmacies in all of Germany's major cities. In Latvia, as well, the pharmaceutical business developed quite rapidly. The first pharmacy in Riga was opened in 1357 in the main city square. It remained in operation until 1758. The second oldest pharmacy in Riga was established in 1570. The third pharmacy in Latvia opened its doors in 1578 in *Jelgava*.

Around 1800 Latvia had more than 30 pharmacies. Beginning in the late 19th century, the country's network of pharmacies expanded to include rural regions, as well. There was very rapid development of the network of pharmacies, as well as of the pharmaceutical industry, during the 20 years of Latvia's independence between the two World Wars, and the Pharmacy Law which Latvia adopted at that time was considered to be one of the most progressive in Europe. A successful industry of manufacturing drugs also sprang up.

All of Latvia's pharmacies were nationalised in 1940, and this destroyed the network of private pharmacies that had existed. The entire system of pharmacies was centralised.

When Latvia's independence was renewed, the network of private pharmacies and wholesalers of medicines reappeared. Today there are some 650 pharmacies in Latvia, and they have been certified in accordance with the relevant European standards. A new Pharmacy Law has been adopted.

Latvia has a wealth of traditions in the area of associations of pharmacists. The first such organisation was established in 1803 by Davids Hieronims Grindelis, while the second, established by Janis Hertelis, followed in 1885. There were several organisations of this kind in later years, but in 1937, President Karlis Ulmanis ordered that they all be merged into the Latvian Pharmacists Association. During the Soviet period, the Latvian Scientific Association of Pharmacists was in operation. The new Latvian Pharmacists Association was established in 1994, and today it has more than 850 members.

One of the first private wholesalers of medications in Latvia was *Farmserviss*, Ltd. and here we see its senior pharmacist, Irena Feldmane.

The general director of the State Drug Agency, Janis Ozoliņš, heads up the process of registering drugs in Latvia

The deputy State secretary of the Ministry of Welfare, Talis Talents, directed the Department of Pharmacy after 1992, but in 1999 he was replaced by Juris Bundulis

The president of the Latvian Pharmacists Association, Aigars Eniņš, at the "Green Pharmacy" which the society established in 1994. The first society of pharmacists in Latvia was founded in 1803

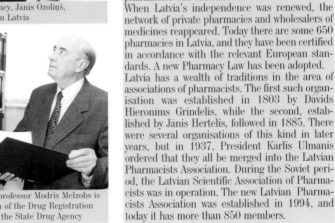

Pharmacology professor Modris Melzobs is the chairperson of the Drug Registration Commission of the State Drug Agency

The *Kamelijas* pharmacy on *Brīvības iela* in Riga is one of the largest pharmacies in Latvia, and it is open around the clock. Latvia's pharmacies are rich with traditions, courtesy and professionalism of the pharmacists. There are about 650 pharmacies in Latvia each of them lead by a professional pharmacist

The staff of the Drug Price Agency. Director Daiga Behmane is seated to the right. The Agency manages Latvia's system of compensation for the purchase of drugs, as well as the list of drugs to which the compensation system applies. The goal is to ensure that all of the residents of the country have access to equal health care, promoting the effective and rational use of drugs and control over the State's expenditures in this area. Each year the State spends approximately 2 lats per resident on the purchase of drugs

A meeting between representatives of the *Berlin-Chemi Menarini Group*, which was the market leader among manufacturers of drugs in Latvia, and representatives of the company's co-operation partner, the wholesaler TAMRO. From the right: Peteris Krauss, Inta Aboliņa, Alģis Blažis and Juris Cilinskis. Typically the Eastern Europe pharmacology firms account for the majority of sales on the Latvian market

Iveta Streipa is the director of the State Pharmacy Inspection, which controls the operations of pharmacies, wholesalers and manufacturing companies in this sector. The Inspection works for regulation of the drug market. For years mainly the less- quality production of the USSR and India were sold in Latvia. At present the sale is open only for registered drugs confirming the Latvian standards.

A complex of buildings at *Vāgnera iela* 13/15 in Riga which is an architectural monument today is the heart of public pharmaceutical activities in Latvia. A branch of the Stradiņš Museum of the History of Medicine is located here, and the Latvian Society of Pharmacists finds its home in the building

Nikolajs Zuments and a tablet manufacturing machine that was imported from Germany in 1938

The director of *MedPro*, Vairis Buļs, helps his company maintain its positions in the market

OLAINFARM

The *Olaines Ķīmiski farmaceitiskā rūpnīca* went on line in 1972. Initially the company produced biologically active substances through industrial and semi-industrial synthesis, but later it also began to produce ready-made drugs in the form of tablets, capsules and sterile powders. Today the stock company *Olainfarm* manufactures 60 different kinds of drugs from various pharmacological groups, as well as 20 drug substances. In 2000, the company was preparing to release 12 new kinds of drugs.

The laboratory of the stock company *Olainfarm*

The president of SC *Olainfarm*, Valeri Maligin

Executive board chairman Peteris Stupans and general director Vitalijs Skriveris of SC *Grindex*, seen here at a ceremony to honour the opening of the SC *Grindex* homepage on the Internet, have always emphasised that the company's main aim is to expand its market share

GRINDEX

Latvia became known around the world in the 1970s when the Latvian Institute for Organic Synthesis developed an important series of new drugs. In order to manufacture these drugs and to develop the necessary technologies, an experimental factory was set up at the institute, and over the course of time it turned into one of Latvia's most important producers of drugs, the company that is known as SC *Grindex*. Today the public stock company *Grindex* is the largest pharmaceutical enterprise in the Baltic States. It develops and manufactures drugs and their active components, and it sells products in the Baltic States, Japan, Western Europe, Russia and the CIS. It also is a co-operation partner for international pharmaceutical firms in the Baltic region.

SC *Grindex* offers 110 different drugs on the market – drugs to treat heart and circulatory disorders, psychotherapeutic medications, anti-cancer treatments, gastroenterological medications, pain relief medications and anti-fever substances, as well as vitamins and tonics. SC *Grindex* and the Institute for Organic Synthesis have collaborated in the development of several original products, including *Mildronāts* to treat heart and circulatory disorders, *Ftorafūrs*, which is an anti-cancer treatment, and *Foridons*, which fights calcium build up.

SC *Grindex* works with some of the world's leading pharmaceutical companies – *Taiho* in Japan, *Johnson & Johnson* in the United States, *Merck Generic* in Great Britain, *Legosan* in Sweden and *Sanofi* in France.

In 1998, SC *Grindex* received a Latvian Quality Award for the all-encompassing quality control system that it uses. SC *Grindex* produces its drugs fully in accordance with Good Manufacturing Practice standards.

The chairman of the public SC *Grindex* council, Valdis Jākobsons, is one of the most distinguished participants in the Latvian pharmaceutical industry – a sector in which he has worked for more than 30 years. Valdis Jākobsons set up an award that is named after the first Latvian natural scientist, Davids Hieronims Grindelis, and this prestigious medal has been awarded since 1995 to Latvian and foreign scientists, pharmacists and physicians. Each year on the anniversary of the birth of the distinguished chemist and pharmacist, flowers are laid at the entrance to his family's chapel at the Martiņš cemetery

A packaging line for tablets at the company. Its facilities conform to the most severe international standards, as well as to the Good Manufacturing Practice standards, which prevail in the industry. This means that every employee who is involved in the manufacturing of drugs must be highly responsible and precise in his or her work

Veterinary medications are also produced in Latvia. The *Sigfarm* factory in *Sigulda* for many years was the leading producer of such medications in the USSR. In 1991, a pharmaceutical laboratory for natural substances was set up in *Sigulda*. It is called *Fitosan* Ltd., and it works to produce medications and biological feed supplements for grass-feeding mammals, which are appropriate for Latvia's conditions. The company specialises in the treatment of various disorders in dairy cows, and it has done extensive research in pharmacology and pharmaceutics, especially focusing on natural resources in Latvia and establishing the facilities to produce the related medications. The senior researcher at the facility is Professor Jānis Vētra, who has worked for years in the field of veterinary medicine

A division where infusion liquids are produced

RĪGAS FARMACEI-TISKĀ FABRIKA

Galenical preparations have been of great importance in Latvian medicine for centuries, and the stock company *Riga Farmaceitiskā fabrika* is the leading manufacturer of such galenical pharmaceutical products in the Baltic States. The factory was opened in 1950, and today it produces a variety of galenical tinctures, drops, extracts, syrups, medications dissolved in alcohol or oil, pastes, creams, liniments and packaged medicinal plans and complex teas – more than 120 items in all. 70% of the raw materials that are used at the factory come from Latvian farmers or from Latvia's fields and forests. The Manufacturing Development Department seeks to improve and modernise the methods whereby drugs are produced and their quality is evaluated. New recipes for medications and production methods are developed. Over the last decade, pharmacies in Latvia and Estonia have received several new products from the SC *Riga Farmaceitiskā fabrika* each year.

The magazine *Aptiekāra padoms* (*Advice to the Pharmacist*) and its editor-in-chief, Gita Krastiņa

Professional books on drugs and their use are published by the publishing house *Nacionalais Medicinas apgāds*, and they used by doctors and patients alike

MUSEUM OF RĪGA'S HISTORY AND NAVIGATION

The oldest museum in the Baltics was founded and named after N. Himsel in 1773 by a decision of the City Council of Riga, because the essence of the exhibition was an artifact collection of natural science, history, and art, left by doctor Nikolaus Himsel from Riga. The history of the museum is attached to the Research Association of History of Russian – Baltic Provinces (founded in 1834) and work of the Natural Scientist Association (founded in 1845).

The museum was moved to the Dome Square vicinity at its present location in 1891 and renamed to Museum of Riga. Later the rest of N. Himsel's collections were passed on to the museum. There are about 80 important collections, providing historical details of Riga. The most important ones are the collection of archaeology and ancient artifacts with more than 130 000 items, the collection of numismatics (more than 70 000 items), the collection of length and weight measurements, records of trade organizations, imported artifacts, providing a view on Riga as a trade center. There are more than 6000 items in the collection of heraldry, showing changes in the political life of Riga. There are many household items, pictures and city plans, there is a unique collection of illegal revolutionary banners and flags – illegal spread-sheets, slogans, material, connected with Riga people's resistance movements against different political authorities.

An exposition in the Museum of Riga's History and Navigation

Museum of Riga's History and Navigation, exposition – *Artist Julius Gotfried Siegmund and his time*

An exposition in the Museum of Riga's History and Navigation – *Middle Age Riga*

HISTORY MUSEUM OF LATVIA

A fragment of an exhibition – *Sacral Art* – the collection of wooden sculptures is unique on the scale of Europe and gives a wide understanding of the development of wood curving art in churches between the XIV and the beginning of the XX century

An exhibition in the History Museum - *Lifestyle of peasantry at the end of the XIX and the beginning of the XX century*

The History Museum of Latvia is located in the Riga Castle. It is the keeper of the largest material culture heritage of the Latvian people. The museum was founded in 1869; unique archeological, ethnographic, numismatic, and historical artifact collections are found there. An exposition of ancient history of Latvia as well as exhibitions of the collections, are on display.

NATURE MUSEUM OF LATVIA

The section of entomology provides information on insect structure, diversity, and ecology

The president of the Natural Scientist Association and the head of the Nature Museum of Latvia, Karl Reinhold Kupfer (1872 - 1935)

Bird egg files

An exposition of birds

The Nature Museum of Latvia located at *Krišjāņa Barona iela* 4, is the oldest and richest in collections of all the north and east European museums of natural science. The beginnings of it are found in exhibitions of Natural Scientist Association at the beginning of the XVIII century, the collections of which were later passed on to the city of Riga and became the core of the Nature Museum of Latvia. The museum is at it present location and lay-out since 1951; there is a wide range of gathered geological, botanical, entomological, zoological, anthropological, etc. material.

A band of students of natural science

An opening of a flower exhibition in summer of 1999. First from left – the director of the museum – Māra Eipure

The Rainis Literature and Art History Museum at *Pils laukums* 2 in Riga, and the director of the Museum, Ivars Zukulis

The *Tadenava* homestead in *Jekabpils* District is where Rainis spent the first four years of his life (1865-1869)

The *Berķenele* home in *Daugavpils* district where Rainis lived from 1872 to 1881

Rainis spent a period of time after he completed high school (from December 1883 until August 1884) at the remote *Jasmuiža* estate which was leased by his parents, and he also spent summer holidays there when he was at university (1884-1888)

The Rainis and Aspazija memorial summer home at *Plieksāna iela* 5/7 in *Majori*, City of *Jūrmala*

One of the rooms in the *Majori* summer home where Rainis spent the last years of his life (1927-1929)

The Janis Akuraters Museum at *O. Vācieša iela 6a* in Riga

THE RAINIS LITERATURE AND ART HISTORY MUSEUM

The beginnings of the museum which is named after Latvia's most distinguished poet, playwright and politician Rainis (his real name was Janis Plieksāns, 1865-1929) date back to 1925. Today the Rainis Literature and Art History Museum (*Raiņa Literatūras un mākslas vēstures muzejs – RLMVM*) is one of the largest museums in Latvia, and there is a basis for speaking of a 10 museum association, in which the central focus is on Latvian cultural history with three main dominants – literature, the theatre and music. Each of the associated museums provides information about a significant stage in Latvian cultural life, actively trying to popularise humanitarian ideas in present-day society.

The collection of the *RLMVM* and the history of literature exposition are located in the heart of Old Riga, in the Riga Castle, right next door to the offices of the President of Latvia. In the ancient rooms of the castle, the museum displays its basic collection, providing an all-encompassing view of Latvian literary life, beginning with feudal culture and continuing to the mid-20th century. In two halls of the castle, as well as in an adjoining building, there are various thematic exhibitions, and these allow the visitor to learn about unique and interesting aspects of literary life in the past and in the present. Tours are available, and museum employees often travel outside of the museum to lecture and to organise literary afternoons or meetings with authors. The museum has a cinema in which documentary films about various aspects of culture and distinguished persons, as well as film versions of great literary works are shown. Similar activities take place at the various branches of the *RLMVM*.

Today the museum's collection contains nearly 600,000 units, and it is a unique collection of original materials from Latvia's cultural history. The museum has a reading room in which people can study any part of the vast collection. In addition to the work of collection, storage and research, the museum feels that it is one of its primary goals to ensure public access to the collection. Each year more than 100,000 units of the collection are used for one purpose or another.

The Janis Rozentals and Rudolfs Blaumanis Museum at *Alberta iela* 12, Apartment 9, in Riga

The Krišjānis Barons Museum at *K. Barona iela* 3, Apartment 5, in Riga

Janis' School in *Piebalga*

OCCUPATION MUSEUM OF LATVIA

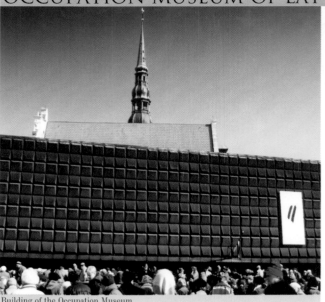

A display of weaponry

The head executive of the Occupation Museum of Latvia, Gundega Feldmane-Zans

Exposition – A model of Gulaga barracks

The museum of the 50 years of occupation of Latvia is in the former Riflemen Museum, *Strēlnieku laukums* 1. The museum building was built on foundations of houses destroyed during the World War II in Old Riga and served the system of soviet propaganda for a long time by falsification of historic facts. The documents and records of individual testimonies unveil a gloomier period of Latvian history, beginning with the soviet occupation in 1940 – an occupation by Germany – and the return of the soviet army. Several hundreds of thousands of people were destroyed or deported from Latvia.

Building of the Occupation Museum

An exposition hall of the museum

THE LATVIAN WAR MUSEUM

Exposition of weapons' collection

Director of the War Museum, Aija Fleija

Museum building – *Pulvertornis* (Powder Tower) and its adjunction

The Latvian War Museum is located in *Pulvertornis* (Powder Tower), built in the 14th c., as a crucial part of the old fortification system of Riga. The museum was founded in 1916 and closed in 1941. It served other purposes during the years of the soviet occupation and was turned back into a War Museum in 1990. The exposition material concerns Latvian riflemen, fights for freedom, Latvian army from 20's to 40's, the World War II, and other themes of military history.

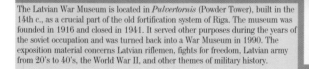

An exposition of the museum – *The proclamation of Latvian state and liberation fights 1918-1920*

MUSEUM OF DECORATIVE AND APPLIED ART

The Museum of Decorative and Applied Art is located in the oldest stone building still preserved in Riga – formerly St. George's, a part of the Sword-brothers' Order Castle. The museum stores and exhibits Latvian professional and applied artwork from the last century up until today. Exhibitions of decorative and applied art by both Latvian and foreign artists is displayed in the exhibition hall. The museum was founded in 1989.

MOTOR MUSEUM

The Motor Museum of Riga is one of the most popular museums in Latvia despite its young age. It was built in 1989 in special design. It is located in *Mežparks*. Several hundred vehicles, bicycles, and motorcycles have found their permanent home in the museum. Such unique samples of car engineering as the 16-cylinder *Auto Union* by *Porsche*, the fire-truck manufactured in *Russo Balt* factory in Riga 1912, as well as cars that belonged to soviet leaders: Stalin and Brezhnev.

The director of the Motor Museum, Edvīns Liepiņš

Priedes inn

ETHNOGRAPHIC OPEN-AIR MUSEUM OF LATVIA

The Ethnographic Open-Air Museum was founded in 1924 and is one of the oldest and richest museums in Europe. Houses, farm-steads, craftsmen workshops, fishermen huts with household artifacts from all parts of Latvia are arranged according to the regions. There are inns, windmills, as well as several churches in the museum. Services are still held in *Usma* Church.

On the first weekend of June, exhibitions and markets of applied arts take place every year in the The Ethnographic Open-Air Museum. Masters of fourteen different crafts work at the museum: blacksmiths, spoon-carvers, weavers, potters, beekeepers. Folklore and other festivals often take place in the museum.

A craftsman homestead from Latgale

A barn from *Cēsis* district, *Vaive Sķesteri*, built in the last quarter of the 18th century

A barn from *Valmiera* district, *Ungurpils Sipoli*, built around 1830. *Auseklis*, the poet lived in the house in 1850

A peasant homestead from Latgale complemented with storehouses from the southern and central parts of Latgale, built at the beginning and the middle of the 19th century

A barn from *Daugavpils* district, *Liksna Oglenieki* village, built in the 30's of the 19th century

A barn from *Bauska* district, *Ceraukste Ribas*, built in 1755

A barn from *Dižļiķi*, *Kuldīga* district, built in 1767

A homestead of a wealthy peasant from Zemgale (the second half of the 18th to the middle of the 19th c.), composed of characteristically representative houses of *Bauska* district

Ate Mill Museum in *Alūksne* district

Memorial Museum of Rudolfs Blaumanis, *Braki*, *Madona* district, *Ergļi*

An exposition of Fishery Museum of the former collective farm *Uzvara* in *Jūrmala*

Museum of Muenhausen in *Limbži* district, 53. km on Riga-Tallinn highway located in the former *Duntes* inn building. The museum is open since 1983

Museum of *Dobele's* History on *Dobele* island, founded in 1969

An exposition of Memorial Museum of *Ojārs Vācietis* with his writing-table and a draft of the last poem

Richard Wagner (1813-1883) worked in Riga from 1837 until 1839

Fyodor Chialiapin (1873-1938) visited Riga five times

Leo Blech (1871-1958) was the conductor of the Latvian National Opera from 1937 until 1941, and he was also a composer

Professor Pauls Jozuus (1873-1937), a faithful colleague of Jazeps Vitols and rector of the Latvian Conservatory from 1935 until 1937, with his wife

A group of musicians in Latvia in the 1920s – Jēkabs Karkliņš (1867-1960), Janis Zalitis (1884-1943), Jazeps Vitols (1863-1948), Arturs Bobkovics (1885-1959) and Teodors Reiters (1884-1956)

MUSICAL TRADITIONS IN RĪGA

The earliest known musical group in Latvia was a choir founded by German Crusaders in 1216. Another choir was established at the Dome Church in Riga in 1240. Its members, according to historians, were students from the Riga Dome School, who learned Gregorian chants in Latin. Riga, as a city of the Hanseatic League, became acquainted with the music of many lands. Latvian music for many centuries was an oral tradition which was passed down from generation to generation.

Beginning in the 14th century, Riga had a city musician, who had four assistants. All five men were civil servants, and every morning and every evening they played a choral from the tower of St. Peter's Church. On Tuesdays, Thursdays and Sundays they performed religious music from the tower of the city hall. The city's musicians played the trumpet, the bassoon and the horn. Music became part of weddings held at the Great Guild as early as the 14th century.

The first pipe organ in Latvia was installed at St. Jacob's Church in 1392, and St. Peter's got its organ in 1465. Indigenous Latvians were far more active in singing than in playing instruments – at the spring, summer and winter solstice celebrations in particular. National instruments included the stringed *kokle* and the pipes known as *dūdas*. Instrumental music developed very intensively in the 17th century, and by the mid-18th century Riga was certainly the center of musical life for the entire Baltic region. The Riga Musical Society was established in 1760, and it organized concerts of symphonic and chamber music. In 1782 the Riga City Theater was opened, and opera was often on its stage. The repertoire kept up with the times, and operas by Mozart, Benda, Cherubini and others were performed. Mozart's *Abduction from the Seraglio* was performed in Riga in 1785 – three years after its premiere in Vienna. Beethoven's *Fidelio* was staged in 1818. Of particular importance to Riga's operatic world was the presence in the city of Richard Wagner from 1837 until 1839. The most popular operas of the day – works by Bellini, Meyerbeer and Auber were staged by Wagner, who also presented regular concerts of symphony music both at the Riga City Theater and at the House of the Blackheads, which quickly developed a reputation as Riga's best concert hall. Nearly all of Europe's leading 19th century musicians visited Riga at one time or another. *Norway's Paganini* – the violinist Ole Bull – visited in 1838. Franz Liszt was in the city in 1842. During the 1830s, many of the continent's most outstanding vocalists performed in Riga, including Henriette Sontag, Angelica Catalani, Anna Milder and Wilhelmine Šredere-Defrinte. Particularly beloved in Riga was Anton Rubinstein, who between 1844 and 1880 performed in the city no less than 15 times. In 1880 Rigensians celebrated an amazing Basque violinist called Pablo Sarasati, and five years later Sergei Rachmaninov, still very young, came to the city's attention. Many famous composers visited Riga. Robert Schumann arrived when his wife, the pianist Clara Schumann, was performing in the city. Berlioz presented his own music, battling – so reports tell us – with a less than obedient orchestra and a less than full hall. Fyodor Chaliapin arrived in Riga at the height of his fame in 1910, and returned later. Conductor Emil Cooper brought the Riga Opera Choir to Berlin specifically for one of Chaliapin's guest performances in 1928. The German author of the opera *Tiefland*, Eugen D'Albert, visited Riga in 1931 to get divorced for the 5th time and married for the 7th time. His romantic intentions ended tragically, and the composer left Riga in a flower-bedecked coffin.

Riga was never forgotten by the famous people who visited.

THE BEGINNINGS OF LATVIAN NATIONAL MUSIC

The Latvian musical intelligentsia emerged fairly spontaneously as part of the Latvian national awakening. The first Latvian composer with a higher education in music was a graduate of the St. Petersburg Conservatory of Music, Andrejs Jurjans. He was born in 1856, when indentured servitude was still the rule in Latvia, but in 1880 he introduced Latvian audiences to symphony music with a suite called *Latvian Dances*.

The first professional Latvian musicians were trailblazers as teachers, organists and choir conductors. Janis Cimze ran a teachers school in *Valmiera* and later in *Valka* (1839-1881), and he trained more than 400 teachers with good musical skills. A second school for teachers operated in *Irlava*, Kurzeme, where the instructor was Janis Betiņš (1830-1912). One graduate of the Cimze school was Karlis Baumanis (1835-1905), author of the Latvian national anthem. The people known as *Cimze's boys* were very active in collecting Latvian folklore and in laying the foundations for Latvia's choral culture.

In the 19th century, there were no schools of music in Riga, and talented young people went abroad. Ernests Vigners entered the Moscow Conservatory in 1873, while Andrejs Jurjans (1856-1922) finished the St. Petersburg Conservatory with three degrees – in organ, composition and French horn. He attended the conservatory between 1880 and 1882). His brothers followed in his footsteps, and the Jurjans French Horn Quartet was famed throughout the Russian Empire.

In 1886 Jazeps Vitols was graduated with distinction from the composition program at the St. Petersburg Conservatory, and he was invited to stay at the school as an instructor. Ludvigs Betiņš (1856-1930) was also a graduate of the St. Petersburg Conservatory, later served as a professor at the Moscow Conservatory, and was one of the most highly talented organ and piano virtuosos of his day. Latvian musicians in the late 19th century were eager collectors of the cultural treasures of the Latvian nation, composing new adaptations of folk songs and popularizing them. In the 1890s Jurjans began to collect what turned out to be six volumes of *Latvian National Music Materials*, which were released between 1894 and 1926.

A new generation of talented musicians appeared in the early 20th century, among them Emilis Melngailis, who focused on Latvian folk songs and national music. Emils Darziņš brought tragically romantic notes to Latvian music. He died young, just like Mozart, leaving behind a series of beloved choral and solo songs, as well as his world-famous *Melancholy Waltz*. Alfreds Kalniņš who, like Melngailis and Darziņš, studied in St. Petersburg under Rimsky-Korsakov, composed operas, cantatas, symphonies, suites, chamber music and choral songs. He was also Latvia's most distinguished organist in his time.

Janis Cimze (1814-1881) laid the foundations for musical education among Latvian teachers

Teachers at the Vidzeme teachers school are seen here tending to their gardening

Jazeps Vitols and his students at the St. Petersburg Conservatory in 1909

Ernests Vigners (1850-1933) – conductor, composer and pedagogue, founder of the Riga Institute of Phonology

Emilis Melngailis (1874-1954), composer, folklore specialist, conductor, critic and outstanding collector of Latvia's cultural treasures

Alfreds Kalniņš (1879-1951) – composer and outstanding organist

Emils Darziņš (1875-1910) – author of unforgettable choral and solo songs

A celebration of the 50th anniversary of Jazeps Vitols' entry into the world of professional musicians at the National Conservatory in Latvia in 1937

The men's choir for Wagner's *Tannheuser* in 1919, when the Latvian National Opera had just been reopened

Alīda Vāne and Mariss Vētra in *Tannheuser*

The first Latvian opera – Alfreds Kalniņš' *Baņuta* – was performed in 1920 and starred Dagmara Rozenberga (center)

Adolfs Kaktiņš as Rigoletto, 1919

Milda Brehmane-Štengele as Salome, 1923

Wagner's *Valkyrie*, at the opera performed in 1963, with Maigurs Adermanis as Votans and Arturs Frinbergs as Siegmund

Žermena Heine-Vāgnere and Anna Ludiņa in Verdi's *Aida*, 1953

The world-famous soloists Jānis Zābers and Pēteris Gravelis are seen here as Rudolf and Marcel in Puccini's *La Boheme*

Kārlis Zariņš has been a leading tenor at the Latvian National Opera for decades

British composer Benjamin Britten in Riga in 1964, directing a performance of *The Little Chimneysweep* in Riga with conductor Edgars Tons

Edgars Vardaunis (1910-1999) was a set designer who served as the chief artist of the Latvian National Opera from 1983 until 1990

Director Jānis Zariņš (1893-1979)

Operas and ballets were often staged at the castle of the dukes of Courland in *Jelgava* in the early 18th century. Individual troupes of performers visited Riga from time to time during that period, but once the Riga City Theater was opened in 1782, operas and other musical performances in German became regular events. In August 1863 the theater moved to the building which now houses the Latvian National Opera. It was a German theater, but among the performers were Latvian vocalists Malvīne Vignere and Jekabs Duburs. In 1912 Pāvuls Jurjāns created a Latvian opera troupe, which continued its work until World War I. In 1918, the troupe was gathered back together in St. Petersburg by an attorney called Andrejs Fridenbergs, as well as conductor Teodors Reiters and composer Jāzeps Vītols. They helped many of the artists to return to Latvia. The troupe arrived in Riga in august 1918, and on October 15, in what is now the Latvian National Theater, the first post-war performance (of Wagner's *The Flying Dutchman*) went on stage. In January 1919 the opera moved to its current home, performing Wagner once again (on January 21). It was in the summer of 1919 that the troupe was given the name National Opera of Latvia.

During the years of Latvian independence the opera was led by chief conductor Teodors Reiters, and its artistic level was very high indeed. World-class soloists included Milda Brehmane-Štengele, Ada Benefelde, Rūdolfs Bērziņš, Mariss Vētra, Arturs Priednieks-Kavara, Herta Luse, Adolfs Kaktiņš, and others. The first Latvian opera, Alfreds Kalniņš' *Baņuta*, was debuted in May 1920, followed by other operas by Jānis Mediņš, Jāzeps Mediņš and others. The Latvian National Opera staged the world's leading operas by Mozart, Verdi, Puccini, Wagner, Tchaikovsky, Strauss and others – more than 100 operas in all. Famous soloists and conductors (including Emil Cooper and Leo Blech) visited the opera.

At the end of World War II, many of the leading performers of the opera fled to the West, but during the Soviet occupation others took their place, eagerly trying to preserve the traditions of the opera. Leonīds Vīgners, who ran the opera from 1944 until 1949, staged major performances. The work of conductor Edgars Tons (1954-1967) cannot be forgotten, and the professional work of Rihards Glazups, Jāzeps Lindbergs and director Jānis Zariņš was highly praised. Many outstanding soloists have performed at the opera – Žermena Heina-Vāgnere, Anna Ludiņa, Elfrīda Pakule, Pēteris Gravelis, Miķelis Fišers, Alexander Dashkov, Jānis Zābers, Laima Andersone-Silare, Kārlis Zariņš, Guri Antipov, etc. New Latvian operas by Marģers Zariņš, Imants Kalniņš, Pauls Dambis and others were staged, and the opera's repertoire included both classical and modern operas. Wagnerian traditions were always preserved in the work of the theater.

After a full restoration of the opera's building in 1995, the theater launched a new phase of activity. A new generation of performers took its place on the stage in Latvia and throughout Europe. Today soprano Inese Galante, tenor Ingus Petersons, bass Egils Siliņš, baritone Aleksandrs Poļakovs, soprano Inga Kalna and a few others are so popular in Europe that they are seen in Latvia only as occasional guests.

In the late 1990s colorful performances of Aida, Nabucco, Alcina, Salome and other operas were the work of conductors Gintars Rinkevičs and Aleksandrs Viļumanis, as well as director Guntis Gailītis. These performances won praise not only in Riga, but also throughout Europe. Many outstanding foreign soloists have been delighted to perform on Riga's stage. A new tradition is the annual opera festival in Sigulda which is organized by physician Dainis Kalns every summer. The opera stages open-air performances in other places in Latvia, too.

The main hall of the Latvian National Opera after reconstruction, 1995

Solveiga Raja in *Don Carlos*

A view of Donizetti's *Milas Dzēriens*, starring Inese Galante and Ingus Petersons

A view from Verdi's *Nabucco* with Samsons Izjumovs in the title role

Vienna Opera soloist Egils Zariņš and Inga Kalna at the *Sigulda* opera festival

Conductor Aleksandrs Viļumanis

A view of Bizet's *Carmen*

Soloists Jānis Sproģis, Inese Galante and Aivars Kranemanis

Guntis Gailītis has directed many opera performances

Norwegian soloist Sisele Kirkebu and Ingus Petersons at the *Sigulda* opera festival

Janis Norvelis

Evita Garanča

A view from Handel's *Alcina*

The parade of choruses started from the building of Riga Latvian Association towards *Ķeizardārzs* during the I General Song Festival of Latvia

Dressed up for the VII Song Festival of Latvia. Awards were granted for ethnographic costumes during the first period of independence

V General Song Festival of Latvia, 1990

Program of the I General Song Festival of Latvia in 1873

VI General Song Festival, 1926

Teodors Kalniņš (1890-1962), leading director

Leonīds Vīgners, leading director, composer

Haralds Mednis, leading director

Gunārs Ordelovskis (1927-1990), the leading director of the united orchestra

Song festival on the large arena in *Mežaparks*

Regional song festivals are popular, in which all the choruses from the region take part; only the best choruses are permitted to the general song festivals. Regional song festival of Latgale, *Ludza*

Chamber-chorus *Vecrīga* in the parade during the first Nordic song festival in Denmark

The tradition of song festival – collective singing of choruses was wide-spread in the countries around the Baltic Sea in the 19th c. – in Germany, Sweden, Finland, Denmark and elsewhere, however the tradition was soon lost as the society split due to political or religious contradictions. The survival of the festivals in the Baltic states is a historical phenomenon. The chorus movement was an important element of unity for the small Baltic nations, giving a chance to express their national belonging and keep their national identity amidst other, strange cultures by awakening the feeling of pride over national virtu in both the singer and the listener.

The movement of song festivals was started by concerts of the united men's choruses in *Dikļi* in 1864 followed by the first song festival of Kurzeme in 1870 in *Dobele*. The repertoire was chiefly composed of church songs. The collective singing of Latvians was organized by folk-teachers prepared by Cimze's seminar; the singing associations played a role in refining the tradition.

The I General Song Festival of Latvia took place in Riga, 1973. The festival was organized by Riga Latvian Association. The concerts of the I General Song Festival of Latvia took place in *Ķeizardārzs* and the Dome Cathedral. 45 choruses and the orchestra of *Irlava* teachers' seminar took part. There were *song wars* as well. There were church songs, Latvian folk songs by Cimze, Franz Schubert, F. Abta, original songs by Karlis Baumanis. Indriķis Zīle and Jānis Bētiņš were the leading directors. Already the first song festival in *Dikļi*, 1864 and the I General Song Festival in Riga, 1873, were a symbolic from symbolic form of the national unity. In all of the first five song festivals (1873-1910) folk songs were the holding core that withstood the dissolving forces, which showed out to be fatal to the tradition in other countries. The four song festivals during the period of independence (1926-1938) revealed the rapid developments of professional musical culture of the new state. In all of the festivals, directors and song authors was the greatest creative power of the state, the musical elite. Unfortunately, the tradition was subdued to the interests of the ruling ideology in the X Song Festival of 1938, when the slogans of the authoritarian regime were proclaimed.

The tradition of song festival was not broken by the soviet authorities, although the idea of the festival was ruthlessly manipulated with. The ten song festivals during the period of soviet occupation (1948-1985), which were now joined by dance festivals, were always accompanied with a certain portion of expressions of national self-assertion and protest, despite elements of the forced-on alien ideology.

The tradition of song festivals was preserved by the Diaspora of the Latvians in exile with an even greater care. It was a spiritual link with the homeland, a way of keeping faith in the resurrection of freedom. The first song festival abroad, took place as soon as 1946 still in the harsh environment of refugee camps and later continued all over the world where Latvians had settled. The song festival of 1990, was also the peak of the third *Atmoda* (awakening) movement, while the XXI and the XXII festivals (1993, 1998) were celebrated in an independent state.

A song festival parade

Song festival, 1998

Choristers dressed in folk-costumes

The parade of the XXII Song Festival in 1998 is passing the sun symbol, which was raised in honor of the song festival on the spot previously occupied by a statue of Lenin

Jurjān's Days in *Meņģeļi*

Dita Kalniņa during *Jurjān's* Days in *Meņģeļi*

Chorus *Dzintars*, a winner of many international awards, one of the best female choruses in the world

The legendary Latvian chorus directors are the leading directors in a song festival, brothers – Imants and Gido – the Kokari

Janis Dūmiņš, leading director

The *Iron Lady* of Latvian leading directors – Ausma Derkevica

Pauls Kvelde, leading director

Edgars Račevskis, leading director

Daumants Gailis, (1927–1991) leading director

Maris Sirmais, leading director

Eduards Gravitis, chorus director

Agita Ikauniece, chorus director

Janis Zirnis, chorus director

Anna Jansone, chorus director

Juris Kļaviņš, leading director

Janis Grigalis, chorus director

Raimonds Igolnieks, director of the united orchestra

Vilis Kokamegi, director of the united orchestra

Tereze Broka in action

A festival event in *Dziesmu svētku parks* (Song Festival Park) during the XX General Song Festival in 1990

Jānis Ivanovs (1906-1983),
most excellent composer – symphonist

Ādolfs Skulte (1909-2000),
an excellent composer and pedagogue

Pēteris Plakidis, composer

Maija Einfelde,
composer with an international approval

Pēteris Vasks, world-famous composer

Talivaldis Deksnis, organist

Tālivaldis Ķeniņš,
a Latvian composer
from the USA

Pauls Dambis, composer

CONCERT LIFE IN LATVIA

Concert life at the end of the century lost its seasonally. Festivals change one another frequently, guests come and go, contests are received with tense interest. Riga is rich in concert halls each with its own acoustics, a face, even its own audience. The most significant concert hall is the Great Guild, a building in English neo-Gothics style from 1859, built around the historic core of Münster's hall and bride's chamber from the 14th c. Here the National Symphonic Orchestra performs concerts mostly of symphonic music.

At its beginnings, in 1925, supported by Radio Latvia (and the director Arvids Parups), the orchestra was a quite puny band of 16 musicians. Later with professor Jānis Mediņš in the lead (1928 - 1944), it grew to 40 members still joining with the National Opera Orchestra on concerts craving more responsibility. During the after war period, lead by Leonīds Vīgners, Edgars Tons, Vasili Synaiski, Pauls Megi, and currently by Terye Mikelsen, the orchestra has become a strong collective with a high professional level. It has been confirmed by concerts with famous soloists and lead directors as well as by guest concerts in Germany, France, England, Switzerland, Spain, and elsewhere.

The National Opera Hall in Riga is reserved for special concert events, the likes of anniversaries. The finals of international musical competitions are held in Riga, large events of oratorios and cantatas, because the chorus *Latvija*, directed by Maris Sirmais, is famous in Europe for the uniquely wide repertoire as well as the refined sound of vocals. The Dome Cathedral with its large organ (124 registers, 6712 pipes) is a regular place for organ concerts and festivals. The large room with its peculiarly high level of reverberation requires a special choice of repertoire. It suits well the music of the old masters. Radio Latvia Chorus (directed by Sigvards Kļava and Kaspars Putniņš), sometimes called the chorus with the absolute pitch often perform in *Dome* with music by both the old and the contemporary composers. The voices of Riga Dome Boys' Chorus (directed by Jānis Erenštreits) may also be heard here. Thanks to their qualities, the chorus has attained approval not only in Europe, but also in America and Japan. Recently artists have grown fond of another place suited for music - an ancient building of Riga - St. John's Church. Concerts of chamber-music take place in Wagner's Hall, which has been renovated in the City Theater House built in the 18th c., where Richard Wagner once worked. Concerts also take place in the hall of *Ave Sol* and in Music Academy on regular basis.

Chorus *Latvija* has attained approval in all of Europe's largest musical centers by mastering oratorios

National Symphonic Orchestra of Latvia

A center of musical importance in Latvia is *Liepāja*, where philharmonic was founded as early as 1886 and was the oldest establishment for music in the Baltics. The School of Music and its orchestra (directed by Valdis Vikmanis) became the musical heart of the city after the World War II. The orchestra became an independent unit (directed by Imants Resnis) in 1987, took an active part in the music life of Latvia, and has been on tours in Spain, Sweden, Malaysia, and elsewhere.

Riga Dome Boy's Chorus

Maris Villerušs, cellist

Concert in Riga Dome

Bill Clinton was pleased
with the performance of Latvian jazzmen

Mariss Jansons, the director of the Symphonic Orchestra of Oslo

Violinist Rasma Lielmane and piano-player Ventis Zilberts

The world-famous violinist Gidons Krēmers has formed a chamber-orchestra CREMERata BALTICA in Riga

The pedagogical staff of Latvian Conservatory in the 1920's

ACHIEVEMENTS OF LATVIAN MUSICIANS IN THE WORLD

Ilze Urbane, flutist

Ilze Graubiņa, professor, piano-player and pedagogue, a descendant of the famous family of musicians, the Graubiņi

After the reclaim of independence, with a possibility of participation in the global music life, the high professional level of our musicians, of both soloists and collectives was truly discovered. Latvia is proud of achievements of her choruses, which almost always come back with Grand Prix from international competitions (*Ave Sol*, *Dzintars*, *Kamēr*, etc.). Latvian opera singers win competitions and sing on the most famous stages of the world (Inese Galante, Ingus Petersons, Inga Kalna, Edgars Siliņš, Krišjanis Norvelis, Elīna Garanča, and others). The Finnish director J. Kangass has let the Nordic audiences discover the consistence of music by Pēteris Vasks. The composer was given the award of Herdera in *Vienna*; the American magazine Review placed his music in its musical elite of author-discs; the 2nd symphony by Vasks is played in Alberthall, London; magazine *Bilboard* call it the best music, while the violin concert *Tālā gaisma* (*Distant Light*) in artist's record, dedicated to Gidons Krēmers, became a best-seller in disc format and the composer has been named as one of the best of his generation.

The director Neme Järvi presented to the world the 4th symphony by Imants Kalniņš in its original version, which had been altered by the soviet censorship. After its success in the USA, the symphony could be heard in Riga, in its original intent.

Maija Einfelde succeeded in winning in composition contest out of 299 contestants in the USA with a chorus cycle *Pie zemes tālās* (*In Distant Land*), an inspiration from *Saistītais Promtejs* (*The Bonded Prometheus*) by Eshils. It is presented to the world in a CD format by Radio chorus. Thanks to this victory, the *15th Psalm of David* re-mastered by M. Einfelde is now sang by four choruses in Europe and America. It is described as a radiant piece by world critics.

Latvian-grown musicians of great fame attained in international competitions are: Ilze Graubiņa, Rasma Lielmane, Uldis Sprudžs, Ilze Urbane, Juris Žvikovs, Juris Abols, and others. Valdis Zariņš has been the first violin in Latvia for more than thirty years, an excellent interpreter of violin-parts by both foreign and Latvian composers, also a prominent concert-master in the Symphonic Orchestra of Oslo. The soloist of French horn, Arvīds Klišans has had great success on many tours. Even vocalists have been awarded: the British Bruce-Miller's award was given to Inga Kalna, the Finish *Grand Prix* of Hellin was received by Elīna Garanča, Egils Siliņš has won in nine international contests.

Violinist Baiba Skride, the winner of the prestigious Paganini competition

Valdis Zariņš, professor, virtuoso of violin

Our organists: Aivars Kalejs, Jevgeņija Lisicina, Talivaldis Deksnis, Agnis Stepiņš, Larisa Bulava, and other have played on world-famous organs.

The achievements of our directors cannot be put in few, simple words. It is no strange coincidence that the Great Musical Award of Latvia, started in 1993, has been given to Leonids Vigners, Haralds Mednis, and Ausma Derkevica for lifetime contribution.

MUSICAL EDUCATION

Latvian sense of music and will of singing has been expressed by craving for musical education ever since the times of teachers seminars in the 19th c. Statistics show that every seventh Latvian sings in a chorus, a plays in an orchestra or a band. There are more than hundred musical schools, eight colleges, music is taught in the University of Pedagogics and in institutes, however the center of musical education in Latvia is the Musical Academy of Latvia.

More than 5500 students have graduated from the Musical Academy (Conservatory) since its foundation in 1919. About 450 students acquire knowledge in the sections of piano and organ, string, blow and beat instruments, composition, musicology, vocals, and musical pedagogics.

The Conservatory, founded and led (1919 - 1935; 1937-1944) by the Latvian musical classic, Jazeps Vitols, shaped the musical foundations of the new Latvian state. The graduates from class of Vitols were composers and the next generation of pedagogics: Pēteris Barisons, Jēkabs Graubiņš, Adolfs Skulte, Janis Ivanovs, Lucija Garuta, Valentins Utkins, and the composers taught by them – Volfgangs Dārziņš, Helmers Pavasars, Bruno Skulte, Marģeris Zariņš, and others.

The Musical Academy may be proud of the many new and middle generation composers brought up by it: Imants Kalniņš, Pauls Dambis, Pēteris Vasks, Pēteris Plakidis, and first of all, the present principal of the Academy, Juris Karlsons. The graduates of the Academy are directors of orchestras and choruses of the Republic, soloists of the National Opera, a diverse league of orchestra musicians (3 symphonic orchestras), members of different chamber-bands, and a large number of musical pedagogics.

Ever since the times of foundation, pedagogical work at the Academy was done hand in hand with concert activities. Concerts take place in the great hall, the organ hall, and chamber-halls of Musical Academy on regular basis. Students acquire practical skills in the symphonic orchestra and the study chorus. The Musical Academy may be proud of the respectable international contests, bearing the name of Jazeps Vitols.

The network of musical schools is of no less significance in finding and developing new talents. Achievements of the students in international competitions is a confirmation of their high professional level. Some of the most excellent of our musicians were educated in the Musical School of Emils Dārziņš: Valdis Zariņš, Ieva Graube, Ilze Urbane, and Baiba Skride. The years spent in the school are unforgettable to world celebrities like Gidons Krēmers, Mihails Maiskis, and others.

The musical schools and colleges of districts and towns of Latvia are centers of regional importance, the managers of cultural events.

Students of the Music Academy of Latvia in front of a wall-painting of the founders of musical life in Latvia

The traditional Festival of the Ancient Music in *Rundāle* Castle

Sanita Šablovska, piano-player

Juris Karlsons, the principal of the Musical Academy of Latvia

The professional groom of Latvian musicians – the Musical Academy of Latvia

A fulfillment of dreams of Raimonds Pauls, the popular Latvian composer and deputy of *Saeima*. A musical center *Vernisāža*, named after the composer, is now open in the heart of Riga. *Vernisāža* is a popular establishment for culture and entertainment with a bar, a theater, an art gallery, and a nightclub

Imants Kalniņš and among his people during *Imanta* Days in *Piebalga*. From left: actor Artūrs Skrastiņš, actress Rezija Liepiņa, *Saeima* deputy and composer Imants Kalniņš, singer Krists Kalniņš. Imanta Days draw thousands of people from all over Latvia

In 60's and 70's the Latvian stage was dominated by REO with Margarita Vilcāne and Ojārs Grīnbergs

Nora Bumbiere – an unbeatable vocalist of Latvian pop music

Mirdza Zīvere and Imants Vanzovičs from *MODO* led by Zigmars Liepiņš in the middle of 80's

Vocalist Viktors Lapčenoks has spent thirty years on Latvian stage

Olga Pīraga, the most popular jazz singer, an owner of a silky voice

Jumprava

The popular festival of *Liepājas Dzintars* has taken place for more than quarter of a century. Thousands of youths from all over Latvia go to *Liepāja*

Adrians Kukuvass and Raimonds Bartaševičs from *Menuets*, 25 years of music by Imants Kalniņš

Zigmars Liepiņš wrote his first rock opera *Lāčplēsis* in 1990, during the time of Awakening. The opera gained an enormous support, it was played more than 100 times

Zigmars Liepiņš, composer, president of radio *SWH*

Zigfrīds Muktupavels

Maija and Jānis, the Lūsēni. *Bildes'99*

Pits Andersons

Kaspars Dimiters. *Bildes'99*

Pērkons and the organizer of *Bildes'95*, Tija Auziņa

Juris Kulakovs, composer

Olga Rajecka

Arnis Mednis

Ainars Mielavs

The beginning of 60's may be regarded as the starting point of contemporary Latvian pop music, when a further development of German hits resulted in band formation with composers and players. Raimonds Pauls has been the leading authority since then. With the increase of western influence, youths' bands started to compete with the established hit music, starting by copying English and American music. *Revengers* is considered the first rock group in the USSR, started in Riga in 1962. Despite all kinds of soviet ideological obstacles, the first bands playing original music started to appear at the end of 1960's – *Katedrāle* and 2xBBM with Imants Kalniņš, which were followed by many others amongst them, the legendary *Menuets*, still rather active.

Liepājas Dzintars was the fist important music festival in the USSR and took place in *Liepāja* in the beginning of 70's. The performers of songs by Raimonds Pauls gained immense popularity: Margarita Vilcāne, Ojārs Grinbergs, Nora Bumbiere, Viktors Lapčenoks, and others. Many of the historically important Latvian bands – *Līvi*, *Sīpoli*, *Pērkons*, and others made their first acts during the decade. Although musicians still had to put up with persecutions by culture bureaucracy, the progress of music was unstoppable. The prohibition of the band *Pērkons* may be mentioned as a unique fact, its repertory did not comply with the soviet ideology because of the disorders caused by the youths' audience during the concerts. The band continued under the name of *Padomju Latvija* (Soviet Latvia), and the bureaucrats were unable to abolish a band with such a prestigious name. The band *Zodiaks* with Jānis Lusens playing in a style of electronic 80's disco sold their albums in over 20 million copies. *New Wave* pioneers, *Elpa* and *K. Remonts*, the underground bands of *Dzeltenie Pastnieki*, *Zig Zag*, electro-pop stars *Jumprava*, the classic rock n' roll band *Arhīvs*, soul and rhythm & blues unit *Odis* should be mentioned among others. *Eolika*, *Dālderi*, and *Credo* were very popular, as well as *Remix* and *Opus* with Zigmārs Liepiņš. The music and art festival *Bildes* takes place in Latvia every year since 1985, where the musicians pick up pencils and brushes and try their skills in fine arts along with their customary habit of playing, while artists, architects, actors, and journalists sometimes try to be musicians for a while. Almost all the distinguished Latvian musicians as well as many promising beginners have tried the stage of *Bildes* during these years.

Samples of almost all common styles of world music are represented by Latvian music in 90's, everything from *post punk* to *acid jazz*, the most distinct names being *Jauns Mēness*, *Prāta Vētra*, *Linga*, *Time After Time*, *100. Debija*, *Iļģi*, *Fact*, *Lādezers*, *Bet Bet*, as well as singers Igo, Agnese, Olga Rajecka, Laima Vaikule, and others. Most of these bands and soloists have played in many countries in the world, yet the most famous one abroad is still the patriarch of Latvian song, Raimonds Pauls (who ran for president of the state in 1999), his records have sold in more than 30 million copies.

Eolika

Lādezers

Gvido Linga

Liepājas brāļi

Composer Valts Pūce and *Marana*, all time best group vocals in Latvia

Remix

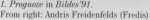

1. Prognoze in *Bildes'91*.
From right: Andris Freidenfelds (Fredis)

Kaspars Upacieris (Ufo). *Bildes '94*.

Ufo and Fredis is more than just music, it is a phenomenon and a happening. The two host a radio show *BB brokastis* every week day from 6 to 10 AM, which is amusing and listened to by almost everyone in Latvia. Its essence is witty dialogue

Līvi have played hard rock in *Liepāja* for more than quarter of a century. The most recorded band in Latvia

Time after time

FACT

100 debija

Agnese

Prāta Vētra is the most famous band at the end of the millennium

Every oppressed nation finds hope in music. Love, desire for freedom, and the Latvian spirit were delivered by the music of *Čikāgas piecīši* in an interpretation of hit and folk music. The records of music by *Čikāgas piecīši* were recorded from tape to tape and listened by Latvian families on every special occasion. One could be arrested for issuing this music. *Čikāgas piecīši* played on the large stage of *Mežaparks* in 1989, they had aged and their voices were husky, but at last they faced their audience in their homeland

Country band *Jūlijs* play traditional Latvian hit music rhythms and works by national composers on weddings, festivities, baptisms

Andris Kārkliņš or Andris de Letone is one of the most popular *flamenco* guitarists. Having spent most of his life in exile, he has now returned to his homeland

Imants Skuja, a great musician plays saxophone for official banquets, but most often – in front of the supermarket *Centrs*, in Vienna or Berlin during summers

The Latvian ballet troupe is directed by a former lead dancer from the ballet, Aivars Leimanis

Aivars Leimanis as Grenguar in *Notre Dame*

In 1918, a man called Voldemārs Komisārs, who had fought in the Latvian War of Independence and received the highest military honour, the Order of Lāčplēsis, began establishing Latvia's national ballet. Komisārs had a vision – that the Latvian ballet would be as outstanding as the *Bolshoi ballet* in Moscow. In 1935, the first Latvian national ballet, *Victory of Love*, was produced, and six months later it was performed before a delighted audience on the stage of the Stockholm Royal Opera. King Gustav VI of Sweden was among the audience, and he presented the choreographer and the lead dancer with the Swedish Royal Order of Vasa.

In 1955, after a troupe from Latvia performed at the Bolshoi in Soviet-era Moscow, the distinguished prima donna Maya Plisetska wrote: "I have encountered ballet at the highest world standard!" Latvian dancers received all of the leading soviet prizes and medals – the Order of Lenin, the Order of Stalin, etc.

The Western world knows the wonder of a number of ballet dancers who were born and raised in Riga – Māris Liepa, Alexander Godunov, Mikhail Baryshnikov and others. Riga is indeed the ballet metropolis of Northern Europe for the 20th century. The ballet stage in Riga has seen performances by such world famous geniuses of the ballet as Marius Petipa, Anna Pavlova, Mikhail Fokin, Olga Spesivtseva and Maya Plisetska. A national school of ballet was founded in 1932, and it trained numerous generations of dancers for the Latvian National Opera.

The Latvian ballet has performed in more than 30 other countries, and it has been viewed in such centres of the arts as Paris, Rome, Berlin, Stockholm, Helsinki and Salzburg.

Since 1993, the head of the troupe has been a former soloist from the Latvian National Opera ballet and a graduate of the famed Moscow *GITIS* state school of theatre, Aivars Leimanis. Currently the troupe has 70 professional dancers. The repertoire includes traditional favourites such as *Swan Lake*, *The Enchanted Princess*, *Giselle*, *Sylphide* and others, as well as Latvian ballets and such modern productions as *Tchaikovsky*, by the St. Petersburg choreographer Boris Eifmann, and *Romeo and Juliet* from Moscow's Vladimir Vasiliev.

A scene from Tchaikovsky's *Swan Lake* in the 1920s

Velta Vilciņa and Haralds Ritenbergs in *Spartacus*

Aleksandrs Lembergs and Ināra Gintere

Zita Errsa and Gennadij Gorbanov in *Romeo and Juliet*

Julija Gurvicha and Aleksei Avechkino in *Swan Lake*

Lita Beiris and Māris Liepa

Osvalds Lemanis

Helena Tangijeva-Birzniece

Aleksandr Godunov

Arvīds Ozoliņš and Anna Priede dancing the ballet *Bakchirskaya Fountain*

A fragment from "Scheherezade"

Mikhail Baryshnikov

A fragment from *Tchaikovsky*

A scene from the ballet *Yellow Tango*

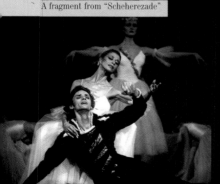

A fragment from *Giselle*

A fragment from *Copelia*

Inese Dumpe and Andrejs Rumjancevs in *Giselle*

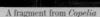

Inese Dumpe and Andrejs Rumjancevs in *Copelia*

Elza Leimane, recipient of numerous international ballet awards

er which demonstrates experimental and new dances which merge elements of folklore and ethnography with modern attempts to create new dances.

The Latvian folk dance is a lively form of cultural tradition. The collection and scientific study of dance-related folklore began in the late 19th century. In the 1920s, materials concerning the dancing traditions and the systematization of relevant choreography were published, and this launched the process of choreographing and publishing new dances.

Public interest in folk dancing in Latvia is durable, and this has become the most common form of amateur cultural activity. Dance groups become particularly active as song and dance festivals approach, but folk dance performances are a regular part at various public events, concerts, competitions and festivals in Latvia and abroad. The activities of folk dance groups help to preserve the creative spirit of participants, as well as the ongoing life of the tradition of folk dancing. Today there are some 825 dance groups with some 20,000 participants in Latvia. Dance traditions are very powerful in Latvia, and folk dances are truly original. It must be noted that Latvian dancing, of course, has been influenced by the dancing of other cultures, as well.

In 1937, the Latvian Home Guard organized a folk dance and gymnastics festival which was attended by 20 folk dance troupes with 720 dancers. The dance troupe from the Home Guard unit which served Latvian Railways won the competition at the event. In 1948, a major dance performance was staged as part of the 11th Song Festival, and this performance is now seen as the first national dance festival. These festivals are theatrical, and they have become a traditional way of demonstrating Latvian dances.

Many of the true leaders of Latvian folk dancing went into exile at the end of World War II, and Latvian folk dancing developed along separate paths in Latvia and in other countries – the United States, Great Britain, Canada and Australia in particular. Since 1934, books about ethnographic Latvian dances, adaptations of same and new dances have been published in Latvia and in exile. The most important of these books are *Latvian Folk Dances* by Johanna Rinka and Janis Osis, and *Latvian Games and Game Dances* by Harijs Suna.

Since 1977, the Latvian Academy of Music has had a Department of Choreography, where more than 100 choreographers, ensemble instructors and dance festival organizers have received their academic education.

There have been 11 dance festivals so far, and smaller events are held in Latvia's districts and regions. Festivals are held for dancers of various generations, including schoolchildren, and there are special events for trade school students or university students.

The national dance festivals involve some 10,000 dancers who join together in youth, adult and senior citizens' dance troupes. Usually there are two programs – one that features the various regions of Latvia, and anoth-

Imants Magone, choreographer and chief director of dance festivals

Uldis Steins, choreographer and chief director of dance festivals

Ingrida Saulite, choreographer and chief director of dance festivals

Kokle – latvian national musical instrument

Uldis Žagata, choreographer and chief director of dance festivals

Ādolfs Alunāns (1848-1912), father of Latvian theatre

Jēkabs Duburs as *Shylock* in William Shakespeare's *Merchant of Venice* (1897)

Lilija Ērika as *Spīdola* in Rainis' *Uguns un nakts* (1911)

Dace Akmentiņa as *Mirdza* in Aspazijas' *Vaidelote* (1894)

Eduards Smiļģis and Rainis (1920)

Lilija Štengele

Berta Rūmniece as *Mother Indrāne*, Aleksis Mierlauks as *Father Indrāns* in Rudolfs Blaumaņis' *Indrāni* (1920)

Mihails Čehovs as *Hamlet*, Lilija Ērika as *Ophelia* in William Shakespeare's *Hamlet* at the National theatre (1932)

Scene from William Shakespeare's *Othello* at the *Dailes* theatre (1937)

Eduards Smiļģis as *Faust*, Lilita Bērziņa as *Gretchen* in *Faust* (1940)

Velta Līne as *Nora*, Berta Rūmniece as *Anna* in Henrik Ibsen's *A Doll House*, production at the *Drāmas* theatre (1950)

The Chronicle of Indriķis testifies that the first theatre performance in Riga took place in 1205. This was organised by priests to further the spread of christianity. Based upon stories from the Bible the performance was held in the open in front of the church.

In the following centuries, the people of Riga became acquainted with the many forms of theatre popular in Western Europe: mystery plays, harvest plays and others. From the 17th century, Riga was visited by professional travelling comedy troupes from England, Holland, Germany and Italy. In the 1760s, the first permanent German theatre was performing in Riga. In 1772, the arts patron baron Von Fitinghof built the first brick theatre at *Vāgnera iela* 4. Performances were held four times a week and the repertoire included plays by Gotthold Lessing, Johan Wolfgang Von Goethe, Johann Christoph Friedrich von Schiller and Pierre-Augustine Beaumarchais. From 1837 to 1839, musical productions were organised by Richard Wagner. In 1863, a new theatre was built, which since 1919, has served as the Latvian National Opera.

German theatre has a large influence on the formation of a professional Latvian theatre. The performances and repertoire of German actors became the model for the first Latvian actors. Of significant importance is the folkloric heritage as the Latvian folk traditions contain many elements of theatre, especially in the mummeries and wedding games.

The first known Latvian organised theatre took place in the summer of 1818 in a barn at the *Dīkļu* manor. A 17 year old servant, Jānis Peitans, translated and produced Schiller's play *The Robbers* and he himself played the role of Karl More.

The official date for the birth of Latvian theatre is traditionally seen as 2 June 1868, when at the Riga Athletics Society hall (*Turnhalle*) the play *Žūpu Bērtulis* (*Bertulis the sot*) was performed. In turn, on 24 June 1869, as the foundation stone for the Riga Latvian Society was laid, the first Latvian original one-act play *Paša audzināts* (*Raised by himself*) by Ādolfs Alunāns was performed. Alunāns is seen as the father of Latvian theatre. He was the first professionally educated Latvian actor, director, dramatist and theatre critic. He managed the Riga Latvian theatre from 1870 to 1885. During his time Berta Rūmniece, who was the first performer of the Mother Indrāne role, commenced her acting career. In later years, the management of the theatre changed many times (Hermanis Rode-Ēbelings, Pēteris Ozoliņš), and a strong, new generation of actors was developed. Two stars particularly shone – Dace Akmentiņa and Jūlija Skaidrīte. From professional actors, Jēkabs Dubrs and Aleksis Mierlauks developed into excellent directors. The theatre developed in close interaction with play writing. On to the theatre boards appeared the heroes of the plays of Rūdolfs Blaumanis, Anna Brigadere and Aspazija.

At the beginning of the 20th century, several new theatres were established. The brothers Teodors Amtmanis and Alfrēds Amtmanis-Brieditis, who were of significant importance to the development of Latvian theatre, began their theatrical careers at the *Jaunais* (*Newest*) Latvian theatre. The new theatre's fate was intertwined with the social and political events of the age. In 1905, it became a meeting place of revolutionaries and so the authorities closed it down.

In 1908, the *Jaunais* (*New*) Riga theatre was opened. Performances at the theatre reached a then unheard of high quality in which all the components of theatre were blended: direction (Aleksis Mierlauks, Jēkabs Duburs, Teodors Amtmanis), scenography (Jānis Kuga, Arturs Cimermanis, Pēteris Kundziņš), acting and others. In the serious theatre repertoire, alongside master actors, new actors bloomed the talents of Lilija Ērika, Biruta Skujeniece, Mirdza Šmithene, Eduards Smiļģis and others. The first plays of Latvia's national poet Rainis received particularly strong acclaim from audiences *Zelta zirgs* (*The Golden Horse*), *Uguns un nakts* (*Fire and night*), *Indulis un Ārija*, *Pūt, vējiņi!* (*Blow, winds!*).

The Russian theatre opened in Riga in 1883. With the founding of the independent Latvian State, theatre received significant organisational and material State support.

On 30 November 1919, the Latvian National theatre was opened. It has always tried to maintain a repertoire of original Latvian plays. The directors of the National theatre (Aleksis Mierlauks, Alfrēds Amtmanis-Brieditis, Jānis Zariņš, Ernests Feldmanis and others) have always been defenders of the realism principle. The National theatre troupe has always formed brilliant personalities. At the beginning of the 1930s, escaping from the Soviet regime, to live permanently in Riga, came the world famous Russian actor, director and teacher Mihails Čehovs. Here he founded his own studio, produced plays and played leading roles both at the National theatre and the Riga Russian theatre.

On 19 November 1920 a second theatre opened in Riga – *Daile* theatre. Its founder, Eduards Smiļģis was an experimenter, a searcher of new ways in the art of direction. Closest to the signature of the Dailes theatre were the world's classics – romantic works by Johann Christoph Friedrich von Schiller and Viktor Hugo, the tragedies and comedies of William Shakespeare, the destiny plays of Rainis. Visually impressive performances were created in collaboration with scenograph Jānis Muncis, later Oto Skulme. The music for many performances was composed by Burhards Sosārs.

The destruction of the Latvian State in 1940, deportations, war, the German and the second Soviet occupations – all took their toll of Latvian theatre. Many excellent theatrical artists became refugees. They formed the nucleus of Latvian theatre-in-exile, preserved Latvian culture and protected the Latvian heritage abroad. After the war, Latvian theatre had to withstand never before experienced ideological pressures, which particularly affected theatre repertoires. In this situation, Latvian theatre many times took on the noble mission of protecting the ideal of personal freedom and of keeping hope alive. For many years, Latvian theatre was the only place where one could hear the Latvian language.

An important part of the repertoire of the *Drāma* theatre (as the National theatre was called during the Soviet period) was Alfrēds Amtmanis-Brieditis' productions of Latvian prose works (Andrejs Upītis – *Zaļā zeme*

Elza Radziņa and Karlis Sebris in *Mīļais melis* (*Loving liar*) at the *Drāma* theatre (1962)

Evalds Valters - 100 years old (1894-1994)

Scene from *Vecā jūrnieka ligzda* (*The Old Sailor's Nest*), production at the *Liepaja* theatre

Arnolds Liniņš (1930-1998)

Arlija Pelše as Golda, Jurijs Jurovskis as Tevje in Šalom Aleiham's *Tevje – pienvedējs* (*Tevje – the milkman*), production at the Russian Drama theatre (1958)

Harijs Liepiņš as *Hamlet* in William Shakespeare's *Hamlet* (1959)

Žanis Katlaps as Jazeps in Rainis's *Jāzeps un viņi brāļi* (*Joseph and his brothers*) (1956)

Lucija Baumane as Neze, Dina Kuple as Irma in Gunārs Priedes' *Centrifūga* (*Centrifuge*) at the *Jaunatne* theatre (1985)

Lidija Freimane as Berta, Janis Osis as Ceplis in the dramatisation of Pāvils Rozitis' book *Ceplis* at the *Drāma* theatre (1953)

Aleksandrs Bojarskis as Talbergs in Mihail Bulgakov's *Turbīnu dienas* (*Days of the Turbines*) at the Russian Drama theatre (1977)

Vija Artmane as Juliet, Eduards Pavuls as Romeo in William Shakespeare's *Romeo and Juliet* at the *Daile* theatre (1953)

Antra Liedskalniņa as Blanche in Tennessee William's *A Streetcar Named Desire* at the *Drāma* theatre (1969)

Vera Singajevska as Karlson in Astrid Lindgren's *Brālītis un Karlsons, kas dzīvo uz jumta* (*Brother and Karlson who lives on the roof*) at the *Jaunatne* theatre (1968)

Janis Kubilis as Louis XIV, Alfreds Jaunušans as Moliere in Mihail Bulgakov's *Moliere* at the *Drāma* theatre (1978)

Uldis Pucitis as Cilvēks in *Mistērija par cilvēku* (*Mysteries about humans*) at the *Jaunatne* theatre (1974)

Alfreds Amtmanis-Briedītis at rehearsal

Vija Artmane as Elizabeth, Arturs Dimiters as Cecil in Ferdinand Brukner's *Elizabeth – Queen of England* at the *Daile* theatre (1980)

Nikolajs Murnieks on his 70th birthday together with his wife Irmgarde Mitrēvice (1974)

Alfreds Amtmanis-Briedītis as Čugunovs and Anta Klints as Kuparina in Alexander Ostrovsky's *Vilki un avis* (*Wolves and sheep*) at the *Drāma* theatre (1945)

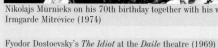

Fyodor Dostoevsky's *The Idiot* at the *Daile* theatre (1969)

Uldis Dumpis as Lilioms in Ferenc Molnar's *Liliom* at the *Drāma* theatre (1974)

Lasma Kugrēna as Alē, Lidija Freimane as Elionora in James Goldman's *The Lion in Winter* at the *Drāma* theatre (1980)

Scenography by Andra Freiberga for the *Valmiera* theatre production (1997) of Anton Chekhov's *Ivanovs*

Pēteris Lūcis (1907–1991)

William Shakespeare's *Midsummer Night's Dream* at the *Daile* theatre (1978)

Adolfs Alunans' *Seši mazi bundzenieki* (*The Six Little Drummers*) at the *Valmiera* theatre (1955)

Jānis Samauskis as Podkoļosins, Edmunds Freibergs as Kočkarjovs, Velta Straume as Agfja in Nikolay Gogol's *Marriage* at the *Valmiera* theatre (1970)

(*The Green land*), Pāvils Rozītis – *Ceplis* and others). A phenomena is the Rudolfs Blaumanis' play *Skroderdienas Silmačos* (*Days of the tailor at Silmačī*) which for tens of years lives on in the repertoire of the theatre, playing to packed houses every time. In the post-war period alongside such master actors as Berta Rūmniece, Anta Klints, Lilija Erika, Emma Ezeriņa, Jānis Osis and Žanis Katlaps, many talented new actors emerged – Alfreds Videnieks, Alfreds Jaunušans, Kārlis Sebris, Lidija Freimane, Velta Line, Elza Radziņa, Jānis Kubilis. In the 1960s – Antra Liedskalniņa, Uldis Dumpis, Ģirts Jakovļevs, Astrida Kairiša, and others.

In the middle of the 1950s Jaunušans debuted as a director, from 1966 to 1987 he worked as theatre's artistic manager (Tennessee William's *A Streetcar Named Desire*, Ferenc Molnar's *Liliom*, Alfred de Misset *Lorenzaccio* and others). In 1987, Mihails Kublinskis took over as the theatre's artistic manager. His main successes were in discovering the right plays for brilliant acting personalities – Juhan Smul's *Mežoņīgais kapteinis Kihnu Jens* (*The wild captain Kihnu Jens*), Jaroslavs Ivashkevich' *Vasara Noānā* (*Summer in Noāna*), Laslo Gurko's *Elektra – mana mīla* (*Elektra – my beloved*), James Goldman's *The Lion in Winter*, Henrik Ibsen's *Hedda Gabler* and others. From 1989, the theatre was managed by Oļģerts Kroders, but since 1995, the theatre's artistic manager has been Edmunds Freibergs. He has produced many works, which in their time were important and significant in the history of the theatre (*Skroderdienas Silmačos*, *Zaļā zeme*, *Zvejnieka dēls* (*Son of a fisherman*), *Rīga*). A number of talented actors have joined the theatre – Ivars Puga, Ilze Rudolfa, Zane Jančevska,

Daiga Gaismiņa, Indra Roga, Uldis Anže, Ivars Stoniņs.

In the post-war years, Eduards Smilģis compensated for the repertoire forced upon the Dailes theatre with theatrical ideas. His best classical productions (Rainis' *Uguns un nakts*, *Spēlēju*, *dancoju* (I played, I danced), Shakespeare's *Romeo and Juliet*, *Hamlet*, Schiller's *Mary Stuart*, Tolstoy's *War and Peace* and others) are characterised by a monumentalism, a clear interpretation and a romantic uplift. These were produced in close co-operation with scenographs Ģirts Vilks, Oskars Muižnieks, composers Maģers Zariņš, Imants Kalniņš, and movement consultant Erika Ferda.

Graduates of the *Dailes* theatre's Studio II who made a name for themselves included Vija Artmane, Rasma Roga, Harijs Liepiņš, Eduards Pavuls, Valentīns Skulme and others.

Pēteris Pētersons worked in the *Dailes* theatre from 1953 as a director, but from 1964 to 1971 as chief director. His production of *The Good person of Szechwan* (1958) was the first interpretation of Bertold Brecht in the Soviet Union. Peteris Petersons' best productions at the *Dailes* theatre were *Lai top!* (*Let it happen!*) (dedicated to the 100th anniversary of Latvian theatre), Dostoevsky's *The Idiot*, and with the poet Imants Ziedonis *Motocikls* (*Motorcycle*), which began a special poetical form of theatre which was further developed by the *Jaunatnes* theatre. Main actors at the theatre included Dina Kuple, Ausma Kantane, Ilze Vazdika, Olga Dreģe, Uldis Pucītis, Juris Strenga, later – Lilita Ozoliņa, Marina Janaus, Peteris Liepiņš, and others.

In 1971, the management of theatre was taken over by Arnolds Liniņš, in whose time the troupe

Indra Briķe as Larisa, Viktors Čestnovs as Karandiševs in Alexander Ostrovsky's *Līgava bez pūra* (*Bride without a dowry*) at the *Liepājas* theatre (1982)

Mara Ķimele and Juris Bartkevičs

Talivaldis Lasmanis as Vronskis in Leo Tolstoy's *Anna Karenina* at the *Valmieras* theatre (1996)

Zigfrīds Muktupāvels as Dzejnieks, Ligita Jevglevska as Ubadze in Māra Zālīte's *Kaupēn, mans mīļais* at the *Liepājas* theatre (1999)

Bertold Brecht's *Fear and Misery in the Third Reich* at the *Jaunatne* theatre (1985)

Edgars Liepiņš as Tils Pūcesspieģelis in Charles de Costera *Leģenda par Pūcesspieģeli* (*The Legend of Uilenspiegel*) at the *Jaunatne* theatre (1966)

was increased by 3 classes of Studio graduates (Akvelīna Līvmane, Mirdza Martinsone, Esmeralda Ermale, Andris Bērziņš, Harijs Spanovskis, and others). He has earned a permanent place in the history of Latvian theatre with his large productions – Henrik Ibsen's *Brand*, Ferdinand Bruckner's *Elizabeth – Queen of England*, and Rainis' *Jāzeps un viņa brāļi*.

In 1987 Liniņš handed over the management reins of the *Daile* theatre to his successor Kārlis Auškāps who had worked as director since the end of the 1970s, producing William Shakespeare's *Midsummer Night's Dream*, Hermann Hesse's *Steppenwolf*, Alehandro Kasonas' *Rītausmas dāma* (*The lady of the dawn*), and Christopher Hemptona's *Dangerous Liaisons*. Auškāps has been the director of splendid musical theatre productions – Arthur Conan Doyle's *Sherlock Holmes*, and Adolfs Alunāns' *Džons Neilands*. Additions to the *Daile* theatre ensemble in recent years are Indra Briķe, Juris Žagars, Ģirts Ķesteris, Rēzija Kalniņa, Agnese Zeltiņa, Valdis Liepiņš, Artūrs Skrastiņš, and others.

The *Jaunatne* theatre was established in 1941. Important phases in the history of the theatre were the times of directors Pavels Homskis (1951-1959) and Adolfs Šapiro (1964-1992). In the productions by Homskis (Šarls de Kostera's *Leģenda par Pūcesspieģeli*, Truman Capote's *Distance bez finisa* (*Distance without an end*) the important roles were played by Elvīra Baldiņa, Lūcija Baumane, Tālivaldis Aboliņš, Edgars Liepiņš, and Vera Singajevska. Productions by Šapiro include: Maxim Gorky's *Pēdējie* (*The Last*), Anton Chekhov's *Ivanovs*, Henrik Ibsen's *Peer Gynt*, Gunārs Priedes' *Centrifūga*, Bertold Brecht's *Fear and Misery in the Third Reich*, and others for the Latvian troupe; Heinrich von Kleist's *The Prince of Homburg* and A. Vasiļjevs' *Rīt bija karš* (*Tomorrow there was a War*) for the Russian troupe.

Of significance were also the productions of director Nikolajs Šeiko – Carlo Gozzi's *The Green Bird*, Astrid Lindgren's *Brālītis un Karlsons, kas dzīvo uz jumta*, and others. In Pēteris Petersons's productions can seen the search for striking forms – Aleksandrs Čaks' *Spēlē, spēlmani!* (*Play, player!*), A. Majakovskis' *Mistērija par cilvēku*, and others. In the 1960s, actors Anda Zaice, Imants Skrastiņš and other joined the Latvian troupe of the *Jaunatnes* theatre. In the middle of the 1970s – Ilga Tomase, Rūdolfs Plepis, Arija Sturniece and others. While in the middle of the 1980s – Juris Žagars, Maija Apine and others.

Ever increasing organisational and creative problems led to the closing of the *Jaunatnes* theatre in 1992.

Latvian theatre is developing not only in Rīga, but also in *Liepāja*, *Valmiera*, *Jelgava*, *Daugavpils* and elsewhere. In the post-war history of the *Liepāja* theatre, two periods have been particularly productive. During the period of artistic management by Nikolajs Murnieks (1953-1968) the following plays were staged: Vilis Lācis' *Vecā jūrnieka ligzda*, Rainis' *Uguns un nakts, Indulis un Ārija*, and Mihail Sholohovs' *Plēsums* (*Virgin Soil*). From 1974 to 1989, Oļģerts Kroders worked as the chief director and established a serious repertoire – Fyodor Dostoevsky's *Crime and Punishment*, Alexander Ostrovsky's *Līgava bez pūra*, William Shakespeare's *Hamlet*, Jānis Jaunsudrabiņš's *Aija*, and Anton Chekhov's *The Seagull*. The core of the troupe is made up of actors – Vera Šneidere, Indra Briķe, Anda Albuže, Mārtiņš Vilsons, Juris Bartkevičs, Jānis Makovskis and others.

Pēteris Petersons (1923-1998), playwright, director at the *Dailes* theatre

Director at the *Dailes* theatre, Kārlis Auškāps, as Francis Bacon in Ferdinand Bruckner's *Elizabeth – Queen of England*

The *Daile* theatre

Directors Oļģerts Kroders and Edmunds Freibergs

Latvian National theatre

The Eduards Smiļģis theatre museum

Eduards Smiļģis' study

The manager of the Eduards Smiļģis theatre museum, Rita Rotkale

Latvian theatre worker, Zigfrīds Kalniņš (1930-1998)

The *Liepāja* theatre

The *Valmiera* theatre

Latvians have always loved to produce plays, popular are both folk theatres and drama groups. The *Alūksne* district *Jaunanna* theatre (current players pictured above) has been playing for some 150 years.

Richard Harris' *Meitenes, mūsu uznāciens* (*Girls, We're On*) at the *Daile* theatre (1999), costumes by Večella Varslavane

Lilita Ozoliņa as Alice, Josifs Rafalsons as Edgars in August Strindberg's *The Dance of Death* at the Russian Drama theatre (1996)

The progress of the *Valmieras* theatre was, for many years, guided by its chief director Pēteris Lucis (1957-1991). Very popular were productions of Latvian classics, which could be performed in the open-air – Vilis Lācis' *Zvejnieka dēls*, Augusts Deglavs' *Rīga*, Pāvils Rozītis' *Valmieras puikas* (*The Boys of Valmiera*), Voldemārs Sauleskalns' *Meldermeitiņa* (*The Miller's Daughter*), Jēkabs Janševskis' *Dzimtene* (*Fatherland*), and Ādolfs Alunāns' *Seši mazie bundzenieki*. Together with Lucis have worked three, very different, directors: Oļģerts Kroders (William Shakespeare's *Hamlet*, A. Tolstoy's *Sāpju ceļi* (*Painful Roads*), Rūdolfs Blaumanis' *Pazudušais dēls* (*Prodigal Son*)); Māra Ķimele (Nikolay Gogol's *Marriage*, Jean Anouilh's *Medea*, Anton Chekhov's *Uncle Vanya*, Dale Wasserman's *One Flew over the Cuckoo's Nest*, Rainis' *Pūt, vējiņi!*); and Valentīns Maculevičs (Rainis' *Spēlēju, dancoju*; *Daugava*, William Shakespeare's *Romeo and Juliet*, and Vladimir Mayakovsky *Pirts* (*The Bath-house*). Up to this day the *Valmiera* theatre excels in its actors – Nina Leimane, Roberts Zebergs, Jānis Samauskis, Ināra Ieviņa, Jānis Zariņš, Rihards Rudāks, Skaidrīte Putniņa, Ligita Devica, Dace Eversa, Aigars Vilims and others. In recent years excellent productions have produced by director Felikss Deičs (Leo Tolstoy's *Anna Karenina*, Anton Chekhov's *Ivanovs*, Rūdolfs Blaumanis' *Trīnes grēki* (*The Sins of Trine*), and others).

The artistic level of the Russian Drama theatre was fundamentally raised post-war by the presence of excellent actors (Jurijs Jurovskis, Jekaterina Bunčuka, Nikolajs Barabanovs and others). The real flowering of the theatre is associated with the name of director Arkādijs Kacs' time there (1963-1988). Productions which became events in the life of Latvian theatre included Dale Wasserman's and Joe Darion's *Man of La Mancha*, Maxim Gorky's *On the Bottom*, Alexander Vampilovs' *Duck Hunting*, William Shakespeare's *King Lear*, and Nikolay Gogol's *The Revisor*.

In the life of Latvian theatre have been many important changes over the last ten year period (when this book went to print). New theatres have emerged – the *Jaunais* (*New*) Riga theatre, the *Daugavpils* theatre, the studio theatre – *Skatuve* (*Stage*), the theatrical studio *Mūris* (*Wall*) in *Liepāja*, and others. More frequently than before guest directors and actors are invited to Latvia, theatrical troupes travel for guest performances and have taken part in international festivals. A new generation of talented and promising generation of directors has arisen. The *Jaunais* Riga theatre is led by Alvis Hermanis (*Kā lēna un mierīga upe ir atgriešanās* (*As a Slow and Peaceful River is Returning*), *Marquis de Sade*, *The Seagull*, *Mans nabaga Marats* (*My poor Marat*), *Piķa dāma* (*Queen of Spades*), *Arcadia*, and others). In various styles these directors have also made their marks: Regnārs Vaivars (*Solome*) at the *Jaunais* Riga theatre and *Vecākais dēls* (*Eldest Son*) at the National theatre), Dž. Dž. Džilindžers (*Fernando Krapa vēstules Jūlijai* (*Fernando Krapps letters to Julia*) and together with Kārlis Auškaps *Šveiks* (*Schweik*) at the *Dailes* theatre).

Juris Žagars as Valmont, Indra Briķe as Madame de Tourvelae in Christopher Hampton's *Dangerous Liaisons* at the *Daile* theatre (1996)

Scenography by Gunārs Zemgals for Augusts Deglavs' *Rīga* production at the National theatre (1998)

Programme for the production of Guy de Maupassant's *Bel-Ami* at the *Dailes* theatre (1999)

Kaspars Znotiņš as *Prince Miškins* in Fyodor Dostoevsky's *The Idiot* at the Jaunais Riga theatre (1999)

Director Alvis Hermanis

Ivars Stoniņš as Hamlet, Ivars Puga as King Claudius in William Shakespeare's *Hamlet* at the National Theatre (1997)

Ģirts Ķesteris, Rēzija Liepiņa and Artūrs Skrastiņš in a rock opera version – *Fausts – Deus ex Machina* – of Johan Wolfgang von Goethe's *Faust*

Christopher de Bach
(1768-1824)

Gunars Katkevičs

Ben Said

Albert Salamonski
(1839-1913)

The balancing act known
as the Rolands

In Soviet times, circuses were ordered to create the image of national circuses. In this
photo, you see a performance of the Latvian
epic *Lāčplēsis* at the Riga Circus, with
Lāčplēsis (Boriss Lazarovs) and Laimdota
(Tatjana Lazarova) in performance

Andrejs Cinovskis, member
of the balancing act
known as Brettini

RĪGAS CIRKS

Taisija
Korņiloca,
Aleksejs Dementjevs and
Andrejs Dementjevs with one of their elephants

Mudite Kraukle and a
partner

The father of the European circus, Christopher de
Bach (1768-1824), was born in Kurzeme, it is
thought perhaps a Latvian. At the age of 10 he ran
away from home and joined a travelling circus as
a horseback rider. In 1808, in Vienna, he built an
enormous circus building with 3,000 seats and a
glass cupola over the ring.

Precise information as to when the first circus
performance took place in Latvia is not known,
although an advertisement for a guest performance in 1893, as well as a poster promoting a
circus performance in 1824, have survived to
this day.

The first wooden circus building in Riga was
opposite the *Vērmanes* Garden in 1864,
and a summer circus building was build
on the same site in 1873. It belonged to
a Prussian citizen called Albert Salamonski (1839-1913), who was a member of a very prominent German circus
dynasty and specialised in the training
of horses. The present-day home of the Riga
Circus, which is located between *Garlība Merķeļa
iela* and *Alfrēda Kalniņa iela*, was designed for
Salamonski by the Latvian architect Janis
Baumanis. For the main hall of the circus, as well
as the cupola that rises above it, he initially used
railroad tracks. The first performance in the building was held on Christmas in 1888, and without
any major reconstruction the building has survived
to this day. During the more than 100 years of the
building's life, various aerial tricks have been performed, and there have been other reasons to affix
heavy equipment to the roof cupola. Baumanis'
construction has safely passed the test of time.

Performers from all around the world came to
demonstrate their skills at Salamonski's circus.
The world's first *red-haired* clown, Tom Belling,
performed here, as did the popular Fratellini
Brothers, Anatole and Vladimir Durov, the Tante
Brothers, and others. In 1889, several championships and demonstrations organised by the circus were held in the building, and various residents of Riga took part. Over the course of time,
Riga residents Dmitri Martinov (who was actually
surnamed Žagars), Kristaps Veilands-Šulcs, Janis
Leskinovičs, Klements Buls, Karlis Mikulis, Fricis
Blumbergs and Emīls Griķis all competed internationally in the sport of wrestling.

The residents of Riga received their first taste of
the cinema at Salamonski's circus in November
1895, when *moving pictures* were demonstrated
by the physicist P.V. Dering. The first cinema
showing held indoors was organised in the building
on 29 October 1896.

One of the first internationally known Latvian circus
artists was the juggler Trofim Meier (who performed under the name of Miforts Reims). He debuted in the ring at the Salamonski circus in 1898.
The Latvian circus arts have produced a number of
highly talented performers and very original performances. The balancing act known as the Brettinis
(Alise and Andrejs Cinovksis) toured the world, as
did the roller skater and animal trainer Kārlis Petersons, the juggler Mocardo (Voldemars Šabans),
the acrobats known as the Devers Brothers
(Teodors and Ludvigs Polrube), the clown Koko
(Alfons Lucs), another clown Koko (Nikolajs Poļakovs, who received the Order of the British empire),
and the *white* clown Rolands (Kazimirs Plučs).

A permanent circus collective was established in
Riga in 1955, and its stars were the clowns Anto-
nio (Antons Markuns) and Aleksis Šliškevičs,
Andris Polkmanis and Aleksandrs Slaugotnis, the
manipulators Staņislavs Strods and his son Leo-
nards, aerial performer and dog trainer Aldona
Berķe, juggler Alfons Virkauss, aerial performer
Alīna Viļļa, acrobat Mudite Kraukle, pigeon trainer
Aija Balode, tiger trainer Stepans Deņisovs, aerial
performer Gunars Katkevičs, and elephant trainer
Anatolijs Korņilovs. In the last decade, Latvia's cir-
cus arts have been represented in the world by
Taisija Korņiloca and Aleksejs and Andrejs De-
mentjevs with their elephant act, the clown quartet
Grog (headed by Valerijs Aleksandrovs), cat trainer
Anna Armande, the Boriss Lazarovs riding group,
juggler Kristaps Lipinskis and the Sergei Ivanov
acrobatic trio.

The director of the Latvian Circus is Gunars
Katkevičs.

Circus artist Alfons Virkauss
and daughter Gunta

Clown Aleksandrs Slaugotnis

The Grog group of clowns, from left – Arkadijs
Prudņikovs, Valerijs Aleksandrovs, Arkadijs Oboļevičs
and Marina Aleksandrova

Natalija and Leonards Strods

Lāčplēsis (1930), director Aleksandrs Rusteiķis, camera – Jānis Sīlis

Pēteris Lūcis as Oskars in the screenplay of the novel by Vilis Lācis *Zvejnieka dēls* (*Fisherman's Son*) by Vilis Jānis Lapenieks (1939) – the first professional Latvian feature movie

Budijs Ebsens, American TV and theatre actor of a Latvian origin. His first success was the musicle *Whoopes* in New York. Taking over Broadway in the musicle *Flying Colors* (1933). Together with his sister Vilma starred in the movie *A Broadway Melody*. Have worked with the Norwegian figure skater Sonya Heny, Janet MacDonald and Judy Garland. For the role in the TV serial *Beverly Hillbillies* has been awarded international prizes of TV and theatre

Alda Rutania, ex. Ruta Skrastiņa, an outstanding actress of Latvian origin, participated in the Five-fold Oscar winner *The Deer Hunter (1979)*, and was nominated herself

The first demonstration of moving pictures in Riga took place in 1896. The first documental filming in Riga took place in 1910 when the cameraman Aleksandrs Stanke shooted the opening of monument to Tsar Peter I in Riga. Feature films have been made in Riga since 1913. There was an extensive network of cinemas in the beginning of the XX century in Riga. The first film production company *Latvfilm* was established in 1920. Vilis Segliņš made a movie *Es, karā aiziedams* (*When I Went to War*), Pjotrs Čardiņins made *Laika viesuļi* (*In the Whirlwind of Time*) , *Vilkiem mests laupījums* (*A Loot Left to Wolves*), *Psihe* (*Psyche*) , starring many prominent Latvian actors. The screenplay based on the novel of Vilis Lācis *Zvejnieka dēls* (*Fisherman's Son*), directed by Vilis Jānis Lapenieks featuring Pēteris Lūcis, was of a permanent value.
In the 20 's newsreels were made and always demonstrated before any movie. Several organizations ordered a number of documental films in the 20's and 30's. M. Lapiņš was extremely active to immortalize events of Latvian culture. Latvian first full length sound film *Daugava* was made in 1933. Since 1935 the sound tracks were done with the technology produced by *VEF* factory. *Mūsu pelēkais dārgakmens* (*Our Gray Jevel*) was the first full length popular science film, made by director Voldemars Pūce on the scenario of Jānis Greste.
In the afterwar years feature movies were made

Vilis Jānis Lapenieks (1908-1983), the first Latvian film director and script writer of the movie in 1937 *Tevzemei un brivibai* (*For Fatherland and Liberty*). In 1939 he made the screenplay *Zvejnieka dēls* (*Fisherman's Son*). After emigration he made documental films in Hollywood *Mēs, latvieši, brīvajā pasaulē* (*We, Latvians of the Free World*) (1972), *Tauta tuvumā,*

tauta tālumā (*Near Nation, Far Nation*) (1974), *Kā es māku, tā es maunu* (*I sing as I can*) (1975)

Vilis Lapenieks junior (1931-1989), cameraman. At the age of seven performed Janitis in *Zvejnieka dēls* (*Fisherman's Son*). He studied in Los Angeles and was the leading cameraman in David Wolper enterprise for five years in America. Worked for the Oscar winner movie *Hellstrom's Chronicle*. Later worked in *Universal International, Paramount, Fox* and other studios. He has made documental films about J.F. Kennedy and Lindon Johnson and feature movies about the plane *U-2* and the assasination of J.F.K. After this successful work he was elected as the director of cinematography in the American Association of Cinematography.

in collaboration with Russian colleagues. Director Alexander Ivanov and cameraman Eduards Tise made *Mājup ar uzvaru* (*Back Home with Victory*), Julius Raisman made *Rainis* in 1949. In 1955 Pavels Armands and Leonids Leimanis made *Salna pavasarī* (*Late Frost*). It was the beginning of regular feature films in Latvia. Film director Varis Krumiņš and cameraman Maris Rudzitis made a satyric screenplay based on the work of Andrejs Upits *Cēloņi un sekas* (*Causes and Consequences*) in 1956. The novel of Vilis Lācis *Zvejnieka dēls* (*Fisherman's Son*)

was repeatedly filmed in 1957. The first movie for children was Rita (1957) by Ada Neretniece. The 60's of Riga film studio came with a variety of genres and themes and also with a strict soviet censorship. Leonids Leimanis made his interpretations of the Latvian classic literature authors Rudolfs Blaumanis and Andrejs Upits in the movies *Purva bridējs* (*Wading the Bog*) in 1966 and *Pie bagātas kundzes* (*By the Rich Lady*) in 1969. Aloizs Brenčs is the director of first action film *Kad lietus un vēji sitas logā* (*Rain and Wind Beating at the Window*). The debut of Eriks Lācis and Jānis Streičs in the genre of children films *Kapteiņa Enriko pulkstenis* (*Captain's Enricco Watch*) in 1967.
A some films made in the 70's were never shown on the screen because of censor restrictions. Among the notable works of this period one may make a note of *Abols upē* (*Apple in the River*) by Aivars Freimanis (1974), *Motociklu*

Juris Podnieks (1950-1992), film director and cameraman holding the highest award in Latvian cinematography *Lielais Kristaps*

The legendary cameraman Laimons Gaigals (1922-1990) meeting the great-grandson of Krišjānis Barons

Anšlavs Eglitis (1906-1993), a critic from Hollywood, writer and artist. He has published many books and is known to the English reading public for always being in the Oscar award ceremonies. A member of the *Hollywood Press Corps*. His impressions on cinematography are presented in the book *Lielais mēmais* (The Great Mute), 1972

vasara (*Motorcycle Summer*) by Uldis Brauns (1975), *Ezera sonāte* (*Sonet of the Lake*) by Gunars Cilinskis and Varis Brasla (1976), *Mans draugs, nenopietns cilvēks* (*My friend, a Simple Man*) by Janis Streičs (1975), *Klāvs, Mārtiņa dēls* (*Klāvs, the Martin's Son*) by Oļģerts Dunkers (1970), *Liekam būt* (*To be Unwanted*) by Aloizs Brenčs (1976), *Nāves ēnā* (*In the Shadow of Death*) by Gunars Piesis (1971), *Pūt, vējiņi* (*Blow, Breeze*) (1973), *Ceplis* (*Kiln*) by Rolands Kalniņš (1972) and *Puika* (*Boy*) by Aivars Freimanis (1977) based on the story *Baltā grāmata* (*White Book*) by Janis Jaunsudrabiņš. Aleksandrs Leimanis made the two most popular costume movies *Vella kalpi* (*Valets of the Devil*) and *Vella kalpi Vella dzirnavās* (*Valets of the Devil in Devilmill*) in 1970 and 1972 respectively.
The 80's of Latvian cinema are characterized by new methods of expression and manifold themes. *Tarāns* (*Ram*), 1982 and *Bailes* (*Fear*), 1986 by Gunārs Cilinskis, *Limuzins Jāņu nakts krasā* (*Limousine of Midsummer Night Colour*), 1981, *Svešās kaislibas* (*Alien*

Film director Rolands Kalniņš

Film director Aivars Freimanis

Alberts Jekste (1908 – 1987), designer and producer of filming technologies in Latvia. He founded *Atlantic Film Electronics Ltd.*, 1930–1988 and participated in all *EXPO* exhibions in exile in Canada

Film director Jānis Streičs

Director Boļeslavs Ružs, cameraman Miks Zvirbulis, director Leonids Leimanis in the 60's

Sergejs Eizenšteins (1898–1948), outstanding film director, born un Riga, studied in St.Petersburg, acted in the 1st Workers Theatre in Moscow. World famous for *Battleship Potjomkin* (1925), *Alexander Newsky* (1938) and *Joann the Terrible* (1944 – 1946). Worked with the cameraman Eduards Tise (Ķisis), born in Liepaja

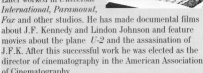

Mihails Šneiderovs (1915–1985), film director and cameraman

Second from left: Mihails Poseļskis, film director and cameraman with Aina Adermane, editor and author of the newsreel *Māksla* (the Art)

Passion), 1983, *Aizaugušā grāvi viegli krist* (*It's Easy to Fall in an Overgrown Ditch*), 1987 by Jānis Streičs, *Īsa pamācība mīlēšanā* (*Brief Instruction in Loving*), 1982 by Imants Krenbergs, *Šāviens mežā* (*Shot in the Forest*), 1983 by Rihards Pīks, *Vilkatis Toms* (*Werewolf Tom*), 1983 and *Fronte tēva pagalmā* (*Battle-front in Fathers Yard*) 1984 by Eriks Lacis, *Spriditis* (*TomThumb*),1985 by Gunārs Piesis are the well known works of this time. Aloizs Brenčs and the cameraman Jānis Mūrnieks made an extremely popular TV movie *Ilgais ceļš kāpās* (*The Long Way in Dunes*) in 1981.

Lomi (*The Catch*) (1969), by director Aivars Freimanis and Ivars Seleckis, camera

Actor Valdemārs Zandbergs in the 80's

Baltie zvani (*White Bells*), 1963, director Ivars Krauklītis, Uldis Brauns, camera

Harijs Liepiņš as Richard in *Es visu atceros, Ričard* (*I remember it all, Richard*). 1966, director Rolands Kalniņš, Miks Zvīrbulis, camera

Divi (*The Two*), 1965, directed by Mihails Bogins, cameraman Rihards Pīks won the award of Moscow Film Festival

Līga Liepiņa and Eduards Pāvuls starring *Pie bagātās kundzes* (*By the Rich Lady*) (1969), dir. Leonīds Leimanis, Mārtiņš Kleins cam.

Alfrēds Videnieks as Vecais Dalda, Ģirts Jakovļevs as Jānis Dalda in *Nāves ēnā*, (the Shadow of Death), dir. Gunārs Piesis

Lilita Ozoliņa as Asja in *Stari stiklā* (*Rays in the Glass*), director Imants Krenbergs, cameraman Māris Rudzītis

Zigrīda Stungure as Madara, Žanis Kopštāls as Migla in *Salna pavasarī* (*Late Frosts*), 1955, by Pāvels Armands and Leonīds Leimanis

Baiba Indriksone as Olita and, Lilita Bērziņa as Mirta in *Limuzīns Jāņu nakts krāsā* (*Limousine of the Colour of Midsummer Night*), 1981, dir. by Jānis Streičs, cam. Harijs Kukels

Vija Artmane as Anna and Aļģirds Paulavičs as Antans *Svešās kaislības* (*Strange Passions*), 1983, dir. Jānis Streičs, cam. Harijs Kukels

Harijs Ritenbergs as Andris and Lolita Cauka as Ruta in *Vella kalpi*, (*Valets of the Devil*), 1970 by Leonīds Leimanis

Evalds Valters as Eidis and Gunars Cilinskis as Rudolfs in *Ezera sonāte* (*The Sonet of Lake*), 1976, directed by Varis Brasla and Gunars Cilinskis

Vija Artmane as Julia Lamberth and Ivars Kalniņš as Tom in *Teātris* (*Theatre*), 1978, director Jānis Streičs

Film director Aivars Freimanis, editor Aina Adermane, cameraman Ruta Urbaste, and film director Ivars Seleckis

Film director Ivars Seleckis

Cameraman Valdis Eglitis

The golden fund of Latvian cinematography since the 60's are documental films. Within the limits of censorship they represent the reality by means of publicity and art. Here *Krasti* (*Beaches*), 1963 and *Gada reportāža* (*One Year Coverage*), 1965 by Aivars Freimanis and cameraman Ivars Seleckis, *Tava algas diena* (*Your Pay Day*), 1971, *Mūžs* (*Lifetime*), 1972 and *Aizliegtā zona* (*Restricted Zone*), 1975 by Hercs Franks, *Valmieras meitenes* (*Girls of Valmiera*) (1970), *Sieviete, kuru gaida* (*Woman for whom to Wait*) (1978), *Meklēju vīrieti* (*Looking for a Man*) (1983), *Maestro bez frakas* (*Maestro without a Tailcoat*), 1985 by Ivars Seleckis, *Dzīve* (*Life*), 1970, *Kristapa mazdēli* (*Kristap's Grandsons*), 1975 and *Četri mekle miljonu* (*Four seeking a Million*), 1979 by Ansis Epners are to be remembered. The influence of Arnis Akmeņlauks, Jevģēnijs Paškevičs, Andris Slapiņš, Mihails Šneiderovs, Biruta Veldre, Laima Žurgina, Talivaldis Margevičs, A. Plaudis on documental cinematography should not be underestimated as well. A lot of documental films were made for TV. Among them – *Rainis trimdā* (*Rainis in Exile*) and *Vētras sēja* (*Seed of Storm*) by Rodrigo Rikards, *Pilsētas portrets* (*A City Portrait*) by Aivars Licis, *Daugavas atslēgas* (*Key of the Daugava*) Guntis Silis and the works of M. Jurjane, V. Znatnaja, S. Rikarde, J. Buka, Andrejs Feldmanis, V. Folkmanis and others.

235 000 000 by director Uldis Brauns, cameras Rihards Pīks, Valdis Kroģis, Ralfs Krumiņš, 1967

Hercs Franks in 1987

Making of a documental movie about the ceramist Izabella Krolle

Augstākā tiesa (*Supreme Justice*), 1987, director Hercs Franks, cameraman Andris Seleckis

Edgars Kauliņš in *Mūžs* (*Lifetime*), 1972, director Hercs Franks, cameraman Kalvis Zalemanis

Director and cameraman Juris Podnieks (1950–1991) with the youngsters from *Vai viegli būt jaunam* (*Is it Easy to be Young?*) in 1985

The team back in *Šķērsiela* 10 years after making the film *Šķērsiela* (*Cross street*)

Producer and cameraman Andris Slapiņš (1949–1991), producer Ansis Epners

Cameraman Dāvis Sīmanis in 80's

Šķērsiela

Award *Lielais Kristaps* in 1998 for the best Latvian documental film

Award *Nike* in 1989 for the best documental film in the USSR

Award *Felix* in 1990 for the best European documental film

Awards to *Šķērsiela*

Arnolds Burovs, producer of animated films

Indars Lācis as Jancis in *Puika* (*The Boy*), 1977, director Aivars Freimanis, cameraman Davis Simanis

From children films *Emīla nedarbi* (*Emil's Rascalities*), 1985 by Varis Brasla and *Saulessvece* (*Candle of Sun*), 1986 by Livija Ločmele are the distinguished ones.

Arnolds Burovs initiated the production of puppet films in *Rīgas kinostudija* in 1964. Now this work is carried on by Roze Stiebra, Dzintra Aulmane, Maija Brence, Laima Eglīte, Juris Dimiters, Daina Lapiņa, Irēna Luse, Miervaldis Polis. The Latvian animated cartoons have a national peculiarity and a high artistic quality.

Andris Rudzinskis as Boņuks in *Cilvēkbērns* (*A Human Child*) form 1991, by Janis Streičs and Harijs Kukels

The team of *Animācijas brigāde* in 1999

In 1966 Arnolds Burovs established the first puppet studio in Rīga and managed it for 25 years. His followers are Janis Cimermanis and Nils Skapāns, artist and script writer Māris Putniņš and the cameraman Peteris Trups. The studio AB produce puppet films on current issues of everyday life. The heroes Munks and Lemijs and the films *Zvēri* (*Animals*) and *Rezgalības* (*Rascalities*) are wide known as the AB studio is an award winner.

Putnu būris (*Bird Cage*) from the serial *Avārijas brigāde* (*Rescue unit*) won the Golden Lynx in Fraiburg in the Festival of Environmental Films in 1999

Putnu dienas (*Bird's Days*) from the serial *Zvēri* (*Animals*) won *Grand Prize* the Silver Goat in the Poznan Festival in Poland in 1999

Lidojam (*Flying*) from the serial *Munks un Lemijs* won the Glass Bear in Berlin Festival in 1995

Cinema *Kino 52*, *Lāčplēša iela* 52/54, Rīga

Cinema *Rīga*, *Elizabetes iela* 61, Rīga

Emīla nedarbi (*Emil's Rascalities*), 1985 by Varis Brasla and Davis Simanis

Arturs Skrastiņš as Beisiks, Romualds Ancāns as Vincents in *Likteņdzirnas* (*Mill of Fate*), 1997, by Janis Streičs

Arturs Skrastiņš, Eduards Pāvuls, Inese Saulīte, Renars Kaupers and director Janis Streičs making *Vecās pagastmājas mistērija* (*Mysteries of the Old Parish House*) in the summer 1999

Arsenāls and *Jūrmalas pērle* are the two well known film festivals in Latvia. The international forum *Arsenāls* takes place every second year since 1986 when for the first time in the USSR it was possible to show the prohibited or *on-shelf* films. The Forum of September 16-24, 2000 will have the themes of Luis Bunhuel and Juris Podnieks *Arsenāls* is a fraternity of different people.

Arsenāls program consists of the central show, panorama, retrospections, Baltic filmshow, comprising 200 films from 40-45 countries. All producers are awarded the Magic Crystal from the Professional guild of Arsenals. The main prize (10 000 USD) is a lottery. The festival jury is from the International Federation of Cinema Critics. The organizers are Riga City Council, Ministry of Culture and the International Centre of Cinematography. The head managers of *Arsenāls* are Māris Gailis and Augusts Sukuts since 1986

Mārtiņš Buclers (1866 – 1944), the first Latvian photographer. He was the one who began to produce photos on plates and paper in Latvia. Latvian Association of Art photography awards the *Buclera premija* for achievements in modern art photography in his memory

Jānis Rieksts (1881–1970), art photographer and portraitist

Vilis Rīdzenieks (1884 – 1962) and Mrs. Rīdziniece. Author of documental pictures and portraits of culture workers.

Mārtiņš Sams (1892 – 1941), the first photo critic and promoter of etnographic photography

Mārtiņš Lapiņš (1873 – 1954), one of the first theatre photographers

Gustavs Žakerts (1887–1945)

Roberts Johansons (1877 – 1959)

Photo studio of T. Bidegs in *Iecava*

Mārtiņš Buclers initiated the foundation of the first Latvian Photographic Society and became its chairman. Here with Roberts Johansons and Andrejs Saulītis on the day of foundation

Fotogrāfu hill in *Sigulda*, 1908

A burning St. Peter's church tower. A Vilis Rīdzenieks photo from the collection *Izpostītā Rīga* (The Ruined Riga), exposition of the Latvian Photography Museum

On the 19th of August 1939 the discovery of daguerrotype was announced in Paris. Already in the following days this message came to Riga. The Rigensians accepted news with enormous interest and enthusiasm. A Riga skyline picture was taken in 1840. It is known that during 1842–1843 there have been active people offering daguerrotype pictures. Museums store pictures from late 1850's, made by Roberts Borhards and Alfons Bērmanis. The first exhibitions and contests of photography in Europe took place in 1860's. It is remarkable that the first Russian contests were usually won by photographers from Latvia.

There are no exact records of the name of the first Latvian photographer. It might be Andrejs Saulītis, Jānis Pavlovskis or Janis Sarkangalvis. Mārtiņš Buclers opened his photographic studio in *Sigulda* in 1897, and he is the one who is recognized as the first artistic photographer in Latvia. The importance of Mārtiņš Buclers on Latvian culture should not be underestimated because he was able to see the artistic potential of photography and used it for storing historical information for the next generations. His book *Fotogrāfija* was published in Latvian in 1904 followed by twenty reissued editions. The distinguished artists of that time are Mārtiņš Lapiņš, Janis Rieksts, Arturs Dulbe, Roberts Johansons, Indriķis Kalcenauss and Eduards Gaiķis. They have made romantic portraits and images of landscapes often using the pictorealistic style and the technology of bromine oil or rubber dichromate. The photographers were engaged both in routine work and creativity. They participated and were recognized in exhibitions. Kārlis Bauls introduced montage, attractive lights and painting on the emulsion of the negative. Among the most outstanding Latvian artists should also be named Gustavs Klucis who often used photography in his monumental works in Russia.

Krišjānis Barons by the *Gūtmaņa* grotto

Kārlis Lakše from *Koknese* worked in a special manner of personal mediative documentation. The well known American photographer Filips Halsmans always stressed his Latvian origin. The start of his professional career in Paris was based on the skills obtained in Riga.

Minokss was designed by Valters Caps who was born in Latvia and lived in Tallinn for a long time. Latvian engineers created a miniature camera in 1932–1933. The factory VEF produced it during 1937–1943. Being a masterpiece of precise mechanics it was admired worldwide. The size of *Minokss* is 7,9 x 2,5 cm, weight - 127 g. The 9.5 mm film has 50 shots. Closure 1/2 to 1/10 sec. For many years *Minokss* was the smallest camera in the world. Latvia produced around 17 000 copies of *Minokss*. In 1943 the Germans brought it to the *Zeiss* factories, from where it was brought to USA as a design of a spying camera

The Bay of Āgenskalns by Mārtiņš Buclers

Egons Spuris (1931–1990)

Viesturs Klimpiņš

Pēteris Jaunzems

Gunārs Binde

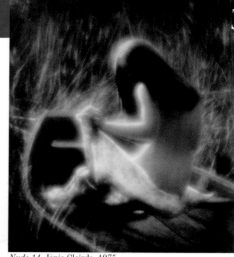

Nude 14, Jānis Gleizds, 1975

Portrait of Inta Ruka, the most well known Latvian photographer of the moment by Egons Spuris

Laiva (The Boat), Vilnis Auziņš, 1980

Laimes lietus (*Happy Rain*) by Valdis Brauns

Vilhelms Mihailovskis

Juris Krieviņš

Ilmārs Apkalns (1931–1997)

Aivis Šmulders

Nude photo by Gunārs Binde

Mana mīla (*My Love*) Leonīds Tugaļevs, 1978

The deportations on June 14, 1941 ruined many works and lives of Latvian photography artists.

The first after-war photo exhibition in Rīga took place only in 1958. It was the time of photography rebirth. Clubs of photo amateurs and exhibitions were organized in Rīga, *Liepāja*, *Cēsis*. A young and talented generation, represented by Gunārs Binde, Ilmārs Apkalns, Egons Spuris marked the quality of Latvian photography during the last 40 years. Aivars Aķis and Huberts Stankevičs took the managerial efforts. Aivis Šmulders, Pēteris Jaunzems, Jānis Gleizds, Vilhelms Mihailovskis, Leonīds Tugaļevs, Valdis Brauns have created a style of their own. Their works could be seen in a variety of amateur exhibitions all over the world. The limitations of the Soviet period, features of national mentality and personal motives have formed a singular Latvian approach for handling the issues of humanity. The emphasis is put on a high level art photography of a rich and complex content and done in half tonalities, lights and shades. The personal position of Egons Spuris was characterized by his desperate wish to show the man, depressed and oppressed by Soviet regime and colourless routine, as a monument of this period. Egons Spuris was the first in Latvia to use photography as an instrument of insight for mirroring oneself.

The industrial landscapes by Valters Ezeriņš, urban photos by Leons Balodis and architecture pictures by Indriķis Stūrmanis were often seen in publications and exhibitions. The professional photojournalism was established in late 80's. The notable photographers Uldis Briedis, Aivars Liepiņš and Ilmārs Znotiņš still work on the visual image of the largest Latvian paper *Diena*. Gunārs Janaitis has been an eminent portrait artist for a long time working with personalities from the Latvian culture life. Uldis Pāže has made a collection of celebrities portraits and is known to make some peculiar staged photos as well. Juris Krieviņš devoted his time to training of young photographers in a studio. However, a formal training and education in the art of photography is not available in any of Latvian universities or colleges.

In late 80's a highly self demanding generation of creative artists, among them, Andrejs Grants, Gvido Kajons, Mārtiņš Zelmenis, Valts Kleins entered the Latvian art photo environment. The photographer Inta Ruka received the highest award of the 48th Venice Biennial for her intuition, love of mankind and stability of style. In 1999 she was awarded the *Spīdola* Prize of the Latvian Culture Capital Foundation for her works. Significantly, the capability of this generation to make a significant contribution to the modern arts scene was initially recognized by the exhibition curators and gallery managers in Europe and America rather than the ones in Latvia.

Sergejs Daugovičs from the University of Latvia has started to collect a theorethical basis of photography

Photographer and researcher of photography Vilnis Auziņš is director of the Museum of Photography

Photo historician Peteris - Korsaks has saved the names of Latvian photomasters from oblivion

Martiņš Zelmenis

Martiņš Krumiņš

August 23, 1987 is the date of the first antisoviet demonstration. Members of the *Helsinki 86* group layed flowers on the Monument of Liberty to remind about the evils of Ribbentrop - Molotov pact. The first person being arrested in the period of Awakening was the photographer Valts Kleins for his attempt to take a shot of this event

Indriķis Sturmanis is notable for portraits and city photos

Marcis Bendiks, an authority among Latvian photographers. During hours of leisure he is the manager of Prime Ministers office or just a bank and organize plenaries in summers

Janis Deinats, Andris Krieviņš, Ainars Meijers, Kaspars Goba, Andrejs Grants, Uldis Briedis and Zigurds Mežavilks

Leons Balodis, the mastermind of Latvian photography is famous for half tonalities and style, and also personal features being a constraint to collaboration with publishers and colleagues

Inclusion of Latvian photos in the exposition *East European year* of the de l'Elysee museum in Lausanne is the quality certificate of professional art. It was followed by the *Ars Baltica* exhibition chain *Attēlu atmiņa* (Memory of Pictures) in several Baltic cities. In 1991–1994 Latvian photos were exhibited in Canadian big cities and galleries of US universities.

Latvians have always been fond of nature and landscape photos. Viesturs Klimpiņš, Maris Kundziņš, Andris Eglitis and Janis Talbergs remain unsurpassed for many years.

The beginning of 90's is notable for the opening of the Photography Museum as an affiliation to the Riga Museum of History and Shipping. It was possible thank to the efforts of Vilnis Auziņš, Livija Blūmfelde, Pēteris Korsaks, Gunārs Janaitis.

The museum has a permanent exposition about the period 1839 -1941. It hosts exhibitions of modern photo art and organizes workshops and conferences on academic studies in this specialty. A number of exhibitions in Vienna, Innsbruck, Vilnius, Moscow and in the two biggest halls of the Bratislava Festival *Mesiac Fotografie* in 1998 are among it's achievements as well as the projects *Latvijas Laiks* (Latvian Time) and *Foto Parāde* (Photo Parade).

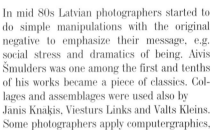

Gunārs Janaitis was the most popular photographer for journals and portraits in the 70's

Valdis Kupris came back to his fatherland

Janis Talbergs, experienced master of landscape photos

In mid 80s Latvian photographers started to do simple manipulations with the original negative to emphasize their message, e.g. social stress and dramatics of being. Aivis Šmulders was one among the first and tenths of his works became a piece of classics. Collages and assemblages were used also by Jānis Knaķis, Viesturs Links and Valts Kleins. Some photographers apply computergraphics, others – virtual reality as a simulation of truth. Aldis Māris Dublāns, Mārtiņš Krumiņš, Aigars Jansons, Arno Antums Jansons have shaped a style of their own. The present trends show the influence of Latvians living abroad Boriss Mangolds, Helēna Hofmane, Ruta Ināra Sniķere and Dace Marga. The names of the very new generation are Arnis Balčus, Gatis Rozenfelds and Ivars Grāvlejs who develop the visual shape of a personal documentation. The Latvian Association of Professional Photographers and the Latvian Association of Photography Artists are non-governmental entities. Photographers are also members of the Associations of Designers and Journalists. Clubs and informal unions of photography are working in Rīga, *Ogre, Talsi, Valka, Daugavpils, Preiļi, Jēkabpils, Liepāja* and *Jelgava*. A nonprofit NGO *ACD Fotoforma* was established in 1999. Works of big volume and high quality are done *Fotocentrs* Ltd., *Valta Kleina fotostudija, J.V.K.* Ltd. and *Fotomaks* Ltd. The development of professional and art photography has reached a stable and multiform dynamics. The professional photography borrows successive findings of art and supports it with technical capacities. Interesting projects from 1999, which approve the artistic and professional potential of Latvian photographers are the exhibition of Juris Kalniņš works in the Jugendstyle building of E.Saarinen's Railway station in Helsinki and the dedication to the 2000 year of Christianity by Andris Tenass, on stage picture collection *Ecce Homo*.

The photos of Imants Predelis in this book tells about music, religion and celebrities

Vējaina diena (a Windy Day) by Aivis Šmulders. 1985

Garā gada kalendārs (Calendar of the Long Year) by Modris Rubenis, 1988

Mazirbe, Aivars Liepiņš

XXX. Gvido Kajons

Pašportrets (Self- portrait), Aldis Māris Dublāns

Pašportrets (Self-portrait), Arnis Balčus

Central Telephone Exchange, Riga, *Kr. Barona iela* 69, Davis Zariņš, 1928

Apartment house, Riga, *Kr. Barona iela* 49, Eižens Laube, 1911

Apartment house, Riga, *Brivibas iela* 68, Alexander Schmaelling, 1903

A prime example of Latvian functional architecture, the former Latvian Stock Bank building, now the *Unibanka*, Riga, *Vaļņu iela* 11, architects Alfred Kars, Kurt Betge, 1931

The German community's architectonic culture also had a national romantic artistic trend, however it was very different from the Latvian. To bring into Latvia the so-called *heimatkunst* or fatherland style at the turn of the century, German architects utilised romanticised renaissance elements: bays, small pane windows, console miniatures in detailed forms.

Functionalism really came into its own only after the World War I, although some new buildings in Riga already showed elements of the style pre-war. Examples of pre-functionalism in Riga are: the *VEF* building (at the time the factory *Union*) designed by the firm of Peter Behrens at *Brivibas iela* 214, courtyard, which forms the factory silhouette, and an apartment building at *Miera iela* 5, which surprises with its contemporary float lines.

Neo-classical features were drawn on the face of Riga by Eižens Pole apartment houses on *Elizabetes iela*, as well as some bank buildings, including the present City of Riga council building. A fine example of the work of an architect is *Kemeri* Hotel, built in 1935.

The world style of *art deco* or the non-functional modernist style could have become grounded in Latvia as well, however Latvian architects respected the wishes of their clients who wanted a neo-classical historical compilation style. Up until the World War II, an international style was continued by Teodors Hermanovskis, a pioneer of the *art-deco* style in Latvia, with the apartment houses at *Marijas iela* 8 and 10, as well as by Pāvils Dreijmanis and Davids Zariņš. The expression of *art deco* in architecture can be seen in the houses built in the suburbs of *Mežaparks*, *Agenskalns* and around *Māras* pond. They are manifestations of new practical architecture, whichwas known as functionalism in Latvia.

However, in the 1930s, the style was criticised in Latvia due to its simple form and international nature. The Baltic German architectural bureau of *Kars & Betge* created the best functional works: the cinema *Aina* (1935), the Latvian Stock Bank on the corner of *Vaļņu* and *Kaļķu ielas* (1931), and the Printers House in *Lāčplēšu iela* (1930). The simple geometrically formed buildings are rationally planned, solidly built and equipped with the most modern engineering equipment of the time. Of the Latvian architects, Aleksandrs Klinklavs worked in the functionalist style up to the second half of the 1930's afterwards followed the prevailing mode of Latvian and monumentalistic architecture.

Monumentalism usually describes the architecture of the Third Reich and its allies. In Latvia, the best examples are the Palace of Justice and the Foreign Ministry building.

Apartment and shop building, Riga, *Marijas iela* 8, Teodors Hermanovskis, 1927

Apartment house, Riga, *Gertrūdes iela* 10/12, Heinrich Sheel, Friedrich Scheffel, 1902

Apartment house, Riga, *Nometņu iela* 47, Wilhelm Bockslaff, 1909

VEF factory, Riga, Heinrich Scheel, 1913

The factory of *Provodņik* (SSC Rigas Elektromašinbuves rūpnica), by engineer Edmund fon Trompovsky, 1894. g.

The section of *Forburga* in Riga, 1913

Māja ar naktssargu (House with a night guard), block house, *Ausekļu iela*, Pāvils Dreijmanis, 1927

The Mortgage Bank, now the City Council of Riga building, Eižens Laube, Augusts Vite, 1913

Aleksandrs Vanags (1873-1919), architect. Some 70 multi-story buildings were built based on his designs, mainly in the national romantic style

Paul Mandelstamm (1872-1941), architect. Some 60 art nouveau and functionalist buildings were built based on his designs in Riga

Eižens Laube (1880-1967), architect. Some 200 multi-story buildings were built based on his designs, mainly in the national art nouveau style

Osvalds Tilmanis (1900-1980), Chief architect of Riga (1934-1950, 1956-1958)

Naval Officers Club building in *Liepāja*. Construction began in 1894 based on a design by the St. Petersburg architect S.P.Galyenzovsky as a temporary building. In 1907, Tsar Nicholas II attended the grandiose opening. The people know it as Koltchak's House, as the Russian general Koltchak briefly stayed there

Cinema in *Jelgava*. An all-Soviet Union standard project, 1950s

VEF Congress Palace, Riga, architect Nikolajs Semencovs, 1960

Modris Gelzis, architect

The Academy of Sciences high-rise, Riga, Osvalds Tilmanis, Vaidelotis Apsitis, Kārlis Pluksne, Vladimirs Šņitņikovs, 1957. Such a building had to be in every larger USSR city and in some satellite country state capitals. Moscow had several of this type of building

Professor Janis Krastiņš, architect

A suburb of *Daugavpils*, 1960s

Zane Kalinka, architect

Professor Ivars Strautmanis, architect

A suburb of *Daugavpils*, 1970s

Gunars Birkerts, an American-Latvian architect. Designer of the Latvian National Library project, pictured near one of his implemented working models – the nearly one kilometre high Domino Pizza Corporation building. The tower of the hotel is at a 15° slope

Andris Purviņš, architect near his implemented project – the Latvian TV building

National conservative architecture most precisely reflected positivist philosophy, under the influence of which the brother's Haralds and Pauls Kundziņš and their students designed their projects.

Modern interpretations allow the architect to be sovereign and to create such truly contemporary buildings as the *Allažu* and *Ikšķiles* churches. Latvia differed from other countries in that patrons of modern art and architecture were almost non-existent. Latvian society was very reserved towards the participation of foreign architects, even regarding the wishes of Estonian and Lithuanian architects in the 1930s to exchange ideas. However, Latvian architects, with good results (1st place in the competition regarding a palace for the President of Lithuania; 2nd place in a competition for a Beauty and Cosmetics Centre in Tallinn) participated in competitions conducted by the other two Baltic States. Latvia, on the other hand, conducted only one international competition – for the best People's House project. The winner, an architect from Dresden in Germany, did not ultimately receive the contract, which was awarded to German architects in Riga.

Soviet authorities required socialistic realism in architecture or retrospectivism – a style similar to neo-eclecticism. Many excellent architects were forced to flee into exile in 1944.

The mandatory use of the dominant USSR standard designs, did not in practice fit into the city historical centres, so, within the framework of the allowed style, Latvian architects attempted to infuse into the socialistic architecture content some nationalistic form. A good example is the Academy of Science high-rise building (the building was built as the *Kolhoznieku nams* (*House of Members of the Collective Farms*), architect Osvalds Tilmanis and others), which in details is very different from the Moscow prototypes, but which has preserved the necessary level of decorativeness.

An international style became the basis of the official doctrines of Soviet architecture for study and acquisition. For Latvia, it was the rehabilitation of the well-known pre-war functionalism. The British architect proclaimed *brutalism* at the beginning of the 1960's, required a much more qualified handwork and individual solutions, and therefore there are almost no explicit brutalism buildings in Latvia.

The expressive strength of neo-plasticism, lay in combinations of large-scale plastic forms. Examples of neo-plasticism in Latvia are the cinema *Oktobris* in *Daugavpils* (architect Oļģerts Krauklis), the hotel *Rīdzene* (Z.Kalinkas, J. Gertmanis, and V. Kadirkov) and the Latvian TV studio high-rise at *Zaķusala* (A. Purviņš, B. Maikre) in Riga.

Most of what was built in the post-war years cannot be looked upon as architecture, but rather as building. A precondition for achievement in the art of building is a good building programme. In some areas of building, for example churches, there was none at all. Almost no banks, cultural and sports facilities, hotels were built.

A particular feature of the 20th century is the widespread construction of multi-story apartment houses. In Sweden, there was a 1 million apartment campaign, in France – a cheap reinforced concrete construction system. In communist Europe, the State also supported everywhere, the cheap construction of apartment houses. The USSR apartment houses were only modular multi-story buildings. Architects could not improve on them even by designing attic floors, as was done in *Mežciems*. This suburb of Riga should have become a positive example, which, similar to *Lazdinai* in Lithuania, could compete for the highest award in the field of art

and architecture. Unfortunately, similarly to other suburbs built in Latvia during the years of occupation, *Mežciems* was not built according to the design by the architect, because the commissioners of the project – State and party nomenclature – refused to build the public buildings and install all the amenities provided for in the design project. The deciding factor was political decisions as to what would be built and what would not.

Examples from abroad stimulated a new, daring and radical approach to the reconstruction of Riga's inner suburbs. Unfortunately, there was a lack of funds for implementation. The most unsuccessful option was put into practice – wooden houses in parts of *Čiekurkalns* were torn down and replaced with the same dreary multi-story apartment buildings – the epitome of the lack of individuality.

In the circumstances of the Soviet authority, the term *national romanticism* was not acceptable and in other parts of the world, the word national also had to be changed for the vernacular or local. Architects in Latvia, in their nationalistic quest, rediscovered the national romantic nature of *Art Nouveau*, as well as Madernieks' angular geometric ornaments. These influences favourably impacted on a whole series of buildings, which the chief architecture theorist at the time, Ivars Strautmanis, called regionalism or regional architecture.

Post modernism arrived in Latvia in the 1970s together with Charles Jenks' books. The best of the buildings built in Latvia reawakened the national consciousness, the historical memory of place and stimulated builders to quality work. Post-modernism freed architects from the stranglehold of Soviet clichés. To be able to orientate oneself in the life of world architecture and art which was promised by apologetics of post-modernism, required wide knowledge and commitment. Without those, it was easy to become the co-author of a mere copy or even worse – a pale imitator.

Following the renewal of Latvian independence, Latvian architects look for their own place in modern Europe. Post-modernism has encompassed the whole of the fragmented world of architecture like a hat. The high-tech style requires precision, which in Latvia, can only be ensured for small scale constructions, because there is a shortage of qualified specialists for large scale design and building. The leading style of the 1990's in interior design is the junk-style. Neurotically romantic and, at the same time, easily recognisable with its refined non-aggressiveness, it fits in well in post-soviet dilapidated environment, which slowly but surely is beginning to recover.

In architecture nothing occurs quickly, especially in Latvia, where buildings are designed and built slower than in other parts of the world. And still, Latvian architecture at this time surprises with daring solutions, which only rarely are implemented at the moment. Uģis Šenbergs' artificial islands project convincingly won in Kobe, Japan international competition. Gunars Birkerts has returned to Latvia and designed the new National Library building. As an example of outstanding Latvian architectural design was the Juris Poga designed USSR exhibition pavilion at the Seville EXPO. At the end of the century, there has been a wood renaissance, not only with the efforts of architect Peteris Blums attempts to preserve the wooden masterpieces of Riga's architecture for future generations, but also modern wood design for individual and row houses. In City centre reconstruction, Zaiga Gaile has shown the vitality of beginning of the century architecture in a new form with her recomstruction of *Berg's Bazaars*.

Skyscraper in the *Citadele*, Rīga. Architect Arturs Reinfelds 1965. Front: multilevel parking facility, architect Juris Gertmanis, 1999

Blocks of apartments houses in *Pļavnieki*, 20th century, 80s

Motormuseum in Rīga, Viktors Valgums, Andris Briedis, 1989

The Art Theatre in Rīga, architects Marta Staņa, Imants Jakobsons, Haralds Kanders, 1959–1975.

Sanatorium *Rīgas Jūrmala*, Modris Ģelzis, Viktors Valgums, Normunds Pavars, 1981

World Trade Centre, the former house of Latvian Communist Party Jānis Vilciņš, Gunars Asaris et al. 1972

Jānis Lejnieks, architector and chief editor of the magazine *Latvijas Architektūra*

Juris Poga, architect and Chairman of the Board of Latvian Architects Association

Communication facility in Cēsis, I. Kiseļovs, S. Gurevičs, 1984

Andris Kronbergs, architect

Peugeot office in Rīga, Andris Purviņš, 1998

Architects Iveta Cibule and Zaiga Gaile have reconstructed the *Berga bazārs* (the Berg's Bazaar)

Ausma Skujiņa, architect

Andrejs Ģelzis, architect

Valdemar's Center in Rīga, architects Visvaldis Sarma, Jānis Norde, Gunta Grikmane, G. Jatnieks, 1999. The first six level building of the post war period with a corner tower. It is constructed from modern materials, but fits in well. It marks the end of the socialistic tradition of Latvian architecture

The supermarket *Pa rokai* in Rīga, architects Ingurds Lazdiņš, E. Timofejevs, 1998

THE VENTSPILS LINEARY CENTRE GAMES

Daiga Dzedone, *Ventspils* chief architect and the author of the Lineary Centre games

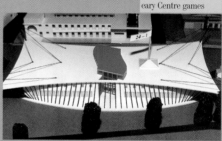

The project *Ventspils Lineārā centra spēles* (VLC, *Ventspils* Lineary Centre Games) was announced in August 6, 1999. It is an avant-gardic principle for design of urban environment, were 13 teams from all Baltic states participated. The boundries of the VLC project include all the 4 km of *Osta* street along the *Venta* river from the old city to the sea. Each team made macket designs for seven topics. The jury and residents of *Ventspils* could choose the most appropriate, interesting and beautiful designs. Internationally recognized architects have made a miraculous vision out of the exceptional place which for many years was hidden under worn-out constructions. *Ventspils* people are looking forward to make it a reality.

THE CASTLES OF LATVIA

The *Araiši* lake castle. The fact that an ancient monument existed on an island in the *Araiši* lake was discovered in 1876 by a nobleman from *Cēsis*, Count Karlis Zivers. He was the first to perform archaeological excavations in the *Araiši* region.

Between 1965 and 1969 and between 1975-1979 there were 10 seasons of archaeological excavations and some three-quarters of the lake castle, which measures some 2500 m² , were investigated. The water in the lake was initially lowered by one meter. Dams were put up around the excavation areas and water that flowed in was pumped out with special machinery. On the island researchers discovered a lake castle that had been inhabited by Latgallian tribes in the 9th and 10th century. The castle had been well fortified, with a complex of residential and public buildings surrounded by a protective wall. It is known that the *Araiši* lake castle was burned down by enemies and was never renewed. The water level in the *Araiši* lake at that time was approximately 1.5 m lower than is the case now. The remnants of ancient wooden buildings have been well preserved in the water, as have various antique objects made from organic materials. Such materials have perished in other environments.

In 1983, the Latvian government decided to reconstruct the *Araiši* lake castle. The reconstruction project was prepared by the archaeologist Janis Apals and architect Dzintars Driba. The foundations of the buildings were restored as copies of the original buildings that had been preserved, while the upper parts were reconstructed after an analysis of various parts of the old buildings that were found, taking into account construction logic and ethnographic parallels. After 1990, the work was done with copies of ancient tools that had been found at the site – narrow-blade iron axes, chisels, shaving knives and wooden clubs. Today the *Araiši* lake castle is a unique open-air archaeological museum, reflecting the lifestyle of ancient Latgallians during the era of the Vikings.

The initiator and organizer of the renovation of *Araiši* Lake castle, Janis Apals

The ruins of the *Koknese* castle, which is one of the oldest and most important castles along the *Daugava* River. It was burned down when Russian Tsar Peter the Great invaded Vidzeme. Today the castle is surrounded by water from the reservoir of the *Pļaviņas* hydro-electrical station

The *Jaunmokas* castle, which was built by Wilhelm Bockslaff, now houses a forestry museum

The *Bauska* castle is the last surviving brick castle built by the Livonian Order between 1443 and 1456 in the southern part of its territory. It was also one of the largest among these castles, and it reflects various eras. The oldest parts of the castle are in carefully preserved ruins, while later sections house the *Bauska* Regional Research Museum

The *Cēsis* castle was built after 1209, and from the 13th until the 16th century it was the residence of the Grand Master of the Livonian Order. The convent-type brick castle has three outer castles. The *Riekstukalns* castle mound, where ancient Liv tribes once lived, is adjacent to the castle

Ruins of the outer walls of the *Ludza* castle, which was built in the 14th century and completed in 1399-1433

Work on the *Turaida* castle began in 1214. The castle has at various times in history been owned by the Bishop of Riga, the Archbishop of Riga, and the Livonian Order. The castle had an irregular, multi-planed design with a tower in the middle of the castle yard. The castle was burned down in 1776. Work on restoring the castle began in the 1970s

The *Vecauce* castle was built in accordance with a design by Fridrihs Augusts Štilers

The *Biriņi* castle, architect Fridrihs Vilhelms Hess

The director of *Rundāle* Castle Museum, Imants Lancmanis

Francesco Bartalomeo Rastrelli built the *Jelgava* castle (1738-1768, which currently houses the Latvian University of Agriculture

The Riga castle is the largest and best-preserved castle in the Baltic region. It is the official residence of the President of Latvia. The cornerstone for the castle was laid on 15 June 1330, by Grand Master Eberhard of the Livonian Order

The *Rundāle* castle is the most significant monument to Baroque and Rococo architecture and art in all of Latvia. The cornerstone for the castle was laid by the Duke of Kurzeme, Ernst Biron, on 24 May 1736. The architect for the castle was the Italian Francesco Bartalomeo Rastrelli, while most of the artists who were involved in the project came from St. Petersburg. Nearly 1,500 men were employed to build the castle. After 1740, when the death of Empress Anna Ivanovna put a halt to the exalted career of the castle's owner, Duke Biron, the duke was arrested and sent into exile. In 1763, Biron was pardoned, and he returned to Kurzeme with Rastrelli. The rebuilding of the *Rundāle* castle took until 1768. The Italian painters Francesco Martini and Carlo Cuki were invited for the interior design, as was a master of decorative work from Berlin, Johann Mikhail Graf. Empress Catherine the Great presented the castle to her favourite, Count Zubov. Until 1920, the castle belonged to the family of Count Shuvalov.

It was only in 1972, that a full restoration of the *Rundāle* castle ensemble was begun. A museum was established in the castle. The castle ensemble covers more than 60 hectares of land and the two floors of the castle have 138 rooms. The galleries of the first floor and the two main stairwells, as well as the Small Gallery remain the only preserved examples of Rastrelli's early style. The most ornate room is the Gold Room, the former Throne Room. The former ballroom, now known as the White Room, is important because of its white stucco relief work and the uplifting mood of the entire room.

The distinguished Latvian artist and cultural worker Imants Lancmanis has been of key significance in the restoration of the *Rundāle* castle.

The *Jaunpils* castle was built in the 14th century and renewed on the basis of a design by the architect Wilhelm Bockslaff

The *Mežotne* castle was built in 1779-1802 after a design by Giaccomo Quarengi and Georg Berlitz. The castle is often used for various celebrations — weddings, birthdays and New Year's eve

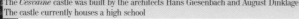

The *Cesvaine* castle was built by the architects Hans Giesenbach and August Dinklage. The castle currently houses a high school

The Riga Cathedral Chapter castle at *Dundaga* was built after 1249. The castle is known for many legends, including the story of the Green Girl ghost who haunts the building.

The *Stāmeriena* castle is known as the former residence of the prominent Italian author, Sicilian aristocrat and European cultural connoisseur Giuseppe Tomasi de Lampedusa (1896-1957). In 1929, de Lampedusa came to Latvia to visit his future wife, *Stāmeriena* Baroness Alexandra von Wolff. A psychologist, she would eventually become the vice president of the Italian Association of Psychoanalysts. Between 1929 and 1939, Lampedusa spent all of his summers, as well as several winters, in Latvia. Lampedusa and the baroness were married at the Church of the Assumption of St. Mary in Riga, which was an Orthodox church (the baroness was Russian Orthodox, while Lampedusa was Catholic). Lampedusa is best known for his novel *The Leopard*, which he wrote in 1955 and 1956 and which made him world famous. The book is seen to this very day as the most intellectual best seller in history. Some of the materials for the book were prepared at the *Stāmeriena* castle.

Weightlifter Jānis Krauze (1894–1919)

Wrestlers Edvīns Beitags (1908–1983) and Alberts Zvejnieks (1902–1987)

Kārlis Kļava (1907–1941), world champion in shooting

Kārlis Vītoliņš started his athletic career in the discipline of so-called "artistic bicycling" in 1896

In 1924 Latvia debuted at the Winter Olympics in Chamonix, France. The delegation had to have at least three people to participate in the opening ceremony – someone to carry the flag, someone to carry the banner with the team name, and at least one athlete. There were only two Latvians at Chamonix, but they were helped out by the Lithuanian delegation – which had just one man

Jānis Daliņš, seen here in a 50-km walk in 1936. He was the first Latvian to set a world record in track and field and to bring home Olympic Medals. A song called "If I had Daliņš' legs …" became popular

The Latvian Olympic team in Atlanta in 1996. The flag is being carried by athlete Einārs Tupurītis

Athletics have always been a part of the life of Latvians. Latvians participate in sports and are fans of leading athletes from the country. Latvian fans are always ready to travel great distances to support their own. They may be typically Nordic in the quiet way in which they do this – they sing and wave flags, but they don't break chairs.

The history of sports in Latvia dates back to the early 19th century, when physical education classes were put on school curricula. These classes were mandatory for boys in the schools of the Riga Educational District after 1889.

The Riga Gymnastics Association was founded in 1862, the Riga Chess Club – in 1869, the Riflemen's Society – in 1866, the Riga Rowing Club – in 1872, and many other athletic organizations – one after the other in later years.

Latvians won their first Olympic medal in 1912 in Stockholm, when Riga resident H. Blauss won a bronze in shooting. Latvia's athletes before and after World War I had the greatest success at world and European championships in wrestling and shooting. The first world champion from Latvia was Lt. Kārlis Kļava, who won the title in shooting at the world championships in Helsinki in 1937.

Latvians were pioneers in bobsled and have done much to improve the sport. The first bobsled tracks in Latvia were built in *Mežaparks* and *Āgenskalns* in the late 19th century, and it was precisely in Riga that many of the criteria for evaluating bobsled events were developed. Nearly a century later, in 1988, Jānis Ķipurs won an Olympic gold (for the Soviet Union) in the two-man bob. Since then another six Latvian bobsledders have won bronze medals.

During the period between the two world wars, Latvians did very well in walking sports. Adalberts Bubenko and the legendary Jānis Daliņš brought home Olympic medals. Daliņš set several world records and created such enthusiasm among Latvians by doing so that now, 60 years later, people still sing: "If only I had Daliņš' legs …".

The war split up the Latvian nation, and many people fled to the West. Those who remained behind lived and competed under foreign flags. The post-war years saw the strong emergence of basketball in Latvia. In the first European championship in basketball, before World War II, the Latvian men's team took gold, while in 1939 in Kaunas it came in second. The ASK men's team from Latvia became Soviet champions in basketball in 1955, 1957 and 1958 and European champions in 1958, 1959 and 1960. The TTT women's team, astonishingly, won the European championship no fewer than 17 times, and star forward Uļjana Semjonova, who received two Olympic golds, is in the Basketball Hall of Fame. Valdis Valters was named Europe's best basketball player several times, Igors Miglinieks played on a Soviet gold medal team, and many other Latvians have done very well in various Soviet teams.

The fact that the Latvian nation was split up was

Jānis and Ilze Kondrāts represented the Australian swim team at the Rome Olympics in 1960 and won gold and silver medals

Jānis Dikmanis was the first president of the Latvian Olympic Committee (1922–1933) and Latvia's only representative on the IOC (1926-1947). He spent the last years of his life in the United States

At the winter Olympic Games in Albertville in 1992, Latvia returned to the Olympic movement after a 56-year pause. The flag was carried by Olympic champion Jānis Ķipurs

The president of the Latvian Olympic Committee, Vilnis Baltiņš (left), is seen here with the president of the IOC, Juan Antonio Samaranch. Baltiņš told the IOC chief that Latvia does a lot of work to develop sports activities among children

seen most vividly in the sport of volleyball. The Olympic gold medal in volleyball in 1980 was won by the soviet team, with Pāvels Seļivanovs as a member. In 1984 America won with Aldis Bērziņš on the team. In 1988 the silver medal was received by Raimonds Vilde and the other members of the Soviet team.

Speed skating traditions came to Latvia via the European victory of Alfons Bērziņš in 1939. His student, Lasma Kauniste, won a European championship in speed skating in 1968. Canadian Latvian Silvija Burka was world champion several times in the 1980s.

Latvian athletes often play with their heads – games which involve teamwork, as well as chess and checkers. In the Chess Olympiad in Paris in 1924, Hermanis Matisons and Fricis Apšenieks took first and second. Latvians have been one of the nations in the world which have worked very hard of chess theory. Mikhail Tal, several times world champion, was the most distinguished Latvian chess player. Latvians win world championships regularly in 100-square checkers. Andris Andreiko won several times in the 1960s, while Zoja Golubeva and Guntis Valneris have been world champions in the 1990s.

There are several kinds of athletic activities that are very popular among everyday Latvians – bicycle riding, boating on rapid rivers, and participation in the sport of orienteering in Latvia's beautiful forests. Basketball competitions are very popular, involving small boys and elderly gentlemen alike. Streetball is played throughout Latvia in the summertime. New sports halls and ice skating rinks are being built. The pride of Latvia's athletic infrastructure, of course, is the bobsled track at *Sigulda*, where the world's best bobsled and luge athletes have trained and competed regularly.

Latvian Olympic Committee president Vilnis Baltiņš receives the official invitation for Latvia to attend the 2000 Summer Olympics in Sydney, Australia

The headquarters of the Latvian Olympic Committee at *Elizabetes iela* 49 in Riga

A UEFA Champions League pre-season game between London *Chelsea* and *Skonto* from Latvia, London, August 11, 1999

The *Skonto* team before a UEFA Champions League pre-season match-up with *Rapid* of Bucharest, August 4, 1999

Andrejs Rubins playing for the Latvian national team in a game against Norway

Latvia's team rejoices after Marians Pahars has scored a goal against the Norwegians

Imants Bleidelis

Mihails Miholaps

Helmuts Balderis Sildedzis is Latvia's all-time great in hockey. he was declared best player and best forward at the world championships in 1976, and he has often been named on imagined world teams. He retired from the game in the early 1980s, but once the Iron Curtain was lifted, in 1988, he went to the United States to play for the *North Stars* of Minnesota. He has trained the Latvian national team and served as director of the Sports Palace in Riga. He is currently a member of the Riga city Council

Latvia's three most popular hockey players from the NHL – defender Sandis Ozoliņš (center), who has been on the NHL All Star Team, Artūrs Irbe (left), several times the NHL's leading goalie who at the world championships in 1990 was named best goalie of the event and who is a regular member of the All Star Team, and Sergejs Žoltoks, who is a starter for the Montreal *Canadiens*. Five or six Latvian hockey players have played in the NHL each year for the last decade

Two Latvian hockey players have won the Stanley Cup – Sandis Ozoliņš with the Colorado *Avalanche* and American Latvian Maikls Knuble with the Dallas *Stars*. Once again – the Latvian nation has been divided up. The children of émigrés from World War II are representing other countries. Maikls Knuble plays for the United States at the Olympics and in world championships

Ice hockey is the team sport in which Latvians have done the best. Latvians played on the Soviet national team for years, and hockey became very popular in Latvia. Boys were happy to train for this very manly sport. Vitalijs Samoilovs played on a gold medal team for the Soviet Union, Helmūts Balderis Sildedzis took home silver. At the Lake Placid Olympics in 1980, the physician and trainer for the victorious American team was Latvian Visvaldis Nagobads.

Hockey becomes more and more popular in Latvia as time goes by. The Latvian team has beaten America, Italy and Germany in world championships and tied with Sweden, Canada and Finland. Between 1997 and 1999 new ice rinks were built in *Liepāja*, *Daugavpils*, *Ventspils* and Riga. The national team usually trains in *Liepāja*, and all kinds of ice skating are very popular among children in that city

The *Skonto* bench erupts in joy after a victory against *Rapid* of Bucharest

The president of the Latvian Soccer Federation and the *Skonto* team, Guntis Indriksons (right) is seen here with star footballer Marians Pahars after he signed an agreement with *Southampton* from Britain's Premiere League, which also employs Imants Bleidelis. Latvians play in leading clubs in Russia, Ukraine, Germany, England and other countries

Unquestionably Latvia's most distinguished tennis player, Larisa Neilande spent 12 years in the pros and won 63 titles, including the doubles championship in the US Open, the French Open, the Australian Open and Wimbledon

American financier and philanthropist George Soros (right) and Latvian Foreign Minister Valdis Birkavs after a tennis match in *Jurmala*. Soros is in outstanding athletic form and beat the minister. Soros has also played against former prime minister Ivars Godmanis, who was quite an athlete in his youth. Apparently George Soros is happy with the quality of the courts at the *Lielupe* Tennis Center where he and the minister played. Many of the world's leading tennis players have visited the facility

The most outstanding Latvian athlete of the 20th century is probably Jānis Lūsis, a javelin thrower who attended four Olympic Games as part of the Soviet team and won one gold medal, one silver medal and two bronze medals. He set two world records and was eight times European champion

Jānis Lūsis is seen here with his son, Voldemars, and with the distinguished javelin trainer Māris Griva. A quarter century after Jānis Lūsis retired from the sport, his son Voldemars has joined the European javelin elite

Jānis Lūsis' wife, Elvira Ozoliņa, won gold in the javelin throw in Rome in 1960

The first Latvian woman to win a gold medal at the Olympics was Inese Jaunzeme, who threw her javelin to gold in 1956. Later she became a distinguished sports physician and taught at the Latvian Academy of Medicine

Voldemars Mazzalitis trained Jānis Lūsis and many other outstanding athletes

Alvis Bērziņš won Olympic gold as part of the American volleyball team

The best Latvian basketball player in all history is Uljana Semjonova, who has won every conceivable title and is seen here next to her photograph at the Basketball Hall of Fame

In the 1980 Olympics in Moscow, Dainis Kūla took gold in javelin – lots of Latvians have been up on that podium

World champions Kristers Serģis and Artis Rasmanis – always first on their motorcycle with sidecar

The Latvian basketball team at the European championships is coached by former Olympic champion Igors Miglinieks. Behind him is assistant coach Raimonds Miglinieks

The basketball legend Aleksandrs Gomeļskis started his markable career of a coach in the Riga ASK. The club won the European Cup of Champions for three times

Europe's best basketball player in 1982 and 1983 was Valdis Valters from the Soviet team, and he is seen here with his sons Sandris and Kristaps. In 1999 Kristaps was recognized as a leading team player at the European Youth Championship

The most outstanding Latvian trainer of all time was Raimonds Karnitis (1929-1999), who trained several world and Olympic championship teams in women's basketball and headed up the TTT team which won the European championship 17 times

One of the most popular athletic events in Latvia is the annual streetball tournament that is sponsored by *Adidas*

Two outstanding Latvian basketball players – Olympic champion Igors Miglinieks and European champion Valdis Valters – play against one another

A new basketball hall in *Ventspils* is one of the most modern facilities of its kind in Northern Europe. The *Ventspils* team has played in European tournaments with good success

The ASK basketball team won the European championship three times

An open air stadium in *Kandava* has a 50-meter pool, areas of track and field, soccer and basketball, and a bicycle track. The *World Latvian Games* have taken place here several times

Bicycling is one of the most popular forms of athletic activity in Latvia. There are professional and amateur competitions alike. The Riga Marathon is run on the first Sunday in June, when anyone who wants to can compete over a 100 km distance. There is also the Keggi Tournament, which involves various distances. Professionals ride a 225 km distance from Rīga to *Alūksne*

The Unity Bicycle Tour takes place in late August every year with the participation of many amateur riders. Here we see the chairman of the Latvian Sports board, Einars Fogelis and Latvian President Guntis Ulmanis (center, with glasses) riding from Riga to *Sigulda* – a distance of some 50 kilometers

World champion Emilija Sonka is retired, but she helps young people to find their right bicycles for them

Alfons Bērziņš, European champion in speed skating in 1939

Silvija Burka and Lāsma Kauniste have both been world champions in speed skating

Lāsma Kauniste skating to her speed skating championship in 1970

If Latvia was not quite the birthplace of the bobsled, Latvians have done a lot to improve the sport. The first bobsled tracks were built in Mežaparks and Āgenskalns at the end of the last century, and criteria for judging bobsled events were developed in Riga

The world champion in academic rowing, Renāte Kokoreviča

Ivans Klementjevs has won Olympic gold in one-man canoeing (1988), as well as silver medals at Barcelona (1992) and Atlanta (1996)

Popular sports in the springtime – the water in the flooded Amata River may be just +4 to +8 degrees Celsius in temperature, but that doesn't keep dozens of men and women from taking to their boats

At the Lake Placid Winter Olympics in 1980, Vera Zozuļa won gold in the luge, while Ingrīda Amantova took bronze

In 1988 Janis Ķipurs received Olympic gold in the two-man bobsled and a bronze in the four-man bob

Raimonds Bergmanis is one of the world's strongest men. Here he is setting a world record in airplane pulling

Viktors Ščerbatihs is one of the world's leading weightlifters in the super-heavy category. In the late 1990s he regularly won silver and bronze medals in major championships

Sandis Prusis piloted this four-man bob in the 2000 season, reaching second place in the world rankings at one point

The Sigulda luge and bobsled track with its artificial ice is, according to bobsled specialists throughout the world, one of the fastest and safest tracks on the planet

The presidium of Latvia's first congress in chess

Zoja Golubeva has won the world championship in 100-square checkers ten times

Andris Andreiko (1942-1976), twice world champion in 100-square checkers

Rolands Upatnieks (1932-1994) was Latvia's leading trainer in winter sports and himself a world record holder in water motor sports. He was a major driving force behind the construction of the bobsled and luge track at Sigulda

Mikhail Tal (1936-1992), formerly world champion in chess and one of the all-time greats in chess and chess journalism

Dana Reizniece, European youth champion and three times Latvia's champion in chess. In 27 games played in the Latvian championships her record is 22:5:0. Here she is demonstrating the so-called Latvian gambit. Few nations in the world live without their own opening moves on the chessboard. The Latvian gambit is played less often than the Sicilian defense, but the Latvia's opening moves always remind viewers that little Latvia, with its 2.5 million residents, has won many chess events, providing the world with grand masters and champions at all levels. In the early 1990s Latvia was among the world's top 10 chess countries

Orienteering is a popular sport in Latvia, and the Kāpa tournament each year brings together orienteering fans from the Baltic States and the Nordic States for four days of competition Here, from the right, are organizers Maris Blodons and Aivars Prošenkovs, and the world champion in senior orienteering, Dr. Peteris Novikovs

Orienteering is a national sport throughout Northern Europe. Every Wednesday from April until October thousands of Rigensians go out on the track, at the Magnets facility, while in other parts of Latvia there are orienteering events just about every day

Thousands of runners participate in various marathon events in Latvia, but the most popular of all is the Folk Song Marathon which takes place on the Biķernieki auto racing track (with a circumference of 5 kilometers) each fall

Vents Balodis, the Minister of environmental Protection and Regional Development

Environmental protection demands in the world grow increasingly strict from year to year, and all of society must be involved in processes that seek to satisfy these demands.

The right of residents to live in a qualitative environment in Latvia is supported through environmental laws, harmonization of Latvian law with EU directives, and implementation of international obligations which Latvia has undertaken. Full harmonization of Latvian law with the requirements of the EU in the area of environmental protection is scheduled to be completed by 2002, and all of the country's environmental laws will go into effect by 2015, taking into account the fact that many aspects of environmental protection are enormously cost-intensive.

The main institution to elaborate and implement environmental policy in Latvia is the Ministry of Environmental Protection and Regional Development. The Cabinet of Ministers approved an environmental protection policy plan in 1995, and two years later the government approved an action program for environmental protection. High-priority environmental problems in Latvia include overgrown bodies of water, degradation of water-based ecosystems, the inadequate quality of water that is used for human consumption, waste management, the influence of transportation on the environment, transfrontier movement of pollution, environmental risks caused by economic activity, reductions in biological diversity in Latvia, and degradation of landscapes. Latvia receives support from governments and environmental protection organizations in Europe and the rest of the world to deal with these problems, and Latvia itself has become increasingly involved in various international activities. Strategies and programs have been elaborated for various sectors of activity such as waste management, water-related programs and efforts to maintain biological diversity.

Between 1992 and 2000 Latvia invested more than 70 million lats in various environmental protection infrastructure projects. Another 40 million lats has been received in technical aid to harmonize legislation, train specialists and conduct pre-analysis of environmental protection projects. The greatest amounts of money have gone toward improving the country's water management system (43 million lats), and toward managing household waste (14 million lats) and hazardous waste (2.9 million lats). The per capita investment in environmental projects in Latvia has amounted to 20,65 lats.

Latvia has signed the Helsinki Convention which deals with the protection of the Baltic Sea environment. Several projects in water management were implemented at the end of the millennium in Latvia's largest cities – Rīga, Liepāja and Daugavpils. A program to manage water systems in all of Latvia's populated places has been introduced in order to deal with various problems that are caused to residents and to the environment by poor-quality and out-of-date water supply and sewage systems. Today more than 60 local governments are part of this program.

Latvia has developed a hazardous waste management strategy and a household waste management strategy. Each year the country produces between 600,000 and 700,000 tons of household waste. Urban waste is collected from 80% of residents. A national investment program on household waste management has been introduced.

The project to set up a proper system for hazardous waste management was launched in 1995 with the aim of establishing a structure that provides for environmentally safe storage and recycling of hazardous waste. Latvia has already collected agricultural chemicals, mostly pesticides, which were left without an owner, and these have been stored at a hazardous waste facility in Gardene. Liquidation of the chemicals has begun. The plan is to build a permanent storage facility for hazardous waste in Latvia by 2001.

A garbage truck owned by the non-profit limited liability company *Northern Vidzeme Waste Management Organization*

The hazardous waste storage facility in *Gardene*

Collecting hazardous waste

In accordance with the Helsinki Convention, purification systems were built in Riga in the 1990s. The Soviet Union ignored the whole issue of environmental protection, and in 1995 Riga was one of the major polluters of the Baltic Sea. Today, however, fully purified water is introduced into the sea

Water purification systems in Rīga are state-of-the-art

A serious problem: A pond at *Inčukalns* into which Soviet-era factories that produced paints and lacquers dumped sulfuric byproducts. Work is being done to liquidate this ecological hazard

In 1998 there was a serious train crash in the town of *Vecumnieki*, and fuel oil leaked from a number of cisterns. Latvia's fire fighters proved their professionalism in averting an ecological tragedy

Collection of mercury light bulbs

Collection of oil products

A high-pressure pipeline in *Liepāja*

Even in the mid-1990s, sewage water from the city of *Cēsis* was dumped right into the *Gauja* River, but today there are modern purification systems in place

A modern sewage water purification plant sits on the seashore in *Liepāja*

Maintenance of safety systems at the *Ventamonjaks* company

EKOLOGISKAIS NAMINS
izstrādāto
eļļu
uzkrātuve

When a train hit an automobile hear the *Līvbērze* station in *Jelgava* district, eight cisterns of diesel fuel ran off the tracks. There was an enormous fire which required 14 hours to extinguish. The catastrophe caused serious environmental damage

Collection and recycling of hazardous waste such as batteries, pesticides and plastics

The city of *Ventspils* was a major ecological hazard in the late 1980s, but today it is the world's cleanest oil transportation terminal. In this photograph we see a facility which cleans bilge water from ships

Parliamentary speaker Anatolijs Gorbunovs signs the 1992 Rio de Janeiro convention on environmental protection

A meeting of environmental ministers from the Baltic Sea states at the American consulate in St. Petersburg, 1990

Glass that is aimed for recycling programs is collected at *Griziņkalns*

Glass that is collected from household waste is melted down

The scene after a leak of oil from the Butinge (Lithuania) oil processing terminal. The seashore in Kurzeme is often polluted with oil products, which cause enormous damage to water birds. There is always a careful effort to collect injured or killed birds

There have also been minor instances of oil leakage at the Riga, *Liepāja* and *Ventspils* ports. Port administrators monitor such incidents very carefully, seeking to avert any problems. There are heavy fines for those who are guilty of oil spills, and there are intensive clean-up efforts

The collection of oil products at the Riga port

Inese Vaidere, Environmental Protection Fund executive director Valdis Kaprālis, Environmental Protection and Regional Development Minister Vents Balodis and an assistant to the minister, Inita Daņiļeviča, are on the front ranks of environmental protection efforts in Latvia

The board of the Environmental Fund, which is financed with money from the natural resources tax and supports environmentally important projects

Latvia can be proud of its natural beauty – large areas of virtually untouched forest, a pristine shoreline and a low level of pollution. Environmental problems in Latvia are concentrated in major industrial centers, transportation networks and the territories which were left behind by the Russian armed forces.

Latvia has a long-term (25-30 years) environmental protection policy plan which is aimed at preserving the country's biological diversity, as well as Latvia's characteristic and beautiful landscapes. The law *On environmental protection* sets out the main missions for environmental protection – to protect the genetic fund, biotopes and varied landscapes in the country. Specific natural territories that are to be protected are listed in a separate law, which sets out the way in which such territories are specified and safeguarded. An agreement that was concluded between Latvia and the member states of the European Union in 1995 also speaks to cooperation in environmental protection.

Parliament in Latvia has ratified a number of international conventions, including the 1992 Rio de Janeiro convention on biological diversity, the 1971 *Ramsare* convention on wetlands, especially those in which water birds live, the 1975 Bern convention on European nature and habitats, and the Washington convention of 1973 on international trade in endangered animals and plants.

Nature reserves in Latvia are territories which are untouched or little touched by human activity. Latvia has five nature reserves – *Moricsala*

Air pollution is a key issue for Latvia's energy sector. The use of heavy fuel oil, which is environmentally harmful, is being reduced, and natural gas is being used increasingly to produce heat. The smokestacks of major boiler houses have been equipped with air filters

A modern boiler house in *Strenči* with high-quality air filters. The level of air pollution and heat runoff at the facility is in line with the spirit of the Kyoto Convention on reducing heating energy volumes

0   40 km

National Park (NP)
Scientific Reserve (SR)
Biosphere Reserve
Protected Landscape

(1912), *Slītere* (1921), *Grīņi* (1936), *Krustkalni* (1977) and *Teiči* (1982). National parks are large territories which are of national importance for a variety of reasons – landscapes that are pristine or little touched by man, areas of a variety of biotopes, or places with cultural and historical monuments. These are locations in which there is not only environmental protection, but also scientific research, education for groups of visitors, and various leisure activities. The *Gauja* National Park (1973) and the *Ķemeri* National Park (1997) are the country's two national parks. Also in 1997, the Northern Vidzeme Biosphere Reserve was set up.

Latvia also has 22 nature parks, of which the best known are the *Tērvete* Nature Park and the nature park *Daugavas loki* (Rings of *Daugava*). Latvia has some 190 natural monuments, 211 restricted areas, and six regions where landscapes are protected. In the interest of preserving diversity in nature, Latvia seeks to protect wild plants and animals in their natural habitats, as well as in biotopes that have been specifically created for this purpose.

Forests cover much of the territory in Latvia that is under environmental protection. Once land was privatized in the 1990s, many restrictions on logging were lifted, and a comparatively strict regime continues to exist in only 2-3% of the country's forested territories. Specific protection is afforded to more than 90 swamps, or some 12% of Latvia's total swampland. Because meadows are often mowed, strict protection alone does not guarantee the preservation of meadows. In reserves they grow over, but in other kinds of territories their mowing is to be supported and is part of the environmental protection plans of several specific territories. More than 50 lakes are located in restricted areas, and many of them include areas of swampland. Untouched forested islands are found in some of the lakes. Of particular importance are those lakes which are home to freshwater plants of various kinds.

Protection of river valleys, tributaries and riverbeds is implemented largely through restricted areas – nature parks and protective zones around bodies of water. On the seashore and especially in the zone of Latvia's dunes there is a protective regime which applies to the entire Baltic Sea and the Bay of Riga. There are several zones which enjoy special protection. The system cannot, however, handle the increased level of recreational activity on Latvia's beaches.

Latvia is home to 27,443 known species of plants and animals. Of these, 907 (3.3%) are rare and protected. Those species of plants and animals that are in particular danger of extinction are listed in the Latvian *Red Book*.

A great deal of attention is devoted to educating young people about environmental protection in Latvia

People who toss their garbage in random areas are a major problem

The *Janvāri* area of a waste dump in *Talsi*

The nuclear reactor of the Latvian Physics Institute at *Salaspils* was shut down in 1999

Mines from World War II are detonated in the Bay of Riga, 1996

KRUSTKALNI

MORICSALA

Ospery

The *Krustkalni* nature reserve is located in the *Madona* district, covering part of the *Madona-Trepe* bank and the *Dūķi-Svēte* lowlands. The size of the reserve is 2,902 hectares, and it was established in 1977. *Krustkalni* is administratively subordinated to the *Teiči* nature reserve. The territory is crossed by the *Svētupe* river, with its tributary, the *Niedruško* river. The Western edge of the reserve is bounded by the *Nirīte* river. There are 13 lakes on the reserve, the largest of which is *Svēte* Lake. There are also many freshwater streams. The best known among them are the *Krāka* streams on the shores of *Svēte* Lake. The reserve boasts an enormous variety of vegetation. Dominated by pine and fir forests, in places it also has leafy trees, including some wide-leaf varieties. Nearly all of the forest-growth conditions that are present in Latvia can be found in the reserve. Drained forests, dominated by pine trees and swamp birches, cover much of the land. There are few meadows and few swamps as such; mostly there are grassy or crossing swamps. Some 760 different kinds of ferns and blooming plants, as well as some 150 varieties of moss have been specified in the reserve. There is also a large variety of orchids in the reserve – some 17 varieties at all. Mushrooms, algae and lichens in the area have not been studied extensively. Animals in the region are mostly typical of mixed forests in Northern Europe – moles, shrews, beavers, otters, European minks, snipes, jays, etc. All told some 40 species of mammals (representing 70% of Latvia's fauna), 140 species of birds, six different amphibians and five reptiles have been found. There are 21 different species of fish in the waters of the reserve. The 40-50 species of vertebrates are particularly rare, and they require special protection. Some 4,300 invertebrates from 22 orders are known to live in the reserve.

The *Moricsala* nature reserve is located on an island in the *Usma* lake, named after the Saxonian Moritz. Being found in June 6, 1912, it is one of the two eldest in Europe. Foundation of the reserve was initiated by prof. bot. Karl Kupfer. The island was supervised by the Riga Society of Natural Science. It's goal was breeding of rare and endangered species, but it never became true. After World War II cut wood on the island.

In 1910 the reserve covered 83 ha. Today it includes two islands – *Moricsala* (83 ha) and *Lielalksnīte* (33 ha) and the *Liziķerte* bay (702 ha). In *Moricsala* you can find 2/5 of all the Latvian plants, although the collection itself is not a unique one.

SLĪTERE

The *Slītere* nature reserve is located in the *Talsi* district and covers a territory of 15,037 hectares; it was founded in 1921. There are three zones in the reserve – one that is under strict protection, one which is under variable levels of protection, and one which serves as a buffer zone. The reserve features a wide variety of natural conditions. Most of the territory is located along Latvia's seashore lowlands, and some 200 hectares are in the Northern Courland highlands. There are seven territorial natural areas in the reserve. 70% of the territory is forested. The reserve is home to virtually all of the forest types known in Latvia, while some 20% of the territory is covered by swamps. Flora at *Slītere* include some 860 ferns and blooming plants, 128 varieties of mosses, 455 kinds of mushrooms and 195 different kinds of lichens. Several plants that are found in the *Slītere* reserve have not been seen anywhere else in Latvia. There is also a wealth of fauna at the reserve, including 40 species of mammals (including 11 that are endangered) and 130 species of birds. One specific area of the reserve features Latvia's highest known density of nesting pairs – 1,080 pairs of birds per square kilometer. Among the animals at *Slītere* are several extremely rare reptiles, including the European swamp turtle and the glossy snake.
In 1992 the reserve was heavily damaged in a fire which burned some 3,300 hectares of swampland and surrounding areas. Plants in swamps, however, regenerate easily, although in dryland areas around the swamps the process is occurring far more slowly. The *Slītere* nature reserve is open only to specialists and only with the permission of the reserve's administration.

Vilnis Skuja

TEIČI

Established in 1982, the *Teiči* nature reserve covers 18,967 hectares, almost all of it (18,670 hectares) made up of a huge swamp between the *Aiviekste* river and *Lubāna* Lake. The *Teiči* swamp began to form some 10,000 years ago, when a lake appeared in the local lowlands. The lake began to grow over 7,500 to 9,000 years ago. The average depth of the swamp is only 3.5 meters, although in places the depth reaches 9.5 meters. The total area of lakes is 394 hectares, and 16 of the lakes are larger than 5 hectares. There are also several rivers.
The *Teiči* reserve is divided up into three territories, and one-quarter of the total area is under strict protection. Specialists have found 14 lichens, 27 mosses, nine ferns and 141 seed plants in the swamps, as well as pine trees and rare swamp birches. The midget birch, *Betula nana L.*, which is extremely rare, is protected by law. Many kinds of invertebrates and 180 species of birds are found in the region. Among mammals there are wolves, badgers, foxes, forest martens, otters, mink, beavers, shrews, bobtails, etc.

Ospery baby

THE ĶEMERI NATIONAL PARK

Young Black Storks

The Great Heath of *Ķemeri* with hundreds of tiny lakes

The *Ķemeri* National Park was established in 1997 under the auspices of a project developed by the Latvian Nature Fund and the European Natural Heritage Fund (EURONATUR). The park is under State protection and was established in order to protect the complex environmental structure of the area, the valuable cultural and historical monuments, natural spas, the development process of mineral waters and medicinal mud, and to promote a sustainable economy.

The *Ķemeri* National Park takes up part of seven parishes and two towns in three administrative districts of Latvia. Several geological structures come together in the area. The seashore lowlands are bordered by the *Krāči* hills, the *Zaļā* dune and a row of other dunes which mark the shores of the ancient Littorina Sea. As the earth rose in ancient times and the sea receded, lagoon lakes – the *Kaņieris* lake, the *Duņieri* lake and the *Sloka* lake among them – emerged along the seashore. The Ice Age left the Northern Kurzeme plicated hills, the highest of which is the *Milzkalns* hill. At the foot of the hills is the 30 meters deep *Valgums* lake, which boasts of a wealth of fish. The *Ķemeri* or Great Heath features many swampland lakes. As the dolomite bedrock in the area interacts with the swamp water, the result is sulphurous springs that are extensively utilised for curative treatments in the *Ķemeri* spas.

The great biological diversity in the *Ķemeri* National Park occurs because of the variety of biotopes in the region, each with its own society of plants and animals. Nearly all of the plants, which are found in Latvia, can be encountered at the *Ķemeri* National Park, including 25% of the plants, which are in Latvia's *Red Book* of endangered flora.

Among the animals that live in the *Ķemeri* National Park are wolves, moose, wild boar, red deer stags and roe, otters and beavers. Among the birds to nest in the region are the rare and endangered black stork, the common crane, the bittern, the whimbrel, the corncrake, the lesser-spotted eagle, the white-tailed sea eagle, the eagle owl and the nightjar.

The *Kaņieris* lake – part of the *Ramsāre* restricted area

A swamp pine

The *Kalnciems* rock quarry today is popular place for recreation. Socialdemocratic political prisoners worked here in 1930's

Sulphur ponds. Thanks to the mild climate and sulphurous water, Ķemeri has been popular place for recreation and treatment for three centuries, a favorite place of tsars of Russia an Prussia

The sundew – a plant that eats insects

The beach at *Lapmežciems*

Blossoming heather

Young wasp buzzards

The information centre and administrative building of the National Park, which can be reached at *Meža māja, Jūrmala*, LV-2012, Latvia

Forest on fire

Mute swans on the wintertime seashore

The Orthodox Church of St. Peter and St. Paul in the *Ķemeri* Park

The *Ķemeri* sanatorium

National Park director, Andris Liepa

The *Ķūķu* rock

The *Gauja* National Park provides facilities for etnography, nature protection and leisure activities. Every year a baloon festival is organized in capital city of the park, *Sigulda*. Talis Puķītis, the Mayor and Jānis Strautmanis, his deputy take care of the balance between this and other recreation events and the ecology.

Nowhere else in Latvia are there so many precipices, ravines, streams, sandstone cliffs and caves in one place than is the case in the ancient valley of the *Gauja* River and its tributaries. In order to protect this unique spot of nature, the *Gauja* National Park was established on September 14, 1973. It covers 92,048 hectares of territory, including the *Gauja* River valley, which reaches a depth of 85 meters in the park itself and has a width that ranges between one and 2.5 kilometers. The sandstone of the *Gauja* valley dates back to some 370 or 380 million years ago, during the Devonian era of geology. Nearly one-half of the *Gauja* National Park is covered with forest, mostly pine trees and fir. There are also large tracts of oak, aspen and elm. A wealth of flora and fauna is found in the large Suda swamp with its many lakes and ponds.

The *Gauja* National Park is extremely varied in terms of its biological elements. Specialists have identified 876 types of vascular plants. In some cases, the park provides Latvia's only habitat for a certain kind of plant. The *Gauja* National Park provides nesting grounds for eagle-owls, nuthatches, black storks and white-backed woodpeckers. There are also significant populations of otters and beavers in the park.

Many of the valley's caves are important wintering spots for bats. *Gauja* and its tributaries are one of the few remaining spots in the Baltic region with natural spawning grounds for lampreys and various salmon-like fish.

There are many cultural and historical monuments in the *Gauja* National Park – ancient castle mounds, graveyards and cult facilities. There are palaces built by conquerors, churches and baronial estates. There are vivid examples of national construction styles, artistic monuments and testaments to the region's history – more than 500 culturally and historically significant objects in all.

The residents of the *Gauja* National Valley have traditionally been specialists at various trades – rafters, chair-makers, beekeepers, pottery-makers, weavers, and producers of canes and barrel hoops. These ancient crafts are an important part of the region's cultural history.

The ancient *Gauja* valley and its surroundings are a popular tourism spot. The area around the town of *Sigulda* is known as the Switzerland of Vidzeme. There are various recreational facilities in the valley – at *Līgatne*, in *Āraiši*, on the shores of the *Amata* River, and near the *Sietiņiezis* rock. There are camping grounds and water tourism facilities. Many people have come to love the *Gauja*, the *Brasla* and the *Amata*.

A threshing barn at the *Rožkalni* homestead of *Raiskums* parish

Preparing dough for bread

A continuous cement bridge built in 1937 by the architect Karlis Gailis, crossing the *Gauja* River at *Sigulda*

A river-crossing facility at *Līgatne*

The *Raganu katls* (Witch's Pot) valley

The *Gūtmaņa* cave

The *Kraukļi* gorge

National Park director Janis Strautnieks   The *Auciems* saloon

A ceiling painting at the *Ungurmuiža* estate

The *Ungurmuiža* estate

The *Lysichinon kamtchatica*

The *Daugava* or snow-drop anemone (*Anemone sylvestris*)

The small yellow lady's-slipper (*Cypripedium claceolus*), part of the National Botanical Gardens' collection of rare and threatened plants

The pasqueflower (*Pulsatilla*), part of the National Botanical Gardens' collection of rare and threatened plant

The National Botanical Gardens in Latvia date back to the activities of a gardening company run by Kristen Wilhelm Schoch, which began work in the town of *Salaspils* in 1898. Wilhelm Behr ran the company until 1918, and then its owner became Pēteris Balodis. He had worked in the company previously and ran it until 1944. The Botanical Gardens as such were established in 1965, and in 1992, they were given the status of National Botanical Gardens.

The primary function of the gardens is to establish, identify and classify the collection of plants. The expositions and collections of the gardens are of decorative, botanical, economic and educational importance. The gardens have 15,000 different species, sub-species, varieties and forms of plants, and this makes the gardens one of the largest dendrological sites in the Baltic area. The gardens cover 129 hectares, and 60% of the territory is taken up with permanent plant expositions. The National Botanical Gardens work to introduce and acclimatise new plants and to develop new varieties of plants. The gardens have established a scientifically controlled genetic fund of local and foreign plants. The formation of various collections and expositions, the cultivation of Latvia's rare or threatened plants, as well as dendrological research, development of methods for improving the vegetative and generative aspects of plants and other work is carried out. In the photograph above, the staff of the National Botanical Gardens with director Kārlis Buivids in the middle of the front row.

The astilbe (*Astilbe*)

The large-berry cranberry (*Oxycoccus macrocarpus*)

The virgin's bower (*Clematis Minister*)

A promising hybrid of loganberries

The common sea buckthorn (*Hippophae rhamnoides*)

The gardens' collection of succulents has been formed since 1957, and it contains more than 1,500 varieties of plants and decorative forms

The *Actinidia polygama*

The gardens' collection of grasses has more than 550 varieties of grasses. The National Botanical Garden plants and restores grassy areas all over Latvia, including seeding of areas, as well as laying down turf

The gardens' collection of Gerbera (*Gerbera jamesnii*) has 150 different varieties, including 32 that were developed locally

The gardens' collection of coniferous trees has 600 varieties and decorative forms

A selection of Chinese asters (*Callistephus chinesis*)

Bladderwort (*Utricularia*)

Lesser Butterfly Orchid (*Platanthera bifolia L.*)

Ferns (*Filicales*)

Snowdrop Anemone (*Anemone sylvestris L.*)

Forest Lilacs (*Syringa L.*)

Cornflag (*Gladiolus imbricatus L.*)

Cross-Leafed Heath (*Erica tetralix L.*)

Iris Siberian (*Iris sibirica L.*)

Spreading Pasqueflower (*Pulsatlla patens (L.) Mill.*)

Myrtle (*Myrica gale L.*)

Violets (*Viola L.*)

Lady's Slipper (*Cypripedium calseolus L.*)

Interrupted Club-Moss (*Lycopodium annotinum L.*)

Horsetail (*Equisetum telmateia Ehrh.*)

Yellow Foxglove (*Digitalis grandiflora Mill.*)

Swordflag (*Iris L.*)

Wild Orchid (*Dactylorhiza baltica (Klinge) Orlova*)

Willows with Mistletoe (*Viscum album L.*)

Daphne (*Daphne mezereum L.*)

Columbine (*Aquilegia L.*)

MAMMALS

Northern bat (*Eplesicus nilssoni*)

Elk (*Alces alces*)

Arctic hare (*Lepus timidus*)

RĪGA ZOO

Kiangs herding in *Liepāja* district

Riga Zoo is one of the most remarkable cultural entertainments in Riga. It was founded on the 18th of October 1914 as the first zoo in north Europe.

Riga Zoo is now a member of the Association of European Zoos and Aquariums. Many animal dwellings, which were in bad condition during the Soviet years have been rebuilt. They are now suited to the needs of animals and convenient to the visitors.

Riga Zoo covers an area of 16.4 hectares. There are more than 400 species in the collection, 115 species of mammals, more than 100 species of birds, about 100 species of amphibians and reptiles. There are 2200 animals in Riga Zoo.

Riga Zoo specializes in preservation of nature; more than 40 species found in the zoo are in the *Red Book* of the world, the *Prjevalska* horses, which are no longer found in the wild. Tree frog has been reintroduced in Latvia under the supervision of Ronalds Greiziņš, the director of Riga Zoo. A branch was opened in *Kalvene* parish, *Liepāja* district, were *kiangs*, *Prjevalska* horses, brown bears, and other rare animals are bred in natural habitat.

The mammal fauna of Latvia started to develop after the glaciers retreated about 10 –12 thousand years ago. Species abundant in the whole of Palaeoartic (the largest part of Eurasia), e.g. wolfs, common foxes, badgers, weasels, as well as the mixed species of western Paleoarctic, e.g. common mole, common shrew, red squirrel spread evenly in Latvia. Elements of taiga fauna – arctic hare, lynx, and flying squirrel now on the verge of extinction are more common in the northeastern part of the state. The density of species of European broad-leave forest populations (polecat, pine marten, roe deer) and those of steppe (common vole, brown hare) is greater in the southern part of Latvia. The differences of regional faunas decreased as time passed and human activities increased.

69 species are registered in Latvia today, more than 62 of which live and bread permanently in the territory of the state. We are hoping to find 5 – 6 more species in Latvia, because judging from information of their spread in neighboring countries there are reasons to believe that their areas cross the borders of our state. The last extinct species in Latvia are considered to be harbor porpoise (*Phocaena phocaena*), which was still found in Riga Bay and along the coast of the Baltic Sea in the beginning of the XX century and European mink (*Mustela lutroela*), which has not been reported only in the last few years. There are three species newly introduced to Latvian fauna: raccoon dog (in the wild since 1948, incomer since 1943), American mink (*Mustela vison* – introduced by fur-animal farms, and immigrated from neighboring countries, reported in wild for the first time in 1944), and muskrat (*Ondatra zibethica*; immigrated in 60's from Belorussia, Lithuania, and Estonia, where it had lived for a longer time – since 1953, 1954, and 1948 respectively). The large number of beavers (reintroduced in Latvia in 1927), otters, wolves, and lynx is not characteristic for the rest of Europe and is a peculiarity of Latvia.

27 species have been protected by the law since 12 year ago. There are 17 mammal species of game.

The most notable researcher of Latvian fauna was Edgars Tauriņš (1907 – 1989), who wrote the book *Latvijas Zīdītājdzīvnieki* (Latvian Mammals) in 1982. The Terriological Society of Latvia was founded in 1996 in order to bring closer the work of mammal researchers and individuals interested in it.

Wild boar (*Sus scrofa*) with piglets

Remarkable Baltic zoologists: professor Erik Kumari (1912 – 1984) from Estonia, assistant professor Egons Tauriņš (1907 – 1989), and Kārlis Vilks (1900 – 1993)

Red deer (*Cervus elaphus*)

Badger (*Meles meles*)

Grey seal (*Halichoerus grypus*)

Otter (*Lutra lutra*)

Common fox (*Vulpes vulpes*)

Common shrew (*Dryomys nitedula*)

Pine marten (*Martes martes*)

Racoon dog (*Nyctereutes procyonoides*)

Beaver (*Castor fiber*)

Brown bear (*Ursus arclos*)

Lynx (*Lynx lynx*)

Wolf (*Canis lupus*)

Roe deer (*Capreolus capreolus*)

The dragonfly (*Odonata*)

The caddisfly (*Trichoptera*)

The European earwig
(*Forficula auricularia*)

The cockroach (*Ectobius sp.*)

Men who was active in the establishment
of post-war zoology in Latvia was Zandis
Spuris (1923-1998), who focused on
dragonflies

The locust (*Acrididae*)

The stink bug (*Graphosoma lineatum*)

An aphid (*Aphidodea*)

The green lacewing (*Chrysopa*)

The large red leaf-cutting beetle
(*Melasoma populi*)

The leaf-cutting beetle
(*Cryptocephalus sp.*)

The golden rose beetle
(*Cetonia aurata*)

The ichneumon-fly (*Ichneumonidae*)

Olga Kračalova (1916-1988), Antonija
Kumsare (1902-1982) and Ruta
Laganovska (1927-1995) were all
prominent insect and plankton
researchers in Latvia

A female *Leptura melanura*

The June beetle (*Rhizotrogus solstitialis*)

The *Sinodendron cylindricum*

The ground beetle (*Carabus nemoralis*)

Bruno Bērziņš (1909 - 1985), Professor
of the Latvian University and the
University of Lund, one of the distinguished zoologists is known for his studies in ornithology and entomology

The click beetle (*Ampedus sp.*)

The robber fly (*Asilidae*)

The bee (*Apoidea*)

A female *Leptura melanura*

The poplar hornet clearwing
(*Sesia apiformis*)

The *Plebejus sp.* butterfly

The noctuid moth (*Deltote bankiana*)

The comma butterfly (*Polygonia c-album*)

The mosquito
(*Culicidae*)

The *Euphydryas maturna* butterfly

Spanworm's moth
(*Perizoma parallelolineata*)

The *Limenitis camilla* butterfly. The species
is included in the Latvian *Red Book*

The heath fritillary butterfly
(*Meltitaea athalia*)

The cocoon of a small
tortoiseshell butterfly
(*Aglais urticae*)

The caterpillar
of a gray farfalla
moth (*Saturnia
pavonia*)

Osprey (*Pandion haliaetus*)

Lapwing (*Vanellus vanellus*)

Great Crested Grebe (*Podiceps cristatus*)

The founder of Latvian Center of Ornithology, Nikolai von Transehe (1886-1969) together with Reinis Sinats published the book *Latvijas putni* in 1936

Teal (*Anas crecca*)

Latvia is in a location where many climate zones meet, therefore Nordic species like Crane, Arctic Tern, Ural Owl, Great Snipe, Parrot Crossbill, Dipper, southern species like, Penduline Tit, Roller, Hoopoe, as well as eastern species like Citrine Wagtail, White-winged Black Tern, and Marsh Sandpiper are found here.

More than 50 million birds of 300 species nest, pass through, or spend winter in Latvia.

One of the four most important tracks of bird migration cross Latvia, therefore many species are more abundant here than one might expect. There are many important places of resting in Latvia of many species of geese, swans, and waders, as well as cranes, and thousands of birds can be seen together in springs and falls in these places. More than 20 thousand such places have been identified with the help of the international organization of birds' protection, *BirdLife International*. There are more than 60 important birds areas in Latvia. Their protection is one of the key functions of the Latvian Ornithological Society for the present moment and the nearest future.

Most of these sites are marshland areas: shallow overgrown coastal lakes, large raised bogs, and floodplains of rivers. The sites are also the key areas for nesting of many species. Many species endangered in Europe have remained in great numbers in Latvia: about 2400 pairs (13% of the total population) of Lesser Spotted Eagles nest in Latvia, 750 – 900 couples of Black Storks, more than 30 thousand pairs of Corncrakes, and others. Many species are abundant here in winter, which nest elsewhere. More than half a million Long-tailed Ducks spend the winter in Riga Bay.

There are also large populations of resident species in Latvia, mostly in the forests: more than 2000 pairs of white-backed Woodpeckers, a similar number of Three-toed Woodpeckers, a large number of Black Woodpeckers, and other.

Cranes (*Grus grus*)

Penduline Tit (*Remiz pendulinus*)

Common Whitethroat (*Sylvia communis*)

Whooper Swan (*Cygnus cygnus*)

Coastal lakes and other marshland areas are important not only for resting while migrating, but also for nesting of many waterfowl – Grebes, Grey Heron, and different sorts of ducks. Ducks gladly nest in the protection of gulls

Arctic Tern (*Sterna paradisaea*)
The species nesting in Latvia spend the winter everywhere from west Europe (Lapwing) to South Africa and the Antarctic coast (Arctic Tern)

Grey Heron (*Ardea cinerea*)

Little Gull (*Larus minutus*)

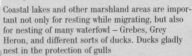

A colony of Black-headed Gulls (*Larus ridibundus*)

Many species of birds became very rare during 50's to 70's due to human activities (degradation of biotopes, thoughtless agricultural policy). Less than 1% of the former Latvian population of rollers has remained; hoopoe is also very rare

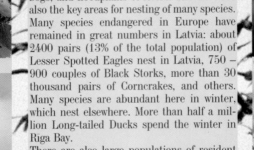

Roller (*Coracias garrulus*)

Citrine Wagtail (*Motacilla flava*)

Kestrel (*Falco tinnunculus*)

Hoopoe (*Upupa epops*)

Latvian bird rings have an inscription *Latvia Riga*. The rings are developed in the Ornithological laboratories of the Institute of Biology; they have a plasticine inline and may be used for ringing of new-hatched ducklings, giving wider possibilities of bird research. The veteran researcher in Ornithological Laboratory of Science Academy Pēteris Blūms manages the introduction of the method in North America

Harold von Laudon (1876 – 1951) is one of the most famous ornithologists and collectors of biological material in the Baltic States

White-winged Black Tern (*Chlidonias leucopterus*)

Several exotic species nest in Latvia – Citrine Wagtail (*Motacilla flava*), Marsh Sandpiper (*Tringa stagnatilis*), and White-winged Black Tern (*Chlidonias leucopterus*), which are not found in the rest of Europe or nest there very rare

Black Stork (*Ciconia nigra*). Some of the species endangered on world or European scale, which nest in Latvia in great numbers are Black stork, Lesser Spotted Eagle, Corncrake, White-backed Woodpecker, and Great Snipe

The king of Sweden is interested in ornithology and supports bird protection. He expressed the desire to see the nesting sites of Black Storks during his visit in Latvia. Unfortunately the visit took place in time when the young ones had left the nests already and the older birds did not stay in the nests because of all the security personnel hiding in the woods and the large escort of the king. The director of the Ornithological Society Māris Strazds is showing a nest of the Black Stork in the National Park of *Ķemeri*

Lesser Spotted Eagle (*Aquila pomarina*)

Swedish eco-tourists are watching a Spotted Eagle in the National Park of *Ķemeri*.
A continual flow of eco-tourists enters Latvia from different European states to see for themselves life of rare and protected birds and animals. Many of the best nature photographers come here to *photo-hunt*

Goosanders (*Mergus menganser*) in winter

Long-tailed Duck (*Clangula hemalis*)

Parrot Crossbill (*Loxia pytyopsittacus*)

White-backed Woodpecker (*Dendrocopus leucotos*)

Jay (*Garrulus glandarius*)

Black Woodpecker (*Dryocopus martins*)

Yellowhammer (*Emberizidae citrinella*)

Pied Wagtail (*Motacilla alba*) is the national bird of Latvia, it is abundant and well known by the people. Pied wagtail is on the logo of the Ornithological Society

Tree Sparrow (*Passer montanus*)

Collared Dove (*Streptopelia decaocto*)

Black grouse (*Tetrao tetrix*) on lek

Corncrake (*Crex crex*)

Great Snipe (*Gallinago media*)

Goldeneye (*Bucephala clangula*)

Approbation of the artificial nesting sites for mallards successfully used in America

Harijs Mihelsons (1930 – 1981) researched ecology of mallards and hole-nesters populations

A mixed couple of a Grey Heron and a Great White Heron tending the young ones near *Engure* Lake in 1997

The first orrery in the world, built specially for researching bird migration, is built by LU Institute of Biology in *Rauda* perish, *Tukums* county

Ornithological coop (*Pape* parish, *Liepāja* county) allows to catch up to 54 000 birds and 4000 bats in one season. Up to 200 long-eared owls are caught in one night

Professor Jānis Vīksne, the director of the Ornithological Laboratory of LU Institute of Biology, has researcher ecology of Black-headed gull population

The boathouse station owned by the Ornithological Laboratory of the LU Institute of Biology in *Engure* Lake is one of the three sites of Ramsare convention. Stationary researches of ecologies of bird populations have been conducted here since 1958. The researches have been conducted together with scientists from USA, Sweden, France, and other countries since 1991

Latvia's forests have emerged over the course of the last 12,000 years. If initially the dominant flora were dryads, i.e., creeping dwarf shrubs of the rose family, as well as dwarf birches, then over the course of the centuries various kinds of trees began to appear, and eventually dominance was taken over by the birch tree. Latvia's climate became warmer in the period between 7,000 and 9,000 years ago. Pine trees appeared, and vast stands of broadleaf trees and broadleaf fir trees developed, reaching their apogee five or six thousand years ago. Increased precipitation levels improved the ability of fir trees to grow. Three or four thousand years ago the area of oak tree forests was halved, and the fir tree represented between 30% and 40% of all forest growth. During the last three millennia the climate has once again turned drier, and the presence of the fir tree in Latvia's forests has declined again, while the number of pine trees has increased. Between the 15th and 19th century, the climate was relatively cool, and the significance of broadleaf trees in Latvia's vegetation all but collapsed. Agricultural work over the course of many centuries had led to serious soil erosion and deterioration, and because people commonly harvested oak trees for building purposes, the spread of broadleaf trees and associated flora and fauna diminished.

Vegetation in the 19th and 20th century was significantly affected by economic processes. Vast broadleaf and fir forests in Latvia are all but gone, and only fragments of their former glory remain. Only in a few parts of Latvia do oak or elm trees proliferate. Around *Kuprava*, *Žiguri* and the *Balvi* district linden trees are dominant, while in Southwestern Latvia one often sees the ordinary hornbeam.

Approximately one-half of Latvia's forest consists of pine trees, and the greatest stands grow in the sands of the Baltic Sea shore, as well as farther inland. In terms of their composition and phytocoenotic character, these are forests reminiscent of the Southern taiga, with growths of boysenberries, blackberries, blueberries, marsh tea, moss and other plants on the forest floor.

The main pioneering species of tree in Latvia is the birch, and as natural forests are restored, it has become the dominant tree in between 40 and 80% of areas which had previously been lost to harvesting, wind storms or fires. The aspen has become less common in secondary forest growths, while the black alder has become more common, especially in fallow land and on grazing pastures.

Without human interference, basic tree species reappear in secondary forests only over the course of a long period of time, and less than fully valuable growths are common. A lot of work is being done in Latvia to plant large areas of pine and fir, and targeted harvesting of trees is done in order to improve the quality of forested areas.

Forests along the seashore are of major importance in reducing damage caused by wind, especially in the sense of erosion. They are also appropriate for research into the structure and evaluation of natural and anthropogenic forests, and that is precisely why the *Slītere*, *Griņi* and *Moricsala* nature reserves are there.

A different kind of forest exists in the lowlands of Eastern Latvia. 40% of the trees in these forests are pine trees, but there are many more firs and birch trees. In the *Aiviekste* and *Pededze* valleys, fragments of once-vast stands of oak trees survive. The Vidzeme heights and the *Gauja* lowland are rich in forests – pines, firs and, less commonly, birches. There are fewer forests in Latvia's four major highlands and in the Zemgale flatlands – the latter territory having been used for agriculture since time immemorial. Where broadleaf forests once stood, there is now farmland, although stands of birches and white alders serve to brighten up the landscape and to protect the earth against wind erosion. Currently forests cover approximately 40% of Latvia's territory – some 28,000 square kilometers in all.

Forests in Latvia are classified on the basis of the fertility of the earth and the structure of moisture in the area. More than one-half of the total territory of forest in Latvia is made up of dry-land forests which are valuable and easy to manage. Mineral nourishment for trees and other plants contributes to highly productive stands of various kinds of trees. Latvian specialists classify dry forests into various country-specific types – the *sils*, the *mētrājs*, the *lāns*, the *damaksnis*, the *vēris* and the *gārša*.

BALTIC SEA

RIGA GULF

ESTONIA

RUSSIA

LITHUANIA

BELORUS

Senior forest ranger
Arnis Melnis

The *sils* is a forest that grows on relatively infertile quartz sand, with a shallow active stratum in the earth. Scrappy pines grow in the *sils*, fir trees do poorly, and the ground cover is rich in heather and lichen.

The *mētrājs* is a forest which grows on poorly fertile sandy soil, with a shallow active stratum. There are both pines and fir trees in these forests, with whortleberry, grasses and moss on the ground.

The *lāns* grows on sand with a low mud content. There may be a sub-stratum of clay. Firs and pines are found here, and the ground cover is of blackberry, eagle ferns and grasses. At the second level we find moss.

The *damaksnis* has various types of soil of mechanical content with a high mud content. Pine and fir grow here, with blackberries, broadleaf plants and green mosses on the ground.

Vēri grow on clay that is well aerated and acidic, with no carbonates in the topsoil. Healthy stands of fir are found here, and the ground is covered with sorrel, blackberry and grasses. Grasses quickly cover any areas in which the trees are chopped down.

The *gārša* grows on clay and sand with a high mud content with carbonates in the topsoil. Hardwood trees and firs grow here for the most part, and the ground is covered with broadleaf plants which cover up any empty areas. The basic species of tree in the *sils*, *mētrājs* and *lāns* is pine. The fir tree can compete in the *damaksnis*, and sometimes there are *damaksnis*-type forests with only firs. The *vēris*, however, is the most appropriate type of forest for fir, and the largest amounts of fir wood can be harvested there.

The *gārša* is an interesting type of forest, because mineral nutrition and intensive decomposition of organic substances are present. The *gārša* over the course of time has become a forest of hardwood trees – oak, elm, maple and other trees.

Latvia also has interesting wet forests, where swamps emerge during damp climactic periods and recede when conditions are dryer. The air, plant and water regime in such areas is unstable, and if conditions are present for a long period of time, it takes radical shifts in the environment for the conditions to move in one direction of the other. Swamps usually take over fields and areas where trees have been harvested when the process begins. There are very few untouched areas of wet forest in Latvia. Nearly everywhere we see ditches and efforts to regulate river flows. During Soviet years, there was very careful reclamation of wet forests, but because the men who did the work were paid for quantity, not quality, nearly three-quarters of the reclamation ditches that were dug in the 1980's were non-functional. This has led to the preservation of wet forests in Latvia, because ecosystems were allowed to develop naturally.

The types of wet forests in Latvia are the wet *grīnis*, *mētrājs*, *damaksnis*, *vēris* and *gārša*.

The wet *grīnis* has infertile and degraded soil, often with an iron pan. Pine trees grow there, but there are few or no lower trees in these areas. The ground is covered with heather, moss and sphagnum.

The wet *mētrājs* grows on poorly fertile sand. Fir grows at the upper level, but lower levels are sparse. Blueberries, heather, mosses, sphagnum and other plants are found on the ground.

The wet *damaksnis* has sand which is of average fertility, sometimes containing a stratum of clay. There are pines and fir on the second level and buckthorn at the lower level, with berry bushes, couch-grass and other plants on the ground.

The wet *vēris* has sand and clay in the ground of average fertility. there are firs, with buckthorn and osier at the lower level and blackberries, couch-grass and sedge on the ground.

The wet *gārša* has fertile soil of various mechanical content and carbonates in the topsoil.

Beavers were reintroduced in Latvia in 1930's, after being completely wiped in the beginning of the 19th century. Their numbers have increased now, their dams provide water supply for forests, but flood the lower areas

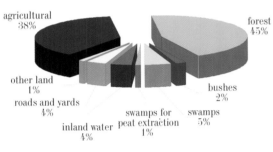

agricultural 38%
forest 45%
other land 1%
bushes 2%
roads and yards 4%
swamps for peat extraction 1%
swamps 5%
inland water 4%

Land use in Latvia
Agricultural land 38%, other land, roads and yards, domestic waters, swamps for peat extraction, swamps, bushes, forest

A tower of fire lookout

A view over *Mežole* forests from fire lookout

The reintroduced beavers also cause damage to the forests

President Guntis Ulmanis helps with forest restoration

The deputy state secretary of the Ministry of Agriculture, Arvids Ozols

There are firs and elms, many kinds of bushes and broadleaf plants and ferns on the ground.

A third group of forests in Latvia consists of swamp forests, where peat mosses are deep and the roots of trees do not reach the mineral soil below. The critical boundary is usually at a depth of 30 centimeters. Groundwater levels in swamp forests are high, and sometimes there is flooding. The water regularly floods the root horizon of trees. When the climate is in a dry period, the process of swamp development slows down, but swamps never recede. Tree growth is poor. In terms of the potential for tree growth, swamp forests are divided up into *purvājs*, *niedrājs*, *dumbrājs* and *liekņa*.

The *purvājs* has a wet and infertile stratum of pine and cotton-grass sphagnum peat, often with burning horizons. There are sparse growths of pine, small fir trees and swamp birches. Heather is on the ground, but there are few other plants.

The *niedrājs* has a wet level of wood and sedge peat with sphagnum in the topsoil. There are pines and swamp birches, with sickly fir trees at the second level. Buckthorn, juniper and low birches are present at the lower level, with sedge, reeds, ferns, mosses and sphagnum on the ground.

The *dumbrājs* has a wet and potentially fertile soil containing sedge, wood and peat moss. Swamp birch and the black alder are found here, with a second level of fir and a lower level of buckthorn and osier. Wet growth broadleaf plants, sedge and ferns are found on the ground.

The *liekņa* has a fertile and nutrient-rich soil, and birch and black alder peat moss is present because of the effect of groundwater. There are large and beautiful black alders, along with less common birches and elm. Underneath there are buckthorn, osier and various bushes.

Drained forests are also common in Latvia. Drainage and reclamation are processes with which Latvia has a great deal of experience. Moss swamps and bogs are not drained during forest reclamation and are left alone. Drainage is prohibited in approximately one-third of Latvia's swamps at this time. The size of preserved swamp forests and swamps is adequate, and correctly done drainage of forests usually does not have any serious effect on the water regime of these territories.

There are two kinds of drained forest ecosystems – *āreņi* and *kūdreņi*.

Āreņi are drained wet forests in which the stratum of peat is not deeper than 20 centimeters. A heather *ārenis* has an infertile level of sand, and the topsoil is acidic. After intensive drainage, the soil which is uncovered is tilled before forest planting. Pines do well on such land. There is little growth at the lower level, and heather covers the ground.

A bilberry *ārenis* has relatively infertile sand soil, often with a stratum of rust. Fine pine trees grow here, as do fir trees at the second level. Sparse juniper and osier are found down below.

The narrowleaf *ārenis* has clay and sand in the soil. The topsoil has extremely nutritious humus. There are large and beautiful pine trees and fir trees, as well as birch trees in such areas. Below there is osier, along with blackberries, couchgrass, ferns and green mosses.

The broadleaf *ārenis* has soil with various mechanical content. Fir grows very well here, along with softwood deciduous trees and osier, blackberries and ferns down below.

Kūdreņi are drained swamp forests with a peat depth of more than 20 centimeters. Tree roots do not reach the mineral soil, but the depth of the peat stratum does not affect the productivity of trees.

A heather *kūdrenis* has an infertile and highly acidic level of peat. Pine is of average quality here, and one also finds swamp birch. There are few other plants.

A bilberry *kūdrenis* has peat that is of average fertility and acidity . Fine pine trees grow here, with occasional fir trees in the mix. Swamp birch is found in those *kūdreņi* which are left wild, and osier and juniper grow on the ground.

The narrowleaf *kūdrenis* is home to very productive pine and fir tree stands, with birch present in wild forests. The broadleaf *kūdrenis*, by contrast, has a very fertile and nutrient-rich stratum of sedge and wood peat, and with rational management one can grow very productive stands of fir there. The undergrowth in these fir forests is scant, while under deciduous trees it can be fairly thick. Many eutrophic species of shrub are found.

Latvia's forest placement is closely linked to the geological and morphological structure of the country's various territories, as well as with the activities of mankind over the millennia in clearing fields, pastures and meadows. The largest territories of untouched forest are found in soil which is infertile and wet and is therefore not appropriate for agriculture. More fertile areas and well-drained territories have long since lost their forest cover and have been transformed into pastures and meadows.

Agriculture was first brought to dry and high areas, and then lower areas were cleared, too. Once soil was used up, the forest reclaimed it. Many rural homesteads and villages in Latvia have been destroyed by war and epidemics over the centuries, and in remote areas of forest where there are no signs of settlement, one can sometimes see evidence that pastures and other clearances were once present. People who lived in the forest always sought out the most fertile areas of land for their fields and the most highly productive lowlands and forest meadows to grow hay. Fields and meadows which are located far from villages, roads and electricity lines are no longer appropriate for mechanized agriculture or livestock breeding, and the forest is reclaiming such territories. In places where trees are not planted in a purposeful way, the land is fallow and birch, white alder and shrubs take over. That is why poor quality trees and bushes became so very common in Latvia in the late 1980's and early 1990's.

THE KALSNAVA ARBORETUM

The *Kalsnava* Arboretum in *Madona* district boasts one of the largest scientific collections of trees and bushes in the Baltic States. It was opened in 1975, and over the course of time, some 2,200 taxa were planted, and long-term scientific research is done.

THE TREE PLANTATION

The tree plantation is a special area in *Kalsnava* where trees, bushes and other plants are grown. The facility grows forest trees, fruit trees and decorative trees alike. Plants in the tree plantation are grown both from seeds (the generative process) and from shoots (the vegetative process) – layering, cuttings, grafting and meristem cultures. Plants are grown both with covered and uncovered root systems. The facility can provide all sizes of plants, from very small to very large – various methods of planting are available.

A display of low-growing decorative plants at the *Kalsnava* facility

THE SC LATVIJAS FINIERIS AND ITS TREE PLANTATION

The stock company SC *Latvijas Finieris* (or Latvian Plywood) has actively participated in the renewal of Latvia's forest resources since 1996, both through working on forestry selection and on providing financing for the process. The company set up its own tree plantation in 1998 and 1999. The company also works with the *Kalsnava* plantation. Together with the Latvian Cultural Fund, SC *Latvijas Finieris* provides support on a competitive basis to farmers who want to plant forest trees on their unused agricultural lands.

Plants grown by SC *Latvijas Finieris*

The view from the *Kalsnava* Arboretum – in the background (15 kilometres in a direct line) is Latvia's highest hill – *Gaiziņkalns*

Each year this Virginia snowflake tree blossoms to great beauty at *Kalsnava*

A container of black alders – ready for planting

The *Kalsnava* Arboretum has one of the most complete collections of fir trees in the world

The *Kalsnava* forest plantation

Decorative mountain pine trees

Modern technologies to grow forest plants are used at *Kalsnava*

Oast house in *Kalsnava*

The directors of the stock company SC *Latvijas Finieris*

A plantation run by SC *Latvijas Finieris*

A birch tree ready for planting

The hothouses of SC *Latvijas Finieris*

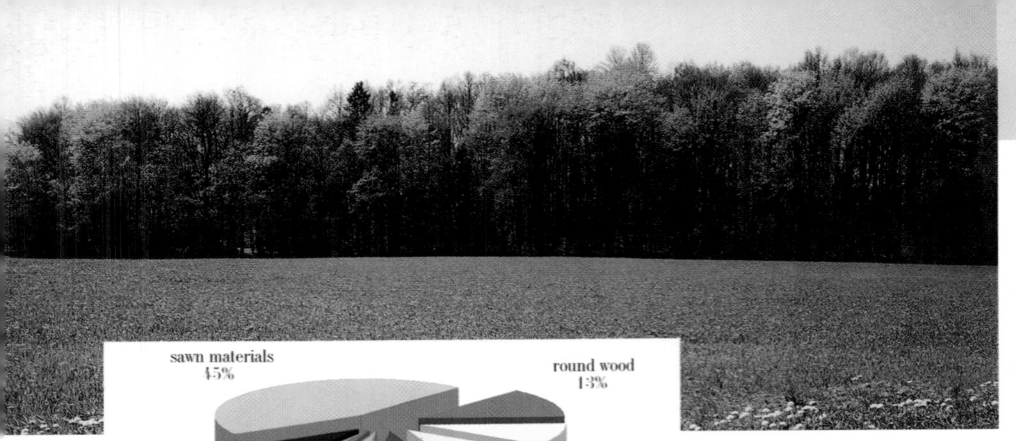

FORESTRY POLITICS IN LATVIA

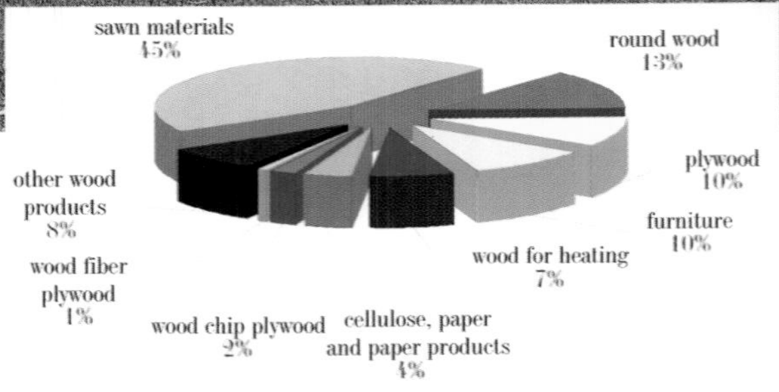
sawn materials
45%
round wood
13%
plywood
10%
furniture
10%
wood for heating
7%
cellulose, paper
and paper products
4%
wood chip plywood
2%
wood fiber
plywood
1%
other wood
products
8%

The export structure of wood in Latvia

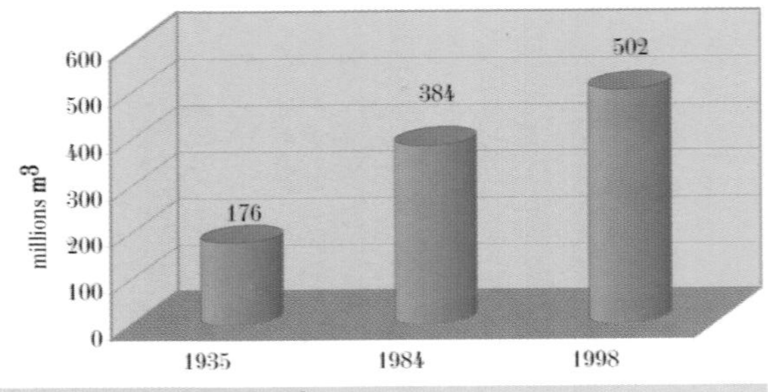
600
500
400
300
200
100
0
millions m3
176
384
502
1935
1984
1998

Total forest growth, million m^3

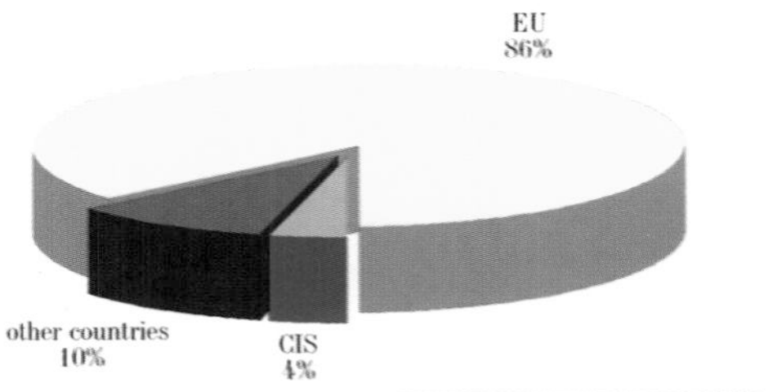
EU
86%
other countries
10%
CIS
4%

Export by country – EU, CIS, other countries

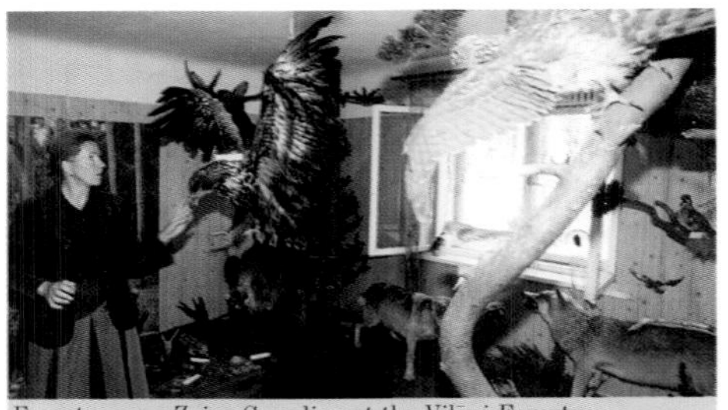

Forest ranger Zaiga Graudiņa at the Viļani Forestry Industry Museum

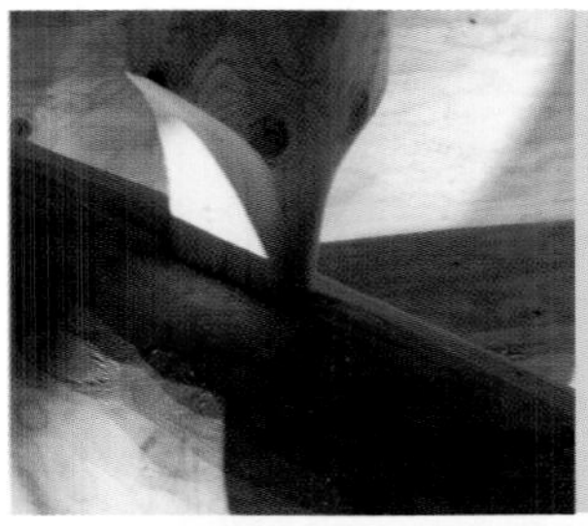

Wood has returned to construction sites after the period of 50 years of Soviet occupation, when it was completely replaced by concrete

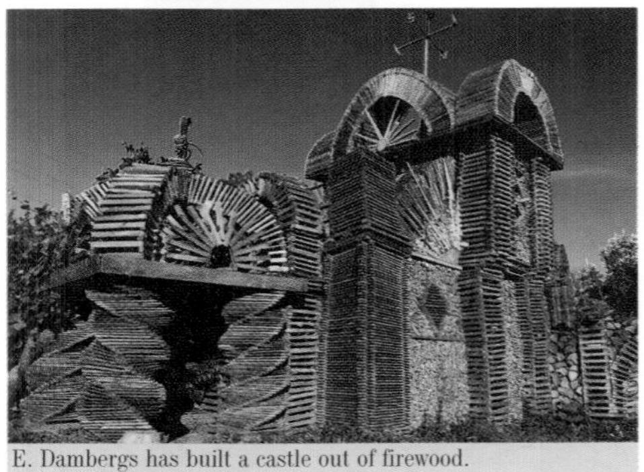

E. Dambergs has built a castle out of firewood. The peculiar structure has attracted many tourists

Forests are Latvia's leading natural resource. Forests cover 3 million hectares, or 45% of the country's territory. It is expected that eventually forests will cover between 50 and 55% of land in Latvia at the expense of inefficient or non-efficient areas of land. Wood and furniture represent 40% of Latvia's exports. In order to ensure the sustainable development and profitability of the forestry sector, Latvia takes good care of its forests. Government policies specify that the value of the forest cannot decline, and profits must be earned from the forest. Forestry policies are aimed at maintaining the biological diversity of the forest, at proper management of the forest, and at taking full account of the importance of the forest ecosystem in local and global processes. It is necessary to balance out the interests of the public and the owners of forests in the use of forests, and proper labor relations in the forestry sector must be promoted. The government's forestry policy provides that forested territories will not be diminished, while productivity and value will increase. That is why the forestry policy also provides for the planting of forests on unused land.

The regional structures of the National Forest Service do the work through smaller structures which, in turn, employ forest rangers. Each regional forestry structure manages an average of 50,000 hectares of forest and supervises 91,000 hectares. The local structures manage and supervise 6,800 and 12,200 hectares respectively, while forest rangers are responsible for 1,000 and 1,800 hectares of forest respectively. The regional structures monitor the implementation of forest-related laws in the country's forests, the way in which the forests are managed, and the way in which the resources of the forest are used or sold.

The information which is needed in order to govern and manage the forest is prepared by the National Forestry Institute, which inventories forests and produced management plans.

More than 50% of forest territory in Latvia belongs to the state, 40% are privately owned, while the remainder are owned by local governments and other entities. In terms of ecological and economic importance, 12% of Latvia's forestland is protected, and all activities in these territories are subordinated to environmental protection concerns. Another 18% of forests are under a less protected regime, but activities seek to merge environmental protection and wood production interests. The remaining 70% of forests are economic in nature, and the purpose of activities in the forests is to produce wood and wood products. There are some areas of forest which are under specifically strict production – 8.6% of total forest territory in all.

60% of Latvia's forest territory is covered with conifer trees and 40% with deciduous trees (65% of deciduous trees in Latvia's forest are birch trees). The presence of conifers has declined from 78% of all forestland in 1942 to 60% in 1995. The proportions of deciduous trees, especially birch, have expanded accordingly . This is because birch and white alder took over former agricultural lands in the post-war period.

Climate and geographic conditions in Latvia, as well as the extent to which land is used or left alone, have led to a situation in which species of birds and mammals which are endangered or completely absent from other countries are still viable in Latvia. Examples include the black stork, the lesser eagle, the whiteback woodpecker, the crane, the beaver, the otter, the wolf, the lynx and the brown bear.

Environmental protection and other protective regimes have been specified for approximately 8% of Latvia's territory, and nearly 7% of are territories which are under specific environmental protection. More than 90% of the protected territories are covered with forest or swamp ecosystems.

Since 1990, regional forest monitoring has been done in Latvia to evaluate the health of forested territories. The objective is to specify changes in these processes and to find the main factors which affect the health of forest. Defoliation and other processes are common in the crowns of the trees, and damaged trees are registered. There is evidence that the health of conifers in Latvia is improving.

Each year some 1,200-2,400 hectares of forest are lost to pestilence, forest fires, excessive moisture (most often due to territories that are flooded by beavers), wind damage, animal damage and disease. There is evidence that the greatest damage is caused by various pests which attack coniferous trees. Between 1993 and 1998, there were an average of 755 forest fires per year in Latvia, with average damage to 0.7 hectares of forest. Burning of old grass was by far the most common cause of forest fires (90% of all instances).

Seed plantations appeared in Latvia in the 1960s. Today there are 759 hectares of pine seed plantations, 116 hectares of fir seed plantations, 5 hectares of birch seed plantations, and 50 hectares of other species seed plantations. In 1998 a new and modern pine cone drying facility and a new regional forestry structure were opened. One cone drying facility can handle 30 kilograms of seed in every 24-hour period. The company also has a new seed storage freezer for coniferous and deciduous tree seeds.

Tree planting materials are grown at 15 state-owned, nine leased and 10 private tree farms with a total territory of 517 hectares. Between 24 and 25 million pieces of planting materials are grown each year. 15-16 thousand hectares of forest are restored each year. Coniferous tree growths are usually restored artificially, while deciduous growths are more commonly restored naturally.

In the early years of forest growth there is careful agricultural and technical tending of the trees. Trees are culled in a purposeful way with the aim of establishing the proper mix of species and number of trees to ensure enough growing space for each tree. When trees reach a height of nine meters, there is another process of culling which is aimed at ensuring the quality of the remaining trees and at earning the first profits from the growth.

The total length of roads in Latvia's forests is 14,700 kilometers, or 0.84 kilometers per 100 hectares of forest.

Nearly one-half of all forests in Latvia have at one time or another been excessively wet, and 41% have been drained to one extent or another. Drainage has led to a productivity increase of two times among birch trees, three times among pine and four times among fir trees.

There are 60 fire fighting facilities in Latvia's forests with access to 90 specialized fire trucks and other resources. There are 200 towers in Latvia's forests for fire lookout.

Harvesting volumes in Latvia's forests increased from 4 million cubic meters in 1992 to 10 million in 1998. Each year some 4.5 million cubic meters of trees are harvested in state-owned forests. This is done on the basis of long-term agreements and tree auctions. The assortment of cut trees depends on market demand. Round trees for sawing along the length represent 28-36% of all cut wood, round trees for peeling represent 6-8%, paper wood and technological wood represent between 25 and 50%, depending on the year, round trees to be used in round form represent 0.5-1%, and firewood represents 10-25%.

Culling and harvest methods in Latvia's forests are designed to be as environmentally friendly as possible, preserving both forest ecosystems and natural diversity. In order to reduce damage to trees and undergrowth, careful work is done to install four-meter technological corridors for motor vehicles at a distance of every 30 to 40 meters of forest.

Approximately one-half of the prepared wood materials in Latvia are processed by companies, while the remainder come from farmers and small rural enterprises.

Since the restoration of Latvia's independence, the wood processing industry has undergone rapid development. Several new sawmills have been built and existing ones have been modernized. A new veneer factory has gone into operation, and furniture is produced from wood plates and plywood. The production of large-format plywood, laminated and colored wood fibers and wood chip plywood is expanding. The processing of wood materials is improving, and the quality indicators of products are harmonized to international regulations and requirements. This ensures greater competitiveness of the products in the international market. Vertical integration between wood processing and forest management operations is improving. Between 1994 and 1999, the amount of sawn wood in Latvia increased nearly fourfold, the production of plywood expanded by 2.5 times, and the production of wood fiber plywood expanded nearly twofold. The capacity of sawmills exceeds available wood resources, so there is much competition among companies in the field. The use of sub-products from the sawmill industry for heating fuel is expanding.

A new Latvian Forest Law was adopted in 1999, which states that Latvian state forests are managed by state enterprise SC *Latvijas Meži*.

The largest timber producer in Latvia is *Nelss* Ltd., *Skaļi* Ltd., *Wika-Wood* Ltd., SC *Inčukalns Timber*, *Gaujas koks* Ltd., *Rēzeknes MRS*, *CED* Ltd., *Balvi Holm* Ltd., *Smiltenes MRS* Ltd., *Holzwerke Lubāna* Ltd., etc. The largest sawmills specialize in standardized production mostly for exporting. The leader in plywood production is SC *Latvijas finieris*, which produced a total of 130 thousand m³ in 1998. *Latvijas finieris* also produces bent and glued components, furniture, does plywood onlay and cut out.

Reloading of timber in a section of *Liepāja* port

Resin collection

Processing of timber

Hauling of timber with the wood-tractor *TIMBERJACK-810*

Hauling with a timber freight *VOLVO*

Processing of timber

Soil processing with the help of a *TIMBERJACK-1210* wood-tractor equipped with a cutter *TTS-Delta*

Soil processing with the help of a *TIMBERJACK-1210* wood-tractor equipped with a cutter *TTS Delta*

Soil processing with the help of a *TIMBERJACK-1210* wood-tractor equipped with a cutter *TTS Delta Combi II*

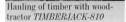
Hauling of timber with wood-tractor *TIMBERJACK-810*

Hauling of timber with wood-tractor *TIMBERJACK-810*

TIMBER EXPORT

Timber is shipped by special dry-freight ships in the Baltic Sea

The 330 m long docks with a gauge of 12.5 m under construction

The most notable achievement of Latvian timber industry during the last 10 years is the ever rapidly increasing export to West Europe. *Linda grupa* is a timber industry concern with a total turnover of USD 60-80 million; it rents 28 hectares of land in the territory of Riga free port, and realizes the largest shipping project of timber in the Baltic States.

The first round of construction, docks of a combined length of 330 m with a gauge of 12.5 m, will be finished in 2000. 10 hectares of storage areas and 3000 m² of warehouses will be completed in order to ensure a continuous flow of cargo.

The annual capacity of the port is gradually increased to 1-1.3 million m³.

The work of loading will be done with the help of mobile freighting and hauling equipment, as well as a special beltline to loading wood for heating. There is also a plan to use gantry-cranes and lay tracks along the docks. All the cargo intended for shipping will be transported by means of lorry or railroad to the terminal on *Krievu sala*. A railroad derivation has been opened connecting the main railroad and the docks. New lorry and train accommodation roads will be built to suit the plans of *Krievu sala* development. Specialized terminal of timber export makes the process of loading faster and fulfills the necessary requirements for storing and loading of this cargo. It also attracts timber transit from Russia and Belorussia, thus making a contribution to the state budget through taxes and toll.

A modern complexion of timber processing with desiccation installments and steam-shops will be built in a territory adjacent to the docks during the period until the year 2003. It will provide markets with competitive production.

A railroad derivation will increase timber transit from Russia and Belorussia to West Europe

Jānis Ķirsis, the president of *Linda grupa* with the new port in *Pārdaugava* in background

A view from the *Daugava* River of the Ruhendorff saw mill (later the *Venta* and *Benka* mill), one mile upriver from Riga at the *Krusts* tavern. Drawing by Johann Brotze in 1781

The opening ceremony of the Olympics in Sydney in the year 2000 will include the arrival of Captain James Cook in Sydney harbour. The Australians wanted to build Cook's ship as closely as possible to the original, so all of the wood was purchased and processed in Latvia. As was the case in the 18th century, the year 2000 version of Cook's ship will be made of Latvian wood, and the proud masts will be made of Latvian pine

A rafter on the *Daugava* at the beginning of the 20th century

Rafting is one of the older crafts in Latvia

Rafts coming from the top of the *Daugava* each year delivered thousands of cubic meters of wood to Riga

Historically, timber has always been the cornerstone of Latvian exports. Through ports in Riga, *Ventspils* and *Liepāja*, wood has been exported for many centuries. The exported timber has come from Latvia's own forests and from trees, which have been transported from the vast regions of Russia; rafted down the *Daugava* River in earlier years, while later transported by rail or road.

Of all the timber, which was exported from Riga, for many centuries, the most valuable was that used for ship's masts. Woodsmen sought out the very best pine trees for masts and spars – trees that were straight and not damaged in any way by rot or pests. The forests at *Pope* and *Zlēkas* were particularly renowned for their mast timber. Latvian timber was exported not only for shipbuilding, but also for the manufacture of windmill blades throughout Europe. The second most valuable timber product was oak, rough-hewn in rectangular lengths between 14 and 15 feet, which were known as *vancoši*. These were also used in shipbuilding, while poorer-quality *vancoši* were used to produce barrels for beverages.

Most of the European ships that plied the world's oceans were built of Latvian oak, which was more resistant to the sea plants that attached themselves to the bodies of ships. Nearly all of the sails of European ships were raised on masts made from Latvian pine. The ships sailed by Columbus, Magellan and Cook were all built of Latvian oak and pine.

Other products that were exported from Latvia included willow ash and the expensive substance called potash or calcium carbonate. Potash was used to produce glass, glue, paper, soap, textiles and porcelain.

Tar, which was obtained in special ovens and ditches through the burning of various kinds of trees and their stumps, was also in high demand. Two cubic meters of wood were needed to prepare one barrel of tar. Charcoal for blacksmiths was a secondary product in this process. In Latvia, the tar was prepared mostly by farmers. When tar was boiled, pitch was also obtained. When birch and aspen were steamed in dry heat, another type of tar, used in the treatment of leathers, was obtained.

As early as the 16th century, Latvia was exporting logs, round billets and square-sawn timber. Other construction materials, which were widely exported, were rafters, boards and slats, usually of oak or fir.

Between 1636 and 1640, the export of planks for barrels expanded enormously. These planks were prepared of wood that was left over from the production of *vancoši*. Oak barrel planks from Riga were used to make barrels for herring, salt and other dry goods, but in Europe the barrels were mainly used to store wine. In

the 17th century, oak trees were barbarously destroyed in Latvia, as members of the aristocracy cut down many oak groves in order to acquire profits.

In the 17th century, timber for ship's masts was exported mostly to Holland, England, France and Spain. The traders who were engaged in this business were among the wealthiest in Riga. Most of them were ethnic Latvians. As they accumulated money and wealth, they became members of the city's upper classes – some in the 17th century, but most toward the end of the 18th century. The Šteinhauers family was the most significant in this area. At the *Hermeliņi* baronial estate, Janis Šteinhauers operated a wood mill with 33 saw-frames. Between 1673 and 1777 this mill processed logs worth 61 500 thalers and sold them to foreigners for 75 000 thalers. There were also sawmills at *Ķengarags*, *Mūkusala* and *Lucavsala* near Riga.

The extent to which trade took place in Riga was largely dictated by capital from Holland and England. In order to reduce the shortage of funds, the Russian Empress Anna Ivanovna in 1735, established a trade treasury in Riga, to which was issued an interest-free loan of 100 000 thalers which had to be repaid in 10 years. This was the first bank in Russia at the time, and one result of this was that forest products began to be utilised for the manufacture of goods on site in Latvia. Vodka and beer breweries, for example, needed firewood in vast quantities, and the finished products were exported to various Russian provinces, St. Petersburg, Lithuania, Belorussia and Sweden.

The Duke Jēkabs of *Kurzeme* established a shipyard near *Ventspils*. In 1676, the *Krūnšerns* shipyard was established at *Kundziņsala*. Ernst Matthew Dannenstern established a shipyard at *Fossala*. He also owned a saw mill and built more than 10 ships that were used to actively trade wood, grain and other products in Riga, as well as in Kurzeme. The *Zasulauks* paper mill opened in Riga in the 1760s.

Riga's first true competitor in timber exports appeared only in the late 18th century, when Canadian wood began to flow into the market. Riga remained the most important city for timber exports in Europe, however, because it had the best access to waterways and the best system for rafting wood along the *Gauja* and *Daugava* rivers. Each year some 20 000 rafts of logs travelled to Riga along the *Daugava*, 900 rafts along the *Gauja* and 700 rafts along the *Lielupe* River. The rafts were made of logs lashed together in a structure that was called a *plenica*. The *plenicas* were tied one to other so that they could move. Small rafts consisted of five or six log *plenicas*, whilst larger rafts consisted of *plenicas* of 20 or 30 logs. When rafts were floated along smaller rivers, two *plenicas*

were tied together, while the *Daugava* River was wide enough to accommodate rafts of as many as 20 *plenicas*. In 1860, when the need arose in Europe for railroad ties, this increased the demand for Latvian wood substantially. During the period of Latvian independence between 1920 and 1940, timber was actively exported. Some 60% of Latvian wood went to England. Other significant customers included Belgium, France, Germany, South Africa, Turkey and Japan.

The owner of *Nelss* Ltd., Uldis Asars, is seen here at the Rīga port from which the company's products depart for England

Another owner of *Nelss* Ltd. is Andris Sihtors, and he is seen here at the *Aizkraukle* sawmill – the largest facility of its kind in all of Latvia

Of Latvia's export volume in 1999, 38% was taken up by the timber industry. The first companies in this field of activity emerged as soon as the Soviet Union collapsed in 1991, and over the course of just a few years they developed quality, precision and work organisations that were a pleasant surprise indeed to partner companies in the European Union.

The largest wood processing company in Latvia at this time is *Nelss* Ltd., a sawmill, which began its work in *Aizkraukle* in 1993. Since 1994, it has been using state-of-the-art technologies in its work. Specially dried timber is prepared specifically for the British market. The sawmill covers 25 hectares, and the drying kilns can handle up to 1,500 cubic meters of timber at a time. The company exports approximately 120,000 cubic meters of timber each year. *Nelss* Ltd. also exports similar volumes of non-dried timber, as well as 40,000 cubic meters of pallet materials annually. The company contributes approximately 8-10% of the timber that is used in construction in Great Britain each year. Some 500 people are employed at *Nelss* Ltd., 400 of them at the sawmill alone.

Some 1,000 cubic meters of timber products are exported every day

The *Aizkraukle* sawmill covers 25 hectares of land

Packaged dried timber

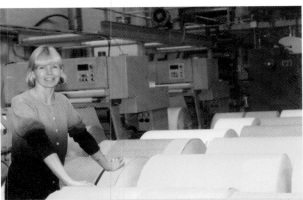

The sawmill can handle 500 cubic meters of sawn timber each day

THE PAPER MARKET

In Soviet times paper was delivered to Latvia in a centralized way from factories elsewhere in the Soviet Union. The paper was distributed according to national plans and was usually of fairly poor quality. True, Soviet-made cellulose was used to produce paper in *Līgatne*, *Jugla* and *Jaunciems*. Until the early 1990s cellulose was produced by a factory in *Sloka*, Latvia, but the process created enormous ecological problems for the spa town of *Jūrmala*. At this time work has almost been completed on planning a new and grand cellulose factory in *Preiļi* district, which will allow Latvia to become a leading exporter of cellulose. Paper today is produced in Līgatne and cardboard – in Rīga – but most of the paper and paper products sold in Latvia are imported from Scandinavia.

The *Upis* wholesale base supplies printing materials, office supplies and paper for retailers all over Latvia. The director of *Upis*, Maris Znotiņš is seen with marketing director Edvins Ginters

Paper is provided to Latvia's printing industry by leading Scandinavian paper factories. All three of the concerns in the *Trebruk* group – Munkedals, Hafrestroms and Kostrzyn – produce paper of faultless quality, and their outstanding services and special attitude toward clients have been known to printers in Latvia for 10 years already. The representative of *Trebruk* in Latvia is Ruta Svaža. Today all of Latvia's leading and most beautiful books are printed on *Trebruk* paper

An important supplier of paper in Latvia is *Modo Paper*, which provides all kinds of Scandinavian-made paper to the printing industry, as well as to retailers

Plywood from Latvia is exported to 35 countries in the world

An export facility for sawn-timber products in *Milgrāvis*

Lignums is the largest plywood factory in the world

Plywood is used in home construction

Interior decoration with plywood

Transportation of wood materials

Use of wood products in interiors

Office furniture

Inside the *Lignums* factory

Office furniture

Non-traditional wood products

Curved glued furniture parts for export

90% of the furniture produced by *Daiļrade* Ltd . is exported to the Western Europe and the Baltic States. This furniture is well received there due to the strength of the material, good quality and competitive price

The production of plywood is the very best use for Latvian-grown birch wood. In fact, the *Latvijas Bērzs* (Latvian Birch) factory, which was established in 1873, is the world's second-oldest producer of plywood.

In 1937, there were 16 veneer factories in this sector in Latvia, and they produced 95,000 cubic meters of plywood each year. The majority of this timber – 76,000 cubic meters – was exported to 46 countries, including 28,000 cubic meters to England.

Since 1992, the plywood industry in Latvia has consistently developed and expanded. Output of glued materials (plywood and curved glued billets) increased to 155,000 cubic meters in 1999. Major companies in the sector include SC *Latvijas Finieris*, SSC *Vulkāns*, *SAGA* Ltd. and others.

In 1996 SC *Latvijas Finieris* merged with the *Hapaks* company, which produces decorated plywood and plywood billets of various types, configurations and sizes. The company's products are exported to 35 countries, especially England, Germany, the Netherlands and Denmark. Sales volumes in Latvia have also expanded. The factory's output is used in construction, machinery building and furniture production.

By participating in the regeneration of Latvia's forestry resources, the company is seeking to promote closer co-operation among forest growers, producers and members of the timber products industry. The aim is to promote the ongoing development of the forestry sector.

By planting forests on land that is no longer used for agriculture, the State is creating favourable conditions for environmental improvements in rural areas. At the same time, it is improving the availability of raw materials for the veneer industry. There are 23 enterprises in Latvia which grow trees professionally, and in 1998 they grew more than 11 million firs, 13 million pines, 521,000 birch trees and small volumes of other trees – all fully in line with prevailing standards.

This is the largest factory for corrugated cardboard in Latvia. The director of *StoraEnso Packaging*, Viesturs Tamužs

The management of *StoraEnso Packaging* (*Pakenso Baltika*) on the day of the opening of the enterprise in 1996

StoraEnso Packaging employs some 80 people

Pulpwood destined for *StoraEnso Mežs* is re-loaded at the *Jaunmilgrāvis* Port. The deputy executive director of *StoraEnso Mežs*, Vilnis Freimanis

StoraEnso Packaging (*Pakenso Baltika*) plant is ceremoniously opened by the director of the Latvian Privatisation Agency, Jānis Naglis, and the Finnish Minister for Trade and Industry, Antti Kalliomäki

The *StoraEnso Packaging* plant. These rolls contain the raw materials for the production of corrugated cardboard

Large foreign companies readily make investments in the forestry industry of Latvia. This is associated with the good condition of Latvian forests, excellent Latvian timber products, and the high level of work performance and knowledge of Latvian forest and timber workers. The largest investor (at time of writing), who has invested in wood processing, as well as paper and carton product manufacture, is the *StoraEnso Group*.

StoraEnso Group is one of the world's leading companies in the forestry industry. The company was formed in 1998 after the merger of Finland's *Enso* and Sweden's *Stora*. The company is a leading producer of magazine and newspaper print, writing paper and packaging paper in the world. *StoraEnso* also is a leading supplier of sawn timber.

StoraEnso has four subsidiaries in Latvia – *StoraEnso Packaging* (which is the only producer of corrugated cardboard in Latvia), *StoraEnso Mežs* (the leading purchaser and exporter of pulpwood in Latvia), *Papyrus* (paper wholesaler), and *Puumerkki Latvia* (which distributes wooden doors and parquet floors in Latvia).

The company operates on the basis of unified principles – ecological, social and economic sustainability. The goal is to provide a wide range of consumer goods in such areas as printing materials, packaging materials and construction materials. All of the company's products have one thing in common – they can be recycled, they are environmentally friendly, and they are safe in terms of user health.

StoraEnso Packaging is the oldest of the subsidiaries, beginning work in Latvia in 1994 with the name *Pakenso Baltika*. It specialises in the production of cardboard. The factory in Latvia is the most important of all of the plants in the Baltic region. *StoraEnso Packaging* uses technologies that are environmentally harmless and modern. Corrugated cardboard is produced without any production waste. The company has a turnover of some 6 million lats per year. Over the course of five years, *StoraEnso Packaging* has won high recognition, including the Latvian Quality Prize, the ISO 9001 certificate, and other awards. Some 80 people work at the corrugated cardboard plant.

StoraEnso Mežs was founded in 1997 and is a supplier of pulpwood and cellulose materials in Latvia. In the future, the company is planning to expand its operations in Eastern Latvia, and offices have been opened in *Rēzekne* and *Madona*.

Papyrus is a company that sells some 2,000 tons of paper per year in Latvia. The largest clients of this wholesaler are the *Jāņa Sēta* and *Preses Nams* publishing houses, the *Saeima* and two mobile telephone companies, *Latvijas Mobilais Telefons* and *Baltcom*. *Papyrus* sells various kinds of paper and cardboard produced in Finland, Germany and France.

Puumerkki Latvia began operations in Latvia in July 1999. The company exports various wood materials to Finland, including Latvian-produced chipboard and plywood. From Finland the company imports exterior and interior doors, parquet floors, sauna equipment and other materials. *Puumerkki Latvia* sells its products exclusively on a wholesale basis.

StoraEnso shares are sold on the Helsinki and Stockholm stock exchanges. The company's market value is assessed at EUR 5.8 billion. Latvia highly values investors who invest in Latvia's traditional production sectors, including wood processing. Therefore, the Government of Latvia is always interested in Latvia's co-operation with the *StoraEnso Group*.

Corrugated cardboard is a no-waste production process. All trimmings are recycled

The opening of *StoraEnso Packaging* (*Pakenso Baltika*) was attended by (from the left) the director of Stora Ltd. *Enso Packaging*, Viesturs Tamužs; the director of *Stora Enso Pakenso*, Markku Pentikäinen; the Finnish minister for Trade and Industry, Antti Kalliomäki; the general director of *StoraEnso*, Jukka Härmälä, and the general director of the Latvian Privatisation Agency, Jānis Naglis

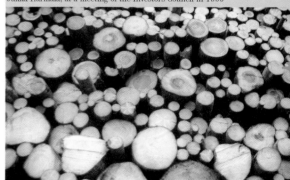

The development opportunities in the timber industry were discussed by the Latvian Prime Minister, Andris Šķele and Jukka Härmälä, at a meeting of the Investors Council in 1999

StoraEnso Mežs is the largest exporter of pulpwood and wood chips in Latvia

The director of *StoraEnso Packaging* (*Pakenso Baltika*), Viesturs Tamužs, with Latvian Prime Minister Andris Šķele at the opening of the enterprise

McAbols is a company which prints high-quality products of various kinds. It specializes in *Hexachrom* printing. Company officials Artis Erglis and Artis Kalniņš are seen in the photograph

The printing house of the stock company *Diena* is specialized in the printing of color daily newspapers with rotation offset printing presses

The newspaper *Lauku Avīze* opened a new and modern printing press in *Rēzekne*, where it produces newspapers and books. Politicians Māris Gailis (center, in overcoat) and Ernests Jurkāns (second from the left) are seen visiting the new facility

Fine work is done on modern *Heidelberg* printing presses by the publishing house *Premo*, which is run by Kristīne Kalniņa

The publishing house and printing company *Apgāds Mantojums* Ltd. designs and prints publications for cultural and scientific institutions, as well as advertising materials. Front row: director Māris Deģis. Second row: printers Normunds Juška and Ivars Lukins. Third row: executive director Uldis Tilgass and printing press director Agris Ķirsons

The largest printing house in Soviet-era Latvia was privatized, and now *Kvadra Pak* Ltd. and the stock company *Kvadra Print* produce high-quality large printing projects, printing cardboard as well as paper and working with offset, deep print, silk screening and other techniques

The printing industry in Soviet times was very strictly monopolized and supervised by censors Soviet standards provided for a small printing house in every region of the USSR to print local newspapers. Riga had several printing houses, by contrast, each with its own specialization. Among the major ones were the Sample *Paraugtipogrāfija* and the *Preses nams*, both of which were privatized successfully during the early years of Latvia's independence.

In May 1990, when Parliament declared Latvia's sovereignty within the soviet Union, the Press Building was taken over by Soviet special forces which remained there to protect the publishing of Communist Party publications until August 1991, when the Soviet Union collapsed. This was an unexpected stimulus for the printing industry in that anyone who wanted to print a book, newspaper or magazine had to think about where it would be done, from where the paper would come, and how the entire process could be ensured. Printing presses were imported from the United States, Denmark and Sweden, although many were old and not really appropriate for modern use. It was, however, precisely in the printing industry that the first steps toward a market economy were taken most swiftly. Soon enough companies were taking out loans, installing machinery and catching up with technological processes elsewhere in the world with astonishing speed. In 1995 Latvia's printing industry was already much more modern than was the case in other countries of the Baltic Sea region, because only the most modern repro equipment was purchased, along with state-of-the-art *Macintosh* computers and *Heidelberg* offset printing presses. If in 1992 Latvia's most beautiful magazines and books were printed in Germany or Finland, then in 2000 publishers from Germany and Finland are printing their products in Latvia.

Today there are some 150 printing-related companies in Latvia with total turnover of some 36 million lats per year. In terms of groups of products, 15% of the process is taken up by newspapers, 25% by magazines, 20% by books, 25% by labels and packaging, 10% by advertising publications and 5% by other kinds of work. The largest printers in Latvia are the stock company *Preses nams*, *Apgāds Jāņa sēta* Ltd., *Kvadra Pak* Ltd. and the stock company *Kvadra print*, the stock company *Diena*, *Talsu tipogrāfija* Ltd., *Jelgavas tipogrāfija* Ltd., *Madonas poligrāfists* Ltd. and *Apgāds Krauklītis* Ltd.

Latvians are a nation that reads a very great deal. In 1939 there were more newly published books per capita in Latvia than in any other nation in the entire world. Denmark was close behind. Latvians are still in the top 10 in this regard, and forecasts are that they'll be back at the top of the heap by the year 2005.

In terms of the number of daily newspapers published in Latvia each day, the level is close to Western European standards. In European leader Denmark there are 30.8 newspapers printed per 100 residents each day, while in Latvia the figure is 23.8.

Printers in Latvia are represented by the Latvian Association of Printing Companies, which is run by president Aivars Zvirbulis. The association publishes a specialized journal. Executive director Ieva Bečere is seen to the right

Stock company *Preses nams* board members Viesturs Grinbergs, Zane Cīrule, board chairman and president Ivars Zariņš, and Janis Blaževičs

Aivars Prošenkovs is director of printing for the stock company *Preses nams*, and he is also the executive director of *Apgāds Jāņa sēta* Ltd.

Aivars Zvirbulis, founder and operating director of the *Jāņa sēta* publishing house and a strategic consultant to the president of the stock company *Preses nams*

An *Edale E510* printing press which can print on metal and plastic surfaces

Eastern Europe's largest and most successful printing house is the stock company *Preses nams*, which employs 1,300 people. The company emerged when two of Latvia's leading printing operations merged. The building which houses the company, as well as the offices of a number of newspapers and magazines, was built in the center of Riga in 1976 and was privatized in 1998. The stock company *Ventspils Nafta* bought the majority share. The company immediately launched a program of development, and modern printing systems were installed. In 2000 the company bought out its largest competitor, *Apgāds Jāņa sēta* Ltd. The founder of that company, Aivars Zvirbulis, had initially founded *Jāņa Sēta* because, as the owner of an art gallery, he needed someplace to print exhibition catalogues. Eventually, however, *Jāņa Sēta* expanded, producing maps and providing other printing services. Today the quality of the printing process is dictated by four new *Heidelberg* printing presses, of which the largest is the *Heidelberg* Speedmaster 102-8-PH+L, with a capacity of 7,000-10,000 two-sided pages per hour. Between 1994 and 1999 the company's turnover increased by 9.5 times.

Since their merger, the stock company *Preses nams* and *Apgāds Jāņa sēta* can provide local clients with the full cycle of print-related production, starting with design, image scanning, preparation of films and color printouts for pre-printing approval, the printing itself and all kinds of post-printing services – cutting of labels in any shape, binding of magazines and books, etc. The facility prints a number of Latvia's leading newspapers, and it exports 40% of its output.

A *Solna G6* printing press at the *Preses nams* facility

Preses nams is located in *Ķīpsala*

A *Heidelberg* printing press at a printing house in *Cēsis*

A *noble elm* in *Indāni* with a trunk circumference of 6.5 meters

This lonely pine tree in *Ape* has been there for more than two centuries

A noble linden tree at *Ziemupe*

A unique elm tree near the *Imula* cliff in Latvia

A noble oak tree in *Krimulda* parish

The pride of the *Kalnamuiža* Park in *Smiltene* – this magnificent pine tree

This juniper tree is the largest in the Baltic States. Its trunk circumference is 2.7 meters. This juniper tree is being measured by Guntis Eniņš a prominent biologist and well known public figure

The Latvian word *dižkoks*, or *noble tree*, is used to refer to particularly old and thick trees that are of great scientific, cultural, historical or aesthetic significance. These trees are protected by the State, and they are an indispensable component of the Latvian countryside – an important element of the nation's pride.

Staņislavs Saliņš laid the foundations for research into the *noble trees*, and in 1960 he recommended that the basic criterion for the specification of a *dižkoks* be the circumference of the trunk of the tree at a height of 1.3 meters from the ground. The minimum circumference for national *noble trees* is 5 meters for oaks and willow trees, 4 meters for linden trees, ash and elm, 3.5 meters for maples and black alders, 3 meters for pine trees, firs and birch trees, and 0.8 meters for juniper trees.

The thickest known oak tree in the Baltic States is the *Kaive noble oak* in *Tukums* district. The circumference of its trunk is a full 10 meters. Latvia has approximately 200 times more *noble trees* than do other countries in the region. Indeed, Latvia can be seen as something of a miracle land in terms of these magnificent trees. For 50 years, Latvians protected their trees from the violent economic methods of the communist regime. Even during land reclamation processes, the trees were protected.

Today, however, many of the *dižkoks* are threatened by the fact that agricultural lands are being abandoned. Trees, which once grew in pastures or fields, are now being surrounded by forest, and they are dying. Not always, though. There is a special public organisation in Latvia which was founded by Latvia's most famous living poet Imants Ziedonis and the biologist Guntis Eniņš that works to clear areas around the *noble trees*, thus preserving them for future generations.

A noble elm tree with a hollow on the *Gauja* bank

Latvia's most magnificent oak tree is found in the village of *Lejaspuņģi* in *Cēsis* District

Latvian President Guntis Ulmanis (third from left) plants an oak tree together with Estonian President Lennart Meri (second from left) and Russian Prime Minister Viktor Chernomyrdin (to the right of Ulmanis). Perhaps some day it will be a noble tree?

Two fir trees, grown together like Siamese twins

Ciemiši elm tree is the greatest one in Latvia

A noble maple tree in *Tukums* district

This old oak tree is still alive

An enormous oak at *Iesalnieki*

The oldest pine tree in Latvia is thought to be not less than 346 and perhaps as much as 360 years old

A massive oak tree near a tourism facility in the *Abava* Valley

State Geological Service – Sabine Cibele, Marina Častņikova, Vizma Karkliņa, Ludmila Barsukova, Maris Segliņš, director Rudīte Aņikejeva, Vladimirs Medko, Skaidrīte Klints, Sergejs Koņevs, Inga Gavena

A uncovered brown coal segment

A flooded for gravel quarry

Skaņaiskalns hill near Salaca

Gravel stones

Tērvete hill castle

Sand washouts

The first books about Latvian geology and geography were written by August Hupel in 1774 in Riga and by Jacob B. Fischer in 1778 in Leipzig. The great collector of Latvian folklore, Krišjānis Barons, in 1859 wrote a book with the title *Mūsu tēvu zemes aprakstīšana* (*A Description of Our Fatherland*). This was the first book on Latvian geography written by a Latvian. In 1920, a Physical Geography department was established within the Faculty of Mathematics and Natural Sciences at the University of Latvia under the leadership of Reinholds Putniņš. In 1923, a Geography Society was founded in Riga and in 1935, a Geography Institute.

Planned geological investigations began in Latvia in 1936 with the founding of the Riches of the Earth Research Committee, which in 1939 became the Riches of the Earth Research Institute.

In 1944, following the occupation of Latvia by the USSR, the former Faculty of Mathematics and Natural Sciences was re-organised as the Faculty of Biology, Geology and Soil Sciences, as well as a Faculty of Geography. In 1951, the Faculty of Geography was abolished. In 1946, the Geology and Geography Institute was established at the Latvian SSR Academy of Sciences, and in 1952 was re-organised as the Geology and Mineral Deposits Institute, but in 1961, it was renamed the Geology Institute. In 1957, a Geology and Protection of Subterranean Depths Administration was established at the Latvia SSR Council of Ministers.

For hundreds of years, the basic task of geology has been to provide information regarding possible mineral deposits and the possibilities for extracting them. In the second half of the 20th century, geology has more and more turned to the sustainable development, and rational utilisation of the subterranean depths and its wealth, as well as its maximum protection from the negative impact caused by the activities of human beings.

In the post-war years geological investigation was organised by centralised USSR geological structures to find, investigate and acquire mineral deposits. All the materials of geological investigations, especially maps were compiled in Russian, were regarded as top secret and were available to a very narrow circle of people.

The secretiveness and the unavailability of information has created myths and uncertainties regarding the geological foundations of Latvia, and a lack of understanding regarding the significance of geological information. The environment in particular is affected by this lack of understanding as the sitting of waste disposal sites in areas which, from a geological point of view, are utterly unsuitable, for example, in *Getliņš* and *Kūdrs*. An especially tragic case is the *Inčukalns* sulphuric acid gaudron waste disposal site. The largest mistakes due to a lack of knowledge of geological information from the Soviet period are: the establishment of a chemical industrial plant at *Olaine*; the baseless decision to develop the water supply of Riga utilising surface waters, as well as the fixing of the Latvian and Lithuanian sea border, which entailed renouncing fairly high level researched petroleum reserves.

Many authorities engaged in the investigation or extraction of mineral deposits in Latvia including the USSR Army. Much of the working materials and information acquired by them came in to the hands of authorities outside the territory of Latvia, and some of the information is for all practical purposes lost.

Following the renewal of Latvia's independence citizens regained the ownership of land, but together with this, the owners acquired the subterranean depths of their properties. The process of renewing land ownership was so complicated that often it resulted in an attitude of *its mine, I can do what I like with it*. This attitude together with a lack of knowledge of the geological foundations has created contradictions between the utilisation and protection of the subterranean depths of the land. Nature does not acknowledge man-made borders and mineral deposits, swamps and other geological formations lie across the properties of many owners. The borders of the Baltic Artesian Basin are one not only beneath land belonging to several owners, but also across different national borders.

In the years since the renewal of independence, various companies have become established who attempt to perform various kinds of geological services, for example, investigations, drilling, etc. However, most work without a knowledge of the subterranean depths and are of poor quality. The more successful companies have been established based on privatised State enterprises, and by acquiring new technologies, ensuring a quality standard of service. In preparing a unified national policy and development strategy for the utilisation of the of the subterranean depths, it turned out that information regarding the characteristics and resources of the subterranean depths, and the possibilities of their utilisation, its targeted acquisition, modern processing and presentation in a user-friendly manner may significantly increase the economic potential of the State and promote regional development.

The Latvian *Valsts ģeoloģijas dienests* (*VĢD*) (*State Geological Service*) has been established under the supervision of the Ministry of Environmental Protection and Regional Development. Its main directions include the development of a national subterranean depths management policy, the regulation and supervision of the targeted investigation and utilisation of the subterranean depths, and ensuring the storage, supplementation, systematisation, use and publication of geological information. In 1996, the Law On the Subterranean Depths was adopted, but in 1997 Cabinet Regulations regarding the utilisation of the subterranean depths, regarding nationally significant minerals and deposits, as well as regarding procedures for the utilisation of parts of the nationally significant subterranean depths.

Life has forced the *VĢD* to begin its activities with a Geology in Society programme. It had to prepare and distribute various geologically orientated information in order to provide to potential users of the subterranean depths with professionally prepared, quality geological information, to acquaint the general public with the basic requirements in the field of rational utilisation and protection of the subterranean depths. The main direction of the activities of the *VĢD* is to investigate the resources and useful characteristics of the subterranean depths, including the preparation of basic geological information for the needs of the general public and State institutions, as well as evaluate the geological process and quality of the subterranean depths. The Service ensures the storage and utilisation of geological information, performs the licensing of the utilisation of the subterranean depths. The *VĢD* participates in the im-plementation of several international projects, and it is a member of the Union of European State Geological Services, as well as the World Hydro-geological Association. Closer international co-operation is realised with the Nordic countries and Baltic State geology services. The *VĢD* also closely co-operates with all levels of local government, ensuring that they have the necessary geological information, as well as providing consultation regarding the rational utilisation and protection of the subterranean depths. The geo-chemical mapping on scale 1:500 000 and the renewal and publication of national geological maps on scale 1:200 000 has been performed, as well as the investigation of the sources of underground water reserves for small towns, and the inventorisation of underground water reserves. A mineral deposits register has been established and the mineral deposit reserves balance has been renewed.

Mineral deposits are a combination of natural minerals and rocks, hydrogen carbons and underground waters, either of non-organic or organic origin, in the earth's crust, which, with modern technical and technological means it is possible to extract and utilise in the economy. The location of mineral deposits is determined by the geological structure.

Latvia's geological section is formed by crystalline base rock and platform cover. The crystalline base rock is very uneven and in a jagged way falls away in direction from northeast to southwest. The base rock is made up of very deformed pre-Cambrian granite, gneiss, gabbro and crystalline slate, the depth of which varies from 340-350 meters in Latvia's north-east to up to 1923 meters in the south-east part. Rich deposits of iron ore and signs of other metal ores are associated with the base rock. Taking into account the great depth (688 meters around *Staicele* and 945-1117 meters around *Garsene*), it is not economically feasible to utilise these high quality magnetite iron ore deposits.

The base rock covers several ages of platform cover, which form various layers of sedimentary rocks and quaternary deposits. Beneath the sedimentary rock cover signs of brown iron ore, mineral waters, thermal waters, petroleum, phosphorite and poly-metal ores have been determined. The invaluable importance of the Cambrian sandstone is as a collector layer for the installation of natural gas reservoirs. Throughout the territory of Latvia the Silurian sedimentary rocks cover the Devonian sedimentary rocks – sandstone, clay, dolomite, marl, gypsum and aleirorite, which is sometimes exposed in the banks of the *Gauja*, *Salaca*, *Daugava*, *Venta*, *Abava*, and other rivers.

In broad lowland areas, they are found beneath a thin layer of quaternary deposit cover. Devonian sedimentary rock strata contain quality building raw material deposits: dolomite – for the production of road metal and decorative slabs, *kvarca* sand – for glass manufacture and the making of moulds, gypsum and brick-making clay. In Devonian sedimentary rocks can be found significant underground-pressurised water, fresh water and mineral water resources. In the south-west of Latvia, the Devonian sedimentary rock covers Carboniferous, Parma, Triassic and Jurassic sedimentary rocks – limestone, clay, sandstone, dolomite and aleirolite. With these are associated limestone and *kvarca* sand deposits and small brown coal deposits. In nearly the whole of the territory of Latvia, pre-quaternary base rocks are covered in varying depths by quaternary deposits. This has been washed away only in some areas of the seacoast, in river valleys and ravines. The maximum thickness of the quaternary deposits (208-310 meters) is in buried ancient valleys, with which often are associated reservoirs of underground drinking water. In the flat lowlands and mildly undulating areas, the quaternary deposit cover is thin (up to 10-20 meters), but in more hilly areas it is of average thickness (20-50 meters), and in some areas up to more than 50 meters. In the Kurish and North-western Vidzeme highlands, the quaternary deposits are between 20 and 50 meters. In the hilly areas of these highlands it grows to 50-100 meters, but the lowlands and mildly undulating areas it does not exceed 20 meters. In Vidzeme, *Alūksne*, Latgale and *Augšzeme* highlands, especially in the inner part, the thickness of quaternary deposit cover is 60-170 meters.

The main reason for the formation of the quaternary cover is glaciers, their streams of melting water and basin deposits, which were formed in the Ice Age. Deposits from the last continental Ice Age formed the majority of the quaternary deposit cover. Important reserves of sand, gravel and quaternary clay are a result of the last Ice Age. Following the Ice Age important deposits of peat, sapropel, as well as many fresh water limestone deposits.

Often the positive glacial relief forms – hills, banks and ridges – are a result of the melting glacier water deposits being folded and pushed together under the impact the glacier's deforming action. These deformations can most often be seen in hilly highland areas and lowland undulating flat lands, where the folded and pushed together melting glacial water stream deposits – gravel and sand or isolated sedimentary rocks – form hills, banks and ridge cores and often uncover their tops, exposing moraines – stony sandy lime or sandstone, as a non-porous layer of continuous cover. Therefore, moraines on the surface normally are uncovered on hillsides of glacial origin, and continuous layers are mostly formed only in hollows between hills, and in broader territories – in flat land areas.

The most important deposits of sand and gravel can be found in the highlands districts, in ancient buried valleys and in glacial relief forms in more segmented lowland areas, where the quaternary deposits are thicker. The main concentrations of stoneless clay and peat are in the lowlands.

The quaternary deposit cover formation characteristics needs to be taken into account when building and examining the problems of soils, subterranean depths and ground waters. In the rural areas, the quaternary underground waters, mainly its upper levels or ground waters, are widely utilised for the water supply. It should be noted that in many places a significant thickness of quaternary deposit strata restricts the possibilities for utilising the prequaternary deposits mineral deposits.

Sand quarry

Extracting gravel in the *Talsi* area

An earthquake is almost impossible in Latvia. Cave-ins in Latvia are caused by underground gypsum deposits being washed-out

Daudas waterfall near *Sigulda* – the highest in Latvia

Man-made caves as storage cellars in *Līgatne* sandstone cliffs. In later years, the river flooded and the caves pictured are no longer utilised

Red cliffs near *Salaca*

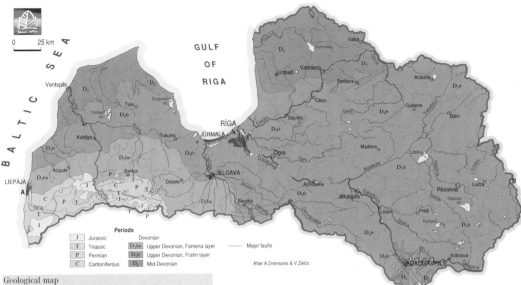

Periods

J	Jurassic
T	Triassic
P	Permian
C	Carboniferous

Devonian
D₃fm Upper Devonian, Famena layer
D₃fr Upper Devonian, Frahn layer
D₂ Mid-Devonian
— Major faults

After A.Dreimanis & V.Zelčs

Geological map

Liepas trees on a clay deposit

Fresh water limestone

Sandy loam deposit
Fresh water limestone in *Mores* parish
Silt
Streaked clay at *Lode*
A quarry at *Tērvete*

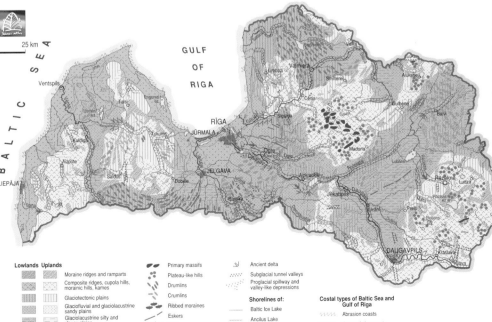

Lowlands Uplands

Moraine ridges and ramparts
Composite ridges, cupola hills, morainic hills, kames
Glaciotectonic plains
Glaciofluvial and glaciolacustrine sandy plains
Glaciolacustrine silty and clayey plains
Offshore plains of early phases of Baltic Sea

Primary massifs
Plateau-like hills
Drumlins
Crumlins
Ribbed moraines
Eskers
Flutings
Karst and suffosian sinkholes and collapse sinks

Ancient delta
Subglacial tunnel valleys
Proglacial spillway and valley-like depressions

Shorelines of:
Baltic Ice Lake
Ancilus Lake
Litorina Sea

Costal types of Baltic Sea and Gulf of Riga
Abrasion coasts
Accumulative coasts

After A.Dreimanis & V.Zelčs

Geo-morphological map

Imants Zauls atop Mt. Everest. Although Latvia does not have high mountains, and *Gaiziņš* hill is only 311.6 meters high, Latvians are mad on mountain climbing. The person who has been most times atop Mt. Everest, who has more often climbed over 8000 meters is a Latvian called Ed Viesturs who lives in Canada

Teodors Ķirsis atop Mt. Everest. An unusual Latvian pastime is to attempt to climb not only the highest mountains in each continent (because that is being done by Ilgvars Pauls), but the second, third highest mountains in each continent

Bruno Šules was the first person to bicycle down Europe's highest mountain Mt. Elbruss' Eastern (5621 meters) and Western (5642 meters) summits

Guntis Eniņš makes a contact tracing of the *Dinamarka* border stone in *Lēdurga* parish

The *Daviņas upurakmens* (sacrificial stone) with many hollowed out holes

The ancient *Lipinit robežakmens* (border stone) at *Liepna*, with an engraved message stating that the borders of Russia, Poland and Sweden are located at this place "for eternity"

The *jūdžakmens* (only mileage) stone that has been preserved in Latvia

A memorial stone commemorating a house that sank into a lake

Ancient sun wheel crosses carved in dolomite from the *Putraskrogs* burial grounds near the *Daugava* River. Today they are at the *Kalnazieds* Museum

The *Ivāni* "devil's stone", known as the Devil's Seat

The *Gārsene dižakmens*, which resembles a stone post or menhir

Latvian tradition contains the concept *dižakmens*, which could be literally translated as "noble stone". The word is used to refer to very large rocks on dry land or in the sea. According to the methodology developed by specialists, a *dižakmens* of national significance is a rock, which has a volume greater than 10 m³ above ground. A *dižakmens* of local significance is one with an above ground volume of between 7 and 10 m³. When *dižakmens* are being evaluated, measurements are taken of their width, length, height, circumference and volume. There are some 200 *dižakmens* of national significance in Latvia, and 31 of these are protected by law by the State.

The largest land-based rock in Latvia is the Great rock of *Nīcgale*, which is 3.5 m high, 10.4 m long and 10 m wide. It has a circumference of 31 m, and the volume of the visible portion is greater than 170 m³.

The Giant stone of *Kapsēde* has a volume of 155 m³. It is thought that the largest land-based rock in Latvia was once located in the *Daugava* River near *Krāslava*. It was considerably more than 30 meters in circumference and three meters high. The stone was blown up in 1818 to ensure better shipping conditions on the river.

The sacred rock of *Pērkons*, which is in the northern part of the *Liepāja* lake, was also more than 30 meters in circumference, with a height of at least four meters. It was blown up in 1841 to provide materials to build a highway.

The largest known sea-based rock in Latvia is located 100 m offshore at *Pāvilosta*. It is some 3.5-m high, and approximately 2 m of the rock can be seen above the waves.

The *Melķitari muldakmens* (trough rock) with a deep cavity at its top that has a capacity of 80 l. In ancient times the water was thought to be sacred water from heaven

A stone boulder reminiscent of a mushroom at the *Džūkste* cemetery

The Great stone of *Pāvilosta* is the largest *jūrakmens* (sea-based rock) in Latvia, located some 100 m from the shore

The *dižakmens* of *Džūkste* parish

A sea-based stone near *Kurmjrags*

The *svētmeitas akmens* (stone of the Holy Daughter) near what was once the frontier between Poland and Sweden, near *Mērsrags*

A sea-based stone that looks like a sculpture

The *Nīcgale dižakmens* is the largest in Latvia

The 23 m long *Gudzonu* cave

Eņģeļu (Angels) cave on the shore of the *Salaca* River

Caves are cavities and passageways of various origins that are found in the upper strata of the Earth's crust. In order for a cavity to be considered a cave by speleologists, it must be large enough for a person to get in and move around. Natural caves are divided into groups – caves formed by water erosion, by underground streams, by abrasion, and tectonic caves. All of these types of caves are found in Latvia.

In Latvia, in accordance with the recommendations of speleologist Guntis Eniņš, only those caves, which are at least three meters in length, are registered. There is information about some 250 natural caves in Latvia. There are also a similar number of man-made caves, especially in the sandstone rocks around the town of *Līgatne*. Man-made caves in that area are used as cellars for the storage of food products. Latvia's caves are protected as important geological and geomorphologic objects, which have great scientific, educational and aesthetic value. They are also protected as zoological objects in which endangered species of bats spend the winter, as well as botanical objects which have a number of rare plants – many species of lichens, algae, ferns and mosses can be found in caves. Some caves are protected as archaeological monuments. At least 27 *Velnalas* (devil's caves) and *Upuralas* (sacrificial caves) in Latvia are known to have been sacred locations for the ancient Latvians. People have hidden in caves during wars, riots and revolutions. Researchers are also interested in caves as hydrological objects, because springs flow out of them. There are also caves in Latvia with lakes and flowing rivers.

The flooded entrance to *Vējiņu* cave and biologist Andris Urtans, who is deputy director of the North Vidzeme Biosphere Reservation

The 48 m long *Lielā Laņģu* cave with a fast-flowing spring

Special protection is given to some caves that are important geological objects. These caves are not named; this one is called simply Cave X, and it is 330 m long

Taking contact rubbings of ancient rock carvings in *Pēterala* cave

Kalējala cave near *Lenči*

Gutmaņala cave was an ancient sacred place for Livs

Lielā Velnala ("Great Devil's") cave near *Sigulda*

At the entrance to several *Līvu Upuralas* (sacrificial caves)

Gaisa caves in the Black cliff on the shore of the *Brasla* River

The old *Ainaži* breakwater has served Latvian fishermen for centuries, but during Soviet times it was allowed to fall into disrepair

The harsh winds which blow from the sea on the shores of the Baltic Sea are tolerated best by certain species of pine, which is why pine forests cover nearly all of the seashore in Latvia. Meadows are not particularly lush because the earth at the seashore is not very rich in nutrients

The *randu* meadows at *Kuiviži* and *Salacgrīva* are the largest seashore meadows in the world. They feature a large variety of plant life – some 600 species in all, of which 36 are rare and endangered. The Baltic Sea, and especially the Bay of Riga, is the sea with the lowest salt content of any sea or ocean in the world. Because of this comparatively low salt content, meadows often stretch into the sea in Latvia

President Vaira Vīķe-Freiberga and the European commander of NATO, Gen. Wesley Clark, at the seashore in *Jūrmala*

The steep shore at *Ulmale*

The new *Ainaži* breakwater on the border between Latvian and Estonia

A Latvian performer of Indian dances, Vija Vetra, is seen here dancing at *Kurmrags* near the sea in Vidzeme

The cliffs along the Baltic Sea shore come in a wide variety of colors

The seashore at *Jūrkalne*

An iceberg on the coast in Vidzeme

Kaltene is the most stretched out (7 kilometers) fishing village on the shore of the Bay of Riga. Long ago the forest around *Kaltene* was rich in so-called mast pines, which have few or no branches and were an enormously lucrative export product for Western Europe

Former Prime Minister and successful entrepreneur Maris Gailis is the skipper of the yacht called *Milda*, which is capable of circumnavigating the globe. The Riga port, as well as smaller ports in Latvia, are always ready to welcome sailors to port

The beach at *Dubulti* is always popular during the summertime for Rigensians and their guests alike

The *Rigas jurmala* sanatorium is a popular hotel and rehabilitation facility right at the edge of the sea

The *Vidlauči* sea rock near *Saulkrasti*

The Ainaži maritime school was founded by Krišjanis Valdemars in 1864, and it was the first maritime school at which men could get an education in the Latvian language. It served as the impetus for the development of a network of maritime schools all along the Baltic Sea shore. Today the building houses a maritime museum

The world's largest four-mast wooden barge *Sedovs* in the waters of the Bay of Riga

The earliest recorded mention of the settlement called *Daugavgriva* dates back to 1205. The lighthouse at the place where the *Daugava* River flows into the sea has been sacked several times and then rebuilt. The first map on which the lighthouse appears was produced in 1536

The lamp of the *Slitere* lighthouse

Fishermen at *Ragaciems*

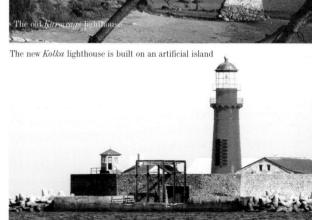

The old *Kurmrags* lighthouse

The new *Kolka* lighthouse is built on an artificial island

The *Roja* port. *Roja* was first mentioned in documents of the Livonian bishopric in 1387. The *Roja* river has been used for shipping since ancient times, and the shoreline features so-called *devil's boats*. Between 1908 and 1910 a protective dam was built 1.5 kilometers off the shore, but it has not survived. Reconstruction at the port started in the 1930s and continued, off and on, until 1972

The world's largest tankers dock at the *Ventspils* port

The Blue Flag attests that a seashore or beach is in conformity with global ecological standards, and even the world's leading beaches have to work hard to get this recognition. Here *Ventspils* Mayor Aivars Lembergs and Inese Vaidere raise *the Blue Flag* in their city. In Soviet times *Ventspils* was a highly polluted and ecologically hazardous city, but the energetic efforts of the City Council have led to a situation where *Ventspils* is the most environmentally clean oil transit port in the world

Hydrographic map

0   30 km

THE GAUJA

The *Gauja* is the longest river in Latvia – 452 kilometers, including 20 kilometers marking the frontier between Estonia and Latvia. The *Gauja* twists and turns through Northern Latvia – its length is 5.5 times larger than the direct-line distance from source to mouth. The river flows into the Bay of Riga. Tributaries include the *Tirza, Mustjegi, Brasla, Bija, Abuls, Rauna* and *Ligatne* rivers. The *Gauja* has a sandy bottom, and it is rich with shoals, islands, twists and landslips along the shores. There are many ancient branches. The river runs particularly fast at the *Sinole, Sikšņi, Strenči* and *Ķūķi* rapids. In the springtime the river often cuts a new bed into the region. Lampreys are harvested in the lower reaches of the *Gauja*, and much of the river flows through the *Gauja National Park*. Along the shores of the river are cities such as *Strenči, Valmiera, Cēsis* and *Sigulda*.

The ruins of the 12th-century *Ikšķile* Church now stand in the middle of the reservoir of the *Daugava* hydroelectric station

THE DAUGAVA

The *Daugava* is Latvia's largest river. Known as the *Zapadnaja Dvina* in its upper reaches, the river flows through Russia, Belarus and Latvia. Its source is in the *Valdai* highlands, and it flows into the Bay of Riga. The total length of the *Daugava* is 1,020 kilometers (357 kilometers in Latvia). Tributaries include the *Meža, Ogre, Drisa, Disna, Aiviekste* and *Dubna* rivers. The bed of the river includes field stones and dolomite cliffs. There are many islands and branches. During spring floods the river rises to 10 meters at *Jēkabpils* – 6.5 meters above its normal height. There are four reservoirs on the *Daugava* – at *Daugavpils, Pļaviņas, Ķegums* and Riga. Among the cities to line the river's shores are *Krāslava, Daugavpils, Līvāni, Jēkabpils, Pļaviņas, Aizkraukle, Ogre* and Riga. The Riga Port is located at the mouth of the *Daugava*.

The *Gauja* in *Taurene* parish, where it originates from *Lode* Lake

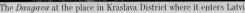

The *Gauja* at *Vireši*

The *Daugava* at *Skrīveri*

The *Daugava* at the place in Krāslava District where it enters Latvia

Rafts in the *Daugava* River at *Dunava*

The *Daugava* near *Slutišķi, Daugavpils* district

The *Gauja* at the *Strenči* bridge

The *Lielupe* at the place where it empties into the sea

A white dune

The *Lielupe* in *Jelgava* district

THE VENTA

The *Venta* flows out of *Veņi* Lake in the Žemaitija highlands of Lithuania. It enters Latvia along the *Venta-Usma* lowlands, ending in the seashore lowlands. The *Venta* is 346 kilometers long (178 kilometers in Latvia), and its tributaries include the *Abava, Vadakste, Zaņe, Ciecere, Liekne, Varduva* and *Virviča* rivers. There are quite a few islands. The width of the river is an average of 60 meters in its middle reaches and between 100 and 140 meters in its lower regions. There is a waterfall at *Kuldīga* and a two-meter rapids at *Ventspils*. The Venta valley from *Kuldīga* to the *Abava* river is a protected territory, as are the *Venta* and *Šķērveļa* river valleys, the Venta rapids, the area around the *Brieži* rapids, and a nature reserve near the *Riežupe* tributary.

The *Venta* rapids at *Kuldīga* include Europe's widest waterfall

The *Abava* river

The *Jumprava* cliffs on the shores of the *Lielupe* in *Bauska* district

The *Memel* – one of the two rivers that make up the *Lielupe*

The *Salaca* river

The *Imula* river

The *Vaive* river at *Priekuļi*

THE LIELUPE

The *Lielupe* originates near the town of *Bauska*, at the confluence of the *Memel* and *Mūsa* rivers. It flows along Latvia's southern lowlands, ending up in a parallel flow along the seashore before it empties into the Bay of Riga. The Lielupe is 119 kilometers long, and tributaries include the *Svēte, Svitene, Islīce, Vircava, Platone, Sesava, Garoze* and *Veciecava* rivers. The upper part of the river flows through an ancient valley, and there are small rapids here and there. At *Jelgava*, a branch called the *Driksa* sets apart an island that is 4.5 kilometers long. The *Lielupe* used to flow into the *Daugava* River, and the old bed of river is now known as *Buļļupe* river. The present-day mouth of the river emerged around 1755. Near its mouth, the *Lielupe* is joined to *Babīte* Lake by the *Gāte* and *Spuņņupe* rivers. There is extensive flooding on the *Lielupe* in the spring, and polders and dams have been built to protect territories against this problem. The river is navigable in its lower and middle reaches. *Jelgava, Kalnciems* and *Jūrmala* are on its shores.

Floods on the *Misa* river

The *Abava* river

The *Vaidava* river at *Ape*

The *Bārta* river

The *Pededze* river

The *Aiviekste* river

The *Mordanga* group of lakes is located near the *Venta* and *Usma* rivers

Rušona Lake

Kalsnavas Lake

Araišu Lake

Burtnieku Lake

Liepājas Lake

Cirīšu Lake near *Aglona*

A lake near *Abeļi* in *Talsi* district

A lake near *Zvirgzde* in *Bauska* district

Papes Lake

A swan nesting in the middle of a lake

Zvirgzdi Lake

Adamovas Lake

Ineša Lake

Kāla Lake

Pulgošņa Lake

Čertoka Lake

Ummis Lake in Riga district

Water surfers on *Ķīšezers* lake in Riga

Rāznas Lake

The First Land Reform

Land is mostly owned by the aristocracy,
later also by peasant farmers.

1804–1860

Also peasant farmers are given the right to buy land.

Owned by the aristocracy, the State,
the church, cities and other owners

Only 36 peasant farmers

1861–1913

Owned by the aristocracy

Owned by farmers 48% | 39%
13%
Owned by the State, churches,
cities and other owners

The Second Land Reform

1920–1939

Land is property

Private property society

Owned by the State, churches,
cities and other owners

70% | 30%

Owned by farmers

The Third Land Reform

Land is only used collectively.
There is no private property.
All land is nationalised.

1940–1988

Used by State forests,
cities and other users

59% | 41%

Used by kolhozes and sovhozes

Lielais Stalins—komunisma saule!

The Fourth Land Reform

First Phase

Land is transferred to lawful owners

1989–1992

Used by State forests,
cities and other users

48% | Use by farmers 25%
27%

Used by statutory companies

Second Phase

Ownership rights to land are guaranteed.
The second phase of land reform is to last for 10-15 years.

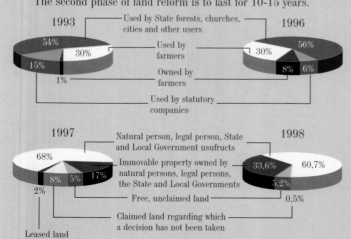

1993 | 1996

Used by State forests, churches,
cities and other users

54% | 30% | 56%
15% | Used by farmers | 30%
1% | | 8% | 6%

Owned by farmers

Used by statutory companies

1997 | 1998

Natural person, legal person, State
and Local Government usufructs

68% | Immovable property owned by natural persons, legal persons, the State and Local Governments | 33,6% | 60,7%
8% | 5% | 17% | 5,2%
2% | Free, unclaimed land | 0,5%

Leased land

Claimed land regarding which
a decision has not been taken

The fourth major land reform in Latvia's history began in 1992, and its initiator was then Prime Minister Ivars Godmanis. Land that had been under the control of *kolhozes*, *sovhozes*, State and Local Government structures was returned to its lawful owners – citizens who owned it prior to the 1940 Soviet occupation, or the heirs of these citizens. Over the course of eight years, the first phase of the land reform was completed. Only 330,000 hectares of land (5% of the total territory of Latvia) was not claimed by anyone. It is expected that most of this land would also be sub-divided in the near future.

The land reform was performed by land commissions in accordance with legislation, but this process was co-ordinated and its legality was ensured by the Central Land Commission (*Centrālā zemes komisija* – CZK). Its members include 8 members of the *Saeima*, as well as 13 representatives from various Ministries and other government structures. The CZK prepares, examines and proposes draft laws that are associated with land reform, as well as taking decisions that regulate the procedures by which relevant laws are implemented. In addition, the CZK co-ordinates and controls the work of the land commissions, examines disputes regarding land and land leasing payments. It also grants ownership of land that has been purchased, if area to be granted exceeds the maximum amount specified by law, and restores ownership rights to land or grants compensation in those cases when people have missed the deadline for submitting documents that affirm ownership or inheritance rights to land, but in rural areas, also when the term for submitting an appropriate application has passed. The CZS also considers issues concerning the cash payments for land ownership compensation certificates, as well as provides written responses to people who ask questions about their rights and performs other explanatory work as well. The CZK also organises and participates in seminars on various land reform issues.

The CZK is entitled to issue, in conformity with legislative enactments, instructions to legal persons, Local Governments and State authorities.

The Central Land Commission of the Republic of Latvia

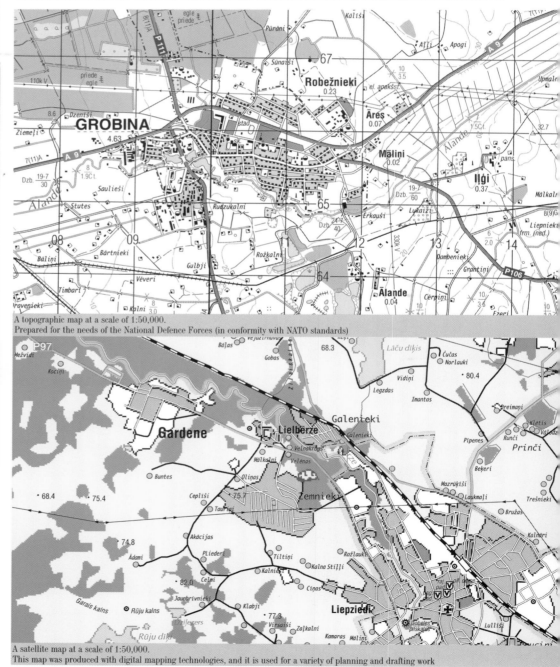

A topographic map at a scale of 1:50,000.
Prepared for the needs of the National Defence Forces (in conformity with NATO standards)

A satellite map at a scale of 1:50,000.
This map was produced with digital mapping technologies, and it is used for a variety of planning and drafting work

The State Land Service (SLS – *Valsts zemes dienests*) performs tasks that are associated with the administration of land, land reform and privatisation of land.

The law *On the Establishment of the State Land Service* was adopted on 15 December 1992. Mr. Guntis Grūbe was appointed General Director of the SLS. It is a government authority, which is subordinated to the Cabinet and is under the supervision of the Ministry of Justice. Much work has been invested in bringing order to land ownership rights. Of Latvia's overall land area, 98% (at time of writing) is included in the State Immovable Property Cadastre – a total of 6.45 million hectares, and 37% of this land is registered as private property.

Following the completion of the work of the city and parish land commissions, the SLS also took over their functions, and now examines boundary disputes associated with land ownership or usufruct.

The basis of the State Land Service structure is eight regional divisions (Greater Riga, Zemgale, Southern Kurzeme, Northern Kurzeme, Vidzeme, Middle *Daugava*, Latgale and Southern Latgale), and it has branches in the country's district centres, as well as in Riga and *Jūrmala*. The preparation of Service strategies, as well as organisational and methodological management is performed by the State Central Land Service, located at *11. Novembra krastmala* 31, Riga. The SLS has access to the most modern surveying equipment, computer equipment and software. Geodesic and land surveying work is done with computerised equipment and global positioning systems. In cartography, the latest photogrammetrical and orthophotomapping preparation technologies are used.

The General Director of the State Land Service, Guntis Grūbe, presents a report to a meeting in Riga of senior officials from the UN European Economic Commission Land Administration

Surveying work with computerised theodolite

An astrolabe with telescope, late 19th century

A triangulation theodolite from the 19th century

A computerised theodolite

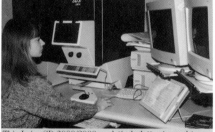

This Leica SD 2000/3000 analytical plotter is used to produce three-dimensional digital vector maps

The State Land Service co-operates with America's National Satellite Enterprise and Mapping Agency

The Latvian-Estonian border

LR VALSTS ZEMES DIENESTS

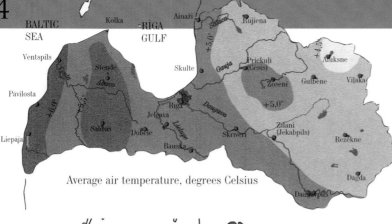

Average air temperature, degrees Celsius

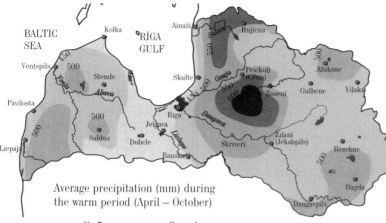

Average precipitation (mm) during
the warm period (April – October)

Average precipitation (mm) during
the cold period (November – March)

Latvia's average annual air temperature is 5.6 degrees Celsius. The absolute maximum recorded air temperature occurred in the town of *Jelgava* on 13 July 1994 – +36 degrees. The lowest temperature on record is –42.9 degrees, recorded in the town of *Zoseni* on 31 December 1978. The average amount of precipitation that falls on Latvia each year is 657 mm, while the 24-hour maximum rainfall on record was 160 mm on 9 July 1973, in *Ventspils*, followed by 136 mm on 14 July 1982, in *Bauska*.

The average annual wind speed in Latvia is 3.9 meters per second, with a maximum speed registered in *Ainaži* in November 1969 – 34 meters per second. The fastest wind gust on record occurred in October 1967 in *Liepāja* – 48 meters per second. Latvia's deepest snow cover was determined in *Stende* in March 1940 – 86 centimetres.

The director of the Latvian State Meteorological Service, Andris Leitass

The Latvian State Hydro-Meteorological Administration is charged with providing adequate information about weather and climate-related conditions, as well as about the condition of the surrounding environment in Latvia. Observations are taken by a 23-station network that is located throughout Latvia. The main observational parameters are: atmosphere pressure, air temperature, humidity, precipitation, the characteristics of the snow cover, if any, soil temperature, cloud cover, visibility, as well as other atmospheric phenomena. Data is collected around the clock, without any interruptions.

At 13 of the stations agro-meteorological observations specifically for farmers are made: developmental phases of plants, the condition of grain plants and vegetables, their development and increased mass, soil moisture, frosts and thaws.

By the year 2001, together with the completion of automation, the level of observations and meteorological data in Latvia will be fully in conformity with European standards.

In order to compile a weather forecast aerial observations are performed, which collect ongoing information about air temperature, humidity, atmospheric pressure, as well as the direc-

tion and speed of the wind at various heights above the ground.

A hydrogen balloon is used to lift a probe to a height of up to 30 kilometres above the Earth. It is mounted with measuring instruments which collect data regarding air temperature, humidity and pressure, and it also contains a special transmitter which sends the data by radio signals to a receiver that is back on the ground. The location co-ordinates of the probe can be determined with the assistance of a special satellite-based navigation system.

Hydrological observations are done at 57 facilities, specifying the water level, through flow, water temperature, icing conditions and ice thickness. Hydrological observations are also done at 10 specifically chosen facilities on the shores of the Baltic Sea and the Bay of Riga, collecting data about the water level, water temperature, waves and ice-related phenomena.

The third major area of activity for the Administration is monitoring the quality of Latvia's environment. The quality of air and water, as well as the existing level of pollution that is carried across extensive distances – all of these are closely linked to the various processes that occur in the atmosphere and in various bodies of water.

One of the largest environmental programs involves ongoing observation of the quality of Latvia's above ground waters. There are two internationally important stations located in Latvia, which monitor the processes of atmospheric pollution movement across large distances. One of the stations is in *Rucava*, the other – in *Zoseni*. The operations of the stations are integrated into the European Monitoring and Evaluation Program (EMEP).

Air quality is determined by stations that not only make ongoing measurements, but also ensure automated data processing and analysis. There are two such stations in Riga and they perform uninterrupted air pollution control in the suburbs of *Kengarags* and *Imanta*. Two other such stations are located in *Daugavpils* and *Valmiera*.

Two measuring stations that operate around the clock are located in *Saldus* district – near the *Mažeiķi* oil refinery in Lithuania. The purpose

Senior weather forecaster Rasma Kleinberga

The deputy director of the State Meteorological Service, Inita Stikute

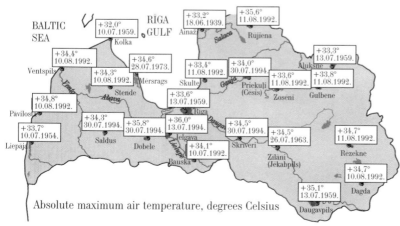

Absolute maximum air temperature, degrees Celsius

Absolute minimum air temperature, degrees Celsius

is to obtain objective information about the effect of that enterprise on Latvia's environment and on the health of its residents.

All of the world's meteorological services are unified in a long-term global weather research program known as the World Weather Watch, or WWW. This program provides for regular and synchronised collection of data from thousands of observation points around the globe – both on dry land and on the sea, as well as high up in the air and in outer space. The information is collected and processed quickly via the Global Telecommunications System (GTS). Access to the global telecommunications network in Latvia is provided through a rapid communications channel between Riga and Norrköping. Information is exchanged without interruption and all around the clock. Data from network stations are transmitted to an administrative telecommunications centre in Riga once every three hours. The information is coded in the form of a synoptic telegram and transmitted from all of the stations at once. At the Centre, it is automatically correlated into a unified exchange file and sent to the regional centre in Norrköping.

In Offenbach, Germany and Redding, UK, work is done to develop specialised atmospheric and synoptic process models. Latvia receives the information that it needs for forecasts via three different satellite channels.

Weather forecasts in Latvia, its major cities, its ports, the central part of the Baltic Sea and the Bay of Riga are prepared for every successive 24-hour period, as well as for a longer range of 3-5 days. The forecasts prove to be true approximately 92% of the time. Data that is received from the various meteorological stations is collected in a specialised climate database. The database also records information regarding changes in water processes in Latvia's rivers. Given the fact that these observations are done frequently and that data have been collected now for many years, it can safely be said that in terms of information volume, this is the largest database in Latvia. The Meteorological Service has meteorological and hydrological data dating back to the last century, and there are even a few records from the 17th century.

Latvia was admitted to the World Meteorological Organisation (WMO) on 14 June 1992. The State Hydro-Meteorological Administration was designated the authorised institution in Latvia, and this allows it to participate in international processes on equal terms with the 179 other countries that are members of the organisation. Latvia has undertaken obligations to participate in several international programs. Ozone measurement data from the *Rucava* observation station are sent to the WMO data centre in Tokyo, which measures the greenhouse effect. The *Skulte* station measures the overall amount of ozone in the atmosphere, and this information is regularly sent to the World Ozone and Ultraviolet Radiation Data Centre in Canada.

Latvia's State Meteorological Service employs 520 specialists who represent 33% of all of the personnel in the Ministry for Environmental Protection and Regional Development.

A light recording device at an air quality observation station

Southern Scandinavia at sunset as seen in a photograph taken from a satellite

Clouds above Eastern Europe photographed from a satellite

A worker at the meteorological station measures the air temperature

A measuring system to determine the height of clouds

The *MILOS 500* automated meteorological station

THE ENVIRONMENTAL DATA CENTER

Data processing; at centre is the director of LVDC, Ilze Kirstuka

Chemical analysis

The management of the Data Processing Division

Biological analysis

Air analysis

Latvia's Environmental Data Centre (*Latvijas Vides datu centrs* – LVDC) operates under the control of the Ministry for Environmental Protection and Regional Development. Its aim is to organise a unified information system in the area of environmental data, as well as a system of laboratories to test the quality of the environment that conforms to EU standards.

The LVDC provides data and information to State and local government institutions, international organisations and institutions, business companies and private individuals. It also provides the network facility functions for the European Environmental Agency in Latvia.

The Latvian Environmental Data Centre is divided into two major structural units – the Laboratory Division and the Data Processing Division. The latter division works to develop databases and data processing programs and to establish and service a Geographic Information System that is appropriate for client requirements. Thematic maps are drawn, environmental information and data is collected, processed and prepared (statistical, cadastral, monitoring), and studies and research projects on various aspects of the environment are conducted.

The Laboratory Division takes samples and tests purified and unpurified waste water, surface, underground and drinking water, the soil, the air, various emissions and radioactive radiation. It also evaluates other laboratories for accreditation purposes, and it organises comparative inter-laboratory testing programs.

Sulphur dioxide emissions into the atmosphere in 1998 (tons)

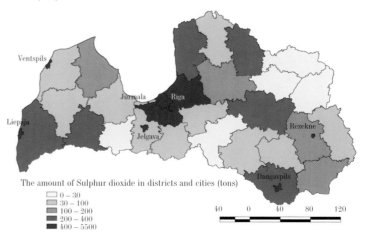
The amount of Sulphur dioxide in districts and cities (tons)

- 0 – 30
- 30 – 100
- 100 – 200
- 200 – 400
- 400 – 5500

STARLIT SKY

Meteorite of *Baldone*

Total eclipse of the sun

Total and partial eclipse of the moon

Founders of Latvian astronomy:
professor Karlis Šteins and professor Janis
(1911-1938) Ikaunieks (1912-1969)

A satellite image of Latvia

Everyone interested is welcome to the observatory
dome of Latvian University for viewing the starlit sky.
The background sky of the photography is a rare
nature phenomenon - silvery clouds

Astronomy students being introduced to planets

Riga-open astronomy contest attracts many young
students from all over the country every year

Astronomic research has been carried out since
long ago in Latvia in cooperation with European
countries. Movement of the smaller cosmic bodies of the solar system has been researched
under the supervision of Karlis Šteins. In
recognition of the achievements of Latvian
astronomers, several small planets – *Latvija*,
Rīga, *Krišbarons* and others – are now recognized by names associated with Latvia.

With the help of up-to-date satellite lazerprojector – telescope – exact coordinates and
movements of tectonic plates can be measured. Astronomers receive images of Latvia
that may be used to ecologically monitor terrain and marine.

Research in astrophysics was lead by Janis
Ikaunieks. It was carried out in Latvia with the
largest Smith system telescope in the Baltic,
the mirror lens of it being 120 cm in diameter.
By researching chemically unusual stars – car-
bonic stars – answers are searched to general
questions on star evolution and space development. One tenth of all carbon stars were discovered in Latvia.

The former soviet army base used for military
purposes is now changed into a radio-telescope and serves for science in *Irbene*, district
of *Ventspils*.

Special attention is directed towards promotion
of science and education. Latvia is among the
few countries in the world where astronomy is a
separate subject in schools. Astronomy is studied in the Latvian University. The magazine
Zvaigžņotā Debess (*Starlit Sky*) introduces
reader to the current developments in astronomy. There are public demonstrations of star-
gazing and a Space Research Museum in Riga.

Lazerprojector in the observatory of
Latvian University

Swedish-Latvian astro-
physicist, professor of
Lund University,
Dainis Draviņš

People watching the *Hayle-Bopp* comet gathered in *Vērmanes*
Garsen in April 1997

Maris Abele, telescope
constructor, winner of the
Great Award of Latvian
Science Academy

The astronaut of the Soviet Union, Anatolii Solovjov, has taken
part in space missions on several occasions, was born and raised
in *Bolderāja*. Photo: A. Solovjov and children in the Museum of
Medicine History in 1998

House of Fridrich Cander (Riga, *F. Candera iela* 1)
houses a museum now

Fridrich Cander (1887-1933),
a constructor of rockets and
aviation engines, one of the
founders of astronautics

Radio-telescope in *Irbene*

Baldone observatory and Smith system telescope

THE CREATORS OF THIS BOOK

Pēteris Apinis, text and idea

Mārtiņš Zunde, technical aspects of the work

Maija Šetlere, organisation of the office and a woman who knows everything about everything in this book

Anna Šmite, who ensured that the data in this book are encyclopaedia-precise

Alda Zunde, responsible for the outstanding design, painting and colours of the book

Anita Kamenščikova, who ran the financial aspects of this project

The *Nacionālais medicīnas apgāds* publishing house which published this book is housed in the *Cat Building* at *Meistaru iela* 10. Architect Friedrich Scheffel constructed the building in 1909 as a residential and commercial building. The collective, which produced this book spends its days in the reconstructed attic of the building, almost directly below the cat in the foreground and among the roofs of Old Rīga.

Lauris Filics, who photographed all of the people on this page in the same place and with the same light

Kārlis Streips, who translated quickly and precisely and was not shy about pointing out shortcomings

Viesturs Pauls Karnups, who edited the English translation

Henrijs Rusis, who translated and edited a great number of scraps

Ilze Stengrevica, edited English texts in Foreign Ministry

Ieva Marga, who assisted in editing and translating English texts

Dace Liela painted the people on the cover of the book

Valdis Stals, who did research on historical facts in the country's archives

Maija Staceviča, computer specialist with the diligence and precision of a bee

Zanda Birze, who never gets upset if something has to be done over

Armands Ezeriņš, who kept everyone surprised over the fact that the computers always worked

Vilnis Vikmanis is friends with his computer whether awake or asleep

Ginta Kulīte, outstandingly good in the Latvian language

Ginta Poriete, also outstandingly good in the Latvian language

Māris Ošlejs produced the audio disk, and his optimism stretches across the National Academic Choir

Ojārs Spārītis – more than just a professor of art and Minister for Culture

Vladislavs Volkovs handled all of the texts that nobody else wanted to fuss with

Jurģis Dzenis scanned all of the photographs in a medically scientific atmosphere

Aiva Koļesņikova processed the pictures

Inguna Draviņa transcribed recorded interviews

Daina Freimantale is a virtuoso on the computer keyboard

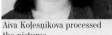

Ginta Lūse provided medical harmony

Benita Feldmane ensured that there were some leisure activities, too

Roberts Klotiņš is a doctor with the philosophy of modern technology and the Internet

Inga Jermacane offered polite answers to pushy and aggressive questions on the telephone

Uldis Usitis was our herald in Parliament and government

Edgars Vasiļevskis is an anaesthesiologist among book publishers

Gaļina Korhova battles the eternal shortage of money in the treasury

Ruta Millere, director of the *Jāņa Sēta* printing house in *Cēsis*. In this picture we see the printers of the book

Biruta Kravale: "It's impossible to find this book format!" (She usually says that after the book has already been found)

Arno Licis, much to the surprise of everyone in *Silakrogs*, can still prepare book out of small sheets of paper

Inga Dundure's smile is the bridge between the client and the printing house at *Preses nams* and *Jāņa sēta*

The financial and printing face of *Jāņa sēta* is represented by (seated) Janīna Blūma and Ingrīda Grasmane and (standing) Līga Lāce, Maija Liepa, Baiba Vasiļevska, Diāna Brauča and Sanita Kaļvane

The layout and design team at *Jāņa sēta* – (front row) Agnis Auns, Dace Ābola, Mārtiņš Znotens, Elīna Kļaviņa and Juris Kļaviņš; (second row) Guna Dubrovska, Ēriks Nuķis, Irīna Indulēna and Kārlis Jakādelis

CONSULTANTS AND SPECIALISTS

Construction engineer Pāvils Abramovs; Dr. sci. Andris Akermanis; music historian Diāna Albina; Naturalization Board director Eižēnija Aldermane; choreographer Maruta Aluta; Dr.hab.mat. Agnis Andžāns; State Geology Service director Rudīte Aņikejeva; public relations specialist Kārlis Anitens; informatics specialist Andris Anspoks; journalist Baldurs Apinis; public relations specialist Haralds Apogs; attorney Romāns Apsītis; Professor Ēriks Kārlis Ārons; publisher Arvīls Ašeradens; advertising specialist Modris Atpils; advisor to the chairman of the *Liepāja* City Council Olita Augustovska; cultural specialist Tija Auziņa; Latvian Photography Museum director Vilnis Auziņš; State Revenue Service board chairman Raitis Averāts; businessman Aleksandrs Aļeksejevs; businessman Vladimirs Balakins; national affairs specialist Aina Balaško; veterinarian Maira Balode; Environmental Protection and Regional Development minister Vents Balodis; Rīga City Council Transportation Department Commission chairwoman Linda Baltiņa; Latvian Olympic Committee chairman Vilnis Baltiņš; Latvian Cultural Fund board chairman Pēteris Bankovskis; businessman Vladimirs Barinovs; Rabbi Natans Barkans; Dr.sci. Pauls Barons; academician Jānis Barzdiņš; the director of the Latvian History Museum, Inga Baumane; Professor Mirdza Baumane; businessman Edvīns Beriņš; journalist Agita Bērziņa; the president of Latvijas *Unibanka*, Andris Bērziņš; the mayor of Rīga, Andris Bērziņš; the foreign minister of Latvia, Indulis Bērziņš; the director of the Labor Inspection Department, Jānis Bērziņš; the director of the Culture Capital Fund, Māris Bērziņš; builder Marģeris Betmetis; the director of the Public Relations Department of the Interior Ministry, Normunds Beļskis; Justice Minister Valdis Birkavs; education specialist Juris Birznieks; tourism specialist Santa Boka; the president of the stock company *Latvijas finieris*, Juris Biķis; architect Pēteris Blūms; the general director of the VOVA agency, Ināra Bluķe; the president of the Latvian Association of Physicians, Viesturs Boka; the director of the chancellery of the president, Mārtiņš Bondars; lawyer and businessman Aivars Borovkovs; architect Māris Bože; journalist Mairita Brice; the general director of the National Real Estate Agency, Kalvis Bricis; regional development specialist Normunds Broks; architect Normunds Broks; Dr.sc.ing. Jānis Brūnavs; Professor Kārlis Buivids; journalist Ilze Būmane; the minister for state governance and local government affairs, Jānis Bunkšs; radio journalist Sendija Burka-Šaicanova; public relations specialist Harijs Burkovskis; marketing specialist and businessman Ervīns Butkēvičs; businessman Nikolajs Butvillo; businessman Andrejs Ceplītis; the president of the Rīga Stock Exchange, Uldis Cērps; historian Zigrīda Ciematniece; businesswoman Monika Cikla; journalist Lelde Ciklīte; the chairman of the Latvian Elections Commission, Arnis Cimdars; information specialist Indra Čekstere; the chief auditor of the Republic of Latvia, Raitis Černajs; Dr.sc. Andris Čikuts; Border Guard Gen. Gunārs Daboliņš; Parliament deputy Guntis Dambergs; architect Juris Dambis; insurance specialist Juris Dambis; advertising manager Andrejs Dārziņš; road building specialist Jānis Daukšts; the board chairman of the stock company *Latvijas gāze*, Adrians Dāvis; businessman Jānis Dāvis; Dr.oec. Andris Deniņš; informatics specialist Māris Detlavs; the general director of the Latvian postal service, Aivars Droiskis; historian Kristīne Ducmane; journalist Uldis Duka; the director of the Railroad Inspectorate, Andris Dunskis; an advisor to the president, Dace Dūze; photo editor Andris Eglītis; collector Voldemārs Eihenbaums; ecologist Indulis Emsis; the chairman of the Constitutional Court, Aivars Endziņš; the president of the Latvian Association of Pharmacists, Aigars Eniņš; biologist Guntis Eniņš; film director and professor Ansis Epners; folklorist Helēna Erdmane; sports historian Aija Erta; the general director of the Latvian Development Agency, Māris Elerts; the president of the Latvian Mortgage and Land Bank, Inesis Feiferis; the executive director of the Latvian Occupation Museum, Gundega Feldmane-Zans; Professor Ruvins Ferbers; the director of the *Miss Latvija* Bureau, Inta Fogele; the director of the Sports Board, Einārs Fogelis; film director Hercs Franks; journalist Aivis Freidenfelds; historian Artis Freimanis; businessman Kārlis Freimanis; Parliamentary deputy Jānis Gaigals; businessman Māris Gailis; director Guntis Gailītis; economist Jānis Galviņš; businessman Valdis Garoza; regional development specialist Ivars Gaters; the director of the *Tērvete* Sanatorium, Miķelis Gediņš; construction specialist Vija Gēme; journalist Kaspars Goba; the director of a marketing communications agency, Vladis Goldbergs; plant breeder Guntis Grants; folklore specialist Maruta Grasmane; the commander of the National Armed Forces, Raimonds Graube; Professor Oļģerts Grāvītis; businessman Valdis Grimza; the executive director of the Rīga City Council, Andris Grīnbergs; agronomist Māris Grīnvalds; journalist Sergei Grodnikov; the general director of the National Land Service, Guntis Grūbe; the director of the Sports Museum, Dzintra Grundmane; customs specialist Ingrīda Gulbe-Otaņķe; the senior notary of the National Company Register, Māris Gulbis; the prorector of the Latvian Academy of Medicine, Marina Gulmane; the chairman of the Supreme Court, Andris Guļāns; the chairman of the Latvian Securities Market commission, Viktors Gustsons; foreign affairs specialist Armands Gūtmanis; the administrative director of Latvian Railways, Juris Iesalnieks; the chairman of the *Jelgava* City Council, Uldis Ivans; journalist Laila Ivāna; the president of the DT Media Group, Māra Jakobsone; the director of the National Construction Inspectorate, Leonīds Jakobsons; lawyer Vija Jakobsone; the Director of State Inspection of Construction, Leonīds Jakobsons; Dr. Ruta Jakušonoka; the director of the Transportation Bureau, Gvido Janēvičs; journalist Kārlis Jansons; librarian Gunta Jaunmuktāne; the chairman of the Latvian Association of Local Self-Governments, Andris Jaunsleinis; businesswoman Margarita Javiča; journalist Anna Joffe; businessman Harijs Jordāns; publisher Jānis Juška; businessman Kaems Benjamins; the director of the Land Book of Latvia, Inese Kalniņa; tourism specialist Aivars Kalniņš; the director of the National Civil Service board, Armands Kalniņš; composer Imants Kalniņš; Dr.hab.ing.sci. Mārtiņš Kalniņš; the director of the Latvian Institute, Ojārs Kalniņš; the director of Rīga's parks and gardens, Agnis Kalnkaziņš; builder Valdis Kalnozols; Agriculture Minister Aigars Kalvītis; economist Gaļina Kaņējeva; the executive director of the Latvian Environmental Protection Fund, Valdis Kaprālis; professor and composer Juris Karlsons; Dr.sc.ing. Edvīns Karnītis; philologist Viesturs Pauls Karnups; the director of the Rīga Circus, Gunārs Katkēvičs; the director of the *Dobele* Selection Station, Edīte Kaufmane; advertising specialist and businessman Gintārs Kavacis; Dr.oec. Ojārs Kehris; the board chairman of the Latvian Maritime Fund, Vilnis Ķeris; bibliographer Velga Kince; the general director of the National Sanitary Border Inspectorate, Jānis Kinna; insurance specialist Igors Kiršbaums; agronomist Andris Kiršentāls; Dr.biol. Ilze Kirstuka; Professor Abrams Kleckins; businessman Vilnis Klibiķis; road building specialist Jānis Klismets; musicologist Arnolds Klotiņš; journalist Dita Kļaviņa; businessman Askolds Kļaviņš; the deputy chairwoman of the Latvian Association of Local Self-Governments, Olga Kokāne; businessman Uldis Kokins; businessman Valdis Kokle; the general director of Radio Latvia, Dzintris Kolāts; academician Rihards Kondratovičs; the commander of the Home Guard, Jānis Kononovs; businessman Sergei Konopijev; businessman Vladimir Kornilov; the director o f the Latvian office of the World Federation of Free Latvians, Linda Kovaļevska; businessman Valerijs Kozlovs; journalist Līga Krapane; Dr.oec. Aivars Krastiņš; the director of the Council of Europe Information Center, Uldis Krastiņš; Parliamentary deputy Guntars Krasts; advertising specialist Iveta Krauja; art specialist Solvita Krese; academician Jānis Kristapsons; Defense Minister Ģirts Valdis Kristovskis; archivist Silvija Križevica; the general director of the stock company Latvian Roads Directorate, Olafs Kronlaks; businessman Ojārs Krūmbergs; surveyor Aivars Krūmiņš, senior *GNP* inspector Jānis Krūmiņš; attorney Marcis Krūmiņš; the chairman of the Latvian Jewish Community, Grigorijs Krupņikovs; the president of *Latvijas Loto*, Maija Kuble; businessman Arnolds Kublinskis; the president of the Latvian Chamber of Industry, Viktors Kulbergs; the coordinator of the Non-Governmental Organizations Center, Laila Kundziņa; publisher Alfrēds Kundziņš; Dr.hist. Mārtiņš Kuplais; lawyer Gunārs Kusiņš; the director of the European Integration Bureau, Eduards Kušners; collector Gunārs Kušķis; journalist Dita Kļaviņa; businessman Askolds Kļaviņš; a member of the National Radio and Television Council, Dace Ķezbere; presidential assistant Evija Ķeniņa; Dr. Jānis Ķisis; businesswoman Iveta Lāce; the director of the National Museum of Art, Māra Lāce; Parliamentary deputy Rišards Labanovskis; public relations specialist Marika Lagzdiņa; regional policy specialist Ērika Lagzdiņa; businesswoman Selga Laizāne; businessman Valērijs Lappo; the state secretary of the Ministry of Agriculture, Jānis Lapša; customs specialist Aināra Latkovskis; Professor Ilmārs Lazovskis; Professor Pēteris Laķis; architect Ēriks Lēdis; a departmental director at the Transportation Ministry, Vigo Legzdiņš; ballet director Aivars Leimanis; Parliamentary deputy Kārlis Leiškalns; the director of the National Meteorological Board, Andris Leitass; architect Jānis Lejnieks; road engineer Valdis Lejnieks; the chairman of the *Ventspils* City Council, Aivars Lembergs; businessman Kārlis Licis; art historian Sarmīte Līdaka; the press secretary of the Rīga Zoo, Ingmārs Līdaka; the director of the Auto Museum, Edvīns Liepiņš; actress and businesswoman Marina Lipčenko; an advisor to the director of the Rīga Circus, Lolita Lipinska; information specialist Anita Ludziša; the director of the Road Traffic Safety Directorate, Andris Lukstiņš; Economics Minister Vladimirs Makarovs; Dr. Ieva Marga; Docent Aivars Markots of the Faculty of Geography of the University of Latvia; diet specialist Antoņina Masiļune; journalist Una Meistare; businessman Juris Mendziņš; veterinarian Gundega Mičule; journalist Māris Millers; beekeeper Andrejs Mizis; energy specialist Kārlis Miķelsons; the deputy chairman of the Rīga Latvian Association, Edgars Mucenieks; Parliamentary deputy Linards Muciņš; businessman Ivars Muzikants; journalist Ilze Nagle; the general director of the Latvian Privatization Agency, Jānis Naglis; businessman Juris Naglis; the director of the Welfare Department of the Rīga City Council, Valdis Nagobads; energy specialist Aivars Nātre; architect Anita Neilande; geologist Uldis Nulle; the press director for the Bank of Latvia, Kristaps Otersons; public activist Agris Olmanis; Professor Uldis Osis; culture organizer Māris Ošlejs; energy specialist Aleksandrs Ošs; public affairs specialist Margita Otto; the press secretary to the National Treasury, Anita Ozola; pharmacist Jānis Ozoliņš; forest specialist Jānis Ozoliņš; businessman Leonards Ozoliņš; the board chairman of the Rīga Central Market, Aivars Ozols; forest specialist Arvīds Ozols; hunting specialist Egils Ozols; Dr. Jānis Ozols; businessman Uģis Ozols; journalist Juris Paiders; the executive director of the Latvian Cultural Fund, Inese Palma; Parliamentary deputy Andrejs Panteļejevs; publisher Māris Pavasars; journalist Leonards Pāvils; the director of the Latvian State Radio and Television Center, Māris Pauders; businessman Dainis Peimanis; historian Elmārs Pelkaus; the director of the Rīga Cinema Museum, Inga Pērkone; historian Pārsla Pētersone; railroad specialist Jānis Pētersons; the state secretary of the Transportation Ministry, Uldis Pētersons; cultural worker Sarmīte Pīka; Parliamentary deputy Rihards Pīks; businesswoman Inga Pinne; health promotion specialist Ineta Pirktiņa; businessman Andris Plezers; advertising specialist Māris Plūme; Parliamentary deputy Aija Poča; Dr. Egita Pole; businessman Almants Polikevičs; public relations specialist Inese Pommere; the president of the *Rīga* airport, Dzintars Pommers; Maj. Voldemārs Pozņaks; the president of the Rīga Passenger Port, Zigmārs Priede; journalist Santa Puče; book publisher Dace Pugača; the general director of the Latvian Confederation of Employers, Ilgvars Pukainis; the chairman of the Latvian Association of Free Labor Unions, Juris Radzevičs; journalist Olafs Pulks; the director of the Rīga Museum of History and Shipping, Klāra Radziņa; journalist Ilmārs Randers; Parliamentary deputy Romualds Ražuks; businessman Gundars Riekstiņš; film critic Dita Rietuma; the board chairman of the Bank of Latvia, Ilmārs Rimševics; the director of the Choreography School, Haralds Ritenbergs; advertising specialist Andris Romanovskis; businesswoman Anna Romašenoka; the director of the Insurance Supervision Inspectorate, Gvido Romeiko; the director of the Smiļģis Theater Museum, Rita Rotkale; *Kandava* Mayor Dainis Rozenfelds; businessman Ivars Roķis; the Rev. Juris Rubenis of the Lutheran Church; the chairman of the Latvian Radio and Television Council, Ojārs Rubenis; Rīga City Council deputy Maija Rubīna; the director of the Latvian Gaming Business Association, Raits Rudovičs; the head of the Rīga office of the City of *Liepāja*, Irēna Rudzāte; the president of the stock company *Staburadze*, Ivars Rudzītis; businessman Māris Rudzītis; plant breeder Jānis Rukšans; the director of the Goethe Institute, Ronalds Ruprehts; energy specialist Uldis Sakne; Dr. Juris Salaks; Professor Gundega Samoviča; the director of the *Ventspils* Free Port, Imants Sarmulis; businessman Atis Sausnītis; businessman Juris Seilis; the editor of *Lauku Avīze*, Viesturs Serdāns; the chairman of the *Liepāja* City Council, Uldis Sesks; agronomist Jānis Sietiņsons; the head of the National Employment Service, Andris Siliņš; finance consultant Elmārs Siliņš; journalist Jānis Siliņš; baker Normunds Skauģis; prosecutor general Jānis Skrastiņš; businessman Viktors Skrebels; the president of the stock company *Ventamonjaks*, Krists Skuja; businessman Druvis Skulte; businessman Pēteris Sliede; fashion designer Asnāte Smeltere; publisher Mairita Solima; the general director of the State Revenue Service, Andrejs Sončiks; businessman Ivars Sormulis; Professor Ojārs Spārītis; finance consultant Armīns Sproģis; Parliamentary deputy Oskars Spurdziņš; the director of the Training Center, Ilmārs Stabrovskis; advertising specialist Kristīne Staļbovska; economist Lilija Stelpe; the director of the Latvian Food Center, Olafs Stengrēvics; historian Ojārs Stepens; professor and historian Aivars Stranga; the director of the Road Traffic Department, Tālis Straume; the deputy chairman of the *Sigulda* City Council, Jānis Strautmanis; *Lattelekom* president Gundars Strautmanis; *Gauja* National Park director Jānis Strautnieks; farmer Kārlis Strazdiņš; the director of the Latvian Association of Ornithologists, Māris Strazds; film director Jānis Streičs; the director of the international cinema center *Arsenāls*, Augusts Sukuts; journalist Ivars Svilāns; Dr. Regīna Svirska; the director of the Catastrophic Medicine Center, Mārtiņš Šics; librarian Inga Šildere; advertising manager Egils Šķele; Prime Minister Andris Šķēle; Dr.geogr. Pēteris Šķiņķis; culture manager Egils Šefers; architect Uģis Šenbergs; the procurement director for the stock company *Ventspils nafta*, Ēriks Šerstņevs; a senior specialist at the Finance Ministry, Jānis Šints; Professor Māris Šlokenbergs; public relations specialist Ingrīda Šmite; the general director of the National Social Insurance Agency, Inese Šmitiņa; teacher Juris Šmits; businessman Guntis Indriksons; businesswoman Elita Šņepste; Parliamentary deputy Jāzeps Šnepsts; Professor Ausma Špona; Professor Ina Šteinbuka; beekeeper Juris Šteiselis; journalist Dzintra Šubrovska; the deputy state secretary of the Welfare Ministry, Tālis Talents; businessman Viesturs Tamužs; businessman Aivars Taurenis; the executive director of the Soros Foundation Latvia, Vita Tērauda; businessman Uģis Tētiņš; Parliamentary deputy Aivars Tiesnesis; businessman Viesturs Tīle; businessman Uldis Tilgass; the director of the National Standards Supervision Inspectorate, Ivars Tiltiņš; journalist Uldis Tīrons; journalist Ieva Tīruma; the general director of Latvian Television, Rolands Tjarve; Professor Andris Tomašūns; radio engineer Kārlis Ulāns; former President Guntis Ulmanis; an advisor to the chairman of the *Ventspils* City Council, Ramona Umblija; scientist Evalds Urtāns; businesswoman Aija Ušča; the deputy director of *Invest Rīga*, Aldis Vaivars; the chairman of the Totalitarian Regime Crime Commission, Dainis Vanags; businessman Jānis Vārna; businesswoman Evija Vaščenko; journalist Klāss Vāvere; magazine editor Aivars Vegners; the director of the National School of Administration, Gunta Veismane; the governor of the National Treasury, Aivars Veiss; the deputy director of the Social Insurance Department, Olita Veldre; plant breeder Aldonis Vēriņš; artist Edgars Verpe; Professor Marģeris Vestermanis; composer Ivars Vīgners; the director of the Latvian National Library, Andris Vilks; astronomer Ilgonis Vilks; economist Pēteris Vilks; journalist Irina Viņņika; businessman Vilis Vītols; Dr.iur. Vitolds Zahars; medical historian Solveiga Zālīte; the general director of the Civil Aviation Administration, Andris Zalmanis; historian Artūrs Zalvteris; computer specialist Dzintars Zariņš; the president of the stock company *Preses nams*, Ivars Zariņš; mountain climber Imants Zauls; the press secretary to the Road Traffic Safety Department, Viktors Zaķis; the director of the Latvian Maritime Administration, Bruno Zeibiņš; Admiral Gaidis Zeibots; a member of the Council of the Bank of Latvia, Valentīna Zeile; fire-fighter Valdis Ziberts; the chairman of the Central Housing Privatization Commission, Ziedonis Ziediņš; the deputy director of the parliamentary chancellery, Valdis Ziemelis; the minister for cooperation with international financial institutions, Roberts Zīle; journalist Egils Zirnis; the general director of Latvian Railways, Andris Zorgevics; the director of the Rainis Museum of the History of Literature and the Arts, Ivars Zukulis; journalist Ieva Zvidre; the director of the Latvian Fire-Fighting Museum, Velta Žerdiņa; the director of the Central Statistical Board, Aija Žīgure; the president of the stock company *Rīgas siltums*, Aris Žīgurs.

Latvia's riflemen's monument is devoted to the heroism of Latvian riflemen during World War I. Here the artists have brought it to life by depicting three men with whom the work of the riflemen is associated. In the front is Oskars Kalpaks, the first commander of the Latvian army. To the right is Fridrihs Briedis, a military specialist and diplomat who was killed by the Soviet bootlickers. To the left is actor Ēvalds Valters, who was a rifleman when young and who lived to the age of 101, spending almost all of his life on stage and never ceasing to be both active and stylish. After 50 years of Soviet occupation it was he who first raised the independent Latvian flag above the tower of the Riga Castle.

Anatolijs Gorbunovs, minister of transportation at this writing, is a statesman who was beloved in Soviet times and during the country's independence

Emils Dārziņš a composer in the early 20th century.

Vilhelms Purvītis, a painter who was the founder and director of the Latvian National Museum of Art.

Playwright and novelist Rūdolfs Blaumanis.

Painter Kārlis Padegs. monument to the pain stands at an edge of t Vermanes Park in Rig created by sculptor A Vārpa and depicted her

Einārs Repše, president of the Bank of Latvia, successfully helped Latvia to move from the Soviet ruble to one of the world's strongest currencies, the lats.

Jānis Lūsis won three Olympic medals in javelin, set several world records and was European champion four times.

Raimonds Pauls, a virtuoso pianist and composer known throughout Eastern Europe, served as Latvia's first post-occupation minister of culture.

Jānis Stradiņš, chemist and historian, president of the Latvian Academy of Sciences and scion of a distinguished family of Latvian scientists.

Pēteris Vasks, a composer known throughout the world.

Imants Kalniņš a beloved composer and politician.

Wilhelm Ostwald, a professor of chemistry at the Riga Polytechnical Institute who won the Nobel Prize in physics (as a German) in 1909.

Liga Berziņa, a Latvian beauty.